UNDERSTANDING THE
OLD
TESTAMENT

ABRIDGED FOURTH EDITION

BERNHARD W. ANDERSON
Emeritus, Princeton Theological Seminary

Assisted by KATHERYN PFISTERER DARR
Boston University School of Theology

 PRENTICE HALL Upper Saddle River, New Jersey 07458

Library of Congress Cataloging-in-Publication Data

Anderson, Bernhard W.
   Understanding the Old Testament / Bernhard W. Anderson. —
Abridged 4th ed.
     p.   cm.
   Includes bibliographical references and index.
   ISBN 0-13-948399-3
   1. Bible. O.T.—History of Biblical events.   2. Jews—History—To
70 A.D.   I. Title
BS1197.A63 1997
221.6—dc20   96–31386
                                       CIP

Editorial Director: *Charlyce Jones Owen*
Acquisitions Editor: *Angie Stone*
Director of Production and Manufacturing: *Barbara Kittle*
Production Editor: *Harriet Tellem*
Manufacturing Manager: *Nick Sklitsis*
Prepress and Manufacturing Buyer: *Lynn Pearlman*
Creative Design Director: *Leslie Osher*
Art Director: *Anne Nieglos*
Interior Design: *Paula Martin* and *Maureen Richardson*
Cover and Insert Design: *Jeannette Jacobs*
Cover Art: *Detail of Town of Lachish (Judean father with two sons)* © *British Museum*
Photo Research: *Francelle Carapetyan/Image Research*

©1998 by Prentice-Hall, Inc.
Simon & Schuster/A Viacom Company
Upper Saddle River, New Jersey 07458

Printed in the United States of America

This book was set in 11/13 Garamond by Pine Tree Composition
and was printed and bound by R R Donnelley & Sons. The cover
was printed by Phoenix Color Corp.

10 9 8 7 6 5 4 3 2 1

ISBN 0-13-948399-3

Prentice-Hall International (UK) Limited, *London*
Prentice-Hall of Australia Pty. Limited, *Sydney*
Prentice-Hall Canada Inc., *Toronto*
Prentice-Hall Hispanoamericana, S.A., *Mexico*
Prentice-Hall of India Private Limited, *New Delhi*
Prentice-Hall of Japan, Inc., *Tokyo*
Simon & Schuster Asia Pte. Ltd., *Singapore*
Editora Prentice-Hall do Brasil, Ltda., *Rio de Janeiro*

*To My
Esteemed
Teacher,
James
Muilenburg*

CONTENTS

ILLUSTRATIONS AND AIDS

A major source used in the preparation of maps has been *The Westminster Historical Atlas to the Bible*, Revised Edition, Copyright 1956 by W. L. Jenkins, The Westminster Press.

COLOR INSERTS

CHRONOLOGICAL CHARTS

KEY CHARTS
AND TABLES

DEFINITIONS

PREFACE

Since the first edition of this book was published several decades ago, the field of biblical studies has changed significantly in response to archaeological research, new methods of study, and the reevaluation of past accomplishments. Like other areas of scholarly research, biblical study is characterized by pluralism of approach and interpretation. Despite changes in the field, however, this book is in its fourth edition, suggesting that its approach offers an inviting path into the study and appreciation of the Hebrew Bible, known in the Christian community as the Old Testament.

From the first, the aim of this book has been to interweave the elements of historical study, archaeological research, literary criticism, and biblical theology by viewing the history of ancient Israel as story—from its crucial beginnings in the Mosaic period to the flowering of its literature in the late period of biblical Judaism, the so-called Maccabean period. Indeed, all four editions have begun with the theme of "the story of our life."

At the same time, I have tried to avoid any tendency to shift exclusively to "story," downplaying the closely related dimension of "history," or to study books of the Bible only in their final literary form, neglecting the history of their traditions. In the ongoing discussion, I remain convinced that the best way to understand the faith of ancient Israel is to use an approach that takes into account the interrelated dimensions of story and history, of tradition history and final literary formulation.

Thus, despite fresh nuances and appropriate modifications in each edition, the basic outline of the book has remained essentially the same. The exposition begins with the formative event of the Exodus and its corollary, the Sinai covenant, then traces Israel's life story through the years to the dawn of the Common Era, when Jews and

Christians appropriated the scriptural heritage of ancient Israel in differing ways in the Talmud and New Testament, respectively.

This paperback version is an abridgment and updating of the fourth edition, which continues in use. With the assistance of others, I have endeavored to abridge without affecting the content and style of the original. Also, I have sought to bring the discussion up-to-date by adding new footnote materials, by completely reworking the selected bibliography at the end, and, in some instances, by making minor changes in the text. The most significant revision occurs in Chapter 16, "The Praises of Israel," which has been recast.

As in previous editions, I call the reader's attention to several basic matters:

1. A footnote at the beginning of each chapter lists appropriate readings in the Old Testament. Keep in mind that this book does not substitute for reading the biblical material. On the contrary, the Bible as it has been said, throws a lot of light on the commentaries!

2. Source footnotes are not excess baggage. Though you might skip them on first reading, they provide important documentation that could invite further study on your part. Moreover, they bear witness to the fact that biblical interpretation occurs in an ecumenical circle—one that includes Jewish, Protestant, and Catholic representatives. Bracketed numbers in footnotes refer to the Selected Bibliography at the end of the book. The Bibliography lists complete information on publications, with entries arranged under general topics (such as Biblical Criticism [595–599]) and book chapters.

3. Translations of biblical passages are identified by an appropriate abbreviation (for example, NRSV for New Revised Standard Version). When no abbreviation is given, the translation is the author's.

4. The discussion conforms to current standards of inclusive language with respect to men and women, Jews and Christians, believers and seekers. Whenever appropriate, I provide translations in nonsexist language. To be faithful to the Hebrew text, however, I retain masculine language with respect to God. Though the holy God of the Bible transcends sexuality (a point that became clear in the encounter between Yahwism and Canaanite religion), the biblical texts express God's personal relationship with the Israelite covenant community—and with all human beings—in a particular language that reflects the social and historical situation of the time.

5. The dating of events is one of the most difficult problems in the study of the Old Testament, for we are dealing with a long sweep of time before modern calendars existed. For the sake of consistency, I have adopted the chronology given in John Bright, *A History of Israel* [110]. To promote greater inclusiveness, I use B.C.E. (Before the Common Era) and C.E. (Common Era) instead of B.C. and A.D., the traditional Christian distinctions.

A project of this magnitude is possible only because of the creative work of many persons who have influenced me, directly or indirectly. Time would run out if I attempted to list all the people to whom I am indebted: my teachers, especially James Muilenburg; my colleagues in various colleges, universities, and theological schools; theologians with whom I have been in dialogue, including G. Ernest Wright, Will Herberg, and Abraham Joshua Heschel. I also want to express appreciation to many students, both at the undergraduate and graduate levels, whose feedback has contributed to my understanding of scripture.

As in the fourth edition, so also in this paperback version, I have been singularly fortunate in having the assistance of my colleague at Boston University School of Theology, Katheryn Pfisterer Darr. She has helped in the initial stage of abridgment, in updating footnotes, in reworking the selected bibliography, and above all in selecting and arranging illustrations. At numerous points she has enriched the discussion with perceptions that reflect the burgeoning field of women's studies.

My thanks also go to the publisher, Prentice Hall (Simon & Schuster) for the technical execution of this project and particularly to Ted Bolen, former Religion Editor in Humanities, who patiently persisted until this project was launched. Above all, I am grateful to my daughter, Carol Anderson Hanawalt, who has performed a major role in the production of the paperback version. Indelibly imprinted upon the book in its final form is her expert work of editing and abridgment that has been accomplished with keen sensitivity to the style and content of the original. Finally, I want to thank my granddaughter, Gwyneth Catlin, for her skilled copyediting while transcribing changes at the computer.

We now approach the year 2000 and the new horizons that lie beyond. How far the history of this book will extend into the future is undeterminable; it is my hope, however, that this abridged and updated paperback version will help the book to enjoy a future of continuing usefulness.

Bernhard W. Anderson

INTRODUCTION

THE STORY OF A PEOPLE

Memory is one of humanity's supreme endowments. Each of us acts today and hopes for tomorrow in the light of past experiences that have been woven into a life-story. When we want to know someone, we ask that person to tell us something about his or her life, for in this way personal identity is disclosed. To be a self is to have a personal history. This is what defines one's uniqueness.

In a larger sense this is true also of human communities, especially those in which people are bound together primarily by shared experiences rather than by natural factors like blood and soil. National self-consciousness finds expression in the remembrance of events people have lived through that have given them a sense of identity and destiny. If, for instance, a visitor from outer space were to ask why America is a *United* States rather than a mixed multitude, Americans would probably tell about the migration of the Pilgrims to the New World, the Revolutionary War, the Declaration of Independence and the first Congress, the Civil War, and more recent events that have thrust the nation into the arena of world politics. To be an American is to share a particular history, whose events are retold and relived from generation to generation. In like manner,

Biblical Readings: For a good introduction to Israel's life-story, read the recitations found in the book of Psalms (such as Ps. 78, 105, 106, 135, 136) and the psalm in Exodus 15:1–18.

peoples of all nations remember and celebrate events that contribute to their national identity.

THE SENSE OF TRADITION

The Jewish people are often characterized by their sense of tradition, a theme celebrated in the Tevye stories of Sholom Aleicheim and popularized in the musical, *Fiddler on the Roof.* In many respects, such as national origin, the Jews have always been a diverse people. But all Jews share a unique memory that reaches back through a long chain of tradition to the stirring events of the Hebrew Bible—events that formed them as a people with a sense of identity and vocation. Whenever the Passover is celebrated, the Torah is read in the synagogue, or parents instruct their children in the tradition, this shared identity is kept alive.

Christians, too, have a strong sense of tradition. The Christian church is diverse culturally, socially, and to a considerable extent theologically. But, like the Jews, Christians comprise a distinctive community with a memory that reaches back over the centuries to the story recounted in the Bible. To be sure, Christian tradition focuses on the historical career of Jesus of Nazareth—his life, death, and resurrection as told in the New Testament. These events, however, are viewed as the *climax* of the historical drama set forth in Jewish Scriptures or, in Christian terms, the Old Testament (Luke 24:13–27, 44–47). Christians express their faith in many ways, but all share in telling "the old, old story" to which the Old and New Testaments of the Christian Bible bear witness.[1]

Muslims also have ties to the Judeo-Christian tradition. Though Islamic faith centers on its founder and supreme prophet Mohammed (about 570–632 C.E.), Muslims trace their ancestry to Ishmael, son of Abraham and Hagar (Gen. 21:9–21). Significantly, each of the three great monotheistic religions—Judaism, Christianity, and Islam—claim Abraham as their common ancestor, and trace the beginning of their story to this ancestor's experience of God.

....

DEFINITION: "HEBREW BIBLE"

Strictly speaking, "Old Testament" is the Christian title of the first volume of a two-volume Bible consisting of Old and New Testaments. In scholarly circles, however, this title has been paralleled with or even superseded by the neutral designation "Hebrew Bible," which has the advantage of being descriptive of a body of ancient literature, without regard to particular religious claims whether Jewish, Christian, or Moslem.

[1]See H. Richard Niebuhr, *The Meaning of Revelation* [199], chap. 2.

The term "Hebrew Bible" is useful but not altogether adequate. For one thing, not all of the Hebrew Bible is written in Hebrew. Some texts (for example, part of the book of Daniel) are in Aramaic. In addition, there is some disparity between the number and order of books in the Old Testament and the Hebrew Bible. As can be seen from the Jewish Publication Society translation (JPSV), the Hebrew Bible excludes a number of writings (called "apocryphal" by Protestants and "deuterocanonical" by Catholics) often found in the Old Testament. The early Christian community read Jewish scripture in the Greek translation known as the *Septuagint*, which included these extra writings. Even when these writings are excluded or relegated to a separate section, as in many modern translations, the Old Testament follows the book order of the Septuagint (see pp. vi–vii).

In deference to long-established general practice, we continue to use "Old Testament" in this study, though also "Hebrew Bible" where appropriate.

THE HEBREW BIBLE AND THE OLD TESTAMENT

"Old Testament" is a widely used designation for the Hebrew Bible, the scriptures of ancient Israel. Keep in mind, however, that the distinction between "Old Testament" and "New Testament" is a Christian one, based on a passage from the prophet Jeremiah (Jer. 31:31–34). For the Jewish community, there is only one Testament or "Covenant," namely the Hebrew Bible. Today the Jewish people refer to their scriptures as *TANAKH*, an acronym made up of the initial consonants of the three major divisions of the Hebrew Bible: *Torah* ("Law"), *Nebi'im* ("Prophets"), and *Kethubim* ("Writings").

In the accompanying chart, you can see that the Hebrew Bible is fundamentally the same as the Christian Old Testament, although the arrangement differs. To understand the Hebrew Bible, imagine three concentric circles. The inner circle, the Torah, presents the basic story of the people and includes laws to guide them in living. The next circle, the Prophets, is a critical commentary on the life of the people to whom the Torah is given. The outer circle, the Writings, is a diverse and open-ended collection that broadens out from Israel's worship and festal celebration to wisdom reflection.

Notice that the Christian Bible, after the first five books (Torah), displays a different order and, in some cases, additional content. These differences are partly accounted for by the fact that the early Christians were a Greek-speaking community who read the Hebrew Bible in Greek, particularly in a translation begun in the third century B.C.E. in Alexandria, Egypt, called the *Septuagint*. As the chart shows, the Septuagint places the prophetic writings last (Haggai, Zechariah, Malachi); while the Hebrew Bible concludes with the Writings (ending with 1–2 Chronicles). Moreover, this translation includes a number of works that are not part of the Hebrew Bible, though these works once enjoyed considerable favor in Jewish circles.

The use of the Septuagint in Christian worship has led to some disagreement over the number of books in the Christian Old Testament. The translators of the Septuagint

The Books of the Old Testament

		Christian Bible		
	Hebrew Bible	Protestant		Roman Catholic[a] and Orthodox[b]
Torah	1. Bereshith ("In the beginning")[c]	1. Genesis		1. Genesis
	2. Shemoth ("Names")	2. Exodus		2. Exodus
	3. Wayiqra ("And he called")	3. Leviticus	Pentateuch	3. Leviticus
	4. Bemidbar ("In the wilderness")	4. Numbers		4. Numbers
	5. Debarim ("Words")	5. Deuteronomy		5. Deuteronomy
Nebi'im (Prophets) Former	6. Yehoshua	6. Joshua		6. Joshua
	7. Shofetim ("Judges")	7. Judges	Historical	7. Judges
	8. Shemuel	8. Ruth	Books	8. Ruth
	9. Melakim ("Kings")	9–10. I and II Samuel		9–10. I and II Samuel
		11–12. I and II Kings		11–12. I and II Kings
		13–14. I and II Chronicles		13–14. I and II Chronicles
		15–16. Ezra and Nehemiah		15–16. Ezra and Nehemiah
		Apocryphal		17. *Tobit*
		Apocryphal		18. *Judith*
		17. Esther		19. Esther[d]
Latter	10. Yeshayahu	18. Job		20. Job
	11. Yirmeyahu	19. Psalms		21. Psalms
	12. Yehezqel	20. Proverbs	Poetry	22. Proverbs
	13. Tere Asar ("Twelve")		and Wisdom	
	Hoshea	21. Ecclesiastes		23. Ecclesiastes
	Yoel	22. Song of Solomon		24. Song of Solomon
	Amos			
	Obadyahu	Apocryphal		25. *Wisdom of Solomon*
	Yonah			
	Micah	Apocryphal		26. *Ecclesiasticus* (Wisdom of Ben Sirach)
	Nahum			
	Habaqquq			
	Zephanyah			
	Haggai			
	Zekaryahu			
	Malaki			
Kethubim (Writings)	14. Tehillim ("Praises")	23. Isaiah		27. Isaiah
	15. Iyyob	24. Jeremiah		28. Jeremiah

The Books of the Old Testament (*cont.*)

	Hebrew Bible	Protestant	Christian Bible	Roman Catholic[a] and Orthodox[b]
			Prophetic Writings	
Festal Scrolls	16. Mishle ("Proverbs of")	25. Lamentations Apocryphal		29. Lamentations 30. *Baruch* including "The Letter of Jeremiah" (R.C. only)[c]
	17. Ruth 18. Shir Hashirim ("Song of Songs")			
	19. Qoheleth ("Teacher")	26. Ezekiel		31. Ezekiel
	20. Ekah ("How") (Lamentations)	27. Daniel		32. Daniel[d]
	21. Ester	28. Hosea		33. Hosea
		29. Joel		34. Joel
		30. Amos		35. Amos
	22. Daniel	31. Obadiah		36. Obadiah
	23. Ezra-Nehemyah	32. Jonah		37. Jonah
	24. Dibre Hayamim ("Chronicles")[e]	33. Micah		38. Micah
		34. Nahum		39. Nahum
		35. Habakkuk		40. Habakkuk
		36. Zephaniah		41. Zephaniah
		37. Haggai		42. Haggai
		38. Zechariah		43. Zechariah
		39. Malachi		44. Malachi
		Apocryphal		45. *I Maccabees*
		Apocryphal		46. *II Maccabees*

[a]In this column deuterocanonical books are italicized. The spelling is that of the Common Bible rather than the Douay-Rheims Bible (1609/10) which was based on the Vulgate.

[b]Note that item 30 was not included in the Old Testament canon established for Orthodox churches at the Synod of Jerusalem in 1672 C.E.

[c]In the Hebrew Bible books are often titled by opening or key words.

[d]Two books of the Roman Catholic canon, Esther and Daniel, are larger than their counterparts in the Protestant and Jewish canons. This surplus material is included in the Protestant Apocrypha as Additions to Esther and Additions to Daniel (The Story of Susanna, The Song of the Three Children, and The Story of Bel and the Dragon). The Prayer of Manasseh, also found in the Apocrypha, is not included in the Roman Catholic canon.

[e]The number twenty-four is reached by counting as one book each of the following: I and II Samuel, I and II Kings, I and II Chronicles, the Twelve (minor prophets), and Ezra-Nehemiah.

added extra books that helped fill the gap between the restoration of the Jewish community under Ezra and Nehemiah (fifth century B.C.E.) and later rabbinical and Christian periods. Ever since the Reformation, however, Protestants have restricted the Old Testament canon to the number of books in the Hebrew Bible. The extra books in the Septuagint have been relegated to a separate section of the Bible called the "Apocrypha" (meaning hidden or secret writings), with an explanatory note that they deserve to be read but are not equal to the rest of the Scriptures. The Roman Catholic Church eventually gave most of these books official canonical recognition, but only after a long period of uncertainty.[2] As a result the Roman Catholic canon, when compared with the Protestant (and Jewish) canon, is seven books longer. Eastern Orthodox churches also recognize almost all of the extra books.

One should not overestimate these differences, however. Despite the problem of fixing the outer boundary of the Old Testament, it is clear that Jews, Protestants, and Catholics share substantially the same body of sacred literature.[3]

This sacred library is in many respects very diverse. The Greek words *ta biblia,* "the books," from which our word "Bible" comes, suggest the diversity of the literature. But the Hebrew Bible, or Old Testament, is not a mere collection of books under one cover. The various writings bear witness to the unique historical experiences of a particular people, "Israel," from their beginning shortly after 2000 B.C.E. to the period of the Maccabean Revolution about a century and a half before the "Common" (or "Christian") Era. The Hebrew Bible is the life-story of Israel, "the people of God." Jews and Christians might differ in their understanding of the outcome of this historical drama, but they agree on the unique character of the history with which the Bible deals.

DEFINITION: "ISRAEL,"   "COMMON ERA"

The term "Israel" is important to our study, and deserves some thought. Today this term refers to a modern state in the Middle East. In the context of the Old Testament, however, "Israel" cannot be reduced to nationhood. This term—once applied to a covenant people before they made the transition to a monarchic state—is more inclusive and, in the last analysis, transcends political, cultural, and racial categories. The apostle Paul spoke of the Christian community as being essentially related to and indeed part of Israel, the people of God (Gal. 3:7, 9, 14, 29; see especially Rom. 9:11).

Since the term "Israel" transcends politics and even ethnic divisions, it is appropriate in our study of the Old Testament to shift from the traditional calendar terminology, B.C. ("Before Christ") and A.D. ("In the Year of the Lord") to the inclusive B.C.E. ("Before the Common Era") and C.E. ("Common Era").

Today we take for granted a calendar that has, in fact, a long and complicated history. Julius Caesar introduced a "Julian" calendar, based on 365 days in the year with a leap year of 366 days every fourth year. This calendar marked time *anno urbis conditae,* "from the foundation of the city [of Rome]." In the year 525 C.E. a learned monk, Dionysius Exiguus, proposed a different chronology that set the year 1 at the presumed date

[2] In Catholic usage *protocanonical* refers to the books whose place in the canon was never challenged, and *deuterocanonical* refers to those recognized only after a period of hesitation and debate. The criterion of canonicity used by the Council of Trent (1545–63 C.E.) was that of long use in the church, as evidenced by the presence of the books in the Latin Vulgate. See *The New Jerome Biblical Commentary* [15], pp. 1035–43, 1051–54.

[3] See Daniel J. Harrington, S.J., "Introduction to the Canon" in *The New Interpreter's Bible*, I (Nashville: Abingdon Press, 1994), pp. 7–21.

of the birth of Jesus. Different methods of calendar reckoning continued to be used throughout the Middle Ages, and it was several centuries before a standard calendar was adopted.

THE STORY OF THE BIBLE

Leaving aside the prologue to this historical drama (Gen. 1–11), the biblical history—reduced to its barest skeleton—can be summarized as follows:

GENESIS 12–50 Shortly after the turn of the second millennium B.C.E., Israel's ancestor, Abraham, migrated from Mesopotamia into the land of Canaan, otherwise known as Palestine. The "patriarchs," or ancestors of Israel, moved about in the hill country of Canaan, with Abraham, Isaac, and Jacob succeeding one another. Eventually, during a time of famine, Jacob's family migrated to Egypt.

EXODUS–DEUTERONOMY After enjoying initial favor in Egypt, the descendants of Jacob were subjected to forced labor by Pharaoh. Under the leadership of Moses (about 1300 B.C.E.), and favored by an extraordinary series of events, they escaped into the desert of the Sinaitic Peninsula, where they became a community with a single religious allegiance. Unable to enter Canaan from the south, they spent a long time (forty years) in the wilderness and eventually made a roundabout journey through Transjordan.

JOSHUA, JUDGES Under the leadership of Joshua, the Israelites crossed the Jordan from their base in Transjordan, carried out a swift military conquest, and claimed the land as their own. During this time (the "Period of the Judges"), they waged ceaseless wars of defense to maintain their hold on the "promised land."

1–2 SAMUEL, 1–2 KINGS (1–2 CHRONICLES) In time, enemy pressure became so intense that a monarchy was established. Under the great kings David and Solomon (1000–922 B.C.E.), Canaan became an Israelite empire that took its place proudly among the nations. At Solomon's death, the United Kingdom split into two kingdoms of the North (Ephraim) and South (Judah). These kingdoms, by virtue of their strategic location in a buffer zone between Mesopotamia and Egypt, were drawn into the Near Eastern power struggle. The Northern Kingdom fell under Assyrian aggression (721 B.C.E.). The Southern Kingdom, after more than a century of vassalage to Assyria, fell victim to the Babylonians when they wrested control from Assyria. Jerusalem fell to the Babylonians in 587 B.C.E., and many people were carried into captivity.

EZRA, NEHEMIAH Under the benevolent rule of the subsequent Persian empire, the exiled Israelites were permitted to return to their homeland, where they rebuilt Jerusalem and the temple and resumed their way of life. The restoration took place chiefly under the leadership of Ezra and Nehemiah (about 450–400 B.C.E.).

1, 2 MACCABEES After more than two centuries of Persian rule, Palestine came within the orbit of Greek control under Alexander the Great (332 B.C.E.). Alexander's policy of imposing Hellenistic cultural uniformity was continued by those who inherited his divided empire, especially by the Seleucid rulers of Syria. When one Seleucid king forced this policy on the Jewish community, open revolution broke out under the leadership of the house of the Maccabees (168 B.C.E.). The Hebrew Bible breaks off suddenly at this point (the book of Daniel), though the story continues in the apocryphal, or deuterocanonical, book of 1 Maccabees. The revolt led to a period of Jewish independence, ultimately eclipsed by the next world empire—that of Rome. Subsequent events described in the Christian New Testament all take place in the vast arena of the Roman empire.

From a secular viewpoint, this history is no more unusual than the courageous stories of other small nations caught in the whirlpool of world politics. In this sense, Israel's history is a minor sideshow in the larger history of the ancient Near East, its culture overshadowed by the more brilliant cultures of antiquity. *But the Old Testament does not purport to be simply a book of secular history or culture.* It is *sacred* history to both Jews and Christians, because in these historical experiences, as interpreted by faith, the ultimate meaning of human life is disclosed. From Israel's standpoint, this history is not an ordinary story of wars, population movement, and cultural advance or decline. Rather, Israelite interpreters perceived in these historical events a unique disclosure of God's activity, the working out of God's purpose in the career of Israel. This faith transfigures Israel's history and gives the Bible its peculiar claim as sacred scripture.

For this reason, we cannot begin to understand the Old Testament if we regard it merely as great literature, interesting history, or the development of lofty ideas. The Old Testament presents the story of God's participation in the history of a particular people. To be sure, all human history is the sphere of God's sovereignty. But God became particularly involved in the career of a comparatively obscure people, thereby initiating a historical drama that has changed human perspectives and altered the course of human affairs.

The Scroll of the Prophet Isaiah was found in Cave I at Qumran in 1947. In the left-hand column, to the left of the black blot, the text (reading right to left) says: "A voice cries: 'In the wilderness prepare the way of the Lord'" (Is. 40:3; cf. Mark 1:3). From such a scroll Jesus read in the Nazareth synagogue (Luke 4:16–30). Notice the scribal corrections of the text, the sewing together of the parchment sheets, and the soiled outer side of the scroll caused by handling. Until the discovery of this scroll, our oldest known manuscript of the Hebrew Bible of any extent was no earlier than the ninth century C.E. The Qumran scroll dates from the second century B.C.E.

THE CRUCIAL EVENT

When we seek to understand the meaning of our individual life stories, we do not actually begin with birth or infancy, even though a written autobiography might start there. Rather, we view or re-view our early childhood in the light of later experiences that are impressed deeply in memory. Analogously, Israel's life-story did not begin with the time of Abraham or even the Creation, although the Old Testament in its present form starts there. Rather, Israel's history had its true beginning in a crucial historical experience that created a self-conscious historical community—an event so decisive that earlier happenings and subsequent experiences were seen in its light.

This decisive event—the great watershed of Israel's history—was the Exodus from Egypt. Even today the Jewish people understand their vocation and destiny in the light of this revealing event. Jews recall and make contemporary the Exodus as they celebrate the Passover. This act of worship is not just a form of archaism—a retreat from the present into the unrecoverable once-upon-a-time. Rather, believing Jews see themselves as participants in that experience. The event of the past enters into the present with deep meaning.

Down through the ages, the story of the deliverance of slaves from the yoke of Pharaoh, and their march through the wilderness toward a promised land, has had powerful appeal to the religious imagination of many oppressed groups.[4] The habit of regarding the Exodus as a paradigm—"a mould in which other stories of rescue from ruin may be cast"—goes back to the Hebrew Bible itself, where the Exodus story forms the basic "pattern of deliverance" to which all other liberation motifs are accommodated.[5] The Exodus was regarded as the clue to who God is and how God acts to deliver the downtrodden and oppressed. More than that, it provided the model for how the people of God should seek justice in society as the only appropriate response to the liberation they had experienced (Mic. 6:1–8).

This note is struck again and again in the literature from the period before the fall of the Israelite nation in 587 B.C.E., the so-called "pre-exilic" period. Notice that the prophets of this period do not even mention the migration of Abraham, as related in Genesis 12. Instead, they trace the historical beginning of the Israelite people to the Exodus, when God acted on their behalf and laid upon them lasting obligations to God and fellow human beings. In the eighth century, Amos reminded his hearers that Israel was bound together as a "whole family" by God's act of deliverance from Egypt (Amos 3:1–2), and he rebuked the people for forgetting the great events in which their God became known to them (Amos 2:9–11). Hosea, his contemporary, traced Israel's "call" to that same event:

> When Israel was a child, I loved him,
> and out of Egypt I called my son.
>
> —HOSEA 11:1 (NRSV)

According to Hosea, Israel's knowledge of God is based on the Exodus event:

> Yet I have been the Lord your God
> ever since the land of Egypt;
> you know no God but me,
> and besides me there is no savior.
>
> —HOSEA 13:4 (NRSV)

---

[4]See James Hutchison Smylie, "On Jesus, Pharaohs, and the Chosen People: Martin Luther King as Biblical Interpreter and Humanist," *Interpretation*, 24 (1970), 74–91. Among Latin American liberation theologians, see J. S. Croatto, *Exodus: A Hermeneutics of Freedom* [240]. In *Exodus and Revolution* (New York: Basic Books, 1984), Michael Walzer treats the Exodus as an ancient story of revolution that is "continuously reinvented."

[5]David Daube, *The Exodus Pattern in the Bible* (London: Faber and Faber, 1963), p. 11.

The prophet Ezekiel put the matter emphatically:

> Thus said the Lord God:
> On the day that I chose Israel, I gave My oath to the stock of the
> House of Jacob; when I made Myself known to them in the land of Egypt, I
> gave my oath to them. When I said, "I the Lord am your God," that same
> day I swore to take them out of the land of Egypt into a land flowing with
> milk and honey, a land which I had sought out for them, the fairest of all
> lands.
>
> —EZEKIEL 20:5–6 (JPSV)

And in many psalms, composed for use in worship, the liberation from Egyptian bondage provides the motive for service of God and the basis for future welfare.

> Hear My people, and I will admonish you;
> Israel, if you would but listen to Me!
> You shall have no foreign god,
> you shall not bow to an alien god.
> I the Lord am your God
> who brought you out of the land of Egypt;
> open your mouth wide and I will fill it.
>
> —PSALM 81:9–11 (JPSV; NRSV
> 81:8–10)

Other passages in the literature of the prophets and the psalms stress the pivotal significance of the Exodus.[6] The theme still reverberates in literature composed late in the Old Testament period, such as Daniel 9:15 and the Wisdom of Solomon 15:18–19:22.

THE HEART OF THE PENTATEUCH

The same accent is found, though not so obviously, in the section of the Hebrew Bible regarded as most authoritative by Jewish tradition: the books of Genesis, Exodus, Leviticus, Numbers, and Deuteronomy. The Hebrew word for these five books is *Torah,* often translated as "Law" but better rendered as "Teaching"—that is, the divine guidance or direction that God gives the people in their historical pilgrimage. Scholars refer to these books as the Pentateuch, a word based on the Greek *he pentateuchos biblos,* "the book of the five scrolls." Scholars also refer to the first six books of the Old Testament (the Pentateuch, plus the book of Joshua) as a unit called the Hexateuch.

As it now stands, the Pentateuch begins with an extended prologue to the Exodus story: the account of primeval beginnings (Gen. 1–11) and the stories of the Israelite

---

[6]See Amos 9:7; Hosea 2:14–15; 12:13; 13:4; Micah 6:4; Jeremiah 2:2–7; 31:32; Psalms 66:6; 78:18–53; 136:10–11.

retrospective

ancestors (Gen. 12–50). Actually, when we begin with Genesis and read to the book of Exodus, we are reading the story backward, as it were, for the period before Moses was remembered and interpreted in the light of the Exodus event that created the people Israel, just as Americans view Columbus's voyage and the landing of the Pilgrims in the light of the decisive historical event of the Revolutionary War. In a later time of theological reflection, Israel could trace its history back beyond the Exodus to the first Hebrew, Abraham, and could portray its "call" (election) in the story of Abraham's migration into the Land of Promise (Gen. 11:31–12:9). But actually the call of Israel was based on the Exodus, the "root experience" enshrined in the memory of the people.[7] One must regard the book of Genesis as a prologue to the moment when the curtain rises on the scene of Hebrew oppression in Egypt at the beginning of the book of Exodus.

Even in the earliest period, long before Israel's history was composed as a written epic, Israelites celebrated the Exodus story in poetry and song. An excellent example is the ancient poem found in Exodus 15:1–18, the "Song of the Sea." In this poem, which displays the influence of Canaanite style and mythology,[8] the poet extols "the glorious deeds" of the God of Israel, who liberated a fugitive people from Pharaoh's army and guided them into the land of Canaan. Here we find Israel's primary confession, later elaborated in epic narrative and poetry (see Pss. 77; 114).

The centrality of the Exodus in Israelite epic tradition is evident in a liturgy found in the book of Deuteronomy, which received its present form after the fall of Jerusalem in 587 B.C.E. The liturgy is couched in relatively late "Deuteronomic" style, yet the content, in the judgment of some scholars, might be much older. The passage is a confession of faith to be made when presenting the first fruits of the harvest at the sanctuary:

> My ancestor was a wandering Aramean who descended to Egypt. There he
> sojourned with a small band and there he grew to be a great, powerful, and
> populous nation. But the Egyptians maltreated us, humiliated us, and
> imposed upon us heavy servitude. Then we cried to Yahweh, the God of
> our ancestors; and Yahweh heard our cry and saw our affliction, our trouble
> and our oppression. Yahweh caused us to go out of Egypt with a strong
> hand and an outstretched arm, with great terror, with signs and wonders,
> and brought us to this place and gave us this land, a land flowing with milk
> and honey.
>
> —DEUTERONOMY 26:5–9;
> see also 6:20–23

---

[7]On Israel's "root experiences" (Exodus and Sinai), see Emil Fackenheim, *God's Presence* [241].
[8]See Frank M. Cross, "The Song of the Sea and Canaanite Myth," *Canaanite Myth and Hebrew Epic* [129], pp. 112–44; also Patrick D. Miller, Jr., *The Divine Warrior in Early Israel* [245].

This "historical credo" is not a private prayer but a confession of faith made in a setting of worship.[9] The worshiper identifies with the story that the community tells, as evidenced by the use of plural pronouns: "The Egyptians maltreated *us* . . . *we* cried to Yahweh . . . and Yahweh heard *our* cry." Notice that only brief reference is made to the ancestral period (the patriarch Jacob is called "a wandering Aramean"). The confession dwells primarily on liberating events at the time of the Exodus and concludes with a grateful acknowledgment that the God who delivered a people from bondage also led them into "a land flowing with milk and honey." One might say that the entire Hebrew Bible is a symphonic exposition of the major themes enunciated at the beginning, when Israel entered upon the historical stage as a people.

Blaise Pascal, a French philosopher of the seventeenth century, once observed that the God of the Bible is "the God of Abraham, Isaac, and Jacob," not the God of philosophers and sages. This is true in the sense that biblical faith is fundamentally historical in character. It is concerned with events, social relationships, and concrete situations, not abstract values and ideas existing in a timeless realm. The God of Israel is known in history—a particular history—through socially conditioned relations with Sarah, Abraham, and Hagar; Isaac and Rebecca; and Leah, Jacob, and Rachel. Trying to reason away the essential historical content of biblical faith, says one Jewish interpreter, is like paraphrasing poetry: "Something called an 'idea content' remains, but everything that gave power and significance to the original is gone."[10]

We must realize, then, that Israelites understood the history of God's dealings with their ancestors in the light of the crucial, revealing event of the Exodus. As a psalmist testified:

> Yahweh achieves righteousness,
> > and justice for all who are oppressed.
> To Moses Yahweh made known his ways,
> > his deeds to the Israelite people.
>
> —PSALM 103:6–7

Throughout the generations Israel praised God as the Holy One who brought a band of slaves out of Egypt, formed them into a people, and gave them a future (Exod. 20:1). The Exodus is the central moment in Israel's history, its true beginning, the time of its creation as a people. Here began the purposive movement of events that later made it possible to see all history and nature embraced within the divine design. So deeply was

---

[9]This was the view of Gerhard von Rad, who maintained that examples of "the short historical credo" (Deut. 6:20–25; 26:5–10; Josh. 24:2–13) form the thematic nucleus from which the epic tradition evolved. See his study, "The Form-Critical Problem of the Hexateuch" [191], pp. 1–27 (summarized in the introduction to his commentary on Genesis [305], pp. 13–24). Some scholars have questioned the antiquity of this creedal statement; e.g., J. P. Hyatt, "Were There an Ancient Historical Credo in Israel and an Independent Sinai Tradition?" in *Translating and Understanding the Old Testament* [181], pp. 152–70.

[10]Will Herberg, "Biblical Faith as Heilsgeschichte: The Meaning of Redemptive History in Human Existence," in *Faith Enacted as History* [198], pp. 32–42.

the Exodus etched on Israel's memory that the maturing faith of the people was essentially a reliving and reinterpretation of this historic event.

A LOOK AHEAD

Our exploration of the Old Testament begins, appropriately, with the Exodus. It will be helpful, however, to view this event in the context of ancient Near Eastern history and culture during the second millennium B.C.E., and to consider events of the ancestral period which, at least in retrospect, the Israelite people regarded as preparatory to the Mosaic period. The next chapter, therefore, considers the prologue to the Exodus: the story of Israel's descent into Egypt and oppression under the Pharaohs. Successive chapters will take up the deliverance from Egypt and making of the covenant, the conquest of Canaan, the rise of the monarchy, and the nation's involvement in the vortex of world struggle. In other words, the outline of our book is based on Israel's historical career. No other approach does justice to the historical character of Israel's faith.

This approach demands that we keep several things constantly in mind. First is the importance of literary criticism, for important episodes in biblical history have been handed down through different narrative traditions, reworked by editors at a much later time. Second, we must consider Israel's relation to the political, sociological, and cultural situation in the ancient world. This requires looking beyond the biblical text to other historical sources and to the important contributions of archaeology and the social sciences. Third, we must never lose sight of our central task: the exposition of Israel's faith. Many books on the Old Testament treat these three elements—literary development, historical study, and theology—separately. We will attempt to weave them together in fugue-like fashion as the story of God's dealings with Israel unfolds chapter by chapter.

Our attention will focus on the community of Israel, known as "the people of God." Individualism, in the modern sense of the word, has no place in the mainstream of Israel's faith. To study isolated personalities like Moses or to deal with abstracts like "the idea of God" is to miss the point of the Old Testament. Personalities and ideas must be considered in relation to the corporate experiences of Israel in the drama of its history.

Our task, then, is to understand the biblical message in its dynamic context of culture, politics, and geography. We will enter into the concrete life situations out of which the various writings have come, and try to understand what the writers were saying to their times. To help you become familiar with the biblical setting, pictures and maps are provided, along with chronological charts showing how Israel's sacred history was tied to international affairs of the ancient Near East.

One final word: If we are to enter sympathetically and imaginatively into the Israelite community and relive its sacred history, there is no substitute for reading the Bible itself. The purpose of this study is to aid in understanding the Bible—not to urge mastery of another book about the Bible. The literal meaning of "understand" is "stand under." By reading the selected Bible passages listed at the beginning of each chapter, you will "stand under the Bible," and the light it sheds on the meaning of human life can fall directly on you.

Note: Unless you can read the Old Testament in the original Hebrew, it is advisable to consult more than one English translation, preferably selected from the following:

> The New Revised Standard Version (NRSV)[*]
> The Revised English Bible (REB)
> The New Jerusalem Bible (NJB)
> TANAKH[**]: Translation of the Jewish Publication Society (JPSV)
> The New American Bible (NAB)
> The New International Version (NIV)

[*]Scripture quotations marked NRSV are from *The New Revised Standard Version of the Bible*. Copyright 1989 by the Division of Christian Education of the National Conference of the Churches of Christ in the U.S.A. Used by permission. All rights reserved.
[**]TANAKH is an acronym based on the initial letters of the three parts of the Hebrew Bible: *Torah* (Teaching), *Nebi'im* (Prophets), and *Kethubim* (Writings).

PART I

If you will obey my voice and keep my covenant, you shall be my own possession among all peoples; for all the earth is mine.
—Exodus 19:5

THE CREATION OF A PEOPLE

CHAPTER 1

THE BEGINNINGS
OF ISRAEL

A stirring historical drama unfolds in the book of Exodus. The protagonist is Yahweh, the God of Israel, who intervenes on behalf of a helpless band of slaves. The plot, developed through a succession of suspense-filled episodes, is God's contest against Pharaoh, the mightiest emperor of the day. The denouement comes when, only moments from capture, Israel's pursuers are swallowed up by the waters of the Red Sea. The leading theme of the drama is the action and triumph of Israel's God.

Viewing the Exodus story as a historical "drama" rather than as a colorless, factual report will help us to enter more imaginatively and sympathetically into its spirit. Drama emphasizes involvement: It purports to tell *our* story. In this way the Israelites retold and relived the Exodus story down through the generations. Some think that Exodus 1–15 reflects an old Passover narrative recited annually in connection with the feast that celebrates Israel's deliverance from Egypt.[1] We need not think, however, that the story was invented as a "cult legend" to explain the feast. In all probability, the narrative is based upon real historical experiences. But because the story was remembered

Biblical Readings: In this and the following two chapters, attention will focus on the stories of the Exodus and Sinai Covenant, found in Exodus 1–24 and 32–34. At this point you should become familiar with the prologue to these events as related in Genesis 12–50.

[1]This is the view of Johannes Pedersen, *Israel* [136], III–IV, pp. 384–415, 728–37, accepted with considerable modification by Martin Noth, *Pentateuchal Traditions* [76], pp. 65–71.

and retold in the cult (worshiping) community, it is written in the confessional language of worship, not in dispassionate prose. Its purpose is to communicate the meaning of the story or history that the worshiping community shares and celebrates.

DEFINITION: "STORY"   AND   "HISTORY"

There is a fine line between "story" and "history." In some modern languages one word covers both, as in the German *Geschichte* or French *histoire*. Check the dictionary for the ancestry of the English word "story" and its relation to "history."[2]

If "history" means a detached report of events, the biblical story is not history. If "story" means a tale spun out of the imagination, the biblical history is not story. We are dealing with a history-like story, or a story-like history, and there is no razor sharp enough to separate these dimensions of the biblical narrative. Keep this in mind throughout our study, especially in the chapters that deal with the origin of Israel.[3]

THE NATURE OF THE TRADITION

To begin our study of the Old Testament, or Hebrew Bible, it is appropriate to let the text make its own first impression. Read the biblical story as a whole, including the prologue (Gen. 12–50) and main body (Exod. 1–15). The so-called "first naiveté" of this initial encounter allows us to reread the text later, after critical study and reflection, with "second naiveté" or postcritical understanding.[4] Just as the analysis of a Beethoven symphony can lead to deeper musical enjoyment of the performed work, so critical study of the Bible can lead to rereading and rehearing the biblical narrative with enhanced appreciation.

When, after this initial encounter, we turn to the parts and details of the biblical story, various literary problems become evident. These include repetitions, stylistic peculiarities, and inconsistencies in the biblical text that are difficult to account for if one assumes a single, human author. Moses has been regarded as the traditional author of the Pentateuch, which is sometimes called the "Five Books of Moses." But as early as the twelfth century C.E., the medieval Jewish scholar Ibn Ezra brooded over certain passages that seemed to imply a later date. This rabbi suspected that the statement in Genesis 12:6—"At that time the Canaanites were in the land"—implied a time after Moses when the Israelites were actually in the land and the native Canaanites had ceased to be

----

[2]On the ambiguity of the words "history" and "historical," see Will Herberg, "Five Meanings of the Word 'Historical,'" in *Faith Enacted as History* [198], pp. 132–37.

[3]See further James Barr, *Story and History in Biblical Theology* [201].

[4]The critical rereading of Scripture is discussed in B. W. Anderson, "Tradition and Scripture in the Community of Faith," *Journal of Biblical Literature* 100 (1981), 5–21 (especially p. 16).

a separate people. Earlier rabbis, writing in the Talmud, questioned whether Moses really wrote the account of his own death and burial (Deut. 34:5–12), suggesting that perhaps Moses' epitaph was written by Joshua, his successor.

The clearest evidence of diversity is the occurrence of the same material in different versions. We find an example of this right at the beginning of the Bible, where the opening account of creation (Gen. 1:1–2:3) is paralleled by another creation story, written in a different literary style and with a different sequence of events (Gen. 2:4b–25). In the Abraham cycle (Gen. 12–25) there are two accounts of God's covenant with Abra(ha)m[5] (Gen. 15, 17), and on two different occasions (Gen. 12:10–17, 20:1–18) the patriarch tells a "white lie" that almost gets his wife, Sarah, into trouble with a foreign king. It is hard to believe that Abraham learned nothing from the first experience; moreover, the same story is told about Abraham's son, Isaac (26:6–11). Turning to the Exodus story, we find two names for one sacred mountain (Sinai, Horeb) and two versions of the Ten Commandments (Exod. 20 and Deut. 5). In addition, there are two versions of the call of Moses and the appointment of Aaron, one taking place in the land of Midian (Exod. 3:1–4:17) and the other in Egypt (Exod. 6:2–7:7). The first account vividly depicts Moses' encounter with God in the wilderness and their question-and-answer dialogue. The second account, in a different literary style and with a different theological perspective, gives more emphasis to Aaron's role in the story (compare Exod. 4:14–17 and 7:1–6). As we will see, these two versions also differ on when the cultic name, Yahweh, was introduced.

How can we account for these—and other—irregularities, discrepancies, and repetitions? Before proposing a possible answer to this question, we will look at three major types of material in the Pentateuch.

First, one need only glance through the book of Deuteronomy to find many exhortations by Moses in an impassioned "sermonic" style. Deuteronomy 30:15–20 is a good example. Long, verbose sentences, characteristic words and phrases, and urgent appeals to be faithful to the covenant with Yahweh characterize this "Deuteronomic" (D) style, not found to any extent elsewhere in the Pentateuch.

Second, a scan of the remaining four books of the Pentateuch reveals large sections dominated by priestly interests such as genealogies, institutions (Sabbath, circumcision, sacrifice), and other cultic matters. Material of this sort is concentrated in the last part of Exodus (Exod. 25–40, minus chapters 32–34), the book of Leviticus, and much of the book of Numbers. But we find it also in the book of Genesis (for instance, the creation story in Gen. 1:1–2:3) and in the second account of God's covenant with Abraham (Gen. 17). Indeed, Priestly (P) material provides the framework for the final form of the Pentateuch—or more exactly the Tetrateuch (first four books), since

---

[5]The name *Abraham* is a dialectical variant of *Abram*, the more original form. See Gen. 17:1–8 for a harmonizing explanation of the two names in the tradition.

⚔ The Source Hypothesis

			Oral Period c. 1200–1000 B.C.E.
Old Epic	J	A Judean source, presumably written during the United Monarchy, which prefers to use the divine name Yahweh (sometimes spelled Jahweh).	c. 950
	E	An Ephraimitic or North Israelite source which favors the use of the divine name Elohim ("God").	c. 850
Deuteronomic Tradition	D	A tradition, best represented in the book of Deuteronomy, which reflects the literary style and theology prevalent at the time of Josiah's reform (621 B.C.E.).	c. 650 and later
Priestly Work	P	A literary corpus, marked by the style and cultic interests of the priestly circle of Jerusalem, which became prominent in the period after the fall of Jerusalem in 587 B.C.E.	c. 550 and later

Deuteronomy seems to stand by itself. A finely wrought literary style, special vocabulary of words and phrases, and distinctive theological point of view mark the Priestly work. Compare, for example, the Priestly style of the account of Moses' call in Exodus 6:2–7:7 with the earlier account in Exodus 3:1–4:17.

After we take away Deuteronomy and the Priestly sections, there is still a third type of material to be accounted for. What is left appears to be the remains of an Old Epic narrative, presented in a lively storytelling style with considerable human interest. You can get a feeling for this epic tradition by reading the paradise story (Gen. 2:4b–3:24), the story of the testing of Abraham (Gen. 22:1–19), or the story of Moses at the burning bush (Exod. 3:1–4:17).

Based on the critical labors of more than two centuries of intensive study, the dominant theory held by Jewish, Protestant, and Catholic scholars is that the Pentateuch is a composite work, one in which various literary strands have been artistically combined during the course of transmission through the generations. According to this hypothesis, several traditions coexisted in ancient Israelite society and were eventually blended to form the Pentateuch, the five scrolls of the Torah. We have already identified these traditions in a preliminary way: the "Deuteronomic," "Priestly," and "Old Epic" traditions.

The widely accepted *source hypothesis* further differentiates the Old Epic tradition into two parallel strands that reflect the division of Israel after King Solomon's time into Northern (Ephraimitic) and Southern (Judean) regions. This view maintains that the literary traditions reflect historical stages in the development of the Pentateuch. Strands of tradition were interwoven at each stage until the Pentateuch reached its present and final form about 400 B.C.E., the time when, under the leadership of Ezra, the Torah became the constitutional basis of the restored community of Israel.[6]

Keep in mind that this kind of source analysis is hypothetical, and is being tested continually through scholarly study and debate. A vulnerable point is the Old Epic tradition, specifically the division of the narrative into Yahwistic [J] and Elohistic [E] strands, and the dating of each. Some scholars maintain that the hypothesis, stated this way, puts too much emphasis on "documents" or "sources" and fails to do justice to the dynamic oral tradition that preceded, and later accompanied, writing.[7] Others question the need to divide the Old Epic tradition into separate strands, suggesting instead that a single tradition was enriched or supplemented in the course of transmission. In the face of differing scholarly opinions, the proper response is not to throw up one's hands in despair. Rather, we should realize that the Torah (Pentateuch) is a very subtle and complex body of literature that challenges the exercise of all the "heart, soul, and strength" (Deut. 6:5) if one is to enter into its meaning.[8]

We will not go further into this type of biblical criticism here. It is enough to say that source analysis, in its own way, emphasizes the enduring importance of the Exodus story in the life of the Israelite community. The various inconsistencies, repetitions, and stylistic differences reflect ways in which the story was retold, reworked, and reinterpreted in different historical periods and life situations. This literary "mosaic" preserves the fundamental tone of the Mosaic tradition, and resounds with the overtones of meaning experienced by the community throughout the generations.

THE ORAL TRADITION

Even if we assume that the Pentateuch is composed of several literary traditions, this kind of analysis is only a provisional starting point for understanding the dynamic of the Torah tradition. Behind the earliest *written* stages of the Exodus story (possibly dating from the period of the Israelite monarchy) was probably a long period of *oral* tradition handed down by poets and storytellers. Even after it was given written form in court or priestly circles, the oral tradition persisted among the people. This is difficult

---

[6]See Chapter 5 for further discussion of the formation of the Israelite epic, Chapter 7 for discussion of the Yahwist (J), and Chapter 9 for the Elohist (E). Chapter 11 discusses the Deuteronomist (D) and Chapter 13 the Priestly work (P). For brief introductions to Pentateuchal criticism, see N. C. Habel, *Literary Criticism of the Old Testament* [69]; also E. A. Speiser, *Genesis* [307], pp. xxii–xxvii; *Jerome Biblical Commentary* [15], pp. 1–6; and Joseph Blenkinsopp, "Introduction to the Pentateuch" in *The New Interpreter's Bible*, I (Nashville: Abingdon, 1994), pp. 305–18.

[7]This is the view of the so-called Scandinavian school; see Bibliography [81–84].

[8]The listings in the Bibliography under "Biblical Criticism" [49–108] are intended to help the student who is ready to go further into this matter. Note especially the work of Hermann Gunkel (1862–1932), who pioneered in the study of the preliterary (oral) tradition by examining the genres of oral tradition and the history of their transmission in various stages of composition.

for us to imagine, for since the time of the Renaissance our culture has placed a great premium on printed words. When we picture the "book" of Exodus, we are apt to think of an author who, after first consulting available sources in the library, sits down to write for a reading public. In antiquity, however, only a few could read and write, and traditions were often passed on through oral performance on ceremonial or informal occasions.

In its written form the Pentateuch reflects a long history of oral recitation. This oral tradition might be compared to Bedouin recitations of generations of family history,[9] or the "singer of tales" in Slavic society.[10] Undoubtedly the early period of Israel's life (before 1000 B.C.E.) was a creative time when the story of Israel was rehearsed and elaborated by the various tribes, each with its own experiences and traditions. Many irregularities and diversities that scholars have tried to explain by literary analysis are probably vestiges of the period when the tradition was transmitted by word of mouth, in song and story.

The main outlines of the later Pentateuch probably began to take shape during this early oral period, as skilled narrators recreated and improvised on the great themes of the Israelite story:

1. The promise to the ancestors.
2. The liberation of Israel from Egyptian bondage.
3. The manifestation of God (theophany) at Sinai and the giving of the law.
4. The providential guidance in the wilderness.
5. The inheritance of the promised land.

Reinterpreted, expanded, and handed down to posterity through oral tradition, these themes were blended into a great historical epic even before they took shape in written form.[11]

Thus the Pentateuch is the end result of a long and dynamic process, from the time the Israelite story was shaped orally and enriched with specific narrative contributions from the various tribes, on to the time when it was given literary form in various

---

[9]For a helpful discussion of the relation between literary sources and preliterary oral tradition see Roland de Vaux, *History* [111]. K. A. Kitchen, *The Bible in Its World* [123], pp. 66–68, gives interesting examples from the second millennium of the reliable transmission of traditions across several centuries; see the rejoinder by Ronald S. Hendel, "Finding Historical Memories in the Patriarchal Narratives," *Biblical Archaeology Review* 21:4 (July/August 1995), 52–59, 70–71.

[10]See the illuminating work by Albert B. Lord, *The Singer of Tales* [294], which studies Homeric literature (the *Odyssey* and *Iliad*) in light of the oral performance by Yugoslavian singers.

[11]This is the position of Martin Noth, a leading advocate of the *traditio-historical* method, which attempts to trace the process by which units (genres) of oral tradition evolved into the literature of the Pentateuch. See Noth's basic work, *A History of Pentateuchal Traditions* [76], and the introductory essay by B. W. Anderson that places Noth's approach in the context of twentieth century biblical criticism. A succinct discussion of this method is found in Walter E. Rast, *Tradition History and the Old Testament* [78]. The implications of this approach are elaborated in Douglas Knight, *Tradition and Theology in the Old Testament* [158].

circles during the monarchy, and finally to the time when these literary strands were brought together by Priestly writers in canonical form. Sometimes different traditions stand out clearly, as with the Priestly and Old Epic versions of creation. But very often these traditions cannot be disentangled, especially in the Exodus story—not just because the final editing was so skillful, but because each circle of storytellers drew upon a common oral tradition.

THE NARRATOR'S POINT OF VIEW

Two problems have already arisen in our study of the biblical text: (1) there are narrative irregularities and dissonances that suggest diverse literary traditions; and (2) the literary traditions are removed from the time of the Exodus by a period of several centuries, bridged primarily by oral transmission. There is a third problem: The Exodus story, both in its original oral form and its written version, does not pretend to be objective history. It is obviously an interpretive account of events which, viewed from another standpoint, might be presented in quite a different manner.

In the biblical narrative, God appears as the main actor. (Indeed, for the Christian community this is a "good story" or a "God-story"—the original meaning of the Anglo-Saxon *god-spel* or "gospel.") But the fact that this story is told to confess faith in God does not necessarily discredit its historical value. Modern historians recognize that there is no such thing as uninterpreted history. History is not a series of naked facts arranged in chronological order like beads on a string, nor is it possible to recover an event as a kind of "thing in itself" after all interpretation is stripped away. An event is a meaningful happening in the experience of a people, and history is the narration of these experienced events—events so memorable that they are preserved in oral tradition and written record. Accordingly, any historical account is selective and interpretative. Historians do not report everything. They select only those events that are meaningful or history-making to them or the community they represent.

Some events have a public meaning that anyone in the immediate vicinity can discern. In the United States, for example, the Civil War is perceived as a political struggle to preserve the unity of the nation at a time when slavery was a divisive issue. Of course, historians differ in their assessments of the historical data and the place of the event in the whole context of American history. There might be different nuances of interpretation, depending on whether the historian comes from the South or the North. As a political event, however, the war has a public meaning that can be appreciated by any people who have struggled to preserve national unity or overcome the divisions of race or class.

Abraham Lincoln, however, perceived another dimension of meaning in the conflict: God's judgment on both the North and the South for their involvement in slavery. To Lincoln the war was not just a political event with a public meaning, but an event with divine meaning when viewed in the perspective of religious faith. His Second Inaugural Address raises important questions for the historical interpreter. Did God's judgment really find expression in the tragedy of the Civil War? Is the historical view too narrow if we fail to see God at work in human affairs? Is history not just the narration of human deeds, but of divine activity as well?

When we deal with the event of the Exodus, the question of *meaning* is put in its sharpest form. From one standpoint, the Exodus was a political event: the liberation of a band of slaves from Pharaoh's yoke. This was its public meaning, and so viewed, it can be described externally and compared with similar political events in the lives of other peoples. But to the biblical narrators, who spoke out of a community of faith, the Exodus was pregnant with divine meaning. What happened was not just the escape of fugitives from slavery, but God's liberation of oppressed slaves and God's creation of a people out of chaos. The Exodus was a "root experience" that disclosed the saving power of the God who is holy, who completely transcends the human world.[12] It was the sign of God's historical presence, of divine intervention in an apparently hopeless human situation. The Exodus story deals with history in a different dimension than ordinary politics.

To speak of history "in a different dimension" should not suggest that the biblical story belongs in some Olympian realm far removed from the ordinary affairs of human life, or that the story can be treated merely as the poetry of faith, with no direct connection to historical fact. This would be a grave misunderstanding of biblical history. To be sure, the biblical narrative is embellished imaginatively to communicate the astounding wonder and revelatory power of the event. Underlying this narrative, however, is the belief that *God becomes known in the concrete affairs and relationships of people.* No external history can demonstrate that the Exodus was an event of divine liberation. Yet for Israel, this "political" event was the medium through which God's presence and purpose were disclosed. God's revelation did not come like a lightning bolt out of the blue. It came *through actual events*, to persons who perceived in these shared experiences a divine dimension of meaning of which others were unaware.

Thus the story of Israel's beginnings does not belong to a completely different sphere from that of the historian. On the contrary, we must take into account the historical concreteness and actuality of the Israelite story if we are to do justice to the narrative of God's dealings with Israel. Before examining the Exodus story more closely, we will consider what bearing the archaeological exploration of the ancient Near East has on our understanding of the Old Testament. Archaeology can help place the period of Israel's ancestors and the Exodus itself against a broad cultural horizon and in a meaningful historical context.

---

[12]Emil L. Fackenheim, *God's Presence in History* [241]. Fackenheim regards Exodus and Sinai as "epoch-making events" with three dimensions: (1) they are decisive past events; (2) they have a public, historical character; and (3) they are reenacted in the community of faith as a present reality.

THE PROLOGUE TO THE EXODUS

The account in the opening chapters of the book of Exodus is linked closely with the history and religion of the ancestral period—the period covered by Genesis 12–50. This continuity is indicated (1) by a reference to events that transpired after the death of Joseph, one of the twelve sons of Jacob (Exod. 1:8), and (2) by the vivid story of the theophany (manifestation of God) in the episode of the "burning bush," when God addresses Moses with the words: "I am the God of your father, the God of Abraham, the God of Isaac, and the God of Jacob" (Exod. 3:6). These narratives, at least in their present form, regard the "Period of the Ancestors" as prologue to the liberating event of the Exodus.

What can be said about the historical antecedents of the Exodus? This is an extraordinarily difficult question, for two reasons. First, the story of Israel's beginnings has come to us through a long process of oral and written tradition, shaped to confess faith in God. This is clearly the case with the narratives about the prehistory of Israel in Genesis 12–50, which belong to the Old Epic tradition. Not only is the prior saving purpose of the God of the Exodus traced back through the whole course of ancestral history, but even the idea of the unity of *Israel, the people of God,* is extended to the time of Abraham, Isaac, and Jacob—that is, to a time well before Israel came into existence as a tribal confederacy in the "Period of the Judges," about 1200–1000 B.C.E. (see Chapter 6). This extending of a pan-Israelite consciousness back into the "Period of the Ancestors" results in an over-simplified picture, something like a historian tracing the conception of the *United* States back into the period before the Revolutionary War when, as a matter of historical record, there was no sense of national unity. Not surprisingly, some scholars are skeptical about the historical reliability of the biblical traditions concerning the pre-Mosaic period. In their view, the scriptural portrayal of the ancestral period is "story," not history in the usual sense of the word.[13]

Second, our knowledge of Israel's ancestors comes from the biblical story/history itself, written in a time far removed from the events described. It would be helpful if archaeology could provide external sources that confirm these events. However, we cannot expect archaeology to prove that the biblical story is true just as written. Archaeology is a scientific discipline that seeks to avoid partisan philosophical or theological interests. As a science, it deals with evidence presented in the field, and so far has provided only general and circumstantial information bearing on the ancestral period.[14]

---

[13]This skeptical view was first espoused in the nineteenth century by Julius Wellhausen (*Prolegomena to the History of Israel*, 1878), and has been revived by T. L. Thompson, *The Historicity of the Patriarchal Narratives* [217], and J. Van Seters, "Abraham," in *History and Tradition* [218]. For critical rejoinders see among others K. A. Kitchen, *The Bible in Its World* [123], chap. 4; J. T. Luke, *Journal for the Study of the Old Testament* 4 (1977), 35–47; H. Cazalles, *Vetus Testamentum* 28 (1978), 241–55; and Nahum Sarna, *Biblical Archaeology Review* 3 (1977), 5–9.

[14]On the task and limitations of archaeology, see William G. Dever in *Israelite and Judaean History* [112], pp. 71–79. See also R. de Vaux, "On the Right and Wrong Uses of Archaeology," *Near Eastern Archaeology in the Twentieth Century: Essays in Honor of Nelson Glueck* (Garden City, NY: Doubleday, 1970), pp. 64–80; and G. E. Wright, "What Archaeology Can and Cannot Do," *Biblical Archaeologist* 34 (1971), 70–76.

Despite these difficulties, the narratives in Genesis probably reflect to some degree the life and times of Palestinians in the early second millennium (about 2050–1550 B.C.E.), the period archaeologists define as the Middle Bronze Age. The "history" of Abraham, Isaac, and Jacob in Genesis 12–35 seems to preserve faint echoes of clan movements and social relationships, later understood as a preparation for the decisive event of the Exodus and the formation of the people Israel.[15]

To consider this prologue to the Exodus, we must turn our attention to the area known as the *Fertile Crescent,* the arc of fertile land that skirts the Arabian desert, reaching from the Persian Gulf up through the alluvial plain of the Tigris and Euphrates Rivers, curving around through Syria and Palestine, and continuing toward the Nile in Egypt (see map, p. 28). This cradle of ancient civilization had been a scene of human activity for centuries before the appearance of the Hebrews who became the ancestors of Israel.

The ancestral history begins in "Ur of the Chaldeans" (Gen. 11:28) in the southernmost part of Mesopotamia. To be sure, there is some textual uncertainty about this, because the Septuagint (the Greek translation of the third century B.C.E.) speaks only of "the land of the Chaldeans," and other biblical passages place the ancestral home in Haran in northwest Mesopotamia. However, the original location at Ur is firmly fixed in the Hebrew Bible, not only in Genesis 11:31 (credited to Priestly tradition) but also in Genesis 11:18 and 15:7 (Old Epic tradition). So it is best to follow the more difficult reading given in the Hebrew text—difficult because it has Terah, the father of Abra(ha)m, move his family from Ur near the Persian Gulf all the way to the city of Haran on the bend of the Euphrates in northwestern Mesopotamia, some 600 miles away. From Haran, Abraham migrated into Canaan (the earlier name of Palestine). Stopping first at Shechem (Gen. 12:9), a great Canaanite commercial center, he moved down through the central hill country and eventually settled in southern Canaan, near Hebron. Abraham was succeeded by his son Isaac, and Isaac by his son Jacob, whose twelve sons bore the names later given to the twelve tribes of Israel.

The Bible describes these ancestors as living peacefully on the fringes of the native Canaanite population, although they maintained contact with relatives back in Haran and secured wives there rather than mixing freely with the Canaanites (Gen. 24, 29). Their social organization was not a political government (a state or nation), but a clan or extended family with a chieftain at the head. In this family story various troubles developed, such as the quarrel between Isaac's twin sons, Jacob and Esau, and the rivalry between Jacob and his Aramean father-in-law, Laban. These troubles came to a climax in the rivalry among Jacob's twelve sons. Jealous of Joseph, his brothers conspired to send him to Egypt. There Joseph rose to the position of prime minister, the most influential post next to that of Pharaoh. Then, in a time of famine, Jacob's family migrated

---

[15]Leading advocates of this position are the historians Roland de Vaux [111] and John Bright [110]. See Kenneth A. Kitchen, "Genesis 12–50 in the Near Eastern World," in R. S. Hess and others, eds., *He Swore an Oath: Biblical Themes From Genesis 12–50* (Cambridge: Tyndalehouse, 1993), pp. 67–92; and "The Patriarchal Age: Myth or History?," *Biblical Archaeology Review,* 21:2 (March/April 1995), 48–57, 88–95.

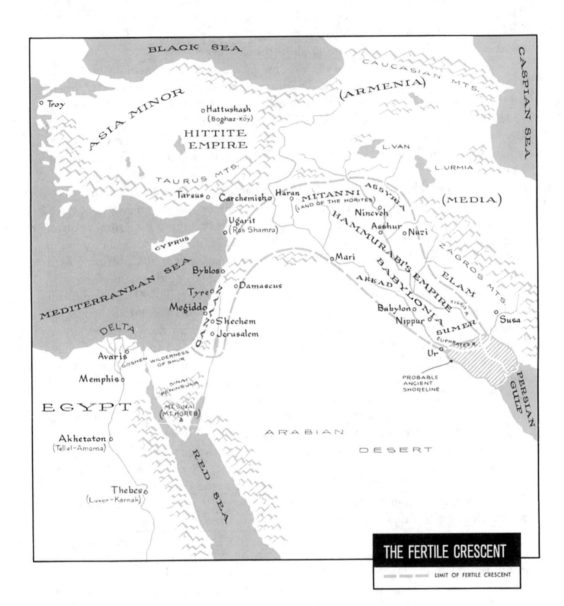

BLACK SEA

CASPIAN SEA

CAUCASIAN MTS.

(ARMENIA)

ASIA MINOR

o Troy

o Hattushash
(Boghaz-Köy)

HITTITE
EMPIRE

L. VAN

L. URMIA

TAURUS MTS.

ASSYRIA

(MEDIA)

Tarsus o

Carchemish o

Haran
o

MITANNI
(LAND OF THE HORITES)

Nineveh

Ugarit
o (Ras Shamra)

HAMMURABI'S EMPIRE

Asshur
o

o Nuzi

ZAGROS MTS.

CYPRUS

o Mari

ELAM

MEDITERRANEAN SEA

Bybloso

BABYLONIA

TIGRIS R.

Tyre o

o Damascus

AKKAD

Megiddo o

Babylon o

Susa
o

o Shechem

Nippur o

SUMER

DELTA

o Jerusalem

EUPHRATES R.

Avaris o

GOSHEN

WILDERNESS
OF SHUR

Ur o

PROBABLE
ANCIENT
SHORELINE

Memphis o

SINAI
PENINSULA

PERSIAN GULF

EGYPT

MT. SINAI
(MT. HOREB)

ARABIAN

Akhetaton o
(Tell el-Amarna)

DESERT

RED SEA

Thebes o
(Luxor-Karnak)

THE FERTILE CRESCENT

LIMIT OF FERTILE CRESCENT

to Egypt, where they settled in the Delta area near Pharaoh's capital and received the bounty of Joseph's wise administration. The book of Exodus takes up the story at this point, stating that Hebrew fortunes changed when an Egyptian king came to power who "did not know Joseph."

POPULATION UNREST IN THE FERTILE CRESCENT

The study of international developments that mark the transition from the Early to Middle Bronze Age in the Fertile Crescent has shed considerable light on Israel's ancestral period. Archaeologists have excavated Ur, Abraham's ancestral city at the southern end of the Euphrates River. This and other archaeological discoveries, especially in northern Mesopotamia around Haran, have helped acquaint us with the early ancestral period. We will take a brief look, then, at the situation in Mesopotamia as it might have appeared in the dawn of recorded history. A number of peoples were on the move, in particular the Amorites, Hurrians, 'Apiru (Habiru), and Arameans.

THE COMING OF THE AMORITES

During the third millennium (3000–2000 B.C.E.), the alluvial plain of the Tigris and Euphrates was the scene of a struggle between two powers, Sumer in the south and Akkad in the north (see map, p. 28). For much of this period, the Sumerians maintained a brilliant civilization in Mesopotamia (about 2850–2360 B.C.E.) based on a loosely organized system of city-states. This was a relatively prosperous and secure period when agriculture, urban life, industry, and the arts flourished.

Then, in the twenty-fourth century B.C.E., Sumer came under the control of a Semitic people known as the Akkadians. Their dynamic leader, Sargon I of Akkad, has been called the first empire builder of history. His empire lasted for almost two centuries (about 2360–2180 B.C.E.), reaching its zenith with the spectacular accomplishments of Sargon's grandson, Naram-Sin. In this period the city of Ebla, a rival to Akkad located in northern Syria, rose to commercial and military power and then was destroyed, apparently by Naram-Sin. Excavations at the site (Tell Mardikh) have uncovered a cache of some 16,000 tablets that throw light on the early background of the Bible.[16] At first it was thought that the tablets contained creation and flood stories, personal names known also in Israel's patriarchal traditions (Abram, Ishmael, and Israel), and place names familiar in biblical tradition (Hazor, Megiddo, Jerusalem, Lachish,

---

[16]The royal palace of Ebla with its library was discovered in 1974–75; see the account by Paolo Matthiae, *Ebla: An Empire Rediscovered*, trans. Christopher Holme (Garden City, N.Y.: Doubleday, 1980). For a brief introduction, see K. A. Kitchen, "Ebla—Queen of Ancient Syria," *The Bible in Its World* [123], chap. 3.

The Victory Stele of Naram-Sin (twenty-third century B.C.E.), the grandson of Sargon I. With his soldiers, the Akkadian king triumphantly ascends a mountain whose peak almost touches the stars, while his victims, the mountain-dwelling Lullubians, fall beneath his feet or plunge headlong from the cliffs.

Gaza). Subsequently, however, much of the claimed evidence of biblical connections seems to have evaporated.[17] The Ebla evidence is too early to throw direct light on the ancestral period, but it helps us to understand its linguistic and cultural background.

In another swing of the political pendulum, the Sumerians returned to power when a barbarian invasion from the Zagros mountains brought an end to Akkadian rule. Ur-Nammu, founder of the so-called Third Dynasty of Ur (2060–1950 B.C.E.), made Ur a thriving commercial center and adorned the city with an impressive ziggurat, or tiered temple-tower, the remains of which can still be seen (see picture, p. 150). Even more significant was Ur-Nammu's code of law, the oldest one discovered to date.[18] But the Sumerian revival was brief, ending about 2000 B.C.E. with a devastating attack by Elamites, who stormed down from their mountainous homeland (modern Iran) into the coveted Mesopotamian plain.

DEFINITION: "SEMITE,"   "SEMITIC"

The terms "Semite" and "Semitic" are sometimes used to refer to the Jewish people, but this is an unwarranted reduction. In the modern world the Semitic family includes peoples who live in Turkey, Lebanon, Syria, Iraq, Jordan, Israel, Arabia, and North Africa. Thus the term is regional and ethnic—certainly not racial. Semite originally referred to Shem, one of the three sons of Noah (Gen. 9:18). In the table of peoples found in Genesis 10, Noah's descendants are broadly classified according to language groups and geographical areas, the Japhethites belonging to a northern area (southern Europe, Asia Minor), the Shemites being situated in the center (Fertile Crescent and its fringes), and the Hamites being located to the south (northern Africa). Curiously, this table links the Canaanites with Ham, even though they are Semitic.

Scholars use the word "Semitic" more precisely to refer to ancient peoples who spoke related languages. These peoples are subdivided into general geographical groupings: East Semitic (Akkadian, that is Babylonian and Assyrian), Northwest Semitic (including Phoenician/Canaanite, Aramaic, and Hebrew), and Southern Semitic (including Arabic and Ethiopic).

During the next two centuries various petty states struggled to achieve power. In this period of confusion, a horde of seminomadic Semites flooded the country from the Arabian desert, the cradle of all Semitic peoples including the earlier Akkadians. With amazing political energy they overran all of Mesopotamia, establishing dynasties in practically every major city. Because their center of power lay in the northwest (Upper Mesopotamia and Syria), they were known as *Amurru* (Amorites), an Akkadian term meaning "Westerners."

For a time the city of Mari, near the border between modern Syria and Iraq, was the center of Amorite rule. A vivid picture of the so-called "Mari Age" (about

---

[17]See Alan Millard, "Ebla and the Bible—What's Left (If Anything?)," *Bible Review*, 8:2 (April 1992), 18–31, 60.
[18]See James B. Pritchard, ed., *Ancient Near Eastern Texts Relating to the Old Testament*, 3rd ed. with supplement [1], pp. 523–25.

The Pre-sargonic Man is a gypsum statue of an offering bearer from Mari and stands 23 centimeters tall. Note the striking juxtaposition of smooth and deeply textured surfaces.

1750–1697 B.C.E.) was provided by excavation at the site of that ancient city during the years immediately before and after World War II (see Insert 3–1). Archaeologists uncovered the remains of a once-magnificent palace, consisting of about three hundred rooms and covering several acres. Of great interest to readers of the Bible was the discovery of about twenty-five thousand clay tablets containing business and administrative matters. Many contained diplomatic correspondence between the Amorite king of Mari, Zimri-Lim, and officials in surrounding states.

The Mari documents illuminate the cultural backgrounds of the early ancestral period. Strikingly, they mention biblical names like Ishmael and possibly Levi. Benjamin appears as the name of a warlike band of tribes, and Peleg, Serug, and Nahor—names in Abraham's genealogy (Gen. 11:10–16)—are given as the names of towns in the neighborhood of Haran. Further, the phenomenon of prophecy, which loomed large in Israelite society (see Chapter 8), was known at Mari.[19]

Eventually leadership shifted to the city of Babylon, where Amorites established the First Babylonian Dynasty. Their greatest king was Hammurabi (about 1728–1686

[19]See Abraham Malamat, *Mari and the Early Israelite Experience* (Oxford University Press: British Academy, 1989).

B.C.E.), who conquered Mari in 1697 B.C.E. Within a short period of time, the Amorites extended their influence from Mesopotamia down through Syria and Palestine, where they came to be the dominant element of the Canaanite population.

Some historians believe that Abraham's migration into Canaan as portrayed in Genesis 12:1–6 was connected in some way with the Amorite infiltration into Mesopotamia and Syria.[20] In this view, Abraham lived during the eighteenth century B.C.E. and might have been a contemporary of the Amorite king, Hammurabi. Haran, Abraham's home town (if not his birthplace), was an Amorite settlement in this period. Amorite personal names, such as Benjamin (*Binu-yamina*), Jacob (*Ya'qub-el*), and Abram (*Abamram*), probably do not refer to the biblical characters themselves, but they certainly point to a common Semitic background.

According to some scholars, Israel's ancestors could have brought traditions from their Amorite homeland that were later transformed and incorporated into the religious epic now found in the biblical primeval history (Gen. 1–11): stories of the Creation, the Garden of Eden, the Flood, and the Tower of Babel. The creation story known as *Enuma elish*, as well as the flood story preserved in the Gilgamesh Epic, both come from the time of the First Dynasty of Babylon.[21] These stories show formal similarities to the biblical accounts, although there is a world of difference between them (see Chapter 7). Furthermore, the prototype of the biblical "Tower of Babel" (Gen. 11:1–9) is the ziggurat (tiered temple-tower) of the city of Babylon, one of the famed wonders of the age of Hammurabi (compare the Ur ziggurat, p. 150). This tower was known as *Etemenanki*, "The House of the Terrace-platform of Heaven and Earth."

The Hebrews might have learned Mesopotamian law in their Amorite homeland. More likely, however, they were influenced by the famous Code of Hammurabi through the Canaanites among whom they later settled. A copy of the code can be seen today in the Louvre Museum, inscribed on a huge black stele beneath a relief that shows Hammurabi standing before Shamash, the sun god who controlled cosmic order and justice. One of the most brilliant achievements of Hammurabi's empire, this code (which incorporated elements from previous codes, including that of Ur-Nammu) improved and standardized the administration of justice. It set the basic pattern of jurisprudence for centuries to come, and influenced Israelite law, known as the Covenant Code, in both style and content (see Chapter 3).

THE HURRIAN MOVEMENT

Into the political vacuum caused by the downfall of the Sumerian dynasty of Ur came the Hurrians, possibly related to the Horites (or Hivites) mentioned in the Hebrew

---

[20]The leading proponent of the Amorite hypothesis is Roland de Vaux; see his *History* [111], chap. 7. This view is also forcefully advocated by John Bright in his *History* [110], chap. 2, and is cautiously supported by William G. Dever, *Israelite and Judean History* [112], pp. 70–120. But compare Kyle McCarter, *History of Israel*, ed. G. Herschel Shanks [117], chap. 1.

[21]See Pritchard, *Ancient Near Eastern Texts* [1], pp. 60–99, 501–07.

The Stele of Hammurabi is a monolith nearly eight feet tall, inscribed with a code of laws. The relief at the top depicts Hammurabi, King of Babylon, standing before the sun god Shamash, who extends a rod and ring, symbols of royal authority to the worshipping king.

Bible. Even before the turn of the second millennium B.C.E., this non-Semitic people started to push down from the Caucasian mountains of Armenia into the plain of the Tigris and Euphrates. Unlike the Amorites, they came not as military conquerors but as infiltrators in a steady, ever-increasing stream. At first they settled in northern Mesopotamia, around Mari and Haran, but by the time of Hammurabi they had spread through the entire area. By the fifteenth century they were the majority population, with great political power, in a new state in Upper Mesopotamia known as Mitanni.

Adept in the use of new instruments of war such as the composite bow, the Hurrians clashed frequently with Egyptian armies that advanced into Canaan, Syria, and Upper Mesopotamia. Indeed, Hurrians migrated into Canaan in such numbers that Egyptians, from the time of the Eighteenth Dynasty, referred to the area as Hurru (Hurrian) land. Almost nothing was known of the Hurrians before 1919 C.E., when

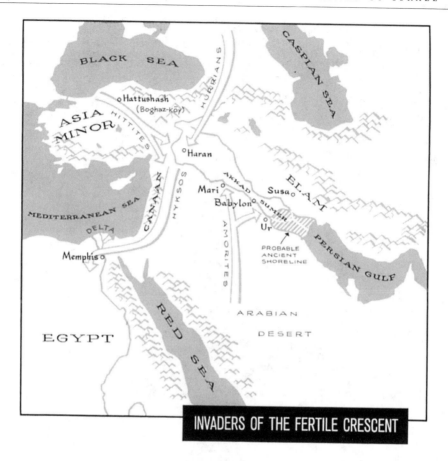

INVADERS OF THE FERTILE CRESCENT

thousands of clay tablets dating from the time of the Mitannian kingdom (about 1500–1370 B.C.E.) were discovered at the Hurrian city of Nuzi, located east of the Tigris River.[22] More recently, archaeologists working in northeastern Syria near the Turkish border have reported the discovery of what might be the ruins of the "lost" Hurrian capital, Urkesh.[23]

THE HITTITES

Even before the rise of the Hurrian kingdom of Mitanni, a people known as Hittites established a vigorous nation in the region of present-day Turkey (see Insert 3–2; 4–1a,b,c). From time to time they ventured from their mountain-locked homeland in

---

[22]For alleged parallels between social customs and family law of Nuzi and the period of Israel's ancestors, see the useful summary by George Ramsey, *The Quest* [116], chap. 2, especially pp. 29–33.

[23]See John N. Wilford's report, "The Lost Capital of a Fabled Kingdom Found in Syria," *The New York Times* (November 21, 1995).

Anatolia (Asia Minor) to expand into Mesopotamia, Syria, and Palestine. Eventually they vied with Egypt for control of the Fertile Crescent. In the heart of their rugged land, atop an impressive height, they built their lofty capital of Hattushash, and not far away they carved upon the walls of a rock-sanctuary scenes of their major deities and of lesser gods marching in procession. In 1907 excavation of the Hittite capital, now called Boghazköy, uncovered evidence of the former glory of this Hittite empire. Massive for-

This bronze statuette from the Hittite Period depicts a deity in combat and stands about 7 inches tall.

tifications and impressive structures were found, including a library that contained a code of laws and treaties with other peoples (see Insert 4–1a, b, c). The biblical tradition that Abraham purchased his burial cave from some Hittites (Gen. 23) suggests that their influence extended as far south as Canaan.

THE ʿAPIRU

Clearly, the ancestral period was a time of unrest, when many peoples mingled in the Fertile Crescent. Canaan was indeed "the land of the Canaanites, the Hittites, the Amorites, the Perizzites, the Hivites, and the Jebusites" (Exod. 3:17).

Of particular interest in documents of the second millennium are numerous references to ʿApiru (*Habiru*), a comparatively inconspicuous people scattered through Asia Minor, Mesopotamia, Syria, Canaan, and Egypt.[24] The term does not refer to an ethnic group, though apparently many Semites were involved. Rather, it refers to a social stratum of people who lacked citizenship in the established nations of the Near East. The ʿApiru were "wanderers" or "outsiders" who lived a rootless existence on the fringes of society. Like modern gypsies or migrant workers, many of them moved from place to place with their families and possessions. They formed guerilla bands that attacked caravans or raided villages, hired themselves out as mercenary soldiers, and sometimes were forced into slave labor on public projects. It was not unheard of for one of the ʿApiru to rise to a position of leadership in an established nation.

There might be some connection—though this is a matter of dispute—between the terms ʿApiru and *ʿibri* ("Hebrew"), found almost exclusively in biblical materials dealing with the period before David. Whatever the connection, scholars agree that the term ʿApiru in Mesopotamian and Egyptian texts of the second millennium does not refer specifically to those Hebrews who were relatives of Abraham and who eventually understood themselves to be "Israelites" (*Benê Yisrael*).[25] Rather, the biblical Hebrews belonged to a larger class of rootless people to whom more established groups applied the descriptive term ʿApiru.

The description of Abraham, the traditional ancestor of those Hebrews who became Israelites (Gen. 14:13), fits this picture. He is regarded as a "sojourner" (Hebrew: *ger*) in the midst of the established peoples of Canaan. With his family and flocks, he moved from place to place seeking seasonal pasture in the sparsely settled hill country of Canaan, eventually pitching his tent at Mamre, near the place where Hebron was later established. The same picture is given of his son and grandson, Isaac and Jacob. Like true ʿApiru, the patriarchs shunned the settled life of cities and, with few exceptions (such as Gen. 33:10; 26:12), did not sink their roots long enough in one place to own land or to farm the soil. Their life probably resembled that of the seminomads por-

---

[24]A fundamental study of this question is Moshe Greenberg, *The Hab/piru* [211]. See also R. de Vaux, *History* [111], pp. 105–12, 209–16.

[25]See Definition, p. 31.

trayed on the wall of the tomb of Beni-Hasan in Egypt (see pictures, pp. 154–155). In this mural, dating back to a time before Abraham (nineteenth century B.C.E.), a family enters Egypt on foot, clad in garments of many colors, with their children and goods carried on donkeys.

THE APPEARANCE OF THE ARAMEANS

One more people deserve mention, though admittedly its appearance in Israel's ancestral history is a bit puzzling. As we read the biblical story, we hear again and again about the land of Aram (modern Syria) and its people, the Arameans. We learn that Abraham sent his servant to the ancestral home, located in "Aram of the Two Rivers" (Aram Naharaim, or Mesopotamia; Gen. 24:10). The Jacob cycle, and other stories, refer to "The Plain of Aram" (Hebrew: *Paddan Aram*), the country to which Isaac sent his son Jacob to find a wife (Gen. 28:2. 5–7). Jacob's father-in-law, Laban, is repeatedly called "the Aramean" (Gen. 25:20, 28:5). The difficulty here is that Aram did not emerge on the political scene until the twelfth century B.C.E., when the people of Israel, after the Exodus from Egypt, were settling in Canaan. This suggests that the ancestral history embraces two widely separated movements: the Amorite infiltration that occurred after the downfall of the Ur regime (about 2000 B.C.E.), and the appearance of the Arameans following the collapse of the Hittite and Egyptian empires (about 1200 B.C.E.). How are we to understand the relation between the "Amorite" Abraham and the "Aramean" Jacob?

In answer to this question, some scholars maintain that the ancestral tradition is late and has historical value only for the time when it was composed. The link between Israel's ancestors and the Arameans, they argue, is much stronger than the link with the Amorites. Thus, the patriarchal tradition in Genesis has to be moved forward from the Middle Bronze to the Early Iron Age (about 1200 B.C.E.).[26] This extreme view would place the ancestors of Israel after the time of Moses—an unsatisfactory outcome if we are to regard the ancestral period as a historical prologue to the Exodus.

A more constructive solution to the Aramean problem is possible if we consider the following. Today we usually refer to the ancient setting of the Fertile Crescent as the "Near East" or the "Middle East," using language that reflects our modern vantage point. Similarly, the narrators of the patriarchal history probably used the language of their time to refer to the ancestral period. Some historians argue forcefully that the "Arameans" referred to in the Hebrew Bible are a later phase of an early Amorite ("proto-Aramean") stock, mentioned in various extra-biblical texts. Keep in mind that

---

[26]See Siegfried Hermann, *History* [113], pp. 41–55, who maintains that the table of peoples in Genesis 10 supports this conclusion; and W. Malcolm Clark in *Israelite and Judaean History* [112], pp. 142–48. Others date the composition of the story in the time of the monarchy (T. L. Thompson [217]) or even later (J. van Seters [218]).

the incursion of the Amorites into the Fertile Crescent was not an isolated event, but a complex rhythm of migrations, wave upon wave, over a long period of time. The ancestral narrative of a back-and-forth migration from Haran to Canaan, for the purpose of keeping in touch with Mesopotamian relatives, perhaps reflects the ethnic continuity from Amorites to Arameans. Quite properly, then, Israelites remembered Jacob as "a wandering Aramean" in their confession of faith (Deut. 26:5).

This discussion points up another important matter. The story of Israel's ancestors was related from the vantage point of the time of the Israelite Tribal Confederacy (about 1200–1000 B.C.E.), when Aram and other mentioned peoples (such as Moab and Ammon in the Abraham/Lot narrative, Edom in the Jacob/Esau story) were political powers. By referring to these peoples, the narrators contemporized a story being told and retold as "the story of our life." We will return to this matter when we consider the formation of the Israelite epic during the period of the Tribal Confederacy, two centuries before David (see Chapter 5).

THE GOD OF ISRAEL'S ANCESTORS

There is reason to believe that the story of Israel's ancestors (Gen. 12–50), though understood in the light of later experiences, reflects to some degree the cultural background of the millennium starting with Hammurabi's reign (second millennium B.C.E.). The evidence is as follows.

First, ancient documents recovered at Ebla and other sites suggest that many parents in this period gave children names such as Abram, Benjamin, Michael, and Ishmael.

Second, Israel's ancestral tradition depicts social customs and legal usages that are much more in harmony with Mesopotamian practice during the second millennium than with Israel's life during the monarchy. For instance, Mesopotamian law codes specified the rights of inheritance for children born to a man who had more than one wife (compare Jacob's relation to his two wives, Leah and Rachel, as well as the handmaids, Bilhah and Zilpah); and ancient jurisprudence under certain circumstances protected the inheritance rights of a child born to a "slave wife" (consider Abraham's reluctance to cast away his son Ishmael born to Hagar, Gen. 21:10–11).

There is a third, more cogent kind of evidence. The religion of Israel's ancestors—the worship of "the God of the fathers"—authentically belongs to the period that preceded Moses. Of course, given that the traditions of Genesis were revised in the light of the Exodus and the Sinai covenant, we cannot know exactly what the religion of Israel's ancestors was. Still, many statements in the book of Genesis, when considered against the background of the culture of the Fertile Crescent, help us to understand the probable character of religious beliefs before Moses.

To jump ahead for just a moment: Joshua 24 describes a great assembly at Shechem where Joshua summoned the people to renew their allegiance to God whose power and purpose were manifested in the Exodus and the guidance into the land of Canaan. Specifically, the people were challenged to "put away the gods which your ancestors served beyond the [Euphrates] River and in Egypt" (Josh. 24:14b; also verse 2). This passage suggests that Israel's ancestors had been under the influence of prevailing religious views throughout the Fertile Crescent, from Mesopotamia to Egypt. Accordingly, the Exodus was not just a flight from political oppression. It was also a departure from the religions of the ancient world, that is to say, from ancient myths that established a particular relationship between the social and divine order. Moses had led the people in this kind of exodus, even as Abraham earlier had followed a divine command to depart from Mesopotamian culture. At Shechem, Joshua was inviting a later generation to join those who exited from the old and entered into the new.

Studies in the history of religions, especially those that deal with mythical symbolism,[27] help us to understand Joshua's challenge to the people. At issue was not just "the service of other gods" (polytheism) versus the service of one God revealed in the Exodus—though this was clearly important. Rather, the choice was between two different views of reality, one expressed in the myths of Mesopotamia, Canaan, and Egypt, and the other in the Israelite story or *mythos* that Joshua recited to the people (Josh. 24:2–13).

A main concern of ancient Mesopotamian mythology was to ensure that human society was integrated into the divine order of the cosmos. To this end the spatial organization of human empires was regarded as a reflection of the order of the cosmic sphere, where the supreme god presided over the heavenly council. Like the heavenly sphere, the social order was threatened by powers of chaos evidenced in violence, social change, and the cyclical recurrence of winter. Religion provided hope for salvation when, at the temple site or *omphalos* ("navel," "sacral center")—where heaven and earth meet and divine power flows into society—the social order was periodically renewed through mythic recitation and ritual drama. A high point was the New Year festival when the king, serving as the representative of the victorious deity Marduk, reenacted the annual victory of the powers of creation over the powers of chaos.[28]

The view of a divine order reflected in the order of society also characterized Egyptian culture, where Pharaoh was regarded as the "image" or representative of the creator-God, through whom the divine *Maat* ("order," "justice," "truth") was mediated to society. This view, in contrast to the more democratic view of the heavenly council in Mesopotamia, endowed Pharaoh with absolute authority. The harmonization of Egyptian

---

[27]See Bibliography under "Ancient Religion" [138–145].

[28]An interesting comparison can be made between the view presupposed in the Babylonian creation myth, *Enuma elish*, and that of the creation story found in Genesis 1:1–2:3. See B. W. Anderson, *Creation versus Chaos* [146], especially chap. 1, and *Creation in the Old Testament* [132], especially the essay by Hermann Gunkel, chap. 1.

society with the divine order produced a static and stable civilization that survived without essential change, despite a succession of dynasties, for more than two thousand years.

Against this background, the phenomenon of Israel represented a distinct break with the culture of the ancient Near East. When the ancestral Hebrew wanderers left Mesopotamia, they brought with them their own religious beliefs and practices, including the worship of their chief God, Shaddai (Gen. 17:1; 23:3; 35:11; 43:14; 48:3). Perhaps of Amorite origin, this divine name means "the Mountain One"—the exalted deity who dwells on the cosmic mountain—and could have provided a natural point of contact between the ancestral religion and the worship of El, the supreme father-god of the Canaanite pantheon. In pre-Israelitic times, El was worshiped at particular sanctuaries in Canaan under compound epithets: *'El Bethel* ("God of Bethel") at Luz (Gen. 31:12; 35:7; compare 28:19); *'El 'Elyon* ("God Most High") at Jerusalem (Gen. 14:18–20); *'El 'Olam* ("Everlasting God") at Beer-sheba (Gen. 21:33); *'El Roi* ("God of Seeing") at a sacred place in the southern wilderness (Gen. 16:13). Israel's ancestors might have identified their God with El in his various manifestations, using the epithet *'El Shaddai.*[29]

In spite of affinities between native religion and the worship of "the God of the ancestors," there were differences that over time became profoundly significant. One difference is implicit in the use of the name "Shaddai" in the book of Genesis, where it is associated with a covenant relationship between God and the ancestors. For example, Genesis 15:7–21 describes a curious incident: Abraham cuts some animals in two, placing half of the carcasses over against the other half. After the sun sets, an eerie darkness falls over the place, and "a smoking fire pot and a flaming torch"—representing the presence of deity—passes between the pieces. This account, though overlaid with later theological interpretation, preserves a very ancient ritual of covenant-making in which the deity makes a binding commitment, sealed by the power of a curse, to fulfill a promise. If we appeal to the ancient Mari texts, which mention the sealing of treaties (covenants) by killing an ass (a practice echoed in Jer. 34:18–19), this strange narrative seems to mean that the covenant partner, by passing through the bloody corridor, submits to the curse of becoming like the divided animals if the covenant obligation is ever violated.

The account in Genesis 15:7–21 emphasizes an important characteristic of the religion of Israel's ancestors: the practice of entering into a personal relationship or "covenant" with the deity. We learn that Abraham entered into relationship with the God known as the "Shield" of Abraham (Gen. 15:1), Isaac with "the Fear [possibly Kinsman] of Isaac" (Gen. 31:42, 53), and Jacob with "the Mighty One of Jacob" (Gen. 49:24). In each case, the family deity enters into a personal relationship with

---

[29]See de Vaux, *Ancient Israel* [111], pp. 289–94, for a discussion of the veneration of the supreme God ('El) at the sanctuaries of Shechem, Bethel, Mamre, and Beer-sheba; also essays 2 and 3 in Frank M. Cross, *Canaanite Myth and Hebrew Epic* [129], pp. 13–75.

the patriarch, making demands and promises; and in each case, the deity is designated by the name of the person who received the revelation: the God of Abraham, the God of Isaac, and the God of Jacob. In the early tradition the deity was associated with a particular patriarch ("the God of your father"; Gen. 26:24; 28:13). Later, the three family cults were combined into one with the formula "the God of the ancestors [fathers]."[30]

The religion of Israel's ancestors is also characterized by strong clan or family solidarity. Even individual names suggest the close personal relationship between the clan and the deity who was regarded as "father," "brother," or patron of the "family": For example, the name "Ab-ram" contains the element *'ab* ("father") and means "the (Divine) Father is exalted." Names of this type reflect a vivid awareness of the deity's involvement with the ancestral family, to the extent that "the God was the unseen head of the house; its members, the members of his family."[31]

The ancestral religion also expressed faith in the God who makes promises and guides into the future, like a shepherd leading a flock (Ps. 23). Jacob prayed to the God "before whom my fathers Abraham and Isaac walked, the God who has led [Hebrew: "shepherded"] me all my life long to this day, the angel who has redeemed me from all evil" (Gen. 48:15–16). This nomadic faith differed markedly from the religions of sedentary peoples of the Fertile Crescent—religions that bound a cult to a sacred location. In Canaan, a sanctuary like the one at Bethel was regarded as the very "gate of heaven" (Gen. 28:17) where the deity became manifest in a special way. We know from the book of Genesis that Israel's ancestors visited these ancient Canaanite places (Shechem, Bethel, Beer-sheba), but these visits were part of an itinerant life style. The "God of the ancestors" was not bound to a place. Instead, the shepherding deity uprooted Abraham from his homeland, leading him and his descendants along new paths to new places, always holding before them the promise of land and posterity.

In the narrative traditions of Genesis, the ancestors are described as wanderers and adventurers who, in response to a divine summons, make pilgrimages into the unknown and the uncertain. As we have already noted, the story of God's call to Abraham and the resulting migration from Mesopotamia is colored by later theological reflection. Nevertheless, some dim apprehension of divine guidance and historical pilgrimage must lie behind the Exodus account that Moses, in the dark period of the oppression of Abraham's descendants in Egypt, was addressed by "the God of your ancestors, the God of Abraham, the God of Isaac, and the God of Jacob" (Exod. 3:6, 15).

---

[30]See H. G. May, "The God of My Father—A Study in Patriarchal Religion," *Journal of Bible and Religion*, IX (1941), 155–58, 200.

[31]John Bright, *History* [110], p. 99, gives illustrations of names compounded with "father" (*'ab*), "brother" (*'aḥ*), and "kindred people" (*'amm*). He points out that these types of names were common in the Amorite population.

THE DESCENT INTO EGYPT

Toward the end of the book of Genesis we find the story of Joseph's rise to power in Egypt and the friendly reception of Jacob's family into the Delta area during a time of famine. Egyptian history from the period of the second millennium B.C.E. gives examples of non-natives who attained government positions. In the fourteenth century, Pharaoh Akhnaton promoted a Semite named Tutu to a high position that entitled him to act as the representative of the crown in certain areas, such as the inspection of public works. In scenes reminiscent of Joseph's success (Gen. 41:41–43), murals on the walls of Tutu's tomb in El Amarna show him being given a gold chain by Pharaoh, riding in Pharaoh's chariot, and being acclaimed by the people, who prostrate themselves before him. An inscription states that Tutu was "the superior voice in the whole country" and that, among his duties, he received foreign delegations and conveyed their words to the palace.[32] Thus, we can believe that a Hebrew like Joseph might have been elevated to political leadership in Egypt.

To be sure, the biblical story about Jacob and Joseph contains elements of folklore. The motif of the false accusation of adultery with Potiphar's wife, for example—after Joseph had in reality rejected her sexual advances—is also found in the Egyptian "Story of Two Brothers" (about 1225 B.C.E.).[33] Though based on oral tradition, the Joseph story of the Hebrew Bible probably comes from the period of Solomon, when relations with Egypt were close—a fact that helps to account for the Egyptian color of the narrative, including the mention of Egyptian names and titles, dream interpretation, and embalming. Taken by itself, the story is a piece of great literature, a historical novel set in the second millennium B.C.E. whose creative artistry has captured the interest of modern writers like Thomas Mann.[34] Within its biblical context, however, it serves as a transition from the ancestral period to the Mosaic age, and is governed by an overarching theological purpose (see Chapter 5).

THE HYKSOS INVASION

Earlier, we considered two great waves—the Amorite and Hurrian—that surged into the Fertile Crescent shortly after the turn of the second millennium B.C.E. In the wake of these and other political disturbances came another tidal wave, the Hyksos invasion that swept down through Syria and Palestine into Egypt. The Hyksos (an Egyptian word meaning "rulers of foreign countries") were a diverse people: many seem to have

[32]Cited by de Vaux, *History* [111], p. 284. The murals are reproduced and discussed by N. de G. Davies, *The Rock Tombs of El Amarna*, VI (London, 1908), 7–15, 27, plates xi–xx.

[33]See Pritchard, *Ancient Near Eastern Texts* [1] pp. 23–25.

[34]Thomas Mann, *Joseph and His Brothers* (New York: A. A. Knopf, 1948). For a literary approach to the Joseph cycle, see W. L. Humphreys, "Joseph and His Family: A Literary Study," in *Studies in Personalities of the Old Testament* (Columbia: University of South Carolina Press, 1988).

been Semites, but some were Hittites and Hurrians. Unlike Hurrians who came earlier from the Caucasian highlands, however, the Hyksos were bent on conquest. With a swift and powerful military weapon, the horse-drawn chariot, they invaded Egypt at a time of political weakness and overthrew the native rulers. Their invasion of Egypt took place about 1720 B.C.E. Later, the Egyptian historian Manetho (about 275 B.C.E.) recalled with horror the Hyksos invasion in the reign of Tutimaeus (probably Thirteenth Dynasty), when cities were burned and temples "razed to the ground."

During the seventeenth century B.C.E., the Hyksos dominated Egypt. The rulers of the Fifteenth and Sixteenth Dynasties, who were all Hyksos, established a powerful empire that included Palestine and Syria. Archaeological excavation shows that during this period Shechem was a Hyksos fortress, equipped with the characteristic ramparts introduced by the Hyksos to ward off attack by horse-drawn chariots.[35] Eventually an Egyptian revolution broke out and, about 1550 B.C.E., Ahmose I, the founder of the brilliant Eighteenth Dynasty, overthrew the hated foreign regime. The city of Avaris was captured, the routed Hyksos were pursued into Palestine, and cities like Shechem were overthrown. The ensuing Egyptian revival, especially under the ambitious Pharaoh Thutmose III (about 1490–1436 B.C.E.), extended Egypt's sway throughout Palestine and Syria.

The account of the Hebrew descent into Egypt accords well with the history of this period. Seminomads in Palestine, a land that depended on seasonal rainfall, would naturally turn their eyes in time of drought toward Egypt, where the periodic overflow of the Nile irrigated the land. We know from Egyptian records that it was the practice of Egyptian officials to allow hunger-stricken people from Palestine and the Sinaitic peninsula to enter the Delta frontier. In about 1350 B.C.E., one Egyptian frontier official sent word to Pharaoh that nomads "who knew not how they should live, have come begging a home in the domain of Pharaoh . . . after the manner of your father's fathers since the beginning."[36] We can believe that under similar circumstances Jacob's family was forced to settle in the eastern part of the Nile Delta ("the land of Goshen").

It is tempting to connect the story of the descent of Jacob and his family into Egypt with the Hyksos movement. One small but significant detail suggests this possibility: According to the biblical narratives, the Hebrew settlement in Goshen (*Wadi Tumilat*, called "the land of Rameses" in Gen. 47:11) was "near Pharoah's court" (Gen. 45:10; 46:28ff.). Before the Hyksos period the Egyptian capital had been at Thebes. The Hyksos, however, built their capital, Avaris, in the Delta or Goshen area. When Ahmose expelled the Hyksos and destroyed Avaris, the capital was moved back to Thebes. The nearby location of Pharaoh's court in the Joseph story suggests that Hebrew settlement in Egypt took place during the Hyksos period. Supposing this is true,

---

[35]Consult G. Ernest Wright, *Shechem* [284], chap. 5.
[36]See Pritchard, *The Ancient Near East in Pictures* [1], pp. 14–20.

Insert 1-1 The Near East as seen from the Gemini II spacecraft while circling the earth in 1966. In the center of the picture is the Sinaitic Peninsula; below this is the Gulf of Suez and above is the Gulf of Aqabah. Extending north from the Gulf of Aqabah is the valley of the Dead Sea and further north still is the Sea of Galilee. The Jordan valley, which runs between these two bodies of water, provides the eastern boundary of the Holy Land; and the Mediterranean Sea *(upper left)* forms the western boundary.

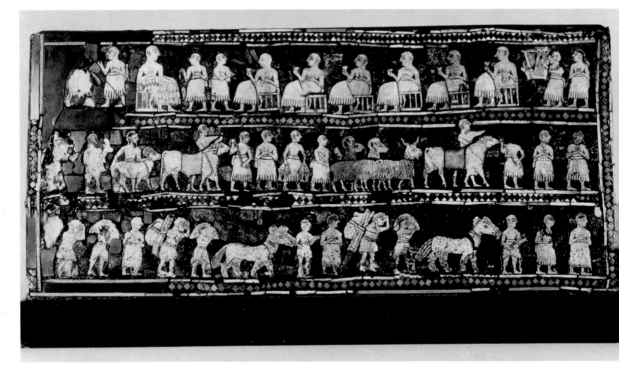

Insert 2-1 The Royal Standard of Ur, a mosaic made of shell, blue lapis lazuli, and red stone (jasper?), depicts a victory celebration. In the top row of the panel the king (the larger figure), surrounded by attendants, sits facing six distinguished guests, possibly military commanders, who join the feasting with upraised cups. To the right stands a lyrist and a black-haired woman, apparently a singer. The middle and lower rows show food, animals, and other spoils of war being brought to the king. The entire standard measures 22" x 9" (2600–2450 B.C.E.)

we might imagine that the Pharaoh who favored Joseph was a Hyksos king, perhaps a Semite himself and therefore hospitable to other Semites.

There is no clear evidence to support this view, attractive and plausible as it might be.[37] Neither the Joseph story nor the early chapters of the book of Exodus explicitly name a reigning monarch. Moreover, our historical knowledge of the Hyksos regime in Egypt is scant, and nothing in Egyptian records now available suggests the figure of Joseph as prime minister under Pharaoh. Because the biblical account depicts a peaceful migration into Egypt, the Hebrew settlement in the Delta area could not have been a part of the Hyksos invasion. But there might be a connection between these events. Israel's ancestors could have entered Egypt in a series of migrations, beginning during the early period of Hyksos domination. Undoubtedly the biblical tradition, for the sake of presenting a vivid, straightforward story, has telescoped events that took place over a long period of time, and has simplified issues that were actually very complex.

THE OPPRESSION IN EGYPT

Returning to the first chapter of the book of Exodus, we learn that after Joseph's death the family of Jacob lost favor in Egypt, owing to a change of administration. "Now there arose a new king over Egypt, who did not know Joseph" (Exod. 1–8). As a result, the Hebrews were reduced to the status of slaves and were put to work building the store cities of Pithom and Rameses in the Delta.

THE PHARAOH OF THE OPPRESSION

Unfortunately, the biblical account does not identify the Pharaoh whose change of political policy resulted in the oppression of Semites in the Delta region. Some historians believe that the account at the beginning of the book of Exodus points back to the beginning of the Eighteenth Dynasty, when Ahmose I expelled the Hyksos and, as a symbol of his new nationalism, moved the capital back to the city of Thebes. In this view many Semites, including the relatives of Jacob, survived Ahmose's purge and remained

---

[37]This view is defended by G. Ernest Wright in *Biblical Archaeology* [125], pp. 54–58. There are, of course, other possibilities for reconstructing the historical background of the patriarchs. Some historians such as C. H. Gordon, in *Introduction to Old Testament Times* (Ventnor, NJ: Ventnor Publishers, 1953), pp. 75, 102–4, place the ancestors in the period after the expulsion of the Hyksos (after 1500 B.C.E.), specifically during the disturbances of the Amarna Age (see pp. 113–114) and the establishment of such small states as Aram, Edom, Moab, and Ammon. This would explain why the book of Genesis makes no reference to the Egyptian domination of Canaan, but the view hardly does justice to the Amorite connections of Abraham. Other historians modify this view by connecting Abraham with the period of Hammurabi and Jacob with the Amarna period. See, for example, H. H. Rowley, *From Joseph to Joshua* (London: Oxford University Press, 1950), chap. 3, who specifically connects Joseph with the time of the Amarna king Akhnaton (1364–1347 B.C.E.). As Rowley admits, however, this requires a radical separation of Abraham (and Isaac) from Jacob and Joseph. For an updated discussion see George Ramsey, [116], chap. 3.

in the Delta. There they fell victim to the oppressive policies that accompanied Egyptian revival during the Eighteenth and Nineteenth Dynasties. During this period (the fifteenth through the thirteenth centuries B.C.E.) the Pharaohs needed cheap labor for their ambitious projects. According to Egyptian documents, they conscripted the service of *'Apiru* (*Habiru*)—a term we have seen is not necessarily limited to the biblical Hebrews. This view, however, leaves a significant time gap between Exodus 1:8 (Ahmose, the "king who did not know Joseph") and the narrative beginning in Exodus 1:9 about slave labor at Pithom and Rameses, fortified cities rebuilt around the turn of the thirteenth century. The statement in Exodus 12:40 that "the time that the people of Israel dwelt in Egypt was four hundred and thirty years" gives some slim support to this view: If this statement refers to the total time the Hebrews lived in the Delta area and not just to the years of oppression,[38] and if the date of the Exodus is reckoned to be about 1290 B.C.E., it brings us back to approximately the time of the Hyksos invasion (1290 + 430 = 1720 B.C.E.). The situation of Egypt might have been something like this:

Period of favor: c. 1720–1552	HYKSOS RULE *XV to XVI [XVII]* *Dynasties*	Capital at Avaris
Period of disfavor: c. 1552–1306	EGYPTIAN REVIVAL *XVIII Dynasty*	Capital moved to Thebes

Period of the Exodus:
  Seti I (c. 1305–1290)
  Rameses II (c. 1290–1224)
  (Pharaoh of the Exodus)
Period of the Conquest:
  Merneptah (c. 1224–1211)
	EGYPTIAN REVIVAL
	XIX Dynasty
		Capital at
		Avaris

This is all quite uncertain, and understandably historians are reserved about associating the descent of Jacob's family into Egypt with the Hyksos invasion, making Ahmose I the new king who was unfavorable to Joseph. The situation becomes much clearer, however, when we come to the period of the Nineteenth Dynasty, which began toward the end of the fourteenth century B.C.E. The account at the beginning of the book of Exodus apparently presupposes this period, when the Egyptian court was moved once again from Thebes to the Delta frontier to place the Pharaohs in a better position to regain their Asiatic empire, which had slipped out of control during the so-called Amarna period (see pp. 113–114). Seti I (about 1305–1290 B.C.E.), the first

---

[38]However, one can interpret Exodus 12:40 to refer only to the years of oppression, as in Genesis 15:13. The Greek version of the this passage in the Septuagint complicates the matter by saying that the Israelites lived in Egypt *and in the land of Canaan* 430 years, covering the whole period from the call of Abraham to the Exodus (see also Gal. 3:17). All of these figures must be weighed against archaeological and biblical evidence.

strong king of the Nineteenth Dynasty, began the reconstruction of the old Hyksos capital, Avaris. The project was continued by his son Rameses II (about 1290–1224 B.C.E.), who renamed the capital Pi-Rameses, the "House of Rameses." The Egyptians also carried out a building program at *Pr-Itm* (Pithom), west of Lake Timsah in the same region where Joseph's brothers were said to have settled. These cities are specifically mentioned in Exodus 1:11, which recounts that Hebrew slaves were employed in their construction. Egyptian documents also record that these Pharaohs used *'Apiru* in public projects.

Despite the problem of relating Joseph to a particular Pharaoh, the opening chapters of the book of Exodus seem to have as their background the situation in Egypt under the Nineteenth Dynasty, specifically under the oppressive regimes of Seti I and Rameses II. Although scholars cannot pinpoint a definite date, many believe that the Exodus took place early in the reign of Rameses II (about 1280 B.C.E. or shortly afterward); (see Inserts 5–1 and 6–1) whose mummy is on display at the Cairo Museum.[39] The next Pharaoh, Merneptah (about 1224–1211 B.C.E.), bragged about victory over Israel in Canaan about 1220, establishing that the Israelites were already present, though not settled, in the land at that time (see pp. 117–118).

The biblical narratives, while reflecting the sober realities of this political situation, interpret these realities through the eyes of Israelite faith. Many other peoples, and many other *'Apiru*, were involved in the disturbed political situation of the Fertile Crescent during the second millennium. But only the Hebrews who stood in the circle of Moses experienced the depth of historical meaning that led to the remembering and eventually the writing down of their historical traditions. Historical investigation can help us to understand that the biblical story was intimately tied up with political and social developments of the time. It takes religious imagination, however, to go beyond the externals to the inner meaning of the events that Israel proclaimed in the exalted language of worship. The significance of the Exodus is determined not by its date, but by its place in the unfolding of the divine purpose in human affairs. In the next chapter, we turn directly to Moses and the drama of liberation in which he played a decisive role as leader and interpreter.

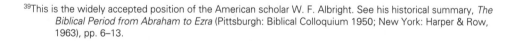

[39]This is the widely accepted position of the American scholar W. F. Albright. See his historical summary, *The Biblical Period from Abraham to Ezra* (Pittsburgh: Biblical Colloquium 1950; New York: Harper & Row, 1963), pp. 6–13.

Chronological Chart 1

B.C.E.	Egypt	Palestine and Syria	Mesopotamia (and Asia Minor)
2000 to 1900	XII Dynasty	Egyptian Control	Third Dynasty of Ur (c. 2060–1950) Hurrian Movement Amorite Invasion
1900 to 1800	XII Dynasty		First Babylonian Dynasty (c. 1830–1530)
1800 to 1700	Hyksos Invasion (c. 1720)	Abraham	The Mari Age Hammurabi (c. 1728–1686)
1700 to 1600	Hyksos Rule (XV to XVI Dynasties) XVII (Theban) Dynasty	Hyksos Control Descent of Jacob family into Egypt	Decline of Babylonia
1600 to 1500	XVIII Dynasty: Ahmose (c. 1552–1527) Expulsion of Hyksos	Egyptian Control	Old Hittite Empire (c. 1600–1500)
1500 to 1400	Thutmose III (c. 1490–1436)		Kingdom of Mitanni (c. 1500–1370)
1400 to 1300	Amenhotep III (c. 1403–1364) Amenhotep IV or Akhnaton (c. 1364–1347)	Amarna Age (c. 1400–1350) Egyptian Weakness	New Hittite Empire (c. 1375–1200) Rise of Assyria (c. 1356–1197)
1300 to 1200	XIX Dynasty: Seti I (c. 1305–1290) Rameses II (c. 1290–1224) Merneptah (c. 1224–1211)	Egyptian Revival (The Exodus, c. 1280) Israelite Conquest (c. 1250–1200) Merneptah's Victory (c. 1220)	Assyrian Dominance

(Middle Bronze Age) spans 2000 to 1700.
(Late Bronze Age) spans 1500 to 1200.

Note: The date of Hammurabi is still uncertain. Some scholars put him in the nineteenth century—that is, the early Amorite period. Others argue for a date in the seventeenth century—the period of Babylonian decline. The former suggestion would not affect our basic outline.

CHAPTER 2

LIBERATION FROM BONDAGE

In their fundamental confession of faith, the ancient Israelites affirmed that the God whom they worshiped "heard our voice, and saw our affliction, our toil, and our oppression" and, in a never-to-be-forgotten act, "brought us out of Egypt with a mighty hand and an outstretched arm, with great terror, with signs and wonders" (Deut. 26:5–9; see 6:21–25). Israel understood its history as originating in a marvelous liberation from distress and oppression. A dispirited band of slaves, bound together only by their common plight, would never have become a "people"—a covenant community with a sense of historical vocation—had God not acted to help them out of a seemingly hopeless situation. The verbs of the narrative sweep to a climax: God heard, God saw, God rescued.

In this chapter and the next, we turn to the narratives in the book of Exodus that elaborate the theme of the Exodus and its sequel, the covenant at Sinai. Consider first the story recounted in Exodus 1–15. In their present form these chapters clearly constitute a dramatic unity, despite some inconsistency and repetition inherited from oral traditions and from the literary reworking of these traditions in various circles. The major elements of the story are:

Biblical Reading: This chapter deals with the section of the biblical narrative in Exodus 1–15.

1. The oppression of Jacob's descendants in Egypt (Exod. 1).
2. The rise of Moses: his infancy, early life in Egypt and Midian, and his call and commission (Exod. 2:1–7:7).
3. The contest with Pharaoh (Exod. 7:8–10:29), culminating in the final plague of the death of the firstborn and the celebration of the Passover (Exod. 11:1–13:16).
4. The flight from Egypt and victory at the Sea (Exod. 13:17–14:31).
5. A concluding hymn of triumph in two versions: the "Song of the Sea" (Exod. 15:1–18) and the "Song of Miriam" (Exod. 15:19–21).

Consider the plot of this drama, a mighty contest between two opposing powers. On one side is "the God of the Hebrews," represented by Moses and his assistant, Aaron. On the other is stubborn Pharaoh with his crafty magicians and all the imperial power and glory of Egypt. Notice that Moses' God does not enter into conflict with the gods of Egypt (mentioned only in Exod. 12:12) but with Pharaoh, who presumptuously supposes that he can determine the course of history. To be sure, this is not a case of ordinary human arrogance. Egyptians believed Pharaoh was the embodiment of deity, possessing superhuman wisdom and absolute power.[1] At the time of our story, Pharaoh Rameses II had shifted his political center to the Delta area to strengthen his hold over Egypt's Asiatic empire (see pp. 45–47). The construction work at Pithom and Rameses, where *Habiru* were employed as state slaves, was part of his grandiose political ambition.

The narrative presupposes that the God who speaks and works through Moses is fully in control, for the whole earth belongs to Yahweh (Exod. 9:29). Nevertheless, the story is told in a way that creates dramatic suspense. The initial moves are made by Pharaoh, who first attempts to crush the Hebrews' spirit by imposing hard labor and then, in a desperate act of genocide, commands that all their newborn males be killed. Even at this stage, the king's sovereignty is implicitly threatened, for by a strange turn of events the infant Moses is rescued from the Nile by an Egyptian princess and taken to the palace to be raised under Pharaoh's nose! This is the Moses who, nurtured by Egyptian culture and empowered by a divine commission, is destined to become leader of the people and challenge Pharaoh in the name of "the God of the ancestors." In a series of episodes the narrator heightens the dramatic suspense. Each visit to Pharaoh accentuates the crisis; each plague increases the gravity of the situation in Egypt. Finally, Pharaoh relaxes his stubborn hold on the Hebrews. In a moment of weakness, he allows them to leave, only to change his mind and send his warriors in hot pursuit. The denouement comes when the Israelites, trapped between the Egyptian forces and the watery expanse ahead of them, are marvelously delivered as the waters close in on their

---

[1]Egyptian kings were regarded as the divine sons of the supreme god of Egypt, the sun-god Re or Amon. A typical letter to Pharaoh begins: "To my king, my lord, my sun-god" (for example, see Amarna Letter No. 288 in Pritchard, *Ancient Near Eastern Texts* [1], p. 488).

pursuers. The powerful dramatic qualities of this story have stirred the imagination down through the centuries.

THE ROLE OF MOSES

The Exodus story is not a heroic epic told to celebrate Moses as liberator of the people. The narrator's primary purpose is to glorify the God of Israel, the "Divine Warrior" whose strong hand and outstretched arm won the victory over Pharaoh and his hosts. Nevertheless, Moses plays an essential role in this story. Through Moses, the political leader, the people are brought out of the land of Egypt. Through Moses, the mediator between God and the people, the meaning of the crisis and the miraculous act of deliverance are declared. While brooding over the fate of the people during his exile from Egypt, Moses has a revealing experience in a lonely mountain spot in the Sinaitic wilderness. With new understanding he returns to Egypt, where he rallies the people and announces the meaning of subsequent events. We turn now to the narratives that deal with Moses in Exodus 2–4.[2]

MOSES' BACKGROUND

Everything we know about Moses is contained in the biblical narratives. Even this knowledge is limited because the narrators were not interested in Moses' biography. Although Moses is an imposing historical figure, the story focuses not so much on Moses' personality as on the God who prepares and summons him to be the agent in the accomplishment of the divine purpose.[3]

The tradition that Moses was raised and educated in Egyptian circles is probably authentic, though colored with elements of folklore. The story of a baby in a basket of bulrushes (Exod. 2:1–10), for example, is reminiscent of a similar legend about Sargon of Akkad (see p. 29–31). In an inscription, Sargon says that his mother gave birth to him in secret, placed him in a basket of rushes sealed with bitumen, and cast him adrift on the river. Akki, the drawer of water, lifted him out of the water and reared him as his son. From this humble beginning Sargon rose to be mighty king of the city of Agade, from which Akkadians drew their name.[4] Moreover, the motif of the adoption of the infant Moses by Pharaoh's daughter (Exod. 1:7–10) is strikingly paralleled in an ancient Mesopotamian legal text. This text stipulates that a foundling shall be turned over to a

---

[2]See Michael Fishbane's perceptive essay, "Exodus 1–4: The Prologue to the Exodus Cycle," in *Text and Texture: Close Readings of Selected Biblical Texts* (New York: Schocken, 1979), pp. 63–76, and J. Cheryl Exum, " 'You Shall Let Every Daughter Live': A Study of Exodus 1:8—2:10," *Semeia* 28 (1983), 63–82.

[3]In this connection, see Gerhard von Rad's illuminating little study, *Moses* [249].

[4]See Pritchard, *Ancient Near Eastern Texts* [1], p. 119.

Slaves Making Bricks for Pharaoh are shown in a tomb painting from the period of the Eighteenth Dynasty. The clay is moistened by water drawn from the pool (left), kneaded with the aid of small hoes, and carried in baskets to the brick makers, who shape it in rectangular moulds. After the bricks are laid out to dry in the sun (just right of the pool), they are carried away. Notice the two dark-skinned taskmasters who oversee the work. These scenes illumine the story of how the Hebrews made "bricks without straw" during the oppression in Egypt.

nurse paid to suckle the child, and that after a three-year period of guardianship, the child shall be adopted and educated as a scribe.[5]

Clearly, various elements of popular imagination influenced the tradition of Moses' birth and his nurture in Pharaoh's court. Moses' name, however, authenticates his Egyptian upbringing. To be sure, the Israelite storyteller, by a play on words, tries to derive the name Moses (Hebrew: *Mosheh*) from a Hebrew verb meaning "to draw out" (*mashah*). The narrator even says the Egyptian princess knew enough Hebrew to explain the name this way (Exod. 2:10). But this is an example of the popular explanation of names based on assonance, or similarity of sound (like taking the meaning of the name Abel from the verb "to be able"). Actually *Mosheh* is the Hebrew form of an Egyptian verb *mose*, meaning "is born." It appears frequently in theophorous (referring to a deity) names such as Tuth-*mose* ("the god Toth is born"), Ptah-*mose*, or Ra-*meses* (Rameses). Royal children born on the anniversary of a deity were named in this fashion, and Pharaohs of the Nineteenth Dynasty were sometimes referred to in the shortened form "Mose," without the name of the deity.[6] Other members of Moses' tribe, the tribe of Levi (Exod. 2:1), had Egyptian names such as Merari and Phinehas (6:16, 25). Also, the name Aaron is possibly Egyptian.

Despite his upbringing in Pharaoh's court Moses strongly identified with his Hebrew kin, as is shown vividly in the story of his impulsive reaction on seeing an Egyptian taskmaster beating a Hebrew slave to death (Exod. 2:11–15). Rumor of the slaying spread quickly and, fearing the wrath of Pharaoh (probably Seti I), Moses fled for his life—not to return until Seti's successor, Rameses II, took the throne (Exod. 2:23;

[5]See Brevard S. Childs, "The Birth of Moses," *Journal of Biblical Literature*, 84 (1965), 109–22, and his discussion of Exodus 2–4 in *The Book of Exodus* [238].
[6]See R. de Vaux, *History* [111], p. 329; also D. M. Beegle, *Moses* [234], pp. 53–55.

4:18–20). Moses took refuge in "the land of Midian," an area of the Sinaitic Peninsula occupied by Midianite shepherds.[7] There, after showing kindness to women at a well, he received hospitality in the tent of "the priest of Midian" and eventually married one of the priest's daughters, Zipporah (Exod. 2:15–22). Various traditions surround the name of Moses' father-in-law, called at different times Jethro (Exod. 3:1; 18:1), Hobab (Judg. 4:11), and Reuel—though perhaps Reuel was the head of the clan and father of Jethro (Exod. 2:18; compare Num. 2:14). In any case, Moses' connection with the Midianites is authentic.

THE BURNING BUSH

While tending the flocks of his father-in-law in the Midianite wilderness, Moses stumbled upon "the mountain of God." The story of Moses' encounter with "the God of the ancestors" in that sacred place, and of the intense inner struggle his God-given task aroused, is one of the masterpieces of the Pentateuch (Exod. 3:1–17). One must read this narrative with imagination and empathy, as a piece of poetry, for it expresses a dimension of meaning that cannot be confined within the limits of precise prose.

....

DEFINITION: "HEBREW"

Today the term "Hebrew" is often used to refer to the Jewish people or to their classical language, Hebrew. It once had a much wider meaning, however.

In the Old Testament/Hebrew Bible the term appears frequently in the Joseph story (see Gen. 39:17; 40:15; 41:12), the Exodus story (see Exod. 1:16; 2:7; 3:18; 5:3; 7:16), and the story of the Philistine wars (see 1 Sam. 4:6; 13:19; 14:11). Outsiders generally use "Hebrew" to refer to the Israelites, and Israelites use the term when speaking to outsiders. Unlike "Israel," however, "Hebrew" does not imply a sense of communal solidarity. There were Hebrews who were not members of the Israelite community.

[7]Geographers usually locate Midian in Arabia to the southeast of the Gulf of Aqabah (see map, p. 70). Because of their roving way of life and their special interest in copper resources, however, the Midianites extended their power into the southern part of the Sinaitic Peninsula. See *Westminster Historical Atlas* [41], p. 38.

Abraham is called a Hebrew only once, in a peculiar tradition concerning his wars with the kings of the east (Gen. 14:13). "Abram the Hebrew" (*'ibri*) was a descendant of Eber (*'eber*), introduced in the genealogy of Genesis 10:21. In that geneaology, however, Eber is the ancestor of other peoples as well: Arabs, Arameans, Moabites, Ammonites, and Edomites. Moreover, documents of the second millennium B.C.E. (such as the Amarna Letters) contain numerous references to *'Apiru* (*Habiru*) as a floating class within the population (see pp. 37–38).

This suggests that the term "Hebrew" was at one time more inclusive than in the biblical narratives, where it refers specifically to Hebrews who were slaves in Egypt and eventually became the community known as Israel. Later the term came to be associated only with the biblical Hebrews or Jewish people (see Jonah 1:9). The Apostle Paul insisted he was "a Hebrew born of Hebrews" (Phil. 3:2).

A critical reading reveals various irregularities: For example, Moses' father-in-law is called Jethro, not Reuel or Hobab; the sacred mountain is explicitly called Horeb, not Sinai;[8] and there is some alternation in the names used for the deity. To account for these disparities, scholars have theorized that separate literary traditions were woven together[9] and that the narrative also bears the marks of an earlier oral tradition. In any case, the story comes to us in its final form as a superb example of narrative art.

The story belongs to a narrative genre that portrays the divine calling and commission of a prophetic figure. Some of its features parallel the account of Jeremiah's call and commission (Jer. 1:4–19): the expostulation with God, the assurance of the divine presence, and the "sign" (the almond rod and the boiling pot). Because the story deals with an inner event, namely, a person's vocation or calling from God, attempts to rationalize the burning bush are beside the point. Whatever Moses saw, it signified to him that he was in the presence of the Holy. The wilderness spot was transfigured into a sacred place, a sanctuary where sandals must be removed. The description of Moses' response to this divine manifestation is terse (Exod 3:6): "Moses hid his face, for he was afraid to look at *'Elohim* [deity]."

The experience of the "holy," which both fascinates and repels, is a well-known phenomenon in the history of religions.[10] For Moses, however, the Holy is not a numinous, suprarational mystery or *mysterium tremendum,* but is associated with the God of Abraham, Isaac, and Jacob. In this theological context, holiness is divine power that breaks into the human world, to upset Pharaoh's oppressive regime and deliver a band of helpless slaves.

Notice how the narrator quickly shifts attention from sight (the bush that does not burn) to sound (God's voice heard by Moses). The way God speaks provides clear

---

[8]Perhaps the narrator intends to make a veiled allusion to the alternate name of the mountain, Sinai: The word for "bush" (Hebrew: *s*^e*neh*) can be understood as a word-play on *Sinai.*

[9]See the supplement to Martin Noth's *Pentateuchal Traditions* [76], pp. 261–76, for an analytical outline of the Pentateuch based on source analysis.

[10]See Rudolf Otto's classical work, *The Idea of the Holy* [143]; and John Gammie, *Holiness in Israel* (Minneapolis: Fortress Press, 1989).

evidence that the problem of the Hebrew slaves in Egypt lay heavily upon Moses' heart. (Recall that Moses fled Egypt after an outburst of anger that led to the murder of a slave driver.) God's words have *historical* meaning. Several verbs describe the divine intention: "I *have seen* the affliction of my people . . . and *have heard* their cry . . . I *know* their sufferings, and *have come down to deliver them* . . ." (Exod. 3:7–8). In contrast to the God of philosophers such as Plato and Aristotle, the God of Moses is not aloof from the human scene or apathetic about human suffering. Rather, the "God of pathos," as Abraham Heschel observes, is sensitive to the human condition and participates in human affairs with saving power.[11] In this narrative we come to the very heart of Israel's historical faith.

Moses' encounter with God sharpened his sense of identity and made him acutely conscious of the demands of the historical hour. In the "I-thou" dialogue, Moses was given a task and was summoned to take part with God in the historical drama: "Come, I will send you to Pharaoh . . ." (Exod. 3:10). With religious insight and sensitivity, the narrator describes Moses' uneasiness about the call and the protests he offers in an attempt to stay on the comfortable sidelines of history.

THE DISCLOSURE OF GOD'S NAME

Among other things, Moses protests that if he were to go to the Hebrews in Egypt and tell them about his experience at Sinai, he would need to know God's name (Exod. 3:13). In antiquity this was a vital question, not just because of the popular belief that many gods existed, but because a name expressed the character or identity of a god (or person). This way of thinking might seem strange today, for in modern society names are often just convenient labels used to distinguish one person or thing from another. Like Shakespeare's Juliet we are apt to ask, "What's in a name?" Moreover, in some religions the very notion of the name of God makes no sense, for the Ineffable cannot be defined or limited within the realm of sensory experience. Surely Moses could have used any current title (such as Shaddai, El, Baal, Re) without substantially altering the meaning of his report.

To the ancient Israelites, however, a name was filled with power and vitality.[12] At the human level, the name represented one's innermost self or identity. Consequently, naming a child was a significant event; and if someone went through a transforming experience (as Jacob, Gen. 32:27–28) that person often received a new name. To know someone personally, it was necessary to know that person's name. Analo-

---

[11]See the illuminating discussion of "the pathos of God," including the "passion" of wrath and mercy, judgment and compassion, by Abraham Joshua Heschel in *The Prophets* [352], chaps. 12–14.

[12]See the discussion of "Name" by Johannes Pedersen in *Israel* [136], pp. 1–11, 245–59. For a similar conception in African society, see E. B. Idowu, *Olódùmarè: God in Yoruba Belief* (London: Longmans, Green and Co., 1962), chap. 4.

gously, it was exceedingly important to know the name of God (again, think of Jacob's nocturnal wrestling in Gen. 32:27, 29), not only in order to establish a personal relationship with the deity, but, above all, to "call upon the name of Yahweh" in worship (see Ps. 116:12–14).

At first glance, one might assume that Moses' question about God's name was a concession to the polytheism of the ancient world. In an environment where many divine powers were present, some known and some unknown, people naturally would want to know which god had chosen to favor them or which god they might have offended.[13] The Exodus 3 narrative, however, rises above this level of popular belief. Clearly the narrator wants us to know that the God who spoke long ago to the ancestors was the same God who confronted Moses in this new situation and announced the divine plan to intervene on behalf of Hebrew slaves. Moses' question, then, amounted to an attempt to know the identity of God. It was tantamount to saying: "Who are you?"

THE GREAT I AM

At this point we come to one of the most cryptic passages in the Old Testament. The account contains no less than three repetitive introductions to God's answer to Moses' question.

Exodus

3:13   Moses said to *'Elohim* [God], "All right, when I go to the Israelites and say that the God of their ancestors has sent me to them, they will ask me, 'What is his name?' and what am I going to say to them?"

14a   *'Elohim* replied to Moses, "*'ehyeh 'asher 'ehyeh*" ["I am who I am" or "I will be who I will be"].

14b   And he [*'Elohim*] said, "*'ehyeh* ["I Am"] has sent me to you."

15a   Again *'Elohim* said to Moses, Thus you shall say to the Israelites, 'YHWH [JPSV, NRSV: *The Lord*], the God of your ancestors, the God of Abraham, the God of Isaac, and the God of Jacob has sent me to you.'

15   'This is my name for all time, and this is how I am to be designated for generations to come.'"

··

DEFINITION: "JEHOVAH," "THE LORD"

The personal divine name YHWH, cryptically referred to in Exodus 3:13, has an interesting history. In the biblical period the Hebrew language was written only with conso-

---

[13]See the ancient Sumerian "Prayer to Every God" in Pritchard, *Ancient Near Eastern Texts* [1], pp. 391–92. The supplicant, not knowing what god he has offended and why he is suffering, addresses any god and all gods whether known or unknown.

nants. Vowels were not added until the Common Era, when Hebrew was no longer a living language. On the basis of Greek texts, which use both vowels and consonants, scholars believe that the original pronunciation was "Yah-weh." Notice the shortened form of the divine name in the exclamation, "Halleluyah" (from the Hebrew *hallelu yah*, "Praise Yah").

Because of its holy character, the name Yahweh was withdrawn from ordinary speech during the period of the Second Temple (about 500 B.C.E. and later). Another Hebrew word—a title, not a personal name—was substituted: *Adonai*, or "(The) Lord," a name still used in synagogues. Scholars who translated the Hebrew Bible into Greek (the Septuagint) in the third century B.C.E. adopted this synagogue convention and rendered YHWH as (*ho*) *kurios*, "(The) Lord." From this Greek translation the practice was carried over into the New Testament.

The word "Jehovah" is an artificial form that arose from the combination of the consonants YHWH with the vowels of Adonai, written under or over the Hebrew consonants to indicate pronunciation. This hybrid form is often attributed to Peter Galatin, confessor of Pope Leo X, in a publication dated 1518 C.E., but in actuality it can be traced back to a work by Raymond Martin in 1270.[14]

Jewish reverence for the divine name has influenced numerous modern translations, including the Septuagint. These translations follow the ancient synagogue practice and substitute *Adonai* (translated "El Señor" in Spanish, "Der Herr" in German, "The Lord" in English, and so on). Here we will use the presumed original form, "Yahweh" (as does the New Jerusalem Bible).[15]

Notice that the direct answer to Moses' query about how he should answer the "Israelites" in Egypt (Exod. 3:13) comes at the conclusion of this passage (Exod. 3:15). In the intervening verse 14, with its separate sections (a and b), the tradition connects the consonantal form YHWH, the special name for the God of Israel, with the Hebrew verb translated "I am" (or, "I will be"). In Hebrew *'ehyeh* ("I am") is the first person singular of the verb *h-y-h*, in its older spelling, *h-w-h* ("to be"). YHWH is the third person singular of the same verb, "he is" or "he will be." The first person form is used in verse 14 because God, when speaking personally, says "I am."

Even in English translation the repetition in verses 14 and 15 seems awkward: "*'Elohim* said," "And he said," "*'Elohim* again said." It suggests that originally Moses' question in verse 13 was followed by the clear answer in verse 15: The personal name of "the God of the ancestors" is Yahweh. If so, we might conjecture that at some point in the history of the tradition the explanation of the divine name given in verse 14 was incorporated into the story.[16] In any case, this is the only place in the Hebrew Bible where there is an attempt to explain the name on the basis of the verb "to be." Scholars, in

[14]See the *Jewish Encyclopedia*, VII (1904), p. 88.
[15]See further B. W. Anderson, "Taking the Lord's Name in Vain," *Bible Review* (June 1995), 17, 48.
[16]This view is held by Martin Noth, *Exodus* [247], p. 80, and R. de Vaux, *History* [111], p. 350.

turn, have made many attempts to explain the explanation! We will briefly consider three interpretations.

One interpretation attempts to go behind the present reading (vocalization) of the consonants as handed down in Jewish tradition and spelled out around 700 C.E. by rabbinical scholars known as the Masoretes. In this view, the divine name YHWH was based originally on a causative form of the verb "to be," namely, "he causes to be" or "he creates" (*yahweh*). This interpretation requires no change in the Hebrew consonants of the verbs in verse 14 and only a slight change in the vowels written in later (*'ahyeh* instead of *'ehyeh*). Moreover, it explains the divine name as it was probably originally pronounced: "Yahweh." Thus the enigmatic expression emphasizes God's creative activity: "I cause to be what I cause to be," or, "I create what I create." In other words, natural phenomena and historical events have their origin in the will of God who is Creator and Lord.[17]

A second interpretation is based on the present reading of the text, that is, the simple form of the verb translated "I am." This is the case with the Greek translation in the Septuagint: *Ego eimi ho ōn* ("I am the One who is"). Some scholars object that this interpretation might introduce a philosophical notion of God's *eternal being* alien to the Israelite way of thinking. Ancient Greeks, who struggled philosophically with the problem of the Changing and the Changeless, would have favored the view that God's being is not essentially affected by the flux and flow of time. Israelite interpreters, on the other hand, were concerned about God's historical activity and the movement of God's purpose toward a temporal goal—not about the divine being or essence within the Godhead. This point deserves consideration. If, however, the verb "to be" is understood in a dynamic sense (as in the phrase, "it came to pass") and if the declaration in verse 14 is read in its narrative context, one can find here an emphasis on the divine *will*: Yahweh's zealous activity and exclusive claim of sovereignty. In this view, Yahweh is "the only one who exists for Israel." Unlike the gods of Egypt and Canaan, who were involved in the cyclical phenomena of the natural world, Yahweh is the transcendent God whose sovereign will is manifest in a succession of events moving toward a goal.[18]

A third and most probable interpretation is also based on the present reading of the text, although the simple form of the verb is translated in the future tense ("I will be"). According to this view, one must understand the declaration in verse 14 in its immediate context, where the God of the ancestors promises to be with and go with Moses: "I will be with you" (Exod. 3:12), "I will be with your mouth" (4:12, 15), or "I

---

[17]This view was championed by W. F. Albright, *From the Stone Age to Christianity* [127], pp. 258–61. It is supported by his students D. N. Freedman, "The Name of the God of Moses," *Journal of Biblical Literature,* 79 (1960), 151–56; D. M. Beegle, *Moses* [234], pp. 69–73; and Frank M. Cross, "Yahweh and the God of the Patriarchs" [209]. Cross gives the theory a new twist by regarding Yahweh as a cult name of the high God El.

[18]See R. de Vaux, "The Revelation of the Divine Name YHWH," in *Proclamation and Presence* [180], pp. 48–75; reprinted with some changes in *History* [111], pp. 349–57.

will be your God" (6:7). The divine name signifies God whose being is turned toward the people; is present in their midst as deliverer, guide, and judge; and is accessible in worship. While giving the divine name (self), Yahweh nevertheless retains the divine freedom that eludes human control: "I will be gracious to whom I will be gracious, and will show mercy upon whom I will show mercy" (Exod. 33:19). Yahweh's name cannot be taken in vain—that is, used for human purposes (Exod. 20:7). The enigmatic words in Exodus 3:14 might reflect God's reticence about revealing the divine name.[19] The answer to Moses' inquiry into the mystery of the divine nature (Name) is somewhat evasive lest the people, knowing the Name, try to hold God under magical control (see Gen. 32:29; Judg. 13:17–18) and make God "their God" in a possessive sense.[20] The God who speaks to Moses is the Lord, not the servant of the people.

THE ORIGIN OF THE YAHWEH CULT

Moses was to tell Pharaoh: "Yahweh, the God of the Hebrews, has met with us" (Exod. 3:18). Though it is difficult to explain the name Yahweh on the basis of verses 13 and 14, we can at least ask the question: Where did this name come from? How does it happen that Yahweh, rather than some other name, is the personal name of "the God of Israel"?

Careful reading reveals that the Exodus 3 narrative alternately uses two terms for deity: the general term translated "God" (Hebrew: *'Elohim*; Exod. 3:1, 4, 11–13) and the special Hebrew word "Yahweh" (Exod. 3:2, 4, 7, 15). This leads many scholars to conclude that the narrative interweaves traditions so closely that they can hardly be separated.[21] Indeed, the discovery of this same alternation of divine names in the book of Genesis gave impetus to the study of the Pentateuch in the eighteenth century. The Creation narrative (Gen. 1:1–2:3) consistently uses the name Elohim, but the Garden of Eden story (Gen. 2:4b–3:24) uses Yahweh (in combination with Elohim). The alternation of names, along with apparent differences in style, theological idiom, and the presence of repetitions and inconsistencies, led to the hypothesis that various "sources" were woven together in the Pentateuch.

The alternation of divine names might reflect separate traditions with differing views as to when the name Yahweh was introduced. According to one passage in the book of Genesis, the worship of Yahweh reached back into the period before the Flood, to the generation of Enosh, the grandson of Adam:

---

[19]Johannes Pedersen remarks in *Israel* [136], I–II, p. 252: "If one is to enter into relation with somebody, he must know his name, and if he knows it then he may use it and exercise influence over him."

[20]See Martin Buber, *Moses* [235], pp. 51–55, and the restatement of this view by Gerhard von Rad in *Moses* [249], pp. 18–28.

[21]On the basis of source analysis, Exodus 3:1–8 belongs to J with the exception of the second half of verse 4, where the word "God" (*'Elohim*) is suddenly introduced, and verse 6. Exodus 3:9–15, which begins with a duplication of the statement that *'Elohim* has heard the people's cry (compare J in verse 7), belongs to E. See the supplement to Noth's *Pentateuchal Traditions* [76], p. 267.

> At that time it became customary to call upon the name of Yahweh.
> —GENESIS 4:26b

In this Old Epic tradition, Yahweh appears to Israel's ancestors beginning with Abraham (Gen. 12:7). Other traditions, however, refrain from using the name Yahweh in the period covered by the book of Genesis, insisting that the name is primarily associated with the revelation to Moses. The Priestly (P) account of Moses' call puts the matter emphatically:

> And God ['*Elohim*] said to Moses, "I am Yahweh. I appeared to
> Abraham, to Isaac, and to Jacob as God Almighty ['*El Shaddai*], but by my
> name Yahweh I did not make myself known to them."
> —EXODUS 6:2–3 (compare GENESIS 17:1)

Apparently the passage in Exodus 3:13–15, where Moses asks for the name of "the God of the ancestors," reflects an ancient oral tradition in which the name Yahweh was unknown.[22] Some argue that the passage does not say Moses received a new name for God, but only a new explanation for a name already known during the ancestral period. But the words of verse 15, "This is my name for all time, and this is how I am to be designated for generations to come," seem to introduce a new name into the circle of Moses. Moreover, the statement in the second version of Moses' call (Exod. 6:3) leaves no room for doubt.

Thus we have two distinct traditions. According to one, God was known and worshiped as Yahweh from the earliest times. According to the other, the cultic name was introduced in the period of Moses. Which is right?

One tradition (usually identified as the Yahwist, or J) underscores the *theological* conviction that Yahweh, the God of Israel, is actually Sovereign of all history and creation. This tradition, by tracing worship of Yahweh back to the remote beginnings, places the Israelite story in an ecumenical perspective. Efforts have been made to show that this tradition is also *historically* correct in the sense that the name Yahweh was actually in use in the pre-Mosaic period, perhaps among the Amorites or in patriarchal clans—but the results are inconclusive.[23] The other traditions (E and P) seem truer to the actual situation when they suggest that the name became commonly accepted during and after the time of Moses, a time when parents began giving their children names compounded with an abbreviated form of the name Yahweh (such as Joshua, meaning "Yahweh is salvation"). Names of this type are not found in the pre-Mosaic period in the biblical traditions, suggesting that the name Yahweh gained currency in the time

[22]Literary critics generally assign this passage to the Elohistic (E) tradition, which at this point echoes ancient oral tradition more clearly than the parallel Yahwist (J) tradition, in which Yahweh is identified as "the God of the fathers." See Brevard Childs, *Exodus* [238], pp. 64–70.

[23]See especially Frank M. Cross, "Yahweh and the God of the Patriarchs" [209]; also Bright, *History* [110], pp. 151–52, and de Vaux, *History* [111], pp. 338ff.

of the Exodus. According to one hypothesis, Yahweh was formerly the mountain god of the Kenites, a clan of the Midianites. Moses was initiated into the Yahweh cult through his marriage to Zipporah, daughter of "the priest of Midian." While tending his father-in-law's flocks in Midianite territory, Moses received a commission from Yahweh at the mountain of Horeb (Exod. 3:5), supposedly a Midianite holy place. Moses then returned to Egypt, where he acquainted his kin with the previously unknown deity and rallied them to return with him to the mountain to worship Yahweh.[24]

The truth is we are not sure from what source Moses received "Yahweh" as the name of God. The significant point here is not where the name came from, or even its literal meaning, but what the name stood for in the worship of Israel from the time of Moses. Regardless of whether the name originated among the Amorites, patriarchal clans, Midianites, or some other people, we must recognize that "Yahweh" meant something radically different to the Hebrews who followed Moses out of Egypt. Whatever its literal meaning, which we cannot recover with certainty, the name was filled with a new meaning at the time of the Exodus. For the Israelite people, the name Yahweh had just one meaning: "I am Yahweh your God, who brought you out of the land of Egypt, out of the house of bondage" (Exod. 20:2).

THE CONTEST WITH PHARAOH

The central theme of the story in Exodus 3 and 4 is Yahweh's commission to Moses: "Come now, I will send you to Pharaoh that you may bring forth my people, the Israelites, out of Egypt" (Exod. 3:10). Like the prophets who followed him, Moses is portrayed as one *sent* to deliver a message in the name of Yahweh, the Sender. A key passage in the Exodus story makes the role of the messenger (prophet) clear:

> You shall say to Pharaoh:
>   "This is what Yahweh says:
>   'Israel is my first-born son.
>   I tell you to let my son go that he may serve
>   [worship] me.
>   If you refuse to let him go,
>   then I am going to slay your first-born!'"
>   —EXODUS 4:22–23

---

[24]The Kenite hypothesis is usually associated with Karl Budde; see his *The Religion of Israel to the Exile* (New York: G. P. Putnam's Sons, 1899), chap. 1. For a defense of this hypothesis see H. H. Rowley, *From Joseph to Joshua* (Chap. 1, fn 37), p. 149. For a vigorous criticism see James Theophile Meek, *Hebrew Origins*, Harper Torchbooks (New York: Harper & Brothers, 1960), chap. 3, and Martin Buber, *The Prophetic Faith* [313], pp. 24–30.

It is appropriate, then, for Hosea to state years later:

> By a prophet Yahweh brought up Israel out of Egypt,
>   and by a prophet Israel was protected.
>
> —HOSEA 12:13

Exodus 4:22–23 anticipates the final round in the struggle between Yahweh and Pharaoh. The narrator introduces the passage by stating that even when Moses performs the "wonders" Yahweh has put in his power, they will have no effect because Yahweh will "harden" Pharaoh's heart. In the perspective of the narrator, Yahweh is completely in control—indeed, everything is foreknown and foreordained! No attempt is made to resolve the paradox of human freedom and divine sovereignty. The text states repeatedly that Yahweh hardened Pharaoh's heart, but also that Pharaoh hardens his own heart—that is, his obstinacy expresses his own will (Exod. 8:15, 32; 9:34). The narrator tells the story in a way that glorifies the God of Israel: Pharaoh is given a lot of rope, so to speak, but he cannot run beyond the bounds of Yahweh's sovereign control (compare Romans 9:17). Indeed, the story has a didactic purpose: to teach future generations of Israel how Yahweh "made a toy" of the Egyptians by performing "signs" among them, "so that you may know that I am Yahweh" (Exod. 10:2; also Deut. 6:20–25).

THE PLAGUES AGAINST EGYPT

According to the story, Moses' first audience with Pharaoh is a complete failure (Exod. 5:1–6:1). Pharaoh regards the slaves' petition for a leave of absence to celebrate a feast for Yahweh in the wilderness as an alibi (which it probably was). He declares that he knows no god named Yahweh, and that he has no intention of letting his slaves go (Exod. 5:2). Instead, he gives orders to increase the workload: The slaves must not only produce the same quota of bricks each day, but also scout around and find the straw used as binding material.

What follows is the story of ten plagues that Yahweh inflicts on Egypt to break the will of Pharaoh (Exod. 7:8–11:10).[25] Many readers have difficulties with the Exodus story at this point. How could this have happened? The story makes the repeated claim—one that is hard to believe—that none of the plagues touched Israel in the land of Goshen. In a miraculous fashion Yahweh "made a distinction" between the Hebrews and the Egyptians (Exod. 8:23) so that not even a dog growled against the people of Israel (11:7–8). Before we discuss this question of miracle, however, consider the nature of the story.

Remember the motive for remembering and writing down these traditions. The Israelites did not have our kind of historical curiosity. Their narratives were not meant

---

[25]The material in Exod. 6:2–7:7 is a Priestly (P) recapitulation of the story of Moses' commission and the appointment of Aaron. It summarizes the Old Epic (JE) narrative in 3:1–6:1.

The Temple of Karnak has 134 of these massive pillars in its Hypostyle Hall. On the north wall of this temple built by Rameses II in the thirteenth century B.C.E., appears the Karnak List, which refers to Shishak's invasion of Palestine (c. 918 B.C.E.).

retrospective accounts

to be objective, photographic reports; rather, they preserve the memory of events as experienced and interpreted within the community of faith. The supreme event to which the narratives bear witness—God's liberating action on behalf of slaves in bondage—belongs to a dimension of history that modern historians are not generally willing to consider. The happenings described in biblical narratives could have been interpreted differently by people who stood outside the community of faith. For the people of Israel, however, these events were seen as the acts of Yahweh.

For all this, we need not conclude that the Exodus account is fiction. After all, God's actions take place within concrete situations and actual crises. Therefore, we must take the biblical account seriously, albeit critically. The wisest course lies between a naive, unquestioning acceptance of the record as it stands, and an equally dogmatic rejection of the whole tradition as having no credibility. One scholar points out that "none of these plagues, except the last, contains anything strange or abnormal; all are events which naturally take place at the end of the inundation of the Nile."[26] But this still leaves an important question unanswered: How do events "which naturally take place at the end of the inundation of the Nile" come to signify the redemptive action of God?

THE NATURE OF THE TRADITION

Even if this dramatic story reflects natural phenomena known in Egypt, such as the blood-red Nile caused by red soil carried at flood season, scourges of frogs and grasshoppers, or the desert wind (sirocco) that blackens the sky with sand, many elements of popular folklore are clearly present. The serpent rod is a good example. In one passage (Exod. 4:2–5), Moses casts his rod on the ground and it becomes a serpent. In another, Aaron does the same thing with the same result (Exod. 7:8–13). Neither action is treated as extraordinary, for the magicians of Egypt, specialists in serpent magic, are said to have accomplished as much by their secret arts: "For each one cast down his rod, and they became serpents" (Exod. 7:12). These and similar features of the account have a meaningful place in the story when read as a dramatic whole, but taken by themselves they are relics of the folklore of Egypt and Palestine.

Keep in mind that the story in its written form is separated by several centuries from the time of Israel's sojourn in Egypt. Even if the oral tradition of Israel authentically preserves the recollection of historical events in the Mosaic period, we still must account for irregularities, repetitions, and differences of interpretation in the written story that presumably arose in the history of transmission. Scholars generally agree that the account of the plagues (Exod. 7–12) received its final form at the hands of the Priestly writers who incorporated the Old Epic tradition (J) into an overall narrative framework that contained other materials preserved in the Priestly circle. There are some differences in the way the story was transmitted. The Old Epic tradition (followed essentially in Ps. 78) recounts eight plagues, while the completed Priestly edition expands the number to ten (as in Ps. 105).[27]

Close study of these traditions reveals differences in content and literary style. In the Old Epic tradition, Moses is the chief actor in Pharaoh's presence while Aaron, if

---

[26]W. O. E. Oesterley and T. H. Robinson, *History of Israel* (Oxford: Clarendon, 1932), I, p. 85. See also J. L. Mihelic and G. E. Wright, "Plagues in Exodus," *Interpreter's Dictionary* [31], III, pp. 822–24, who maintain that there is a natural basis for the first nine plagues even though the tradition has been enhanced in liturgical usage. Similarly Greta Hort, "The Plagues of Egypt," *Zeitschrift für die alttestamentliche Wissenschaft*, 69 (1956), 84–103; 70 (1958), 48–59, maintains that the plagues correspond to a chain reaction of natural events during the seven-month period from August to March; this view is supported by D. M. Beegle, *Moses* [234], pp. 97–118.

[27]The plague of darkness (sandstorm) is attributed to E by some literary critics. J. L. Mihelic and G. E. Wright demonstrate that Psalm 78 in its rehearsal of the Exodus events follows the seven-plague tradition of J, and that Psalm 105 is based on the completed P account of ten plagues. See *Interpreter's Dictionary* [3], III, 822–23.

The Egyptian God Bes (shown here with a lyre) was a household god who guarded people against misfortune, protected children, and also promoted human fertility.

mentioned at all, stands silently by. But in the final Priestly version, Aaron—the recognized ancestor of the Jerusalem priests—always accompanies Moses and acts as priestly spokesman in negotiations with Pharaoh. This view of the relation between Moses and Aaron is evident in the Priestly passage dealing with Aaron's appointment (Exod. 6:28–7:7) and in the introduction to the plagues (7:8–13).

Stylistically, the Old Epic tradition describes the plagues with more restraint than does the Priestly version. For example, the Old Epic account of the locust plague tells how an east wind brought a cloud of locusts and, with a shift of wind, they were driven into the Red Sea. Given that farmers in Egypt and other parts of the world have often witnessed such a plague, the miracle here is not the natural event itself but the fact that Moses predicted it and that it came at a particular time with a particular meaning. The Priestly version, on the other hand, tends to heighten these miracles by putting greater stress on the wonder-working power of the rod. Furthermore, Moses is overshadowed by the Priestly figure, Aaron. Yahweh commands Moses: "Say to Aaron, 'Stretch out your rod . . .'"; and Aaron wields the rod with the most marvelous results (as in Exod. 8:16–19).

THE HISTORY OF THE TRADITION

Literary criticism is important here because it allows us to view the story in its present form as the end product of a long history of transmission, reaching back into the oral stage when the story was told, improvised upon, and retold. In all likelihood the original nucleus of the account was an ancient Israelite story told to interpret the celebration of the Passover. Even before the period of Moses, shepherds observed this nomadic festival in springtime at the last full moon before setting out for summer pastures. During this nocturnal celebration it was the custom for families to sacrifice a young animal and eat the meat in their tents, along with unleavened bread and desert herbs. The original purpose, echoed faintly in the Old Epic tradition (Exod. 12:21–39), was to secure the welfare and fertility of the flocks when the baby lambs and goats were being born, and to drive away evil spirits (thought to be especially active at such a time). The blood of the sacrificed animal was smeared on the entrance to the tents to ward off the Destroyer (specifically mentioned in Exod. 12:23) who attacked people and animals. In the light of the Exodus, a new understanding of this rite eventually superseded its primitive meaning: The custom of shepherds leaving for summer pastures was reinterpreted to refer to the Hebrews departing for a new land. Yahweh became the Destroyer who spared the blood-marked Hebrew dwellings when "passing over" them, so that no scourge would destroy them (Exod. 12:13 [P]).[28] Some scholars surmise that, in the course of time, nine other plagues were added as a dramatic introduction to the great death plague (an epidemic?) that struck Egypt.[29] After the Israelites settled in Canaan, the nomadic Passover rite came to be connected with the Feast of Unleavened Bread, an agricultural festival celebrated at the barley harvest.[30]

The long history of the story of the plagues becomes evident when one examines literary features of the account as a whole. The story of the first nine plagues (Exod. 7:14–10:29) has literary unity, carefully wrought by the Priestly redactors who incorporated the Old Epic tradition into the final work. This story is governed by an overall scheme, with a clear beginning and a definite finish, and makes use of formulas characteristic of this section.[31]

---

[28]The original meaning of the word translated "Passover" (Hebrew, *pésah*, Greek, *pascha*; compare our adjective *paschal*) is lost. In Hebrew the verbal form means "limp" (compare the reference to a skipping or limping dance in 1 Kings 18:21). In Exodus 12:13, 23, 27 the verb means "to skip by," "to spare."

[29]This is essentially the view of Martin Noth, *Pentateuchal Traditions* [76], pp. 65–71. See also Dennis J. McCarthy, "Plagues and the Sea of Reeds," *Journal of Biblical Literature*, 85 (1966), 137–58, who differs from Noth in some ways but maintains that the plagues developed in the history of the tradition to enhance the core of the story.

[30]On the origin and significance of both feasts, see R. de Vaux, *Ancient Israel* [130], pp. 484–93.

[31]The literary unity of the story of the nine plagues is stressed both by scholars who follow source analysis (such as R. de Vaux, *History* [111], pp. 359–70, and D. M. Beegle, *Moses* [234], chap. 5) and those who do not (such as Umberto Cassuto, *Exodus* [237], pp. 92–135).

Furthermore, the story of nine plagues seems to presuppose that the Exodus was a secret flight, not an expulsion. The narrative concludes at the end of the ninth plague when Pharaoh, firm in his refusal, tells Moses to get out and never see his face again (Exod. 10:27–29). According to one tradition, the Hebrews, having failed in their negotiations, might have slipped away without Pharaoh's knowledge (Exod. 14:5a). On the other hand, the material in Exodus 11–13 stands apart from previous plagues, as suggested by the opening statement that Moses and the people enjoyed great esteem among the Egyptians, even among members of the royal court (Exod. 11:2–3). The story of the tenth plague clearly presupposes that the Exodus was an expulsion: After such a grievous blow, Pharaoh "drove out" the Hebrews. The Egyptians were so glad to get rid of the Hebrews that they gave them whatever they asked for, including jewelry and clothing (Exod. 12:31–36)! The tenth plague is also closely linked to the celebration of the Passover.

In the midst of the crisis, between the announcement of Yahweh's intention (Exod. 11:1–10) and the start of the plague (12:29–32), the narrator pauses to introduce the ancient feast as follows:

Egyptian Plagues and Hebrew Exodus

	Epic Tradition	Priestly Expansion
Announcement of plague	11:1–8	11:9–10
Institution of Passover	12:21–23 (24–27a)	12:1–20, 28
Occurrence of plague	12:29–36	
THE EXODUS	12:37–39	12:40–42
Passover legislation	(13:1–16)	12:43–51
(The two passages in parentheses are in Deuteronomic style)		

In summary, the Exodus story as we know it is the result of a long history of tradition, in the course of which various circles of narrators reinterpreted and embellished the details. From the earliest period the story was rehearsed at the celebration of the Passover, the cultic setting for remembering and elaborating Israel's liberation from Pharaoh's yoke. Eventually, after centuries of transmission, the Priestly writers reworked the traditional story into the final, written version of the dramatic contest with Pharaoh that moves dynamically toward Yahweh's decisive victory.

SIGNS AND WONDERS

We speak of the "plagues" against Egypt, but in fact this word rarely appears in the Exodus story (notably Exod. 9:14; 11:1; compare 8:2). The Exodus narratives usually refer to the so-called plagues as "signs" and "wonders," terms that also appear in the recitations of Psalms 78 and 105 and in creedal summaries (Deut. 26:5–9). This raises the question of "miracle."

In the Hebrew Bible, miracle is not seen or understood as a disruption of natural law.[32] The biblical writers did not think of "nature" or the "cosmos" as an independent, self-operating realm governed by its own laws. Rather, they believed that the God who created the universe is constantly involved in sustaining and maintaining it. Because God has made a covenant with creation, an ecological covenant embracing humans, animals, birds, and the earth itself (Gen. 9:10–17), people can count on regularities such as "seedtime and harvest, cold and heat, summer and winter, day and night" (Gen. 8:22).[33] And because God is constantly active, people can discern God's will even in a "natural" event like the coming of spring rains or the birth of a child. Gilbert Chesterton captures this point of view in his whimsical remark that the sun does not rise by natural law, but because God says: "Get up and do it again!"

Beyond such regularities of nature, however, the Israelites tell of extraordinary events that show God's power to intervene and are therefore special "signs." These signs are not proofs given to convince people once and for all that God is sovereign. As the Exodus narratives demonstrate, the meaning of unusual natural events is not always self-evident to those who witness them. Whom did they really convince? The first two plagues (water to blood, the scourge of frogs) left Pharaoh unmoved because his magicians were able to perform the same feats (Exod. 7:22, 8:7). Beyond that point the Egyptian sorcerers could not go; nevertheless, subsequent miracles failed to convince Pharaoh to let the slaves go. Furthermore, the Israelites who witnessed the signs performed by Moses did not believe him "because of their broken spirit and cruel bondage" (Exod. 6:9). Even after the successful escape across the Sea the Israelites murmured in disbelief and longed for the fleshpots of Egypt. So a miracle, in the biblical sense, is an indication of God's purposive activity, but never a final proof. The miracle is evidence of God's presence and redemptive intention, but is given in an ambiguous way that demands faith and trust.

We cannot be sure about the historical nucleus that lies at the heart of these traditions—traditions elaborated and colored by Israel's faith over many generations. Some miracles are more central to the Exodus story (and more native to the Mosaic period) than others. Because the account is interpretive, it is difficult to separate the central elements of the tradition from later accretions. Nevertheless, Israel's ancient faith undoubt-

matter of FAITH

[32]Martin Buber, in *Moses* [235], p. 76, observes: "Miracle is not something 'supernatural' or 'superhistorical,' but an incident, an event which can be fully included in the objective, scientific nexus of nature and history; the vital meaning of which, however, for the person to whom it occurs, destroys the security of the whole nexus of knowledge for him and explodes the fixity of the fields of experience named 'Nature' and 'History.'"

[33]See B. W. Anderson, "Creation and the Noachic Covenant," *From Creation to New Creation* [146], chap. 9.

edly was based on the experience of events that facilitated the escape from Egypt, events that seemed to signify the work of God. The clearest historical evidence for this is found in the account of the crossing of the Sea, an event fixed firmly in Israel's memory.

....

DEFINITION: "SIGNS AND WONDERS"

In the context of the Hebrew Bible, a "sign" can be defined as visible evidence of the presence and purpose of God. This use of the word does not conform to our distinction between "natural" and "supernatural." In the Exodus story everything that happens is a potential sign, even an ordinary event such as a plague of locusts or some other phenomenon connected with the overflow of the Nile (signs of this type include the rainbow, the heavenly bodies, the birth of a child, or a seeming coincidence in the day's affairs). On the other hand, a "sign" might be an extraordinary event, a sensational wonder like the death of the firstborn in Egypt (signs of this type include the restoring to health of a leprous hand, the turning of water into blood, and the retreat of the sun's shadow on a dial).

This approach to the subject of miracle might not answer all our questions, but it can lead to asking questions in a new way. Basic to Israel's faith is the conviction that God is neither aloof from the world of daily affairs nor bound by an iron chain of cause-and-effect sequences. For the Israelites, God's presence was so immediate that any event—ordinary or extraordinary—could be a sign that God was in their midst. In their view an event was *wonder*-ful or *sign*-ificant not because it defied natural law, but because it testified to God's presence and activity in their midst.[34]

....

THE VICTORY AT THE SEA

The crossing of the Sea is the climactic moment in a series of events that follow the last plague (the death of the Egyptians' firstborn sons). As a result of Moses' prophetic interpretation of the Exodus, the primitive meaning of the ancient nomadic Passover festival was superseded by a radically new understanding, subsequently preserved in all levels of the tradition. The Festival became a time to remember that in the darkest hour Yahweh broke Pharaoh's yoke and graciously delivered the people of Israel:

> When your children ask you, "What does this rite mean to you?" you shall respond, "It is the passover [*pésaḥ*] sacrifice to Yahweh, for he passed over [*pasaḥ*] the houses of the Israelites in Egypt when he struck the Egyptians, but spared our dwellings."
>
> —EXODUS 12:26–27

[34]See further "Signs and Wonders," *Interpreter's Dictionary IV* [31], pp. 348–51.

The Festival of Unleavened Bread (Mazzoth), today closely associated with the Passover, can be traced back to the time when the people left Egypt so hurriedly that there was no time for dough to be leavened (Exod. 12:34, 39). As in the Passover Seder (service) today, ancient Israelites explained this custom to their children by saying: "It is because of what Yahweh did *for me* when I came out of Egypt" (Exod. 13:8).

THE ROUTE OF THE FLIGHT

The people set out from Egypt in haste. According to Exodus 12:37 (also Num. 11:21) there were "six hundred thousand men on foot"—that is, men of military age twenty years and older. If we include women, children, teenagers, and old men, this would bring the total to over two million people! A historian has estimated that a column of this size, marching in single file, would extend at least all the way from Egypt to Sinai and back. The depiction of a mass exodus is a later exaggeration, perhaps based on census figures from a much later time. Certainly it conflicts with the information in Exo-

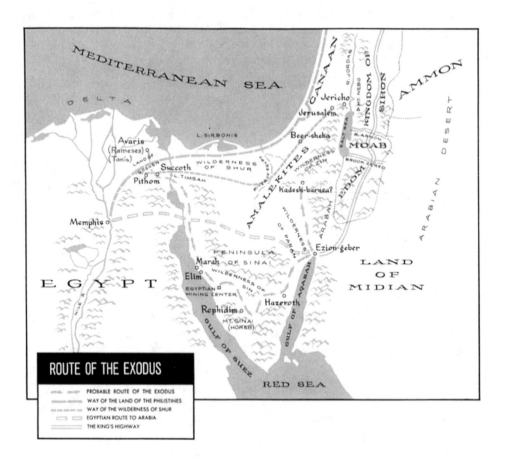

ROUTE OF THE EXODUS

PROBABLE ROUTE OF THE EXODUS
WAY OF THE LAND OF THE PHILISTINES
WAY OF THE WILDERNESS OF SHUR
EGYPTIAN ROUTE TO ARABIA
THE KING'S HIGHWAY

dus 1:15–20 that two midwives were sufficient to serve the whole Hebrew colony. In any case, the Delta area could not have accommodated so many Hebrews and their animals, and the wilderness of southern Canaan could not have supported them. In reality the band of slaves was probably small. The record is correct, however, in stating that they were a diverse group: not only the family of Jacob but a "mixed multitude" (Exod. 12:38) including *'Apiru* of other origins. Keep in mind that it is historically inaccurate to speak of these peoples as "Israelites" at this stage, although the narrative does so repeatedly. Only later, as they shared the experiences of the desert and remembered a common history, were these slaves forged into a *community*, the people Israel. *Community*

According to the story of the nine plagues, Moses repeatedly demanded of Pharaoh that the Hebrews be allowed to make a three-day journey into the wilderness to sacrifice to Yahweh (Exod. 5:3; 7:16; 8:27, and elsewhere). Not even Pharaoh's concession that the Hebrews could make their sacrifice in the land of Goshen (Exod. 8:25) or on the Egyptian border (8:28) was acceptable. This suggests that the original destination of the flight was the sacred mountain where Moses had his experience (see Exod. 3:12)—not the land of Canaan. Only in later retellings did these fugitives look longingly toward the goal envisioned by the present narrative: the occupation of Canaan. This is another indication that the story is told from the perspective of later experience. *retrospective elements*

One passage declares that even the route of escape was providential, for "when Pharaoh let the people go, God did not guide them by the way of the land of the Philistines, although that was close" (Exod. 13:17). This is more evidence of a later retelling, because the expression "the way of the land of the Philistines" is anachronistic (it reflects later usage). The Philistines did not settle that area until around 1200 B.C.E., well after the time of Moses.[35] The route referred to was the main highway leading from Egypt along the Mediterranean coastland, a major commercial and military route heavily fortified with Egyptian outposts. Indeed, the Hebrews would not have had a chance on that road. Their strategy called instead for a more circuitous journey: "God led the people round about by way of the wilderness . . ." (Exod. 13:18). In other words, they left "the land of Rameses" (Goshen), where they had been working, and struck out into the wilderness that today borders the Suez Canal, pausing first at points called Succoth and Etham (Exod. 13:20).

Present biblical texts do not give us a clear picture of the escape route. Some evidence suggests an initial move along a northern route toward Baal-saphon on Lake Sirbonis, a lagoon on the Mediterranean side of the coastal highway. The evidence probably favors a southern route, however—at least for those Hebrews who arrived at Sinai.[36]

---

[35]On the arrival of the Philistines and other Sea Peoples in Palestine, see Chapter 6.
[36]This complex question is discussed in J. L. Mihelic's "Red Sea," in *Interpreter's Dictionary*, IV [31], pp. 19–21; G. Ernest Wright, *Biblical Archaeology* [125], pp. 60–67; and D. M. Beegle, *Moses* [234], pp. 145–58. De Vaux advocates a double exodus, one group taking the northern (Lake Sirbonis) route and cutting over to Kadesh, the other taking a southern route and going directly to Sinai; see his *History* [111], pp. 370–81.

According to Exodus 13:18, the fugitive Hebrews took "the way of the wilderness" that led in the direction of *Yam Suph* (often translated as "Red Sea").

The map shows that this route could not have taken them to the Red Sea, unless we are to suppose that the Egyptian army chased the Hebrews many miles to a point opposite the tip of the Sinaitic Peninsula. True, in some biblical passages *Yam Suph* has a broad meaning that could apply to the Gulf of Suez (Num. 33:10–11) or the Gulf of Aqabah (1 Kings 9:26), two arms of water that extend from the Red Sea. The words were used in this wider sense when the Hebrew Bible was translated into Greek (the Septuagint) in the third century B.C.E., and this meaning was transmitted through the Latin Vulgate. Today historians believe that *Yam Suph,* when used in the context of the Exodus, should be translated "Reed Sea" or "Papyrus Lake." In Hebrew *yam* means "sea" (like the Mediterranean Sea) or an inland body of water (like the Sea of Galilee); *suph* means "reed, papyrus," referring to the reeds that grow around the body of water. The reference was probably to some marshy lake at the northern extension of the Gulf of Suez, around the area of Lake Manzaleh (perhaps Lake Timsah). The Hebrew's route took them into this area. Though we cannot pinpoint the exact location of the crossing, we need not make the story more difficult by supposing that they somehow negotiated the Gulf of Suez where, in fact, reeds do not grow. The account of the miraculous crossing in Exodus 14 speaks only of the sea (*yam*), while the parallel poetic account in Exodus 15 speaks specifically of *Yam Suph.*

The narrative expresses the belief that God was guiding the people on their journey. A passage from the Old Epic tradition says that "Yahweh went before them by day in a pillar of cloud to lead them along the way, and by night in a pillar of fire to give them light" (Exod. 13:21ff.). This language suggests the ancient practice of carrying a burning brazier at the head of a marching army or caravan to indicate the line of march,[37] a practice that fits the description of how the signal, seen by day as a cloud and by night as a flame, moved about as the leader at the head of the caravan changed course. It does not, however, explain every mention of the pillar (such as Exod. 14:19b–20). The fire and cloud might refer to meteorological phenomena, such as electrical rainstorms that often accompanied the hot desert wind (sirocco). If so, the tradition has been enhanced with poetic imagery used in the ancient world to portray divine appearance (theophany) in cloud, fire, lightning, and rain,[38] especially the storm phenomena of the northern mountains (see Ps. 18:7–15). Whatever the case, the narrative affirms that Yahweh was with the people, leading them out of bondage and guiding them toward their destination at Sinai.

---

[37]See, for instance, U. Cassuto, *Exodus* [237], p. 158, and D. Beegle, *Moses* [234], p. 149.

[38]Thomas W. Mann in "The Pillar of Cloud in the Reed Sea Narrative," *Journal of Biblical Literature,* 90 (1971), 15–30, draws attention to poetic parallels in Canaanite literature. See further his *Divine Presence and Guidance in Israelite Traditions: The Typology of Exaltation* (Baltimore: Johns Hopkins University Press, 1977), especially chap. 5, "The Reed Sea and Sinai."

A PATH THROUGH THE WATERS

Realizing that the fugitives were heading toward the Egyptian border, and supposing that they would be "entangled in the land" and "shut in" by the wilderness (Exod. 14:3), Pharaoh sends his charioteers in hot pursuit. The dramatic suspense is now intensified. Trapped between the barrier of the Sea on one side and the Egyptian forces on the other, the panic-stricken Hebrews are on the verge of revolting against Moses and going back to their miserable life in the Delta—"for it would have been better for us to serve the Egyptians than to die in the wilderness" (Exod. 14:11–12). Their murmuring (a frequent theme in the wilderness narratives) contrasts sharply with the indomitable faith of Moses, who believes that the Divine Warrior is fighting for the people (Exod. 14:13–14). From a human perspective it seems to be a "no-win" situation. But the divine imperative is given: "Tell the people of Israel to go forward!"

The ensuing account of the miraculous opening of a path through the waters (Exod. 14:15–31) belongs to the poetry of Israel's faith. The event constitutes, in Emil Fackenheim's words, a "root experience"—an experience celebrated up to the present in the Passover Service as the sign of "a saving Presence" in history.[39] Even historians who are skeptical about many of the ancient Mosaic traditions might admit that at this point we strike "the bedrock of an historical occurrence," an event "so unique and extraordinary that it came to constitute the essence of the primary Israelite confession and was regarded as the real beginning of Israel's history and the act of God fundamental for Israel."[40] The story undoubtedly rests on some actual happening, some experience that aroused ecstatic jubilation and became the undying memory of the people. Yet it is almost impossible to penetrate beyond the language of faith to historical reality. What really happened at the Reed Sea?

One way to approach this question is to analyze the levels of tradition in the prose narrative of Exodus 14. Critics generally recognize that the account in its present form comes from the Priestly tradition (P). The Priestly writers provided the basic narrative pattern of divine command and execution, and enriched the narrative by drawing upon the Old Epic tradition. After separating out the Priestly language and interests, the remaining Old Epic material portrays a crossing facilitated by wind and tide:

> And Yahweh drove the sea back with a strong easterly wind all night
> and he made the sea into dry land . . .
> In the morning watch, Yahweh looked down on the army of the
> Egyptians from the pillar of fire and cloud and threw the Egyptian army
> into confusion. He so clogged their chariot wheels that they drove on only

[39]Emil Fackenheim, *God's Presence in History* [241], pp. 8ff.
[40]Martin Noth, *Pentateuchal Traditions* [76], p. 50.

with difficulty, which made the Egyptians say, "Let us flee from the
Israelites, for Yahweh is fighting on their side against the Egyptians!"
—EXODUS 14:21b, 24–25 (NJB)

Such an occurrence is not impossible in the marshy area of Lake Menzaleh—in fact,
people have witnessed it at other times. The miracle was that it happened at a particular
time and with a particular meaning. To Israel this was not a freak of nature, but a sign
of the saving presence of Yahweh in their midst.

If this event is indeed the substance of the old tradition, the wonder has been
heightened in the course of retelling with the inclusion of other materials, mainly from
the Priestly circle. The expanded version tells how Moses held out his wonder-working
rod and the waters of the sea were divided, allowing the people to pass over on dry
ground while the waters stood up like walls on either side (Exod. 14:21a, 22). When
the Egyptians attempted to follow, Moses stretched out his rod again and the waters
overwhelmed them (verses 23, 26–28). The people of Israel, however, "walked on dry
ground through the sea, the waters being a wall to them on the right hand and on their
left hand" (verse 29).

The value of this kind of analysis is in demonstrating the long history of the story,
from the early oral period when it was told and retold by skilled narrators, to the final
stage of its literary formulation by the Priestly writers. Remember that at no time in
the history of the tradition was the narrators' purpose to give a straightforward account
that would satisfy our later historical curiosity. Their intent was to glorify the God
whose saving presence was marvelously manifested in an unforgettable historical experience.

A HOLY EVENT

The narrative comes to a climax when Miriam, sister of Moses and Aaron, takes a tam-
bourine and, while all the Israelite women follow her with music and dancing, sings an
ecstatic hymn of praise to Yahweh:

> Sing to Yahweh!
>   for he is powerfully ascendant.
> Horse and charioteer
>   he has hurled into the sea.

—EXODUS 15:21

This couplet, one of the oldest pieces of poetry in the Hebrew Bible, probably originated with the actual event it celebrates. At the earliest stage of tradition the song was
attributed to a prophetess, Miriam (Exod. 15:20; compare Judg. 4:4), though at a later
stage Miriam's voice was almost drowned out by a longer poem, the "Song of the Sea,"
attributed to Moses (Exod. 15:1–18).[41] Miriam's song poetically describes the experi-

ence of a "wonder"—an event that was a sign of the redemptive activity of God on be-half of the people. The philosopher Martin Buber speaks of the experience as a "holy event" that was, for those who participated in it, "transparent," permitting "a glimpse of the sphere in which a sole power, not restricted by any other, [was] at work."[42] To be sure, the event occurred in the context of "the objective, scientific nexus of nature and history," as we observed in our discussion of the "high wind" theory (see pp. 73–74). But there is no causal explanation that diminishes the wonder of the event. As Buber observes:

> The great turning-points in religious history are based on the fact that again and ever again an individual and a group attached to him wonder and keep on wondering: at a natural phenomenon, at a historical event, or at both together; always at something which intervenes fatefully in the life of this individual or this group.[43]

Israel's capacity "to wonder and keep on wondering" is evident in other passages in the Hebrew Bible where the miracle at the Sea is rehearsed in such a way as to bring out its rich overtones of meaning. One of these passages is the previously mentioned "Song of the Sea" (Exod. 15:1–18), in which the "Song of Miriam," here transposed into the first person "I will sing . . ." (compare Exod. 15:21), becomes the opening re-frain of a poem that celebrates the events reported in the dramatic prose of Exodus 14. This poem probably comes from the period before David. It is especially significant be- *Miriam's Song* cause it seems to draw on Canaanite mythical views to express the transcendent and wonderful dimension of the event at the Sea: the conflict of the Divine Warrior with adversaries, the building of a temple for the triumphant deity on the sacred mountain, and the celebration of the god's everlasting reign.[44] Yahweh, the victorious Divine War-rior (Exod. 15:2; compare 14:13–14), is supreme in the Heavenly Council of the gods:

> Who is like you in the heavenly council, Yahweh?
>> Who is like you, majestic in holiness?
>> You who are awesome in deeds, who does wonders?
> You stretched out your right hand,
>> Earth swallowed them.
>
> —EXODUS 15:11–12

[41]See B. W. Anderson, "The Song of Miriam Poetically and Theologically Considered," *Directions in Biblical Hebrew Poetry*, Elaine R. Follis, ed., JSOT Supplement 40 (Sheffield, England: JSOT, 1987), pp. 285–302; and Phyllis Trible, "Bringing Miriam Out of the Shadows," *Bible Review*, V:1, February 1989, p. 14.

[42]Martin Buber, *Moses* [235], p. 77.

[43]Martin Buber, op. cit., pp. 75–77. Emil Fackenheim quotes and discusses this passage in *God's Presence in History* [241], pp. 11–14.

[44]See Frank M. Cross, "The Song of the Sea and Canaanite Myth" [129], pp. 112–44, and "The Divine Warrior" [129], pp. 91–111; also Patrick Miller, *The Divine Warrior in Early Israel* [245], pp. 74–128.

The poet goes on to describe a further demonstration of divine power: the guidance of the people to Canaan, depicted as the mythical mountain of the gods (Exod. 15:17):

> In your faithfulness you led the people that you redeemed,
> You led them in your power to your holy abode.
> —EXODUS 15:13

Panic then overwhelms the rulers of Canaan so that they become "still as a stone":

> While your people passed over, Yahweh,
> while your people passed over whom you have created.
> —EXODUS 15:16b (Frank Cross translation)

In this poetic portrayal the Exodus event is more than an act of liberation—it marks the creation of a people. In an early instance of this narrative tradition, the poet attempts to communicate the wonder of the event by drawing on mythical elements to enhance the historical account. Yahweh's adversaries are Pharaoh and his armies, and the Sea is a passive element under Yahweh's control. Later in the history of this (Reed Sea) tradition the Sea comes to represent the mythical powers of chaos Yahweh conquers in order to demonstrate sovereignty over Israel and the world. In this reinterpretation, Yahweh's victory was not over Pharaoh's hosts but over "Sea," the mythical symbol of the chaos and evil that threaten the creation (Ps. 74:12–17; 77:16–20; 114; Hab. 3). The victory *at* the Sea came to be understood as a victory *over* the Sea.[45]

In view of the overwhelming significance of the Exodus in the biblical narratives, it might seem strange that existing Egyptian records make no reference to Moses and the escape of the Hebrews. We are reminded again that archaeology and the study of ancient history give, at best, only circumstantial evidence to support the Israelite record. But the Egyptian silence is not really so strange. We would hardly expect the escape of a band of runaway slaves to figure in the Egyptian annals that record the imperial wars and cultural achievements of the Nineteenth Dynasty. This border incident, which caused scarcely a ripple in Egyptian affairs, held no significance for Egyptian historians. But to the Israelites who participated in the escape and who passed on the story to their children and children's children, this was the most important event of the time. In its light they understood the subsequent events of their history, as well as their prehistory in the ancestral period.

---

[45]On the use of mythical imagery to elaborate the Exodus tradition, see B. W. Anderson, *Creation versus Chaos* [146], pp. 93–109, and various essays in *From Creation to New Creation* [146].

CHAPTER 3

COVENANT IN THE WILDERNESS

Wilderness theme

Deeply etched upon Israelite tradition is the understanding that the people of Israel had their origin in the wilderness. The Exodus narrative tells us specifically that those who followed Moses in the flight from Egypt were a "mixed multitude" (Exod. 12:38) held together primarily by the desire to be free from slavery. Clearly, this motley band lacked the conscious identity, the commitment to a common way of life, and the shared experiences that constitute a *people*, a historical community. In the wilderness of Sinai, however, Moses' followers became "the people of Yahweh": a frequent expression in the Old Testament (see Judg. 5:11, 13) that later influenced the conception of church and synagogue.[1] The Torah tradition testifies that it was in the wilderness that God spoke to Moses, and that the people, submitting to the demand and promise of that Voice, became Yahweh's special people.

Biblical Readings: Primarily Exodus 19–24 and 32–34. A biblical commentary on the whole story, Exodus and Sinai Covenant, is given in the book of Deuteronomy (see especially Deut. 5–28).

[1]The Septuagint uses the Greek *ekklesia* and *synagogé* to translate Hebrew words that refer to Israel as "the people of God [Yahweh]."

GUIDANCE IN THE WILDERNESS

When the Hebrews turned their backs on the land of Egypt, they took a road leading into the wilderness. According to the narratives in Exodus 15:22–19:2, they set out for the Wilderness of Sinai, for Moses had been sent to bring the people to a mountain rendezvous where they might find freedom in serving (worshiping) God (Exod. 3:12).[2] The journey was fraught with hardships and uncertainties. Food and water were scarce, and as though the inhospitable natural environment were not enough, hostile desert tribes roamed the area and resented the intrusion of the fugitives.

The narrators are remarkably realistic in describing what it must have been like to live under such precarious circumstances. These stories do not portray the wilderness as some sort of nomadic ideal. While Israel experienced "grace in the wilderness" (Jer. 31:2), it was also a time of grumbling, revolutionary discontent, internal strife, rebellion against Moses, and, above all, lack of faith. Despite the deliverance from slavery and the marvelous crossing of the Reed Sea, the people complained (Exod. 17:7): "Is Yahweh among us or not?"

SIGNS OF YAHWEH'S AID

The narratives, however, emphasize the positive theme of Yahweh's guidance and gracious aid in the wilderness. First, Yahweh provides daily sustenance, the elemental necessities of food and water. The stories about manna and quail (Exod. 16:1–36) are another example of "miracle"—signs of God's presence in ordinary events (see pp. 66–69). Manna is a sweet, sticky substance produced by insects that suck the tender twigs of tamarisk bushes in the desert region. This "honeydew excretion" falls to the ground where, in the hot desert air, the drops quickly evaporate, leaving a solid residue. During the day ants carry off the sweet grains, but overnight the grains accumulate and can be gathered by early risers for food. The Hebrews were evidently unfamiliar with this desert substance. The word "manna" is based on the question, *man hu'*, Hebrew for "What is it?" (Exod. 16:15). Moses answers, "It is the bread that Yahweh has given you to eat" (compare John 6:31). In Arabic *man* is still the name for these plant insects, and their honeydew, regarded as a great delicacy, is called *man essimma* or "manna from heaven."[3]

As for quails (Exod. 16:13; compare Num. 11:31–34), large flocks migrate over the region in spring; and the exhausted birds are easily caught. Some modern readers

[2]On Moses as political leader see Aaron Wildavsky, *The Nursing Father: Moses as a Political Leader* (Tuscaloosa: University of Alabama Press, 1984).

[3]F. S. Bodenheimer, "The Manna of Sinai," in *The Biblical Archaeologist*, X (1947), 2–6; reprinted in *The Biblical Archaeologist Reader*, I [119], pp. 26–80.

might regard such life-saving phenomena as a sign of good fortune, or "luck." To the Israelites, however, they were signs of Yahweh's daily providence.

Second, Yahweh provides divine guidance in the fierce struggle against hostile desert tribes. Chief among these were the Amalekites who claimed the desert oases in the Negeb, the southern wilderness of Canaan. The battle against the Amalekites (Exod. 17:8–16) made a deep impression on the Hebrews and initiated a long and bitter feud (see 1 Sam. 15; Deut. 25:17–19). This story from the Old Epic tradition gives us our first glimpse of Joshua, who "mowed down Amalek and his people with the edge of the sword" (RSV, Exod. 17:13). Though it includes fanciful features like the magic power of Moses' rod, the narrative probably rests on an actual experience and was another event that sharpened the historical awareness of Israel's faith. Moreover, the idea of a "holy war" led later prophets such as Isaiah to demand faith in Yahweh who alone gives the victory (see Isa. 7:7–9).

MURMURINGS IN THE WILDERNESS

Alongside the positive theme of Yahweh's gracious response to the needs of the people *being tested* during their wilderness sojourn is a negative one: The people persistently murmured against Yahweh and against Yahweh's servant, Moses. The wilderness period was, according to Deuteronomic interpretation, a time when the people were "tested" to see if they lived in complete and daily dependence upon Yahweh's providing mercy (Deut. 8:3, quoted in part in Matt. 4:4). But it was also a time when the people put Yahweh to the test, demanding proof that their God was actually present. Manna did not satisfy those who remembered a better diet in Egypt, including fish, cucumbers, melons, onions, and garlic (Num. 11:4–6). Israel's grumbling occurs time after time in the stories dealing with the wilderness. Indeed, in the present arrangement of the Pentateuch this grumbling intensifies after the Sinai sojourn:

ISRAEL'S MURMURINGS IN THE WILDERNESS

Exod. 15:22–26	Brackish water at Marah
Exod. 16:2–3	Longing for the fleshpots of Egypt
Exod. 17:2–7	Water complaint at Massah and Meribah
Sinai Sojourn	*(Exod. 19:1–Num. 10:10)*
Num. 11:4–6	Complaint about manna
Num. 12:1–2	Criticism of Moses for marrying a Cushite wife
Num. 14:2–3	Complaint against the leadership of Moses and Aaron
Num. 16:12–14	Accusation made by Dathan and Abiram
Num. 20:2–13	Complaint about wilderness life
Num. 21:4–5	Impatience during the march through Transjordan

Mount Sinai, the traditional "Mount of Moses," is located in the mountainous tip of the Sinaitic Peninsula.

As stories were handed down from generation to generation, these murmurings were probably accentuated in some circles.[4] Nevertheless, the tradition undoubtedly preserves the memory of real struggles in the wilderness. Even though Moses interpreted events as "signs" of divine guidance and aid, it was difficult for people to believe in Yahweh as they moved from the relative security of life in Egypt to the uncertainty of life in the wilderness. What is remarkable is that Israel's story-tellers were so candid about the people's lack of faith at the beginning of their historical sojourn. Even Moses was judged for his wavering faith and was not permitted to enter the Promised Land. Where else has a people had the courage to say that its origin was characterized by weakness, if not failure? This is another reminder that Israel told its history not from the standpoint of human achievement, but in awareness of God's searching judgment.

THE ARRIVAL AT SINAI (HOREB)

Despite enemy attack, lack of food and water, and the murmurings of the people, the indomitable Moses led the Hebrews on until at last they staggered into the oasis of Sinai. Here they were able to reflect upon the experiences that had brought them together, and to understand in a deeper way the nature of the community into which they

---

[4]George W. Coats emphasizes this point in *Rebellion in the Wilderness* [254]. Relying on Psalm 78, Coats believes that the murmuring tradition was a polemic of Jerusalem priests against the Northern Kingdom of Israel. See also Brevard Childs, *Exodus* [238], pp. 254–64.

had been called—a community based on the covenant relationship between Yahweh and the people. *Covenant*

In Israel's traditions, the scene of the establishment of this (Mosaic) covenant was located at "the mountain of God" (Exod. 24:13; also 3:1)—called Horeb in some circles and Sinai in others.[5] Unfortunately, we cannot determine the geographical location of the sacred mountain though some identify it with *Jebel Musa*.[6] Those who handed down the tradition were not interested in geography but in the covenant made in the wilderness after the Exodus from Egypt. Throughout subsequent generations it became increasingly clear that the covenant was the basis of Israel's existence as a people.

DEFINITION: "COVENANT"

Today the word "covenant" refers to "a binding and solemn agreement" made by two or more parties and involving mutual responsibilities. Examples might be a marriage covenant, an agreement among members of a religious body, or a treaty between sovereign political powers.

Some scholars believe the Hebrew word *b^erîth*, translated "covenant," derives from the Akkadian (Babylonian) word *birîtu*, meaning "fetter" or "bond." Whatever the case, the Hebrew Bible uses the word to describe a binding relationship based on commitment—that is, a relationship involving promises and obligations and having the quality of constancy or durability. The friendship between Jonathan and David was based on covenant (1 Sam. 18:3). Covenants were made between heads of families such as Jacob and Laban (Gen. 31:44–50), and between socio-political groups such as the conquering Israelites and the Gibeonites (Josh. 9:3–27) or David and the elders of Israel (2 Sam. 5:3). Often a solemn oath gives force to the covenant (Gen. 26:28; compare 31:49–50); sometimes the word "oath" is used instead of "covenant" (Josh. 9:20).

Israelite traditions give differing views of the covenant between God and Israel, depending on whether the interpreter wants to emphasize God's being bound to Israel *unconditionally*, or Israel's being bound to God *conditionally*. Both views of the covenant of divine grace entail human responsibility, but the conditional interpretation emphasizes Israel's success or failure in meeting its obligations.[7]

THE SINAI NARRATIVES

In the present arrangement of the Pentateuch, the Israelites arrive at Sinai in Exodus 19:1 and do not break camp until Numbers 10:11. The intervening material, which includes the last half of the book of Exodus, all the book of Leviticus, and the first ten

---

[5]The name Sinai appears in Old Epic (J) and Priestly (P) traditions, while the name Horeb was favored in Northern circles represented by the Elohist stratum (E) and Deuteronomy (D). A northern (Ephraimitic) tradition portrays Elijah making a pilgrimage to "Horeb, the mountain of God" (1 Kings 19:4–8).

[6]The identification of the sacred mountain with Jebel Musa is defended by G. E. Wright in *Biblical Archaeology* [125], p. 64; *Westminster Historical Atlas* [41], pp. 38–39; Y. Aharoni in B. Rothenberg, *God's Wilderness*, trans. Joseph Witriol (London: Thames and Hudson, 1961), p. 170; *Macmillan Bible Atlas* [35], map 48.

[7]See further George E. Mendenhall, "Covenant," in *Interpreter's Dictionary*, I [31], pp. 714–23.

chapters of the book of Numbers, is set at Sinai. Thus a large part of the Pentateuch deals exclusively with incidents and laws associated with Israel's Sinai encampment. Moreover, this block of material is inserted right into the heart of another body of narratives dealing with Israel's experiences in the wilderness, as the following outline shows:

A.   Israel in the wilderness: Exodus 15:22–17:16[8]
     [Israel at Sinai: Exodus 19:1 to Numbers 10:10]
B.   Israel in the wilderness: Numbers 10:11 to 20:22

Note: In the Hebrew Bible the title for the book of Numbers is $B^{e}midbar$ ("In [the] Wilderness").

Notice that some stories in part B of the outline seem to be located in the same general area (Kadesh) as those of part A. We will consider this later along with the question of whether the Sinai covenant tradition is separate from the Exodus-Conquest tradition.

 Much of the material in this long Sinai section belongs to the relatively late Priestly tradition (P), as evidenced by the interest in cultic matters such as the tabernacle, sacred objects (especially the Ark), ordination to the priesthood, and various kinds of sacrifices. All the book of Leviticus and the first ten chapters of Numbers (except the last few verses, Num. 10:29–36) are Priestly material, as is a significant portion of the Exodus material (Exod. 25–31 and 35–40). The rest of the Exodus material (Exod. 19–24 and 32–34, roughly speaking) belongs to the Old Epic tradition—the so-called J and E sources that are almost inseparable.[9]

This is not to say that the Priestly material has no historical value. Though not written down until the period after the fall of the nation in 587 B.C.E., the Priestly Work (P) undoubtedly preserves many ancient recollections. In the study of biblical traditions, it is axiomatic that *the date of a writing is no sure index of the age of the traditions it records.* This is also true for the Old Epic (J and E) tradition. Though presumably written down in the period of the monarchy (after David, about 1000 B.C.E.) some Old Epic material in the book of Exodus goes back to the time of Moses, and some reflects Israel's life in the agricultural setting of Canaan (the time of Joshua and later). We will consider some of this Sinai material, such as the agricultural laws preserved in the Old Epic tradition (Exod. 20:23–33:23) and the institutions of the Priestly Work, in Chapters 4 and 13.

---

[8]Exodus 18 is apparently out of order, for it locates Jethro's visit to Moses at "the mountain of God" (verse 5); but according to the present arrangement, the Israelites reached the mountain in Exodus 19:1–2.

[9]Deuteronomic (D) material is not present in any significant degree until the book of Deuteronomy. For a source analysis of materials dealing with Sinai, see the supplement to Martin Noth's *Pentateuchal Traditions* [76], pp. 270–73.

THE COVENANT AT SINAI

Exodus 1–24 deals with two series of events. First is the deliverance from Egypt and its sequel, the guidance through the wilderness. Second is Yahweh's revelation at Sinai, the giving of the Law, and the making of the covenant. In the story as it has come down to us, these two series are inseparably related. The first is preparation for the second (see Exod. 3:12), and the second is based theologically on the first.

THE "EAGLES' WINGS" PASSAGE

A small literary unit at the beginning of Exodus 19 stresses the essential connection between the Exodus and Sinai traditions. This passage (Exod. 19:3b–6) serves as a transitional link, occurring right after the notice in 19:1–2a (derived from the Priestly itinerary) that Israel arrived at Sinai about three months after leaving Egypt. In it Yahweh is portrayed as carrying the people, like an eagle lifting its young, toward the mountain rendezvous. Notice the rhythmic style and balanced unity: *transition*

> Thus you shall say to the house of Jacob,
> and tell the Israelites:
>
> "You have observed what I did to Egypt,
> and how I carried you on eagles' wings,
> bringing you unto me here.
>
> Now, then, if you will only hear my voice,
> and keep my covenant,
> You shall be to me[*lî*] a special possession among all peoples,
> for [*kî*] to me [*lî*] the whole earth belongs,
> and you shall be to me [*lî*] a kingdom of priests.
> and a holy nation."
>
> These are the words you shall speak to the Israelites.
> —EXODUS 19:3b–6

Literary critics maintain that this passage stands by itself, with a beginning formula ("Thus you shall say . . .") and a conclusion ("These are the words you shall speak . . .").[10] Notice the parallel structure (one line's thought is echoed and balanced

---

[10]See James Muilenburg, "The Form and Structure of the Covenantal Formulation," *Vetus Testamentum*, 9 (1959), 347–65. Martin Buber discusses the theological significance of this passage in *Moses* [235], pp. 101–9.

in the next) and the climactic use of "for" (Hebrew: *kî*), which provides the theological basis for the calling of Israel. In the original Hebrew there are assonances and recurring words used for emphasis (such as *lî*, "to me"). The carefully chiseled form and rhythmic style of this independent unit suggest that it might have been shaped by catechetical usage, perhaps in connection with services of covenant renewal.

The restrained and simple style of the passage expresses a mature theological reflection on the meaning of Israel's special calling (election). That calling is grounded in the Exodus event: the manifestation of God's action in delivering Israel from Egyptian bondage ("you have seen what I did"). But Yahweh's initiative placed the people in a decisive time, summoning them to a task within the divine purpose. At Sinai all the people experienced what Moses had sensed earlier at that same sacred mountain—the call to take part in Yahweh's historical plan. This had far-reaching implications for the future. Whether in fact these people would be the people of Yahweh depended on the condition, "if you will only obey my voice and keep my covenant." In order to become Yahweh's personal "possession" (the Hebrew word means "personal property"), the people must have a special vocation: the ordering of life according to Yahweh's sovereign demands.

Here we find a characteristic of Israel's faith that we will come back to later: the strange combination of the universal and the particular. Yahweh's sovereignty knows no boundaries, for "all the earth is mine" (Exod. 19:5b). But from many peoples Yahweh singles out one people, not for privilege but for a task. They are to be "a kingdom of priests"—that is, a community separated from the world and consecrated to the service of God (compare 1 Peter 2:5, 9).[11]

After this theological overture, the narrative goes on to describe the divine appearance (theophany) on Sinai and the giving of laws binding upon the covenant people (Exod. 19:9–20:20). This passage suggests to some scholars that Sinai was once a volcanic mountain or that the theophany was accompanied by a violent thunderstorm (see verses 16–19). More likely, however, the narrators use traditional storm imagery— "earthquake, wind, and fire" (compare 1 Kings 19:11–13)—to describe the awesome divine holiness and majesty of God's manifestation to the people. Significantly, Israel adopted religious metaphors not from the serene aspects of nature's beauty, but from the violent storm that shakes the earth, overwhelming people with an awareness of the transcendence and holiness of God and a sense of the frailty and precariousness of human life (see Isa. 2:12–22; Ps. 29).

---

[11]The expression translated "kingdom of priests" is not altogether clear. It might express Israel's uniqueness, that is, its separation from the profane and its peculiar belonging to God; so William L. Moran, in *The Bible in Current Catholic Thought*, ed. J. L. McKenzie (New York: Herder and Herder, 1962), pp. 7–20. Or it might mean that Israel is "a kingdom set apart like a priesthood" for a special service; so R. B. Y. Scott in *Oudtestamentische Studien*, VIII, ed. P. A. H. de Boer (Leiden: Brill, 1950), pp. 213–19. The verse seems to affirm that Israel's priestly role is to minister on behalf of the nations before Yahweh (compare Gen. 12:3).

THE RATIFICATION OF THE COVENANT

The Old Epic tradition portrays the ceremony of covenant making in an important chapter (Exod. 24) that blends two ancient strands of tradition. In one strand (Exod. 24:1–2, 9–11) the covenant is consummated with a sacred meal on top of the mountain. The participants in this "summit meeting" are the "distinguished ones" or representatives of Israel: Moses, the Priestly Aaron and his two eldest sons (compare Exod. 6:23), and seventy elders. The unusual statement, "they beheld God and ate and drank," suggests that the presence of the holy God was so real that, like Isaiah, they envisioned the heavenly king enthroned in cosmic majesty (Exod. 24:10; compare Isa. 6:1–3). Yet despite the warning that no human being could see God and live (Exod. 33:20; compare Isa. 6:5) they suffered no harm. In its own way the story deals with a fundamental theme of Israelite tradition: the presence of the transcendent God in the human world. *transcendence & immanence*

In the other strand of Old Epic tradition (Exod. 24:3–8) the entire assembly of Israel takes part in a covenant ceremony at the foot of the mountain. In this case the covenant is sealed with a sacrifice. Moses builds an altar and sets up twelve pillars to represent the twelve Israelite tribes. Animals are sacrificed: half the blood is dashed against the altar as a symbol of Yahweh's participation in the rite, the other half is put into basins. Acting as covenant mediator, Moses reads to the people "the book of the covenant." After the people pledge to accept and obey Yahweh's demands, Moses dashes the blood upon them saying, "Behold the blood of the covenant which Yahweh has made with you in accordance with all these words."

The traditions thus describe two different ceremonial means of concluding the covenant. Sharing a common meal was one way to seal a covenant, as we know from the contract that Jacob made with Laban (Gen. 31:46, especially verse 54). Making a covenant by sacrifice was also a familiar practice in ancient society. The Mari tablets (see pp. 31–32) refer to the consummation of a treaty or covenant alliance with the sacred rite of "killing the ass" (compare Gen. 15:7–21 and especially Jer. 34:18–19). Though the ritual is not exactly the same, Exodus 24 reflects the ancient belief that sacrificial blood has the power to bring together two parties in sacred covenant. *NT. Jesus*

Even more important, the two strands of tradition presuppose different understandings of the covenant itself. In one tradition, the people are involved only through their representatives; in the other, the people participate directly. In one, the ceremony apparently imposes no stipulations; in the other, the covenant rite includes the reading of requirements (particularly Exod. 19:5, "*if* you will obey my voice and keep my covenant . . .").[12] Both these covenant conceptions were deeply rooted in Israel's his-

---

[12]Source critics usually assign the mountaintop ceremony (Exod. 24:1–2, 9–11) to the Yahwist Epic (J) and point out that in this tradition the covenant law is not introduced until 34:10–28. The ceremony at the base of the mountain (24:3–8), which might have included the Decalogue (Exod. 20:1–17), is often assigned to the Elohist (E). See Murray L. Newman, *The People of the Covenant* [262], who maintains that the two covenant traditions, with their different theological emphases, originated at Kadesh in two different but related groups.

tory, and both were important for understanding Yahweh's relationship with the people. Therefore they were brought together in Exodus 24.

The Old Epic tradition thus included ceremonies for sealing the covenant and, at least in some passages, emphasized the keeping of laws as the condition for a continuing covenant relationship. But the Priestly writers played down these features when they incorporated this tradition in the final form of the Torah (Pentateuch). The Priestly traditionalists had no doubt about the validity of the Sinai covenant; they included *in toto* the Old Epic material found in Exodus 19–24. At the same time, they subsumed the Sinai covenant under the theology of the "everlasting covenant" (*bᵉrîth 'ôlām*)—that is, a covenant established by God *in perpetuity* regardless of human performance. In the Priestly scheme, the ecumenical covenant with Noah (Gen. 9:1–17) and the special covenant with Abraham (Gen. 17) belonged to this type of "everlasting" covenant. This allowed the Priestly writers to embrace the Sinai covenant within the "everlasting covenant" that El Shaddai (Yahweh) had made with Abraham and his descendants (Gen. 17:7–8), and even to regard the Sinaitic covenant itself as a "perpetual covenant" (*bᵉrîth 'ôlām*), the sign of which is the Sabbath (Exod. 31:12–17). The Priestly writers base the deliverance of the people from Egyptian bondage on Yahweh's "remembrance" of the covenant with Abraham, Isaac, and Jacob (Exod. 2:24; 6:2–8), and view the establishment of the cult at Sinai (Exod. 25–31, 35–40) as the fulfillment of Yahweh's pledge to be God to the people (Gen. 17:7) and to "tabernacle" in their midst (Exod. 29:45–46).

Notice that the Old Epic tradition, in contrast to the Priestly tradition, insists that the covenant contains a *conditional* element that the people must take with the utmost seriousness (see especially Exod. 19:3b–6; 24:3–8). This view is expressed by later Israelite prophets who announced the people's failure to obey Yahweh's voice and threatened them with divine judgment for breaking the covenant. The two understandings of the covenant—the conditional and the unconditional—stood in tension with one another throughout the history of Israel's traditions.[13]

COVENANT AND LAW

In the Old Epic tradition, the making of the covenant included the announcement of covenant stipulations. Exodus 24:3–8 begins:

> Moses came and told the people all the words [*dᵉbarim*] of Yahweh, and all the ordinances [*mishpatim*]. Then all the people, answering with one voice, said: "All the words [*dᵉbarim*] that Yahweh has spoken we will do."
> —EXODUS 24:3

---

[13]An excellent discussion of the Mosaic covenant is Jon Levenson, *Sinai and Zion* [159], especially Part I.

Clearly, this passage refers to the Ten Commandments or "Ten Words" introduced earlier in the narrative (Exod. 20:1–7)—specifically designated as "words" (*deḇarim*) in 20:1. But the covenant service also included the reading of "ordinances" (*mishpatim*). This seems strange, because the people respond by saying that they will obey the "words," and these "words" figure throughout the following service (Exod. 24:4, 7, 8). Apparently an editor wanted to insert the "ordinances" found in Exodus 21–23 (the so-called Covenant Code) and slipped in the loosely hanging phrase "and all the ordinances" at the end of the sentence. Originally, however, the "book [or document] of the covenant" Moses read to the people (Exod. 24:7) probably contained the Ten Commandments.[14]

By inserting law collections from later times and circles into the story of Israel's sojourn at Sinai, later editors emphasized the contemporaneity of the covenant for new generations:

> Yahweh, our God, made a covenant with us in Horeb. Not with our ancestors did Yahweh make this covenant, but with us, we who are here, all of us who are alive today.
>
> —DEUTERONOMY 5:2–3

In this way editors also gave Mosaic authority to later covenant laws. A number of separate bodies of law have gravitated to Mount Sinai.

Bodies of Legal Material in the Pentateuch

At Sinai:

1. The Decalogue	Exodus 20:1–17 (repeated in Deut. 5.6–21)
2. Civil and religious laws, often called the "Covenant Code"	Exodus 20:22–23:33
3. A set of ritual laws, often thought to be another decalogue	Exodus 34:10–26
4. Priestly legislation:	
Cultic instructions	Exodus 25–31 (executed in Exod. 35–40)
Priestly laws	Leviticus 1–18, 27
The Holiness Code	Leviticus 19–26
Priestly supplements	Numbers 1–10

After Sinai:

1. Priestly supplements	Numbers 28–31, 33–36
2. Deuteronomic Code	Deuteronomy 12–26
3. Laws sanctioned by a curse	Deuteronomy 27

[14]The civil and religious laws in Exodus 20–23 are often called "The Covenant Code" on the basis of the phrase in 24:7, "The Book of the Covenant." This is inaccurate, but it is possible these laws were promulgated in later covenant services (see Chapter 4). See Paul D. Hanson, "The Theological Significance of Contradictions within the Book of the Covenant," in *Canon and Authority: Essays in Old Testament Religion and Theology*, ed. George W. Coats and Burke O. Long (Philadelphia: Fortress, 1966) pp. 110–31.

The present diverse form of the Pentateuch shows how successive generations continued to respond to Yahweh's covenant demand under changing historical circumstances. The Priestly legislation found in Exodus 25–31 bears the stamp of later times. The Covenant Code, for the most part, betrays the interests of an agricultural rather than a wilderness environment (see Chapter 4). Moreover, the group of ritual laws in Exodus 34:10–26 reflects a Canaanite background. By a process of reduction, not much is left that comes from the time of Moses.

Does this mean that no specific laws were transmitted from the Mosaic period? Some scholars answer this question in the affirmative. However, studies of the form and content of laws in the Pentateuch indicate that the Jewish tradition tracing the covenant law—particularly the Decalogue—back to Moses is fundamentally authentic.

ABSOLUTE LAW AND CASE LAW

The Pentateuch contains two general types of law: conditional (or case) and absolute (or apodictic).[15] *Conditional law* has a characteristic pattern: If *this* happens, then *that* will be the legal consequence. A case can be carefully defined to include various subconditions, as in modern law books. This type of law is found in ancient law codes such as the Code of Hammurabi, in the legislation of the so-called Covenant Code, and in the legal corpus found in Deuteronomy 12–26.

Absolute law, on the other hand, has no "ifs" or "buts." This type of law is unconditional and stated in sharp, terse language. You can immediately see the difference between the two types of law by comparing the casuistry of the law about buying a Hebrew slave (Exod. 21:2–6) with the staccato command: "Whoever curses his father or his mother shall be put to death" (Exod. 21:17). Absolute law seems more characteristically Israelite in that it expresses the unconditional demands of the covenant. Law of this type might well go back to the wilderness period. Unlike the casuistic "ordinances" in Exodus 21–23, the Decalogue does not necessarily presuppose an agricultural society as do, for instance, the laws dealing with an ox (Exod. 21:28–36) and those dealing with damage done to a vineyard or grain field (22:5–6).[16]

Thus there is reason to believe that the Ten Commandments in Exodus 20:1–17 come from Moses. In Hebrew they are called "the Ten Words." Several command-

---

[15]This form critical distinction was made by Albrecht Alt in his important study of "The Origins of Israelite Law," first printed in German in 1934 and now available in *Essays on Old Testament History and Religion* [128], pp. 101–71. Subsequent studies have modified his thesis by tracing apodictic law to ancient clan circles and by drawing attention to the presence of this type of law in other ancient law codes. See the studies on the Ten Commandments by J. J. Stamm and M. E. Andrew [265], Brevard Childs, *Exodus* [238], pp. 385–439, and Walter Harrelson, *The Ten Commandments and Human Rights* [255].

[16]The Covenant Code also contains a few sharply stated unqualified laws of the apodictic type; compare 21:15–17. Usually, however, these laws are not cast in the "thou shalt" form of the Decalogue, but in Hebrew begin with a participial word (meaning the one who does something) and conclude with strengthened verbal forms that demand the death penalty absolutely.

ments are two or three words; others are much longer in present form but were undoubtedly expanded as they were handed down. Originally, all Ten Commandments were probably terse, absolute demands of the apodictic type. The original set of laws was probably something like this:[17]

1. I am YHWH your God, you shall have no other gods before me.
2. You shall not make for yourself any graven images or any likeness.
3. You shall not swear falsely by the Name of YHWH your God.
4. Remember the Sabbath day to keep it holy.
5. Honor your father and your mother.
6. You shall not commit murder.
7. You shall not commit adultery.
8. You shall not steal.
9. You shall not bear false witness against your neighbor.
10. You shall not covet.

Except for numbers 4 and 5, these commandments are a series of prohibitions. Each begins with a verb in the second person singular, indicating an address to each member of the covenant community. One might view these Mosaic commandments, with their predominant "don'ts," as restrictive in a negative sense often associated with biblical religion. Actually, the intention is just the opposite. The Decalogue stakes out "the basic conditions for inclusion in the [covenant] community."[18] Within this constitutional framework, however, there is wide latitude for freedom of action and for interpretation of obligation to God and to one's fellow human beings. Indeed, the purpose of case law was to spell out the implications of the apodictic commandments in the changing and complex situations of Israel's life. Eventually the commandments were reduced to two, stated in positive form: "You shall love Yahweh your God with all your heart, and with all your soul ["being"], and with all your strength" and "You shall love your neighbor as yourself" (Deut. 6:5; Lev. 19:18b; compare Mark 12:28–31). But even these positive commandments leave it up to the people to decide, within the context of the community and its traditions, what the absolute law means in specific situations.

---

[17]See Moshe Weinfeld, "What Makes the Ten Commandments Different?" *Bible Review*, VII:2 (April 1991), pp. 35–41; in greater detail, "The Decalogue: Its Significance, Uniqueness, and Place in Israel's Tradition," in *Religion and Law: Biblical-Judaic and Islamic Perspectives*, ed. Edwin R. Firmage and others (Winona Lake, IN: Eisenbrauns, 1990). Roman Catholics, Eastern Orthodox, and Protestants (Lutheran and Reformed) differ on the way the Ten Commandments are to be numbered. D. M. Beegle (*Moses* [234]) tabulates these differences (p. 217) and discusses the meaning of the commandments (pp. 218–34); see also Ronald Youngblood, "Counting the Ten Commandments," *Bible Review*, X:6 (Dec. 1944), 30–35.

[18]Weinfeld [169], p. 37.

TREATY AND COVENANT

The Law was thus intended to be the social expression of the covenant bond. The term "covenant" (Hebrew *bᵉrîth*) was often used for a political treaty, as is still the practice today. We are told that Solomon negotiated with Hiram, king of Tyre, to supply timber for the building of the temple, and that "the two of them made a treaty" (literally, "cut a covenant"; 1 Kings 5:26b). The concept of "covenant" was drawn from the field of politics and used as a model for expressing God's relationship with Israel. Of course, the parties in the covenant between God and Israel were not equal. Hence it is Yahweh who "cuts" the covenant.

A study of international treaties of the late second millennium B.C.E., found chiefly in Hittite archives, has thrown new light on the relationship between covenant and law.[19] Scholars distinguish two types of covenants in the Hittite treaties: parity and suzerainty. A *parity* covenant is reciprocal: Both parties, being equal in rank, bind themselves to each other through bilateral obligations. The *suzerainty* covenant is more unilateral: It is made between a great king (suzerain) and a vassal, the head of a subordinate state. The suzerain "gives" a covenant to the vassal, and within this covenant the vassal finds protection and security. As the subordinate party the vassal is under obligation to obey the commands of the suzerain, whose words are spoken with majesty and authority.

The suzerainty covenant in no way diminishes the sovereignty of the great king, but at the same time is not just an assertion of power over an inferior, as though the vassal were forced to obey. The most striking aspect of the suzerainty covenant is the attention given the king's deeds of benevolence on behalf of the vassal, deeds that evoke a response of grateful obedience. This treaty form contains six characteristic features:[20]

1. *Preamble.* Here the great king of the Hittite realm gives his name and sovereign titles, for example, "Thus speaks the Sun, Mursil, the Great King, the king of the country of Hatti, the favorite of the god Teshup, the son of . . . ."
2. *Historical prologue.* The suzerain proceeds to rehearse antecedents to the treaty, especially deeds of benevolence performed on behalf of the vassal. Thus the vassal's motive for obligation is gratitude.

---

[19]See the basic work by George E. Mendenhall, *Law and Covenant in the Ancient Near East* [260], and his more recent article on "Covenant" in *Interpreter's Dictionary* [31]; see also Klaus Baltzer, *The Covenant Formulary* [252]. A good general introduction to the subject is Delbert Hillers, *Covenant* [256].

[20]For an example of the suzerainty treaty, see the "Treaty between Mursilis and Duppi-Tessub of Amurru" in Pritchard, *Ancient Near Eastern Texts* [1], pp. 203–205. No. 4, which is missing in this example, is not always present in the treaty form. Other examples of the treaty form, both biblical and extrabiblical, are given in J. Arthur Thompson, *The Ancient Near Eastern Treaties and the Old Testament* (London: Tyndale Press, 1961).

3. *Stipulations imposed on the vassal.* Most important, the vassal is required to take an oath of loyalty, pledging not to recognize the sovereignty of other powers and vowing to aid the king in time of war.

4. *Attention to the treaty document.* Copies of the treaty must be preserved in the temples of both countries, and the treaty must be read publicly in the vassal state once a year.

5. *Witnesses to the treaty.* Although the gods of both countries are invoked as witnesses, precedence is given to Hittite gods. Included among the witnesses are natural powers such as heaven and earth, winds and clouds, mountains and rivers.

6. *Sanctions.* Blessings are bestowed on the vassal who obeys the treaty, but curses await the vassal who is unfaithful. The king offers protection within the terms of the treaty, but the threat of judgment, even total destruction, falls upon a vassal-state that violates the treaty.

The striking correlation between this treaty form and the Mosaic covenant in Exodus 19–24 leads some scholars to argue that it must have been the model for the biblical portrayal of Yahweh's relationship with the people. Some of the treaty elements present in the Old Epic tradition are:

1. The preamble is suggested in God's self-identification ("I am Yahweh, your God," Exod. 20:1).

2. The historical prologue can be found in the affirmation that Yahweh delivered the people from Egyptian bondage (Exod. 20:2; compare 19:4).

3. The decalogue in Exodus 20 provides stipulations, written down by Moses in "the book of the covenant" and read in the hearing of the people (Exod. 24:4a, 7).

Items 4 through 6 of the suzerainty treaty form are not present (of course, we would not expect the witness clause—at least in the same form—because Yahweh does not recognize other "gods"). Moreover, critics of this hypothesis point out that the Sinai narratives have elements not found in the Hittite treaty, especially the theophany to the people and the ceremony of the sealing of the covenant.

It is conceivable that Moses became acquainted with this treaty form in Egypt, which had a long history of dealing with the Hittites, and used it to interpret Yahweh's initiative in freeing the people.[21] But the treaty analogy would not have been meaningful to wanderers in the wilderness. The suzerainty treaty form belonged to a world of settled peoples with defined political relations, far removed from the realities of the Sinai sojourn. This way of thinking probably had its greatest influence later on, when

---

[21]John Bright, *History* [110], pp. 149–57, argues that the "overlord" (Hittite) covenant type was known to the founders of Israel. See also D. M. Beegle, *Moses* [234], pp. 204–13.

the Israelites had settled in Canaan and were beginning to adjust to the political realities of the ancient world.[22] We will return to this matter when we consider Israel's occupation of Canaan in Chapter 4.

One thing is clear: The Mosaic covenant was in no sense a parity contract between equal and mutually dependent parties. It was a relationship between unequals—between human beings and God, whose majesty is revealed in awesome thunder and lightning. As a sovereign confers relationship on a people, God *gives* the covenant to Israel. In this view, Yahweh was not legally bound to Israel: Yahweh freely initiated the relationship and, as prophets like Hosea and Jeremiah pointed out, was free to terminate the relationship, with the result that Israel would no longer be "the people of God" (Hos. 1:9). Israel, on the other hand, was bound to Yahweh, the Liberator who had performed "mighty acts" on its behalf. Israel's pledge of obedience, as expressed in the covenant ceremony ("All the words that Yahweh has spoken we will do"), was a response to Yahweh's gracious initiative and an expression of gratitude for Yahweh's marvelous goodness. Salvation was the basis for obligation.

In the Mosaic covenant tradition, the relationship between God and people is analogous to that of sovereign and servant. Significantly, the unconditional obligations set forth in the Ten Commandments begin with a brief historical prologue: "I am Yahweh your God, who brought you out of the land of Egypt, out of the house of bondage" (Exod. 20:2). Thus the Law was preceded by the remembrance of what God had done.

EXODUS AND COVENANT

In the present arrangement of the Pentateuch, Exodus is followed by Sinai covenant. Does this sequence result from *editorial arrangement* of the traditions, perhaps under the influence of the suzerainty treaty form, or from the people's *historical memory* that Sinai really did come after the Exodus in the experience of those who followed Moses out of Egypt? There is reason to suppose the connection is purely formal (editorial). We have seen that a large block of Sinai material seems to be inserted into, and interrupts, a sequence of narratives dealing with Israel's experiences in the wilderness, especially at the oasis of Kadesh located about fifty miles south of Beer-sheba (see pp. 86–88). Accordingly, some historians argue that the fugitives from Egypt went directly to this oasis, and that the Sinai sojourn pertains to a different group.[23]

Also, typical Israelite confessions of faith, which are considered to be early in thematic content (Deut. 26:5–9; 6:20–25; Josh. 24:2–13), conspicuously omit mention of

---

[22]Discussions of this subject are summarized in Dennis J. McCarthy, *Old Testament Covenant* [259]. See also R. de Vaux, *History* [111], pp. 439–52.

[23]The strict separation of these materials has been challenged by R. de Vaux, *History* [111], pp. 401–19, who argues that there were actually two exoduses. One group ("exodus-expulsion") took a northern route along the coast and then veered to Kadesh. A little later, under Moses, another group ("exodus-flight") took a southern route which led first to Sinai, then to Kadesh.

the Sinai covenant. These confessions, which epitomize the sacred history, concentrate on the beginnings of the ancestral history, the deliverance from Egyptian oppression, and the entrance into the Promised Land. Some scholars interpret this silence to mean that originally the Exodus-Conquest story and the Sinai story were separate traditions, based on events experienced by different groups and commemorated on separate cultic occasions. Eventually, they maintain, these groups pooled their traditions into a unified epic, and, through the creative artistry of the author known as the Yahwist (J), the Sinai covenant material was neatly inserted into the heart of the expanded sacred history.[24]

Advocates of the suzerainty treaty hypothesis, however, are right in calling attention to the essential connection between the Exodus and the Sinai law, as indicated in the Ten Commandments (see Exod. 20:2; also the "Eagles' Wings" passage, 19:4–5). The Sinai covenant was not one of Yahweh's mighty acts, but rather Israel's *response* to those actions. This could explain why it is not mentioned in some of the confessional summaries and in early poetry like the "Song of the Sea" (Exod. 15:1–18).[25] We know that Joshua's rehearsal of the sacred history is part of a service that included the making of a covenant and the reading of the law (Josh. 24:25–28). Moreover, the historical recitation in Deuteronomy 6:20–25 is explicitly intended to be a response to the question about the meaning of God's giving the law to Israel.

When we search back through the chain of tradition to the time of Israel's beginning, we find ourselves in a misty area where uncertainties abound. Nevertheless, the tradition as a whole stems from "root experiences": "the saving experience" (Exodus) and "the commanding experience" (Sinai).[26] From the very first, divine grace and divine demand—in Jewish terms, *haggadah* ("narrative") and *halakah* ("commandment")—were inseparably connected in Israel's experience. Thus there is good reason to affirm that the sequence of the Exodus narratives is historically correct: The Sinai covenant actually took place *after* the Exodus in the experience of a single group of Hebrews. In accordance with Moses' prophetic interpretation, the people accepted the

---

[24]This view is set forth by Gerhard von Rad in his essay on the form-critical problem of the Hexateuch [191]; see also his commentary on *Genesis* [305], pp. 13–24. Martin Noth accepts von Rad's position in general, but instead of stressing the literary work of the Yahwist (J), he maintains that the unification of the two separate themes, Sinai and Exodus, took place in the previous oral period and thus belonged to the *Grundlage* (basic epic) that underlies the literary sources. See his *Pentateuchal Traditions* [76], pp. 46–51, 59–62; *History* [115], pp. 126–37.

[25]This point is emphasized by Artur Weiser, *The Old Testament: Its Formation and Development*, trans. from the 4th German ed. by Dorothea M. Barton (New York: Association Press, 1960), pp. 83–99, and is further strengthened by Herbert H. Huffmon in "The Exodus, Sinai and the Credo" [257]. Walter Beyerlin also makes a strong argument for the common origin of the Sinai and Exodus traditions in his study of the Sinaitic traditions [253].

See also J.P. Hyatt, "Were There an Ancient Historical Credo in Israel and an Independent Sinai Tradition?" in *Translating and Understanding the Old Testament* [181], 152–70. Hyatt, along with a number of scholars, questions the antiquity of the creedal confession isolated by G. von Rad and doubts that it is a full expression of Israel's faith. E. W. Nicholson, *Exodus and Sinai* [246], also argues for a historical connection between the events.

[26]See Emil Fackenheim, *God's Presence in History* [241], chap. 1.

covenant obligations out of gratitude for what Yahweh had already done on their behalf.

THE BREAKING OF THE COVENANT

So far we have focused on the Sinai narratives in Exodus 19–24. After an interlude of Priestly material, the Old Epic tradition continues in Exodus 32–34.[27] These chapters begin with the dramatic episode of the Golden Calf and culminate with a reissuing of the commandments and a reaffirmation of Yahweh's covenant with Israel.

The story of the Golden Calf (Exod. 32) serves an important function in the larger Pentateuchal narrative. The impatient murmuring of the people is a recurrent theme in the wilderness stories (see pp. 79–80). In this instance, they are restive because of their leader's long absence on the mountaintop. Supposing that something has happened to Moses, the people ask Aaron to make them "gods ['elohim] who shall go before us."[28] Using the people's gold earrings, Aaron casts the image of a golden calf and announces a festival. The ensuing "feast to Yahweh," with sacrifices, eating and drinking, dancing, and perhaps sexual orgies (verses 5–6), probably reflects the local Canaanite culture with its emphasis on sexual vitality and fertility. The story goes that when Moses came down the mountain and saw this wild spectacle he was overcome with anger, smashing the tablets on which the Decalogue was written to dramatize that the covenant had been broken.

Striking similarities between this story and the account in 1 Kings 12:25–33 illustrate how the Mosaic traditions were reinterpreted in new situations in Israel's history. The 1 Kings account reflects a political situation after the death of Solomon when the United Kingdom was split into the Northern Kingdom of Israel (Ephraim) and the Southern Kingdom of Judah. Jeroboam I (about 922–901 B.C.E.), the first king of the Northern Kingdom, set up golden bulls at two shrines, Dan and Bethel, in order to consolidate his kingdom. The king's announcement, "Behold your gods, O Israel, who brought you up out of the land of Egypt" (1 Kings 12:18) is the same as that of Aaron in the Golden Calf story (Exod. 32:4)! Clearly the narrator, whose loyalty was to the Southern Kingdom, wanted to condemn Jeroboam's innovation by likening it to the apostasy that Moses once condemned. Some scholars even maintain that the story of the Golden Calf was created ad hoc as a polemic against the Northern king, "who made

[27]That Exodus chapters 25–31 come from the Priestly (P) tradition is evident from the different style and the concern for cultic matters such as the tabernacle, the Ark, priestly ordination, and so on. The instructions given in these chapters are carried out in chapters 35–40, with considerable repetition of content.
[28]The assumption that polytheism was involved indicates the narrator's bias. Thus the word 'elohim, which can mean either "God" or "gods" in Hebrew, is construed with plural verbs in verses 1 and 4. But the story speaks of only one calf-symbol, and the feast is explicitly called "a feast to Yahweh" in verse 5. The same bias is reflected in 1 Kings 12:28, where 'elohim probably should be translated "God" rather than "gods."

An Israelite bronze bull, dating from the period of the Judges (c. 1200 B.C.E.). Found on a "high place" or cultic site in the hills of Samaria, this figurine (7 inches long, 5 inches high), symbolizing power and fertility, apparently was associated with the worship of Yahweh as well as Baal (cf. Judg. 6:25).

Israel to sin."[29] The story in Exodus 32 probably rests upon a tradition much older than Jeroboam I, however, indicating that some ancient circles believed the bull could legitimately be used to symbolize the supremacy of Yahweh.[30]

Whatever the case, the Golden Calf story sets the stage for the narratives that follow (Exod. 33–34). For a time it seemed that all hope for the future was lost. How could Yahweh accompany such a sinful people without divine holiness becoming a consuming fire? But Moses, the covenant mediator, interceded for the people and received the assurance that Yahweh's name (character, identity) is holy love, which includes both judgment and forgiveness. Yahweh acts in divine freedom: *Moses as mediator*

> "I will be gracious unto whom I will be gracious, and I will be
> compassionate to whom I will have compassion."
> —EXODUS 33:19

[29]This view is championed by Martin Noth, *Pentateuchal Traditions* [76], pp. 141–45. See also his *Exodus* commentary [247], p. 246.
[30]See Frank M. Cross, "Yahweh and El" [129], pp. 73–75, who argues that in Northern circles the Bull was a symbol of the high god *'El*, with whom Yahweh was identified. Bethel, he points out, was an old sanctuary where "Bull *'El*" was worshiped (not Baal, the god of fertility, who was also portrayed as standing on a young bull). Jeroboam's policy was to reestablish the old sanctuary of Bethel, with its *'El* worship, as a rival to the Jerusalem sanctuary.

Forgiveness offers a new opportunity only God can give, evoking awe and wonder (compare Ps. 130:4). In this context appears for the first time a great confession of faith, centering in the "name" of God:

> Then Yahweh passed by before him [Moses] and proclaimed:
> YAHWEH, YAHWEH!
> God who is compassionate and gracious,
> slow to anger and full of steadfast love [*ḥesed*] and faithfulness,
> extending steadfast love to thousands,
> forgiving iniquity, rebellion, and sin,
> but who will definitely not exempt any from punishment,
> visiting the sins of the parents upon the children,
> and to children's children to the third and fourth generation.
> —EXODUS 34:6–7

The narratives in Exodus 32–34 are marked by a sober realism. They show that the Israelites could not claim to be *better* than other nations, either morally or religiously, for they displayed the same weaknesses and strengths found in other peoples. The difference, if any, lay in the extraordinary experience that had formed this people into a community and given them a destiny in the service of God. Moses asks, "Is it not in thy going with us, so that we are distinct, I and thy people, from all other people that are upon the face of the earth?" (Exod. 33:16). The people faced the future with the conviction that Yahweh, their Leader, was going before them. We find here, moreover, an early recognition of what later prophets announced: The covenant that is broken by human folly and rebellion can be renewed only through divine forgiveness (see Jer. 31:34b), which exceeds human expectations and opens a new way into the future.

In Exodus 34:10–28 we find a parallel tradition about the making of the covenant. In this case there are virtually no resemblances to the suzerainty treaty form (see pp. 90–92). The covenant is introduced not with a historical prologue, but with the promise of marvels that Yahweh will accomplish in the *future* (verses 10–11). Moses' impulsive destruction of the first stone tablets provides the occasion for a new edition of the Decalogue, symbolizing the renewal of the covenant. The second set of tablets was to contain "the words that were on the first tablets" that Moses broke (34:1). Strangely, however, the laws found in 34:11–26 display just a few points of contact with the first decalogue (the laws in verses 14 and 17 prohibiting worship of other gods and the making of molten images). Moreover, it is difficult to find exactly ten commandments here, though verse 28 indicates that the new edition was "ten words."

These laws are sometimes referred to as the "ritual decalogue" because of their concentration on cultic matters such as seasonal festivals or the prohibition against the Canaanite practice of boiling a young goat in its mother's milk. For the most part these laws presuppose the later situation of Israel's settlement in Canaan, when agricultural festivals were adopted and some Canaanite practices were repudiated. The present narrative scheme, which includes Moses' breaking of the first tables, makes it possible for this separate set of laws to be included here.

THE MOSAIC FAITH

"A stream never rises higher than its source." We can apply this proverb to the source of Israel's faith in the Mosaic period. In subsequent periods the stream was widened, its channel deepened, and its flow interrupted by many obstacles and cataracts. Prophetic interpreters, however, viewed Israel's greatest moments of worship and prophetic insight as a return to the source: the Exodus and the covenant of Sinai.[31]

We can summarize the main aspects of the Mosaic faith as follows:

1. *The God of History.* As the preface to the Ten Commandments indicates, Yahweh is preeminently the God whose liberating power was revealed in the historical-political event of the Exodus—an event so crucial that it became part of the undying memory of the people. The Israelites were not the only people who witnessed to divine activity in history. Other ancient peoples believed their gods were active in upholding the political and cosmic order.[32] But no other nation of antiquity, as far as we know, viewed divine activity in history as central to the self-understanding of a people and God's relation to them. The passion of this conviction was later expressed by Hosea, who declared that Yahweh is Israel's God "from the land of Egypt," and that besides Yahweh the people "know" no other deity (Hos. 13:4–5).

    Yahweh's power, however, was in no way limited to the historical/political arena. Yahweh's theophany could be portrayed in thunder and lightning; Yahweh could command the wind to drive back the waters of the Reed Sea; Yahweh could inflict plagues to remind even the most hard-hearted that "the earth belongs to Yahweh" (Exod. 9:29; compare Ps. 24:1). But Yahweh was not understood as a natural power—a sun-god, a storm-god, or a god of nature's mysterious fertility. Rather, Israel affirmed that Yahweh could use the powers of nature to achieve a *historical purpose*: to challenge the mighty empire of Pharaoh, to liberate a people from the bondage of slavery, and to open a path through the wilderness into the future. The Mosaic faith has a special interest in historical events, precisely because it rests upon "root

---

[31]See Chapter 8 for a discussion of the story of Elijah's return to Horeb/Sinai (1 Kings 19).

[32]See Bertil Albrektson, *History and the Gods* [221], who argues that testimonies to divine activity in history were not peculiar to ancient Israel. He admits, however, that "the idea of divine acts in history [in Israel on the one hand and in Mesopotamia on the other] may well have occupied a different place in the different patterns of beliefs" (p. 115).

experiences" that bear witness to the God who transcends both nature and history.

2. *The Covenant Relationship.* Israel believed that through these extraordinary events, centering in the crossing of the Reed Sea, Yahweh established a close relationship with a people. To be sure, the narratives do not remove the distance beween God and people. Even Moses, through whose mediation Yahweh spoke to the people, was warned that he could not see Yahweh's "face" (or "presence"), "for a human being may not see me and live" (Exod. 33:20). But the holy God who is "far off" (transcendent) is also "near" (immanent). God takes the initiative to enter into relationship with the people and thus becomes, in a special sense, "the God of Israel." Within this relationship, Israel is like a "first-born son" (Exod. 4:22–23). Israel's gratitude for divine liberation is the primary motive for its response of faith, expressed by obeying the laws of the covenant and facing the future in the confidence that Yahweh would be with, and go with, the people. The covenant relationship—"coexistence with God" as Abraham Joshua Heschel puts it[33]— was the basis of the Israelite community.

3. *You Shall Have No Other Gods.* For Israel there was to be only one God, Yahweh. The first commandment of the Mosaic Decalogue is: "You shall have no other gods before [or besides] me." If other gods existed, as the commandment implies, they were not to claim Israel's allegiance and paled into insignificance before the glory of Yahweh. The contest in the Exodus drama is between Yahweh and Pharaoh—not between Yahweh and the gods of Egypt. Yahweh alone controls the events of history and the powers of nature. Moreover, in Israel's faith Yahweh is not part of a pantheon, even though the idea of the Heavenly Council, composed of the "sons of God" (heavenly beings), could be used to portray Yahweh's cosmic majesty (see Exod. 15:11).

The biblical rejection of a masculine/feminine relationship in the divine nature is evidence of Israel's protest against polytheism. In other ancient religions, major gods were paired with goddesses: for example, Asherah with the high god El, and Ashtarte (Ishtar) with the storm god Baal. In leading Israelite circles, however, as opposed to popular piety, Yahweh was not represented as having a consort or partner. Though numerous passages in the Hebrew Bible use feminine imagery to portray God (see Isa. 42:14–15; 66:13) the narratives suppress any conception of the mother-goddess, an important element in the religions of Canaan, Babylonia, and Egypt (and

---

[33]The main aspects of Heschel's important book, *God in Search of Man: A Philosophy of Judaism* (New York: Farrar, Straus and Giroux, 1955) are presented and discussed in B. W. Anderson, "Coexistence with God: Heschel's Exposition of Biblical Theology," in *Abraham Joshua Heschel: Exploring His Life and Thought,* ed. John C. Merkle (New York: Macmillan, 1985).

probably in popular Israelite religion as well). Israel did not adopt contemporary sexual models for understanding the divine-human relationship, but turned instead to historical-political models such as the liberation from oppression and the covenant or treaty (see Chapter 6).

The second commandment of the Decalogue goes a step further by saying that Yahweh is not to be worshiped in the form of any image or likeness. This was a revolutionary view at the time, for other ancient peoples believed that divine presence was concretely represented in images, both human and animal. Israel affirmed that Yahweh is the Incomparable One who cannot be likened to "anything that is in heaven above, or that is in the earth beneath, or that is in the water under the earth" (Exod. 20:4)—in other words, in the whole realm of creation, pictorially conceived.[34] The only exception to this commandment is the Priestly view that 'adam (human being), consisting of "male and female," is created in the image of God, to represent God's sovereign rule on the earth (Gen. 1:26–28). The Mosaic intolerance of images is given supreme expression in later prophecy (see Isa. 40:18–26).

Was Mosaic religion monotheistic—that is, did it affirm belief in only one God? Perhaps we should not put the question in this way, for Israel's interpreters were not concerned with the abstract issue of whether or not other gods existed. Instead, Israel heard the command that forbade allegiance to other gods. The commandment does not say, "There are no other gods," but "You shall have no other gods."[35] Yahweh made a complete, absolute claim upon Israel's devotion. The earliest way of expressing Israel's sense of divine sovereignty was in terms of Yahweh's "jealousy": We are told in Exodus 34:14 that Yahweh's name is Jealous. This figurative expression underscores the meaning of the first commandment. Yahweh makes an unconditional demand upon the loyalty of the people, a demand put to the test when the Israelites settled in Canaan and faced the temptation of competing loyalties (see Exod. 34:11–16).

---

[34]See Gerhard von Rad, "Some Aspects of the Old Testament World View," in *The Problem of the Hexateuch and Other Essays* [191], p. 147.
[35]See Martin Buber, *The Prophetic Faith* [348], pp. 19–23.

CHAPTER 4

THE PROMISED LAND

The struggle for land has always been a powerful force in history. In the United States, for instance, Americans rehearse in story and song the stirring epic of immigrants who landed on the Atlantic seaboard and pushed the frontier to the shores of the Pacific. The other side of the story is that the native Indians were tragically dispossessed and almost exterminated. Despite this injustice, in times of thanksgiving Americans affirm their belief that God was guiding the "pilgrim feet" of the colonists. The song "America, the Beautiful" celebrates these early settlers "whose stern, impassioned stress, a thoroughfare for freedom beat, across the wilderness."

From earliest times the Fertile Crescent was the scene of fierce struggles for the land. This coveted area was periodically invaded by peoples from Arabia, Asia Minor, the Caucasian highlands, and Egypt (see Chapter 1). With its strategic geographic location, Palestine was inevitably drawn into the incessant conflict.

Into this dynamic arena came the Hebrews. Like other 'Apiru in the ancient world, they were at first a landless people, part of a floating population that included various unsettled groups in society. Their struggle to obtain land and fulfill their historical destiny entailed much suffering and bloodshed and the suppression of native Canaanite culture. But throughout this struggle they held the firm conviction that

Biblical Readings: Numbers 11–14, 18–24, and 32 (mainly Old Epic narratives); also the narrative of the conquest in Joshua 1–12 and the account of the Shechem assembly in Joshua 24.

Yahweh, their God, was with them in the midst of conflict, leading them victoriously into the land.

A LAND FLOWING WITH MILK AND HONEY

"The guidance out of Egypt" and "the guidance into the arable land" were inseparably linked in the faith of ancient Israel.[1] This is evident from a passage in the book of Deuteronomy that deals with religious instruction of the younger generation.[2] To explain to their children the motive for obeying the commandments, parents are to recite the events that happened "for us"—that is, all generations past and future:

> Once we were Pharaoh's slaves in Egypt,
> and Yahweh brought us out from Egypt with a mighty hand.
> Before our very eyes Yahweh displayed great and ominous signs
> and wonders against Pharaoh and all his court.
> Us he brought out from there so that he might bring us in, to give
> us the land which he promised by oath to our ancestors.
>
> —DEUTERONOMY 6:21–23

This same sequence of events is found in the liturgical recitation in Deuteronomy 26:5–9 (see pp. 12–13). While offering the first fruits of the harvest at the pilgrimage festival (Feast of Weeks or Pentecost) the worshiper gratefully confesses that Yahweh not only "brought us out of Egypt with a mighty hand and an outstretched arm," but also "brought us to this place, and gave us this land, a land flowing with milk and honey." Anyone who has been in Palestine, with its abundance of rocks on every hand, might wonder at the extravagant description of "a land flowing with milk and honey." But in ancient times milk and honey in abundance signified the blessings of Paradise. To wanderers who had lived in the barren wilderness, Canaan was a veritable paradise (see Deut. 8:7–10).

The liturgy in Deuteronomy 26:5–9, with its harvest festival setting, clearly dates from a time well after Israel had settled in Canaan and had made the transition to agriculture. Some scholars believe, however, that the promise of land was part of the ancestral tradition ("the faith of the ancestors"; see pp. 39–42). The Pentateuch in its present form emphasizes this theme in stories of the ancestors. Yahweh says to Abram: "To your descendants I will give this land" (Gen. 12:7)—a promise that was reaffirmed to Isaac and Jacob and renewed in the time of Moses. Thus Canaan came to be known as "the Promised Land." We must remember, however, that these traditions were written down

---

[1]Martin Noth, in *Pentateuchal Traditions* [76], pp. 51–54, stresses that "the constitution of a 'free' Israel on its own soil" was implicit in the primary theme of the Exodus.
[2]In this connection see Walter Brueggemann, *The Land* [268], pp. 14–39.

after the occupation of Canaan was an accomplished fact. Whatever the promise of the land meant in the "period of the ancestors," the tradition was recast in the light of the Exodus event.

The affirmation of Yahweh's gift of the land is the high point in the rehearsal of Israel's sacred history and, as such, is given great prominence in the Pentateuch—especially in the book of Joshua (Hexateuch), which deals with the conquest of Canaan.[3] True, this theme is colored by Israelite nationalism, which accounts in part for its important place in the narrative. But even the great prophets, who vigorously attacked Israel's proud nationalism, affirmed their belief that the gift of the land was the supreme sign of Yahweh's benevolence toward the people:

> It was I [Yahweh] who brought you up from the land of Egypt,
> and for forty years led you in the wilderness,
> > to take possession of the land of the Amorites.
> > —AMOS 2:10

The prophets Hosea (Hos. 2) and Jeremiah (Jer. 2:7; 3:19) make similar statements about Yahweh's gift of the land. The book of Deuteronomy, which purports to be a sermon given by Moses on the eve of the invasion of Canaan, describes the land as Israel's "inheritance," received from Yahweh.

Considering the terrible suffering involved in the conquest of Canaan, especially for the defeated Canaanites, it is difficult to understand the Israelite conviction that God actually took part in the struggle. Nevertheless, Yahweh is portrayed as a God of "holy war" who ruthlessly demands the sacrificial destruction (Hebrew: *ḥérem*) of Israel's enemies (see Definition, p. 128). The book of Joshua bristles with theological difficulties. We must keep in mind that in Israel's faith God is not aloof from history, but rather takes part in the human struggle, guiding and shaping the course of human affairs according to divine purpose. In Israel's experience the conquest of Canaan did not happen by accident or by the assertion of superior human power. It occurred within the providence of God. Therefore, the land was not a possession to boast about, but a gift to be received with humility and gratitude (Josh. 24:13).[4]

We consider next the narratives that deal with Israel's sojourn in the wilderness, the preparations for invading Canaan, and the long circuit through the countries of Transjordan. The books of Numbers (starting with Num. 10:11), Deuteronomy, and Joshua cover this period of Israel's history. We will defer discussion of some of these materials to later chapters: Chapter 11 for the book of Deuteronomy (D); and

---

[3]Gerhard von Rad referred to the liturgy in Deuteronomy 26:5–9 as "the Hexateuch in miniature"; see *The Problem of the Hexateuch and Other Essays* [191].

[4]On the problem of the land, especially the dispossession of the natives, see B. W. Anderson, "The Promised Land," *Bible Review* IX:1 (February, 1993), 4; also "Standing on God's Promises," in *Problems and Perspectives of Biblical Theology*, essays in honor of J. C. Beker, ed. by Ben Ollenburger and others (Abingdon, 1995).

Chapter 13, for the Priestly (P) material in the latter half of the book of Numbers and (possibly) the last part of the book of Joshua. In this chapter we will focus primarily on the Old Epic tradition of the book of Numbers (Num. 11–14, 20–24, 32) and the story of the conquest in the book of Joshua (Josh. 1–12).

FORTY YEARS OF WANDERING

According to tradition, Israel spent forty years wandering in the wilderness south of Beer-sheba. In the Bible the number forty is often a stylized expression for a full genera-tion and sometimes means only "a long time" (see 1 Kings 19:8, where Elijah is said to journey into the wilderness forty days and forty nights). In this case, however, the num-ber is probably about right. We are told that none of the adults who left Egypt entered Canaan; all died during the sojourn in the wilderness (Num. 14:26–35; 26:63–65). It was a new generation, under the leadership of Joshua, that was privileged to set eyes on the promised land.

THE SOJOURN AT KADESH

The narratives in the Pentateuch concentrate on the sojourn at Mount Sinai: The Is-raelites arrive at Sinai in Exodus 19:1 and break camp (ten months and nineteen days later) in Numbers 10:11. All the intervening material deals with the given laws and in-stitutions by which the covenant people are to live. The Israelites undoubtedly spent the greater part of their wilderness sojourn at a desert place called Kadesh or Kadesh-barnea (Num. 13:26; 20:1, 16; Deut. 1:46). This site is identified with an oasis watered by three springs in the barren Negeb about fifty miles south of Beer-sheba.[5] Some of the traditions about episodes in the wilderness have their original setting at Kadesh, said to be eleven days' journey from Sinai (Deut. 1:2) on the edge of territory controlled by Edom. This is probably the setting of some material placed before Sinai (Exod. 15:23–18:27),[6] and is clearly the setting of much of the post-Sinai material found in Numbers 11–20 (from the Old Epic tradition except for Num. 15 and Num. 17–19, which come entirely from Priestly tradition).

The sojourn at Kadesh had a profound influence on the people later known as Is-rael. Some historians even argue that Kadesh, not Sinai, was the original destination of the Hebrews who fled from Egypt, and that their basic community life, administration of law, and style of worship were established at this oasis. Some support for this hypoth-

---

[5]See Y. Aharoni, "Kadesh-Barnea and Mount Sinai," in B. Rothenberg, *God's Wilderness,* trans. Joseph Witriol (London: Thames and Hudson, 1961), pp. 117–40.

[6]Note that Exod. 15:23–27 relates a murmuring experience at Massah and Meribah, presumably two of the springs of the Kadesh area. The incident is paralleled in Num. 20:2–13, where the location is clearly Kadesh (or Meribath-Kadesh, Deut. 33:5). Some maintain that all the material in Exod 15:23–18:27 be-longs to Kadesh, but this is doubtful.

esis can be found in Judges 11:16–18, which jumps from the Exodus to Kadesh in one sentence without any reference to a stop at Sinai. This argument from silence is dubious: The same telescoped summary is found in Numbers 20:14–16, where Moses sends a message to the king of Edom. In this case and in Jephthah's later message to the king of Ammon (Judg. 11:12–28), it was appropriate to mention only those matters that were politically relevant. The historical situation was more complex than what we can gather from the biblical account, which magnifies the revelation at Sinai and emphasizes Moses' leadership. The Hebrews who fled Egypt might have followed a southern route that took them first to Sinai and then to Kadesh. When they arrived at the oasis, they could have come into contact with other Hebrews who had come down from Palestine earlier or who had left Egypt under other circumstances.

The narratives in Numbers 11–20 renew the theme that, in spite of Yahweh's providence, the people continued to murmur and occasionally rebelled against Moses' leadership. The manna of the desert was not good enough for those who remembered the highly seasoned diet in Egypt (Num. 11:4–6). A revolt was instigated by Moses' own brother and sister, Aaron and Miriam (Num. 12)—suggesting that Miriam played a more important role in early Mosaic tradition than is evident from the present Priestly edition of the Pentateuch.[7] Korah stirred up factional strife in Moses' tribe of Levi to renew the revolt on a larger scale, and Dathan and Abiram aroused other tribesmen against Moses (Num. 16). Little is known about the years of Israel's sojourn in and around Kadesh, but the tradition affords vivid glimpses of how the people were united through bitter struggle and suffering.[8]

The "rabble" (Num. 11:4) under Moses' leadership did not become a stable, unified community overnight. While the centripetal force of Yahweh's liberating action pulled the people toward a center of common covenant allegiance, powerful centrifugal forces pulled them away from that center: tribal rivalry, power struggles for leadership, hunger and thirst, and the human incapacity for faith. At the oasis of Kadesh-barnea these two forces came into sharp conflict. The covenant bond could easily have dissolved in the disruptive tensions of the wilderness. To later Israelites, however, who looked back on the desert experience from the perspective of covenant faith, it seemed clear that through these trials Yahweh was uniting and disciplining the people for the historical task ahead. A later Deuteronomic discourse affirms this truth:

> You must remember the entire journey that Yahweh, your God,
> caused you to take during these forty years in the wilderness in order to
> make you feel humble, to test you so as to know what is in your heart—
> whether you would keep his commandments or not. Yahweh humbled you
> and let you get hungry, giving you manna to eat which you did not know

---

[7]See B. W. Anderson, "Miriam's Challenge," *Bible Review*, X:3 (June, 1994), 16; also Phyllis Trible, "Bringing Miriam Out of the Shadows," *Bible Review*, V:1 (February 1989), 14–25, 34.

[8]On the "controversy at Kadesh," see Murray L. Newman, *The People of the Covenant* [262], chap. 3. The murmuring narratives are discussed by George Coats, *Rebellion in the Wilderness* [254].

and your ancestors had not known, in order to make you realize that it is not by bread alone that a human being lives, but rather it is by every utterance of the mouth of Yahweh that a person lives.

—DEUTERONOMY 8:2–3

THE HOLY ONE IN THE MIDST OF ISRAEL

According to ancient tradition, two sacred objects signified Yahweh's presence in the midst of the people: the Tent of Meeting and the Ark of the Covenant.

The *Tent of Meeting* is first mentioned in connection with the sojourn at Sinai (Exod. 33:7–11) and later in connection with Kadesh and the wilderness (Num. 11:16–17, 24–26; 12:1–8; see Deut. 31:14–15). In addition, the Priestly (P) tradition gives an elaborate description of this tent or "tabernacle" in Exodus 26–27 and 35–38. Though much of the Priestly description reflects later theological and cultic development, it probably preserves reminiscences of the ancient wilderness sanctuary, which resembled the red leather tent-shrines known among ancient Semites.[9]

We are told that Moses pitched the Tent outside the camp and would go there to encounter Yahweh, who descended from heaven in a pillar of cloud to the door of the tent and spoke with him "face to face, as a man speaks to his friend" (Exod. 33:11). The Tent was the place of "meeting" with the deity, where one could seek an oracle or proclaim Yahweh's word to assembled Israel. Those with difficult problems would go out to the Tent, where Moses would bring their petitions before Yahweh. In this way, we can imagine, the covenant law was expounded and expanded.

The *Ark of the Covenant* is described in the Priestly Writing in Exodus 25:10–22 and 37:1–9, which probably relies on ancient tradition. Originally, the Ark seems to have been a portable throne on which Yahweh was believed to be invisibly enthroned. As we have seen, Mosaic religion strictly prohibited worship of Yahweh in the form of a visible image (see p. 99). Nevertheless, the people firmly believed that God was present in their midst, enthroned on the Ark that was carried before them in wandering or in battle. One of the oldest fragments of the Pentateuch is the "Song of the Ark":

As the ark set out, Moses would say:
"Rise, Yahweh, may your enemies be scattered
and those who hate you flee at your approach!"
And when it halted, he would say:
"Come back, Yahweh,
to the countless thousands of Israel!"

—NUMBERS 10:35–36 (NJB)

[9]See Frank M. Cross, Jr. "The Tabernacle," in *The Biblical Archaeologist*, X (1947), 45–68. Reprinted in *The Biblical Archaeologist Reader*, I [119], pp. 201–28.

The Old Epic tradition at one time might have described the construction of the Ark. Indeed, according to a tradition in Deuteronomy (Deut. 10:3–5), Moses constructed an ark of acacia wood at Sinai to hold the tablets on which the Decalogue was inscribed.[10]

Nowhere does the Old Epic tradition state that the Ark was placed inside the Tent of Meeting. This striking coincidence has led some interpreters to conclude that the two cultic objects were originally independent, each the focus of a particular theology and each identified with a separate group of people. In this view, the Tent represented a theology of "manifestation" (the transcendent God from time to time appears to Moses and the people) while the Ark stood for a theology of "presence" (Yahweh is present in the midst of the people). The Tent was supposedly the shrine of a "Southern" group (especially the tribe of Judah), and the Ark was identified with a "Northern" group (the Joseph tribes that Joshua led into Canaan). These cultic objects went their separate ways in the history of the traditions until the Priestly writers united them with the statement that Moses put the Ark inside the Tabernacle at Sinai (Exod. 20:2–3, 21; see also Exod. 25:22; Num. 7:89).[11] But there is only slight evidence for this view in the Old Epic tradition. In the early monarchy the Ark was stationed in a "tent" (2 Sam. 7:2; also 6:17). This might indicate that David conservatively maintained a cultic arrangement going back at least to the time of the former Tribal Confederacy, when the Ark was stationed at Shiloh (1 Sam. 1–5; compare Ps. 78:60).[12]

During the sojourn in the wilderness, especially at Sinai and Kadesh, the people undoubtedly borrowed patterns of worship from other ancient peoples who also had sacred objects like the Tent and the Ark. Under Moses' interpretation, however, these objects came to express the distinctive faith of Israel: the worship of Yahweh as the transcendent God in heaven who, without any limitation upon divine sovereignty, is also present in the midst of the people. It is interesting that it was a Midianite, Jethro, who proposed a scheme for administering laws that would ease Moses' responsibilities as leader (Exod. 18:13–27). This story also indicates Israel's indebtedness to its neighbors.

A FOOLHARDY ATTACK ON CANAAN

Eventually desert hardships and lack of living space compelled the Hebrews to look elsewhere for a home. A group of spies set out from the Kadesh base to survey the hill country of Canaan in the vicinity of Hebron, directly to the north (Num. 13 and 14). This reconnaissance team brought back a report that the land was fertile, "a land flow-

[10]The Old Epic tradition about the construction of the Ark apparently has been replaced by the fuller treatment found in Priestly tradition (Exod. 25:10–22).

[11]This is the view of Gerhard von Rad, *Old Testament Theology*, Vol. I [163], pp. 234–41. Murray Newman, in *The People of the Covenant* [262], pp. 55–71, maintains that two different covenant theologies were associated with the Tent and the Ark respectively and traces the separation of these cultic shrines to a major controversy at Kadesh.

[12]Frank M. Cross, in "Ideologies of Kingship in the Era of the Empire" [129], p. 242, states emphatically: "The Ark had always been associated with a tent shrine, wherever it wandered, wherever the central sanctuary was established."

ing with milk and honey." The scouts also reported that the land was strongly fortified and that the inhabitants were of such great stature that "we seemed to ourselves like grasshoppers, and so we seemed to them" (Num. 13:32–33).

Opinion was sharply divided over whether to try to enter Canaan from the south, with some people in favor and some so discouraged that they proposed finding a leader to guide them back to Egypt. Finally it was decided that a risky attack was preferable to wandering for a lifetime in the wilderness. This foolhardy move lacked divine sanction, for Moses and the Ark of the Covenant remained at Kadesh. The result was what might be expected: The Hebrews were decisively repulsed by the Amalekites of the Negeb and by Canaanites of the hill country in the vicinity of Hormah, a few miles east of Beer-sheba (Num. 14:39–45).[13]

Too weak to break through the fortresses guarding the southern approach to Canaan, the Hebrews had to seek another way to escape from the wilderness. There was only one other route: a long circuit through the country of Transjordan.

DETOUR VIA TRANSJORDAN

The rest of the book of Numbers deals with the Hebrews' advance along "the other side of the Jordan" (Num. 32:19) in order to invade Canaan from the east. This route was also beset with many hazards, for Transjordan was occupied by settled peoples who resented the appearance of a band of armed intruders.

The Hebrews faced obvious tactical problems (see map, p. 120). Just south of the Dead Sea and directly opposite Kadesh-barnea was Edom, traditionally related to Israel through Esau, Jacob's twin brother (Gen. 36). Just above Edom lay Moab, bounded on the north by the river Arnon and on the south by the brook Zered. Above Moab was Ammon, on the edge of the Arabian desert. In biblical tradition Moab and Ammon were distantly related to Israel through Lot, the nephew of Abraham (Gen. 19:30–38). To the west of Ammon lay the Amorite kingdom ruled by King Sihon, bounded by the river Arnon to the south and by the river Jabbok to the north. Still farther north lay the land of King Og, known as Bashan.

Whether these countries were nations with flourishing populations at this time is open to question. Existing archaeological evidence indicates that Moab and Edom did not achieve national unity until a later period.[14] Both peoples, however, are mentioned

---

[13]Another account of the battle of Hormah, though misplaced and perhaps relating to another situation (see Judg. 1:16–17), is found in Numbers 21:1–3. When the king of Arad (a Canaanite city in the Negeb) heard that the invaders were attempting to move north into Canaan, he sent out an army to intercept them, but this time the tables were turned. The account of the decisive victory of the Hebrews provides an explanation for the name of the city Hormah (from *ḥērem* ["destruction"], the Hebrew word for the sacrificial ban).

[14]See Hayes and Miller, *History* [112], pp. 258–59. For a discussion of literary and archaeological evidence bearing on the three kingdoms from about 1200 B.C.E. to 300 C.E., see Burton MacDonald, *Ammon, Moab and Edom: Early States/Nations of Jordan in the Biblical Period* (Amman, Jordan: Al Kutba, 1994).

The King's Highway seen from the air as it runs north to cross the Brook Zered. The Israelites attempted to use this ancient caravan road during their detour via Transjordan (Num. 20:17). Paved by the Romans, the road has remained visible in its outline through the centuries. The rectangular structure beside it is the ruin of an ancient guardpost.

in early Hebrew poetry ("Song of the Sea," Exod. 15:15) and in Egyptian texts from the thirteenth century B.C.E.[15] We can assume that other *'Apiru* groups were in the process of establishing themselves in the area at the time when those Hebrews who came to be known as Israel were seeking a homeland.

DISPUTES OVER THOROUGHFARE

According to Numbers 20:14–21, Moses sent messengers from Kadesh to the king of Edom requesting permission to travel on the King's Highway. This ancient route, now followed by a modern road in that area, linked Syria and Ezion-geber, the seaport town located on the Gulf of Aqabah. From Ezion-geber the road ran north through Moab and the Amorite land of King Sihon, skirted the border of the kingdom of Ammon, and continued up through the territory of King Og (Bashan) to Damascus, the capital of Aram or Syria. In spite of Moses' promise that the Hebrews would stay on the highway, turning neither right nor left, the suspicious Edomite king refused to grant them

[15]Hayes and Miller, *op. cit.*, pp. 250–51.

Insert 3-1   The Mari Woman with Headdress. A gypsum sculpture (6" high) of a woman from ancient Mari (twenty-fourth century B.C.E.). She wears a tall headdress; and traces of bitumen "eyeliner" still enhance her eyes, once inlaid with lapis lazuli pupils. A hole at the base of the neck suggests that the head was once attached to a body.

Insert 3-2   Hittite gold pendant (less than 2") of a child sitting on a woman's lap. Note her broad headdress and earrings, as well as the formal poses assumed by both figures.

Insert 4-1a The Hittite capital of Hattushash lies on the ridge *(right)* that slopes down to the modern city of Boghaz-köy; the rugged terrain enhanced its defenses.

Insert 4-1b The Lion Gate at Hattushash stands in the Hittite capital's ruins.

Insert 4-1c Excavated ruins of the fortified upper part (acropolis) of the Hittite capital.

passage. As a result they traveled along the western border of Edom, turning east at the boundary brook Zered in order to skirt Moab.

As the Hebrews approached the territory of the Amorite kingdom of Sihon, Moses again sent messengers asking for permission to use the King's Highway. The king not only refused, but also sent an army to crush the invaders (Num. 21:21–32). The result was Israel's first major military victory: So decisively did the Hebrews defeat the Amorites that they took possession of the whole kingdom. The taste of victory spurred them to move farther north, where they met and defeated King Og of Bashan, a gigantic man whose main claim to fame was his unusually large and sturdy bed (Num. 21:33–35; Deut. 3:1–11). According to the narrative, the Hebrews took possession of a large strip of land in Transjordan, including the lands of Sihon and Og. They were now encamped in "the plains of Moab" (Num. 22:1)—the Moabite lowlands just across the Jordan River from Jericho. The stage was set for a bold thrust into Canaan from the east.

THE ORACLES OF BALAAM

At this point the narrator inserts the story of Balaam, a Babylonian diviner summoned by the king of Moab to pronounce a potent curse against the victorious Israelites (Num. 22–24). The story has elements of popular humor, as when Balaam's ass—a "dumb" beast—speaks out in protest of his master's harsh treatment. The story's main feature is not the "talking ass," however, but what Balaam said as a prophetic spokesman of God. Ancient peoples believed that words spoken as a curse or as a blessing had power to achieve the desired result (as illustrated in the story of Jacob, who "steals" the deathbed blessing of Isaac from his older brother Esau; Gen. 27). Balaam was invited to stand on a hilltop in view of the Israelites and say, with a force greater than any show of military power, "Let them be damned." But the tradition affirms that even a foreign diviner like Balaam had to obey the dictates of Israel's God, despite King Balak's promises of a good fee and great honor:

> How can I curse whom God does not curse,
> and how can I damn whom Yahweh does not damn?
> For from the top of the rocks I see them,
> from the hills I observe them
> behold, a people living apart,
> not counting themselves among the nations.
> Who can count the dust of Jacob?
> or number the mass of Israel?
>
> —NUMBERS 23:8–10

The oracles of Balaam, which in this poetic form might date back to the thirteenth or twelfth century B.C.E., express the passionate faith of the victorious Israelites. In this view Israel is seen not as a nation, but as a unique people set apart by Yahweh (compare Deut. 7:6). No magic or divination could avert the blessing that Yahweh had chosen to bestow upon them.

We find a more refined expression of Israel's covenant faith in the last book of the Pentateuch, Deuteronomy (see Chapter 11).[16] This book is cast in the form of a farewell address by Moses, given in the plains of Moab just before the Israelites crossed over the Jordan to storm the land of Canaan. Moses rehearses the stirring events of Israel's history—the Exodus, the making of the covenant, the wandering in the wilderness, the victories in Transjordan—in order to exhort the people to remember all that Yahweh has done for them and be faithful to their covenant obligations amid the temptations of Canaan. In its present form, the address comes from a time centuries after Moses. It shows, however, how this "sacred history" was kept alive in Israel's memory and was reflected upon with deepening insight through the generations.

THE INVASION OF CANAAN

The book of Deuteronomy ends with an account of the death of Moses and the elevation of Joshua as his successor (Deut. 34). In this abrupt manner the Torah or Pentateuch breaks off. Obviously, the story is not meant to end here, for the climax toward which the narratives of the Pentateuch point still lies in the future: fulfillment of the promise of "inheritance" in the land of Canaan. Moses' death on Mount Nebo, in full sight of the Promised Land, occurs just as the Israelites are poised to attack.

The story resumes in the book of Joshua. This is the first book in the second major division of the Hebrew Bible, known as the Prophets. As we have seen earlier (see chart pp. 4–5), the canon of the Prophets is subdivided into two sections, each containing four scrolls. The first is known as the Former Prophets, the second as the Latter Prophets. In the rest of this chapter we consider the first book of the Former Prophets, Joshua.

You might wonder why the book of Joshua, with its emphasis on historical narrative, is considered "prophecy." The reason is that Joshua, along with the other books of the Former Prophets, is governed by an interpretation of Israel's history that was profoundly influenced by the great prophets of the eighth and seventh centuries B.C.E. This theology of history was championed by Deuteronomistic historians who reworked Israel's traditions in the period shortly before and just after the fall of the nation in 587 B.C.E. The characteristic style and viewpoint of these historians, illustrated in the sermonic material in the opening chapters of Deuteronomy, pervade the books of the Former Prophets. Since Deuteronomic (D) material is not found to any significant degree

---

[16]With few exceptions, the rest of the book of Numbers comes from the Priestly tradition and deals largely with ritual matters.

in the books of Genesis through Numbers, one can regard all the material found in Deuteronomy through 1–2 Kings as a comprehensive history that begins with the end of the Mosaic period and interprets the events of Israel's history to the time of the fall of the nation.[17]

THE LAND OF CANAAN

The first verses of the book of Joshua (Josh. 1:1–9) are written in the style, and from the theological perspective, of the Deuteronomic writers. Yahweh summons Joshua to lead Israel across the Jordan into the Promised Land, a land extending from the southern wilderness to the high Lebanon ranges to the north, and even beyond to the river Euphrates (see Gen. 15:18). Yahweh tells Joshua that this segment of the Fertile Crescent will be Israel's on one condition: that the people obey the "book of the law" (the Deuteronomic Law) and study it diligently (Josh. 1:7–9). This is the Deuteronomic formula for success and failure. Obedience to Yahweh's commands will be rewarded with victory and prosperity; disobedience will bring the divine judgment of suffering and failure. This succinct doctrine of reward and punishment, which runs through the whole Deuteronomistic History, might go back to ceremonies of covenant renewal when formulas of divine blessings and curses were solemnly recited (see pp. 90–92).

Important as it was, other factors besides faithful obedience to the covenant contributed to Israel's success in Canaan. The historical situation in the Fertile Crescent facilitated the Israelite advance: the lay of the land, the Canaanite culture, the political relation of this strategic corridor to the political powers in Egypt and Mesopotamia. The time was right, and years of experience in the wilderness had prepared and disciplined Israel for a bold venture. This does not deny Israel's doctrine of providence, the conviction that "Yahweh your God is with you wherever you go" (Josh. 1:9). To appreciate the significance of this doctrine, however, one must view it in the wider perspective of archaeology and ancient history. Before continuing with the narrative of the conquest in Joshua 2–12, we will consider the situation in Canaan.

THE LAY OF THE LAND

To start with, one must have a general idea of the geography of Canaan, or Palestine as it was later called.[18] The most striking topographical feature is the central backbone of hill country lying between the deep cleft of the Jordan and the Mediterranean coastland (see map inside book cover). The hill country is divided in the area of Mount Carmel

---

[17]This widely accepted view was advanced by Martin Noth in *The Deuteronomistic History* [278]; see various essays in *Heritage of Martin Noth* [77]. See also the discussion in Chapter 6 (with Definition, p. 166) and Chapter 11.

[18]See *The Harper Atlas of the Bible* [39], *The Macmillan Bible Atlas* [35], or one of the other atlases listed in the Bibliography [35–41].

by a valley known as Jezreel (or Esdraelon),[19] which gives access to the Jordan Valley. In ancient times, the main military and commercial highway from Egypt to Mesopotamia ran along the coast, then turned into the Valley of Jezreel and veered northward to Damascus. Located along this route were important fortified cities such as Megiddo, which guarded the pass leading from the southern coastal plain into the Valley of Jezreel. Many ancient and modern battles have been waged for control of this strategic pass and for the fertile valley.[20]

The advancing Hebrews stationed themselves in "the plains of Moab"—a lowland area in the Jordan Valley. This valley is part of a deep geological rift that starts with the Kara Su valley in modern Turkey, runs down through the Beka Valley between the Lebanon and anti-Lebanon ranges, extends through the Dead Sea (1285 feet below sea level), and follows the Arabah valley toward Egypt. In this great rift lies the Jordan River. Fed by springs at the base of Mount Hermon, the river follows a serpentine course to the Sea of Galilee and eventually enters the Salt Sea (Dead Sea), where a heavy saturation of salt prohibits marine life or surrounding vegetation. In between Mount Hermon and the Dead Sea the Jordan Valley is lush with vegetation, though terribly hot in summer. Understandably, the Hebrew pilgrims looked with envious eyes toward the highlands of Canaan, beyond the west bank of the Jordan.

The Canaanite hill country can be divided into three areas. To the north, beyond the valley of Jezreel, lie the mountains of Galilee. To the south is the hill country of Judah that fades into the southern wilderness (the Negeb) not far beyond Beer-sheba. In between is the central hill country of Ephraim (Samaria), whose major center in antiquity was Shechem, situated in the pass between Mount Gerizim and Mount Ebal (see Insert 8–1). This strip of central hill country, from Mount Hermon to the Judean wilderness, was the scene of the Israelite struggle.

The broken terrain of Canaan was not well-suited for the establishment of a strong, centralized government such as was achieved in the plain of Mesopotamia or the valley of the Nile. In the period of the Israelite settlement, Canaan was divided into autonomous city-states (fortified cities surrounded by satellite cities or villages). Most city-states were concentrated in the coastal plain and in the valleys of Jezreel and Jordan, which contained the best farmland. Cities located in these plains could be defended by chariots and other heavy military equipment, whereas the central hill country was vulnerable to guerrilla attacks.

Canaan was politically important because it lay in a strategic corridor between Egypt and Mesopotamia. Possession of this corridor was indispensable for any nation seeking to extend its control through the Fertile Crescent. Since approximately 2000 B.C.E. Canaan had been either nominally or actually under Egyptian control. This con-

---

[19]In Greek the name Jezreel was corrupted to "Esdraelon," a term used to designate the western part of the valley.

[20]Archaeologists will revisit this important site; see Israel Finkelstein and David Ussishkin, "Back to Megiddo," *Biblical Archaeology Review* 20:1 (Jan/Feb 1994), 26–43.

trol weakened temporarily when, in the latter part of the eighteenth century B.C.E., a flood of Hyksos swept into Egypt and seized power (see pp. 43–45). The expulsion of the Hyksos by Ahmose I, however, renewed Egypt's determination to regain control of its Asiatic empire.

Pharaohs of the early Eighteenth Dynasty (1570–1310 B.C.E.) carried out extensive military campaigns in Canaan and Syria, strengthening Egyptian outposts such as the one at Beth-shan in the upper Jordan Valley. Egyptian officials policed and exploited the country under Pharaoh's authority, requiring local Canaanite rulers to pay tribute and supply laborers to work on Egyptian projects.

THE AMARNA AGE

Eventually Egyptian control over Canaan weakened again, especially during the reign of Pharaoh Amenhotep IV in the fourteenth century B.C.E.—the so-called Amarna Age.[21] Archaeologists have excavated the library of the Egyptian monarch's capital and found many documents that shed light on Egyptian foreign affairs in Canaan during this turbulent period. Unlike his predecessors of the Eighteenth Dynasty, Amenhotep IV was less interested in pursuing an aggressive foreign policy than in effecting a religious revolution in Egypt, introducing a kind of monotheism based on worship of the sun disc Aton. To dramatize the break with the established priesthood of the high god Amon, he changed his name to Akhnaton (meaning "The Splendor of Aton") and built a new capital called Akhetaton ("Horizon of Aton") near modern Tell el-Amarna. Owing to their preoccupation with domestic affairs, the Egyptians quickly lost control of the situation in Canaan.

Akhnaton's archives contain correspondence from a number of Canaanite kings that gives a vivid picture of the disorder.[22] Apparently these city-state rulers were taking advantage of Egyptian weakness to advance their own political purposes, though they continued to proclaim their loyalty to the Egyptian crown. The corruption of Egyptian officials contributed further to the confusion and intrigue. Correspondence from a certain 'Abdu-Heba, Egyptian ruler of Jerusalem, mentions the devastating effect *'Apiru* raids were having on Egyptian control in Canaan.[23] He complains that he is not to blame for the loss of Egyptian land, for "like a ship in the midst of the sea" he is surrounded by opposition on every hand. The situation, he says, is one of anarchy, and "now the 'Apiru capture the cities of the king." In desperation he exhorts "Let the king take care of his land!" and adds that even a garrison of fifty guards would help considerably.

---

[21]The Amarna Age covers the reigns of Amenhotep III (about 1403–1364 B.C.E.) and Amenhotep IV (about 1364–1347 B.C.E.). See chronological chart, p. 48.
[22]These texts are found in Pritchard, *Ancient Near Eastern Texts* [1], pp. 483–90; see also *The Amarna Letters*, ed. and trans. by William F. Moran (Baltimore and London: Johns Hopkins University Press, 1992), and T. O. Lambdin, "Tell el-Amarna," *Interpreter's Dictionary* IV [31], pp. 529–33.
[23]Pritchard, *op. cit.*, Letters 286–290, pp. 487–89.

Amarna Letter no. 68, one of the 380 tablets found at Tell el-Amarna in Egypt, dates from the mid-fourteenth century B.C.E. In it, Prince Shuwardata of Hebron informs the Pharaoh (called "king") of his desperate plight and requests a large force to deliver him.

It is tempting to surmise that the Amarna letters refer to events described in the book of Joshua, but this is not the case. The term *'Apiru* had a broad meaning, as we have seen (see pp. 37–38). In the Amarna period these restless, rootless elements of society had gained sufficiently in numbers and strength to function as a revolutionary force. The *'Apiru* raids of the Amarna period have nothing to do with the Israelite conquest, though conceivably some of the *'Apiru* who entrenched themselves in the hill country and took control of a large area of central Canaan might have been related to followers of Joshua who entered the country more than a century later. The Amarna letters refer bitterly to a certain Lab'ayu, Canaanite ruler of Shechem, who is accused of turning over his land to the *'Apiru*.[24] We are about to see that it was precisely in the Shechem area that Joshua met with no resistance, and where he apparently made a covenant alliance with Hebrew relatives and others who had not been in Egypt.

[24]Pritchard, *op. cit.*, Letter 289, p. 489.

Pharaoh Akhnaton and his wife, Nefertiti, offering a libation to the sun god Aton, represented by the solar disc. Each of the rays streaming from the sun ends in a hand opened caressingly, and the two hands just above the faces of the royal pair hold a hieroglyph meaning "life."

EGYPT'S NEW BID FOR POWER

The Amarna Age of Egyptian weakness in Canaan soon came to an end. Akhnaton's successors removed all traces of his monotheistic "heresy" and began to restore order and prosperity within Egypt's borders. This brief respite ended when the Hittites, against whom the Egyptians and the Mitannians had formed a treaty of mutual protection, rose to world power under the leadership of the great king Shuppiluliuma (about 1375–1335 B.C.E.). Aided by the disruptive attacks of the *'Apiru* and the intrigue of Canaanite rulers, the Hittite empire was extended into Syria, Phoenicia, and even into Canaan itself. This new development occurred at approximately the time of an enormous revival of Egyptian power under the Pharaohs of the Nineteenth Dynasty, especially Seti I and Rameses II, whom we have already met in connection with the Exodus.

The military showdown between the two powers came in the fifth year of the reign of Rameses II (1290–1224 B.C.E.). The Egyptian army, under the personal command of Rameses, was ambushed and severely mauled by the forces of the Hittite king Muwatallis (about 1306–1282 B.C.E.) in the vicinity of Kadesh on the Orontes River in Syria. With typical modesty, Rameses claimed that by his personal valor he saved his army from the trap and even won a whopping victory, the report of which he published and illustrated on the walls of temples along the Nile, including the famous temple at Abu Simbel[25] (see Insert 6–1). The military stalemate ended when Rameses II and the Hittite king Hattusilis (about 1275–1250 B.C.E.) agreed to a peace treaty, copies of which have been discovered in both countries. Throughout the rest of Rameses' long rule the Hittite boundary remained north of Mount Lebanon, and Canaan was again under the hegemony of Egypt.

Rameses' son Merneptah (about 1224–1211 B.C.E.), however, was faced with a threat far more serious than the Hittites. The Amarna period brought a great surge of population into the area of the Aegean Sea, the arm of the Mediterranean that reaches up between Greece and Anatolia (Turkey). Bands of these homeless peoples swept into Asia Minor, where they eventually brought the old Hittite empire to an end. Others overran the island of Crete, eclipsing the Minoan civilization, and moved on to Greece where they merged with the indigenous population. Still others sailed to and took control of Cyprus, then moved on to the mainland of Syria-Palestine, where they conquered important cities such as Ugarit (Ras Shamra; see pp. 169–171). Other waves of peoples pounded against Egypt, some coming by sea and others by land. The "Peoples of the Sea," as they are called in Egyptian documents, were known by an assortment of names: among them were the Peleset (Philistines), the people who later gave Canaan the name "Palestine."[26]

---

[25]Pritchard, *op. cit.,* [1], pp. 255–58.

[26]See *People of the Sea: The Search for the Philistines* (New York: Macmillan, 1992) by Trude Dothan and Moshe Dothan, archaeologists who have concentrated on Philistine history and culture; also, Avner Raban and Robert R. Stieglitz, "The Sea Peoples and Their Contribution to Civilization," *Biblical Archaeology Review* 17:6 (Nov/Dec 1991), 34–42.

This Profile of a captured Philistine appears on a wall of the mortuary temple of Pharaoh Rameses III at Medinet Habu in the Theban necropolis in Egypt.

Merneptah held back this population surge during his brief reign, but pressure increased, especially during the reign of his successor Rameses III (about 1183–1152 B.C.E.). On the walls of his temple of Medinet Habu at Thebes, Rameses III described the threat: "They laid their hands upon the lands as far as the circuit of the earth, their hearts confident and trusting: 'Our plans will succeed!'"[27] Rameses III checked the coalition's attempt to penetrate Egypt by pushing the Philistines back onto their beachhead on the coast of Canaan. This effort exhausted Egyptian power, however, and in succeeding centuries Egypt never regained its former glory.

The movement of the Israelites under Joshua into the hill-country of Canaan took place against this background of political turmoil and social upheaval. The powerful Pharaoh Rameses II was on the throne, but already his hold on Canaan was beginning to slip because of Hittite incursions from the north. Egypt found it increasingly difficult to cope with the volatile situation in Palestine. The invading Hebrews, according to the

[27]Pritchard, *Ancient Near Eastern Texts* [1], pp. 262–63.

biblical account, moved into the central hill country, avoiding contact with Canaanite strongholds and Egyptian outposts on the plains. But at one point Merneptah had to act: About the year 1220 B.C.E. he set up a victory stele on which he claimed to have quelled unrest in the lands of Syria and Palestine, as well as in Libya (see Insert 8–2). His hymn of triumph contains these poetic lines:[28]

> Israel is laid waste, his seed is not.
> Hurru is become a widow for Egypt.

This highly significant text contains the earliest reference to Israel outside the Bible. It locates Israel in Palestine, but speaks only of a people, not a nation. The translator notes that "the word 'Israel' is the only one of the names in this context which is written with the determinative of people rather than land. Thus we should seem to have the Children of Israel in or near Palestine, but not yet as a settled people."[29]

Obviously the Egyptian military claim was exaggerated. Whatever happened in the encounter between Israelites and Egyptians, the biblical account passes over the incident in discreet silence. Merneptah could not give further attention to the matter, for his energies were diverted by the greater problem of resisting other invaders—the "Sea Peoples" who threatened his country in great numbers. The stage was set for Israel to inherit the Promised Land.

ISRAEL'S CONQUEST OF CANAAN: THE DEUTERONOMISTIC VIEW

Joshua 1–12 sets forth a dramatic story of the Israelite conquest of Canaan. The reader is told that the whole land fell to Joshua in three swift, decisive military campaigns.

The first campaign gave the Israelites a firm foothold on the western side of the Jordan River, which was dammed at Adam (modern ed-Damiyeh), presumably by one of the landslides that occur in the geological rift followed by the river.[30] After crossing the dry river bed with the Ark carried before them, the people encamped at Gilgal (Josh. 3–5). From this base in the Jordan Valley they laid siege to Jericho, which reportedly fell early in the morning to the sound of trumpets (Josh. 6). Spurred by this victory, a military force climbed the West Bank, where they captured the city Ai by subterfuge (Josh. 7:1–8:29). (Nothing is said about the conquest of nearby Bethel; compare Judges 1:22–26.) Apparently meeting no resistance in the central hill country, the Is-

---

[28]Pritchard, *Ancient Near Eastern Texts* [1], pp. 376–78. The Egyptians referred to Palestine as "Hurru," that is, the land of the Hurrians (see pp. 33–35).
[29]Pritchard, *op. cit.*, p. 378, note 18.
[30]Nelson Glueck, *The River Jordan* (New York: McGraw-Hill, 1968), p. 118.

raelites moved north as far as Shechem, where Joshua built an altar on a mountain over-looking the city (Josh. 8:30–35).

In the second campaign the victorious Israelites penetrated the southern hill country. Near the fortress of Jerusalem, which they seem to have bypassed temporarily, the Israelites were tricked into making a treaty with four federated cities, chief among them Gibeon (Josh. 9). As a result of this treaty, the Gibeonites were threatened with reprisals by a coalition of Canaanite kings led by Adonizedek, king of Jerusalem; however, the Israelites moved swiftly to their defense. In a quotation from a lost book of Israelite poetry, "The Book of Jashar" (see also 2 Sam. 1:18), Joshua wished that the sun and moon would stand still so his soldiers might have enough time to finish the battle decisively (Josh. 10:12–13a):

> "Sun, stand still over Gibeon,
> and moon, you too, over the Vale of Aijalon!"
> —JOSHUA 10:12b (NJB)

The narrator who quoted from this old work apparently took the poetry literally (see Josh. 10:13–14)—as have many interpreters of biblical scriptures—and commented that the sun and moon actually stopped in their course. This would mean that the earth ceased to rotate for almost a whole day! The purpose of the quotation, however, was to testify that Yahweh, the Divine Warrior who commands the host of heaven, was fighting for Israel (Josh. 10:14; compare Judg. 5:20).

The Israelites moved on to further conquests of the city-states of Libnah, Lachish, Eglon, Hebron, and Debir (Kiriath-sepher), bypassing some heavily fortified towns like Gezer and Beth-shemesh (Josh. 10:16–43). The account also states (Josh. 10:33; also 16:10) that forces from Gezer attempted to intercept the Israelites and were defeated.

Finally, in the third campaign the Israelite forces won significant victories in the northern hill country, above the Valley of Jezreel in an area known as Galilee (compare Isa. 9:1). Here Joshua triumphed over a coalition of northern kings (Josh. 11:1–9). Above all, he won a decisive victory at the fortified city of Hazor, which was destroyed and burned (Josh. 11:10–15).

In short, Joshua, the leader of united Israel, masterminded an effective strategy from a military base at Gilgal and, in three lightning campaigns into the center (Josh. 7–9), the south (Josh. 10), and the north (Josh. 11) took complete possession of Canaan in a short time. At least three fortified cities (Jericho, Ai, Hazor) were burned to the ground. In their inexorable advance the Israelites destroyed the resisting Canaanites with the edge of the sword. The "whole land" was given to them in a holy war "because Yahweh, the God of Israel, fought for Israel" (Josh. 10:42). The account's conclusion (Josh. 11:16–23) summarizes the thoroughness of the conquest.

The style and theological viewpoint of the Deuteronomistic historians dominate the story in Joshua 1–12 and Joshua's farewell address in Joshua 23. Undoubtedly these

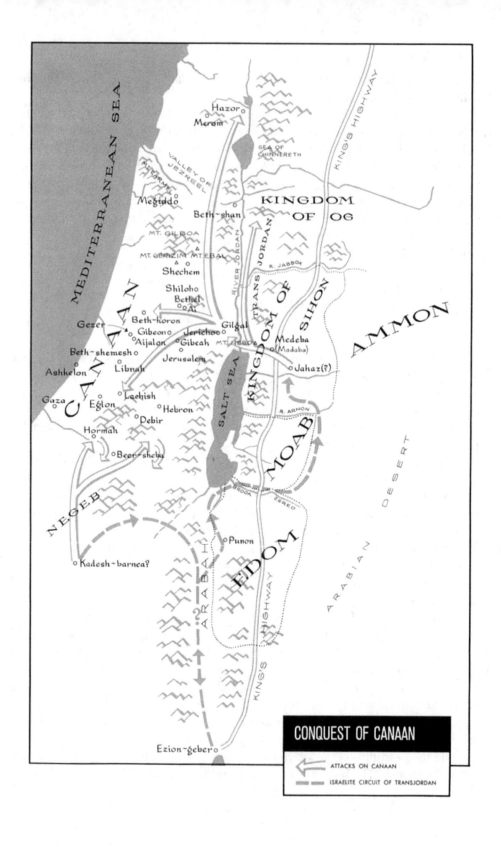

MEDITERRANEAN SEA

CANAAN

KINGDOM OF OG

AMMON

KING'S HIGHWAY

VALLEY OF JEZREEL

MT. CARMEL

Megiddo

Beth-shan

SEA OF CHINNERETH

Hazor

Merom

MT. GILBOA

MT. GERIZIM MT. EBAL

Shechem

Shiloh

Bethel

Ai

RIVER JORDAN

TRANS JORDAN

R. JABBOK

KINGDOM OF SIHON

Beth-horon

Gibeon

Jericho

Gilgal

Gezer

Aijalon

Gibeah

MT. NEBO

Medeba
(Madaba)

Beth-shemesh

Jerusalem

Libnah

Jahaz(?)

Ashkelon

Lachish

Eglon

Gaza

Hebron

Debir

SALT SEA

Hormah

Beer-sheba

R. ARNON

MOAB

NEGEB

BROOK ZERED

Punon

EDOM

ARABAH

Kadesh-barnea?

KING'S HIGHWAY

ARABIAN DESERT

Ezion-geber

CONQUEST OF CANAAN

ATTACKS ON CANAAN

ISRAELITE CIRCUIT OF TRANSJORDAN

historians drew from older traditions: tribal stories, cultic legends, and perhaps material from the Old Epic tradition found in the books of Genesis, Exodus, and Numbers. The historians took the theme of the promise of the land to Israel's ancestors and the Mosaic tradition of covenantal obligations and showed how they were marvelously fulfilled in the time of Joshua. These writers seem to have been carried away by religious enthusiasm, however, because their account makes the historical realities of the invasion of Canaan appear much simpler than they actually were. Joshua did not make a clean sweep of the land, for the aging Joshua is told that "there remains yet very much land to be possessed" (Josh. 13:1–7). In his farewell address Joshua exhorts the Israelites not to join "the remnant of these nations left here among you" or else "Yahweh your God will not continue to drive out these nations before you" (Josh. 23:12–13). Much work remained before the Israelites could claim, as the Deuteronomistic historians do in a climactic moment, that "the land had rest from war" (Josh. 11:23).

AN ALTERNATIVE VIEW OF THE CONQUEST IN JOSHUA AND JUDGES 1

A more complex picture appears when we compare the Deuteronomistic view of the conquest with statements found elsewhere, especially in the first chapter of Judges. The account in Joshua 10:36–37 states that Joshua destroyed the city of Hebron, but in Judges 1:10 the city is said to have been taken by the tribe of Judah. Joshua 10:38–39 reports that Joshua took the city of Debir (or Kiriath-sepher), while Joshua 15:13–19 and Judges 1:11–15 give credit to a Calebite named Othniel. Moreover, the book of Joshua mentions that the Israelites were unable to expel the Canaanites from a number of cities, including Jerusalem (Josh. 15:63), Gezer (16:10), Beth-shean, Taanach, and Megiddo (17:11–13).

Indeed, Judges 1 gives a completely different picture of the invasion. Despite the victory announcement in the book of Joshua, Judges 1:1 reports that the first question asked after Joshua's death was: "Who shall go up first for us against the Canaanites, to fight against them?" The ensuing account of independent tribal actions is fragmentary and at times puzzling: For example, Judges 1:8 credits the tribe of Judah with capturing and burning Jerusalem (but compare this with verse 21!), though we know from other sources that this fortress was not captured until David's time (2 Sam. 5:6–7). Moreover, the account is not consistent with the Deuteronomistic view that the land was conquered by Israelite forces acting under the single military command of Joshua. Judges 1:9–20 attributes the capture of Hebron and Debir, associated with Caleb and Othniel (as in Josh. 10:36–37), to the leadership of Judah and Simeon. And Judges 1:22–26 reports that the house of Joseph conquered Bethel, the city near Ai not mentioned in connection with Joshua's first military campaign. In general, this account stresses the incompleteness of the occupation of the land (see Judges 1:19, 21, 27–29).

Critical historians have argued persuasively that these scattered statements in Judges 1 are fragments of an older, more reliable epic tradition (J) that preserves a different view from that of the Deuteronomistic historians. In this tradition, the Israelite occupation of Canaan was remembered as a complex process that occurred over a long period of time, with tribes acting alone or in groups under widely separated circumstances. Some tribes came from the south through Arad and Hormah, others from the east across the Plains of Moab, and still others settled in the land during the ancestral period. When the tribes were subsequently unified within the covenant community of Israel, various tribal traditions were combined in the account of an all-Israelite conquest under Joshua.

EVIDENCE FROM ARCHAEOLOGY

Archaeological investigation sheds some light on the period of the Israelite conquest.[31] Keep in mind, however, that archaeology does not attempt to prove or disprove the biblical record. It is, at best, a science that describes what is found and offers hypotheses to be tested in scholarly debate.

In archaeological terms we are dealing with the transition from the Late Bronze (LB) Age (about 1550–1200 B.C.E.) to the Early Iron (Iron I) Age (about 1200–900 B.C.E.). We have seen that the fourteenth and thirteenth centuries B.C.E. (the Amarna Age) were marked by political upheaval and social turmoil (see pp. 113–114). This ferment was intensified by major technological advances: the use of iron instead of bronze for tools and weapons, waterproof plaster-lined cisterns for storage of rainwater (allowing people to move away from springs and streams), and terraced hillsides for cultivation of crops.

The picture provided by archaeology is blurred. There is evidence (such as layers of ash) that some fortified cities were violently destroyed during this period: Bethel in the central hill country (a city Joshua did not take), Lachish in the south, and in the north Hazor, "the head of all those kingdoms" (a city Joshua is said to have burned).[32] Yet other fortified cities reportedly taken by Joshua were not destroyed in this period. Joshua 6:24 claims that Jericho was burned to the ground. On the basis of archaeological evidence, however, the wall of Jericho that supposedly "came tumbling down" in Joshua's time actually dates back to the third millennium B.C.E. and was destroyed in the middle of the sixteenth century (perhaps in connection with expulsion of the Hyksos from Egypt). This would mean that in the time of Joshua the mound of Jericho was in ruins.[33] Ai, reportedly burned by Joshua (Josh. 8:19–20), was also apparently in ruins

---

[31]For discussions of the complex archaeological evidence, see J. Maxwell Miller in Hayes and Miller, *History* [112], pp. 252–79; Philip J. King, "The Contribution of Archaeology to Biblical Studies," *Catholic Biblical Quarterly*, 45 (1983), 1–16; and more recently, G. W. Ahlström, *History* [109], chap. 7.

[32]See Yigael Yadin, *Hazor* [285].

[33]Kathleen M. Kenyon, *Digging up Jericho* [272]; also "Jericho," in D. Winton Thomas, *Archaeology and Old Testament Study* (Oxford: Clarendon, 1967), pp. 164–75.

The Mound of Jericho shows this deep cut made by archaeologists at the site of the oldest city of Palestine. The upper edge of an excavated stone tower runs across the base of the photo. Dating back to about 7000 B.C.E., this circular structure was part of the city's defense system in the Stone Age. One level of occupation was built upon another through the centuries until the city came into the possession of Israel, though the story of Joshua's conquest is archaeologically enigmatic. In the background is the traditional Mount of Temptation.

at the time of the Israelite invasion. Indeed, the archaeological record at Ai suggests there was a gap in occupation from about 2400 B.C.E. to 1200 B.C.E. (Early Bronze to Iron I), and that even during the Iron Age this settlement was small and unfortified.[34] Late Bronze archaeological evidence from Gibeon is negligible, although the city apparently gained importance during the twelfth century B.C.E.[35]

[34]J. A. Callaway, "New Evidence on the Conquest of Ai," *Journal of Biblical Literature* 87, (1968), 312–20; also "Was My Excavation of Ai Worthwhile?" *Biblical Archaeology Review,* 11:2 (March/April 1985), 58.
[35]Pritchard, "Archaeology and the Future of Biblical Studies," *The Bible in Modern Scholarship* [185], pp. 313–24.

THE NATURE OF THE ISRAELITE OCCUPATION

Not surprisingly, the ambiguous biblical account and blurred archaeological record have led scholars to a number of different conclusions about the Israelite "conquest." Three views or "models" deserve attention: (1) gradual infiltration; (2) military invasion, and (3) peasant revolution.

Gradual Infiltration. This view maintains that a history of Israelite "settlement" took place over several generations and was not completed until the time of David. Initially there was no military assault on the land—only gradual infiltration as pastoral nomads from the desert to the east and south of Canaan moved into the sparsely settled hill country in search of pasture for their flocks and cattle. As a rule, the nomads lived on good terms with the Canaanites and even intermarried with them. There were occasional clashes but no serious conflicts until the eleventh century B.C.E. (the time of the Judges), when the expanding Israelites moved beyond the hills into the fertile plains where strong Canaanite cities were located.

In this view, the story of Joshua's swift conquest is a product of the religious imagination of the Deuteronomistic historians who sought to stress Yahweh's mighty power. Studied critically, Joshua 1–12 proves to be a chain of etiological stories intended to explain such things as the existence of "the Ai" (Hebrew: "the ruins") or the subordinate status of the Gibeonites ("hewers of wood and drawers of water," Josh 9:21). Indeed, some scholars have questioned whether Joshua was really the successor of Moses, and have suggested that originally Joshua was only a local Ephraimite tribal hero whose fame grew as his people ("the house of Joseph") gained prominence. Eventually the folk tales were embellished and exaggerated until at last Joshua became the hero of united Israel, upon whom the mantle of Moses fell.[36]

This view, while attractive, suffers from serious weaknesses. First, the Israelites were probably not pastoral nomads who came in from the desert, but agriculturalists accustomed to village life.[37] Second, archaeological evidence for the violent destruction of Canaanite cities in the thirteenth century is considered to have little bearing on the biblical account. Third, this view reduces the tradition etched on Israel's memory—that Yahweh brought the people out of Egypt and led them victoriously into Canaan (Josh. 24:5–13, Amos 2:9–10, and elsewhere)—to a purely "confessional" or ideological claim.

Military Invasion. This view, while admitting that Joshua 1–12 presents a glorified account, takes seriously the biblical tradition that the Israelites made a "forced entry" into Canaan. The Deuteronomistic historians intended not to give a colorless, factual report,

---

[36]See especially Albrecht Alt, "The Settlement of the Israelites in Palestine," *Essays* [128], pp. 133–69. This view is championed by Alt's student, Martin Noth, in his various writings, including *Pentateuchal Traditions* [76], pp. 71–74, and *History* [115], pp. 68–84. It is also maintained by Yohanan Aharoni, an archaeologist who claims to have found evidence for a long period of peaceful settlement in the north (Galilee); see "The Israelite Occupation of Canaan," *Biblical Archaeology Review* 8:3 (May/June 1982), 14.

[37]The notion of Israelite pastoral nomadism has been severely criticized by Norman Gottwald, *The Tribes of Yahweh* [271], pp. 435–63; see also Marvin Chaney, "Ancient Palestinian Peasant Movements and the Formation of Premonarchic Israel," in *Palestine in Transition* [270], pp. 41–44.

but to proclaim to the Israelite community the dramatic story of the victory of Yahweh, the Divine Warrior. They telescoped the account of the invasion by attributing to Joshua feats that were actually carried out by others, and by reporting modest gains as decisive victories. But this does not undermine the central claim of the book of Joshua: that the warlike Israelites, probably spearheaded by the Joseph tribes and the tribe of Benjamin, succeeded in wresting a good part of the central hill country from the Canaanites.

Archaeological excavation gives some support to this view of military conquest: There is evidence that some Canaanite cities were violently destroyed in the late thirteenth century, though not necessarily at Israelite hands. Lachish and Hazor, cities reportedly attacked by Joshua, actually did fall in that period. Other cities such as Bethel, Debir, and Eglon also fell at that time. Presumably some cities taken in the thirteenth century were retaken later. This would account for the fragmentary reports in Judges 1, which in this view is not a remnant of "the lost J [Old Epic] account of the conquest," but an anthology of material from differing dates and circumstances.[38]

Challenging this view is the archaeological evidence that two cities allegedly burned to the ground by Joshua—Jericho and Ai—were actually unfortified at the time. A British excavation conducted during 1930–1936 set the date of the violent destruction of Jericho, apparently by earthquake, at about 1385 B.C.E., suggesting a connection with the activity of the 'Apiru invaders described in the Amarna letters. But subsequent excavation has led archaeologists to conclude that, in contrast to the cultic account in Joshua 6, "the Jericho of Joshua's day may have been little more than a fort."[39] According to one proposal, based on an archaeological survey of the tribal territory of Manasseh, the Israelite settlers entered Palestine north of Jericho opposite Shechem and gradually moved south. The Jericho tradition might have been created to minimize the role played by Northern tribes and to magnify the role of the Southern tribe of Judah.[40]

Scholars who support the military view suggest that Joshua's conquest of Ai, "the ruin," might have been confused with nearby Bethel, which actually was destroyed in the same period (see Josh. 12:16; Judg. 1:22–26). This would explain why the Canaanite city of Bethel, which lay directly on Joshua's path, is not mentioned elsewhere in the account of his first military campaign. But there is no evidence for this. Indeed, one historian has flatly stated that "in no instance has archaeology been able to prove that a city was destroyed by incoming Israelites."[41]

---

[38]W. F. Albright's view of the conquest has been defended and elaborated by G. Ernest Wright in "The Literary and Historical Problem of Joshua 10 and Judges 1," *Journal of Near Eastern Studies*, V (1946), 105–14, and *Biblical Archaeology* [125]. See also A. Malamat, "Origins and Formative Period," in *The History of the Jewish People*, ed. H. H. Ben-Sasson (London/Cambridge: Weidenfeld and Harvard University Press, 1976), pp. 1–87, who discusses the biblical account from the standpoint of military feasibility.

[39]G. E. Wright, *Biblical Archaeology* [125], p. 79; also Kathleen Kenyon's account of the excavation in *Archaeology in the Holy Land* [122], pp. 209–12. For further discussion, see Bryant G. Wood, "Did the Israelites Conquer Jericho? A New Look at the Archaeological Evidence," *Biblical Archaeology Review*, 16 (March/April 1990) and the ensuing debate in the Sept/Oct issue of *Biblical Archaeology Review*, 16.

[40]Adam Zertal, "Israel Enters Canaan: Following the Pottery Trail," *Biblical Archaeology Review*, 17:5 (Sept/Oct 1991), pp. 28–47.

[41]G. W. Ahlstrom, *History* [109], p. 348.

Peasant Revolution. This view holds that the conquest was not an invasion from the outside but an uprising inside the land of Canaan, inspired by faith in Yahweh, the liberating God of Israel. The social revolution actually began in Transjordan, where the Israelites joined with restive elements to overthrow the kingdoms of Sihon and Og. Migrating Israelites then carried the revolution to the west bank of the Jordan, where they joined with 'Apiru eager to overthrow the city-state system maintained under Egyptian hegemony. These dispossessed and discontented elements of society (see pp. 113–114) would have sympathized with Joshua and his followers, and in their own way abetted the sociopolitical upheaval. So regarded, the conquest was really not a military conquest but a "peasants' revolt against the network of interlocking Canaanite city-states."[42] The conflict was essentially between the villages, where the peasants were subject to taxation, and the cities where Canaanite kings ruled.

This intriguing view illuminates several aspects of the biblical account. It might explain why some cities (such as those in central Canaan around Shechem) fell to Israel without any reported military attack; why there is no archaeological evidence of the destruction of some cities claimed by the revolutionaries; and why some Canaanite elements (such as the Gibeonites) hastened to join the Israelite cause. The story of Rahab, the prostitute who hid spies sent to Jericho by Joshua (Josh. 2), suggests that there might have been widespread collusion between "outside agitators" and restive elements of the Canaanite population against the royal power structure.[43]

But this view also has difficulties. There is no *explicit* indication of a peasants' revolt in any of the biblical traditions of the books of Joshua and Judges.[44] Furthermore, the hypothesis does not do justice to the reality of entrenched political power, for human history shows that an establishment (in this case, the Canaanite city-state system) does not surrender its hold without a military struggle. This view downplays evidence for the violent destruction of cities in the Canaanite hill country during the late thirteenth century B.C.E. and discounts the biblical claim of a military invasion from the east under Joshua.

THE WARS OF YAHWEH

These three models of the "conquest"—gradual infiltration, military invasion, and peasant revolution—suggest that the Israelite occupation of Canaan was far more complex than one might gather from an initial reading of the biblical narratives. One eminent

---

[42]George E. Mendenhall advances this view in "The Hebrew Conquest of Palestine," *Biblical Archaeologist* 25 (1962), 66–87; reprinted with slight revision in *The Biblical Archaeologist Reader* [119]. The view has been adopted and championed by Norman K. Gottwald, *The Tribes of Yahweh* [271], who understands the revolution in Marxist terms as a class struggle between peasants and their feudal overlords in the Canaanite city-states. See B. W. Anderson, "Mendenhall Disavows Paternity of Gottwald's Marxist Theory," *Approaches to the Bible* [104], pp. 114–19.

[43]See Marvin Chaney, "Ancient Palestinian Peasant Movements," in *Palestine in Transition* [270], pp. 68–69.

[44]See, for example, Alan J. Hauser, "Israel's Conquest of Palestine: A Peasants' Rebellion?" and the ensuing responses from other symposium participants (Thomas L. Thompson, George E. Mendenhall, Norman K. Gottwald) in *Journal for the Study of the Old Testament* 7 (1978), 2–52.

historian, John Bright, maintains that all three models must be considered. He assumes that to some degree the conquest was an "inside job": Large numbers of Hebrews were already long settled in Palestine, and they joined with other Hebrews coming from the desert. This coming together struck the spark that ignited Palestine, and out of the resulting revolution emerged the Tribal Confederacy known as "Israel." But, according to Bright, "it was not simply a matter of local uprisings" for "there were military operations on a larger scale as well." Indeed, the revolution was "a bloody and brutal business," as the Bible confirms. A decisive campaign by Joshua in the thirteenth century smashed into the hill country and "broke the back" of Canaanite resistance, burning some cities to the ground and bypassing or neutralizing others. Perhaps during this upheaval the Pharaoh Merneptah, who claimed to have defeated "Israel," found it necessary to intervene on behalf of Canaanite overlords in the latter part of the thirteenth century B.C.E. In Bright's view, however, the Israelite conquest was not a *blitzkrieg* (swift victory) but "a seesaw struggle that went on for years."[45]

Note that the Israelites were successful mainly in the hill country, where their relatively simple methods of warfare could be used to advantage in the broken terrain. Even the Deuteronomistic historians do not claim that the Israelites attacked major Canaanite strongholds and Egyptian outposts located along the coastal plain and in the Valley of Jezreel. This silence might be explained in the statement:

> Yahweh was with Judah and he took possession of the hill country,
> but he could not dispossess the inhabitants of the plain because they had
> iron chariots.
>
> —JUDGES 1:19

Because Israel's armaments were ineffective against the weapons of the Iron Age, the Israelites had to follow up their assault on the hill country in the thirteenth century with a continuing struggle for possession of the land after Joshua's death. The Deuteronomistic historians recognized that there was much to be done in the remaining centers of Canaanite resistance (Josh. 13), though this side of the picture is not presented in full. Sometimes individual tribes in local areas continued the assault. Meanwhile, the conquest of the Canaanites was facilitated by treaty, intermarriage, and the absorption of city-states into the Israelite confederacy.

The complex question of the emergence of Israel in Canaan in the thirteenth and twelfth centuries B.C.E. will be discussed for years to come. Whatever the nature of the Israelite "settlement" or "entry," the conviction that it was not achieved by mere military power or strategy was deeply ingrained in Israel's memory. Israel was fighting "the wars of Yahweh." In those stirring times of political and social change, the Israelites recognized the active presence and guidance of Yahweh, who had delivered oppressed

---

[45]John Bright, *History* [110], pp. 140–43. See further the discussion in G. W. Ramsey, *The Quest* [116], chap. 4.

slaves from bondage and in a marvelous way had led them into a land of promise to fulfill a historic role. Faith in the God who actively took part in the historical struggle unified the Israelites and inspired them with tremendous zeal. Against this the Canaanites, split up into city-states, separated by hills and valleys, and lacking a dynamic religious faith, were unable to stand.

DEFINITION: "HOLY WAR"

One cannot equate the view of "holy war" expressed in biblical traditions of the conquest of Canaan with modern conceptions of religiously sanctioned warfare such as the Islamic "holy war" (*jihad*) or the "just war" of Western nations. Even in the context of the Bible, there is a difference between the "holy war" of Joshua's time and the kind of warfare introduced by David and Solomon, which was characterized by military conscription, a professional corps of officers, a standing army, and pitched battles using mechanized equipment.

Holy war in the tribal period was a kind of guerrilla warfare based on voluntary response to a summons in the name of the deity, the Divine Warrior, to whom the tribes owed allegiance. It was sometimes defensive, but often offensive as well. According to Joshua 1–12 and Judges 1, a relatively small band of warriors could succeed by using scare tactics, ambush and other surprise maneuvers, feigned flight, and so on. Viewed religiously, the holy war was to be won not by sheer military force but because God gives the victory: "It was not by your sword or by your bow"(Josh. 24:12b).[46]

A practice of holy war, both in ancient Israel and among other peoples, was the *ḥerem* or "sacrificial ban": the dedication of persons, booty, or cities to God (Josh. 6–7). (Something devoted to God became holy and was withdrawn from common use.) According to the Bible, the *ḥerem* was practiced only in the case of resisting cities (as with Hormah, Num. 21:1–3; the kings Sihon and Og, Josh. 2:10; Jericho, Josh. 6:17; Ai, Josh. 8:24–29; and some southern cities, Josh. 10:28–43). The directive in Deuteronomy 20:16–18 that the Israelites are to destroy utterly the Canaanite cities, sparing nothing that breathed, is an overstatement; Israel's conquest of the land did not involve the wholesale extermination of the Canaanite population. See further the discussion of holy war in connection with Deborah (pp. 177–179) and Saul (pp. 197–198).

THE FORMATION OF THE TRIBAL CONFEDERACY

After Joshua's farewell address (Josh. 23) comes one of the most important chapters in the Hebrew Bible. This chapter, Joshua 24, seems to stand by itself and might well relate an incident that happened earlier in Joshua's career. In the judgment of some literary critics, much of the narrative is based on an old literary stratum (E) that runs

[46]See further Millard C. Lind, *Yahweh is a Warrior* [274].

through the Pentateuch into the book of Joshua. The substance of the narrative, however, apparently dates back to an ancient period when the tradition circulated orally.

THE ASSEMBLY AT SHECHEM

Joshua 24 describes a great convocation at Shechem, a city located near Joseph's grave (Josh. 24:32) and Jacob's well (John 4:6). From at least the beginning of the second millennium B.C.E., Shechem was a great Canaanite city-state strategically located in the narrow pass between Mount Gerizim and Mount Ebal. From this vantage point the Shechemites commanded the highways that ran between the two mountains. Excavations at the site (the modern village of Balatah, near Nablus) have uncovered the impressive remains of the ancient city.[47] A type of rampart typical of the Hyksos indicates that it was once a strong fortress of the Hyksos empire. Evidence of violent destruction in the middle of the second millennium B.C.E. suggests that Egyptians captured the city after Ahmose I expelled the Hyksos from Egypt and extended his conquests into Palestine. In the fourteenth century, as we learn from the Amarna letters, Egypt lost Shechem as a result of Lab'ayu's treaty with 'Apiru. Thus Shechem was the scene of decisive political struggles long before Joshua arrived.

Shechem was also an important religious center. In the acropolis stood a large temple, the temple of Baal Berith ("Lord of the Covenant"; see Judg. 9:4). Today visitors to the ruins can see the foundations of this ancient temple—one of the largest pre-Roman temples in Palestine—and visualize how impressive the shrine must have been in ancient times.

According to the biblical narrative, Joshua gathered the people "before God" at the city of Shechem (Josh. 24:1). In the presence of the assembled Israelite tribes and their leaders, he rehearsed Israel's "sacred history," beginning with the ancestral period and then dwelling on the events of the Exodus and the conquests in Transjordan and the Canaanite hill country (Josh. 24:2–13). After this confessional summary, Joshua challenged the people to decide either to serve Yahweh in sincerity and faithfulness, or to serve the gods their ancestors had served beyond the River (Euphrates) and the gods of the Amorites (Canaanites). With the warning ringing in their ears that Yahweh is a jealous God, a holy God who would not tolerate the worship of "strange gods," the people affirmed their decision to serve Yahweh. Joshua demanded that they put away foreign gods, and the ceremony concluded with the making of a covenant, the giving of law, and the erection of a memorial stone beneath a sacred tree.

Clearly Joshua was not officiating at a covenant ceremony that brought Yahweh and Israel together for the first time. Israel did not become "the people of Yahweh," nor Yahweh "the God of Israel," *at that moment*. Rather, Joshua and the people reaffirmed

---

[47]The first campaign of the American archaeological expedition was directed by G. Ernest Wright in the summer of 1956. See his *Shechem: The Biography of a Biblical City* (New York: McGraw-Hill, 1965).

the sacred covenant made by Israel at Sinai. (That Joshua's rehearsal of the Israelite story makes no reference to the Sinai covenant is appropriate, given that the Sinai covenant was not one of Yahweh's mighty acts but rather a response to those deeds; see pp. 92–94.) The covenant renewal took place in the land of Canaan where the Israelites, in a time of political and economic opportunity, were tempted to violate their covenant obligation and adopt Canaanite religious practices. Joshua's challenge was put with the urgency later voiced by the prophets: "*Today* you must decide!" Yahweh demands exclusive devotion. The people's answer, "We will serve Yahweh, for he is our God" (Josh. 24.16), was a reaffirmation of the Mosaic belief that for Israel there can be only one God.

NEW CONVERTS TO THE MOSAIC FAITH

There was probably more to this ceremony than a renewal of covenant allegiance. One of the strange things about the conquest story is the complete silence about any activity in the area around Shechem. The fact that Shechem was not attacked and was the scene of the tribal convocation suggests that the people in this vicinity were friendly to the invaders, either through kinship or alliance. We have already seen (pp. 113–114) that in the Amarna Age *'Apiru* were active in the vicinity of Shechem and had entered into a treaty with the Canaanite ruler of the city. Before Joshua's time there possibly existed at Shechem some sort of tribal alliance, based on covenant allegiance and the common worship of *'El* (the chief Canaanite deity). Old traditions relate that Jacob purchased land near Shechem where he erected an altar to "*'El*, the God of Israel" (Gen. 33:18–20) and that Hebrew tribes very early attempted to enter into cordial relations with this Canaanite city-state (Gen. 34).

There are faint recollections, then, that some of Israel's ancestors—broadly speaking, the Leah tribes[48]—settled in Canaan at a comparatively early date and did not take part in the Exodus or the wilderness experiences. If the invaders under Joshua—that is, the Rachel tribes of Joseph and Benjamin—found friends or relatives already settled in central Canaan, this explains why there was no conflict in that region. In this case, Joshua 24 describes not just the renewal of the Mosaic covenant but also its extension to other Hebrews new to the community. To them Joshua's words would have had special force: "Choose this day whom you will serve!" If they chose to serve Yahweh, they had to put away all foreign gods, whether retained from the ancestral period or adopted from the Canaanites in whose midst they had been living.

Why did Joshua rehearse for these new converts the stirring events of the Exodus and the wilderness sojourn—events in which neither they nor their immediate ancestors had participated? How could they say, "This is *our* life-story too"? We have seen that, to

---

[48]For Jacob's six sons by Leah, see Gen. 29:31–35; 30:14–20. The duality of the Leah tribes and the Rachel tribes undoubtedly reflects the historical relationships of the tribes in an early period.

be initiated into a historical community and to participate fully in its life, newcomers must share in its memories. Thus to become an Israelite was to appropriate the whole sacred past. It was not just a matter of blood relation: Even Canaanites such as the Gibeonites were absorbed into Israel in the early period. Rather, it was a matter of willingness to identify with the whole drama of Israel's history, to acknowledge the God of the covenant, and to accept the obligations of membership in the covenant community.

The name of this covenant community was Israel. We have already seen that the term *'Apiru* (*Habiru*) had a broad meaning during the second millennium. Moreover, not all Hebrews were Israelites: The Israelites included only those Hebrews who were bound into a covenant alliance. Israel was basically a "folk" or people (Hebrew: *'am*)—not, in the first instance, a racial group or a nation.[49] In the history of biblical traditions, the more general "Hebrews" was eventually superseded by "Israelites" to refer to the particular people whose life-story we have been following. The term "Israel" was used on Merneptah's stele (see pp. 116–118 and Insert 8–2) and gained currency especially during the period of the occupation and the era of the judges.

THE TWELVE-TRIBE CONFEDERACY

One of Israel's preeminent features was its organization into twelve tribes. In the book of Genesis this structure is read back into the ancestral period, in order to unify the traditions and make them relevant to the whole people. Thus the patriarch Jacob is renamed "Israel" after a crucial experience (Gen. 32:28), and is regarded as the father of twelve sons, each one the leader of a tribe (Gen. 29:16–30:24; 35:16–20). In stories dealing with the period before David, the pattern of twelve was so sacred that if one tribe dropped out, a way was found to fill its place. For instance, when Levi lost tribal standing, "the house of Joseph" was split into two tribes, Manasseh and Ephraim (Gen. 48).

Notice that the number twelve, signifying the totality of Israel, was stressed on cultic occasions when the people assembled before Yahweh. During the ceremony of the sealing of the covenant at the foot of Mount Sinai, Moses set up "twelve pillars, according to the twelve tribes of Israel" (Exod. 24:4). Likewise, when the people crossed over the Jordan River from their base in the plains of Moab (a kind of reenactment of the crossing of the Reed Sea), twelve stones were set up in the sanctuary at Gilgal near Jericho to symbolize "the number of the tribes of the people of Israel" (Josh. 4:3, 8, 20).[50] These traditions show that the pattern of twelve was fundamental to Israel's understanding as a worshiping community, bound in covenant to the God who had delivered the people from Egyptian bondage.

---

[49]See E. A. Speiser, "'People' and 'Nation' of Israel," *Journal of Biblical Literature,* 79 (1960), 157–63. Speiser points out that ancient Israelite tradition speaks of "the people of Yahweh" but not "the nation of Yahweh."

[50]According to another version (Josh. 4:5–7, 9) twelve stones were set up in the bed of the Jordan.

At one time some historians saw an analogy to the Israelite tribal federation in the sacral leagues of ancient Greece and Italy. The Greek *amphictyony* was a fixed number of tribes—twelve, in the case of the League of Delphi—loosely bound together by a common religious obligation. A central sanctuary was cared for by each of the tribes in turn, where regular festivals were held and basic laws binding upon all the tribes were administered. The bond holding these tribes together was primarily religious, in contrast to the political basis of a city-state or nation. In times of military emergency, however, when the tribes united to face the common foe, the federation brought about some degree of unity in language, customs, and political interests.[51]

The Greek amphictyony is probably too distant in terms of time and culture to be helpful. One might better seek analogies closer to home in the federations found among Israel's neighbors.[52]

The Ishmaelites were organized into twelve tribes with a tribal prince at the head of each (Gen. 25:12–16), and the Edomites seem to have had a similar tribal system (Gen. 36:10–14). Apparently a confederation of this sort was instituted at Shechem. During the subsequent "Period of the Judges," the tribes of Israel were bound together in a covenant alliance that allowed for considerable autonomy on the part of the twelve participants. The alliance was primarily a theocratic community as indicated by the word *Israel*, which perhaps should be translated: "may God rule." Shechem seems to have been the center of the confederacy for a while. Later the central sanctuary was located at Shiloh, where the Ark was kept and where the tribes assembled for religious festivals. Like the Mosaic covenant, the tribal covenant was based on a rehearsal of Yahweh's great acts on behalf of the people.

THE COVENANT SERVICE

The covenant renewal service described in Joshua 24 contains features that are strikingly similar to the suzerainty treaty form (see pp. 90–92). The parallel is almost exact if one associates the ceremony with other passages describing ritual acts that took place at Shechem, such as Joshua 8:30–35 and Deuteronomy 27. Consider the following elements of the cultic service in which representatives of the tribes "presented themselves before God," probably in the presence of the Ark (see Josh. 8:33):

1.   A preamble to the covenant service in which the covenant-maker begins: "Thus says Yahweh, the God of Israel" (Josh. 24:2a).
2.   A long "historical prologue" cast in the "I-thou" style characteristic of suzerainty treaties, in which Yahweh recalls prior relations to the "vassal"

---

[51]Martin Noth set forth this view in his study of the scheme of the twelve Israelite tribes: *Das System der zwölf Stämme Israels* [322]; see also his *History* [115], pp. 85–108. Various scholars have strongly dissented, such as Harry M. Orlinsky, "The Tribal System of Israel and Related Groups in the Period of the Judges," *Oriens Antiquus*, 1 (1962), 11–20; and G. W. Anderson "Israel: 'Amphictyony' . . ." in *Translating and Understanding the Old Testament* [181].

[52]Roland de Vaux, *History* [111], pp. 695–749, vigorously criticizes Noth's amphictyonic hypothesis and finds analogies in the twelve-tribe federations among Arabs.

(Josh. 24:2b–13). The emphasis is on Yahweh's benevolent deeds on behalf of Israel (chiefly the deliverance from Egypt), which should evoke a response of gratitude and obligation.

3. The fundamental stipulation of the covenant (Josh. 24:14–24): The people are to place their complete trust in their suzerain in remembrance of what Yahweh has done for them—that is, Yahweh's guidance out of Egypt through the wilderness and into the land (verses 16–18). Specifically the people are to have no relations with other divine suzerains ("other gods"), for Yahweh is a "jealous God" who does not tolerate covenant unfaithfulness (verses 19–21). The people must renounce other gods, both those their ancestors worshiped in Mesopotamia and those of the Canaanites (Amorites), pledging themselves to "serve" Yahweh alone (verses 22–24).

4. Joshua writes the covenant stipulations in "the book of the law of God," after publicly proclaiming "statutes and ordinances" (Josh. 24:25–26). The covenant document was perhaps deposited in "the sanctuary of Yahweh" located outside the Canaanite city of Shechem at a sacred oak ("the Oak of Moreh," Gen. 12:6; 35:4). According to Deuteronomic tradition, the covenant law (Decalogue) was kept in the Ark (Deut. 10:5).

5. Instead of invoking various gods as witnesses (ruled out by Mosaic theology), the people are called as "witnesses against themselves" that they have chosen to serve Yahweh (Josh. 24:22). There is another strange "witness," the large stone or pillar Joshua erected in the sanctuary of Yahweh:

> Joshua said to all the people:
> "Look! This stone will be a witness against us, for it has heard all the words that Yahweh has said to us. So it will be a witness against you in case you deny your God."
>
> —JOSHUA 24:27

6. The Shechem ritual included sanctions of divine blessing and curse, according to other passages that seem related to Joshua 24. Joshua writes a copy of the covenant law on stones and, after the Ark has been solemnly carried by the priests, he reads "all the words of the law, the blessing and the curse" (Josh. 8:30–35).

The "law" referred to in Joshua 8 undoubtedly includes the absolute or apodictic law associated with the Mosaic covenant (see pp. 88–89). This type of law is illustrated in some of the twelve curses found in Deuteronomy 27:11–26:

> Cursed be the person who makes a graven or molten image.
> Cursed be the one who dishonors his father or his mother.
> Cursed be the one who removes his neighbor's landmark.
> Cursed be the one who slays his neighbor in secret.

These laws are formulated in the short, categorical manner of the Ten Commandments. To make the law absolutely binding, it is put in the form of a curse that expresses Yahweh's unqualified disapproval of a particular act. The twelve curses surely date back at least to the time of the Israelite Tribal Confederacy. They were recited in connection with a ritual ceremony that took place at Shechem, when the tribes arranged themselves half on Mount Gerizim and half on Mount Ebal.

The suzerainty treaty form, derived from the sphere of international politics, clearly influenced Israel's understanding of its covenant relationship with Yahweh, especially while Israel occupied Canaan. Perhaps the assembly at Shechem provided the pattern for other tribal gatherings at the central sanctuary when the people rehearsed the great story of Yahweh's redemptive deeds, when they listened to the solemn recitation of binding obligations, and when they pledged themselves anew to Yahweh's covenant. Support for this view comes from Deuteronomy 31:9–13, which stipulates that public reading of the law is to take place every seventh year in the autumn (New Year) at the Feast of Booths (see Neh. 8). Since the Feast of Booths was a yearly festival, the sabbatical scheme was perhaps a later modification of the practice of holding a covenant renewal ceremony annually.[53] If so, the Shechem assembly provided a cultic precedent for periodic gatherings of the people during the time of the Tribal Confederacy and later during the monarchy.

THE COVENANT LAW

When Joshua made a covenant with the people at Shechem, he also "made statutes (Hebrew: *ḥoq*) and ordinances (*mishpaṭ*) for them" (Josh. 24:25). "Statute" refers to apodictic covenant law, exemplified by the twelve curses (Deut. 27:15–26) and the Decalogue. "Ordinance" refers to case law, which clarifies the law under certain conditions or circumstances (see pp. 88–89). Since the so-called Covenant Code (Exod. 20:22–23:33) includes both types, and since this code concludes with the promise of Yahweh's blessing and protection, some scholars believe that this was the law Joshua promulgated at Shechem.[54] In any event, the Covenant Code presupposes the agricultural mode of life Israel adopted during the period of the Tribal Confederacy.

Israel's law was covenant law—not "secular" law or even civil law in a narrow sense. Indeed, Israel did not recognize any separation between the secular and religious realms: The whole of life was to be lived under Yahweh's demand within the covenant. This sense of total accountability before God led to an expansion of law in new situations, such as the adjustment to agricultural life in Canaan. Israel borrowed laws from

---

[53]This view was set forth by the Scandinavian scholar Sigmund Mowinckel in *Le Décalogue* (Paris: Librairie Felix Alcan, 1927) and has been adopted with various modifications by other scholars including G. von Rad, *The Problem of the Hexateuch* [191], pp. 20–26; G. Ernest Wright, commentary on Deuteronomy in *Interpreter's Bible*, II [23], p. 326; and Artur Weiser, *The Psalms* [538], pp. 23–35. R. de Vaux criticizes the view in *History* [111], pp. 405–8.

[54]This view is advocated by, among others, R. de Vaux, *Ancient Israel* [111], pp. 221–22.

the culture of the Fertile Crescent and transformed them according to its needs and religious concerns. During the period of the Tribal Confederacy, covenant renewal festivals might have provided the occasion for developing the law as disputes were arbitrated between, or even within, tribes.

Many of the "ordinances" (the *mishpaṭ* case laws) in the so-called Covenant Code (Exod. 20:22–23:33) and the code of Deuteronomy (Deut. 12–26) are similar in form, and largely in content, to legal codes of the Babylonians, Hurrians, and Assyrians. The following example shows the affinity between Israel's legislation and the Code of Hammurabi:[55]

Code of Hammurabi	*Covenant Code*
Par. 120: If a seignior deposited his grain in a[nother] seignior's house for storage and a loss has then occurred at the granary or the owner of the house opened the storage-room and took grain or he has denied completely [the receipt of] the grain which was stored in his house, the owner of the grain shall set forth the particulars in the presence of God and the owner of the house shall give to the owner of the grain double the grain that he took.	Exod 22:7–9 (RSV): If a man delivers to his neighbor money or goods for safekeeping, and they are stolen from the neighbor's house, then, if the thief is found, he shall pay double. If the thief is not caught, the owner of the house shall come near to God, to show whether or not he has put his hand to his neighbor's goods. For any breach of trust, whether it is for ox, for ass, for sheep, for clothing, or for any kind of lost thing, of which one says, "This is it," the case of both parties shall come before God; he whom God shall condemn shall pay double to his neighbor.

The laws in the Hebrew Bible were not copied from the Code of Hammurabi, which presupposed an aristocratic class system that did not prevail in Israel. Moreover, Israel did not accept the view that the state is custodian of the law: In Israel's covenant faith, even kings were subject to the law given at Sinai (see Deut. 17:18–20). Nevertheless, the similarity of form and even of some details indicates that Israel borrowed from a fund of legal tradition known throughout the Fertile Crescent.

There are vast differences between Israelite law and other Near Eastern codes even where evidence of borrowing exists.[56] Israel's law is characterized by a humane spirit, a high ethical emphasis, and a pervading religious fervor. Regardless of its source, the law is set within the "I-thou" of the covenant relationship. As the tribes gathered at their

---

[55]See Pritchard, *Ancient Near Eastern Texts* [1], p. 171.
[56]On the nature of Israelite law, see Martin Noth, *The Laws of the Pentateuch and Other Studies* (Philadelphia: Fortress, 1967); also Paul D. Hanson [178], pp. 110–31.

common sanctuary to rehearse the stirring events of their past and to hear the absolute requirements of Yahweh, the covenant was continually reaffirmed:

> Yahweh did not make this covenant with our ancestors,
> but with us who are here alive this day.
> —DEUTERONOMY 5:3

The language does not exaggerate. In each great covenant-renewal ceremony, such as the one in Joshua 24, the covenant was made contemporaneous. This Deuteronomic passage preserves an echo of the spirit that animated the Tribal Confederacy and infused the expanding laws of the community.

CHAPTER 5

THE FORMATION OF AN ALL-ISRAELITE EPIC

The convocation at Shechem (see pp. 129–131) was a momentous occasion. Joshua 24 tells us it was an all-Israelite affair: Joshua convened "all the tribes of Israel," represented by their leaders, to present themselves "before God" at the sacred shrine. Joshua's address also had an all-Israelite appeal, for in the biblical text the Hebrew pronouns are in the plural: "*Your* [plural] ancestors formerly lived beyond the Euphrates" (Josh. 24:2); Yahweh "fetched *your* ancestor Abraham . . . and led him through all the land of Canaan" (24:3); Yahweh "escorted *your* ancestors out of Egypt, and *you* [plural] came to the sea" (24:6); Yahweh "brought *you* to the land of the Amorites" (24:8) where "*you* crossed the Jordan" (24:11). In short, the people heard from Joshua "the story of *our* life."

The pan-Israelite approach of Joshua's address is an oversimplification: Not *all* the Israelite tribes had experienced *all* the stirring events related here. Some had experienced the events of the Exodus. But of the "Israelites" whom Joshua addressed, some

Biblical Readings: Biblical texts are given in the outlines of the Primeval History (p. 144), the Ancestral History (pp. 152–153) and the People's History, pp. 161–162.

probably entered Canaan from the south, some from the west through Transjordan, and still others were probably already living in the land among the Canaanites. Indeed, even in the ancestral period a proto-Israelite alliance apparently existed in the region of Shechem, organized around the worship of "El [God], the God of Israel" (Gen. 33:18–20). We can best understand Joshua's address as an invitation to various tribes outside the core group to identify with Yahweh, the liberating God of the Exodus. Conversion to Yahwism, which involved discarding previous religious affiliations and pledging loyalty to a single covenant, would result in political unity and social solidarity. The Israelite Tribal Confederacy came into being when the people pledged allegiance to Yahweh, and when Joshua in return made a covenant with the people (Josh. 24:25).

The all-Israelite epic that emerged from this Tribal Confederacy (the "Period of the Judges") provided the basic outline of the Pentateuch. In joining together, the various tribes not only identified with the "core story" of the exodus from Egypt and the guidance into the land, but also brought with them their own traditions. The pooling of narrative resources that began in this period gradually resulted in an expansion and enrichment of the all-Israelite epic, as the story was told and retold throughout the generations. The people confessed that Yahweh, who delivered slaves from bondage and made them a community, was also the God of the ancestors and the Creator who from the very beginning guided the unfolding drama of all peoples who dwell on earth.

Scholars have customarily viewed Israel's national epic as the product of a literary awakening that occurred in the period of the United Kingdom. In this view, an unknown author known as "the Yahwist" (J) composed a masterful prose epic that creatively interpreted Israel's covenant faith to express the new sense of national unity under David and Solomon.[1] When the Davidic monarchy later split into northern and southern kingdoms (Ephraim and Judah), an Elohist (E) version of the epic was composed to express the interests and perspectives of the North (about 850 B.C.E.). These two traditions, J and E, contained overlapping and often inseparable versions of what we call the "Old Epic" tradition.[2]

No doubt the events of the monarchy—the rise of the Davidic empire (about 1000 B.C.E.), its split into two kingdoms (about 922 B.C.E.), the fall of the Northern Kingdom of Ephraim (721 B.C.E.), and the demise of the Southern Kingdom of Judah (587 B.C.E.)—profoundly affected the formation of an all-Israelite epic. Even the Golden Calf story (see pp. 94–95) was retold in the political context of the monarchy, as shown by its echo of cultic reforms introduced by the Ephraimite king, Jeroboam I. Nevertheless, the parallel Yahwist (J) and Elohist (E) versions of the Israelite epic that circulated during the monarchy rest upon a common, basic tradition. There is reason to

---

[1]This part of the Documentary Hypothesis (see pp. 19–22) is adopted by Harold Bloom in *The Book of J*, translated from the Hebrew by David Rosenberg, interpreted by Harold Bloom (New York: Grove Weidenfeld, 1990). Bloom suggests that "J" was a woman who wrote in the early monarchy.

[2]In "The Form-critical Problem of the Hexateuch," Gerhard von Rad stresses the creative accomplishment of "the Yahwist" (*Essays* [191], 1–78). See further Peter Ellis, *The Yahwist* [299].

believe that this tradition *began* to be shaped orally, perhaps largely in poetic form, during the Tribal Confederacy as the tribes came to a new awareness of their unity and solidarity in covenant with Yahweh.[3] In the process of storytelling over many generations the basic narrative outline was further expanded and elaborated, and was eventually written down as the completed Torah.

FROM TRADITION TO LITERATURE

The period from Moses to David was a period of *oral tradition.* This does not mean that, beginning with David (1000 B.C.E.), oral tradition was superseded by literary records, or that before David there were no written records. The matter is not that simple: Even after David's time, many of Israel's religious traditions—stories, hymns, and prophetic oracles—were handed down orally, resulting in a fruitful interplay between the written and the remembered word.[4]

Indeed, the art of writing was known quite early in the biblical period. From the second millennium B.C.E. comes a number of literary works, among them the Canaanite Ras Shamra literature of the fourteenth century (see pp. 169–171). Future archaeological research might show that writing was more common in ancient Israel than the Bible seems to indicate (see Exod. 17:14; 24:4; Josh. 24:25). In any case, there are references to, and quotations from, written sources that no longer exist. One of these is "The Book of the Wars of Yahweh" (Num. 21:14). Another is "The Book of Jashar," parts of which are quoted in Joshua 10:13 (the command for the sun to stand still), 2 Samuel 1:18 (David's dirge for Saul and Jonathan), and possibly 1 Kings 8:13 (Solomon's ritual of dedication).[5]

In general, however, the period before the monarchy was a preliterary one in the sense that poems, proverbs, and stories were inscribed primarily in human memory. Writing played a lesser role, confined for the most part to business and practical affairs. The absence of written records does not mean we are left "in the dark" about this early period. In contrast to our modern reliance on the printed word, ancient peoples practiced the art of "learning by heart" the traditions that were meaningful to them. Storytellers transmitted the Homeric poems orally for generations; Jewish rabbis committed to memory the traditions of the Mishnah centuries before any of them were written down; and the materials of the Christian Gospels circulated orally before they became

---

[3]In *Pentateuchal Traditions* [76], Martin Noth maintains that literary sources such as J and E point back to, and are dependent on, a common *Grundlage* (G), that is an all-Israelite epic tradition.

[4]Some Scandinavian scholars stress the persistence of oral tradition throughout the period of the monarchy and the flowering of literature after the fall of the nation in the sixth century B.C.E. See Ivan Engnell, *A Rigid Scrutiny* [82]; also Eduard Nielsen, *Oral Tradition* [84].

[5]In the Greek translation of the Hebrew Bible (Septuagint) this ancient ritual is said to have come from "The Book of Songs," which by a slight misreading of the Hebrew could have been "The Book of Jashar."

literature. Even today there are Arabs who can recite the whole Koran without faltering, and Brahmins who know the whole Rig Veda by heart. Similarly, in the period before David the religious traditions of Israel were preserved, shaped, and transmitted through oral recitation at great religious festivals and other social gatherings.

THE ORAL TRADITION

Based on research into the history of oral tradition, we can isolate small "memory units" in the biblical tradition and understand their characteristic types or genres. These units of tradition are associated with some act or event that comes out of a living situation. An excellent example is the "Song of Miriam," a spontaneous outcry of praise after a great victory (see pp. 74–77).

A brief summary of these preliterary units of tradition shows that the oral tradition was as diverse and rich as life itself. There were various types of poetic units: songs to accompany work (the "Song of the Well," Num. 21:17–18), songs of taunting victory (the "Song of Deborah," Judg. 5), hymns of praise ("Song of Miriam," Exod. 15:21), and songs of lament (David's dirge for Saul and Jonathan, 2 Sam. 1:19–27). There were various poetic aphorisms: the saying when the Ark was carried (Num. 10:35–36), the saying about the shedding of human blood (Gen. 9:6), the proverb about Saul among the prophets (1 Sam. 10:12), and Samson's riddle (Judg. 14:14, 18). There were all kinds of narratives: stories about creation and primeval history, about a place, a custom, a tribal hero, a cultic practice, or about the idiosyncrasy of a people. Some stories explained origins (etiologies), some were for entertainment, some expressed moods and feelings evoked by daily affairs.

Popular genres are important in understanding Israel's historical experience during this period of song and legend. Today we use the term "legendary" to describe a story or account that lacks historical authenticity. No modern historian would think of writing history in the form of a flood narrative, or the story of Jacob's dream at Bethel, or the Joseph cycle. But ancient sagas often tell us something about history that is missing from a modern "factual" account based on government records, population statistics, war casualties, and so on. A "saga" communicates *history as experienced*—the internal meaning of events. If the deepest dimension of life's meaning is the relation of human beings to God, saga and poetry are exceedingly important ways of telling history.[6]

---

[6]See Definition, p. 19. A fundamental study is *The Legends of Genesis* [291], Hermann Gunkel's preface to his commentary on the book of Genesis. In an introduction to this reprinted work, W. F. Albright points out that, because the English word "legend" is associated with myth or fiction, it is perhaps better to use the old Norse word *saga*, defined as "a prose or more rarely a poetic narrative of historical origin or coloring." For a helpful discussion of the relation of saga to history, see Martin Buber, "Saga and History," in *The Writings of Martin Buber* [289].

THE FORMATION OF AN ISRAELITE EPIC

Some units of oral tradition were non-Israelite in origin and were probably associated with Canaanite shrines taken over by the Israelites. For example, the stories of Abraham's sacrifice of Isaac (Gen. 22) and Jacob's dream at Bethel (Gen. 28) were pre-Israelitic, Canaanite cult legends that meant something completely different in their original versions. These independent units of tradition were not just borrowed—they were *appropriated* by Israel and given new meaning in the Yahweh faith.

The oral tradition emerged in a gradual process that took place over many years. The major catalyst was the Yahweh faith confessed by members of the Tribal Confederacy established at Shechem, in the heart of territory long under the domination of Canaanite culture (see Chapter 4). Israel naturally inherited various traditions from the Canaanites: agricultural laws, cult legends, stories about primeval history, etiologies, tribal tales, and so on. But the Hebrews who came into Canaan brought with them their own shared story—the tradition of events through which Yahweh had delivered the people from Egyptian bondage and had graciously led them through the wilderness into the land. What Israel borrowed was, therefore, transformed into a vehicle for expressing the covenant faith. Popular traditions, inherited from non-Yahwistic sources, were changed to give expression to the meaning of Israel's history as directed by Yahweh.

The oral tradition that preceded the period of the monarchy was not a formless mass, haphazardly thrown together. The story of Yahweh's dealings with Israel, later to assume elaborate form in the great historical narratives of the Hebrew Bible, was beginning to take shape as the tribes wove units of tradition into cycles of stories, stamped with their particular interests and experiences. The annual ceremony of covenant renewal, held first at Shechem and later at the confederate sanctuary of Shiloh, was probably an occasion for the recitation of laws and narratives binding on all Israel. Here the early nucleus of Israelite themes celebrated in story and song (such as Exod. 15:1–18) would be expanded into a great Israelite epic that included the careers of the ancestors, the deliverance from Egypt, the wandering in the wilderness, the giving of the Law at Sinai, and the conquest of Canaan. Shaped by this liturgical usage, Israel's traditions probably reached a unified *oral* form even before the rise of the monarchy.

THE SCOPE OF THE OLD EPIC NARRATIVE

What was the scope of the Old Epic narrative that began to develop during the period of the Tribal Confederacy, a period some scholars regard as the heyday of Israel, "the people of Yahweh"?

Notice that the Old Epic tradition places the Mosaic tradition—Exodus, Sinai, Wilderness, Entry into the Land—in a comprehensive narrative context: one that embraces the unfolding drama of Yahweh's historical purpose from Creation through the occupation of Canaan and beyond into an open-ended future. The drama has three movements or "acts" that follow each other in succession and lead toward a climax:

A. *The Primeval History* (Gen. 2–11),[7] with its own structure and integrity, moves from creation toward chaos (the Flood) and the new beginning after the Flood. This narrative is "ecumenical" (it includes all humankind).

B. *The Ancestral History* (Gen. 12–50), also with its own structure and dynamic, portrays Israel's prehistory through the family stories of the "founding" fathers and mothers. The Joseph story (Gen. 37–50), which has its own integrity, is incorporated into this family history.

C. *The People's History* (Exodus 1 to the opening of the book of Joshua) extends from the oppression in Egypt to the entrance into Canaan. This lengthy narrative constitutes the Mosaic tradition.

Consider the interrelation of these three "histories" or "stories" that make up the all-Israelite epic:

First, each history has its own special character. The Primeval History (A) deals with fundamental human experiences: guilt and punishment, broken relations, the struggle for power, the search for security, and the powers of chaos that threaten the ordered world.[8] There is no mention of Israel, the people of Yahweh, and for the most part the stories presuppose a Mesopotamian setting (Gen. 10:21). The Ancestral History (B) is essentially a family history. With the exception of Genesis 14, Israel's ancestors are not involved in politics but move quietly and peacefully on the fringes of Canaanite society. The People's History or Mosaic tradition (C) plunges immediately into the political sphere as it recounts how enslaved Hebrews were liberated from Egyptian bondage and struggled to possess the land of Canaan.

Second, these three histories are presented from the standpoint of faith in Yahweh, Israel's God. We have seen that the introduction of the sacred Name is connected with the "root experiences" of Mosaic tradition—Exodus and Sinai (see pp. 55–59). Significantly, the Ancestral History tells us it is *Yahweh* who initiates Abraham's migration and gives promises to each of the patriarchs; and in the Primeval History *Yahweh* is creator of the world and director of human history. Indeed, the Old Epic narrative traces the worship of Yahweh to Seth, grandson of Adam and Eve: "At that time people began to invoke the name of Yahweh" (Gen. 4:26b).

In a sense we should read these three parts of the Israelite epic *backward*, as it were—viewing earlier stories through the prism of the crucial historical experiences that created the community of Israel in the Mosaic period. Yahweh's self-revelation in the

---

[7]The first chapter of Genesis is omitted here because, by general agreement, the story found in Gen. 1:1–2:3 comes from the Priestly (P) Work, considered in Chapter 13.

[8]This "mythical" dimension of the primeval history is stressed by Claus Westermann in his essay, "Biblical Reflections on Creator-Creation," in *Creation in the Old Testament* [132], pp. 90–101. See also Susan Niditch, *Chaos to Cosmos: Studies in Biblical Patterns of Creation* (Chicago: Scholars Press, 1985).

Mosaic period cast new light on the ancestral period, making it a period of anticipation and movement toward the inheritance of the Promised Land and Israel's full participation in the divine plan that embraces all nations. That revealing light also fell on the stories of the Primeval History, which portray the potential glory and actual tragedy of human history. These stories prepare for the turning point in the unfolding drama: the call of Abraham.

THE GRADUAL ELABORATION OF THE ISRAELITE STORY

Thus the Israelite epic, initially centered in Exodus and Sinai, probably began to expand during the period of the Tribal Confederacy as the outline was extended back to the beginning of human history and was filled in with materials that once circulated independently. Storytellers reinterpreted the past in a present context: Even the distant Primeval History was adorned with contemporary touches such as the story of Noah's drunkenness (Gen. 9:18–27), which reflects Canaan's subjugation to Israel. These storytellers retold the Ancestral History to make Jacob the eponym for "Israel" (Gen. 32:28) and the father of the twelve sons of the Tribal Confederacy; and they refer to peoples who were neighbors or rivals in the period of the Tribal Confederacy: Arameans (Gen. 25:20; 28:5), Edomites (Gen. 32:3; compare chapter 36), Moabites and Ammonites (Gen. 19:30–38), Philistines (Gen. 21:32; 26:1, 14), and so on (see pp. 38, 39, 116–117).

Thus the Pentateuch in its final form is the end result of a long process of transmission, during which many individuals and groups reinterpreted the sacred heritage for their own times. We have mentioned the Yahwist (J), who retold the Old Epic tradition in the conviction that Yahweh's promises to Abraham were being fulfilled in the time of David and Solomon, and the Elohist (E), whose version of that same epic tradition reflected the interests of the Northern Kingdom. Still later, around the time of the fall of Jerusalem in 587 B.C.E., the Deuteronomistic historian (D) wrote a great historical work based on the core of the book of Deuteronomy, which emphasized Yahweh's deliverance of the people from Egypt and the making of the covenant at Sinai. Later yet, during the period of the exile (about 587–538 B.C.E.), Priestly Writers (P) issued a comprehensive history of God's covenants, beginning with Creation (Gen. 1:1–2:3) and incorporating the old Israelite epic (see Chapter 13). None of these versions, however, depart from the *basic* outline of the ancient Israelite epic inherited from the days of the Tribal Confederacy and early monarchy.

OVERVIEW OF ISRAEL'S EPIC NARRATIVE

We turn now to a direct examination of the Old Epic narrative, with its three "histories" that make up the whole. Our concern is to see how the whole narrative, despite its diversity, coheres as an all-Israelite epic intended to confess faith in Yahweh, the God whose purpose is traceable in a historical drama that extends from Creation to the entry into the Promised Land. We will not attempt to separate the Southern (J) and Northern (E) versions of the Old Epic tradition. These versions could have circulated in tribal groupings within the confederacy from the first, and in any event did not surface until the period of the monarchy. Also we will not attempt to distinguish between traditions present in the earliest stages of growth and those produced at a somewhat later time. It suffices to say that we are dealing with an *evolving* story.

A. THE PRIMEVAL HISTORY

The dramatic power of the Old Epic tradition can be discerned in the way units of tradition have been joined into a comprehensive story. At points it is difficult to separate the Old Epic narrative from the surrounding Priestly (P) material. On the whole, however, the Old Epic narrative stands out sharply enough for us to read it as a continuous narrative. We will consider some of the main episodes in this dramatic account.[9]

THE STORY OF HUMAN BEGINNINGS

The Garden of Eden	Gen. 2:4b–3:24
Cain and Abel	4:1–16
Cain and his descendants	4:17–26
Promiscuity of the Sons of God	6:1–4
The Flood (J and P blended)	
Noah's favor with Yahweh	6:5–8
Into the Ark	7:1–5, 7–10, 12, 16b
The Flood comes	7:17a, 22–23
The Flood abates	8:2b, 3a, 6–12, 13b
Conclusion	8:20–22
Noah's culture of the vine	9:18–27
Noah's descendants	10:8–19, 21, 25–30
The Tower of Babel	11:1–9
The ancestry of Abram (Abraham)	11:28–30

The Primeval History belonged to Israel's basic narrative even in the period of oral tradition. The motifs of Creation, Paradise, the Flood, and the deliverance of humankind from total destruction are common in myths and legends of the ancient Near

---

[9]This outline and those that follow recognize that the Israelite epic comes basically from the Yahwist (J), though no effort is made to separate sharply Northern (E) and Southern (J) versions of the Old Epic tradition or to distinguish between early traditions and later elaborations. For a more refined analysis, see the Supplement to Martin Noth's *Pentateuchal Traditions* [76], or the Appendix to Walter Harrelson's *Interpreting the Old Testament* [11].

An Akkadian Cylinder Seal impression depicts a scene from the Gilgamesh Epic.

East. An ancient Sumerian list of rulers makes a sharp distinction between the period "before the flood" and the period "after the flood" (see Gen. 10:1).[10] Moreover, Israelite narrators probably appropriated the ancient view of a "Golden Age" at the beginning of history, though making it a time when violence (sin) also began to emerge on the earth.

There is a striking parallel between the biblical Flood Story and the famous Gilgamesh Epic, which tells how Gilgamesh, a legendary Sumerian king, tried to discover the secret of immortality from the hero of the flood, Utnapishtim. In Tablet XI, Utnapishtim vividly relates how the gods capriciously decided to destroy humankind in a great flood. However, Ea, the god of wisdom, advised Utnapishtim to build a large boat and take aboard the seed of all living things. The flood came with such destructive fury that "the gods cowered like dogs" and crouched against the walls of heaven, weeping over their decision to destroy humanity. The storm finally subsided on the seventh day, with the boat grounded on the top of Mount Nisir. Seven days later Utnapishtim sent forth a dove, a swallow, and—because these birds found no resting place—a raven. Then he offered a sacrifice of such sweet savor on the mountaintop that "the gods crowded like flies" around it.[11] The similarity of this ancient story to the biblical account shows that Israelite story-tellers borrowed freely from the reservoir of popular tradition as they developed their own Yahwistic narratives.

The stories of the Primeval History are "historical" only in the sense that they plumb the depth of history's meaning and evince those fundamental experiences common to human beings from the very dawn of history. The manner of presentation is

---

[10]"The Sumerian King List," in Pritchard, *Ancient Near Eastern Texts* [1], p. 265.
[11]See Pritchard, *Ancient Near Eastern Texts* [1], pp. 93–97.

poetic or pictorial, for the narrators are dealing with a subject that eludes modern historical and scientific investigation: namely, the ultimate source of the human drama in the initiative and purpose of God.

THE PARADISE STORY

The story of Paradise (Gen. 2:4b–3:24) is filled with images found in ancient folklore—for example, the Tree of Life and the cunning serpent. The story evidently once circulated as the storyteller's answer to several questions: Why are man and woman attracted to each other? Why does social propriety demand the wearing of clothes? Why must there be the pain of childbirth and the misery of hard work? Why do people fear snakes? The Israelite epic also deals with a deeper question: Why do man and woman, God's creatures, refuse to acknowledge the sovereignty of their Creator, with the result that humans are tragically banished from the wholesome life for which they were intended?

The Paradise story in the Old Epic narrative and the Priestly Creation story in Genesis 1 give different accounts of the creation of humankind. The Priestly account affirms that God made 'adam (humanity) in "the image of God," creating *them* "male and female" (implying equality of role). In the Paradise Story, the creation of 'adam takes place in two stages (Gen. 2:7 and 2:21–22), but here as well creation is not complete until man and woman stand in partnership with each other.[12]

The two stories supplement one another in interest, though they differ in many respects. Unlike the Priestly version, the Old Epic narrative does not emphasize cosmic creation—the creation of heaven and earth—but rather the creation of human beings and their earthly environment. The story of 'adam, in the inclusive sense, is down to earth and existential. Human being is made from the soil ('adama, a play on the word 'adam) and returns to the soil at death (Gen. 2:7 and 3:19b). Human being is a special creature of Yahweh, whose breath ("spirit") animates the dust, making it become *nefesh*—a "living being" or "psychosomatic self." (The Greek dualism of a perishable body and a deathless "soul" is alien to the Hebraic view.) Human being is related to the animals who are also "living being" (Gen. 2:19); but humans have the power to name the animals and thus transcend animal being. A three-dimensional being, 'adam exists in relationship with the natural environment, with another human being, and with God.[13] To this human being God speaks—giving a task ("to till and keep the garden") and calling to decision ("You may freely eat of every tree of the garden, but . . ."). The story portrays life, not only as it was in the beginning, but also as it is now.[14]

---

[12]See Phyllis Trible's exquisite treatment of the Paradise story, "A Love Story Gone Awry," in *God and the Rhetoric of Sexuality* [167], chap. 4.

[13]See Martin Buber, *I and Thou* (Edinburgh: T. & T. Clark, 1937).

[14]See the treatment of Genesis 2–3 in various commentaries such as Gerhard von Rad [305], Umberto Cassuto [237], and Walter Brueggemann [300]; see also Michael Fishbane's essay, "Genesis 2:4b–11:32/The Primeval Cycle," in *Text and Texture* [94], pp. 17–39.

The story of Paradise Lost has cast a long shadow over human history. In brief, the story portrays the rebellion of human beings against divine authority and their determination to assert independence by grasping for the fruit of the forbidden tree. In this story, sin is an act of will in revolt against God—the ambition to overstep human status as a creature dependent on God and to become "like God" or perhaps "like the gods," the divine beings in Yahweh's heavenly court (Gen. 3:5; note the "us" in 3:22). The story tells us that this human act of defiance brings in its wake a sense of guilt ("They knew that they were naked," Gen. 3:7; compare 2:25); a futile effort to hide from the inescapable God (Gen. 3:8, compare Ps. 139); attempts to rationalize the act by shifting the blame to someone or something else; the misery of painful birth and of work that becomes drudgery; and finally the banishment from the primeval beauty and harmony of God's garden.

The theme of Paradise Lost is similar to Greek tragedy: Human pride (Greek: *hubris*) prompts human beings in Promethean fashion to assert themselves against Fate (*moira*), with the result that retribution (*nemesis*) comes upon them for a presumptuous deed. There is a profound difference, however. In Genesis, human beings do not revolt against a blind, impersonal fate but against the will of the holy God who chooses to be involved in their history, and whose personal relation with the man and the woman is portrayed with delightful anthropomorphism (as in the vivid portrayal of Yahweh God "walking in the garden in the cool of the day"). *'Adam* is an earthling who is related to the ground, the *'adama*, but also a creature who exists in "I-thou" relationship with the Creator. The primeval revolt against God is an act of violence that disrupts all relationships: with God, with human beings, and with the earth itself. The consequence is that henceforth human beings must live in suffering and anxiety, with the prospect of death hanging over them like a Sword of Damocles.

THE STORY OF CAIN AND ABEL

Banishment from the Garden of Eden begins a period of history in which *'adam* is an agriculturalist, a "tiller of the *'adama* [ground]." The next episode in the Israelite epic narrative is the story of Cain and Abel (Gen. 4:1–16). In this story, which reflects the characteristic animosity between farmer and shepherd, we learn that Yahweh favored the pastoral Abel, who sacrificed the firstlings of his flock, rather than the farmer Cain, who offered "the fruit of the ground [*'adama*])."

There are a few rough edges to the story: For example, as the son of the first human couple, Cain would have had difficulty finding a wife! Nevertheless the story, which might have once circulated independently, now functions in its narrative context to illustrate how things began to go wrong in consequence of the rebellion in the Garden. Just as his parents had presumptuously disobeyed Yahweh, Cain was susceptible to an evil impulse (sin) that crouched at the door like a predatory animal, waiting to spring upon its prey (Gen. 4:6–7). The break-up of the human community is evident in

Cain's irresponsible question: "Am I my brother's keeper?" Again the ground (*'adama*), polluted by murder, is accursed, for from it Abel's blood cries out to Yahweh for retribution (Gen. 4:11; compare 3:17–19).

The narrative tells us that the first city was built by Cain, a murderer (Gen. 4:17). Human culture got off to a bad start! The story is not blind to progress in technology and the arts, however: One of Cain's descendants is Jubal, the ancestor of musicians, and another is Tubal-cain, a forger of the metals that played such an important part in the culture of the second millennium (Gen. 4:21–22). But cultural advance was accompanied by violence, lust, and unbridled passion—a chain reaction of evil going from bad to worse. The last straw, according to the Old Epic scheme, was the violence perpetrated by heavenly beings ("the sons of God"), who had intercourse with beautiful human maidens (Gen. 6:1–4). This archaic story, which on its own defies understanding, functions in this context as final evidence "that the evil of humankind was great in the earth, and that the whole tendency of the thoughts of the human heart was only evil all the time" (Gen. 6:5). Yahweh is described as the God of pathos, "grieved to the heart" about human failure, and resolved to make a new beginning.

THE GREAT FLOOD

Ancient flood stories (such as the Gilgamesh Epic) show that the Mesopotamian plain, subject to annual inundation by the Tigris and Euphrates rivers, has been the scene of floods from time immemorial. In the Israelite Old Epic narrative, however, the Great Flood was not just a natural event. The narrators used ancient popular traditions as a vehicle to express a fundamental conviction of Israel's faith: God's inescapable judgment in human affairs.

There are obvious differences between the biblical story and the Gilgamesh Epic. To be sure, the Israelite narrative has naive anthropomorphic touches, as in the statement that Yahweh shut the door of the Ark (Gen. 7:16b), or that Yahweh smelled the pleasing fragrance of Noah's sacrifice (8:21). But these details, inherited from popular tradition, do not obscure the central view that Yahweh, the sole God (in contrast to Babylonia's many gods), acts in human affairs in a meaningful and consistent way (in contrast to the capriciousness of Babylonian deities).

The narrative imbues Yahweh's judgment with tender mercy. This quality is also evident in the story of Eden, where Yahweh clothed the human couple in skin garments (Gen. 3:21), and in the story of Cain, where Yahweh's wrath was mitigated by putting a protecting mark on Cain's forehead (4:15). Similarly, in the Flood story, Yahweh's judgment upon an earth corrupted by human violence is not the last word, for Noah finds favor in Yahweh's sight. Yahweh takes the initiative by instructing Noah how to make a boat (an ark) and commanding him to take aboard his family and "families" of animals and birds. The ark, tossing helplessly on the rising flood waters, signifies Yahweh's intention to deliver a remnant with which to make a new beginning in history.

The story concludes with the statement that, even though "the imagination of the human heart is evil from youth," Yahweh will never again curse the earth with such a calamity. The new beginning is based not on human possibilities but on Yahweh's grace: Henceforth the regularities of nature—"seedtime and harvest, cold and heat, summer and winter, day and night"—will continue uninterrupted as signs of God's covenant faithfulness (Gen. 8:20–22).

THE TEMPTATIONS OF CULTURE

Divine judgment did not check the evil impulses of the human heart or prevent the breakdown of human culture in the Fertile Crescent. This is the point of the two episodes that follow the Flood in the Israelite epic: the story of Noah's drunkenness (Gen. 9:18–27) and the story of the construction of the Tower of Babel (11:1–9).

We are told that Noah, "a man of the soil ['adama]," was the first to plant a vineyard (the chief symbol of Canaanite agriculture). From the fruit of the vine he made a potent wine, drinking which put him into a drunken, debauched condition that led to one of his sons (Ham, the father of Canaan) committing what was regarded as a sexual abomination. Noah's indignation and subsequent curse on Ham, the father of black-skinned peoples, is not a statement of racial prejudice but a pointed attack on *agricultural Canaan* (represented as a person) with its wine-drinking and sexual abandon. In the time of Noah, so the story implies, the curse on the ground was removed (see Gen. 5:29; also 3:17–19), and Noah himself succeeded as a farmer. But Noah was unprepared for this potent taste of the fruits of Canaanite agriculture. When he saw that he was overcome by the new cultural powers available to him, he pronounced a terrible curse on Canaan.

The narrative tells us that after the Flood the earth was peopled by descendants of Noah's three sons, Shem, Ham, and Japheth, regarded as the ancestors of all ancient nations and social groupings. This brings us to the last story in the Primeval History: the story of the Tower of Babel. Before it was incorporated into the Old Epic scheme, this story circulated independently as an explanation of the origin of diverse peoples and languages. You can sense the independence of this unit by comparing it with the table of Noah's descendants (Gen. 10), which already presupposes the diversity of humankind. Despite its inconsistent beginning ("Once the whole earth had one language and few words"), the narrators have inserted the story here as an appropriate climax to the Primeval History and, at the same time, a transition to the next major section of the Old Epic narrative.

The scene is Babylonia (Shinar) where nomads, wandering in the east, find a plain and begin to establish a settled way of life—the culture for which Babylon was to become famous. Urged by the ambition to achieve political security and fearing social diffusion and diversity, the people decide to build a city and a "tower"—a reference to the ziggurat, or terraced temple-tower, the most famous of which was known as Eteme-

An Artist's Reconstruction of the ziggurat of Ur, based on the restoration suggested by archaeologists who excavated the site between 1922 and 1934. At the top of the artificial mountain constructed with brick stands the temple of Nanna, the moon god who was worshipped at Ur.

nanki in Babylon.[15] The episode provides climactic evidence of the self-assertion that prompted people to revolt against Yahweh—in this instance by resisting the Creator's will for social diversity and seeking to achieve a name, that is, to gain fame for themselves. As in the case of the Flood, Yahweh visits the earth with judgment, terminating the building project and thereby frustrating the people's desire for unity, even unity against God. By means of a Hebrew pun, the word *Babel* is understood to mean "confusion" (compare English "babble"). Thus Yahweh confused language so peoples could not understand one another, and dispersed peoples in various language groups over the face of the earth.[16]

The Primeval History had a sad outcome, for humanity failed to find true wholeness through life in communion with God and in community with fellow human beings. From Cain to the Tower of Babel the human tragedy increased, despite advances in the arts and sciences. History was driven by an "evil impulse" that polluted God's

---

[15]The Greek historian, Herodotus, gives some interesting comments on the ziggurat (*Persian Wars*, 1, 181–82). See R. de Vaux, *Ancient Israel* [111], pp. 281–82, who points out that the ziggurat was actually an artificial mountain with a huge stairway so that, ascending and descending, worshipers and the god could meet.

[16]See further Bernhard W. Anderson, "Unity and Diversity in God's Creation: A Study of the Babel Story," in *Currents in Theology and Mission*, V:2 (1978), 69–81; a shorter version appears in *Concilium*, No. 121 (1977), 89–97.

creation, leaving human beings estranged from their Creator and at odds with one another. Taken by itself, the story is extremely pessimistic, but the Primeval History now forms part of the larger Israelite epic. In this narrative context it serves as a prologue to what follows: the call of Abraham and his venture of faith.

B. THE ANCESTRAL HISTORY

Passing from Genesis 11 to Genesis 12, we leave the nebulous realm of Primeval History and enter the historical arena of the second millennium B.C.E. Like the Primeval History, the Ancestral History (Gen. 12–50) is in the form of a saga. There is an important difference, however. The sagas of the ancestral period are related in some degree to what was going on in the Fertile Crescent at that time (see Chapter 1). Historians can at least attempt to establish some correlation between the Ancestral History and ancient Near Eastern history. None of the episodes of the Primeval History are supported by other historical or archaeological information, with the possible exception of the Table of Nations (Gen. 10), believed by some historians to reflect circumstances in the late second millennium.[17] By and large the Primeval History is "historical" only in the broad sense that it portrays the conflicting realities of human existence, and in the sense that it interprets human history, in all its glory and tragedy, as the drama of God's dealings with humankind.

In stating the matter this way, we are admittedly expressing a modern point of view. The ancient Israelite narrators, and the people who heard their narration, undoubtedly saw dramatic continuity in the progression from Genesis 11 to Genesis 12. The Primeval History portrays the human situation in universal terms: Human beings should live in harmony, security, and mutual welfare—everything connoted by the Hebrew *shalom* ("peace")—but in fact are broken, divided, and scattered over the face of the earth in confusion and strife. This "history" provides the dramatic prologue to the central theme of the other parts of the Old Epic narrative: the particular identity and special vocation of Israel in Yahweh's history-long and world-embracing purpose.

As the following outline shows, the family history of Israel's ancestors concentrates mainly on Abraham, Jacob, and Joseph. Isaac is relegated to a minor role—overshadowed on one side by Abraham and on the other by Jacob—while Joseph is the main figure in the story of Jacob's twelve sons. Nevertheless, the Israelite epic is governed by the schematic sequence that appears at the outset of the Exodus story: Abraham, Isaac, and Jacob. Despite the patriarchal structure of ancient society, women played an important role in the story. This is particularly true of Sarah (Sarai) who, together with her husband Abraham (Abram), ventured into the land of Canaan (Gen. 11:31; 12:5).

---

[17]See Siegfried Herrmann, *A History of Israel* [113], pp. 41–55.

The Family History of Israel's Ancestors*

The Abraham Cycle

The promise to Abraham	Gen. 12:1–4a
Abraham and Sarah in Egypt	12:10–13:1
Abraham separates from Lot	13:2–18
[Abraham's victory: 14:1–24]	[special source]
Yahweh's covenant with Abraham	15:1–21
Ishmael, son of Abraham and Hagar	16:1–14
A son promised to Abraham and Sarah	18:1–16
The Fate of Sodom and Gomorrah	
Abraham's expostulation with God	18:17–33
Lot's deliverance from the holocaust	19:1–29
The birth of Moab and Ammon	19:30–38
Abraham and Sarah in Gerar	20:1–18
Isaac and Ishmael	21:1–21
Abraham's dispute with Abimelech	21:22–34
Abraham's near sacrifice of Isaac	22:1–19
The descandants of Abraham's brother	22:20–24
Finding a wife for Isaac	24:1–67
Abraham's children by Keturah	25:1–6

The Jacob Cycle

Rebekah gives birth to twins	25:21–26a
Jacob steals the birthright	25:27–34
Isaac's journeys	26:1–33
Jacob steals the blessing	27:1–45
Jacob's dream at Bethel	28:10–22
The Jacob and Laban stories:	
Jacob's meeting with Rachel	29:1–14
Jacob's marriage to Leah and Rachel	29:15–30
Jacob's eleven children	29:31–30:24
Jacob outwits Laban	30:25–43
Jacob's covenant with Laban	31:1–55
Jacob prepares to meet Esau	32:1–21
Jacob's wrestling with the angel at Penuel	32:22–32
Jacob's meeting with Esau	33:1–17
Jacob's arrival at Shechem	33:18–20
The rape of Dinah, attack on Shechem	34:1–31
Jacob's return to Bethel	35:1–15
The birth of Benjamin	35:16–21

The Story of Jacob and His Sons

Joseph's dream and its consequences	37:2–36
The Judah and Tamar interlude	38:1–30
The Joseph story continued:	
Joseph's temptation	39:1–23
Joseph's interpretation of dreams	40:2–41:40

The Family History of Israel's Ancestors* (*cont.*)

The Story of Jacob and His Sons

Joseph's rise to power	41:41–57
The brothers' first visit	42:1–38
The brothers' second visit	43:1–34
Joseph tests his brothers	44:1–34
The brothers recognize Joseph	45:1–28
Jacob's family settles in Egypt	46:1–34
Joseph (and Jacob) before Pharaoh	47:1–6, (7–12)
Joseph's agrarian program	47:13–26
Jacob's last wishes	47:29–31
Jacob's death-bed blessing	48:1–22
A poem: Jacob's blessing (and censure)	49:1–28
Jacob's burial in Canaan	49:29–50:14
Joseph's forgiveness and last days	50:15–16

*In this outline no attempt is made to separate putative J (Yahwist) and E (Elohist) elements of the Old Epic tradition or to identify editorial (Priestly) connective tissue. For a refined literary analysis, see the appendix in Martin Noth, *Pentateuchal Traditions* [76], pp. 263–67.

THE PROMISE TO ABRAHAM

The "divine address" at the beginning of Genesis 12 holds the key to interpreting the Ancestral History. From the descendants of those dispersed from the abortive enterprise at Babel, Yahweh singles out one individual and opens a new horizon before him:

> Yahweh said to Abram:
>> Betake yourself from your land, your kindred, and your
>> father's house to the land that I will show you.
> I will make you a great nation; I will bless you
>> and magnify your name so that you will be a blessing.
> Those who bless you I will bless,
>> and those who curse you I will curse.
> By you all the families of the earth will bless themselves.
>> —GENESIS 12:1–3

To possess a land, to become a great nation, to be a blessing to the peoples of the earth: This threefold divine promise runs like a golden thread through the tapestry of the Ancestral History. These three elements—land, posterity, blessing—apparently belonged to ancient ancestral religion, and are highlighted and formalized in the divine addresses (see pp. 39–42) that punctuate the narrative.

Semitic Nomads present themselves to an important Egyptian official. This wall painting from the tomb of Chnumhotep, a noble at Beni-hasan, Egypt, dates back to about the time of Abraham and is considered one of the most beautiful pictures of antiquity. At the rear of the procession are two bearded men: a bowman and a musician. Ahead of them is a line of women and children preceded by a group of bearded warriors, led by the chieftain (bending). The first figure to the left of the oversized official is the Egyptian royal scribe, who holds a document giving details about the immigrants.

YAHWEH'S PROMISES

Abraham's migration initiated a new kind of history: the history of Yahweh's promises to Israel and to other peoples as well. From the beginning of the Primeval History the narrative scope narrows until it concentrates upon the solitary figure of Abraham, the ancestor of the people chosen for a special task in Yahweh's historical purpose.[18] Coming almost immediately after the story of the Tower of Babel, which presents a dark picture of human pride and ambition, the story of the call of Abraham is like a burst of light that illumines the whole landscape. The builders at Babel failed in their ambition to make a name for themselves; in contrast, Yahweh promises to make Abraham's name great (Gen. 12:2; compare 11:4). Israel's greatness will lie not in its ambitions or achievements, but in its witness to the God who acts in history to overcome the confusion, disharmony, and violence of the Primeval History.

....

DEFINITION: "BLESSING"

One dimension of God's promise to Abraham is that of blessing, which is somehow to include other peoples.

In the ancient view, blessing is the imparting of well-being ("peace") and is especially efficacious when given by a person who has superior prestige or power, such as an elder to a child, a king to a subject, or a priest to a suppliant. It is the opposite of a curse, which has negative effects. Some societies still revere the power of the word spoken in blessing (affirmation) or in curse (censure).

In Israel's ancestral period, a blessing or curse was believed to have immediate effect. This explains the importance attached to deathbed blessings (as with Isaac and Jacob)

---

[18]In the Priestly (P) scheme, the writers display through genealogies the same movement from the universal to the particular: Creation-Adam-Noah-Shem (father of the Semites)-Terah-Abraham.

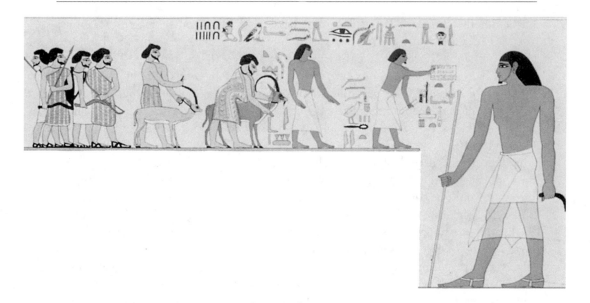

or to imprecations against enemies (Balaam's refusal to curse Israel in the Balaam oracles). Israel's Old Epic narrative, however, institutes a major change: The blessing is postponed to the future, beyond the lifetime of the original recipients. Hence the blessing becomes a *promise*. Postponement of the promise means that the whole ancestral period becomes an interim between promise and fulfillment, with the resulting tensions and anxieties of faith. When the interim seems unbearably extended, people raise cries of lament, as in Psalm 13 ("How long, O Yahweh?") and Psalm 22 ("My God, why have you forsaken me?").

The promise of blessing is ambiguous in one regard, owing to the question of whether to understand the Hebrew verbs in a passive sense ("to be blessed") or in a reflexive sense ("to bless themselves"). This grammatical problem appears from time to time (Gen. 12:3; 18:18; 22:18; 26:4; 28:14). The intended meaning is probably that other peoples will "bless themselves," in the sense that they invoke the name of the God of Abraham or that they say to one another: "May we be as blessed as the people of Abraham." In any case, Israel interpreted the promise to mean that God would bless the nations through—that is, *by means of*—Israel's role and witness. This view, found in the Greek translation of the Hebrew Bible (Septuagint) and in the Wisdom of Ben Sira 44:21, is adopted in the New Testament (Acts 3:25, Gal. 3:8).[19]

In working out the theme of the promise, the narrators of the Old Epic tradition wove together stories that once had completely different meanings. Therefore we can only guess what the ancestors might have been like in their "oldest dress." Evidence suggests that Abraham was once connected with the sanctuary of Mamre, near Hebron;

[19]See further Claus Westermann, *Blessing* [170].

Isaac with the shrine of Beer-sheba; and Jacob with the "house of God" (Hebrew: *beth 'El*) at Bethel. Since each of these places was an old Canaanite shrine that had been taken over by the Israelites, some stories about these three figures might be Canaanite in origin. In any case, we are not dealing with biographies, but with stories in which Israel personified its history. This personification is clear in the case of Jacob and Esau, who represent Israel and Edom respectively (Gen. 25:22–26). Abraham, too, is more than an individual: He is typical of the people of God who venture into the future in faith (Heb. 11:8–10).

During the period of the Tribal Confederacy, narrators gradually harmonized these miscellaneous traditions into the story of a single family bound together by the father-son-grandson sequence: Abraham, Isaac, and Jacob (compare Exod. 3:6). Genesis 15:13–16, where we find references to the duration of the oppression in Egypt and to the Exodus, clearly indicates the retrospective view of this story. In the process of handing down the tradition, the ancestral stories began to take on a unity that did not actually exist at that time. Eventually the story encompassed all of Israel, for from Abraham's seed, in direct succession through Isaac and Jacob, sprang the twelve tribes. Moreover, the ancestors no longer worshipped their gods "beyond the River" (Josh. 24:14): El Olam at Beer-sheba (Josh. 21:33), Baal Berith or El Berith at Shechem (see Judg. 8:33; 9:4, 46), or El Bethel at Bethel (Gen. 35:7). The religion of the ancestors is now the worship of Yahweh, the God of Israel who is also the God of Abraham, Isaac, and Jacob, and indeed the creator of the universe and ruler of human history. In the present form of the narrative, it is Yahweh who appears to each of the ancestors and renews the promise given to Abraham, a promise that has universal implications.

THE TRIALS OF FAITH

In the view of the Old Epic narrative, Israel's ancestors were wanderers toward a goal that Yahweh had set before them. Their history was a pilgrim movement from promise toward fulfillment, not an aimless meandering on the fringes of Canaan. Yet, according to the storytellers, it was not easy for the ancestors to live by the promise, for again and again they found themselves in situations in which the divine promise seemed incredible. At such times their trust in Yahweh was severely tested, and they reached the edge of despair. Each element of the promise—land, posterity, blessing—was almost taken away. In episode after episode the narrative builds dramatic suspense, only to resolve the tension by showing how Yahweh intervened at the critical moment, renewing the promise just when everything seemed lost.

We will see how this theme is worked out by considering the divine addresses to the ancestors:

> To Abraham:
> In Haran before the migration   Gen. 12:1–3
> In Shechem, the heartland of Canaan   12:7

In Canaan after separation from Lot	13:14–17
In Canaan (perhaps at Hebron)	15:4–5 (13–16)
In Hebron before the holocaust of Sodom	18:17–19
To Isaac in Gerar	26:2–5
To Jacob at Bethel [quoted in the Joseph story: Gen. 48:1–4]	28:13–15

ABRAHAM   After migrating from Mesopotamia, Abraham came to Shechem in the heart of Canaanite country. There, at a sacred oak, Yahweh appeared to him and reaffirmed the promise of land to his descendants (*Divine Address*, Gen. 12:7). But after a while Abraham was driven by famine to Egypt, where, to save his life, he ingratiated himself with Pharaoh by an act of deceit involving his wife Sarah. True, his hunger was severe, and it seemed expedient to take things into his own hands rather than to trust Yahweh's providence. But Abraham's act was tantamount to surrendering the promise, even though it brought him great material advantage, for with Sarah (the ancestress of Israel) in Pharaoh's harem there would be no future for Israel. At the last minute, however, Yahweh saved the day and Abraham, despite his rash deed, was sent away from Egypt a rich man (Gen. 12:10–13:2). He returned to Bethel and "called upon the name of Yahweh," as he had done before his Egyptian adventure.

Next, strife between the herdsmen of Abraham and Lot made it necessary for the two relatives to go their respective ways. Lot, the ancestor of Moab and Ammon (Gen. 19:30–38), was free to choose where to go, and the future of Israel depended on his decision. Providentially, Lot chose not the Land of the Promise but the area of the Jordan Valley, whose wicked cities—Sodom and Gomorrah—Yahweh later destroyed by volcanic fire and brimstone (Gen. 13:3–13). Once again Yahweh renewed the promise to Abraham (*Divine Address*, Gen. 13:14–17).

But there was still a major obstacle barring the door to the future: Abraham had no son. His sole heir was Eliezer, his household slave. Again Yahweh renewed the promise that Abraham would have a great progeny (*Divine Address*, Gen. 15:4–5) and that he (through his family) would inherit the land. This time the promise was sealed with a covenant (Gen. 15:7–21). The covenant ceremony is archaic, indicating the antiquity of the material included in the narrative (see pp. 41–42).

ISAAC   It seemed impossible that the promise could be fulfilled, for Sarah was barren. Faith needed more evidence. Taking matters into her own hands, Sarah urged Abraham to have a child by her Egyptian maid, Hagar—only to regret her action and force the maid out of their home. The suspense is heightened when Hagar, at a well in the wilderness, receives Yahweh's promise that she would bear a son to Abraham and that Ishmael (regarded by Muslims as the ancestor of the Arabs) would grow to be a formidable Bedouin, "a wild ass of a man." But Ishmael, conceived in a moment of weakness of faith, could not be the child of the promise, even though Yahweh was deeply concerned for Hagar and her child (Gen. 16). Later, Yahweh appeared to Abraham at the sanctuary near Hebron (by the sacred oak of Mamre; Gen. 13:18) and announced that a son would be born to him. Sarah, who was eavesdropping on the conversation, laughed out loud, knowing she had passed her childbearing years and not believing that with Yahweh all things are possible (Gen. 18:1–16). The incident of Sarah's laughter is one of many puns in the Old Epic tradition: In Hebrew *titzḥaq* means "she laughs," and *yitzḥaq* is "Isaac." The words of the story play on the ludicrous disproportion between the divine promise and the impossibility of the human situation.

Following this announcement is the story of the destruction of Sodom and Gomorrah (Gen. 18:17–19:38). In the preface to this story we hear again the theme that "Abraham shall become a great and mighty nation, and all the nations of the earth shall bless themselves by him" (*Divine Address*, Gen. 18:17–19). Because Abraham had a special relationship with Yahweh, it was proper to take him into confidence about impending developments. Here we find one of the most powerful passages in Scripture (Gen. 18:22–33): Abraham's expostulation with God about the indiscriminate destruction of righteous people along with the wicked ("Shall not the Judge of all the earth do what is just?").

The birth of Isaac, the son of Abraham's and Sarah's old age, is reported briefly in Genesis 21:1–2. This is followed by the story of Abraham's testing (Gen. 22:1–14), which perhaps once circulated as an independent legend to explain the name of a sacred place and justify the commutation of child sacrifice. Whatever its original meaning, this moving story now adds to the suspense in the history of the promise. We are told that Abraham was commanded by God to sacrifice his only son whom he loved dearly—the child of the promise. Abraham undergoes the supreme trial of faith as he prepares to slay Isaac, thereby sacrificing the future of God's people on the altar. Only when the knife is upraised does God intervene! In that critical moment, Abraham spies a ram caught in a thicket, which he offers in place of Isaac. Once again the promise is renewed (*Divine Address*, Gen. 22:15–18).[20]

The dramatic suspense continues in the story of the selection of a wife for Isaac (Gen. 24). Isaac could not marry a local Canaanite woman, for that would presumably contaminate the line of Abraham and bring the promise to naught. Accordingly, Abraham's servant was sent to the ancestral homeland in Mesopotamia (Haran) with instructions to bring a prospective wife back to the Promised Land. Would Abraham's servant find the right maiden? Would Rebekah decide to come to Isaac's country? The story leaves no doubt that Yahweh guides the mission, despite the servant's worrying and doubt. Nothing happens by chance; Yahweh means it to turn out just as it does.

---

[20]See Søren Kierkegaard's exposition of Abraham's "leap of faith" in *Fear and Trembling* (Garden City, N.Y.: Doubleday, 1954); also Erich Auerbach's discussion of Gen. 22 in *Mimesis: The Representation of Reality in Western Literature*, trans. by William Trask (Garden City, N.Y.: Doubleday, 1957), pp. 5–20.

JACOB   Not much is said about Isaac, who seems little more than a replica of his father (Gen. 26; and the *Divine Address*, verses 2–5.) But the drama is reenacted, this time with the spotlight on Jacob.

Like Sarah, Rebekah was barren and would not have presented Isaac with a son if Yahweh had not intervened. But the result is a new complication that almost abolishes the promise. Rebekah conceived two sons: Esau, the father of the Edomites, and Jacob, the ancestor of Israel. Even in the womb they struggled together, as these nations did in real life. Esau won the first round: He was born first, and therefore had a right to be his father's heir (Gen. 25:21–26). But Jacob shrewdly tricks his twin brother out of his birthright (Gen. 25:27–34) and, with the help of his mother, receives Isaac's final blessing (Gen. 27). To appreciate the point of this story, remember the ancient belief that words spoken in blessing (or curse) were immediately effective—they had the power to produce the intended result.[21] And, like an arrow in flight, they could not be retracted. So Jacob, having received his father's blessing, was destined to gain preeminence over Esau (Edom), as Israel later did, especially in the time of David.

In spite of Jacob's coup, however, everything seemed hopelessly lost. What good was the blessing when, because of Esau's hostility, Jacob had to flee to Haran and become an exile from the land on which the promise was to be fulfilled? Jacob's flight gives the narrators a chance to introduce a once independent cycle of legends dealing with Jacob's adventures in the territory of Laban, the ancestor of Syria (Aram). In the words of one scholar, this cycle functions in the Old Epic tradition "like a bridge supported from within by two pillars."[22] At one end the bridge is anchored to the story of Jacob's dream at Bethel (Gen. 28:10–19), and at the other to the story of his wrestling with an Assailant at the river Jabbok (32:22–32).

In the Bethel story, Yahweh appears to the despairing Jacob in a dream and renews the threefold promise given to Abraham: to give Israel the land; to make Israel a great and numerous people; and, through Israel, to bestow blessings upon all the families of the earth (*Divine Address*, Gen. 28:13–15). Assured that Yahweh was with him and would bring him back to the Promised Land, Jacob journeyed to his kin in Haran. There, through Yahweh's providence—not to mention his own shady dealings—Jacob married Laban's daughters, Leah and Rachel, fathered eleven sons, and acquired two concubines, numerous servants, and the best portion of Laban's flocks (Gen. 29:31). With this wealth he managed to escape from the clutches of his wily Aramean father-in-law and prepared to win over Esau with a lavish display of gifts (Gen. 32:1–21).

At the other end of the bridge formed by the Laban cycle is the story at the river Jabbok (Gen. 32:22–32). At Bethel, Yahweh had appeared to Jacob in a nocturnal dream in the time of his despair. Now Yahweh comes in the form of a nocturnal visitor

---

[21]See the discussion of Balaam's oracles, pp. 109–110, also the Definition of "blessing," pp. 154–155.

[22]The figure of speech comes from Gerhard von Rad's commentary on *Genesis* [305], p. 39. We are following his interpretation at this point.

in the time of Jacob's prosperity, when it seemed he could buy his way into the Promised Land by winning Esau's favor. Jacob wrestled until daybreak with the angel (NRSV: "man"; perhaps a night demon in an earlier form of the story). He finally received a blessing, but went away limping, wounded in the combat. Soon Jacob was reunited with Esau and gained access to the Promised Land (Gen. 33).

JOSEPH   From this point the Old Epic narrative moves quickly to the Joseph cycle (Gen. 37–50). This cycle reflects to some degree the historical conditions of the second millennium, when it was not unheard of for a Semite to rise to power in the Egyptian court (see pp. 43–45). Once having circulated independently, the Joseph story is obviously embellished with various popular motifs. For example, the account of Potiphar's wife attempting to seduce Joseph (Gen. 39:7–20) might have been influenced by the Egyptian "Story of Two Brothers," where the same motif appears.[23] Whatever their source, these motifs are skillfully and artistically blended into a story with a single plot that discloses the hidden realization of God's purpose in human affairs. This view is magnificently expressed in Joseph's magnanimous words to his brothers:

> Even though you intended to do harm to me, God intended it for
> good, in order to preserve a numerous people, as he is doing today.
> —GENESIS 50:20 (NRSV)

This passage encapsulates the theme of the Joseph story: Human affairs are not governed by the evil designs of human beings, or by the economic stresses that forced Jacob to migrate to Egypt, but by the overruling providence of God, who works for good in all things (compare Gen. 45:5–7).

When Old Epic narrators incorporated the Joseph story into the Ancestral History, they linked the theme of God's hidden providence with the theme of the divine promise in its threefold dimension: posterity, land, and blessing. Certain narrative touches suggest this function of the story in its larger epic context: for example, Jacob's recollection of Yahweh's promissory address to him at Luz (Bethel; Gen. 48:3–4), and Joseph's reference, just before his death, to the promise made to the ancestors (Gen. 50:24). Indeed, in its present dramatic context the Joseph story hints that the promise made to Abraham—the promise that through Israel the nations would bless themselves—was moving toward fulfillment. Joseph, elevated to the position of prime minister of Egypt, saves the land from famine and brings security and prosperity to the country.[24]

---

[23]See Pritchard, *Ancient Near Eastern Texts* [1], pp. 23–25. The Egyptian seduction story tells of a man's refusal to lie with the wife of his older brother, the wife's false accusation to her husband, and the husband's attempt to destroy his brother for the alleged deed.

[24]See David J. A. Clines, *The Theme of the Pentateuch* [298], who shows that the three-fold promise to the ancestors is carried to partial fulfillment in the completed Israelite epic, the Pentateuch.

C. THE PEOPLE'S HISTORY

From the Joseph story the Old Epic narrative continues the story of Israel's life through the books of Exodus and Numbers (discussed in Chapters 2–4) toward its goal: Israel's occupation of the Promised Land. This part of the Old Epic narrative portrays the shared history of a people, one that has its setting in the ancient world of the Fertile Crescent. At the outset of the People's History the promise was eclipsed, for the descendants of Abraham and Sarah were reduced to slavery—pawns in Pharaoh's game of power who had no future and no hope. But Yahweh, identified as "the God of Abraham, Isaac, and Jacob," remembered the promise to the ancestors and intervened, assuring Moses at the burning bush that the people would be liberated and brought into a land flowing with milk and honey (Exod. 3:7–8).

The People's History (the Mosaic tradition) combines the crucial events of Exodus and Sinai—the experiences in the wilderness and the circuit via Transjordan toward the land of Canaan—to form a dramatic narrative. Moses' career frames this story, from the opening scene of his birth in Egypt to his death within view of the Promised Land.

The Mosaic Tradition*

The Exodus Story

Oppression in Egypt	Exod. 1:8–22
The rise of Moses	2:1–22
Moses' call and commission	3:1–4:17
Moses' return to Egypt	4:18–31
Encounter with Pharaoh	5:1–6:1
Plagues against Egypt (combined with P)	7:8–11:10
The first Passover	12:21–28
Final plague and departure from Egypt	12:29–39
Route of the flight	13:17–22
Victory at the Sea (combined with P)	14:1–31
Song of the Sea	15:1–18 (19)
Song of Miriam	15:20–21

Beginning of Wilderness Wandering

First stations	15:22–27
Quails and manna (combined with P)	16:1–36
Water from the rock	17:1–7
Victory over the Amalekites	17:8–16
Visit of Moses' father-in-law, Jethro	18:1–27

The Sinai Covenant

Theophany at Sinai	19:1–25
The Decalogue	20:1–17
Theophany	20:18–21
The Covenant Code	20:22–23:33

(cont.)

The Mosaic Tradition* (*cont.*)

The Sinai Covenant

Making of the Covenant	24:1–11
Breaking of the Covenant: Golden Calf	31:18–32:35
Covenant renewal	33:1–34:28
Moses' transfiguration	34:29–35

Sojourn in the Wilderness (Kadesh)

Israel on the march	Num 10:29–36
Murmuring in the wilderness	11:1–35
Miriam's punishment	12:1–16
Reconnaissance (combined with P)	13:1–33
Murmuring (combined with P)	14:1–38
Abortive attack on southern Canaan	14:39–45
Revolts against Moses (combined with P)	16:1–50

Circuit via Transjordan

Departure from Kadesh	20:14–22
Battle of Hormah	21:1–3
The bronze serpent	21:4–9
Itinerary	21:10–20
Victory over Sihon and Og	21:21–35
Balak and Balaam	22:1–40
The Balaam oracles	22:41–24:25
Apostasy in Moab	25:1–5
Allotment of land in Transjordan	32:1–42
Moses' death	Deut. 34:1–6

*Here again no attempt is made to separate Yahwistic (J) and Elohistic (E) variations on the epic narrative, or to distinguish between early and later stages of tradition. Note that in this area the Priestly Writers (P) evince greater interest in particular stories, as shown by the blending together of Old Epic and Priestly narratives. For a more refined analysis, see the appendix to Martin Noth, *Pentateuchal Traditions* [76], pp. 267–71, 273–76.

The ancestral stories are mirrors reflecting the interior struggles of people of faith: perplexity about God's hidden ways, the temptation to trust more in human devices than in God's providence, and the alternation of faith and unbelief. The same is true of the People's History that extends from the book of Exodus to the end of the Pentateuch. This history not only recites the crucial events that formed Israel as a people (Exodus and Sinai), but also portrays the realities of human experience: the breaking of the covenant and its renewal in divine forgiveness; the murmurings in the wilderness; the trials of faith when people are faced with great adversity. Through the ups and downs of these human experiences, however, runs the unshakable conviction that Yahweh's promise does not fail. Yahweh is faithful, not capricious. Yahweh's purpose links events into a meaningful history, even when this is hard for human beings to perceive.

Chronological Chart 2

B.C.E.	Egypt	Palestine (and Syria)	Mesopotamia
1200 *to* *1100*	XX Dynasty (c. 1185–1069) Sea Peoples defeated by Rameses III (c. 1175) Egyptian decline	Period of the Judges (c. 1200–1020) Philistines settle in Canaan Battle of Megiddo (c. 1125)	Collapse of Hittite Empire Assyrian decline
1100 *to* *1000*	XXI Dynasty (c. 1069–935) Egyptian decline	Philistine ascendancy Fall of Shiloh (c. 1050) Samuel and Saul (c. 1020–1000)	Brief Assyrian revival Tiglath-pileser I (c. 1116–1078)

(Iron Age)

Like the Ancestral History, the People's History deals with events we might not usually think of as historical. The story has two important dimensions. On the one hand, it is a "God-story" in the sense that Yahweh is an active participant, whose judgment and grace must be reckoned with in daily affairs and in political events. On the other hand, it is the story of a people invited to take part with Yahweh in history's unfolding drama.

The drama moves to its climax: the inheritance of the Promised Land and Israel's rise to the status of nationhood. In the following chapters we will consider this remarkable conclusion, the transformation of "the people of Yahweh" (Hebrew: *'am Yahweh;* Judg. 5:11b) into a great "nation" (Hebrew: *goy;*[25] Gen. 12:2; Exod. 19:6), with a political lifestyle like the surrounding nations.

[25]In the period before David, Israel was basically regarded as *'am Yahweh* (people of Yahweh), not *goy Yahweh* (nation of Yahweh). See E. A. Speiser, "'People' and 'Nation' of Israel," *Journal of Biblical Literature* 79 (1960), 157–63.

CHAPTER 6

THE STRUGGLE BETWEEN FAITH AND CULTURE

Life within the Israelite confederacy was a continual struggle during the period between the death of Joshua and the rise of the monarchy under Saul. Those were "the days when the judges ruled" (Ruth 1:1), the twelfth and eleventh centuries B.C.E. Having won a foothold on Canaanite soil, Israel faced the problem of adjusting to agricultural ways and taking its place among the nations. The Tribal Confederacy, straining under conflict with forces both without and within, was severely tested.

In part, the struggle was for Israel's physical survival. Although the decisive phase of the occupation took place in the thirteenth century B.C.E., the contest for Canaan went on for many years. The Israelites waged their offensive by means of war, treaty, and the gradual absorption of the Canaanites into the Israelite alliance. On a deeper level, however, an even more important battle was being fought between conflicting religious loyalties. In this ideological struggle, the final victory would go to the side that won the allegiance of the people's hearts.

Biblical Readings: The book of Judges (especially 2:6–16:31) and 1 Samuel 1–12. The theological commentary on the meaning of the settlement in Canaan, found in the book of Deuteronomy, is relevant but will be discussed at length in Chapter 11.

TEMPTATIONS OF CANAANITE CULTURE

Throughout the centuries, conquering nations have themselves been molded by the superior cultures they vanquished. In ancient Mesopotamia the brilliant Sumerian culture was overcome by aggressive Semitic Akkadians who, under the leadership of Sargon, established the first empire in history. The Akkadians were, in turn, profoundly influenced by Sumerian culture. Centuries later, Rome vanquished the Greeks and established the famous Pax Romana, a political order unsurpassed by any other world empire. But Rome itself was heavily dependent on the legacy of Greek culture. During the Israelite occupation of Canaan, the stage was set for a similar development. Archaeological excavation in Palestine has shown that Israelite life was crude in comparison to the highly sophisticated, aristocratic culture of Canaan. Would the victor again be overcome by the vanquished?

In some ways, Israel reacted strongly against the culture of the Fertile Crescent. Echoes of antipathy for this culture are found in Old Epic traditions preserved in Genesis 2–11. The story of the Tower of Babel, in its earliest form, expressed scorn for the proud culture of the Fertile Crescent, symbolized by the famed temple-tower (ziggurat) of Babylon (Gen. 11:1–9). In another Old Epic narrative the first city was built by a murderer, Cain, whose anger erupted when his agricultural offering of the "fruit of the ground" was not as pleasing to Yahweh as his shepherd brother's gift, the firstlings of the flock (Gen. 4:1–17). Noah was the first man to till the soil and plant a vineyard— the characteristic crop of Canaan; but this activity led to a revolting spectacle of drunkenness and nakedness. As a result Canaan, the son of Ham, was burdened with a threefold curse (Gen. 9:18–27). A deep-seated aversion to Canaanite culture persisted in some Israelite circles long after the time of the Confederacy (see Jer. 35).

Negative attitudes toward Canaanite culture, however, went hand in hand with the opposite extreme—the wholesale adoption of Canaanite ways. The temptation was great because, contrary to some exaggerated claims of the book of Joshua, Israelite military victories did not exterminate or even significantly reduce the Canaanite population. Moreover, the Tribal Confederacy was constituted at Shechem in the midst of Canaanite culture, and embraced new converts who previously worshiped the "strange gods" of the pre-Mosaic period. The very diversity of the Israelite confederacy would have made it difficult to avoid lapses from the stern demands of the Mosaic faith.

The sermonic warnings of Moses in the book of Deuteronomy, actually written many years later, appropriately emphasize the dangers and temptations of life in Canaan. Israel's transition from a pastoral lifestyle to the sedentary existence of farmers in the Fertile Crescent had fateful and far-reaching implications. Previously, Yahweh had been the God of the wanderers, but now Israel's relationship was to the soil, which had to be tilled. The problem increasingly came to center around the people's relation to nature: the need for rainfall, the dependence on regular change of the seasons, and the concern with fertility. Yahweh's "strong hand and outstretched arm" had proved effective in history. Could Yahweh triumph now in rivalry with gods who controlled the cycles of nature, upon which farmers depended for their existence?

THE DEUTERONOMISTIC INTERPRETATION

The biblical source for our study of the transitional twelfth and eleventh centuries B.C.E. is the book of Judges, the second book in the *Deuteronomistic History* (Dtr). Not all of the present book of Judges belongs to the Deuteronomistic tradition. The preface (Judg. 1:1–2:5; see pp. 121–122) and the appendix (Judg. 17–21) contain valuable information about the period, but stand outside the framework of the Deuteronomistic material in Judges 2:6–16:31.

The Deuteronomistic "theology of history" is found in capsule form in Judges 2:6–3:6. After recapitulating the conclusion of the book of Joshua (compare Josh. 24:28–31 and Judg. 2:6–9), the narrative describes the new situation after Joshua's death. During Joshua's lifetime the people had remained faithful to Yahweh, for they lived under the creative power of "the saving experience" (Exodus) and "the commanding experience" (Sinai). But "another generation grew up after them, who did not know Yahweh or the work that he had done for Israel" (Judg. 2:10). Faith in Yahweh was not belief in a body of knowledge that could be transferred, like a bank account, from parents to children. To *know* (Hebrew: *yada'*) Yahweh means to acknowledge Yahweh personally, to be in covenant relation with Yahweh. The parents' faith does not necessarily become the faith of their children—each generation must either renew or repudiate the covenant in its own way.

....

DEFINITION: "DEUTERONOMIC,"   "DEUTERONOMISTIC"

In studies of the Old Testament or Hebrew Bible, a subtle distinction is made between the adjectives "Deuteronomic" and "Deuteronomistic." *Deuteronomic* refers specifically to the *torah* ("teaching") found in the heart of the book of Deuteronomy (Deut. 5–28). *Deuteronomistic* refers to the style and point of view that characterizes the so-called "Deuteronomistic History," whose authors were influenced by the (Deuteronomic) *torah*. This historical work, to be discussed further in Chapter 11, extends from Joshua through 2 Kings (the so-called "Former Prophets"). See also the Definition, p. 322

....

The Deuteronomistic history of the "Period of the Judges" follows a neat pattern that illustrates a basic theological conviction: Obedience to Yahweh's *torah* leads to welfare and peace; disobedience leads to hardship and defeat. The Deuteronomistic "history lesson" has the following rhythm of events:

1. The people of Israel did what was evil by forsaking Yahweh, who had brought them out of Egypt, and by serving the gods of the surrounding peoples.
2. Therefore Yahweh's anger was kindled against them, and they were delivered into the power of their enemies, who oppressed them.
3. In their affliction, the people cried out in remorse. So Yahweh, moved to pity, raised up a judge who delivered them from their enemies. Throughout the lifetime of the judge, the land enjoyed rest.
4. When the judge died, the people reverted to idolatry. Therefore Yahweh's anger was kindled against Israel, and Yahweh sold them again into the hands of their plunderers.

This is the pattern outlined in Judges 2:6–3:8. Usually a Deuteronomistic summary along these lines appears at the beginning and end of the stories of the major judges: for example, Othniel (see the account in Judg. 3:7–11), Ehud, Deborah (and Barak), Gideon (also called Jerubbaal), Jephthah, and Samson. The stories of the judges, drawn from ancient tribal traditions, are inserted between the summaries like old pictures into a new frame. When read in the Deuteronomistic editorial framework, the history moves in a rhythmic pattern of rebellion and return.

Though the Deuteronomistic scheme does not do justice to the complexity of events in the period of the Judges, it contains much truth. History teaches that the downfall of a people often begins not with external military pressure, but with internal moral and spiritual degeneration. The Deuteronomistic historians emphasized the central truth that Israel's vitality and solidarity lay in a united, exclusive loyalty to Yahweh. While this covenant faith was strong, Israel was in a better position to cope with the in-rush of foreign ideas and armies. When this ethically demanding faith was weakened under pressure from the surrounding culture, Israel became easy prey to its enemies. Undoubtedly Israel would have been lost in the cultural melting pot of the Fertile Crescent had it not been for the political crises that rallied the Israelites to the standard of the Mosaic faith and renewed their loyalty to the God of the covenant.

To appreciate the nature of Israel's struggle, we must know something about the religion of Canaan, described in the Hebrew Bible as worship of the Baals and Ashtarts (Judg. 2:13; 10:6; 1 Sam. 7:4; 12:10). This religion, intimately connected with the land, was the most divisive and destructive threat Israel faced in the period of the Judges.

....

DEFINITION: "BAAL"   AND   "ASHTART"

The title *Baal* (meaning "lord" or "owner") in Canaanite religion designated a male deity who owned the land and controlled its fertility. His female counterpart was *Baalath* ("lady")—also referred to by the personal name, Ashtart. Because these deities were connected with particular localities or towns, one could speak of many Baals and

Ashtarts, as many as the there were towns in the land (Jer. 2:28). But it was also possible to regard these local powers as manifestations of the great "Lord" and "Lady" who dwelt in the heavens, in which case worshipers could address Baal and Ashtart in the singular as cosmic deities.

The myths and rituals of the Canaanite Baal religion existed in varying forms throughout the Fertile Crescent. In Babylonia, for example, the Tammuz cult dramatized the relations between the god Tammuz and the goddess Ishtar (the equivalent of the Canaanite goddess Ashtart). In Egypt the Isis cult was based on worship of the god Osiris (Horus) and his female counterpart Isis (Hathor). The similarities between these religions encouraged borrowing back and forth, for they shared a common concern about the relation of human beings to their natural and cosmic environment.

RELIGION AND AGRICULTURE

Modern farmers, despite their training in the science of agriculture, can still marvel at the strange powers of fertility that work to bring about a fruitful harvest. At such times they are linked with their agricultural forebears, who from time immemorial marveled

This statuette of the Canaanite deity Baal is made of gold and bronze and stands approximately 7.5 inches tall. The combative pose and outstretched arm suggest that the figure was once equipped with weaponry.

at the mysteries of nature. In the Fertile Crescent, where culture was often dependent on the fruitfulness of the soil, people viewed nature's mystery in a religious way.[1] The land was believed to be the sphere of divine powers: The "Baal" of each region was the lord or "owner" of the land. When the rains came, the mysterious powers of fertility stirred again, and new life was resurrected from the barrenness of winter. This astonishing revival of nature, people believed, was due to sexual intercourse between Baal and his partner, Baalath.

Central to Canaanite religious practice was the belief that the whole natural sphere, to which the existence of the farmer was intimately bound, was governed by sexual vitality—the powers of masculine and feminine. Furthermore, farmers were not mere spectators of the sacred marriage. By ritually enacting the drama of Baal, they sought magically to assist the fertility powers to reach their consummation—thereby insuring the welfare and prosperity of the land. This cooperation with the powers of fertility included a rehearsal of the story of Baal's loves and wars in the temple and, in the view of some scholars, a ritual of sacred prostitution in which human partners acted out the union of Baal and Ashtart.[2] The assumption was that when persons imitated the action of the gods, power was released to bring that action about (like the "rainmaker" who, by pouring water to imitate rain, induces the gods to end a drought).

THE RAS SHAMRA EPIC

We get a clear picture of Canaanite religion from the Ras Shamra tablets, discovered in 1929 at Ras Shamra, site of the ancient Canaanite city of Ugarit on the coast of northern Syria.[3] These texts contain ancient myths dating from the Amarna Age (fourteenth century B.C.E.). Just as the Amarna letters give a picture of political conditions in Canaan before the Israelite occupation (see pp. 113–114), so the Ras Shamra texts provide firsthand information about Canaanite religion. In many respects this was a highly developed, sophisticated religion. At the head of the Canaanite pantheon was the high god, El, "the King, Father of Years," whose consort was the goddess Asherah. Next in rank was the great storm-god, Baal, the god of rain and fertility, who, like his father El, took the form of a bull. His consort-sister was the warrior goddess Anath, known for vi-

---

[1]See Tikva Frymer-Kensky, "Asherah and Abundance," *In the Wake of the Goddesses: Women, Culture, and the Biblical Transformation of Pagan Myth* (New York: The Free Press, 1992), pp. 153–61.

[2]Some scholars question whether sacred prostitution actually existed. See M. Hooks, "Sacred Prostitution in Israel and the Ancient Near East," Ph.D. dissertation, Hebrew Union College, 1985; and Phyllis Bird, " 'To Play the Harlot': An Inquiry into an Old Testament Metaphor," in *Gender and Difference* [341], pp. 75–94. Though not confirmed in the Canaanite literature itself, this practice is suggested in the Hebrew Bible (Deut. 23:17–18).

[3]See Pritchard, *Ancient Near Eastern Texts* [1], pp. 129–55. Good introductions to the Ras Shamra literature are: T. C. Craigie, *Ugarit and the Old Testament* (Grand Rapids, Michigan: Eerdmans, 1983); A. Curtis, *Ugarit (Ras Shamra)* (Grand Rapids, Michigan: Eerdmans, 1985). On Canaanite deities, see Patrick Miller, "Aspects of the Religion of Ugarit," in *Ancient Israelite Religion* [121], pp. 53–66.

The Mother-Goddess known as "the queen of wild beasts." This ivory representation (from the fourteenth century B.C.E.) was found in a tomb near Ras Shamra. Two goats stand on their hind legs, apparently reaching for the stalks of grain she has in her hands.

olent passion and brutality. In one text she rejoices at the destruction of people from "the rising of the sun" to "the shore of the sea":

> Beneath her were heads like balls,
>   Above her were hands like locusts.
> She plunged her knees into the blood of warriors,
>   Her thighs into the blood of youths.[4]

---

[4]Quoted from W. F. Albright, *Yahweh and the Gods of Canaan* (Garden City, N.Y.: Doubleday Anchor Books, 1969), pp. 130ff.

The original sequence of these Baal epic fragments is difficult to determine, but the drama apparently opens with an account of the god's victory over the primordial water dragon, known as "Prince Sea" and "Judge River." Next come Baal's preparations to build a temple with the assistance of his sister, Anath. Evidently these plans are interrupted by Mot ("Death"), the god of summer drought, who kills Baal and carries him down to the underworld. When the gods hear that "the lord of the earth" has perished, they mourn deeply; but Anath is seized by a great passion for Baal and searches for him:

> Like the longing [heart] of a wild cow for her calf,
> Like the longing of a wild ewe for her lamb,
>   So was the longing of Anath for Baal.[5]

When at last she finds him in Mot's possession, a furious struggle ensues. Anath kills Mot, Baal is resurrected and put on his throne, and the lovers are reunited. Anath emerges as heroine of the epic, and there is great rejoicing in heaven:

> In a dream, O Kindly One, God of Mercy [?],
> In a vision, Creator of Creatures,
> The heavens rained oil,
> The dry valleys flowed with honey;
>
> So I know
> That Triumphant Baal lives,
> That the Prince, Lord of Earth, is alive![6]

These lines show the connection between the myth of Baal's death and resurrection and the conflict waged in nature as seasons change. Baal personifies the fertilizing powers of springtime; Mot personifies the destructive powers that bring death to vegetation and life. In the ancient view, the farmer's life was caught up in these rhythms of nature—springtime and summer, fertility and drought, life and death. Existence was precariously dependent on the powers of nature, but religion provided a way to control these powers and thereby to insure the fruitfulness of the soil. By reenacting the mythological drama of Baal's death and resurrection in the temple, people sought to release a magical power that guaranteed fertility and well-being.

ATTEMPTS AT COMPROMISE

Here, then, was a practical religion for farmers. In Canaanite religion, one could in effect ensure a plentiful harvest by worshiping the fertility god, Baal—recognized as lord of the earth, owner of the land, giver of rain, source of grain, wine, and oil. To ignore

---

[5]W. F. Albright, *op. cit.*, p. 132.
[6]Translated by W. F. Albright, *Interpreter's Bible*, I [23], p. 261.

the Baal rites in those days would have seemed impractical and even reckless, as if a farmer today were to ignore current agricultural science in the cultivation of the land.

Keep in mind that the Baal religion was also part and parcel of the city-state system of Canaan that, under Egyptian hegemony, maintained order and security in the land. In a sociological sense, Baalism functioned to legitimize the existing social structure, with its power centers in Canaanite cities, and to pacify farmers in the countryside who lived close to the soil and who had to pay taxes to the city-state kings.[7]

Given these conditions, it is not surprising that many Israelites turned to the gods of the land. These people probably did not intend to turn away from Yahweh, the God of the Exodus and the Sinai covenant. Rather, they meant to serve Yahweh and Baal side by side, or to identify Yahweh with Baal, like people for whom "God" symbolizes the values of civil religion. The two religions were not seen as contradictory or mutually exclusive; indeed, there must have been a strong tendency for the two faiths to coalesce in popular worship. Archaeological excavation, for example, has revealed that in the outlying regions of Israel people kept figurines (small statuettes) of the goddess of fertility, Ashtart, indicating that elements of Canaanite ritual and mythology were incorporated into the worship of Yahweh. We know that the Israelites rededicated former Canaanite sanctuaries—like Bethel, Shechem, and perhaps Gilgal—to Yahweh, and adopted the Canaanite agricultural calendar for the timing of pilgrimage festivals (Exod. 34:22–23). Moreover, parents began naming their children after Baal, apparently with no thought of abandoning Yahweh. One of the judges, Gideon, was also named *Jerubbaal* ("let Baal contend" or perhaps "may Baal multiply"). Saul and David, both ardent devotees of Yahweh, gave Baal names to their children.[8] As late as the eighth century, as reported by the prophet Hosea, Israelites actually addressed Yahweh as "Baal" and sought from Yahweh the blessings of fertility by celebrating Baal festival days (Hos. 2:13, 16–17).

At the popular level this syncretism (fusion of different religious forms and views) went on to some degree from the time Israel first set foot on Canaanite soil. Unlike other religions that commingled in the Fertile Crescent, however, Israel's faith was based on the novel belief in a *jealous* God who tolerated no rivals. Israel was to have "no other gods before Yahweh" (Exod. 20:3; 34:14). Therefore, to suppose that Yahweh was lord in one sphere (history) and Baal in another (fertilization of the soil) was a fundamental violation of the meaning of the covenant. Later Israelite prophets saw clearly the basic conflict between the two faiths and threw down the challenge: either Yahweh or

---

[7]The sociological dimension of the struggle between Yahweh and Baal was stressed by George E. Mendenhall, "The Hebrew Conquest of Palestine" [276], also *The Tenth Generation* [188], pp. 174–97. This subject has been treated in depth by Norman Gottwald, *The Tribes of Yahweh* [271]; see especially Part IX.

[8]Two of Saul's children were called Mephi*baal* (Mephibosheth) and Ish*baal*. Jonathan had a son named Meri*baal* (Meribosheth). The Hebrew *bosheth* ("shame") was later substituted by an editor horrified at the presence of "baal" in the names. See 2 Sam. 4:4; 9:6; 21:8; 1 Chron. 8:34. One of David's daughters was named Beeliada (1 Chron. 14:7).

Insert 5-1 Rameses II was Pharaoh of the Exodus. This colossal granite statue shows him wearing the distinctive royal helmet and holding the symbolic scepter.

Insert 6-1 Rameses II's rock temple at Abu Simbel as seen shortly before being cut into huge blocks and reassembled on higher ground above the lake formed by the dam south of Aswan.

Insert 6-1a (Above) Two of the four colossi of the pharaoh which guard the entrance.
Insert 6-1b (Below) A view from the smaller queen's temple toward the king's temple, which—from entrance pylon to the innermost holy of holies—was hewn from solid rock.

Baal. Joshua's appeal at Shechem resounded from generation to generation: "Choose this day whom you will serve!" (Josh. 24:15) There could be no compromise, for Yahweh claimed sovereignty over the whole of life and demanded devotion of the whole heart.

NATURE AND HISTORY

H. Wheeler Robinson observed that "only as a religion has to meet the challenge of its opposite does it discover its own nature and potential strength."[9] Despite popular attempts to blend Canaanite religion and the Mosaic faith, the two were like oil and water. With their radically different understanding of the relation of human beings to the deity, these religions found expression in diametrically different world outlooks.[10]

In the Canaanite view, divine power was disclosed in the sphere of nature— specifically in the mystery of fertility. Sexual relations between a god and goddess ensured the recurring cycle of the seasons, represented mythologically by the annual death and resurrection of Baal. Since the cycle of fertility did not take place by itself through natural law, worshipers sought magically to control the gods and thereby to preserve and enhance the fertility upon which people depended for their existence. Thus Canaanite religion sought to control the gods in the interest of human well-being. With its emphasis on maintaining the harmony and rhythm of the natural order, it was a serviceable tool for the aristocracy who wished to maintain the social *status quo* against disruptive changes (see Insert 7–1). Baalism catered to the natural desire for security in the precarious environment of the Fertile Crescent.

In Israel's faith, on the other hand, divine power was disclosed in nonrecurring *historical* events. These events, primarily the Exodus, were perceived as signs of God's liberation of the people from bondage and God's creation of a covenant community. The revelatory power of these events, as interpreted by prophets like Moses, was sensed by other clans and tribes that had not participated originally in the crucial historical experiences. This "symbolization of historical events," as one scholar observes, "was possible because each group which entered the covenant community could and did see the analogy between bondage and Exodus and their own experience."[11] This analogy was sensed repeatedly in the Period of the Judges, when the Israelites suffered new forms of oppression (see Judg. 6:9).

---

[9]H. Wheeler Robinson, in *A Companion to the Bible*, ed. W. Manson (Edinburgh: T. & T. Clark, 1939), p. 293.
[10]An excellent analysis of ancient religion is found in the writings of Mircea Eliade, especially *Cosmos and History* [138] and *The Sacred and the Profane* [139]. He observes: "The chief difference between the man of the archaic and traditional societies and the man of the modern societies with their strong imprint of Judaeo-Christianity lies in the fact that the former feels himself indissolubly connected with the Cosmos and the cosmic rhythms, whereas the latter insists that he is connected only with History." (*Cosmos and History*, p. vii.)
[11]George E. Mendenhall, "The Hebrew Conquest of Palestine" [276], p. 74.

Nude female figurines bespeak ancient Israel's concern for fertility, successful pregnancy and delivery, and lactation. The armless "Venus of Jerusalem," a well-endowed female figurine from the First Temple period, was found during excavation of an ancient, wealthy district in Jerusalem. Her arms have been restored (note their smoother texture). The figurine with the head missing was found at Beth-shan, in a level dating to the fourteenth century B.C.E. The one with the high headress was found at Megiddo, in a level which dates to the general period 2000–1200 B.C.E.

Israel's identity as a people was tied up with loyalty to Yahweh, as the unique and sole deity. Unlike Baal, Yahweh had no consort, no female counterpart.[12] Moreover, the ethical demands of the covenant precluded worshiping Yahweh in sexual rites (see the Golden Calf episode, Exod. 32) or in religious rituals that attempted to guarantee fertility of soil and womb. As the holy God transcending the human world, Yahweh was beyond sexuality. To be sure, Yahweh was spoken of using masculine terms—a convention that reflects the limitations of grammar as well as the patriarchal structure of ancient society. But we should not overlook the fact that Israel's God-language included feminine, as well as masculine, dimensions.[13] Above all, Yahweh was not a dying-rising

[12]The Hebrew language, in fact, has no special word for "goddess." In the fifth century a Jewish colony in Elephantine, Egypt, did apparently believe that Yahweh had a partner, Anath (see p. 384).

[13]See especially Phyllis Trible, "God," in *Supplement to the Interpreter's Dictionary of the Bible* [32], and *God and the Rhetoric of Sexuality* [167].

god, like Baal, but "the Living God" whose vitality was disclosed in the social arena where human lives touch one another, where injustices oppress and yearnings for deliverance are felt, where people are called to make decisions that alter the course of the future.

Over time the encounter with Baal religion enriched Israel's faith (especially in the prophecy of Hosea; see Chapter 9).[14] Israel's more discerning leaders, however, sensed the fundamental opposition between the stern demands of Yahweh and the erotic Baal religion. In Canaanite religion Israel's faith met the challenge of its opposite, but it took many generations for the strength and uniqueness of Yahwism to be realized.[15]

The first phase of the conflict between Yahweh and Baal was waged during the period of the Judges, when Israel responded to its new environment by turning to the Baal cult for agricultural success. The concern with the problem of fertility, however, did not permit Israel to forget the demands of history, for its existence was threatened by enemies on all sides. The Deuteronomistic History demonstrates that in times of crisis the people turned with renewed zeal to the worship of Yahweh, the God of the covenant. We will briefly summarize the history of Israel during this period (see the Chronological Chart 2, p. 116).

LEADERS IN CRISIS

Israel's invasion of Canaan and expansion in the hill country were made possible by the lack of political interference by any strong power (see pp. 116–118). There is no reference to Egyptian intervention in the book of Judges. After the death of Pharaoh Merneptah in about 1211 B.C.E., Egypt lost control of its Asiatic empire and, with the exception of a brief revival under Rameses III (about 1183–1152 B.C.E.), lapsed into confusion and political impotence. The Hittites, forced to a standstill by the Egyptians, disappeared as a world power at the beginning of the twelfth century B.C.E. In Mesopotamia, Assyria was beginning its rise to power (about 1250 B.C.E.) but as yet posed no threat to the Israelites. Israel's political rivals were all in and around Canaan: the new nations in Transjordan, raiders from the Arabian desert; the Canaanite city-states; and the newly arrived Philistines.

Stories in the book of Judges that depict local conflicts and tribal jealousies of that period are derived from very old sources. The Deuteronomistic historians touched up some of the narratives and added introductory and concluding formulas. But for some reason the narrative of Abimelech (Judg. 9) and the accounts of the so-called minor judges (Judg. 10:1–5 and 12:8–15) were not altered at all. Similarly, no Deuterono-

---

[14]This "crisis due to the conquest" is discussed by Gerhard von Rad in *Theology,* I [163], pp. 15–35. He points out that in the course of the struggle between Yahweh and Baal the Israelite faith adopted new forms of expression and "came more than ever before into its own."

[15]See Martin Buber, *The Prophetic Faith* [313], pp. 70–76.

mistic editing is evident in the material in Judges 17–21. When the Deuteronomistic "framework" is removed, these ancient traditions provide us with information about the period that began with the death of Joshua (about 1200 B.C.E.).

Taken by themselves, the stories illustrate how loosely organized the Israelite tribes were. The present book of Judges relates how twelve judges, in successive reigns amounting to 410 years, held sway over all Israel. This is an oversimplification. Actually tribal leaders arose from time to time in certain trouble spots, in order to relieve the pressure on a specific area (for example, Ehud was a member of the tribe of Benjamin). Sometimes these leaders were able to appeal to other tribes for support, but by and large their leadership was local in character and confined to emergency situations.

Nevertheless, a sense of Israelite solidarity transcended the boundaries of any particular tribe. The Tribal Confederacy (see pp. 128-132) provided a common basis of worship and mutual support: Not only did the tribes gather at the common confederate sanctuary of Shiloh for annual religious festivals (Judg. 21:19; also 1 Sam. 1:3; 2:19),[16] but also in times of emergency they were summoned to concerted action in the name of the God of the covenant. A vivid example is the story of the Gibeah outrage (Judg. 19–21). This disturbing "text of terror" relates how a Levite, incensed at the rape-murder of his concubine by some Benjaminites, cut up her corpse into twelve pieces and sent the parts throughout "all the territory of Israel."[17] The act of dividing the body into twelve parts (compare 1 Sam. 11:7) symbolized the ideal twelve-part structure of the Israelite confederacy. The tribal response was quick and decisive, indicating that the tribes were bound together by a common sense of justice even when the offender was a member of one of their own tribes:

> Thus shall you say to all the Israelites, "Has such a thing ever
> happened since the day that the Israelites came up from the land of Egypt
> until this day? Consider it, take counsel, and speak out."
> —Judges 19:30 (NRSV)

The men of Israel gathered together in the "assembly of the people of God" and resolved to take punitive action, "united as one person."

The Role of the Judge

What was the role of Israel's judges in the Tribal Confederacy? Though translated as "judge" (implying a person who presides in a court of law), the Hebrew word *shofeṭ* is actually closer in meaning to "ruler." For example:

[16]After the central sanctuary was moved from Shechem, Bethel was apparently the confederate center for a time (Judg. 20:26–27). Later Shiloh was selected.

[17]See Phyllis Trible's powerful treatment of this story in *Texts of Terror* [167], chap. 3.

Yahweh is our judge [*shofet*], Yahweh is our ruler,
Yahweh is our king; he will save us.

—ISAIAH 33:22

Hence the statement that so-and-so "judged Israel" has a broad meaning. In the period following Joshua's death, a *judge* was primarily a military champion or "deliverer" (Judg. 2:16). Judges also arbitrated internal disagreements, as did Deborah (Judg. 4:4–5) and the last judge, Samuel (1 Sam. 7:15–17). The authority of a judge could extend beyond the locale of a particular tribe and be recognized throughout the territory of the Tribal Confederacy. It is possible that a judge presided as "covenant mediator" when the tribes convened at the central sanctuary for covenant-renewal festivals.[18]

Unlike the dynastic office of king, which passed from father to son, the office of judge was nonhereditary. Judges were qualified to head the Tribal Confederacy by virtue of the divine *charisma*, or spiritual power, that possessed them. For this reason they have been called "charismatic leaders." We are told, for example, that "the spirit of Yahweh took possession of Gideon" or literally "clothed itself with Gideon," empowering him with an authority recognized not only in his own clan but also in surrounding tribes (Judg. 6:34–35). The legendary Samson story tells how "the spirit of Yahweh came upon him mightily," empowering Samson to tear apart a lion barehanded (Judg. 14:6). Deborah charismatically summoned the tribes of Israel to military action against the Canaanites in the name of Yahweh (Judg. 4–5). Charismatic success in battle or extraordinary physical prowess presumably encouraged members of the various tribes to consult the judge in cases of legal dispute. In this way, Israel's covenant law (see pp. 134–136) was applied and expanded in specific cases.

Contrary to the impression created by the Deuteronomistic historians, the judges did not follow one another in chronological succession. This makes it difficult to outline the sequence of events between Joshua's death and the time of Saul, Israel's first king. Nevertheless, the stories give vivid vignettes of conditions and crises within the Israelite Confederacy during the twelfth and eleventh centuries B.C.E.

THE BATTLE OF MEGIDDO

The Israelites had managed to entrench themselves in the central hill country, but could not dispossess the Canaanites on the plains. The most strategic area under Canaanite control was the Valley of Jezreel, through which the main commercial route ran from Egypt to Mesopotamia. Guarding the pass into the valley was the Canaanite fortress of Megiddo, the scene of many decisive battles. The symbolic importance of this site is

---

[18]Suggested by Martin Noth in "Das Amt des 'Richters Israels,'" *Festschrift A. Bertholet* (Tübingen: J. C. B. Mohr, 1950), pp. 404–17. Noth maintains that the so-called "minor judges" in Judges 10:1–5 and 12:7–15 were actually legal administrators selected by the Tribal Confederacy. But this theory presupposes the dubious view that the book of Judges tells about two different kinds of leaders, whereas the tradition indicates that the two functions, legal and military, were combined in one person.

reflected in the book of Revelation (Rev. 16:16) in the New Testament, where the scene of the final battle is set at *Ar-mageddon* (literally "hill of Megiddo").

While the Canaanites controlled the Megiddo pass they could throttle Israel's economic life. This was the situation, we are told, in the days of the judge Shamgar (see Judges 3:31):

> In the days of Shamgar son of Anath,
> > in the days of Jael, caravans ceased
> > and travelers kept to the byways.
> > —JUDGES 5:6 (NRSV)

Spurred into action by Deborah and under the command of Barak, the Israelite forces met General Sisera's Canaanite army in the vicinity of the fortified city of Taanach (Judg. 5:19), which provides a commanding view of Megiddo and the whole plain of Jezreel. Apparently only half the tribes of the Israelite confederacy responded to Deborah's summons, but victory was theirs that day—thanks in part to a terrific rainstorm that caused the river Kishon to overflow its banks, leaving the Canaanite charioteers helplessly trapped in clay.

The book of Judges gives two accounts of this battle: a poetic version, the "Song of Deborah" (Judg. 5), and a somewhat different prose version (Judg. 4). The "Song of Deborah," one of the oldest passages of poetry in the Hebrew Bible, was probably written by someone very close to the event, perhaps by a participant. Though archaeological research is inconclusive, the poem seems to reflect events that occurred in the latter part of the twelfth century B.C.E. and, in the view of one scholar, has striking affinities with the Canaanite style of the Ras Shamra literature.[19]

Even in translation, the poem vividly communicates the meaning and spirit of the battle at Megiddo. The reader senses the quickened pulse of those summoned to participate in the historic crisis, the "galloping rhythm" that propels events toward the climax of victory, and the fierce zeal of Jael, the tent-dwelling woman who slays Sisera (Judg. 5:24–27). In contrast is the pathos of Sisera's mother, gazing anxiously through the lattice for a son who will never return (Judg. 5:28–30). More than the later prose account, the "Song of Deborah" conveys a sense of history as it was lived.

To the author of the poem, the storm that defeated the Canaanites is a sign of Yahweh's active presence as leader and champion of the people. With passionate faith the poet declares that no array of human forces can stand against Yahweh, the Divine Warrior, who comes to Israel's aid in the fury of a thunderstorm. Even the stars, conceived as Yahweh's heavenly army (host), join in the battle:

> The stars fought from heaven,
> from their courses they fought against Sisera.
> > —JUDGES 5:20 (NRSV)

---

[19]See W. F. Albright, "The Song of Deborah in the Light of Archaeology," *Bulletin of the American School of Oriental Research*, LXII (1936), 26–31.

The song begins and ends with an exclamation of praise. In the poet's experience, it was Yahweh's participation in the battle that made the event historic and momentous.

Deborah's song underscores the chief conviction of Mosaic faith: Yahweh is the "God of Israel" (verses 3, 5) and Israel is "the people of Yahweh" (verses 11, 13). Although there is no specific reference to the covenant, the entire poem is based on the close relationship between God and people. Yahweh is praised as the people's Leader, who comes in an earthshaking storm from Sinai through the region of Edom southeast of the Dead Sea (verses 4–5). The people are exhorted to rehearse the "triumphs" (literally, "righteous deeds") of Yahweh (verse 11)—the mighty acts by which the divine *Shofeṭ* ("Champion of Justice") defends the oppressed. Yahweh is pictured as going forth at the head of the people, with the result that the tribes are summoned to "holy war."[20]

Those tribes who failed to answer the summons, who "did not come to the help of Yahweh . . . against the mighty" (verse 23), are strongly censured for not acting as "the people of Yahweh." Thus the basis of the Israelite community was not just political expedience or family ties, but voluntary dedication to Yahweh, the exclusive Suzerain of the Tribal Confederacy. To the true Israel belong only those clans or tribes who are "friends" of Yahweh (Hebrew: "those who love" Yahweh); they receive a concluding benediction (verse 31). The "Song of Deborah" is clear witness to the historical vigor of Israel's faith.

FOES FROM OTHER DIRECTIONS

The decisive victory over Sisera's army marked the end of united Canaanite resistance to the Israelites, but soon threats arose from other directions. Newly established kingdoms in Transjordan looked jealously toward Israel's holdings in Transjordan and Canaan. Under the leadership of King Eglon, Moabites invaded Israelite territory and took Jericho, "the city of palms." The tide was turned when Ehud delivered "a message from God" to Eglon with a dagger (Judg. 3:12–30). Later the Ammonites attacked Israel both in Transjordan and the Canaanite hill country. This threat was met effectively by Jephthah (Judg. 10:6–12:7)—though at terrible personal cost. The story of Jephthah's sacrifice of his daughter (Judg. 11:29–40) to fulfil a voluntary religious vow is one of the most tragic texts of Scripture.[21]

An even more serious threat was a series of devastating attacks by Midianite raiders who came from the Arabian desert on camels. The use of the camel was new in military tactics: Wild tribesmen of Arabia had learned how to use fleets of camels for traveling long distances to make surprise attacks on settled villages. So effective were the

---

[20]See Definition, p. 128. For further discussion of "holy war," see especially Gerhard von Rad, *Holy War in Ancient Israel*, translated by E. W. Conrad and M. Lattke (Sheffield: JSOT Press, forthcoming) and the introduction by E. W. Conrad; also R. de Vaux, *Ancient Israel* [111], pp. 258–67.

[21]See Phyllis Trible, *Texts of Terror* [167], chap. 4.

raids of these camel-riding nomads that the Israelites had to leave their villages and take to mountain caves:

> For they [the Midianites] and their livestock would come up, and they would even bring their tents, as thick as locusts; neither they nor their camels could be counted; so they wasted the land as they came in.
> —JUDGES 6:5 (NRSV)

In the face of these raids the Israelites could not carry on farming, and were in danger of losing everything they had gained in Canaan. The day was saved under the military leadership of a judge named Gideon, otherwise known as Jerubbaal (Judg. 6–8). Gideon's charismatic zeal for Yahweh was directed against anyone, even members of his own family, who had turned to Baal. Though Gideon's father, Joash, had a Yahweh name (*Yah* [Yo]), he erected a Baal altar with a fertility tree (Asherah) beside it. Gideon destroyed the Baal cult objects and built an altar to Yahweh, much to the displeasure of the citizens of Ophrah (Judg. 6:25–32). This important story shows how deeply the Canaanite religion had infiltrated farmers' lives, and how Israel's strength in times of crisis was connected with a revival of vigorous faith in Yahweh, the God of the covenant. To Gideon's surprise, Yahweh permits a task force of only 300 warriors for the huge offensive against the Midianites. This underscores the point of the narrative: that victory belongs to Yahweh *alone*.[22]

The pressure on Israel was increased throughout the twelfth and eleventh centuries B.C.E. by newcomers known as Philistines, one of a number of "Sea Peoples" who poured out of the Aegean onto the eastern shores of the Mediterranean (see pp. 116–117). Shortly after 1200 B.C.E., the Philistines swarmed into Canaan by sea and by land, establishing a beachhead on the coastal plain (see Insert 9–1). Their natural aggressiveness was augmented by their skill in making instruments and weapons of iron, a trade in which they achieved a virtual monopoly. From their restricted base on the coast, the Philistines moved inland, sweeping away Canaanite resistance and coming into contact with the already entrenched and victorious Israelites.[23] Indeed, the Philistines almost succeeded in making Canaan a Philistine empire, as the name "Palestine" suggests (see Definition, p. 182).

Early in the book of Judges is a brief account of the exploits of Shamgar, who slew six hundred Philistines with an oxgoad (Judg. 3:31). This must have occurred fairly early in the Philistine occupation, for Shamgar is referred to in the "Song of Deborah" (Judg. 5:6). Elsewhere we hear of the Philistines only in passing, until we come to the

---

[22]Compare the biblical story with Paddy Chayefsky's modern interpretation: *Gideon, A New Play* (New York: Random House, 1962).

[23]See Trude Dothan, "What We Know About the Philistines," *Biblical Archaeology Review* 8:4 (July/Aug 1982), 20–44; also Bryant G. Wood, "The Philistines Enter Canaan," *Biblical Archaeology Review* 17:6 (Nov/Dec 1991), 44–52, 89–92.

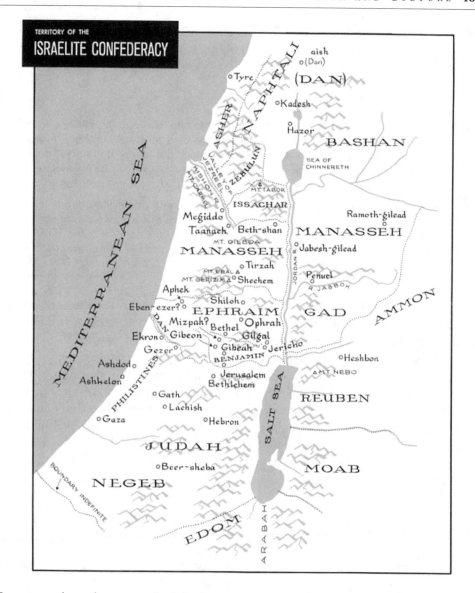

Samson cycle at the very end of the Deuteronomistic edition of Judges (Judg. 13–16). The legendary Samson stories have as their theme the discomfiture of the Philistines by an Israelite strongman whose fatal weakness was women. Though Samson is regarded as a judge, he is not a military leader like the other judges described in the book of Judges: His individual exploits seem designed more to tickle the fancy than to record history.[24]

---

[24]For a sensitive study of the Samson story see James L. Crenshaw, *Samson* [92]; also J. Cheryl Exum, "Literary Patterns in the Samson Saga: An Investigation of Rhetorical Style in Biblical Prose," Ph.D. dissertation, Yale University, 1976.

Viewed theologically, the story of Samson's tragic demise portrays what happens when a person filled with *charisma* disregards Yahweh's guidance to pursue personal whim in a time of crisis.

DEFINITION: "PALESTINE" AND "CANAAN"

A great irony of history is that "Palestine," the name later given to Israel's promised land, derives from the name of Israel's archenemies, the Philistines. In the fifth century B.C.E. the Greek historian Herodotus, sometimes called "the father of history," designated the country south of Phoenicia as "Philistine Syria" (I, 105; II, 104). The Greek term *Palaistina* subsequently came into English through the Latin *Palestina*.

The older name "Canaan," found in the Amarna Letters and other documents going back to at least the fifteenth century B.C.E., might be Hurrian in origin. According to one theory, the name meant "red-purple," a dye produced on the eastern coast of the Mediterranean. The Greek name for Phoenicia, *Phoinike*, also seems to refer to this crimson color (Greek: *phoinix*).

The Samson tales provide a valuable picture of relations between the Israelites and Philistines, probably at the beginning of the eleventh century B.C.E. As the Philistines consolidated their position on the coast, their increasing strength worried the Israelites, who responded in part by spinning yarns that poked fun at their uncircumcised neighbors. There were no pitched battles, however, and no expressions of despair over Philistine ascendancy. The stories probably reflect border incidents that were not sufficiently grievous to disrupt commercial relations between the two peoples. This situation was to change, for by the end of the eleventh century B.C.E. the Philistines controlled all the arteries leading into the Israelite hill country. As things turned out, this was the first stage in an all-out Philistine offensive that sought to destroy, once and for all, the Israelite Confederacy.

THE DECLINE OF THE CONFEDERACY

As political pressure mounted on the Israelites, it became increasingly apparent that the Tribal Confederacy was an ineffective organization for coping with the troubled situation in Canaan. As in the case of the battle of Megiddo, not all tribes responded to the judges' charismatic summons to holy war. The Israelite tribes were not bound together by a centralized government, but by a common devotion to Yahweh, the God of the covenant, and by common religious and legal responsibilities. Thus by its very nature the Tribal Confederacy encouraged a high degree of tribal independence. Yahweh alone ruled the Israelite tribes. The divine rule (theocracy) was manifested through charismatic judges and through priests who attended the central sanctuary, like Eli at the shrine of Shiloh (1 Sam. 1–4). Only when religious festivals were held at the confeder-

Prisoners of Rameses III are shown bound and tied together by a rope around the neck in this relief carved on the wall of a temple at Medinet Habu, near Thebes (Luxor). The structure was erected to celebrate Rameses' victory in repelling the Sea Peoples, one of whom was the Philistines. The figure wearing the feathered helmet (fourth from the left) is one of the Sea Peoples, perhaps a Philistine. The others are Libyan (with pointed beard and side-lock), Syrian (wearing a kilt), Hittite (beardless and wearing a long garment), and on the far right another unfortunate captive from Syria.

ate shrine, or in dire emergencies such as the Gibeah outrage, did the tribes come together "as one person."

This form of organization, at least for a time, spared Israel from the political despotism of the Near East. In times of political crisis, moreover, it threw the people back upon Yahweh, God of the covenant, with a consequent renewal of Israel's distinctive historical faith. For all its merit, however, the Tribal Confederacy was vulnerable to the political forces of the time, as the Philistine menace made clear.

THE SHECHEM EXPERIMENT

The first abortive effort to establish a centralized government was carried out at Shechem, the very place where the Tribal Confederacy had been established in the time of Joshua. The name Abimelech is connected with this attempt, though some precedent had been established in Ophrah, a city located in the hill country north of Jerusalem. This earlier incident involved Abimelech's father, Gideon, whose charismatic leadership had proved effective against the nomadic Midianite raids that devastated Israelite farmers. Because of Gideon's success, and doubtless also because of the increasing Philistine menace, the Israelites offered to crown him king. "Rule over us," they said, "you and your son and your grandson also" (Judg. 8:22). This would have instituted a change from nonhereditary, charismatic judgeship to a hereditary monarchy modeled after the kingdoms of Transjordan, notably Moab and Ammon.[25] But Gideon replied: "I will not rule over you, and my son will not rule over you; Yahweh will rule over you" (Judg. 8:23). His answer was consistent with the foundations of the Israelite theocracy: Yahweh alone was Israel's King, and it was presumptuous for any person to usurp the divine throne.

Gideon had a concubine in the city of Shechem who bore him a son named Abimelech, whose career is recounted in Judges 9. After Gideon's death, Abimelech went to his mother's kinsfolk in Shechem. Pointing out that he was a relative of the Shechemites, he persuaded them that he was entitled to rule over them as king. With money furnished him from the treasury of the temple of Baal-berith ("Lord of the Covenant"), he hired ruffians as his followers and forthwith set out to murder all seventy of his brothers in his father's house at Ophrah. Only the youngest brother, Jotham, escaped. With these rivals out of the way, Abimelech was crowned king at Shechem, possibly near a sacred pillar that still stands in the ruins of the acropolis known as Beth-millo (Judg. 9:6).

This incident did not go without rebuke. Standing on Mount Gerizim overlooking Shechem, Jotham told the famous fable of the trees: Seeking a king to rule over them, the trees asked the olive, the fig, and the vine in turn, finally settling for the bramble, which still grows abundantly in the area (Judg. 9:7–15). The implication was that Abimelech's rule, like the flammable bramble, would be a tinderbox for the fires of revolution. Jotham's pointed attack on Abimelech's kingship expressed the conservative attitude toward monarchy that prevailed in the Israelite Confederacy. It is no surprise that Abimelech's bid for the kingship relied on the financial support of the Baal-berith priests, who would have advocated a Canaanite form of government.

For three years (Judg. 9:22) Abimelech imposed his rule over a considerable territory, with Shechem as the chief city of his kingdom. True to Jotham's prediction, however, revolution broke out in Shechem. Abimelech successfully ambushed the rebels and destroyed the city (Judg. 9:45), probably about 1100 B.C.E. The revolution apparently spread into other parts of his kingdom, however, for he died attacking a fortified tower in the city of Thebez, on the road from Shechem to Beth-shan. According to the tradition, a woman of the town tossed a millstone from atop a tower onto Abimilech's head, crushing his skull and thereby ignominiously ending his rule (Judg. 9:53–54). The Shechem experiment had failed, but it was a fateful harbinger of things to come. The days of the Tribal Confederacy were limited. A stronger form of government was needed.

---

[25]According to the list in Gen. 36:31–39, the kingship of Edom was dynastic. Apparently the petty kings of the Canaanite city states did not establish a hereditary line.

THE FALL OF SHILOH

Israel's last judge was Samuel, whose farewell address to Israel (1 Sam. 12) concludes the Deuteronomistic survey of the period of the Judges. We turn now from the book of Judges to the first twelve chapters of 1 Samuel, referring only to those sections that bear on the collapse of the Tribal Confederacy during the period of Philistine aggression.

1 Samuel 1–3 deals with events at Shiloh, the central sanctuary of the Confederacy to which Israelites customarily made a pilgrimage each year (1 Sam. 1:3, 7, 21) to offer sacrifices to Yahweh. There the High Priest Eli and the boy Samuel were "ministering to Yahweh." In this troubled period there was apparently some hope that the tribes would unite around the priestly rule of Eli and his sons, custodians of the Ark and the sacred oracle. The hereditary rule of priests ("hierocracy") at the confederate sanctuary offered an alternative to monarchy.

A following section (1 Sam. 4:1–7:2) deals with the fortunes of the Ark of the Covenant, which was kept at Shiloh. The Philistines and the Israelites were at war, and the battle was going against Israel. After a serious reversal, Israel's elders suggested that the Ark be brought to the battlefield, as had often been done in the past (see the "Song of the Ark," Num. 10:35–36), so that Yahweh "may come among us and save us from the power of our enemies" (1 Sam. 4:3). When the Ark arrived in the Israelite camp, accompanied by Eli's two sons, its presence caused the raising of a mighty shout "so that the earth resounded." Nevertheless, the panic-stricken Philistines decisively defeated Israel and took the Ark into Philistine territory as a trophy of war.

From this point 1 Samuel contains no other reference to the Israelite sanctuary at Shiloh. Why this strange silence? A passage in Psalm 78 relates how Yahweh forsook "the tent" at Shiloh and delivered "his glory" (the Ark) into captivity (Ps. 78:60–64). Toward the end of the monarchy, when people of the Southern Kingdom put great confidence in the Temple of Jerusalem, Jeremiah reminded them of what happened at Shiloh (Jer. 7:12–14; also 26:6, 9):

> Just go to my shrine that was in Shiloh, where I [Yahweh] once caused
> my name to dwell, and see what I did to it on account of the wickedness of
> my people Israel.
>
> —JEREMIAH 7:12

Archaeological evidence suggests that Shiloh was destroyed in a great catastrophe, probably by the Philistines when they invaded the hill country of Palestine.[26] This would have occurred at the battle of Ebenezer, when the Ark was taken into captivity. In any case, Shiloh disappeared from Israel's history.

---

[26]The archaeological evidence is uncertain, but it is likely that there was destruction by the Philistines. See Israel Finkelstein, "Shiloh Yields Some, but Not All, of Its Secrets," *Biblical Archaeology Review* 12:1 (Jan/Feb, 1986), 22–41.

The Philistine victory struck a devastating blow to the very foundation of the Israelite confederacy. The central sanctuary of Shiloh had been burned to the ground, and the Ark of the Covenant, the ancient symbol of Yahweh's protecting and guiding presence in the midst of the people, had been seized by enemies. The shock and despair these events created among devout Israelites is expressed in the stories that cluster around the fate of the Ark. When the High Priest Eli heard the report of the outcome of the battle of Ebenezer, he keeled over, broke his neck, and died. His daughter-in-law, who gave birth to a son in the fateful hour of Israel's defeat, named the child Ichabod ("the glory has departed from Israel"). This unhappy name testified that the Ark, the seat of Yahweh's presence, had gone into exile (1 Sam. 4:12–22).

Why the Philistines failed to take advantage of their military opportunity, when the mastery of Palestine was almost in their grasp, is something of a mystery. Perhaps there were internal weaknesses in the Philistine alliance of city-states: the Pentapolis comprising Gaza, Ashdod, Ashkelon, Gath, and Ekron (Josh. 13:3). But one factor they could not reckon with was the Yahwistic faith, which showed an amazing resilience and vitality in times of political crisis. Yahweh's control of history was not bound up with any form of political organization, not even the Israelite confederacy. Political defeat was not Yahweh's defeat, even though the people might have thought so in times of despair. Yahweh could discipline the people with political disaster as well as bless them with victory. In Israel's prophetic faith, political crisis was an occasion for the people to search their hearts and renew their allegiance to the God of the covenant. Such a religious renewal took place in the dark hour of Philistine ascendancy.

THE LAST JUDGE OF ISRAEL

The person most instrumental in this religious renewal was the prophet-judge Samuel, unquestionably Israel's greatest spiritual leader since the time of Moses. His career marked the transition from the old type of charismatic leadership to the new prophetic leadership which, from this time on, played an outstanding role in Israel's life. Under his guidance, Israel shifted from the politically inadequate Tribal Confederacy to the more stable government of the monarchy.

Samuel's leadership is portrayed in two types of tradition, both of which describe him as playing an important role in Israel's fateful decision to establish a monarchy. These traditions are easily traced in 1 Samuel 1–12.

One tradition, apparently the first to be written down, is found in 1 Samuel 9:1–10:16 and in 1 Samuel 11. Here we find the engaging story of how Saul, "a handsome young man" who "stood head and shoulders above any of the people," set out to search for his father's lost asses and found a kingdom. The story goes that Saul was on the verge of giving up the search for his father's livestock when, at the suggestion of his servant, he decided to obtain advice from a seer, Samuel—in return, of course, for the necessary fee. Samuel, it turned out, was more than a local seer. He was recognized as the priestly authority in the city, who officiated at a sacrificial rite on a "high place" (shrine). More than that, he was a prophet who, in the name of Israel's God, could appoint a king. Seeing in Saul the man who could save Israel from the power of enemies such as the Philistines, Samuel took the initiative and secretly anointed Saul "prince" over the people.

According to this *Saul Tradition,* Saul was not publicly acclaimed king until he had demonstrated his leadership in a decisive battle (1 Sam. 11). This conflict was not with the Philistines but with the Ammonites, who were expanding in Transjordan and were taking advantage of Israel's preoccupation with the Philistine menace. When the men of Jabesh-gilead, finding themselves overwhelmed by Ammonite forces, asked for a treaty, the Ammonite king contemptuously replied that he would not make a treaty unless the right eye of every Israelite was gouged out. In desperation, the men of Jabesh sent an appeal for help throughout all the territory of Israel. Saul happened to be coming from the field behind some oxen when he heard the report about the Ammonite ultimatum. Suddenly the divine charisma, "the spirit of God," came mightily upon him in a manner reminiscent of the ancient judges. What follows is highly significant:

> He took a yoke of oxen, cut them into pieces and sent these by messengers throughout the territory of Israel with these words: "Anyone who will not march with Saul will have the same done to his oxen! At this, a panic from Yahweh swept on the people and they marched out as one man."
>
> —1 SAMUEL 11:7 (NJB)

Like the severing of a corpse into twelve pieces (see p. 176), this was a symbolic summons to the whole Israelite confederacy to engage in concerted action in the name of Yahweh. Inspired by Saul's *charisma,* the Tribal Confederacy won a decisive victory over the Ammonites. As a result, the Israelite militia offered the crown to Saul. Unlike Gideon, he accepted, and was crowned in Gilgal "before Yahweh."[27]

THE REQUEST FOR A KING

A second *Samuel Tradition* is found in 1 Samuel 7:3–8:22, 10:17–27, and 12. Here the picture of Samuel is somewhat different. Samuel is called not a seer, but a judge—the last and the greatest judge of Israel. His judgeship probably included the settling of legal disputes, for which purpose he made an annual circuit of the shrines at Bethel, Gilgal, and Mizpah (1 Sam. 7:15–17). Samuel also led the Israelites to triumph against the Philistines, although he accomplished this not by military leadership but by prayer and

---

[27]Verses 12–14, which speak of a "renewing" of the kingdom, are an editorial addition to harmonize the story with the account in 10:17–27, which comes from the second (Samuel) source. Similarly, the words "and Samuel" in 11:7 are an attempt to harmonize the two accounts.

sacrificial rite (1 Sam. 7:5–14). Noteworthy is the different way in which this Samuel Tradition deals with the establishment of the monarchy. In the earlier Saul Tradition, we find no divine disapproval of the anointing of a king: Indeed, Samuel, as Yahweh's prophetic spokesman, takes the initiative in selecting Saul. But in the Samuel Tradition, the idea of the monarchy displeases both Samuel and Yahweh. Samuel tried to adapt judgeship to the political situation by changing it from a charismatic office to a hereditary one. He appointed his own sons as judges; however, they did not have the same stature as their father:

> Then all the elders of Israel gathered together and came to Samuel at Ramah. They said to him, "Look, you are old, and your sons do not follow in your footsteps. Now appoint for us a king to rule us [literally "to judge us"] like all the nations."
>
> —1 SAMUEL 8:4–5

The Israelites' attempt to imitate the surrounding nations and establish a stable political government is interpreted as a rejection of Yahweh:

> Yahweh said to Samuel: "Listen to the voice of the people in all they say to you; for they have not rejected you, but *me they have rejected from being king over them.*"
>
> —1 SAMUEL 8:7

Samuel sought to dissuade the people from their plan by warning them of what would happen if they had a king: By centralizing power a king would limit their freedom and subject them to despotic tyranny. But the people insisted, and Samuel grudgingly consented to go along with them. 1 Samuel 10:17–27 reports Samuel's selection of Saul by lot from all the tribes of Israel. According to the Samuel Tradition, Saul was acclaimed king at the city of Mizpah (not Gilgal, as in the Saul Tradition), and Samuel gives his valedictory speech as the last judge of Israel in 1 Samuel 12.

The Samuel Tradition, probably written at a later date than the Saul Tradition, bears the marks of Deuteronomistic revision. 1 Samuel 7:3–4, for example, recalls the Deuteronomistic language found in the book of Judges (including imaginative features like the notion that the Philistines were subdued by a thunderstorm that came in answer to Samuel's prayer). We cannot readily harmonize the different portrayals of Samuel and the attitude toward the monarchy found in the two traditions. This does not warrant the conclusion, however, that the earlier Saul Tradition is the only one that has historical value. Keep in mind this important axiom of biblical study: *The date at which a* *tradition is written down does not necessarily indicate the date at which the tradition originated.* In the case of the Samuel Tradition, the Deuteronomistic historians were working with an older tradition going back at many points to the time of Samuel. We do not know exactly what Samuel's role was. The view, usually based on the Saul Tradition, that he was only a "local seer," has been grossly exaggerated. It is possible that he was last in the succession of Israel's judges, as the Samuel Tradition portrays him.

Moreover, what we know about the Israelite Confederacy lends authenticity to the attitude toward the monarchy expressed in the Samuel Tradition. Gideon had refused the crown for precisely the same reason Samuel opposed the kingship—namely, that Yahweh alone was Israel's king. Jotham's parable of the trees also expressed the distaste for centralized power. Not everyone in Israel agreed, as indicated by Abimelech's experiment with monarchy at Shechem. The Saul Tradition, more favorable to the monarchy, probably emerged from the tribe of Benjamin, where Saul was glorified as a tribal and national hero. The Samuel Tradition, on the other hand, shows the persistence of the more conservative belief of the Israelite Tribal Confederacy.

ISRAEL AND THE STATE

We noted at the beginning of this chapter that the struggle between Israel's faith and Canaanite culture found expression in the temptation to compromise with Canaanite naturalism and worship fertility gods. Now we see that the struggle was waged on a second front, that of nationalism. The cultural situation seemed to demand that Israel become "like the nations" in order to survive. Yet this step, though expedient, threatened to undermine the distinctive character of the Israelite community. From the earliest times Israel was bound together not by human factors such as race, economics, and politics, but by its relationship to Yahweh, the God of the covenant community. Israel was not a "nation" (Hebrew: *goy*) but a "people" (Hebrew: *'am*). While the Tribal Confederacy allowed for some political solidarity, especially in times of emergency, the basis of the organization was a religious covenant. In view of this history, the elders' request for a king was a shocking move, one that threatened to destroy the true identity of Israel as the "people of God."

Accordingly, 1 Samuel views the establishment of the Israelite monarchy in an ambivalent light. The Samuel Tradition is not just a reflection of the later unhappy experiences of the monarchy, but echoes early criticism made by representatives of the Tribal Confederacy. These critics believed that the Israelite state was not founded with divine blessing, but was allowed as a grudging concession to the people. Even the Saul Tradition does not regard the monarchy as a divine kingdom descended from heaven to earth, like a Babylonian dynasty, but as a providential development in history occasioned by the Philistine menace.

The establishment of the monarchy *was* in one sense providential, as the Saul Tradition emphasizes. In retrospect, one could say that events which brought about the collapse of the Tribal Confederacy and the rise of the Israelite state were not completely devoid of divine purpose: God's revelation is relevant to the whole of human life, including economics and politics. Nevertheless, Israel was not allowed to identify a human kingdom with the kingdom of God, for Yahweh alone was King. Israelite kings like David and Solomon, in their consuming ambition to make Israel great in the eyes of the world, sometimes forgot this truth, with the result that prophets arose to remind the people in the spirit of Samuel that Israel's calling was not to be "like the nations" but to be the "people of the Covenant." This conviction was underscored, as we will see, by prophetic criticism of the state and the announcement that the Israelite nation must fall in order that Israel might be reborn.

Admittedly, the ambivalent attitude toward the monarchy, which finds expression in the combined Saul and Samuel traditions, was rooted in Israel's actual historical experience. The early Saul Tradition seems to have been written before Israel had succumbed to the dangers and temptations of becoming like the other nations. It reflects the vigor and vitality of a new beginning, unspoiled by mistakes of the past and the corruption of political power. The monarchy is portrayed as a new possibility graciously offered by God in response to the people's petition, just as Moses was sent in answer to the people's cry of affliction. This tradition regards the anointing of Saul as Yahweh's act of deliverance:

> He shall save my people from the hand of the Philistines; for I have
> seen the suffering of my people, because their outcry has come to me.
> —1 SAMUEL 9:16b (NRSV)

The later Samuel Tradition, on the other hand, looks back to the anointing of Saul through the disillusioning experiences of the period of the monarchy. Like a "prophecy after the event," this account portrays the dire consequences that follow from Israel's decision to have a king like other nations. These unhappy experiences led some prophetic interpreters to conclude that the fateful step had been taken in defiance of Yahweh's will. Just before the fall of the Northern Kingdom in 721 B.C.E , the prophet Hosea condemned the monarchy, seeing in it a rejection of Yahweh as King (Hos. 8:4; 9:15; 10:3, 9). When the Southern Kingdom fell almost a century and a half later (587 B.C.E.), it was clear to discerning interpreters that Israel's history as a kingdom had ended in failure. Because the traditions about the founding of the monarchy date to the time of its end, the negative perception of Israel's attempt to be a kingdom "like the nations" almost drowns out the other, more positive view.[28] Thus Israel's eventual failure as a nation (see Part II) casts its lengthening shadow back across the pages of its history.

---

[28]This point is brought out effectively by Gerhard von Rad, *Theology*, I [163], 324–27.

A star shall come forth out of Jacob, and a scepter shall rise out of Israel.
—NUMBERS 24:17

ISRAEL BECOMES LIKE THE NATIONS

CHAPTER 7

THE THRONE OF DAVID

In the twelfth century B.C.E. forces were set in motion that profoundly affected the whole Fertile Crescent and left a deep impression upon the life and faith of Israel. In archaeological terms, this was the beginning of the Iron Age. The shift from the use of bronze to iron had important economic and political repercussions, somewhat like the changes brought about by the harnessing of nuclear energy in the twentieth century.

The Philistines who came into Canaan around this time quickly capitalized on the new mode of life. They controlled the smelting of the new metal and guarded this monopoly so effectively that other small nations, like Israel, were economically at their mercy. A picture of their stranglehold is given in 1 Samuel 13:19–22, where we learn that the Hebrews had no smiths who could make swords and spears, and that farmers had to go into Philistine country to sharpen their agricultural implements. As long as the Philistines were powerful enough to throttle Israel's economic and political life, Israel had no future. The destruction of Shiloh and the ignominious capture of the Ark were vivid reminders of that fact.

Biblical Readings: This chapter covers the narratives found in 1 Samuel 13–31, all of 2 Samuel, and 1 Kings 1–11. The account is paralleled in the Chroniclers' History (1 Chron. 10–2 Chron. 9), discussed in Chapter 15.

The Philistine blow to the old Tribal Confederacy (see pp. 185–186) was a stimulus for Israel to rally under a new form of political-religious unity: the *monarchy*. Under the leadership of the first kings of Israel—Saul, David, and Solomon—the Philistine stranglehold was broken and the long story of the occupation of Canaan came to an end. The way was opened for a period of economic and political good fortune that enabled Israel to establish a miniature empire extending from Mesopotamia to Egypt. For Israel, the Iron Age was a golden age in which Israel proudly took its place among the nations.

A TIME OF INTERNATIONAL FAVOR

Just as in the earlier occupation of Canaan, the political situation in the Fertile Crescent now favored Israel's expansion. No nation to the north was strong enough to interfere. After the demise of the Hammurabi regime, the Babylonians became politically weak and ignored Canaan for more than a thousand years. Assyria showed signs of imperial ambition during the reign of Tiglath-pileser I (about 1116–1078 B.C.E.), but subsequently sank into obscurity until the ninth century B.C.E., the time of the prophet Elijah.

Israel, then, was safe from the north, and the situation in Egypt was just as propitious. Although Canaan was nominally under Egypt's political control during the Late Bronze Age (1500–1200 B.C.E.), that control vanished during the Twentieth Dynasty, especially after about 1150 B.C.E. During the reign of Solomon there was a brief revival under Shishak I (935–914 B.C.E.), but thereafter Egypt remained politically impotent for more than three centuries.

The account of how Israel attained national unity and extended its political control throughout Palestine and Syria takes place against this favorable international background. The story is stirringly presented in the books of 1–2 Samuel and 1 Kings 1–11, which make up part of the great Deuteronomistic History. Within the Deuteronomistic framework, the historians included materials from different circles of tradition with varying degrees of historical reliability: Recall the account of the establishment of the kingdom (1 Sam. 1–12) with its pro-monarchic Saul Tradition and theocratic Samuel Tradition (see pp. 186–189). Scholars have attempted to trace these traditions through the rest of the books of Samuel, but after the conclusion of the Samuel story the division becomes much less clear-cut. Some material is undoubtedly legendary (such as the story of David and Goliath, 1 Sam. 17), and some reflects a political or theological bias (such as the story of Nathan forbidding David to build a temple, 2 Sam. 7).

Allowing for legendary and theological embellishments, however, the narratives are so vivid and historically authentic that they must have come from a time close to the events described. This is especially evident in the Court History of David (2 Sam. 9–20 and 1 Kings 1–2), a "succession narrative" evidently composed during the reign of David, perhaps by an eyewitness. Scholars regard this narrative, with its unusual realism and fluency of style, as one of the best examples of Hebraic prose in the Hebrew Bible.[1] By contrast, the history found in Chronicles is so dominated by theological bias that the historical picture is blurred, even though some of the traditions preserved in this late work are valuable.[2]

ISRAEL'S RUSTIC KING

The account of Saul's reign in 1 Samuel 13–31 portrays a heroic leader who lived during the period of transition from the collapse of the old Tribal Confederacy to the birth of a new order. Sadly, the historical situation that molded Saul's destiny as Israel's first king also aggravated weaknesses in his personality. His tragic career revolved around the alienation from two persons: Samuel and David.

The narrative portrays Samuel as the last representative of the old Tribal Confederacy, which was gradually collapsing under political pressures. David represents the youth and vigor of the new national order, within which Israel was to find a new formulation of its historic faith. Saul himself belongs more to the old age than to the new. But his rejection by Samuel cuts him off from the sanctions and supports of the old regime, and David's popularity is a constant reminder that Saul cannot enter the new. Caught between these two worlds, Saul's life becomes the arena of an intense psychic conflict—a conflict that eventually leads to his destruction.

Would that we had a historical narrative written in a circle sympathetic to Saul—such as an account composed by a member of Saul's own tribe of Benjamin! In their present form, however, the narratives of 1 Samuel are dominated by the bias of historians of the Southern Kingdom of Judah, who cast Saul in an unfavorable light in order to enhance the prestige of David, founder of the Judean dynasty. Keep in mind that all the traditions of the monarchy were preserved and edited by members of Jerusalem circles sympathetic to David. From a different point of view, Saul might have emerged as a heroic figure who, like Hamlet, was the victim of baffling, uncontrollable circumstances and the dark depths of his own sensitive and passionate nature. The narratives testify that Saul was capable of inspiring great devotion from his followers, even after Samuel deserted him. Moreover, Saul's military successes, though finally eclipsed by the dismal defeat at Mount Gilboa, ended the Philistine monopoly over iron smelting and paved the way for important economic developments in the reigns of David and Solomon. Saul's victories over Israel's enemies were impressive (1 Sam. 14:48), and under his rule the tribes of Israel lived in harmony. Much can be said to Saul's credit.[3]

---

[1]Gerhard von Rad has described this succession document as a new kind of historiography "without parallel in the ancient East." *Theology*, 1 [163], pp. 312–17.

[2]The Chronicler's History, comprising Ezra, Nehemiah, and 1–2 Chronicles, was composed in the post-exilic period and reflects the priestly theological interests of Judaism (see Chapter 15).

[3]The poet Robert Browning treats Saul sympathetically in his poem, "Saul."

This handsome, life-size head of an Ammonite monarch from the ninth century B.C.E. wears both a crown and earrings. Note the stylized locks and facial hair (mustache, beard, and brows).

SAUL'S CHARISMATIC LEADERSHIP

One of the clearest points of contact between Saul and the old Tribal Confederacy was his possession of divine *charisma*, the "spirit of Yahweh" that endowed the judges with the authority of leadership. Saul was acknowledged as leader not through heredity or a military coup, but because the spirit of Yahweh had rushed upon him, allowing him to deliver the city of Jabesh-gilead from the Ammonites (1 Sam. 11:6–7; see p. 187). After this charismatic military feat the people of Israel made him king, hoping he would deliver them from the Philistine oppression. But Saul was more like one of the ancient judges than a king. In fact, the oldest source (1 Sam. 9:16; 10:1) carefully avoids calling him a "king" (Hebrew: *melek*), describing him instead as a "prince" or "leader" (*nagîd*).

Unlike David and Solomon, Saul made no attempt to transform the tribal structure of Israel into a centralized state. He levied no taxes, instituted no military conscription, had no hierarchy of court officials and no harem. His only army was a band of volunteers recruited from his supporters (1 Sam. 13:2; 14:52). Excavations at Saul's

fortress of Gibeah confirm the biblical picture of the "rustic simplicity" of his court.[4]
Saul perpetuated the tribal democracy of the earlier period, claiming authority among
the tribes only because of divine charisma. No wonder he became melancholy when, as
a result of Samuel's rejection and David's growing popular acclaim, the "spirit" seemed
to leave him.

Reading Saul's story we sense that, despite his weakness, he was a man of sincere,
passionate faith in Yahweh. Some interpreters suggest that Saul broke with orthodox
Mosaic faith early in his career and turned toward the worship of the Canaanite nature
god, Baal. We know that Saul, after giving his first son a Yahweh name, Jonathan
("Yahweh [Yo] gave"), gave his later children Baal names (such as Ishbaal, "man of
Baal"). Furthermore, Saul ruthlessly slaughtered the priests of the Eli family who were
guardians of the central sanctuary at Shiloh (1 Sam. 22)—an act that might help explain why Samuel later repudiated Saul. But it is doubtful that Saul was a heretic. Despite his impulsive actions, Saul evidently intended to serve Yahweh with his whole
heart.

Unlike Samuel, Saul was not gifted with profound insight into the meaning of Israel's faith. Rather, Saul's tumultuous life story portrays situations where persons were
called to act in faith, to trust when the odds were desperate, and to make quick decisions and accept the consequences. This story belongs in Israel's scripture not because
of its edifying ideas but because of its vivid, uncensored description of the human situation. True, Saul came under prophetic influence on occasion—to the surprise of his ac-
quaintances, whose incredulous question, "Is Saul also among the prophets?" became
proverbial (1 Sam. 10:10–11; 19:18–24). But Saul was no prophet. Rather, he was a
soldier and leader who lived in a state of constant military emergency ("there was hard
fighting against the Philistines all the days of Saul"). His task was to "fight Yahweh's
battles," which to the people were Israel's battles.

Through these narratives breathes the intensity of Israel's conviction that Yahweh was actively engaged in their conflict. Saul was not deterred by Israel's pitiful
lack of armor, by the handful of recruits who made up his army, or by the numbers
who deserted when the going got rough. What did it matter that the odds were
against him? As his son Jonathan declared before setting out on a daring exploit at
Michmash: "Nothing can hinder Yahweh from saving by many or by few" (1 Sam.
14:6). When the tide of battle turned against Israel, Saul was humble enough to suspect that he had done something to incur Yahweh's displeasure. Saul's concern with
military strategy perhaps limited his view of the divine purpose. Nevertheless, he
deserves credit for coming to realize, through bitter experience, that it was Yahweh
who was in supreme command, shaping history and demanding the people's zealous
devotion.

---

[4]Gibeah was excavated in 1922–23 under the direction of W. E. Albright. Re-excavation of the site in 1964
largely confirmed Albright's results; see Paul Lapp's report in *The Biblical Archaeologist* XXVIII (1965),
2-10.

A HOLY WAR

Saul's devotion to Yahweh was put to the test in an incident related in 1 Samuel 15: the battle with the Amalekites. Many scholars believe this chapter comes from a literary tradition related to the Samuel Tradition (see pp. 187–189). Whatever its source, the story is evidently based on authentic historical memory. The Amalekites, who lived in the Negeb to the south of Beer-sheba, were ancient enemies of Israel whose all-out effort to destroy Israel during the wilderness march still rankled in memory (Exod. 17:8–16). Perhaps some provocation aroused the Israelite's longstanding animosity, such as Amalekite raids upon southern settlements at a time when Israel was preoccupied with the Philistines. In any event, through the prophet Samuel, Saul received a divine command: Destroy the Amalekites utterly—man, woman, child, cattle, and goods!

By present-day ethical standards, this goal of total extermination was a barbarous act (though scarcely less refined than modern warfare). But instead of making a value judgment from our standpoint, we will consider Saul's acts within the religious perspective of ancient Israel. The story tells us that Yahweh takes the initiative, commanding Israel to punish Amalek for its ancient atrocity. In other words, this was not to be a customary military action, but rather a "holy war"—a religious action.

To understand "holy war," recall the period of the Tribal Confederacy and the charismatic summons to battle, as in the "Song of Deborah" (see pp. 178–179 also the Definition, p. 128). The covenant bond imposed certain obligations upon the participating tribes, one of which was to respond to a charismatic leader's summons to rally behind Yahweh who was "going before" the people. Volunteers would "offer themselves willingly" (Judg. 5:2, 9) and consecrate themselves by submitting to such disciplines as sexual abstinence (1 Sam. 21:4-5; 2 Sam. 11:11). Because Yahweh was in the people's midst as military leader, the numbers of fighters and weapons were inconsequential (as with Gideon, see p. 180). The strategy of holy war was to frighten the enemy with the "terror of God," causing them to flee in panic and confusion.

The spoils of a holy war were to be under sacrificial ban (Hebrew: *ḥérem*)—that is, devoted to Yahweh as a holocaust or sacrifice. Because spoils belonged exclusively to Yahweh, it was considered a great sin to take anything for oneself, regardless of personal motive. Thus Achan, who stole precious things from the spoils of Jericho, suffered disastrous results for himself and his family (Josh. 7). To take something from Yahweh's sacrifice was regarded as "breaking faith" (Josh. 7:1), an offense against Yahweh's holiness.

This ancient view helps to explain the seriousness of Saul's offense in taking Amalekite spoil: Saul used his own judgment to decide how far he would go in obeying the stipulations of holy war. After the collapse of the Tribal Confederacy, the concept of "holy war" disappeared.[5] Charismatic leaders were superseded by hereditary monarchs

[5]The concept was revived later, however, by the unknown writer of Deuteronomy (for example, Deut. 7:1–2; 20:1, 21:14). See Gerhard von Rad, *Studies in Deuteronomy* [418], pp. 45–49. The Deuteronomic rules for conducting a holy war were followed in the Maccabean Revolt, and were accepted by the Essene sect of Jews at Qumran (see pp. 575–576).

who, like kings in surrounding nations, fought wars with chariots and infantry and took all the spoils for themselves. In Saul's day, however, the old standard was still in effect. Saul was a charismatic leader who was ordered to destroy the Amalekites completely— that is, to put them under the sacrificial ban (*ḥerem*). So decisively did Saul defeat the Amalekites that they soon vanished from the historical scene. The last reference to the Amalekites is in 1 Samuel 30, when David avenges their raid on a Philistine outpost.

To us, the sparing of Agag might seem humane, and taking the best of the livestock might seem practical wisdom. But in a holy war all spoils belonged to Yahweh. Saul's defect was his refusal to obey Yahweh completely in this situation—an act of disloyalty that polluted the entire Israelite community. Later Saul explains that Agag and the spoils were brought back to be sacrificed. But Samuel, who speaks for the old Tribal Confederacy, is not satisfied:

> Surely, to obey is better than sacrifice,
> And to heed than the fat of rams.
> —1 SAMUEL 15:22b (NRSV)

Because Saul "rejected the word of Yahweh," Samuel declares that Yahweh has rejected Saul as king over Israel. With fierce devotion to Yahweh, the enraged Samuel finishes performing the sacrificial ban: He "hewed Agag in pieces before Yahweh in Gilgal" (1 Sam. 15:33b).

A REJECTED MAN

This story marks the turning point in the narrative cycle that deals with Saul. Clearly, the story is biased in favor of David, the "neighbor" who was better than Saul (1 Sam. 15:28). Not even Saul's confession of sin and plea for pardon could deliver him from the consequences of his deed, which pursued him like a nemesis in the days ahead. Saul's passionate devotion to Yahweh caused Samuel's word of rejection to prey on his mind and drove him to the edge of insanity. Outwardly, he enjoyed some measure of popularity and success for a time, but inwardly his life was distracted and maddened by the thought of Yahweh's rejection.

Two developments pointed clearly to Saul's estrangement from Yahweh. One was the decisive break with Samuel. A narrative more sympathetic to Saul might portray the impulsive acts that led to the final rupture with Samuel in a better light. Saul can be seen as a man of action who did not consider the religious implications of his acts, especially in times of emergency. He summoned the priest Ahijah to obtain a divine oracle, but evidently terminated the investigation abruptly when the military situation indicated that there was no time to wait for Yahweh's answer (1 Sam. 14:18–23). When his hungry soldiers slaughtered cattle and began to eat meat with the blood—ignoring the proper ritual procedure—Saul himself built an altar for sacrifice (1 Sam. 14:31–35). These actions might show only Saul's impulsiveness, rather than a determination to take things into his own hands. Together with the Amalekite episode, however, they convinced Samuel that Saul was out to defy the "rule of God." The prophet broke with the king he had anointed, and "Samuel did not see Saul again until the day of his death" (1 Sam. 15:35). To Saul, the absence of Yahweh's prophet meant the absence of Yahweh. Cast off by God, he was condemned to loneliness within his own tumultuous being.

The other development was the rise of David's star on the horizon. From Saul's vantage point, David must have appeared a threat to his very existence, a threat even greater than the Philistine menace. From the first, Saul's instability was aggravated by David's personal charm, gallantry, and success—all of which seemed directed toward gaining the throne (see 1 Sam. 18:8). How else could one explain David's ability to ingratiate himself with the people, his cunning attempt to marry into the royal family, his friendship with Jonathan, and his favor with the priests of Nob? The more Saul brooded over David's actions, the more he worried that David was a pretender to the throne. And everywhere, David met with success. Saul's plots to humiliate him all turned to David's advantage. Even the women who celebrated Saul's return from battle with music and song reserved their greatest praise for David, Saul's armor-bearer:

> Saul has slain his thousands,
> but David his tens of thousands!
>
> —1 SAMUEL 18:7

The growing conflict was more than a personal rift between two heroic individuals. The divine charisma, the spirit that endowed the old Israelite leaders with authority and strength, had departed from Saul. In Saul's despairing view, it was more and more apparent that David had charisma; we are told that when Samuel anointed David "the spirit of Yahweh came mightily upon David from that day forward" (1 Sam. 16:13). Ironically, Saul is still seen as having charisma, but it is "an evil spirit from Yahweh" that torments him until he is beside himself. Today, Saul's behavior might seem to border on the insane. In ancient times, however, extreme behavior was often seen as a sign that the divine spirit had invaded and was in control of one's being (compare the story of David's feigned insanity in the Philistine court, 1 Sam. 21:12–15). The line separating the spiritual leader from the disordered mind could be a very fine one indeed.[6]

Saul's desperate efforts to find himself again and to recover his kingly prestige proved futile. Haunted by dark moods and inflamed by insane jealousy and rage, he began to suspect the loyalty of his best friends (1 Sam. 22:6–8). He imagined conspiracy on every hand, as shown by his wild command to massacre the eighty-five priests of Nob, who had been kind to David (1 Sam. 22:9–19). Eventually he became obsessed

---

[6]Prophets were sometimes called "madmen" (2 Kings 9:11), and the Hebrew word used in 1 Samuel 18:10 to describe one of Saul's fits (NRSV translates "rave") literally means to prophesy under the influence of the divine spirit. See Simon B. Parker, "Possession, Trance, and Prophecy in Pre-Exilic Israel," *Vetus Testamentum* 28 (1978), 271–85.

with one intention: to hunt David down and kill him. Frustrated in his efforts to track down the fugitive David, he was finally confronted with a concerted Philistine drive into the plain of Jezreel. The Israelite armies, gathered near Mount Gilboa on the southern flank of the pass leading to the Philistine fort of Beth-shan, were panic-stricken at the sight of the large army in the valley below. Saul made one last effort to seek Yahweh's counsel, but no answer came through the usual channels: the sacred lot ("Urim and Thummim"), dreams, and prophetic oracles (1 Sam. 28:5–6). Even though he had banned mediums from the land, Saul secretly visited a necromancer at En-dor, hoping to hear Yahweh's word through the ghost of Samuel, summoned from the underworld.

1 Sam. 28:8–25 gives a moving portrayal of the tragedy of Saul's last hours. Having heard from Samuel a crushing prophecy of doom, Saul goes out into the dismal night—and to defeat and suicide at Mount Gilboa. In a magnificent elegy, once contained in an old collection of Israelite poetry called "The Book of Jashar," David pays immortal tribute to Saul, fallen leader of Israel:

> How the mighty have fallen,
> and the weapons of war perished!
>
> —2 SAMUEL 1:27 (NRSV)

DAVID, ARCHITECT OF THE ISRAELITE STATE

The Philistine victory at the battle of Mount Gilboa was decisive. The Israelite armies were dispersed in leaderless rout, and Saul's decapitated body was impaled on the walls of Beth-shan. The Philistines now controlled the valley route leading from the Mediterranean Sea to the Jordan Valley, and their conquest of Israelite territory was within easy reach. Why did they not follow up their victory by wiping out all pockets of Israelite resistance? One reason, certainly, was the rise of David, one of the greatest military commanders and statesmen of history. With amazing speed David reorganized the Israelite army, dealt a defeating blow to Philistine power, and established a dynasty, or "house," that was destined to last for over four hundred years. An inscription found at the site of the ancient city of Dan, dating from the ninth century B.C.E., makes apparent reference to "the house of David" (*Bytdwd*). If interpreted correctly, archaeologists have found an early reference to the Davidic monarchy outside the Bible.[7]

The story of David's early life is interwoven with the fateful events of Saul's reign (1 Sam. 13–31). In fascinating detail we learn of David's rise from the obscurity of a

---

[7]See "'David' Found at Dan," ed. Hershel Shanks, *Biblical Archaeology Review* 20:2 (July/Aug 1994), 26–39. Some maintain that the inscription refers to a town name; see Philip R. Davies, "'House of David' Built on Sand," *Biblical Archaeology Review* 20:4 (July/Aug 1994), 54–55, and the response by David Noel Freedman and Jeffery C. Goeghegan, "House of David Is There!" *Biblical Archaeology Review* 21:2 (March/April 1995), 78–79.

shepherd's life, his appearance as a harp player in the king's court, his victory over the giant Goliath, his gallant exploits among the Philistines, his adventures as leader of a band of outlaws, and finally, his elevation to the rank of king of Israel. These stories, written to glorify a leader whose personal charm and charismatic power made him a popular idol, have captured the imagination of countless generations. His posterity hailed David as the greatest of Israel's rulers—"a man after God's own heart"—who was both architect of the nation and royal champion of Israel's faith.

This high estimation is all the more remarkable when we consider the true-to-life picture of David presented in the narratives. To be sure, the book of Chronicles, written some centuries later, touches up David's portrait in order to emphasize his better traits (1 Chron. 11–29). The account in the books of 1–2 Samuel and 1 Kings, however—especially the Court History or "succession narrative" in 2 Samuel 9–20 and 1 Kings 1–2—presents David not as an idealized figure up on a pedestal, but as a flesh-and-blood person of extraordinary winsomeness and charm.

There are notable inconsistencies in the narrative, such as the differing accounts of how David was introduced to Saul's court. In one account (1 Sam. 16:14–23) David is summoned as a musician to cheer the depressed king; in the other (1 Sam. 17:1–18:5) he first wins the king's attention by defeating Goliath.[8] Furthermore, 2 Samuel 21:19 attributes the slaying of Goliath to Elhanan from Bethlehem, a detail that casts doubt on the story of David the giant-killer.[9] On the whole, however, the narrative gives an authentic, if somewhat romanticized, account of David's rise from the sheepfolds to the royal throne.

The deaths of Samuel and Saul marked the passing of an era. Under Saul's charismatic rule the tribes had been held together in the loose union of the Tribal Confederacy, with no apparent signs of rebellion. Under David, however, charismatic leadership gave way to centralization of power in the crown. Israel was transformed from a tribal league into a small empire modeled after the surrounding nations. David's problem was to maintain tribal unity under the new nation-state.

DAVID'S RISE TO POWER

David's methods suggest that he was a shrewd politician who stopped at nothing to achieve his political ambitions. At the time of Saul's death David was an exile in Philistia. His first task was to put himself in a strategic position from which he could attain his political goal—to set himself up as ruler over the tribes of Israel. Fortunately, he had prepared the way for readmission to his native tribe, Judah: During his outlaw period in the Wilderness of Judah and in Philistia, David had ingratiated himself with the

---

[8]Notice that in 1 Samuel 17:55–59 Saul questions David about his identity, which seems to indicate that he had not known of him before (compare 1 Sam. 16:17–22).

[9]This discrepancy is smoothed over in 1 Chronicles 20:5, which states that Elhanan killed the brother of Goliath, Lahmi, not Goliath himself.

Judeans by protecting landholders from robbers and dividing the spoils of his raids with the elders (1 Sam. 23:1–5; 25:2ff.; 27:8–12; 30:26–31). It is not surprising, then, that shortly after Saul's death David was anointed king at Hebron, where he reigned for over seven years, evidently as a kind of Philistine vassal.

During this period, however, David had his eye on the whole territory of Israel. The Northern tribes still owed allegiance to Saul's weak son, Ishbaal,[10] a stooge of his army general, Abner. David's Judean forces were under the command of his able general, Joab. Eventually a conflict between the house of David and the house of Saul was touched off by a curious incident by the pool of Gibeon, uncovered by archaeologists in 1956–57.[11] The two army commanders, facing each other from opposite sides of the pool, agreed to a test of strength: Twelve young men would represent each side in a kind of gladiatorial contest. But nothing was settled because the champions only killed each other off. As a result, general fighting broke out between the armies (2 Sam. 2:12–17).

From this time on David's power grew stronger and stronger. The struggle between David and the house of Saul ended when Abner, stinging under a deserved rebuke from Ishbaal, offered to deliver the remnant of Saul's kingdom to David. Part of the deal was for David to receive Michal, Saul's daughter and David's first wife. Motivated chiefly by political calculation, David took Michal into his harem in order to establish a claim upon Saul's throne. Michal's tearful parting from her own husband is described with great pathos (2 Sam. 3:12–16). Saul's male descendants were either liquidated in despotic style or put under careful custody (2 Sam. 21:l–14). At the age of thirty-seven, David became the unchallenged ruler of all Israel.

The Philistines ignored David during his reign at Hebron, perhaps because they regarded him as their vassal and were content for Israel to be divided between the houses of Saul and David. But when David's power increased with the union of all the Israelite tribes, the Philistines decided it was time to act (2 Sam. 5:17). Not much is said about the Philistine wars, but one of David's greatest accomplishments was breaking the Philistines' control over Canaan once and for all (2 Sam. 5:17–25; 21:15–22). Confining the Philistines to the coastal plain, he also waged successful wars against Moab, Ammon, Edom, Amalek, and Aram (Syria), and concluded a treaty with the Phoenician king, Hiram of Tyre. David came to be recognized as the ruler of an empire that stretched from the Lebanon mountains to the borders of Egypt, from the Mediterranean Sea to the Desert of Arabia. Seeing the hand of God in these dazzling achievements, the narrator comments: "David became greater and greater, for Yahweh, the God of hosts, was with him" (2 Sam. 5:10). Never before or after the time of David did Israel exceed this zenith of political power.

---

[10]In the biblical text Ishbaal is called "Ishbosheth." Editors have substituted Hebrew *bosheth* ("shame") for *baal*, the abhorred name of the Canaanite deity.

[11]See James B. Pritchard, *Gibeon: Where the Sun Stood Still* (Princeton, N.J.: Princeton University Press, 1962), pp. 64–72.

The Pool of Gibeon was the scene of a gladiatorial contest, according to 2 Sam. 2:13. First excavated in the summer of 1956, Gibeon was one of four federated cities that entered into alliance with Joshua during his invasion of southern Canaan, and came to be an important Israelite city by the time of the early monarchy.

CONSOLIDATING THE NATION

David was more than a brilliant military commander. Desiring a greater centralization of power in the throne, he took several important and fateful steps to limit the independence of the confederate tribes. In a daring maneuver he captured the old fortress of Jerusalem, despite the boast of its occupants, the Jebusites, that it was an impregnable stronghold. David's men penetrated this stronghold by ascending a water shaft (2 Sam. 5:8) that cut through rock from the Gihon spring outside the walls to the interior of the old city, called Ophel. Consider what David's feat meant at a time when Northern tribes had gathered around the house of Saul and Southern tribes had sworn allegiance to David in Hebron. Jerusalem, bypassed by Israelite forces at the time of the occupation of Canaan, had never been incorporated into the territory of the Tribal Confederacy. In his bid for power David capitalized on the sectional feeling of the Southern tribes; but since his political ambitions also included the North, he wisely sought a place for his capital that was neither "Northern" nor "Southern." By selecting the neutral site of Jerusalem, right on the boundary of the Northern and Southern tribes, he revealed his intention of elevating his throne above all tribal factions.

Jerusalem from the south with the hill called Ophel, the site of David's city, highlighted in the center foreground. Behind the walls can be seen the Dome of the Rock, a mosque built over the site of Solomon's Temple. Ophel slopes off to the deep Valley of Kidron, on the right of which is the modern village of Silwan.

Jerusalem came to be known as "the city of David" (1 Sam. 5:9). In his new capital David assembled a group of courtiers who derived their position from the crown. This was a great change from the days of the Tribal Confederacy, when leadership was based on status in a tribe or on the divine charisma. The administration of law, previously vested in judges or in tribal elders who "sat at the gate," was taken over by the king himself or delegated to royal appointees (see 2 Sam. 14:4–17; 15:1–6). In the case of two royal officials, the Recorder and Secretary (2 Sam. 8:15–18), scholars detect the influence of Egyptian governmental models. Israel was becoming "like the nations," with a special class known as "servants of the king" who exercised power over the people.

If he was to capture the allegiance of all Israel, however, David needed to establish his throne on the religious sanctions and Mosaic traditions of the Tribal Confederacy. He had to demonstrate that his political innovations would not sweep away Israel's sacred heritage, but instead bring it to glorious fulfillment. One of his shrewdest acts, therefore, was to rescue the Ark of the Covenant from its place of oblivion since the fall of the confederate sanctuary of Shiloh, and to bring it to Jerusalem with great pomp and ceremony. On this occasion he came into the city practically naked, "leaping and dancing" before Yahweh with all his might—much to the disgust of his wife Michal (2 Sam. 6:16–23).

With the Ark stationed in a "tent" in Jerusalem, the city of David also became "Zion, City of God." Yahweh's presence once again "tabernacled" in the midst of Israel. Moreover, those priests of the house of Eli (headed by Abiathar) who had survived Saul's bloody purge at Nob were brought to Jerusalem and attached to the royal court. In this way David shifted the religious center of Israel from the confederate sanctuary of Shiloh to the royal shrine in Jerusalem. Some Psalms (see Ps. 24:7–10, 132:6–10) suggest that a "Zion festival" periodically reenacted the bearing of the Ark through the gates of Jerusalem, with Yahweh the "King of glory" invisibly enthroned on it (see pp. 499–503).

David's innovations marked the beginning of a *royal theology:* the view that Yahweh had made a special covenant with David, promising to establish David's throne securely through all generations (2 Sam. 7). A corollary to this view was the belief that Yahweh would favor any king who descended from David.

David's ambitions soared ever higher. Already he had placed the Ark of the Covenant within the Tent of Meeting (2 Sam. 7:2), thus joining together the two major cultic objects inherited from Mosaic times (see pp. 105–106). A tradition preserved in 2 Samuel 24:18–25 states that he purchased (from a citizen named Araunah) a threshing floor north of his palace on which to build an altar to Yahweh. Here David aspired to replace the old Tent with a splendid royal temple patterned after the temples of other nations. Voicing the conservative view of the old Tribal Confederacy, however, the prophet Nathan argued that Yahweh had not dwelt in a "house" since the time of the Exodus but had been "moving about in a tent" (2 Sam. 7:6). David wisely conceded that he was going too far—at least for the time being. He contented himself with building a "tent-shrine" (Hebrew: *mishkan*), perhaps along the lines of the "tabernacle" described in Exodus 25–31 and 35–40.[12] He also reorganized Israel's religion in other spheres, especially music. According to the Chroniclers' History (1 Chron. 25) David organized the musicians into guilds, a credible report in view of David's reputation as a musician (Amos 6:5).

David took other measures to control and modify the Tribal Confederacy. Against the advice of his counselors, he insisted on taking a census of all Israel, an ambitious project that took over nine months to complete. Evidently the census was to be the basis of military conscription, taxation, and forced labor, thus serving notice to all citizens that they owed primary allegiance to the king, not to a tribal unit. The plan

---

[12]The confederate sanctuary at Shiloh must have been a tent (as in Ps. 78:60), not a temple (compare 1 Sam. 1:7, 9). In his essay on "Temples and High Places in Biblical Times" (Jerusalem, 1981), Frank Cross maintains that the tabernacle portrayed in Priestly portions of the book of Exodus (Exod. 25–31, 35–40) reflects the tent-shrine constructed by David. The building of a "house" or temple for Yahweh, in his view, was exclusively Solomon's project.

backfired, however. The people's bitter resentment against the census is expressed in the story of a plague, interpreted as a sign of Yahweh's wrath against the king in the face of which he repented (2 Sam. 24).[13] Nevertheless David introduced the policy of forcing his subjects into work camps (2 Sam. 20:24), a despotic practice that later became a hated symbol of tyranny.

DAVID'S TROUBLES

Not surprisingly, David's initial popularity began to wane. The people became increasingly restive under the yoke of centralized power, and longed for the independence they had enjoyed before Israel became a state.

Outwardly, the Israelite state was brilliant in its achievements, the envy of the surrounding nations, as we learn later from the account of the visit of the Queen of Sheba (1 Kings 10:1–10). David's name was renowned throughout the Fertile Crescent. Jerusalem, whose royal buildings were designed and constructed by the best artisans of Phoenicia, was seen as a monument to David's skill and diplomacy. The commercial wealth of the Near East poured into the kingdom, with the result that the life of the people underwent profound changes. Israel's faith was exposed to a more cosmopolitan atmosphere. New conceptions of property were introduced as commercial entrepreneurs, protected by the king's military power, exploited opportunities in trade.

Even during David's reign there were signs of volcanic rumblings that, at Solomon's death, broke forth with pent-up fury. Absalom, David's son, instigated a revolution in Judah that almost cost David his crown. The Northern tribesman, Sheba, also sounded a call to arms:

> We have no portion in David,
>   no share in the son of Jesse!
> Everyone to your tents, O Israel!
>
> —2 SAMUEL 20:1 (NRSV)

David proved equal to these crises, but they signaled trouble.

David's domestic troubles are recorded in the Court History found in 2 Samuel 9–20 and 1 Kings 1–2.[14] The account is so realistic that it must have come from a contemporary of David, probably a member of his court. The narrator gives us a glimpse into the intrigues of David's own family, and from this biographical angle we learn indirectly about the character of his administration. Unlike the portrait of David found in

---

[13]The Chroniclers' History attributes the temptation to "count the people of Israel" to Satan rather than to David's imperial ambitions (1 Chron. 21:1).

[14]The basic study of the Court History or "succession narrative" is Leonhard Rost, *Succession to the Throne* [344]. Gerhard von Rad builds upon this study in his excellent discussion of "Israel's Anointed" in *Theology*, I [163], especially pp. 306–18.

the Chroniclers' History, the Court History portrays the king in both his strength and his weakness. No attempt is made to depict him as either better or worse than he actually was, or to suppress or distort the facts in the interests of theological bias.

Nevertheless, the Court History is dominated by a religious theme that makes the David story one of the greatest tragedies ever written. The key to the story is the encounter between David and the prophet Nathan (2 Sam. 12), a sequel to David's affair with Bathsheba. David had desired Bathsheba. What was to prevent him, the most powerful man in the land, from satisfying his desire? It was spring and Bathsheba's husband, Uriah the Hittite, was away fighting the Ammonites. David took Bathsheba, only to learn later that she had become pregnant. To make it appear that Uriah was the father, David called him home from battle. But Uriah was a faithful warrior who refused to break the rules of sexual abstinence that applied to a sanctified soldier during holy war (2 Sam. 11:11). David entertained Uriah until he was drunk, hoping to weaken his will. When this attempt failed, he contrived Uriah's death in a manner that would put himself beyond suspicion.

It seemed to be a perfect crime—but, we are told, "the thing that David had done displeased Yahweh" (2 Sam. 11:27). What follows is one of the most dramatic encounters in scripture. The prophet Nathan appears before the king as spokesman of Yahweh, and tells the parable of a poor man's pet ewe lamb that was stolen to provide meat for a rich man's table. Outraged, David declares that the man deserves to die. Nathan's exclamation, "You are the man!" strikes home like a dagger to David's guilty heart. Overcome with shame and remorse he confesses, "I have sinned against Yahweh" (2 Sam. 12:13).

David's penitence, though heartfelt, could not free him from the fateful consequences of his actions. David's lust and murder sets off a chain reaction that corrupts his own sons. The eldest, Amnon, forces his virgin half-sister, and Absalom in revenge assassinates Amnon. Estranged from his father, Absalom foments a revolution and, accidentally caught in the limbs of a tree, is murdered as he dangles helplessly. A poignant passage describes the king's anguished response to this news:

> The king was deeply moved, and went up to the chamber over the
> gate, and wept; and as he went, he said, "O my son Absalom, my son, my
> son Absalom! Would I had died instead of you, O Absalom, my son, my
> son."
>
> —2 SAMUEL 18:33 (NRSV)

To the end of his days David's sons were engaged in intrigue and treachery over the succession to the throne, a dreadful fulfillment of Yahweh's word through Nathan: "Behold, I will raise up evil against you out of your own house" (2 Sam. 12:11). Though surrounded by the glories and wealth of the state he created, the aged David described in 1 Kings 1–2 is a pathetic, brokenhearted figure, seeking in vain to warm himself at the dead embers of his former passions (1 Kings 1:1–4). Under Solomon, son of the fateful marriage with Bathsheba, the United Kingdom is split in two.

This honest portrayal of David's tragedy is a testament to the realism of Israelite faith. In one sense, David was a victim of his own greatness, of an indomitable will that urged him to scale the tempting heights of power. On a deeper level, David was engaged in struggle with the God he sought to serve, the God whose covenant law transcended the practical affairs of daily life. This, at any rate, is the view we are given in the vivid narratives of the Court History. Significantly, the penitential Psalm 51 is described as "a psalm of David, when Nathan the prophet came to him after he had gone to Bathsheba."[15] If David believed that Yahweh, enthroned on the Ark, entered triumphantly into the capital of his kingdom (Ps. 24:7–10), he also had to be ready to hear Yahweh's word of judgment spoken by a prophet. Faith in Yahweh's sovereign rule prevented Israel from following the ancient Near Eastern practice of making royal power absolute or, as in Egypt, deifying the king.

THE IDEAL KING

In time David's weaknesses were forgotten and his greatness extolled. Israel's historians took the view that David, more than any other king, typified the ideal combination of power and goodness. He was remembered as "Yahweh's servant," the God-fearing king who "executed justice and righteousness unto all his people" (2 Sam. 8:15).[16]

According to Nathan's oracle in 2 Samuel 7, the special relationship between Yahweh and David was extended to David's entire dynasty. Recall that David had asked Nathan for divine approval of a plan to build Yahweh a house of cedar, a temple comparable in glory to David's own palace. Yahweh refused, promising instead to make David a "house" (a dynasty) and to establish the throne of his kingdom *forever*, in perpetuity (verses 11b–13). The oracle stated that the Davidic king would be elected to the special relationship of Son of God (verse 7:14a; see Ps. 2:7). Furthermore, though divine judgment would chasten individual kings for their iniquities, Yahweh's *hesed* ("covenant loyalty") would not be withdrawn from the Davidic house (verses 14b–16).

The oracle is colored by the language and interests of the Deuteronomistic historians. Nevertheless the core of the chapter, with its own formal introduction and conclusion, undoubtedly preserves a tradition of royal covenant theology dating back to the early Jerusalem court:

---

[15]Some psalms might have been composed by David, but scholars generally agree that he was not the author of the whole Psalter (see Chapter 16).

[16]See Walter Brueggemann's provocative study, *David's Truth in Israel's Imagination and Memory* (Philadelphia: Fortress, 1985).

Yahweh announces to you that Yahweh will make a "house" for you:

> When your days are completed and you rest with your ancestors,
> > I will raise up after you your offspring, who will
> > issue from your body, and I will stabilize his kingdom.
> He shall build a "house" for my name,
> > and I will establish his royal throne in perpetuity.
> I will be Father to him, and he will be Son to me.
>
> When he does wrong, I will chasten him with the rod of human punishment,
> > and with the stripes of human justice,
> but my loyalty [*ḥésed*] I will not withdraw from him,
> > as I did in the case of Saul, whom I removed before you.
> Before me your house and your kingdom will stand secure perpetually,
> your throne will be established in perpetuity.
>
> > > —2 SAMUEL 7:11b–16

In this tradition, Yahweh's solemn oath to David is *unconditional*, thereby assuring social stability and averting civil crises such as anarchy or revolution following a king's death or assassination. The so-called "Last Words of David" (2 Sam. 23:1–7) reflect this view of Yahweh's "everlasting covenant" (Hebrew: *berîth 'ôlam*). This passage is so old in both style and content that it must have been composed by David or one of his court circle:[17]

> Indeed, my house stands firm before God (*'El*);
> > for God has made a perpetual covenant (*berîth 'ôlam*)
> with me, its terms duly stipulated and secured.
>
> > > —2 SAMUEL 23:5

Just as the Mosaic covenant was influenced by the suzerainty treaty (see pp. 90–92), the Davidic covenant was influenced by Canaanite and other Near Eastern models of kingship and temple. In these models the king was a sacral person, the representative or "son" of God through whom the blessings of the divine order were mediated to society. The temple, founded at the center or "navel" of the world, was the meeting place of heaven and earth where creation was renewed annually in a mythical

---

[17]Gerhard von Rad, *Theology*, I [163], 310–14, maintains that the motif of the "everlasting covenant" found in the "Last Words of David" is actually very ancient and prepares the way for 2 Sam. 7. On this matter, see especially Frank M. Cross, "The Ideologies of Kingship in the Era of the Empire" [129], pp. 219–65. Cross argues that at first the Davidic covenant was "a covenant granted by divine initiative and conditional upon divinely imposed stipulations," and therefore was in line with the conditional (suzerainty) covenant of the Tribal Confederacy. Under Solomon's "Canaanizing despotism," however, it evolved into the unconditional covenant that became "the standard Judean ideology."

   Other scholars maintain that David himself, relying on older covenant conceptions associated with Hebron, advocated an unconditional covenant. See Murray Newman, *The People of the Covenant* [262], chaps. 5 and 6; and Ronald Clements, *Abraham and David* [329].

THE EMPIRE OF DAVID

victory over the powers of chaos. Thus the king was a temple-builder, and the temple was a royal sanctuary where the king performed a cultic role.

These views were modified in the Davidic covenant model, however. Monarchy and temple were not traced back to primordial times "when kingship was lowered from heaven," as in the ancient Sumerian king list.[18] Rather, the Davidic covenant announced that, at a definite stage in Israel's history, Yahweh designated the Davidic king as "the anointed one" (Hebrew: *mashîaḥ*) and the temple of Zion as the divine meeting place (Ps. 132). The Israelite monarchy began providentially in the time of Saul and David, and the temple of Jerusalem first became Yahweh's dwelling place in the time of Solomon.[19] Psalm 78, for example, declares that Yahweh had done something new in the time of David. In this Southern (Judean) view, the Mosaic covenant, identified with the Northern tribes, had ended in failure when the people rebelled and betrayed their Suzerain. Yahweh rejected the North and made a new beginning by choosing Mount Zion as the central sanctuary (Ps. 78:67–69) and by elevating "David his servant" from a shepherd of flocks to shepherd of the people Israel (verses 70-72).

DEFINITION: "MESSIAH"

The term "Messiah" (Hebrew: *mashîaḥ*, Greek: *christos*, English: "Christ") literally means "anointed," reflecting the ancient practice of anointing, and thereby consecrating, a person for an exalted office such as prophet (1 Kings 19:16; compare Isa. 61:1), priest (Exod. 28:41; 29:7) or king (Judg. 9:15 in Jotham's fable).

The anointment of a person to be monarch was an important part of the coronation ceremony, sometimes carried out by a prophet (1 Sam. 10:1; 1 Kings 19:16) and at other times by priests (1 Kings 1:39; 2 Kings 11:12). Anointment made the king a "sacred" person, signifying that the royal office conferred on the monarch a special relationship with God. This explains why David, when given an opportunity to kill Saul, refused to raise his hand against the king, "seeing that he is Yahweh's anointed [*mashîaḥ*]" (1 Sam 24:6, 10).

In the Hebrew Bible the term *mashîaḥ*, when used in royal contexts, always refers to the reigning king, regarded as God's representative in the earthly kingdom. In later literature, beyond the boundaries of the Old Testament and Hebrew Bible, the term took on the meaning of an ideal king or deliverer ("Messiah") who would come to establish God's kingdom on earth. The corresponding Greek term *ho christos* ("the Christ") is used in this sense in the New Testament (as in Mark 8:29).

Just as Israel's covenant faith found new expression within the Tribal Confederacy, so it found new expression within the radically different conditions of the monar-

---

[18]Pritchard, *Ancient Near Eastern Texts* [1], p. 265.
[19]For a discussion of the new "Zion theology," see Bennie C. Ollenburger, *Zion, The City of the Great King* [400], and Jon D. Levenson, *Sinai and Zion* [159], pp. 84–194.

chy. The bitter political experiences of Israel after David's death gave rise to the hope that a "Messiah" of David's lineage would come to reunite the tribes of Israel and restore Jerusalem to a position of prestige among the nations (see Isa. 9; 11). In times of national calamity people prayed ardently to God to remember the covenant with David and to restore the kingdom of Israel. The poignant Psalm 89, for instance, petitions God to look upon the distress of the people and, in divine mercy and power, to fulfill the promise once made to David by the prophet Nathan. When everything seemed lost, the people looked back to the glorious rule of David as the symbol of God's future kingdom on earth. Hence the increasing theological importance of the kingdom, the city of David, the Davidic dynasty, the Temple, and the covenant with David. Indeed, the whole conception of the kingdom of God, so important in both Hebrew and Christian Bibles, was profoundly influenced by Israel's experience as a nation under David.

We must emphasize, however, that this fateful step in Israel's pilgrimage was resisted by conservatives, who feared that the transition from confederacy to monarchy would corrupt the people of Yahweh by making Israel "like the nations." Nathan's prophetic reaction in 2 Samuel 7:1-7 probably reflects authentic tradition even though the chapter (in its present form) comes from a late literary source concerned primarily with the continuance of the Davidic (Judean) dynasty. David succeeded in transferring the traditions of the Tribal Confederacy—Ark, Tabernacle, and priesthood—to Jerusalem, but in the process something happened to the distinctive character of "Israel." Israel was no longer a people of God bound together on the basis of *covenant allegiance* to Yahweh at the central sanctuary. Rather, the people were bound together *politically*, on the basis of a contract between the people and a king who could take a census, exact forced labor, and require submission to his power (2 Sam. 5:3). A deepseated conflict between these two ideas of "Israel" smoldered throughout the history of the monarchy.

SOLOMON IN ALL HIS GLORY

The words of Jesus, "Even Solomon in all his glory was not arrayed like one of these," referring to the natural beauty of the lilies of the field (Matt. 6:29), show how the name of Solomon came to symbolize the wealth and glory of empire. No other king, not even David himself, ascended a higher pinnacle of worldly splendor. Solomon's vast building program, his fabulous wealth and far-flung commercial enterprises, his up-to-date military program, his patronage of wisdom and the arts—all were regarded with awe by his subjects and by visitors from afar such as the Queen of Sheba (see Insert 10–1).

We have seen that in a brief span of fifty or sixty years Israel rose from political obscurity to the rank of a small empire that could command the political attention and economic envy of surrounding nations. Much of the credit was due to the leadership of David, whose reign was for the most part peaceful. Shortly before David's death, however, his empire began to slip out of control as a result of the revolt of Edom and Syria (1 Kings 11:15–25). Solomon, though not a military man like his father, practiced political shrewdness and international diplomacy to carry out and stabilize the policies David had initiated.

The political situation during Solomon's time continued to favor these achievements. Egypt continued to be politically weak, Assyria was not to be a threat for almost a century, and Israel controlled other smaller nations through military action or commercial treaty. The most prominent figure on the political horizon was Hiram I, king of Tyre. As leader of the Canaanite people called the Phoenicians, this monarch had established a vast colonial empire around the Mediterranean. David had entered into alliance with Hiram, however, and Solomon easily maintained that alliance through his military control over land routes. Thus the stage was set for a period of dazzling material prosperity.

THE HISTORIAN'S SLANT

The Court History of David concludes with an account of the intrigues that gave Solomon political power over Adonijah, his half-brother who was first in the line of succession (1 Kings 1–2). Unlike Saul and David, Solomon's claim to leadership was based not on charisma but solely on his birth and the political influence of his supporters. Thus "the kingdom was established in the hand of Solomon" (1 Kings 2:46) by eliminating any possible contenders to the throne. This was the road to power taken by most ancient kings, and in this respect Israel had indeed become "like the nations." Later, the people would look wistfully to a future messianic age when the "spirit of Yahweh" might rest once again upon the king, as it had upon David (Isa. 11:1–2).

The Davidic Court History ends abruptly at the conclusion of 1 Kings 2. Information about Solomon's reign is contained in 1 Kings 3–11, evidently extracted from a now lost royal document known as "The Book of the Acts of Solomon" (1 Kings 11:41). In its present form, however, the account reflects the viewpoint of the Deuteronomistic History (see Definition, p. 166, and Chapter 11): It has the same style of language and thought as the Deuteronomistic sections of Joshua, Judges, and Samuel—especially 2 Samuel 7 (compare 1 Kings 3:3–14; 5:3–5; 6:11–13; 8:14–61; 9:1–9; 11:1–13). Because the Deuteronomistic historians wanted to emphasize their own theological teachings, they selected from the royal annals only what served their purpose, and added interpretive passages.

The Deuteronomistic historians adhered to the view that true worship of Yahweh must be centralized in the Temple of Jerusalem, not in the outlying "high places." As a result, their history glosses over or neglects many of Solomon's acts, and concentrates attention on the building of the Temple. Moreover, they write with the conviction that the Davidic line was the only legitimate one, for Yahweh had promised David that he would build him a "house" (2 Sam. 7). So these historians did not hesitate to touch up

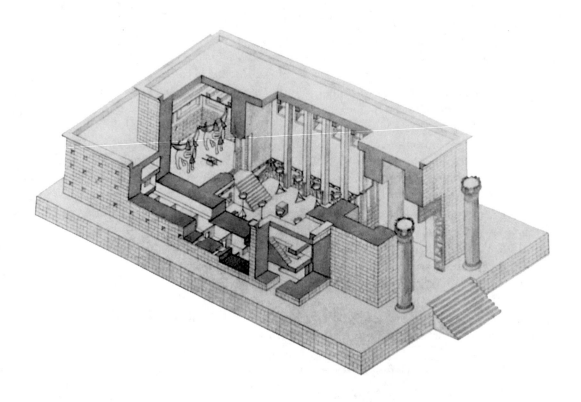

the portrait of Solomon. They apologize for Solomon by saying that at first he had to worship in "high places" because no temple had yet been built (1 Kings 3:1ff.). In the same breath, they maintain that "Solomon loved Yahweh, walking in the statutes of David, his father." This judgment is later qualified (1 Kings 11:4–6), but in general the Deuteronomistic History affirms that Yahweh was gracious to the kings of the Davidic dynasty "for David's sake."

Finally, these historians look back wistfully to the time before the sinful secession of the Northern tribes when the people were united and strong. With a nostalgia for the glorious past, they remember the time when Solomon ruled over all the kingdoms from the Euphrates River to the very border of Egypt, doubtless comparing that ideal situation with the unhappy state of affairs at the time of their writing. Even in the midst of describing an oppressive policy of Solomon, they boast that "Judah and Israel were as many as the sand by the sea; they ate and drank and were happy" (1 Kings 4:20–21). With no apparent fear of exaggeration, they claim that "Solomon excelled all the kings of the earth in riches and wisdom."

In reality, the portraits of David and Solomon—father and son—present a study in contrasts. David, who began as a shepherd and came to the throne after leading the rough life of a warrior, never rose so high that he was cut off from the common people and the traditions of the Tribal Confederacy that nourished him in his youth. Solomon, on the other hand, was born to the purple and never knew anything but the sheltered, extravagant life of the palace. From first to last Solomon ruled with absolute power, caring little about the sacred and social institutions of the former Tribal Confederacy. At

---

Solomon's Temple (upper left): a reconstruction showing the two massive, free-standing pillars flanking the ornamental east door. The Temple was originally built according to Phoenician architectural patterns. In front of the Temple was a courtyard, within which was placed the altar of burnt offering.

The interior of the Temple (lower left): a cutaway drawing by Edward S. Winters. (Since the drawing is isometric, the perspective is slightly distorted.)

The congregation worshipped in the court outside, near the high altar of sacrifice. Like other temples of the Syro-Phoenician region, this one was divided into three parts: the Ulam (vestibule), the Hekal (sanctuary), and the Debir (cellar or inner shrine).

The priest first ascended the ten steps of the Temple, passed through the huge cypress doors guarded by two elaborately adorned bronze pillars, known as Jachin and Boaz, and entered the vestibule. He then passed through another pair of cypress doors into the main sanctuary, about 60 feet long, which contained the sacred furniture: the seven-branched golden candlesticks, the table of showbread, and a small altar. This huge room, 45 feet high, was paneled with cedar and floored with cypress. Its flat roof was supported by huge cedar beams, and the room itself was dimly lit by latticed windows on either side, just below the ceiling. On the wall panels were carvings of palm trees, flowers, chain work, and cherubim.

Just beyond the small cedar altar, which was situated in the center of the main sanctuary and decorated with gold leaf, another series of stairs led up to a raised room, a perfect cube 30 feet squared, access to which was gained through a small double door. This was the Holy of Holies. It was lined with cedar and, having no windows, was pitch dark. In it were the two large cherubim, made of olive wood decorated with gold leaf, standing about 15 feet high. Beneath their outstretched wings stood the Ark of the Covenant, which was regarded as Yahweh's throne. (The above description is based on an article by G.E. Wright, "Solomon's Temple Resurrected," in *The Biblical Archaeologist*, IV [1941]. See also Roland de Vaux, *Ancient Israel* [130], Part IV, chap. 3.)

one point Solomon is said to have chosen God's gift of an understanding heart to judge (that is, to rule) his people, rather than riches and honor (1 Kings 3:3–15). But the actual facts of his administration show that he lacked the common touch. Ambitious and selfish by nature, his lavish court in Jerusalem was a hall of mirrors that reflected the glory and reputation of the great king of Israel. The law in Deuteronomy 17:14–20, which specifies that an Israelite king shall not rule autonomously but shall be guided by the *torah* of Yahweh, must have been composed with Solomon in mind.

A PROGRAM OF BUILDING AND EXPANSION

Thanks to the favorable international situation, Solomon was able to concentrate on an ambitious twenty-year building program. Because the Deuteronomistic historians regard the Temple as the most important part of this program, they give a proportionately large amount of space to the description of its erection, design, and furnishings (1 Kings 5–7). The temple was located on a ridge above and north of the site of the old city on ground that David had purchased for an altar (2 Sam. 24:18–25)—probably the very spot marked today by the sacred rock inside the Mosque of Omar (also known as the "Dome of the Rock," [see Insert 20–1]). It was modest in size (about 90 × 30 × 45 feet), but a great architectural achievement for its time. To consecrate their temple as the central sanctuary, the Israelites brought the Ark of the Covenant from Zion, David's old city, and held an elaborate ceremony in which Solomon himself officiated. The king offered a magnificent prayer—albeit cast in the Deuteronomistic language of a much later time (1 Kings 8:22–53).[20]

The Ark was one of the few points of contact with Israel's Mosaic heritage. By contrast the Temple, designed by Phoenician (Canaanite) architects, represented an invasion of Canaanite culture right into the center of Israel's life and worship.[21] Solomon's bold imitation of foreign ways must have shocked conservative Israelites who cherished the ancestral faith. It was many years before the Temple became the focus of Israelite affection and worship as in many of Israel's psalms (chapter 16).

In broader perspective, the building of the Jerusalem temple was overshadowed by other phases of Solomon's building program. Seven years were spent building the Temple, but thirteen years were devoted to the construction of Solomon's palace, a vast complex that included government buildings, the king's house (about 150 × 75 × 45 feet), and the house of his Egyptian queen. Moreover, outside Jerusalem Solomon built "chariot cities" and other fortifications at Gezer, Megiddo, Hazor, and elsewhere

---

[20]To the Deuteronomistic school of theologians, the idea of Yahweh dwelling in a temple was too limiting (1 Kings 8:27). They overcame this difficulty by saying that Yahweh, who is transcendent and cannot be contained in even the highest heavens, causes the divine "name" to dwell in the temple (1 Kings 8:28ff.).

[21]On the Canaanite architecture of the Temple, see G. E. Wright, "Solomon's Temple Resurrected," *The Biblical Archeologist*, IV (1941), 17–31; and W. F. Albright, *Archaeology and the Religion of Israel* [127], pp. 142-55. R. de Vaux, *Ancient Israel* [130], pp. 312–30, discusses fully the structure, furnishings, history, and theology of the Jerusalem Temple.

(1 Kings 9:15–19).[22] A fleet of horse-drawn chariots enabled him to protect his land and to control the trade routes over which wealth poured into his kingdom from Phoenicia, Egypt, Arabia, and other parts of the world (1 Kings 4:26; 9:10; 10:26). Solomon's traders purchased chariots from Egypt and horses from far off Cilicia (Kue), located in Hittite country. Indeed, Solomon was such a clever horse dealer that his agents exported horses and chariots to other nations at a handsome profit (1 Kings 10:28–29).

An excellent example of Solomon's far-flung commercial enterprises was his construction of a "fleet of ships" at Ezion-geber on the Gulf of Aqabah, an arm of water extending northward from the Red Sea (1 Kings 9:26–28; 10:22). In cooperation with Hiram, king of Tyre, Solomon's ships navigated to distant parts of the Mediterranean, providing Israel with an important seaport that Palestine lacked. The building of the seaport at Ezion-geber was a major political achievement.[23] The Phoenicians, a seafaring people who were ancestors of the later Carthaginians, had already been exploiting the commercial opportunities of the Mediterranean. Solomon's league with Hiram brought wealth into Palestine through Phoenician ports (see 1 Kings 10:22) and enabled him to take advantage of Phoenician maritime skill in exploiting the area of the Red Sea and Indian Ocean.

We read that the Queen of Sheba made a long trip from southern Arabia to visit Solomon (1 Kings 10:1–13). The real purpose of this visit might have been to negotiate a commercial treaty with the Israelite king, whose armies were cutting into the prosperous camel-caravan trade of Arabia. In this case, when the queen "told him all that was on her mind" the conversation must have come around to economic relations between the two countries. Evidently her diplomacy was not in vain, for "King Solomon gave to the Queen of Sheba all that she desired" (1 Kings 10:1–13). Interestingly, rulers of Ethiopia traditionally have claimed direct descent from Solomon through the Queen of Sheba.

RUMBLINGS OF DISCONTENT

Beneath this brilliant spectacle, however, were the rumblings of an approaching catastrophe. Like the great Pharaohs of Egypt, Solomon carried out his program of expansion by means of harsh measures. To pay for his tremendous overhead, he divided his kingdom into twelve tax districts, each with an officer in charge (1 Kings 4:7–19). One of the duties of the governors was to see that the royal larder was amply provided (1 Kings 4:22–28). Historians have argued convincingly that the real purpose behind this administrative organization was to centralize power in the crown, replacing the old tribal system with twelve districts under the direct supervision of royal appointees, two

---

[22]At first it was supposed that Solomon's stables had been excavated in the chariot city of Megiddo. Subsequently this proved to be erroneous; see, however, Graham I. Davies, "King Solomon's Stables—Still at Megiddo?," *Biblical Archaeology Review*, 20:1 (Jan/Feb 1994), 44–49.

[23]Ezion-geber (Tell el-Kheleifeh) was excavated under the direction of Nelson Glueck in 1938–40. See his book, *The Other Side of the Jordan* (New Haven: American Schools of Oriental Research, 1940), chaps. 3 and 4; also his updated discussion in *The Biblical Archaeologist*, XXVIII (1965), 70–87. For later evaluations see Gary D. Pratico, "Where Is Ezion-Geber," *Biblical Archaeology Review*, 12:5 (Sept/Oct 1986), 24ff.; and Alexander Flinder, "Is This Solomon's Seaport?" *Biblical Archaeology Review*, 15:4 (July/Aug 1989), 30ff.

of them sons-in-law of Solomon.[24] The boundaries of several tribal territories were deliberately changed in a move to eliminate the last remnants of tribal independence. In this respect, Solomon abandoned the administrative policy of his father, David, who respected the tribal divisions and the tribal representatives.

Equally oppressive was Solomon's program of forced labor. Though much of the slave labor for his building projects was drawn from conquered peoples, Solomon also brought the lash down heavily upon his own people. In 1 Kings 5:13–18 we learn that 30,000 Israelites were conscripted and sent off to the labor camps in Lebanon one month out of every three. In the north they felled the great cedars of Lebanon, floated them down the Phoenician coast to Joppa, and from there hauled them over the hills to Jerusalem. Eighty thousand Israelites were reportedly put to work in the stone quarries, and 70,000 toiled as burden-bearers. The great Temple was completed at tremendous human cost.

No wonder, then, that the pent-up resentment of the people eventually exploded into revolution. The leader of the revolt was a man Solomon had appointed to supervise one of the work gangs: Jeroboam, son of Nebat, from the Northern tribe of Ephraim. Even during David's reign the Northern tribes, formerly under Saul, had attempted to secede from the united monarchy. Just as the prophet Nathan had led the court intrigue that placed Solomon on the throne, so the prophet Ahijah, from the former confederate center of Shiloh, announced Solomon's fall. Ahijah announced that Yahweh would "rend the kingdom out of the hand of Solomon," leaving only the tribe of Judah under the rule of a Davidic descendant (1 Kings 11:29–39; see Chronological Chart 3, p. 233).

Israel had to relearn under prophetic teaching the truth experienced in the period of Moses and Joshua—namely, the inescapable judgment and mercy of God in the historical struggle. Unlike other religions of the time, Israel's covenant faith did not promote and sanction the harmony of the existing order. Rather, it promoted social change by emphasizing the conflict between God's will and human ambitions, between the kingdom of God and the kingdom of Israel. The God of Israel was involved in the political events that shook the very foundations of the kingdom created by David and Solomon.

SOLOMON'S BROADMINDEDNESS

"Yahweh was angry with Solomon" (1 Kings 11:9; compare 9:1–9). This is the view of the Deuteronomistic historians who pondered the meaning of events during Solomon's reign. Solomon's kingdom was weighed in God's balance and found wanting. The historians were as lenient as they could be, attributing Solomon's defects in part to his dotage: "When Solomon was old, his wives turned away his heart after other gods; and his heart was not perfect with Yahweh his God, as was the heart of David, his father"

---

[24]See G. E. Wright "The Provinces of Solomon," *Eretz Israel*, 8 (1967), 58–68.

(1 Kings 11:4). Solomon's weakness was seen as an excessive broadmindedness, most evident with respect to his harem of "seven hundred wives and three hundred concubines." To be sure, many of his marriages were for the purpose of establishing close political and cultural ties with surrounding peoples. His marriage with Pharaoh's daughter, for example, was a diplomatic union that linked Israel and Egypt as allies and brought Solomon the city of Gezer as a wedding dowry (1 Kings 3:1; 9:16).[25] Since marriages of this type were motivated primarily by political considerations, Solomon willingly allowed his foreign wives to practice their native religions, and he went so far as to build them shrines in his capital city. To the Deuteronomistic historians this was carrying tolerance too far, by giving royal sanction to an idolatrous policy that diluted and perverted Israel's faith.

The record indicates, however, that Solomon's entire reign tended toward religious syncretism—the amalgamation of alien cultural elements with Israel's native traditions. These foreign influences radically changed the character of Israel's life. The former simplicity of Israel's agricultural society was swept away in the wave of Solomonic prosperity, bringing sudden riches and royal favor to a few while others were consigned to abject poverty and royal slavery. Jerusalem, the capital of the kingdom, became a cosmopolitan city into which caravans came from all parts of the world bringing new ideas and practices, along with coveted wealth. Solomon probably regarded himself as a loyal worshiper of Yahweh, but his broadminded hospitality led him to adopt elements of the Baal religion and combine them with his Mosaic heritage. In the Temple, a conspicuous innovation was the "sea" (symbolic of the primeval ocean) supported by twelve bulls (1 Kings 7:23–26), which reflected fertility and mythological motifs of the Fertile Crescent. Apparently the Temple was meant to be a replica of Yahweh's heavenly abode, a microcosm of the macrocosm, in line with the ancient mythical view that a correspondence exists between the earthly and heavenly spheres.[26]

Finally, in his "largeness of mind" Solomon moved beyond the limitations of Israel's Mosaic tradition to pursue the cosmopolitan wisdom fashionable in foreign circles, such as the Egyptian court. Indeed, Solomon was regarded as the patron of Israel's wisdom movement, a movement that played an increasingly important role in Israelite life and thought throughout the period of the monarchy (see Chapter 17). There is good reason to trace the origin of Israel's wisdom movement to Solomon, for the historical Solomon undoubtedly had an avid interest in wisdom. He was a skillful diplomat in negotiating with Hiram of Tyre (1 Kings 5:12; compare 5:7), and apparently was known for his ability to settle local disputes as well. His legendary wisdom is illustrated in the story of two women who claimed the same baby son (1 Kings 3:16–28).

---

[25]On the significance of Gezer and its excavation (with footnote references to archaeological reports), see Hershel Shanks, "Memorandum: Re Restoring Gezer," *Biblical Archaeology Review*, 20:3 (May/June, 1994), 66–69.

[26]See R. E. Clements, *God and Temple* [517], chap. 5; also M. Eliade, *Cosmos and History* [138], pp. 6–20.

Solomon proposed to settle their argument by cutting the baby in two with a sword, giving half the body to one woman and half to the other. At this one woman immediately surrendered her claim and, recognizing a mother's love, Solomon rendered the verdict in her favor. The story ends with the community's reaction:

> All Israel heard of the judgment that the king had rendered; and they stood in awe of the king, because they perceived that the wisdom of God was in him, to execute justice.
>
> —1 KINGS 3:28 (NRSV)

This folktale, one of the finest in the wisdom tradition, must have circulated orally for many years before the Deuteronomistic historians included it as evidence that Yahweh had bestowed the gift of wisdom upon Solomon. The story helps us understand the place of wisdom in ancient Israel. In our way of thinking, Solomon was a shrewd judge of character and knew how to use a little practical psychology when the need arose. But in Israel's view, this kind of insight did not simply come with maturity or as a result of keen observation of human behavior. Israel believed that Yahweh bestowed wisdom upon the sage, just as Yahweh gave "teaching" (Hebrew: *torah*) to the priest or the "word" to the prophet (see Jer. 18:18).

The books of 1–2 Kings preserve other, less legendary information about Solomon's wisdom. One passage (1 Kings 4:29–34) reports that "Solomon's wisdom surpassed the wisdom of all the people of the east [that is, the bedouin Arabs], and all the wisdom of Egypt," as well as the wisdom of the sons of Mahol, who might have been Edomite sages. People from all lands came to hear the wisdom of Solomon, for "he was wiser than anyone else":

> He would speak of trees, from the cedar that is in the Lebanon to the hyssop that grows in the wall; he would speak of animals, and birds and reptiles, and fish.
>
> —1 KINGS 4:33 (NRSV)

This does not mean Solomon was a biologist. The idea is that, by studying the behavior of the natural world, Solomon gained insight into correct human behavior. Ancient peoples did not draw a sharp line between "nature" and human nature. The sage sought to understand the divine order of creation, upon which the well-being of all existence—animal and human—was believed to depend. The profound influence of wisdom upon Israel's worship of Yahweh as Creator is reflected in Psalm 104, which resembles Akhnaton's exquisite "Hymn to the Aton" and parallels the Priestly creation story (Gen. 1:1–2:3).[27]

---

[27]Akhnaton's hymn is found in Pritchard, *Ancient Near Eastern Texts* [1], pp. 369–70. For a discussion of Psalm 104 and creation theology, see B. W. Anderson, *Creation in the Old Testament* [132], pp. 11–14; reprinted in *From Creation to New Creation* [146], p. 86ff.

NEW HORIZONS OF FAITH

Profound changes were taking place in the age of Solomon in every aspect of Israel's life: political, economic, social, and intellectual. Emphasis on wisdom was only one symptom of the transition from the old Tribal Confederacy to Solomon's cosmopolitan royal government. It was no longer possible, at least in the "enlightened" circles of the Solomonic era, to be completely satisfied with the portrayal of Yahweh as a God who took direct part in Israel's history through special appearances, signs, and wonders. Yahweh's presence, according to the new theology, was veiled in the ordinary course of human events in which actions have consequences—a fundamental theme of wisdom literature.

We have already seen this subtler understanding of Yahweh's activity in the Court History of David, where the divine purpose is disclosed through a chain of actions and consequences in the Davidic family. A similar understanding characterizes the Joseph story, apparently shaped in wisdom circles, where Yahweh does not intervene directly or become openly manifest, but is revealed indirectly in the drama of human relations (see p. 160). This is also the case in the book of Ruth. This charming short story, placed in the rural setting of the old Tribal Confederacy ("In the days when the judges ruled . . .") tells how Ruth, a Moabite woman, was providentially led from her native country to Bethlehem of Judah, where she married an influential citizen, Boaz, and became the great-grandmother of David. There are no divine visitations in the story; rather, God's purpose is worked out through the *hésed* ("loyalty") of two women, Ruth and her mother-in-law Naomi.[28] Though probably composed after the period of the United Kingdom, Ruth's story is surely consonant with the spirit of the Age of Solomon.

ISRAEL AS A NATION

The Age of Solomon, then, must be viewed ambivalently. On the one hand, it opened up more spacious horizons than Israel had ever imagined, and revealed Yahweh's providence working in a subtle way through ordinary human experiences. On the other, it was a continuation of the conflict between faith and culture, between Yahweh and the gods—a conflict traceable throughout Israel's history as a nation in Canaan.

The Deuteronomistic historians leave no doubt about where they stand. It was not Yahweh's intention that Israel should become a great nation, as nations measure greatness. Israel was to be separated from other nations by a covenantal allegiance, as affirmed in Solomon's "Deuteronomistic" prayer (1 Kings 8:51, 53). From the first, Israel's covenant emphasized Yahweh's uncompromising, "jealous" demand for absolute loyalty. The people were called to maintain faithfulness to the Mosaic tradition within the cultural crosscurrents of Canaan, where the gods of the Fertile Crescent made an irresistible claim upon people's lives. Motivated by political gain and commercial expan-

---

[28]On "loyalty" (*hésed*), see Definition, pp. 277–278; also Katherine Sakenfeld, *Faithfulness in Action* [165], and Katheryn P. Darr, "'More than Seven Sons': Critical, Rabbinical, and Feminist Perspectives on Ruth," in *Far More Precious than Jewels: Perspectives on Biblical Women* (Louisville: Westminster, 1991), pp. 55–84.

sion, however, the people's faith tended toward tolerance and compromise—the very attitudes encouraged during Solomon's reign. Were it not for the prophets who rebuked and arrested these secular compromises, Israel's distinctive faith would have fallen into the oblivion of other ancient religions. Influenced by the convictions of Israel's prophets, the Deuteronomistic historians insisted that the regime of Solomon stood under divine judgment: Yahweh acted to stir up revolutionary ferment, even to the point of raising up adversaries against Solomon (1 Kings 11:14, 23).

The masterful prose epic of the "Yahwist" (J) viewed Israel's role as a nation in another historical perspective. This work, like that of the "Elohist" (E), probably incorporated parts of an all-Israelite epic tradition formed in the "Period of the Judges" (see Chapter 5). Based on generations of oral tradition nurtured at various tribal shrines (such as the confederate sanctuary at Shiloh), the Old Epic narrative expressed the faith and worship of the covenant community in much the same way the legends of King Arthur mirror the age of chivalry. But just as the age of chivalry came to an end with social changes that brought about the decline of feudalism, so Israel's age of song and legend was superseded by the new way of life in the monarchy. The times called for a reinterpretation of the sacred heritage, one that would express the new nationalism. The Yahwist responded to this challenge by creating a monumental literary and theological work, based on the story of Israel's life inherited from the days of the Tribal Confederacy.[29] (See Chap. 5)

This hypothesis helps to explain why, at the outset of the ancestral history, Yahweh promises Abraham that he and his descendants will become a great "nation" (Hebrew *goy*; Gen. 12:2, 18:18; compare Gen. 17:6, 16). The belief in Israel as the people of Yahweh and Yahweh as the God of Israel was fundamental to the ancient tradition of song and legend (as in the "Song of Deborah," Judg. 5). The Yahwist, however, understands Israel's nationhood in the context of an unfolding plan that embraces *all* nations. In the divine plan Israel's role is to bring blessing upon all the families of the earth—a role emphasized by viewing the call of Abraham in the context of the stories of primeval history. Israel is chosen for a purpose. Yahweh's promise to Abraham will yield benefits for all humankind.

We can understand the circumstances that prompted this historical vision during the Yahwist's time. Under David and Solomon, Israel began to abandon parochial ways of thinking and to welcome influences from the farthest parts of the world. Just when Israel's distinctive faith was in danger of being drowned by the new cosmopolitanism, an unknown writer, the "Yahwist,"[30] reinterpreted the Mosaic tradition in a way that made it profoundly relevant to the larger world in which Israel was to fulfill its task. The breadth of this historical vision was not surpassed until centuries later, when a prophetic poet of the Exile, echoing the Yahwist, proclaimed that in Yahweh's providential plan Israel was to be a "light to the nations" (Isa. 40–55).

---

[29]This is the view of Gerhard von Rad in his commentary on Genesis [305], pp. 13–31. See also Peter Ellis, *The Yahwist* [299], and R. W. Wolff, "The Kerygma of the Yahwist," in *The Vitality of Old Testament Traditions* [70], chap. 3.

[30]Harold Bloom, in *The Book of J*, makes the intriguing suggestion that this unknown writer was a woman.

CHAPTER 8

PROPHETIC TROUBLERS OF ISRAEL

In this chapter we resume Israel's life-story and—against the background of stormy events that followed Solomon's death—consider the rise of the prophetic movement.

Today the terms "prophet" and "prophecy" suggest a variety of meanings: We speak of prophets of the weather, prophets of the news, prophets who champion a social cause. In popular television presentations, prophets are clairvoyants who gaze into God's crystal ball and predict the shape of things to come. This linguistic confusion is an obstacle to understanding the role of Israel's prophets and their remarkable spiritual legacy.

We get some idea of how Israel's interpreters understood prophecy from Exodus 4:14–16 and 7:1–2. These passages use figurative language to describe the relationship between Moses and Aaron: Moses is to act as "God" to Aaron, by telling him what to say, and Aaron in turn will be Moses' "mouth," by articulating Moses' words to Pharaoh (Exod. 4:16). This analogy makes clear the view that prophets are persons *through whom God speaks.* Prophets were called by God, and they received the promise that God's "words" would be put in their mouths (Jer. 1:9).

Biblical Readings: 1 Kings 12 through 2 Kings 8, with special attention to the Elijah stories. The account is paralleled in 2 Chronicles 10–21.

The language prophets used to communicate the divine will helps us to understand their role. Studies of prophetic speech show that both Israelite and non-Israelite prophets often employed a "messenger style" well known in the ancient world.[1] Jacob used this style when, to bridge the distance between himself and his brother Esau, he dispatched messengers to announce his return:

> And Jacob sent messengers before him . . . instructing them,
>> "Thus you shall say to my lord Esau:
> Thus says your servant Jacob, 'I have sojourned. . . .'"
> —GENESIS 32:3–4

To a striking degree, prophetic oracles use the same language. They often begin with the messenger formula "Thus says Yahweh" and conclude with "the oracle of Yahweh" or "says Yahweh" (Amos 1:3–5; Jer. 2:1–3; Isa. 45:11–13). This indicates that prophets understood themselves to be *sent as messengers* to communicate "the word of Yahweh" to the people.[2] Their authority lay not in themselves—in their own religious experience or beliefs—but in the One who had sent them. They had received Yahweh's commission, "Go and say to my people." Accordingly their messages rang with an authority that could shake nations: "Thus says Yahweh!"

The purpose of biblical prophecy was not to communicate information about events in the distant future. To be sure, Israel's prophets often made predictions—some fulfilled and others not—in the conviction that Yahweh was guiding the course of events. But these predictions referred only to an immediate future that impinged on the

---

[1]See Claus Westermann's analysis of the basic forms of prophetic speech [370], pp. 70–91; also James F. Ross, "The Prophet as Yahweh's Messenger" [366].

[2]Martin Noth, "History and the Word of God in the Old Testament" [190], pp. 183ff., discusses parallels to the prophetic messenger speech in texts from Mari. For example, in a dream the god Dagon says to a man: "Now go! I am sending you to Zimri-lim [the king of Mari] and you yourself shall say to him: `Send your messengers to me. . . .'"

present. The prophetic announcement of what God was about to do stressed the urgency of the present. The prophets' task was to communicate God's message for *now*, and to summon the people to respond *today*.

THE BACKGROUND OF PROPHECY

In a broad sense, Israelite prophecy arose in connection with the Exodus, when God not only delivered a band of slaves from servitude but also raised up a leader to proclaim the meaning of that historical experience (pp. 51–55). Thus, at least in retrospect, Moses was called *nabî'* or "prophet" (see Deut. 18:18; Hos. 12:13). In addition, the Hebrew term *nebî'ā* ("prophetess") was used to describe the leadership of two women, Miriam (Exod. 15:20) and Deborah (Judg. 4:4). By the time of Samuel, however, the term *nabî'* was being applied to a special class in Israelite society, one that included the immediate forerunners of prophets such as Elijah.

We first hear of a company of prophets in connection with the Philistines' attempt to overrun the territory of Israel (1 Sam. 10:5–13). Israel's very existence is hanging in the balance: The Philistines had not only destroyed the confederate sanctuary at Shiloh but also captured the Ark. At this time of crisis Samuel, the last judge of the Tribal Confederacy, tries to rally the people to militant devotion to Yahweh, as Deborah had done at Megiddo. Supporting Samuel is a band of prophets who evidently had been active in Israel for some time, judging from the fact that their presence is taken for granted. After anointing Saul as king, Samuel enumerates various "signs" that will show Yahweh's confirmation of his choice of Saul. One is that Saul would come to a place called "the hill of God" (*Gibeath-'elohim*):

> And as you come to the city you will meet a band of prophets coming
> down from the high place [sanctuary], with harp, tambourine, flute and lyre
> in their lead, and they will be prophesying [ecstatically]. Then the spirit of
> Yahweh will overpower you; you will prophesy [ecstatically] with them and
> be changed into another person.
>
> —1 SAMUEL 10:5b–6

SPIRIT POSSESSION

Here the verb "to prophesy" (Hebrew: *hithnabbe'*) has a special meaning: "to behave like a prophet" or "to prophesy ecstatically." For us, ecstatic behavior might suggest a state of emotion so powerful that self-control or reason is suspended.[3] In the Hebrew

---

[3]The word comes from the Greek *ékstasis*, "to set or stand out," thus "to derange" or "be beside oneself."

sense, however, ecstatic prophecy arises not from mere emotional rapture but from the spirit (Hebrew: *rúaḥ*) of Yahweh that falls upon a person, takes control of the center of the self, and makes one an instrument of the divine will. Thus Samuel could promise that Saul would be turned into "another person"—not just Saul the son of Kish, but Saul *possessed* by Yahweh's spirit. Unusual things happened in a prophetic state: In another story we learn how Saul, seized by prophetic ecstasy, stripped off his clothes and lay naked in a stunned condition all day and all night (1 Sam. 19:19–24). Such incidents seem to correspond to prophetic behavior in other cultures where individuals acted in stereotyped ways that would be recognized as the working of the divine spirit.[4]

According to narratives in 1 Samuel, ecstatic prophecy was already practiced in Israel during the days of the early monarchy. Hence we must look farther back to find the origins of this movement. Numbers 11:24–29 tells a curious story about how the spirit of Moses was transferred to the elders of Israel, causing them to "prophesy ecstatically" (*hithnabbe'*). Most scholars, however, view this episode as an anachronism—a description of the Mosaic period that reflects the language and custom of a later time. Most likely, Israel first became acquainted with ecstatic prophecy in Canaan, where it was connected with Baal religion. The Egyptian story of Wen Amon (from the eleventh century B.C.E.) tells of a religious festival in the Phoenician port of Byblos where "the god seized one of [the] youths and made him possessed [he fell into an ecstatic state]."[5] Centuries later, prophets of Baal, imported from Phoenicia, worked themselves into an ecstatic frenzy on top of Mount Carmel as they danced around the altar, cut themselves with knives, and raised their cultic shouts (1 Kings 18:20–29). This type of "ecstatic" prophecy was also known in Asia Minor, from which it spread into the Mediterranean world and later took the form of orgies in the cult of Dionysus.

If the Israelites borrowed ecstatic prophecy from the Canaanites, they transformed what they borrowed. To be sure, there were external similarities that linked the Baal prophets (such as the Mount Carmel prophets in 1 Kings 18) to the Israelite prophets of the early monarchy. Israel's prophets also traveled in companies, responding to inquiries by delivering oracles from God. Prophetic ecstasy was contagious and was often stimulated by the rhythm of music and bodily movements. An interesting passage tells how Elisha, when asked for a word from Yahweh, first summoned a musician: "And when the minstrel played, the spirit of Yahweh came upon him" (2 Kings 3:15). The influence of the divine spirit sometimes stimulated hyperactivity, as in the case of Elijah, who ran before the king's chariot with superhuman energy (1 Kings 18:46). But similarities in behavior are rather superficial. The prophets of Israel were set apart from their Canaanite counterparts by their unique calling as spokespersons of Yahweh, mes-

---

[4]See the important essay by Robert R. Wilson, "Prophecy and Ecstasy: A Reexamination," *Journal of Biblical Literature* 98 (1979), 321–37. He argues that "at least some Israelite possession behavior did in fact follow patterns similar to those found in the possession behavior of modern prophets."
[5]See Pritchard, *Ancient Near Eastern Texts* [1], pp. 25–29.

sengers sent to interpret the promises and demands of the covenant within Yahweh's historical purpose.

Many of Israel's early prophets belonged to guilds or schools known as "the sons of the prophets,"[6] living communally under the leadership of a chief prophet apparently known as "father" (2 Kings 4:1). Elijah and Elisha were evidently leaders of prophetic communities at Bethel, Jericho, and Gilgal (2 Kings 2:3–4; 4:38). Members of these guilds were not tied permanently to any one place but were instead free to travel around and deliver oracles as the occasion demanded. As we know from the story in 2 Kings 4:1–7, women also lived in these prophetic communities.

CULTIC PROPHETS

In addition to the roving bands of ecstatics, there were prophets with closer ties to the great shrines of Israel. Studies have shown that sanctuaries like those at Bethel and Jerusalem employed priests and prophets who served side by side in a joint ministry.[7] These so-called "cultic prophets" had a special role in services of worship: Regarded as experts in prayer, particularly intercessory prayer, they brought the people's petitions before Yahweh. Moreover, as Yahweh's spokespersons, they indicated whether or not an offering was acceptable and communicated the divine answer to a petition. During great religious festivals, such as that of covenant-renewal, they might have played an important part in announcing the demands and promises of the covenant.

These anonymous prophets had a great influence on Israelite tradition, even though their names and oracles have not been preserved. Great prophets such as Elijah might have inherited the forms of oracular speech used to communicate God's "word" from such prophetic ancestors. Oracles of cultic prophets, composed originally for use in situations of worship, might now lie embedded in the body of prophetic literature transmitted under the names of the great prophets. Moreover, some psalms seem to reflect the role of these anonymous prophets in Israel's worship (see Psalm 81:5b–16). In difficult times, when Israel was exposed to dangers from without and within, many of these unknown prophets must have been sincere and passionate interpreters of the covenant between Yahweh and Israel.

PROPHETS AND POLITICS

Prophecy was intimately associated with politics from its first appearance in Israel, as is obvious in the story of Samuel's anointment of Saul (1 Sam. 10). A prophetic band was stationed at "the hill of God," right next to a Philistine garrison, apparently with the

---

[6]"Sons" is an idiomatic way of indicating members of a group or company; thus "the sons of God" (Gen. 6:2; Job 1:6) refers to "members of the heavenly council, heavenly beings."

[7]See especially A. R. Johnson, *The Cultic Prophet in Ancient Israel* [354]; also R. E. Clements, *Prophecy and Covenant* [349], pp. 11–34. A good discussion of various types of "primitive prophets in ancient Israel" is given in J. Lindblom, *Prophecy in Ancient Israel* [355], chap. 2.

purpose of inciting the Israelites to "holy war" against the enemy. Members of this band must have sung and danced with ecstatic fervor, much as singing and dancing are performed in modern Arab circles to arouse patriotic feeling. Like the charismatic judges of an earlier day, the prophets were inspired with enthusiasm.[8] Elijah and Elisha were such vigorous champions of Israel's faith that they were called "the chariots of Israel and its horsemen" (2 Kings 2:12; 13:14).

The early prophets were more than zealous champions of "holy war." Primarily they were called on to deliver Yahweh's word in specific situations. At the time there were three accepted channels for ascertaining the divine will: dreams, particularly those experienced in a holy place; "Urim and Thummin," the sacred dice handled by the priests; and prophecy (1 Sam. 28:6). In times of political crisis the prophet, rather than the priest, was better suited to be Yahweh's spokesperson. A priest could officiate at sacred rites, teach the people the sacred traditions, and manipulate the sacred lot in answer to yes-or-no questions. But the prophet, speaking under the influence of Yahweh's spirit, interpreted the meaning of events and proclaimed God's will in concrete terms.

Devotion to Yahweh, fired by the energy of prophetic enthusiasm, was Israel's bond of unity and strength in its struggle for survival. When Israel became a nation, however, with a monarchic form of government like the surrounding nations, the prophets' role in relation to the political establishment became more ambivalent. Some prophets, like Elijah, stood outside the power structure and were viewed as the king's enemies (compare 1 Kings 21:20). As radical critics of society, they advocated rapid, revolutionary social change. Other prophets operated within the social structure, advocating more orderly social transition.[9] One of these was Nathan, whose oracle concerning Yahweh's covenant with David (2 Sam. 7:11–17) influenced other prophets like Isaiah and had a lasting effect upon Israelite society. At the same time, Nathan did not hesitate to summon the king before the highest tribunal to hear words of divine judgment against the misuse of royal power (2 Sam. 12).

Israel's prophetic movement, then, is inseparably linked to the period of Israel's nationhood, when kings and queens sat upon the thrones of Israel and Judah. The prophets were not mystics or individualists seeking escape from society, but members of communities that kept alive a sacred tradition and gave their support to a prophetic leader. They addressed their oracles to Israel who, though having become a nation (Hebrew: *goy*), was still to be "the people of Yahweh."

Nevertheless, prophets differed in their relation to the structures of power, in the theological accents with which they spoke, and in their judgment on national policy.

---

[8]The word "enthusiasm" comes from the Greek *entheos*, "to be inspired of God." Abraham J. Heschel attempts to distinguish between "ecstasy" and "enthusiasm" in *The Prophets* [352], pp. 326–27; but no sharp line can be drawn.

[9]This is the thesis of Robert R. Wilson, *Prophecy and Society* [371], who draws a distinction between "central" and "peripheral" prophets with regard to their relation to the political establishment.

This led to the question of true and false prophecy: "Who speaks the word of Yahweh?"[10]

THE DIVIDED KINGDOM

At this point in our study we focus attention on developments that took place after Solomon's death, specifically, during the time from the split of the United Kingdom to the revolution of Jehu (about 922–842 B.C.E.). No literature attributed to specific prophets survives from this period. Instead, traditions about the prophets are interwoven with historical narratives in the books of 1–2 Kings, which carry the story of Israel from the end of David's reign to the time just after the tragic fall of Judah in 587 B.C.E.

THE DEUTERONOMISTIC VIEW

The books of 1–2 Kings form the conclusion of the Deuteronomistic History (pp. 110–111),[11] which interprets the history of the monarchy from the standpoint of the Mosaic tradition. In this view, obedience to the covenant (as prescribed in Deuteronomic law) yields the blessings of welfare and peace, and disobedience invites the divine judgment of suffering and even expulsion from the land. To be in covenant with Yahweh requires that the people love Yahweh with their whole being (Deut. 6:4); anything smacking of idolatry must be eradicated from the community. To keep Israel's society pure from contamination by surrounding cultures, the Deuteronomistic historians advocate the centralization of worship in Jerusalem and the closing of all outlying sanctuaries ("high places") where popular syncretism and idolatry flourished. They condemn Jeroboam I, who established rival sanctuaries such as the one at Bethel, and all kings who tolerated these innovations no matter what else could be said to their credit.

Advocates of the royal covenant theology of Judah, the Deuteronomistic historians emphasize Yahweh's everlasting covenant with David and the choice of Zion as the central sanctuary. Their historical perspective is set forth clearly in the summary in 2 Kings 17:7–41, which reviews events from the establishment of the monarchy to the fall of the Northern Kingdom.[12]

Within the Deuteronomistic History, each Northern and Southern king is strictly judged against the standard of covenant obedience. As in the history of the judges (pp. 166–167), the historians follow a formulaic scheme that varies only slightly from case to case:

---

[10]See James Crenshaw, *Prophetic Conflict* [350].

[11]Notice that the Deuteronomic law is specifically mentioned in 2 Kings 14:6; compare Deuteronomy 24:16.

[12]See Frank M. Cross, "The Themes of the Book of Kings and the Structure of the Deuteronomistic History" [129], especially the discussion of the historians' themes, pp. 278–85. He advocates two editions of this history: an original version written just before the fall of Judah, and an updated expansion during the Exile.

Judah	*Israel*
1. In the _____ year of so-and-so, king of Israel, so-and-so, king of Judah, began to reign.	**1.** In the _____ year of so-and-so, king of Judah, so-and-so, king of Israel, began to reign.
2. Facts about his age, duration of reign, name, and queen mother.	**2.** Facts about the length of his reign and the place of his capital.
3. Evaluation of his standing in comparison to "David his father."	**3.** Censure for the fact that "he did what was evil in the sight of Yahweh, and walked in the way of Jeroboam and his sin which he made Israel to sin."
4. "Now the rest of the acts of so-and-so . . . are they not written in the Book of Chronicles of the Kings of Judah?"	**4.** "Now the rest of the acts of so-and-so . . . are they not written in the Book of Chronicles of the Kings of Israel?"
5. Concluding statement that he slept with his ancestors, and so-and-so reigned in his stead.	**5.** Concluding statement that he slept with his ancestors, and so-and-so reigned in his stead.

The Deuteronomistic historians make it plain that anyone interested in learning more about these kings can go to the royal library and consult the archives. Their purpose in writing is to apply the great lessons of the past to their own day, so that those who read or listen might understand and face the present crisis. They want to show that the breakup of the Davidic kingdom did not happen by chance; rather, God was at work in Israel's tragic career, punishing the people for their repeated faithlessness (despite prophetic warnings) and summoning them to turn from their evil ways (2 Kings 17:13). Thus they proceed through the list of kings, painstakingly dating the reign of each king of Israel and Judah through cross-reference to each other—a somewhat confusing procedure made necessary by the absence of a standard calendar. Not one king of Israel escapes the historians' blacklist! The kings of Judah are also judged severely: Only two Southern kings (Hezekiah and Josiah) come off with a clean record; six receive a mere passing grade because they failed to remove the high places; and ten "flunk" because they "did what was evil in the sight of Yahweh."

Fortunately, the Deuteronomists often clothed their historical skeleton with flesh and blood by choosing stories and traditions from other sources. Their account of Solomon evidently drew on royal archives known as "The Book of the Acts of Solomon." They probably had access to temple archives as well. The history of the divided kingdom refers frequently to two sources: "The Book of the Chronicles of the Kings of Israel," and "The Book of the Chronicles of the Kings of Judah." But the Deuteronomists preserved only fragmentary quotations from these royal annals, no trace of which has ever been found. In addition, they incorporated legends drawn from popular tradition, such as the stories of Elijah and Elisha.

SOLOMON'S HEAVY YOKE

The story of the divided kingdom opens in 1 Kings 12: Rehoboam, the son of Solomon, makes a trip into Northern territory to be installed as "king of Israel," though he is already recognized as king in Jerusalem. Here "Israel" refers to the ten Northern tribes—not to the larger unity that David had forged from remnants of Saul's kingdom and his own tribe of Judah. Clearly the policies of David had only superficially healed the deep rift within the covenant community, already evident in the period of the Tribal Confederacy.

The gathering took place at Shechem, a place hallowed with tradition. There, near a sacred tree, Abraham had built an altar to Yahweh (Gen. 12:7). Moreover, in the Jacob cycle treasured in Northern circles, Jacob's first holding in Canaan was at Shechem (Gen. 33:18–20). Above all, Shechem was the place where the Tribal Confederacy had been established (Josh. 24). At this ancient tribal gathering place, the Northern tribes—acting with a show of independence—gathered to make Rehoboam their king. Smarting under the whiplash that Solomon had laid upon them in his labor gangs, the tribes demanded that the yoke be lightened.[13] Solomon's tyrannical policy had fallen most heavily on the prosperous Northern tribes. But Rehoboam, shunning the advice of his older counselors and swayed by the young men around him, gave a harsh reply: "My father disciplined you with whips, but I will discipline you with scorpions" (1 Kings 12:14).

Again the call to revolution resounded, as it had in David's time under Absalom and Sheba. The people's cry harked back to the old days of tribal independence:

> What share do we have in David?
>   We have no inheritance in the son of Jesse.
> To your tents, O Israel!
>   Look now to your own house, O David.
>   —1 KINGS 12:16 (NRSV)

When Rehoboam indiscreetly sent Adoniram, the taskmaster in charge of forced labor, to bring the situation under control, Adoniram was stoned to death. The king jumped into his chariot and hastily fled to Jerusalem. Only the oracle of the prophet Shemaiah (1 Kings 12:22–24) prevented him from precipitating an immediate civil war.

JEROBOAM THE FIRST

At some point in this revolution Jeroboam I, the son of Nebat, decided to "lift up his hand against the king" (1 Kings 11:26). Jeroboam belonged to the Northern tribe of

---

[13]Murray Newman, in *The People of the Covenant* [262], p. 177, points out that the "yoke" the Northerners wanted lightened was theological, too. Unable to accept the royal covenant theology (2 Sam. 7) that promised divine authorization for the Davidic throne and dynasty, they insisted upon limiting the king's sovereignty in the North, in accordance with their Mosaic covenant theology.

Ephraim and had once been Solomon's taskmaster over forced labor in the northern provinces (1 Kings 11:26–28). Now he joined the plot to overthrow the Davidic regime.

Notice that the prophet Ahijah, from the former confederate center of Shiloh, was a chief conspirator in this plot. Pouring fuel on the fires of rebellion, Ahijah prophesied that Yahweh was about to tear the ten Northern tribes from Solomon and give them to Jeroboam (1 Kings 11:29–39). When Solomon crushed the first stage of the revolt, Jeroboam fled to Egypt, where he was given political asylum by Pharaoh Shishak (1 Kings 11:29–40). About 922 B.C.E., at the opportune moment after Solomon's death, Jeroboam returned and was proclaimed king over the Northern tribes. Thereafter these tribes were known as "Israel" or "Ephraim"—as distinguished from "Judah," the tribe (along with Benjamin) that gave allegiance to the Davidic dynasty.

Surprisingly, the empire of Solomon, fortified with the best military equipment of the day and policed by the king's officers, collapsed almost overnight. The political situation at the time undoubtedly favored the Northern tribes (Ephraim) in their secession. Rehoboam surely had the military power to make a preemptive strike against the revolutionaries, and probably would have won had he acted quickly. The fact that he did not was undoubtedly due to a threatened attack from Egypt, which caused him to forget Ephraim ("Israel") momentarily and divert his energies to the protection of his southern and eastern borders. We can infer that the fortifications described in 2 Chronicles 11:5–12 were built in expectation of an Egyptian invasion (2 Chron. 12:2–4).

··

DEFINITION   "EPHRAIM"   AND   "JUDAH"

During the period of the divided kingdom the term "Israel," once used to designate the whole covenant people, was narrowed down to refer only to a political entity, specifically the Northern Kingdom that split off from the Davidic dynasty centered in Jerusalem. Thus the term was nationalized, as has occurred also in the case of the modern state of Israel.

Often, however, the Northern Kingdom is called "Ephraim," after Jeroboam's tribe. The Northern prophet, Hosea, uses both terms (for example, "Ephraim" in 12:1; 13:2 and "Israel" in 10:1; 11:1), showing that the terms can be understood synonymously. Quite apart from ideological claims on behalf of the Northern state, the Northerners undoubtedly believed that they were the true preservers of the Mosaic tradition—one upheld in the time of the Tribal Confederacy under the leadership of Joshua, also an Ephraimite.

The foolish policy of Rehoboam, who sought to crush rebellion within the Davidic empire with extreme measures, exacerbated tensions between Ephraim (Israel) and Judah. But the seeds of this tension can be traced back to the time before the monarchy when the Joseph tribes (Ephraim and Manasseh) had ascendancy over the tribe of Judah. The rise of the tribe of Judah, especially under David and Solomon, temporarily smoothed over but did not eliminate these deep-seated differences.

Despite the schism between North and South, "Israel" retained its ancient meaning of a people united in covenant solidarity with Yahweh. Thus some Israelite prophets portrayed the future as a time when political wounds would be healed and all Israel, Ephraim and Judah, would unite in a community transcending national rivalries (as in Isa. 9, 11; Jer. 31).

Egypt was awakening from three centuries of political lethargy that followed the death of Merneptah in 1211 B.C.E. A new monarch had seized the throne: Shishak (about 935–914 B.C.E.), founder of the Twenty-Second Dynasty. Hoping to regain Egypt's former position of prestige and power in the Fertile Crescent, Shishak reversed the policy of diplomatic subservience that had been in force during the reign of David and most of the reign of Solomon, and began meddling aggressively in Palestinian affairs. During Solomon's lifetime, Shishak had given refuge to political criminals such as Jeroboam of the Northern Kingdom of Israel and Hadad of Edom. The death of Solomon gave Shishak an opportunity to undermine Solomon's empire using the age-old political principle of "divide and conquer." He gladly released Jeroboam to lead the seditionist movement, and began to prepare for his own invasion of Palestine.

Actually, Shishak was no fonder of Jeroboam than he was of Rehoboam. The Egyptian invasion, which came just five years after the division of the United Kingdom (918 B.C.E.), swept like an avalanche over Edom, Philistia, Judah, and Israel alike. In addition to the brief report in 1 Kings 14:25–28, we have the famous Karnak List of Asiatic countries conquered by Egyptian kings. This list was inscribed on the walls of the magnificent temple of Karnak, whose remains still stand outside Luxor.[14]

Chronological Chart 3

B.C.E.	Egypt	Palestine		Phoenicia	Mesopotamia
1000		THE UNITED KINGDOM			
	Decline	David, c. 1000–961		Hiram I,	Assyrian
		Solomon, c. 961–922		c. 969–936	Decline
	XXII Dynasty				
	Shishak I				
	(c. 935–914)				
(*Iron Age*)		Division of the kingdom at			
		death of Solomon, c. 922			
		THE DIVIDED KINGDOM			
	Shishak	*Judah*	*Israel*		
	invades Judah	DAVIDIC DYNASTY:			
	c. 918	Rehoboam,	Jeroboam I,		
		c. 922–915	c. 922–901		
		Abijah (Abijam),			
		c. 915-913			
900		Asa, c. 913–873	Nadab,		
			c. 901–900		

[14]See Pritchard, *Ancient Near Eastern Texts* [1] pp. 242–43, 263–64; also Frank J. Yurco, "3,200-Year-Old Picture of Israelites Found in Egypt," *Biblical Archaeology Review* 16:5 (Sept/Oct 1990), 20–38.

JEROBOAM'S REFORM

While Rehoboam was busy preparing for the threatened Egyptian invasion, Jeroboam took measures to strengthen his Northern Kingdom. The Deuteronomistic historians, who regard Jeroboam as a *bête noire,* give minimal information about his reign. All of 1 Kings 13–14 is a lengthy tirade against Jeroboam's blasphemy in setting up rival shrines in the North. For a more sympathetic understanding of Jeroboam's accomplishments, we must rely on the historical fragment in 1 Kings 12:25–33.

To begin with, Jeroboam strengthened his temporary capital, Shechem, and fortified Penuel on the other side of the Jordan. Both sites figured prominently in Israel's ancient sacred traditions, and were especially identified with the Northern patriarch Jacob (Gen. 32:22–32; 33:18–20; 34). Jeroboam realized that something more than military measures was necessary to consolidate his people. By turning to Shechem, the first center of the old Tribal Confederacy, he capitalized on its religious significance. Jeroboam also knew that the pull toward Jerusalem, seat of Solomon's temple, could easily counteract the political independence of the North. Just as David sought to unify his kingdom by bringing the Ark of the Covenant to Jerusalem, Jeroboam determined to provide a religious foundation in the Northern Kingdom. He set up shrines at Dan and at Bethel, both of which had long been places of pilgrimage, and he established a priesthood that claimed direct lineage from the Mosaic period. Finally, he instituted an annual Fall festival (the Feast of Ingathering or Thanksgiving) comparable to a festival celebrated in Judah at a slightly different time.

The Deuteronomistic historians were horrified at Jeroboam's innovations, especially the setting up of golden bulls in high places outside Jerusalem. Repeatedly they denounce Jeroboam as "the man who made Israel to sin." The account of Jeroboam's religious reforms echoes the story of the worship of the Golden Calf in the wilderness period: "You have gone up to Jerusalem long enough. Behold your gods, O Israel, who brought you up out of the land of Egypt" (1 Kings 12:28; see Exod. 32:4, 8). Swayed by anti-Northern propaganda, the Judean editors probably changed the tradition from "Behold your *God,*" for it is extremely doubtful that Jeroboam intended to introduce polytheism. Rather, Jeroboam could have been returning to an old Northern Israelite tradition in which Yahweh, identified with El ("Bull *'El* "), was represented standing invisibly on the back of a young bull (see pp. 94–95). Scholars who defend Jeroboam argue that the practice was "no more idolatrous than the equally symbolic representation of Yahweh in the Temple of Solomon as an invisible Presence enthroned on the cherubim."[15]

Whatever the case, Jeroboam had no idea of introducing the worship of new "gods." His intention (as the Deuteronomistic historians imply) was to connect the reli-

---

[15]W. F. Albright, *From the Stone Age* [127], pp. 203, 228–30. This view is supported substantially by Frank M. Cross, "Yahweh and *'El* " [129], pp 73–75. For a different assessment of Jeroboam's reform, see Martin Noth, *Pentateuchal Traditions* [76], pp. 141–45.

The Storm God Hadad stands on the back of a bull, holding in each hand a pronged fork representing lightning. This bas-relief, found at Arslan-Tash in northern Syria, comes from the eighth century B.C.E. Jeroboam I may have intended the golden bull to be not an idol but a pedestal on which Yahweh stood invisibly.

gion of the Northern Kingdom with the main stream of Mosaic tradition, the chief theme of which was the Exodus from Egypt. Traditions of the Tribal Confederacy inaugurated at Shechem, the very place Jeroboam chose as his capital, were emphasized more in the North than in the Davidic circles of the South (see Chapter 11). Moreover, in Jeroboam's time the Northern (Elohist) version of the sacred history probably was written to express the nationalism of the independent state (see pp. 260–262).

Even though he intended to renew Israel's devotion to the God of the Covenant, Jeroboam's action in setting up the golden bulls was fraught with serious dangers in an environment where Canaanite religion was all too attractive. In the Ras Shamra literature (see pp. 169–171) the bull was associated not only with 'El, the high god of the pantheon, but also with Baal, the virile god of storm and fertility. Unwittingly, perhaps, Jeroboam encouraged the fusion of Israel's faith with Baal religion. It was a Northern prophet, not a historian from the South, who first denounced the calf of Bethel, seeing in it the seductive idolatry that had perverted Israel's faith since the entrance into Canaan. According to Hosea, Yahweh reacted with loathing and rage to the "Calf of Samaria," the official image of the cult of Israel (Hos. 8:5–6; 10:5–6).

THE RISE OF THE HOUSE OF OMRI

After giving their account of Jeroboam, the Deuteronomistic historians retrace their steps to summarize the reigns of two southern kings, Rehoboam and Abijah (or Abijam), contemporaries of Jeroboam. These kings are dismissed quickly with characteristic Deuteronomistic judgments (1 Kings 14:21–15:8). But the historians do include a notice about Shishak's invasion, excerpted from "The Book of the Chronicles of the Kings of Judah." This event, in the Deuteronomistic perspective, demonstrated Yahweh's retributive action against Rehoboam for his sins.

Next the historians turn to the reign of Asa of Judah, also overlapping the reign of Jeroboam (1 Kings 15:9–24). Asa's reign provides a long dateline of about forty years on which to peg the reigns of the contemporary kings of the Northern Kingdom—Nadab, Baasha, Elah, Zimri, Omri, and Ahab (1 Kings 15:25–16:34). This narrative leads up to the account of King Ahab's reign, into which the Elijah stories have been inserted (see Chronological Chart 4, p. 233).

During these years (about 900–850 B.C.E.) political tensions mounted in Palestine. For fifty years—ever since the split of Solomon's kingdom—Israel and Judah had fought an ongoing civil war. Egypt continued to interfere, and new dangers menaced from the north. Most imminent was the threat of Syria (Aram), whose traditional rivalry with Israel was reflected in the Jacob-Laban stories (Gen. 29–31). No longer subservient to Israel, Syria took advantage of its strategic location at the commercial crossroads of the Fertile Crescent. Syrian kings looked with envious eyes on Israel's territory, especially the territory in Transjordan just south of the Syrian capital of Damascus. Further off, the Assyrian lion, which would ultimately threaten Syria, Israel, Judah, and all the small nations of the Fertile Crescent, was pacing restlessly in its Mesopotamian lair. This lion would roar in about 870 B.C.E., when Ashur-nasirapal (884–860 B.C.E.) marched through northern Syria and subjugated parts of Phoenicia.

SYRIAN AGGRESSION

Trouble was brewing during the reign of Asa of Judah (about 913–873 B.C.E.). Asa was interested in religious reforms, for which he won the qualified praise of the Deuteronomistic historians. Indeed, he probably helped halt the tendency toward syncretism that

Insert 7-1 These Canaanite gold female figurines are rare sheet-gold pendants found in a storeroom at Gezer. These (still stylish!) female figures measure 16.1 and 10 centimeters in height.

Insert 8-1 The Shechem Pass is the strategic gateway to the heart of Canaan. Located at the caravan crossroads between Mount Gerizim *(left)* and Mount Ebal *(right)*, Shechem was the first center of the Israelite confederacy.

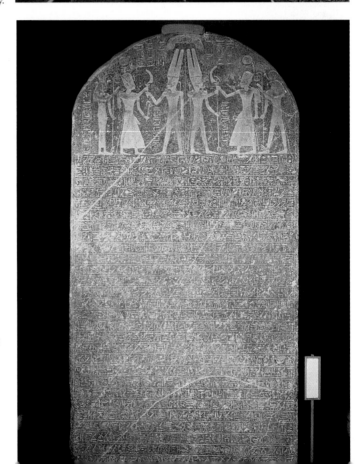

Insert 8-2 The Stele of Merneptah contains the earliest mention of "Israel" outside the Bible. Under the winged sun disc stands the god Amon in double representation. The king is also shown twice, standing before the god with a sickle sword in one hand and a scepter in the other. Behind him stands the goddess Mut *(extreme left)* and the falcon headed god Horus *(extreme right)*.

Mediterranean Sea

Hamath

Arvad (ISLAND)

Byblos

PHOENICIA

Sidon

Zerephath

Tyre

MT. LEBANON

MT. HERMON

ARAM (SYRIA)

Damascus

Dan

Hazor

ISRAEL

GALILEE

VALLEY OF JEZREEL

MT. CARMEL

Megiddo

Jezreel

Ramoth-gilead

Beth-shan

Tirzah?

Tishbeh?

Samaria

Penuel

Mahanaim

Shechem

R. JORDAN

R. JABBOK

AMMON

Shiloh

Bethel

Gilgal

Rabbath-Ammon

Jerusalem

Jericho

Tekoa

VALLEY OF ACHOR

Heshbon

SALT SEA

Gaza

PHILISTIA

Lachish

Hebron

Dibon

Gerar

Beer-sheba

JUDAH

MOAB

R. OF EGYPT

EDOM

ARABIAN DESERT

Ezion-geber

OMRI'S KINGDOM

▬ ▬ ▬ ▬   OMRI TERRITORY

237

had been encouraged under the reigns of Solomon and his immediate successors. He succeeded in shaking himself free from the control of his queen mother, whom he deposed, and he banned the worship of Asherah, the Canaanite goddess she had sponsored (1 Kings 15:13).

Asa had other problems, however, that could not be solved by religious reform. Israel (Ephraim), with whom Judah had waged intermittent war since the division of the monarchy, had become so strong that its king, Baasha, was able to blockade the northern avenues into Jerusalem. Consequently, Asa took a fateful step: He appealed to Benhadad, king of Syria, to join him as an ally against Israel. The Syrian king gladly obliged by invading and devastating Galilee (about 878 B.C.E.), at the same time advancing his own political ambitions. The resulting confusion led to a rapid turnover of Israel's kings through assassination, suicide, and intrigue (one king, Zimri, held the throne only seven days after murdering his predecessor). As often happens in such circumstances, the commander of the army, Omri, emerged from the struggle as the most powerful person. Omri came to the throne by a coup d'état.

The Deuteronomistic historians are unusually severe with Omri, insisting that he "did more evil than all who were before him." The account of his reign is limited to six verses (1 Kings 16:23–28), most of it filled with the usual Deuteronomistic formulas. But if we could look at "The Book of the Chronicles of the Kings of Israel," we would undoubtedly discover a man of tremendous political stature. He was able to do what none of his predecessors had done: establish a dynasty of such prestige that Assyrian kings continued to refer to the Northern Kingdom as "the land of the house of Omri" for many years after his death and the downfall of his dynasty. He initiated a collaboration with Judah that was later strengthened by intermarriage between the two royal houses.

Archaeologists have discovered a great deal more about Omri's reign than we learn from the fragmentary report in 1 Kings. In the Louvre, museumgoers can see the Moabite Stone erected by Mesha, king of Moab (2 Kings 3:4) during the reign of the last king of the Omri dynasty. Mesha reports:

> As for Omri, king of Israel, he humbled Moab many years, for
> Chemosh [the god of Moab] was angry at his land. And his son [or,
> grandson] followed him and he also said, "I will humble Moab." In my time
> he spoke [thus], but I have triumphed over him and over his house, while
> Israel has perished for ever![16]

Not only was Omri successful against the Moabites in Transjordan, but he was also able to keep the Syrians at bay—though at the cost of ceding territory in Transjordan and granting the Syrians commercial concessions in Samaria (1 Kings 20:34). His hand was

---

[16]See Pritchard, *Ancient Near Eastern Texts* [1], pp. 320–21.

The Stele of Mesha (king of Moab in the ninth century B.C.E.), on which the ruler boasts of his victory over the king of northern Israel. Discovered in 1868 at Dibon (Dibhan) in Transjordan, the stone was broken by some Bedouin, and only fragments could be taken to the Louvre for restoration.

strengthened, no doubt, by the close alliance he formed with Phoenicia, following the precedent of David and Solomon. The political union of these two countries with a common interest in holding Syria at bay was consummated by the marriage of Omri's son Ahab to the Phoenician king's daughter, Jezebel (1 Kings 16:31).

In spite of the virtual silence of 1 Kings on Omri's reign, we have reason to believe that under his statesmanship Israel achieved great stability and prosperity. During his twelve-year rule, Israel's political power expanded toward the Mediterranean and into Transjordan. Something like an economic boom must have followed in the wake of his vigorous political exploits, with an inevitable widening of the gulf between the "haves" and the "have-nots"—a situation still evident in Israel's society during the time of the prophet Amos, a century later.

A monument to Omri's political astuteness was his purchase of the hill of Samaria, where he began to build a new capital city that was completed by his son Ahab (1 Kings 16:24).[17] Situated on a hilltop with an excellent view of the surrounding landscape and steep slopes that made capture difficult, the city of Samaria was strategically situated astride the main north-south highway. This enabled the Israelites both to watch for advances from Judah and gain easy access to Phoenicia. Excavation of this once luxurious city has uncovered masonry, fortifications, the palaces of Omri and Ahab, and even ivory inlaid furniture and walls (1 Kings 22:39; Amos 3:15; 6:4). The style of these artifacts suggests that Omri imported Phoenician craftsmen to execute the art and architecture, just as Solomon had done. Henceforth, Samaria was to be the symbol of the Northern Kingdom, as Jerusalem was symbol of the Southern Kingdom.

Omri's son Ahab, also strongly censured in the Deuteronomistic History, apparently continued Israel's material progress. But international troubles were beginning to mount. Although Egypt had sunk again into oblivion, Syria (Aram) was expanding south into Transjordanian territory traditionally claimed by Israel, even advancing to the very gates of Samaria (1 Kings 20). The southern king Jehoshaphat (1 Kings 22:41–46), reversing the foreign policy of his predecessor Asa in order to recover Ramoth-gilead, joined forces with Ahab to fight the Arameans in Transjordan. In this battle, we are told, Ahab lost his life (1 Kings 22).

THE THREAT OF ASSYRIA

Just a few years before Ahab's death, the necessities of politics made Syria and Israel bedfellows. The Assyrians, intent on expanding to the Mediterranean, were beginning to pose a threat to the kingdoms of Syria and Palestine. Syria, the nearest and most vulnerable, was the first to come under attack. The Assyrian king, Shalmaneser III (about 859–825 B.C.E.), supposing the small western states to be easy prey, struck in 853 B.C.E. The battle was fought at Qarqar near Hamath, not far north of Damascus. Joining a coalition organized by Benhadad of Syria, "Ahab the Israelite" brought 10,000 foot soldiers and 2,000 chariots—the greatest number of chariots contributed by any of the allies, according to Shalmaneser's annals.[18] In the usual manner of war communiqués, the Assyrian boasted an overwhelming victory. The victory was perhaps not as decisive as he claimed, for he withdrew and did not appear again in the west for several years. Never-

---

[17]Previously the Northern capital had been located to the northeast at Tirzah. Due to military pressure Omri's predecessor, Jeroboam I, had been forced to move the capital from Shechem to Tirzah (see 1 Kings 14:17; 15:33).

[18]See Pritchard, *Ancient Near Eastern Texts* [1], pp. 278–79.

theless, from this point on Assyria's ambition to rule the Fertile Crescent loomed as the darkest cloud on the political horizon of Israel (Ephraim) and Judah.

Against this background arose a succession of prophets who stood in the spiritual lineage of Moses and Samuel. Some are mentioned only briefly: Ahijah from Shiloh, who led the revolt against Solomon (1 Kings 11:29–39), and Jehu ben Hanani, who pronounced doom against King Baasha of Israel (1 Kings 16:1–4). Three Ephraimitic prophets who lived during the Omri dynasty stand out above the rest: Micaiah, Elijah, and Elisha.

ONE PROPHET AGAINST FOUR HUNDRED

One of the most vivid episodes in the history of prophecy is the story of Micaiah, son of Imlah and a contemporary of Elijah (do not confuse Micaiah with the later and better-known prophet, Micah). The story comes from the closing years of Ahab's reign, and thus would properly follow the Elijah narratives. But we will look at Micaiah first, because his story shows how much the prophetic "schools" or guilds had been nationalized during this period.

There is a connection between the Micaiah story in 1 Kings 22 and the story of Ahab's treaty with Benhadad in 1 Kings 20. The Deuteronomistic historians included these accounts—both drawn from an independent source dealing with Ahab's wars—to show how divine retribution finally fell upon Ahab. Their description of the wars, however, gives us a clear picture of the activity of "the sons of the prophets" (1 Kings 20:35) at a time of military crisis. In the foreground stands Ahab's nemesis, the prophet Micaiah.

1 Kings 20 takes us back to a time slightly before the battle of Qarqar. Although his capital was besieged, Ahab succeeded in turning the tables at the battle of Aphek, forcing a treaty under which the Syrian king agreed to restore cities that Omri had ceded and grant commercial concessions in Damascus. Because he spared the Syrian king, Benhadad, Ahab was sharply rebuked by a member of a prophetic school who stood for the ruthless practice of holy war: the application of the sacrificial ban (*ḥérem*) against the enemy (see Definition, p. 128). Nevertheless, Ahab's covenant with Benhadad was politically shrewd, for the western nations needed to stand together if they were to halt the impending Assyrian advance.

Then came the battle of Qarqar (853 B.C.E.)—discreetly passed over by the Deuteronomistic historians because it did not serve their theological purpose. For three years the military alliance against Assyria had upheld the truce between Israel and Syria (1 Kings 22:1). But the friendship lasted no longer than the crisis. Shortly after the indecisive battle at Qarqar and the subsequent withdrawal of the Assyrians, the two nations resumed their bitter quarrel. The bone of contention was the city of Ramoth-gilead in Transjordan, which Omri had ceded in order to hold Syria at bay. Benhadad had agreed to return the city after the battle of Aphek, but reneged on his promise.

Ahab was eager to repossess Ramoth-gilead, which occupied a strategic position on the north-south commercial and military highway through Transjordan.

Chronological Chart 4

B.C.E.	Egypt	Palestine		Syria	Mesopotamia
		THE DIVIDED KINGDOM			Assyria
		Judah	*Israel*	*Syria*	*Assyria*
900		Asa, c. 913–873	Baasha, c. 900–877		Assyrian Revival
			Elah, c. 877–876		Adad-nirari II, c. 912–892
			Zimri, c. 876 (7 days)	Benhadad I, c. 885–870	Ashur-nasir-apal II, c. 884–860
				Benhadad II, c. 870–842	
			Omri Dynasty: Omri, c. 876–869		
	Egyptian Weakness	Jehoshaphat, c. 873–849	Ahab, c. 869–850		Shalmaneser III, c. 859–825
		Jehoram, c. 849-842	(*Elijah,* c. 850)		Battle of Qarqar, 853
		Ahaziah, c. 843/2	Ahaziah, c. 850–849		
850			Jehoram, c. 849–843/2	Hazael, c. 842–806	

As 1 Kings 22 opens, we see Ahab of Israel and Jehoshaphat of Judah taking counsel on a proposed joint military campaign. One of the accomplishments of the Omri dynasty had been to enter into friendly alliance with the Southern Kingdom, an alliance twice sealed by marriage. In this situation, however, Jehoshaphat's behavior suggests that he was almost a vassal of the more powerful and wealthy Northern Kingdom.

Jehoshaphat declared his willingness to go along with whatever Ahab had in mind, but he slyly hoped that an oracle from Yahweh would render the proposed campaign unnecessary. As was customary with important military decisions, he suggested that they "inquire first for the word of Yahweh." Ahab complied by summoning about four hundred ecstatic prophets. 1 Kings 22:10–12 gives a vivid picture of these nationalistic dervishes working themselves into an ecstatic frenzy, or "prophesying ecstatically" (*hithnabbe*). Meanwhile the prophets' ringleader, Zedekiah, performed a symbolic act intended to dramatize the inevitable defeat of the Syrians. The "sons of the prophets" spoke "with one accord" (literally "with one mouth"), proclaiming that Yahweh's will and the purpose of the king coincided perfectly (1 Kings 22:13). Without any question, these yes-men agreed, Ahab would be successful in a campaign against Ramoth-gilead.

Suspicious of this verdict, Jehoshaphat asked whether all the prophets had been heard from. It turned out that Micaiah had not been called—for obvious reasons. "I hate him," said Ahab, "for he never prophesies good concerning me, but only evil" (1 Kings 22:8). A revealing confession! Nevertheless Micaiah was summoned before the kings, after receiving a stern reminder that the majority was unanimously in favor of the military venture.

Using sarcasm, Micaiah at first mocked and mimicked the optimistic prophecy of the four hundred. But Ahab, knowing that Micaiah was acting out of character, put him under oath to speak the truth in the name of Yahweh. The prophet then delivered two oracles. One was a vision of Israel in leaderless rout, "scattered upon the mountains, as sheep that have no shepherd"—a prediction of the Israelite king's death and the utter failure of the Syrian expedition. The other was a vision of Yahweh presiding over the heavenly court and commissioning a "spirit" to fill the prophets with a lying ecstasy. The reaction to Micaiah's unpleasant prophecy was not surprising: a slap on the face from Zedekiah, and an order snapped out by Ahab to "put this fellow in prison." But Micaiah's prophetic word was later vindicated: Despite Ahab's battle disguise, an archer "drew his bow at a venture" and mortally wounded the king. In a seemingly chance occurrence, Yahweh's word through a prophet was fulfilled, supporting the Deuteronomistic view that, after all, the events were governed by divine providence.

1 Kings 22 gives us a glimpse of a transitional moment in the history of prophecy. Micaiah vowed that "what Yahweh says to me, that will I speak"—even though it was diametrically opposed to the royal view and to the voice of the majority. He proclaimed God's judgment *against* the king—a message of doom—which in time was recognized as one of the badges of a true prophet of Yahweh (see Jer. 28:8–9). With Micaiah, prophecy was no longer the echo of nationalism or the servant of the political establishment. This break with the professional prophets became sharper when Amos later disavowed any connection with the "sons of the prophets" (Amos 7:14). In a deeper sense, however, prophets like Micaiah did not break with Israel's true prophetic tradition, but rather brought alive the ancient Mosaic faith with new meaning and power.[19] This is clear in the case of the greatest ninth century prophet, Elijah (about 850 B.C.E.).

ELIJAH, THE TISHBITE

We now look back from the end of Ahab's life (1 Kings 22) to the fateful domestic crisis that marked the beginning of his reign. Our source for this period is the Elijah cycle, found chiefly in 1 Kings 17–19 and 21. Like the stories of Ahab's wars, this narrative cycle is an independent unit of tradition that was incorporated into the Deuteronomistic History.[20]

---

[19]See the discussion of the Micaiah story by Simon De Vries, *Prophet Against Prophet* [351], especially pp. 33–51.

[20]The Septuagint, the Greek translation of the Hebrew Bible, places chapter 21 immediately after chapters 17–19, suggesting that these four chapters belong together as a single unit.

Notice that the stories lack the characteristic language of the Deuteronomistic historians, and show no concern over the fact that Elijah built an altar on a "high place" (Carmel). Nor is Elijah rebuked for not denouncing the bull cult of Bethel, a subject on which he is completely silent. These are prophetic legends, preserved no doubt in the prophetic community with which Elijah was associated (2 Kings 2:1–18).

The Elijah stories were not meant to be a precise, factual account. Remembered and elaborated in oral tradition, the stories were colored by the imagination and faith of Israel. Though many of them reflect actual circumstances, they mirror primarily the *experienced history* of Israel. Not only do these stories record the terrific impression made by Elijah, the man of God, but they also portray the deepest dimension of Israel's history: the encounter with Yahweh in a time of great political and cultural crisis. This crisis came to a head as a result of the religious and political agenda of Ahab's wife, Jezebel.

The French writer Pascal once said that the whole course of Western history was changed by the shape of Cleopatra's nose. One might also say that the course of Israel's history was profoundly affected by the eccentricity of Jezebel. Remember that Omri, in order to strengthen relations between Israel and Phoenicia, had arranged the marriage of his son Ahab to Jezebel, the daughter of Ethbaal, king of Tyre. The Deuteronomistic historians leave no doubt about their attitude toward this political marriage: We are told that by marrying Jezebel, Ahab actually out-sinned Jeroboam (1 Kings 16:31).

Ahab tried to make his bride at home in the new capital, Samaria, where he was continuing the building program initiated by Omri. Just as Solomon built shrines in Jerusalem for his foreign wives, so King Ahab built a "temple of Baal" equipped with an altar and an image of Asherah, the mother goddess (1 Kings 16:32–33). The Baal in this case was Baal-Melkart, the official protective deity of Tyre and the Phoenician version of the Baal nature religion that had been making subtle inroads into the covenant faith ever since Israel's entrance into Canaan. Notice, however, that Baalism had now also acquired a political drive, for Phoenician imperialism was at its very height in the Mediterranean world. In antiquity, one way to recognize the political supremacy of another nation was to acknowledge and appropriate the religion of that country.

Contrary to the Deuteronomistic judgment of 1 Kings 16:31, Ahab seems to have had no idea of rejecting Yahweh, the God of Israel. He gave his children names containing the sacred element *Yah* (Atal*iah*, Ahaz*iah*, *Jeho*ram), and—as we know from the Micaiah story—he later consulted the prophets of Yahweh. His position was one of tolerance: He merely wanted to give his wife freedom of worship, as Solomon had done with his foreign wives. But Jezebel was a proud, strong woman who stopped at nothing to achieve her goals. A fanatical evangelist for her Phoenician religion, she inevitably came into conflict with the Yahweh prophets, who were equally passionate in their crusade for the covenant faith of Israel. She imported from Phoenicia a large number of Baal prophets and supported them out of the public treasury (1 Kings 18:19). Moreover, she began an aggressive campaign to "cut off the prophets of Yahweh." Taking advantage of the people's easygoing tolerance and religious syncretism, she tried to liquidate every vestige of Israel's traditional faith. The altars of Yahweh were torn down, the prophets were killed, and the remaining loyal adherents were driven underground. It was at this time of crisis that Elijah appeared in Israel to speak "the word of Yahweh."

THE CONTEST ON CARMEL

A paralyzing drought sets the stage for the first story in the Elijah cycle (1 Kings 17, 18). Seen through a veil of legend, Elijah the Tishbite (native of the city Tishbeh in Gilead) appears on the political horizon like a meteor. The dramatic suddenness with which he is introduced suggests the impression he made on his contemporaries. Coming from across the Jordan, where he had lived a rough, seminomadic life on the edge of the desert, he must have been a strange sight in the cultured land of Israel, clothed in a garment of hair, wearing a leather girdle, and displaying his rugged strength (2 Kings 1:8). His movements were so baffling that Obadiah, the king's servant, was loathe to let

This "horned" limestone altar from Megiddo stands 21 inches tall and dates from the tenth to ninth centuries B.C.E. Although its exact use(s) eludes us, the Hebrew Bible provides some clues. In Exodus 29:11–12, for example, the blood of a bull is placed upon the altar's horns. Exodus 30:1–10 describes a horned altar made of wood, on which Aaron is to burn incense; it further specifies that "Once a year Aaron shall perform the rite of atonement on its horns . . . with the blood of the atoning sin offering" (v. 10).

Elijah out of his sight, being convinced that the spirit (or "wind") of Yahweh would whisk him away to nobody-knows-where (1 Kings 18:12). According to legend, his disappearance was just as mysterious as his lightning appearance, for a fiery "sweet chariot" (to quote the American spiritual) swung down and carried him off in a whirlwind to heaven (2 Kings 2:11–12).

Elijah's first act was to announce a drought in the name of Yahweh—a direct challenge to Baal's power over fertility (1 Kings 17:1). The narrative continues with a series of vignettes showing the severity of the famine and the great miracles Elijah reputedly performed. The central concern of the stories is to affirm that Yahweh controls fertility not only in Palestine but also in Phoenicia, the special province of Baal-Melkart. Accordingly, Elijah is shown ministering to a widow in the Phoenician town of Zarephath during the widespread famine.

1 Kings 18 depicts Elijah's dramatic encounter with Ahab. The king's first words ("Is it you, you troubler of Israel?") betray his opinion of this prophetic gadfly, whose seemingly senseless prophecy of drought had so afflicted Samaria that the king and his steward had to scour the countryside to find enough fodder to keep the chariot horses alive. Elijah, however, turned Ahab's words against him: The trouble had been brought about by Ahab's support of the worship of Canaanite "Baals" (1 Kings 18:18)—here regarded as local manifestations of the Phoenician Baal, lord of sky and weather. It is Yahweh, the prophet announced, not Baal, who controls fertility. Elijah challenged the "four hundred and fifty prophets of Baal and the four hundred prophets of Asherah" to a contest on the promontory of Mount Carmel, which juts out toward the Mediterranean Sea.

The dramatic contest between the Baal prophets and the solitary prophet of Yahweh has been set to powerful music in Mendelssohn's oratorio, *Elijah*. Elijah accuses the people of vacillating, of "limping with two different opinions" (NRSV):

> Elijah stepped toward all the people there and said, "How long will you sit on the fence? If [Yahweh] is God, follow him; but if Baal, then follow him."
>
> —1 KINGS 18:21 (REB)

The prophet chastises the people for wanting to keep one foot in the traditional faith of Israel and the other foot in the worship of Baal. This type of syncretism had a long history among the people, encouraged in part by Jeroboam's religious innovations. Owing to Jezebel's program, however, Israel had finally come to the fork in the road. The people would need to choose either Yahweh, the God of the Mosaic covenant, or Baal, the Phoenician god of storm and fertility. Elijah puts the issue of monotheism in practical, not theoretical, terms: "If Yahweh is really God, then follow Yahweh; if Baal, then serve Baal." Deity makes a total claim upon human allegiance. Standing in the tradition of Moses, Elijah portrays Yahweh as the jealous God who will tolerate no rival gods. The name Elijah, meaning "Yah(weh) is (my) God," is highly appropriate for this zealous prophetic champion of the Mosaic faith.

The object of the contest was to determine then and there who was Lord, who had the power to control rain and fertility. Both parties, the Baal prophets and the solitary Yahweh prophet, agreed to perform their respective rites with the understanding that "the God who answers by fire" is God. The Baal prophets lashed themselves into ecstatic frenzy, performed a limping dance around the altar and shouted their ritual cries to Baal. With a touch of humor the narrative tells how Elijah, serenely confident, taunted the Baal prophets with the jest that perhaps the heavens were unresponsive because Baal had "gone aside" (was relieving himself), was on a business trip, or needed to be awakened from a reverie or from slumber. In spite of their ranting and raving, the ecstatic prophets were unsuccessful in eliciting fire. The episode ends with the solemn words: "There was no voice; no one answered, no one heeded" (1 Kings 18:29).

When Elijah stepped forward, his first act was to repair the abandoned altar of Yahweh—a symbolic gesture that boldly reclaimed the cultic site for the God of Israel. Next came what seems a curious ritual (1 Kings 18:32b–35): Elijah, in a threefold ceremony, poured water on the wood until it filled the trench. Why would the prophet pour water on wood if he expected it to be consumed with fire? There have been various fantastic explanations, including the conjecture that the "water" was actually inflammable naphtha from a nearby oil geyser! But the purpose of the act was clearly to bring on rain by sympathetic magic—that is, by imitating the falling of rain.

The upshot of Elijah's ritual is described in 1 Kings 18:36–40. Supernatural fire descends from heaven; the people, awed by the spectacle, exclaim "It is Yahweh who is God"; and the Baal prophets are condemned to the sacrificial ban (ḥérem). Finally, in verses 41–46, the goal of the contest is realized: The drought is ended. Elijah proclaims to Ahab that "there is a sound of the rushing of rain." Another rain ceremony, in which a servant is sent seven times to look toward the Mediterranean Sea while the prophet lies prostrate in prayer, concludes with the announcement that a storm cloud—"a little cloud like a human hand"—is approaching. While the storm gathers and the rain begins to fall, Ahab hurries through the Valley of Jezreel lest his chariot bog down in the mud. Elijah, with a terrific burst of ecstatic energy, runs before him.

The story of Elijah belongs to the poetry of Israel's faith. We should not attempt scientific rationalizations, such as construing the fire falling from heaven to be a bolt of lightning in a thunderstorm. In biblical narrative fire is frequently used symbolically to express the manifestation of God (recall the "burning bush" episode, Exod. 3). Above all, the narrators want to communicate a sense of Yahweh's active presence in the historical situation, as interpreted through the prophetic faith of Elijah.

THE FLIGHT TO MOUNT HOREB

The dramatic description of the contest on Carmel—the participation of "all Israel" (1 Kings 18:19, 20), the people's unanimous confession of faith in Yahweh, and the massacre of the Baal prophets—might give the impression that Baalism was destroyed once and for all. But a few years later there were still enough Baal worshipers to fill a

Baal temple (2 Kings 10:21). Yahweh's victory on Mount Carmel was not the end of the war. Elijah was reminded of this by the fact that Jezebel was still on the throne, threatening to track him down.

The sequel to the Carmel episode is the legend of Elijah's flight from the territory of Ahab and Jezebel into the wilderness of southern Judah, a day's journey south of Beer-sheba (1 Kings 19:1–18). There he threw himself down beneath a lonely juniper tree. With profound insight the narrator portrays the doubt that shadows faith:[21] How could Yahweh really be in control when Jezebel's power was undiminished? Elijah is portrayed as a broken and fatigued man, running for his life and wishing to die because, in his efforts to crush the power of tyranny and idolatry, he had fared no better than his forebears. The miracle story in 1 Kings 19:5–8, however, affirms that in this darkest hour Yahweh did not desert him, but mercifully supplied him with strength for the long journey ahead.

The story tells us that Elijah traveled "forty days and forty nights" (the traditional number for a long period of time) until he came to Horeb (Sinai), the sacred mountain of the covenant. On Horeb a divine visitation (theophany) takes place that clearly echoes the revelation to Moses at Sinai/Horeb. The cave in which Elijah lodged recalls the cleft of the rock in which Moses was sheltered while Yahweh "passed by," showing the divine glory (Exod. 33:18–34:8). The Elijah story also reports that Yahweh "passed by," and that this visitation was accompanied by earthquake, wind, and fire—the traditional phenomena of Yahweh's revelation on the sacred mountain (Exod. 19).

The story is an excellent illustration of "the contemporization of tradition."[22] The sacred heritage is not regarded as a mere relic from the past, but is contemporized to fit the present situation of the people of God. Notice, moreover, that this reinterpretation of the Mosaic tradition almost reverses the traditional theophany. The narrator says that Yahweh was *not* in the earthquake, wind, or fire, but in the lull that followed the tempestuous storm (compare Ps. 107:29). The Hebrew words are usually translated "a still, small voice" and refer to "a kind of silence so intense that you can hear it."[23] The "sound of silence" was perceived to be the voice of the God of Exodus and Sinai who spoke with a new accent in the present.

When Elijah heard this voice of silence, he moved to the entrance of the cave. The ensuing dialogue enhances Israel's Mosaic tradition with new dimensions of meaning. The question addressed to Elijah implied that he had no business in the safe mountain retreat, a fugitive from the places where history was being made. The prophet protested that he had been very jealous (the Hebrew word means both to be "jealous" and to be

---

[21]See Robert Davidson, *Courage to Doubt* [152], pp. 95–99, for an illuminating interpretation of the Elijah narratives.

[22]Contemporizing the sacred heritage is one dimension of the "canonical criticism" advocated by James Sanders in *Canon and Community* [103], especially chap. 2.

[23]R. Davidson, *op. cit.* [152], p. 98.

"zealous") for Yahweh. He had been a *zealot* for the Mosaic tradition, even though the people of Israel, under Jezebel's influence, had "forsaken your covenant,[24] thrown down your altars, and killed your prophets with the sword" (NRSV).

Elijah's brooding over his loneliness and over the threat to his life was challenged by three divine orders, two of which involved fomenting political revolutions. Though two of these commissions were carried out by Elisha, his prophetic successor, their mention here shows that Israel's faith finds expression in action rather than mere mystic contemplation. As in the case of Moses at the burning bush, Elijah realized afresh that Yahweh acts in the historical sphere, summoning a prophet to take part in the divine plan of action. Yahweh's plan called for Elijah to return to the land of Israel to incite a revolution. Elijah was told that although the revolution would make a clean sweep of the house of Omri and its supporters, Yahweh would nevertheless spare a faithful remnant—"seven thousand in Israel, all the knees that have not bowed to Baal."

That Elijah journeyed to Sinai, to the place where Moses had received the revelation from Yahweh after the Exodus, is most significant. In one sense, the whole prophetic movement—with Elijah its great exemplar—was a pilgrimage back to Sinai, to the source of Israel's faith. The prophets did not claim to be innovators with bright ideas that would enable Israel to keep abreast of the onward march of culture. Rather, they demanded that the people return to their religious roots and to the covenant allegiance demanded by a "jealous" Yahweh. They were reformers who took their stand on the ancient ground of Sinai. This return to root experiences was not a timid retreat from the cultural crisis into an idealized past. As we can see from the stories of Elijah, the message of the prophets contemporized the Mosaic past, giving it new vitality and meaning.

THE AFFAIR OF NABOTH'S VINEYARD

The third episode in the Elijah cycle (1 Kings 21) apparently took place some years later. In the city of Jezreel, his second capital, Ahab wanted to purchase a vineyard that adjoined his palace. His terms were generous enough, but Naboth, the owner, refused to sell for the simple reason that it was a family estate. His refusal ("Yahweh forbid that I should give you the inheritance of my ancestors") expressed an attitude toward land that was unique with Israel. Properly speaking, it was not Naboth's "private property" to dispose of as he pleased. It belonged to the whole family or clan who had passed it down from generation to generation as a sacred inheritance. In this view the real owner

---

[24]The Hebrew word translated here "your covenant" is textually insecure; important versions read simply "have forsaken you [Yahweh]" at 1 Kings 19:10:14. Commentators admit, however, that the covenant tradition is implied in the whole narrative. See John Gray's commentary on *I and II Kings* [331], pp. 409–10.

of the land was Yahweh, who had fulfilled the promises made to the ancestors by bringing the Israelites into a country where they could settle down. The various tribes and clans were stewards of Yahweh's property, administering it for the welfare of the whole community in a way that ruled out land-grabbing and private speculation. Naboth was only reaffirming the ancient basis of Israel's land tenure when he insisted that he was not free to sell the ancestral estate.

Ahab, recognizing the validity of Naboth's position, became sullen and refused to eat. But Jezebel, nurtured in the commercial civilization of Phoenicia, had other conceptions of property. Her Baal religion placed no limitations on the exercise of royal power. "Do you now govern Israel?" she asked Ahab. She promised to get Naboth's vineyard for him—in her own way. At her direction, Naboth was accused by two "good-for-nothings" of "cursing God and the king" (blasphemy and treason). With no word of defense on his behalf, Naboth was stoned to death; and evidently his sons were done away with too (2 Kings 9:26). The murder had a pretense of legality, enough to salve the consciences of those who had a hand in the treacherous deed. With Naboth and his sons out of the way, Ahab thought he was free to take possession of the vineyard.

But Ahab had yet to stand before the highest tribunal, for "the word of Yahweh came to Elijah the Tishbite." In the vineyard that Ahab had gone to claim as his own, the prophet and king again came face to face. Like the ground stained with the blood of Abel, this outrageous crime was crying to Yahweh for requital, and the prophet thundered out the impending divine judgment. Stinging under the sharp words of Elijah, this prophetic gadfly, the king could only mutter, "Have you found me, O my enemy?" The story concludes with a vivid description of Ahab's penitence, which reminds us of David's remorse after his encounter with Nathan (1 Kings 21:27–29; most of verses 20b–26 are Deuteronomistic comments).

The Naboth incident is an appropriate preface to the social message of later prophets. Here we see Baal religion and Yahwistic faith in opposition, not in a dramatic contest on Carmel but in the field of social relationships. The great Israelite prophets were champions of the stern ethical demands of the ancient Mosaic tradition, in which Israel's covenant obedience was motivated by gratitude for the great acts of liberation that Yahweh had wrought on behalf of an oppressed people (see Chapter 3). Yahweh had created a covenant community in which every person stood equal before the law—whether rich or poor, king or private citizen. The whole community was responsible to the sovereign will of Yahweh, as expressed in the absolute laws handed down from the wilderness period and refined by legal usage. When a member of the community was downtrodden by the powerful, Yahweh intervened to defend the weak and the defenseless and to restore the order and familial solidarity of the covenant community. Baal religion tended to support the status quo, with the aristocracy on top. But Yahwistic faith, as revived by the prophet Elijah, supplied the energy for a protest against the evils of a commercial civilization and encouraged social reform.

ELISHA AND THE CLOSING YEARS OF THE OMRI DYNASTY

The Elijah legends in 2 Kings 1 and the Elisha cycle (2 Kings 2–9; 13:14–21) represent a different type of prophetic tradition from the great Elijah narratives in 1 Kings. Here we have a collection of wonderful tales: the rolling back of the Jordan by Elijah's mantle, the magical sweetening of water, the deception of the Moabites with a mirage of blood red water, the restoration of the Shunammite woman's child from the dead, the incident of the floating ax head, and so on. Stories like these delighted the popular imagination and no doubt were told and retold by members of the prophetic order with which Elisha, Elijah's prophetic successor, was intimately associated. Fanciful though they are, they show us Elisha as a prophet concerned for the people. They are written with the conviction that "the word of Yahweh (was) with him" (2 Kings 3:12).

In the background of the Elisha stories are the political events that involved Israel during the closing years of the Omri dynasty, especially the reign of J(eh)oram, king of Israel. In this period (about 849–842 B.C.E.) Moab revolted against Israel—a fact confirmed by the Moabite Stone (pp. 238–239).[25] The inscription on this stone makes the extravagant claim that Mesha, the Moabite king, subjected Israel to the sacrificial ban (*ḥerem*) of the god Chemosh, so that "Israel perished forever." The Israelite account reports that the Moabite king sought victory by sacrificing his eldest son to the Moabite god Chemosh upon the city wall. As a result, so the historians interpret, "there came great wrath upon Israel" (2 Kings 3:4–27).

Most of the stories, however, reflect the conditions of the continuing wars between Syria and Israel. An illustration is the charming story of Naaman, commander of the Syrian army. At the suggestion of a little slave girl whom the Syrians had carried off from Israel during a raid, Naaman journeyed into Israelite territory to seek Elisha, where he became convinced that "there is no God in all the earth but in Israel" (2 Kings 5). The story shows how people could believe, even under the trying conditions of war, that the enemy was encompassed within the wideness of Yahweh's sovereignty.

According to the account in 2 Kings 8:7–15, Elisha traveled to Damascus, the capital of Syria. When the ailing King Benhadad heard that Elisha was in the city, he sent one of his officers, Hazael, to ask the prophet whether he would recover. In a prophetic trance, Elisha predicted that Hazael would be the next king of Syria and that he would bring great military calamity to Israel. Under the authority of this prophetic word, Hazael murdered Benhadad the very next day, bringing about one of the revolutions that Elijah was to foment (1 Kings 19:15–16). The second revolution occurred when Elisha summoned one of the "sons of the prophets" to anoint Jehu as king over Israel (2 Kings 9:1–13). With Jehu's rise to power, the Omri dynasty came to an end in a terrible bloodbath, and a new chapter in Israel's history began.

---

[25]In the Moabite text "son" probably means Omri's grandson. The revolt occurred in Jehoram's reign, not Ahab's.

CHAPTER 9

FALLEN

IS THE

VIRGIN ISRAEL

Modern democracies are by definition established on the principle of tolerance, whether toward differing views or toward competing religious loyalties. We might easily sympathize, therefore, with Solomon's cosmopolitanism, or even with the compromising attitude of Ahab's generation, which teetered back and forth between opposing views. But, as we have seen, Israel's prophets attacked the tolerant syncretism of the time and insisted on an ardent devotion to Yahweh. The flame of their conviction was kindled at the ancient sources of Mosaic faith, and burst forth like a consuming fire at a time when the nation was in danger of being engulfed by Canaanite culture.

As we continue our study of Israel's prophetic movement, the spotlight again falls on the Northern Kingdom of Israel (Ephraim), whose prosperity and political power overshadowed that of the Southern Kingdom of Judah. To be sure, in the reign of Jehoshaphat, a contemporary of Omri, Judah enjoyed a resurgence of political and commercial power. The policy of peaceful collaboration with the Northern Kingdom, sealed by intermarriage between the royal houses, enabled Judah to recover from the civil wars that had sapped its energies since the division of Solomon's kingdom. But Judah was the weaker of the twin kingdoms throughout the powerful Omri dynasty and its successor, the dynasty of Jehu. During this time the star of Israel reached its zenith, thereafter to plunge like a meteor into oblivion.

Biblical Readings: The books of Amos and Hosea, and the background material in 2 Kings 9–17 (paralleled in 2 Chronicles 22–25).

In this chapter we will see that the prophets of "the great eighth century,"[1] particularly Amos and Hosea, continued and deepened the reforming zeal of the prophets of the ninth century B.C.E.—Elijah, Micaiah, and Elisha (see Chapter 8). The main sources for our study are a section of the Deuteronomistic History (2 Kings 9–17) and especially the written prophecies of Amos and Hosea.

THE REVOLUTION OF JEHU

Unlike the Southern Kingdom of Judah, which had a single dynasty from the time of David to its end, the political career of Israel (the Northern Kingdom) was characterized by an instability that lasted until the fall of the nation in 721 B.C.E. Unrest and intrigue kept both Jeroboam I and Baasha from founding a dynasty. The dynasty of Omri held power through the reigns of only four kings, and was superseded by the five-king dynasty of Jehu. The difference in the stability of the two kingdoms was rooted in differing ideologies. In Judah the view that Yahweh had made a covenant to maintain the Davidic throne supported the continuity of the Davidic dynasty, providing a basis for the transfer of power from one royal administration to the next. In Israel, however, the persistence of the old "democratic" ideal of the Tribal Confederacy contributed to political instability. Northerners believed that Yahweh's spirit was poured upon an individual, not a dynasty—a view that could foster revolution.

The story of the Jehu dynasty opens in 2 Kings 9. Elisha commissions a member of the band of prophets to seek out Jehu—the army commander who had resumed the attempt to take Ramoth-gilead from Syria—and to anoint him king of Israel. The word of Yahweh, received from an ecstatic "madman" (2 Kings 9:11), was all that was needed to incite a revolt. Supported by the power of the mutinous army, Jehu was proclaimed king with great fanfare.

Jehu's purge of Israel was both thorough and brutal. Memory of the gory details, as given in an old story touched up with a few Deuteronomistic comments (2 Kings 9:7–10a), would send a shudder through future generations. Riding furiously in his chariot, Jehu came to the valley of Jezreel, where Joram, the king of Israel, was nursing wounds received in the Syrian battle. There he sent an arrow through the heart of the fugitive king and, with a sense of poetic justice, ordered that Joram's body be cast into Naboth's vineyard (see pp. 249–250). This symbolic act was no doubt designed to win over the people, who had been suffering under the economic oppression of the nobility and merchant class during the Omri dynasty. But Jehu was not satisfied with purging Israel alone. He murdered Ahaziah of Judah, who had come to visit his sick uncle, and later Ahaziah's brothers, who also came to visit. Jezebel was tossed out of a window and

[1]See the acclaimed essay of Philip J. King, "The Great Eighth Century," *Bible Review*, V:4 (August 1989), pp. 22–33.

mangled beyond recognition. Finally, Jehu had all seventy sons of Ahab decapitated, thus removing all claimants to the throne (see Chronological Chart 5, p. 274).

THE RELIGIOUS SIDE OF THE REVOLUTION

Jehu's revolution was not the usual *coup d'état*. Although the more sensitive Israelites must have cringed at Jehu's brutal excesses and brazen callousness, Jehu sincerely believed that he was carrying out the religious revolution called for by Elijah and Elisha. To be sure, his butchery of the house of Ahab was motivated by political ambition, and he shrewdly capitalized on revolutionary ferment within the army and widespread economic unrest in the land. But he was also influenced by religious considerations, and undoubtedly intended the massacre as an application of the sacrificial ban (*ḥerem*) against an evil family (compare Josh. 7:24–26). Elijah himself, after all, had demanded the ruthless extermination of the prophets of Baal after the Carmel contest.

That the revolution was in part a religious development is clear, not only in Jehu's anointment by an ecstatic prophet, but also in the collaboration of Jehonadab, son of Rechab (2 Kings 10:15–17). Jehonadab headed a family known for passionate devotion to the wilderness tradition and stern opposition to the agricultural ways of Canaan. He was a descendant of the Kenites (Midianites), the nomadic people who influenced and supported Moses during the wilderness period. Jehonadab's descendants of a later generation, known as Rechabites (Jer. 35), perpetuated their ancestors' puritan devotion to the wilderness tradition. Under a vow they took from Jehonadab, they refused to drink wine, cultivate vineyards, build houses, or till the soil. Dwelling in tents, as had their nomadic ancestors, they stood for a pristine form of the Mosaic tradition—one not defiled by the agrarian culture of Canaan.

According to the story, Jehu invited Jehonadab to "come with me, and see my zeal for Yahweh." Jehu showed his zeal by slaughtering the remnants of Ahab's house, according to the prophetic word of Elijah. Jehonadab, a representative of the conservative, nomadic tradition of Israel, endorsed Jehu's purge by riding with him in his chariot. Jehonadab also joined Jehu in exterminating the Baal worshipers (2 Kings 10:18–27). With cunningly concealed sarcasm, Jehu announced that he was planning to make a great sacrifice to the Phoenician deity, Baal-Melkart. But the "sacrifice" turned out to be an application of the sacrificial ban (*ḥerem*) to the devotees assembled in the temple of Baal. The holocaust was completed by burning the "pillar" (perhaps the *Asherah*, an image of the mother goddess), demolishing the temple, and converting the place into a latrine. Notice that the Deuteronomistic historians are somewhat impressed by Jehu's zeal, and not the least bit horrified at the ruthless destruction of the house of Ahab and the Baal worshipers. Despite Jehu's fanatical devotion to Yahweh, however, they denounce him for not removing the idolatrous shrines that Jeroboam I had established at Dan and Bethel.

Jehu's revolution had serious repercussions in the Southern Kingdom of Judah. Jehu had slain the Judean king Ahaziah, whose mother was Athaliah, a daughter of Ahab. Despite Athaliah's Yahweh name (Athal-*iah*, "Yah[weh] is exalted"), she was evidently a devotee of Baal-Melkart and, like Jezebel in the North, had helped promulgate this religion in Judah (2 Kings 11:18). When Athaliah heard of her son's death, she liquidated the male members of the Davidic line and usurped the throne. She missed one member, however: The infant Joash (or Jehoash) was spirited away and hidden by the priests in the Temple. Whereas prophets led the revolution against the Phoenician Baal in the Northern Kingdom, it was the priests who fomented revolution in the Southern Kingdom. Helping them were "the people of the land"—the conservative landowners who lived outside Jerusalem. After a covenant ceremony involving Yahweh and the people on the one hand and the people and the king on the other (2 Kings 11:17), the temple of Baal was destroyed and both Athaliah and the Baal priest Mattan were assassinated. Joash took his place alongside Asa as one of the reforming kings of Judah, winning moderate praise from the Deuteronomistic historians (2 Kings 12:1–3).

PROBLEMS OF FOREIGN POLICY

After the fire of revolution died down in the north, Jehu faced political problems too difficult for him to handle. His cold-blooded murder of Ahaziah had alienated the Southern Kingdom of Judah, and his liquidation of the devotees of the Phoenician Baal had no doubt cut off any support from Phoenicia. Without the political alliances that had helped support the Omri dynasty, the Northern Kingdom of Israel was now more vulnerable to attack from Syria than ever before. The Syrian king Hazael quickly took advantage of the situation, and swept down through Transjordan (2 Kings 10:32–33). In 841 B.C.E., Jehu, anxious to save his throne at any cost, paid tribute to the Assyrian monarch Shalmaneser III, who by that time had recuperated from the battle of Qarqar and was renewing his march into the west. The biblical account ignores this political event, but the famous Black Obelisk of Shalmaneser III depicts Jehu at the head of an Israelite delegation, kneeling before "the mighty king, king of the universe, king without a rival, the autocrat, the powerful one of the four regions of the world"—as Shalmaneser modestly described himself. The inscription records the "tribute of Jehu, son of Omri," for the Assyrians continued to designate Israelite kings as the house of Omri.[2]

The Assyrian advance relieved the pressure on Israel for the time being, for Syria had to meet this threat to its Mesopotamian border. Within a few years, however, internal problems forced Assyria to shelve its plans for expansion into the west. Hazael took advantage of this good fortune (after 837 B.C.E.) by sending his armies in lightning

---

[2]See Pritchard, *Ancient Near Eastern Texts* [1], p. 286.

thrusts to the south (Amos 1:3). During the reign of Jehu's son, Jehoahaz, Israel's army was reduced to a bare minimum: We learn that "the king of Syria had destroyed them and made them like the dust at threshing" (2 Kings 13:7).[3]

Then the tide turned. The Deuteronomistic historians tell us that "Hazael king of Syria oppressed Israel all the days of Jehoahaz; but Yahweh was gracious to them and had compassion on them." When Hazael's son, Benhadad, came to the throne, the new king of Israel, Jehoash (who had the same name as the contemporary Judean king), was able to recover cities previously lost to the Syrians (2 Kings 13:22–25). This turn of affairs was due less to the energetic warfare of Jehoash than to the aggressiveness of a new Assyrian monarch, Adad-nirari III. In 805 B.C.E., Assyria resumed its westward invasion, leaving Syria so crippled that it was no longer a threat to Israel. The momentum of the Assyrian advance was spent in the campaign against Syria, however, and for fifty years Israel did not have to fear invasion from beyond the Euphrates.

With Assyria having troubles at home, and with Syria barely able to stand, J(eh)oash of Israel inherited the most favorable political situation in the entire history of the Northern Kingdom. His program of political expansion was challenged only by the Southern Kingdom of Judah, whose king, Amaziah, insisted on trying to settle a score with the Jehu dynasty. This was a foolhardy move, as we learn from the fable about the thistle and the cedar (2 Kings 14:8–10). The Israelite king soundly whipped the Judean state and reduced it to vassalage, thus preparing the way for the glorious era of Jeroboam II, the greatest king of the Jehu dynasty.

THE AGE OF JEROBOAM II

The Deuteronomistic historians dismiss the reign of Jeroboam II with a scant seven verses, consisting mostly of the usual monotonous formulas (2 Kings 14:23–29). Nevertheless, they excerpt from "The Book of the Chronicles of the Kings of Israel" the notice that Jeroboam "restored the border of Israel from the entrance of Hamath as far as the Sea of the Arabah." The "entrance of Hamath"—the northernmost boundary of Solomon's kingdom (1 Kings 8:65)—refers to the pass between Mount Lebanon and Mount Hermon (located on a map by drawing a line straight across from Damascus to Sidon). The "Sea of the Arabah" refers to the Dead Sea, named after the low desert plain that extends from the Jordan valley to the Gulf of Aqabah. Jeroboam II thus extended his kingdom northward into the orbit of Hamath and Syria, and southward into territory that encroached upon

---

[3]At the same time, during the reign of the contemporary Judean king Joash, the Syrians swept down the Philistine coast and were stopped from attacking Jerusalem only when the royal and temple treasures were turned over to them (2 Kings 12:17–18).

Judah.[4] Never before had an Israelite king held undisputed sway over so large a kingdom. This nationalistic revival was inspired by another prophet: Jonah, son of Amittai, under whose name the book of Jonah was later written (see pp. 546–547).

A blanket of Deuteronomistic silence also falls upon the reign of Azariah (Uzziah), Jeroboam's contemporary in Judah (2 Kings 14:21–22; 15:1–7). Under his reign and that of his son and co-regent, Jotham, Judah also experienced a national revival (2 Chron. 26). Having enlarged and modernized his army, Uzziah carried out conquests on both sides of the Jordan. Moreover, the Negeb to the south was brought into the orbit of Judean control, enabling Uzziah to build Elath (2 Kings 14:22) near Ezion-geber, and to restore the avenues of commerce into the Arabian world that Solomon had opened up two centuries before. Under Jeroboam II and Uzziah, the twin kingdoms of Israel and Judah controlled almost the full sweep of Solomon's empire "from the entrance of Hamath to the Brook of Egypt" (1 Kings 8:65). To be sure, the Southern Kingdom of Judah reached the peak of its political and economic power only after the stronger Northern Kingdom had begun its decline (following the death of Jeroboam II). We will postpone further discussion of Judah until the next chapter, in order to consider the last and most glorious era of the Northern Kingdom of Israel. This period marked the beginning of the classical age of Israelite prophecy.

The Classical Age of Israelite Prophecy*

	North	South
Middle and Late Eighth Century B.C.E.	Amos (c. 750) Hosea (c. 745)	
		Isaiah (c. 742–700) Micah (c. 722–701)
Late Seventh Century		Zephaniah (c. 628–622) Jeremiah (c. 626–587) Nahum (c. 612) Habakkuk (c. 605)
Sixth Century		Ezekiel (c. 593–573) Obadiah (after 587) II Isaiah (c. 540)
Period of Restoration		Haggai (c. 520–515) Zechariah (c. 520–515) Joel (c. 500–350) Malachi (c. 500–450)

*This outline gives the sequence of the prophetic figures, but does not take into consideration the later updating of their prophecy in prophetic circles.

[4]The statement in 2 Kings 14:28, "he recovered for Israel Damascus and Hamath, which had belonged to Judah," is very obscure.

Carved from an elephant tusk, this eighth-century portrait of a woman was discovered at the bottom of a well in Nimrud. It may once have adorned a piece of furniture and is six inches in height.

A TIME OF PROSPERITY

In spite of the silence of the Deuteronomistic historians, we know a great deal about the long reign of Jeroboam II, not only from the books of Amos and Hosea, but also from archaeological findings. Excavations at Megiddo and Samaria (see p. 240)[5] give a vivid picture of the material prosperity and cultural achievement that prompted Amos, a prophet of the mid-eighth century, to denounce "those who feel secure on the mountain of Samaria" (Amos 6:1). Amos, disgusted with the beautiful ivories, the luxurious summer and winter homes (Amos 3:15), the impressive fortifications, and the teeming marketplaces, proclaimed that Yahweh too loathed the whole spectacle (see Inserts 11–1, 11–2, 11–3). The God of Amos is involved in the human situation and reacts with passion:[6]

---

[5]See Kathleen Kenyon, *Archaeology in the Holy Land* [122], chap. 11.
[6]Contrast this view with the "Unmoved Mover" of Greek philosophy, who is apathetic and uninvolved. For a discussion of "the pathos of God," including the pathos of indignation, see Abraham J. Heschel, *The Prophets* [352], especially chaps. 11–12.

I loathe the pride of Jacob,
I hate his palaces,
and I am going to hand over the city [Samaria]
    and all it contains.

         —AMOS 6:8

The books of Amos and Hosea clearly depict the economic injustices that followed generations of intimate cultural relations with the mercantile economy of Phoenicia. During the reign of Jeroboam II, the commercial and colonial activity of the Phoenicians was at its peak in the Mediterranean world, and the Northern Kingdom of Israel shared in the profits that flowed from the exchange of goods and services. Moreover, Jeroboam's conquests in Transjordan (the cities of Lo-debar and Karnaim; Amos 6:13) gave him control of the trade route from Syria and evidently of the commercial highways from Arabia as well. Samaria, his luxurious capital, became a great center of wealth. The price for this prosperity, however, was an oppressive social pyramid with royal courtiers and the merchant class at the top and a great mass of people ground into poverty at the bottom. The heinous crime that Ahab committed against Naboth was perpetrated on a wider scale as economic tyrants, with the sanction of corrupt courts (Amos 5:10–13), "bought the poor for silver, and the needy for a pair of sandals" (Amos 8:6; compare 2:6). Amos believed these crimes would have shocked any of Israel's neighbors with an elemental sense of justice:

Proclaim it to the palaces in Ashdod,
    and to the strongholds in the land of Egypt,
    saying:
        "Gather together upon Mount Samaria,
        and see the terrible disorder in that city,
        and the oppression within it!"
They don't know how to do right,
        Yahweh says,
    they who accumulate violence and force
        in their palaces.

         —AMOS 3:9–10

Amos and Hosea also give a clear picture of popular religion, one that tends to support the Deuteronomistic judgment that Jeroboam II perpetuated the ways of Jeroboam I. In the Northern Kingdom, which was directly exposed to the culture of the Fertile Crescent, Baalism was too deeply rooted to be eradicated even by measures as thorough as those of Jehu. Hosea, a contemporary of Amos, excoriated Israel for supposing that its agricultural prosperity sprang from worshiping the Baals, local representatives of the Canaanite storm god (Hos. 2:2–13). He heaped scorn upon Baal festivals (Hos. 2:13), illicit sexual activity (4:14), sacrifice at the high places (4:13), and the worship of images in the form of bulls (13:1–2)—particularly the golden bull that Jeroboam I installed in Bethel as a symbol of Yahweh's presence (8:5; 10:5).

THE NORTHERN MOSAIC TRADITION

Yahwistic faith was by no means dead during Jeroboam's reign. In centers of worship the Mosaic tradition was kept alive through ceremonies of covenant renewal (like the one inaugurated at Shechem; Josh. 24). In the villages, a class of teaching priests known as Levites proclaimed and expounded the great convictions of Israel's faith. Prophets like Amos and Hosea could appeal to the people on the basis of a common religious heritage. Their task was to recall their hearers to the memory of events all but forgotten, and to beliefs that formed the basis of the community of Yahweh.

In the Northern Kingdom this religious heritage probably found expression in an Ephraimitic version of Israel's sacred history: the so-called "Elohist" (E) narrative. This epic narrative, which survives only in fragmentary form, was presumably composed in the ninth century B.C.E. (possibly in the time of Elijah) to express the national consciousness of the newly formed Northern Kingdom of Israel. Whatever the date of literary composition, the narrative cycle goes back to a common oral tradition that flourished during the Tribal Confederacy. This oral tradition was given a special stamp in the circle of the northern tribes, just as it received a distinctive Judean impression from the so-called Yahwist (J) in the Age of Solomon (see p. 222). By the time of Amos and Hosea (eighth century B.C.E.) this northern

This Assyrian relief from Nineveh depicts two warriors astride a camel. The first directs the camel, the second shoots arrows at the enemy.

version of the Israelite epic was well known in Ephraim (Israel), and was a point of contact when prophets addressed the people (as in Amos 2:9–10; Hos. 12:2–6).[7]

This hypothesis provides another example of how the sacred heritage was contemporized during the people's ongoing history. The Elohist narrative, which rehearses Israel's sacred history with special emphasis on the call to obedient faith (the "fear of God") and the mediating role of the Mosaic prophet, was possibly written down in the time of Elijah, when Israelites were tempted to follow the easy way of religious syncretism. In this case, it would have provided a forceful call to radical obedience and a powerful reinterpretation of the Mosaic heritage.

Whatever the distinctive literary and theological traits of the Ephraimitic (Elohist) and Judean (Yahwist) versions, both traditions agree on the fundamental convictions that bound together the twin kingdoms, Israel and Judah, in the common worship of Yahweh. Sharing these convictions, Amos—a southerner and perhaps a representative of Judean (Zion) theology—journeyed to Bethel in the Ephraimitic hill country to hurl his protest against the people's way of life and to recall Israel to a worship and lifestyle consonant with Mosaic covenant tradition.

....

DEFINITION: "ELOHIST" (E)

The "Elohist" version of the Israelite Old Epic tradition, designated by the letter "E," shows an Ephraimitic, or northern, slant. This is evidenced by the prominence given to northern figures like Joseph, his mother Rachel, and his son Ephraim (Gen. 48:20), and also by the interest in northern shrines like Bethel (Gen. 28:17–22) and Shechem (Gen. 33:18–20). Moreover, the narrative uses a characteristic vocabulary: For example, the sacred mountain is called "Horeb" (the southern or "J" tradition prefers "Sinai"), and the natives of Canaan are referred to as "Amorites" (the southern tradition favors "Canaanites"). Finally, in stories dealing with the pre-Mosaic period the Ephraimite tradition apparently prefers to use the word 'Elohim (instead of Yahweh) for "God."

Literary analysis suggests that southern or Judean editors reshaped the "E" version of the Old Epic tradition, especially after the fall of the Northern Kingdom in 721 B.C.E. These editors gave preference to the southern version of the tradition, with the result that it is often difficult to reconstruct a continuous Ephraimitic (or Elohistic) narrative from the remaining fragments. Indeed, for some time the "Elohist" hypothesis has been regarded as the Achilles heel of the literary analysis of the Pentateuch. Nevertheless, a number of scholars maintain that what is left of the Ephraimitic tradition, even after Judean editing, stands out sharply enough to give some idea of its distinctive character.[8]

In this view, the Elohist narrative starts with the call of Abraham (Gen. 15) and follows the general outline of the Old Epic tradition through the rest of the books of Genesis, Exodus, and Numbers. Special nuances distinguish this tradition: the motif of obedience to or

---

[7]On the message of the Elohist, see Hans Walter Wolff in *The Vitality of Old Testament Traditions* [70], chap. 4.
[8]See Hans Walter Wolff, "The Elohistic Fragments in the Pentateuch," *Interpretation* 26 (1972), 158–73; also *The Vitality of Old Testament Traditions* [70], chap. 4.

"fear of" God (illustrated in the story of Abraham's sacrifice of Isaac (Gen. 22, especially verse 12) and the special status of Moses who, as prophet, acts as the mediator between God and people (Num. 12:7–8; and the presumably Elohist passage, Deut. 34:10–12). The Ephraimitic tradition regards Moses as the prophet *par excellence,* the first in a succession of prophets "like Moses" (Hos. 12:13; Jer. 15:1; compare Deut. 18:15–22).[9]

THE HERDSMAN FROM TEKOA

We know little about Amos, for the book bearing his name stresses his proclaimed "words of Yahweh" rather than biographical details. The book heading (Amos 1:1), added by a later editor, tells us that Amos came from among shepherds of Tekoa, a village lying a few miles south of Jerusalem,[10] and that he was active during the reigns of two contemporary kings, Uzziah of Judah and Jeroboam II of Israel. We could date his career more precisely if we knew the meaning of the chronological reference, "two years before the earthquake" (Amos 1:1; compare Zech. 14:5). In any case, Amos was active in the Northern Kingdom during the height of the reign of Jeroboam II, some time before Jeroboam's death (746 B.C.E.). A date of about 750 B.C.E. fits the conditions reflected in the book.

A prose passage, Amos 7:10–15, gives a clearer picture of Amos' background. It records the dramatic encounter between Amos and Amaziah, chief priest of the Bethel temple—the royal sanctuary Jeroboam I had established as one of the national shrines of the Northern Kingdom. Here we learn that Amos, a native of Judah, had been a herdsman and a "dresser of sycamore trees" (referring to the act of puncturing the sycamore's fig-like fruit to release the insects inside). The appearance of this southerner in the Northern Kingdom discloses that the division between Israel and Judah was primarily political, and that the two nations were actually bound together as one covenant people with a common religious tradition. Amaziah, assuming that Amos was a southern "visionary" (Hebrew: *ḥôzeh*) who earned his living by his religious trade (1 Sam. 9:8; 1 Kings 14:2; 2 Kings 8:8), warned him to return to Judah and there "eat bread" (seek fees for his prophetic oracles). Amos replied:

> I am not a prophet [*nabî'*],
>> Nor a member of a prophetic order;`
> rather, I am a herdsman,
>> and a dresser of sycamore trees.
> However, Yahweh took me from behind the flock,
>> and Yahweh said to me:
> Go! Prophesy to my people Israel.

> —AMOS 7:14–15

[9]See Robert R. Wilson, *Prophecy and Society* [371], pp. 159–66, for a discussion of how the Ephraimitic view of the Mosaic prophet was expanded by the Deuteronomistic circle to mean a succession of prophets "like Moses."

[10]Some scholars believe Amos was at home in the atmosphere of traditional wisdom that was esteemed in nomadic clans and small towns like Tekoa. See H. W. Wolff, *Amos, the Prophet* [382], and Samuel Terrien, "Amos and Wisdom," *Israel's Prophetic Heritage* [174], pp. 108–15.

The meaning of Amos' reply to Amaziah is not altogether clear. The priest recognized Amos to be a "visionary" (*ḥôzeh*), a term used to refer to the prophetic office in southern circles, and told him to go back to Judah where prophets of this type belong. Amos answered by using the word *nabî'* ("prophet"), a northern term used to designate a Moses-like prophet who found support in a prophetic community ("sons of the prophets"). Was Amos merely disavowing that he was a northern (Ephraimitic) prophet like Moses? Or was he saying that he was not a prophet in any sense, northern or southern?[11] Probably the latter: Amos was a layperson whose work had been interrupted by a divine commission that came to him with the irresistible power of Yahweh's spirit (Amos 3:8). In his understanding, this was prophecy of such a different type that the usual terms for "prophet" did not adequately express his task.

Amos was the first in an extraordinary series of prophets whose oracles survive in written form. The prophets who preceded him, like Elijah and Elisha, are known to us only through an oral tradition that preserved the memory of their words and acts. With Amos, however, we have the actual "words that he saw" (Amos 1:1). The book of Amos is a compilation of little units or "oracles" spoken by the prophet on different occasions, and compiled by Amos himself or by the circle of prophets who treasured them. Amos delivered these oracles over a fairly brief span of time during his preaching at Bethel (Amos 7:13) and possibly at Samaria (4:1). He directed his message primarily to the Northern Kingdom but, as a southerner, also had the twin kingdom of Judah in mind (Amos 6:1, 2; 8:14). He was concerned about "the whole family which Yahweh brought out of Egypt" (Amos 3:1).

YAHWEH'S SOVEREIGNTY OVER THE NATIONS

In the age of Jeroboam II, with Syria weakened and the Assyrian lion confined to its distant lair, Israel was able to flex its military muscles and expand. The situation was about to change dramatically. Under Tiglath-pileser III (about 745–727 B.C.E.), the Assyrians would resume their advance into Palestine (as clearly reflected in the book of Hosea). In the time of Amos, however, Assyria's threat to Israel was still only "a little cloud" on the horizon "the size of a human hand" (compare 1 Kings 18:44). Nevertheless Amos saw that trouble was brewing—not just because of Assyria's imperial ambitions, but also because Yahweh was at work in the political arena. Amos shocked his contemporaries with harsh descriptions of brutality by the sword, captivity, desolate cities, and political collapse. His role as a prophet was to interpret these ominous events within the purpose of Yahweh.

The prophecy of Amos opens with an account of "Yahweh's Judgment Against the Nations" (Amos 1:3–2:3). This prologue is perhaps adopted from a cultic "execration"

---

[11]See Robert R. Wilson, *Prophecy and Society* [371], pp. 269–70. Some scholars argue that the reply should be translated in the past tense (see NRSV footnote to Amos 9:14): "I was no prophet, nor a member of a prophetic guild . . ." This would imply that Amos was not a member of a prophetic order when Yahweh called him, but was now a prophet by his own admission.

form used in the Temple to pronounce divine judgment upon the enemies threatening Yahweh's chosen people.[12] But if this is the case, Amos gives the form a new twist. The prophet draws attention by throwing the spotlight of divine judgment upon the small nations surrounding Israel: Syria, Philistia, Tyre, Ammon, Moab.[13] He affirms that Yahweh is sovereign over Israel's enemies and that, because of their military atrocities, a divine fire will break out against their proud palaces and fortifications. Then comes the surprise. What Israel least expected or wanted to hear was the prophetic announcement that the same fire would consume the chosen people of Yahweh during peace and prosperity. At the climax of the series of divine judgments is the startling announcement that Yahweh's wrath is also directed against the people of Israel (Amos 2:6–8).

Amos' affirmation of Yahweh's universal sovereignty clearly points to the covenant tradition in which the prophet was rooted. Though speaking with a disturbingly new accent, he did not claim to say anything new. Echoing Israel's confessional affirmation (Deut. 26:5–9; Josh. 24:2–13), he interpreted Israel's crisis in the light of events enshrined in Israelite tradition, events that had made Israel Yahweh's people with a special task and destiny. He summoned the people to remember their sacred history: how Yahweh had brought them out of the land of Egypt, guided them in the wilderness, enabled them to possess the "land of the Amorites," and raised up prophets and Nazirites to keep them faithful to their God (Amos 2:9–11).[14] In short, the prophet proclaimed the "word of the Lord" within the context of Israel's sacred story, affirming that God speaks in the present through the remembrance and appropriation of tradition.

COVENANT PROMISES AND THREATS

Amos was a vigorous upholder of the Mosaic tradition, as shown by his appeal to the shared Israelite tradition and to the great convictions stamped indelibly on the national epics (J and E) of both the northern and southern kingdoms. The keynote of Amos' prophecy is sounded in Amos 3:1–8, a passage that begins by recalling the crucial event of Israel's history: the Exodus from Egypt. Through Yahweh's action in this event, Israel had become a community—a "whole family" bound together by religious loyalty. Moreover, through this event Yahweh had entered into a covenant relationship with Israel: "You only have I known of all the families of the earth. . . ." The verb "know" (Hebrew: *yada*) refers to the closest kind of personal relationship: In some contexts the

---

[12]See especially A. Bentzen, *The Ritual Background of Amos 1:2–2:16*, Oudtestamentische Studien VIII (Leiden: Brill, 1950), pp. 85–99.

[13]Some scholars question the originality of three oracles—those against Phoenicia (Amos 1:9–10), Edom (Amos 1:11–12), and Judah (Amos 2:4–5)—because they are cast in a somewhat different form and lack a specific portrayal of impending punishment. The oracle against Judah might have replaced an earlier oracle, for it is hard to believe that the prophet would have omitted his own home country.

[14]The Nazirites (literally, "separated ones") were individuals who took special vows of consecration to Yahweh. Their abstinence from wine was a protest against Canaanite culture in the spirit of Israel's wilderness tradition.

verb refers to the intimate union between husband and wife (as in Gen. 4:1). Here, however, it reflects ancient covenant (or treaty) language, in which a suzerain "knows" (that is, enters into covenant relationship with) a vassal, who in turn is obligated to "know" (or recognize the legitimate authority of) the suzerain (see pp. 90–92). This formula—"Yahweh the God of Israel, and Israel the people of Yahweh"—is at the heart of the covenant faith.

Among the Israelite people, however, this conviction led to an attitude that Amos protested with all his might. Reasoning from Yahweh's special calling, the people felt entitled to say: "Therefore, Yahweh will give us prosperity, victory, and prestige among the nations." After all, they thought, the covenant included Yahweh's promises of blessing! Flushed with the national revival and economic boom of the Age of Jeroboam II, they anticipated the "Day of Yahweh"—a festal day apparently celebrated at the turn of each year during the fall covenant festival. In popular belief this day was an anticipation and foretaste of the great "Day of Yahweh," a final climax of history when Yahweh would fulfill the promises of the covenant and crown Israel with glory and honor. The oracle in Amos 5:18–20 says that the people were "desiring" the Day of Yahweh, confident that it would be a day of "light"—a time of victory and blessing. Religion went hand in hand with nationalism. Indeed, at that time there was a great religious revival. Amos paints vivid pictures of people thronging to the shrines to worship (Amos 4:4–5; 5:21–23), although they could scarcely wait for the services to end so they could get back to their money making (8:4–6).

As remembered in the north, however, the Mosaic covenant tradition did not give an unconditional guarantee for the future. It rested upon a fundamental condition: "*If you will obey my voice and keep my covenant, you shall be my own possession among all peoples*" (Exod. 19:5). The covenant included blessings in return for obedience, but it also included threats in the form of curses for disobedience (see pp. 132–134). Standing in this covenant tradition, and aware of its serious threats of divine judgment, Amos reversed the popular logic of his time. Yahweh, he said, has "known" only Israel of all the families of the earth; *therefore*, Israel will be punished for its iniquities. Israel's special calling did not entitle it to special privilege, but only to greater responsibility.

In fact, Amos censured Israel far more heavily than any of the surrounding nations, precisely *because* Israel alone had been called into a special relationship with God. Israel had received, through its historical experience, teaching concerning God's will; yet having seen the light, the people preferred darkness to cover up evil doings. For this reason, Amos proclaimed that the Day of Yahweh would prove to be the night of gloom:

> Disaster for you who long for the Day of Yahweh!
> What will the Day of Yahweh mean for you?
> It will mean darkness, not light,
> as when someone runs away from a lion,
> only to meet a bear;

he goes into his house and puts his hand on the wall,
> only for a snake to bite him.
Will not the Day of Yahweh be darkness, not light,
> totally dark, without a ray of light?

—AMOS 5:18–20 (NJB)

Later, Amos was even more specific: Yahweh, who supervised the affairs of all peoples, was about to raise up a nation to be the instrument of divine judgment (Amos 6:14).

So critical was Amos of the belief in Israel's election that in one passage he seems to renounce the doctrine altogether:

O Israelites, aren't you the same to me as Ethiopians?
> Yahweh says.
Didn't I bring Israel up from the land of Egypt,
as well as the Philistines from Caphtor and the Syrians from Kir?

—AMOS 9:7

Two peoples referred to in this passage, the Philistines and the Syrians, had been Israel's worst enemies. Yet, says the prophet, Yahweh—Sovereign of all the nations—has brought these peoples to their national homelands, just as Israel was brought out of Egypt into Canaan. In this instance the prophet repudiated Israel's notion that Yahweh is a national god to be mobilized for the service of Israel's interests. Insofar as the doctrine of election meant that God serves Israel, rather than that Israel is called to serve God, it was in error.

These somewhat contradictory oracles about divine election (Amos 3:2 and 9:7) were undoubtedly delivered at different times. Amos was not a systematic theologian, but a prophet who spoke the word that needed to be heard at the moment. Even so, one need not assume a fundamental inconsistency between the two statements. Amos says in 9:7 that Yahweh is surely active in the histories of other nations, even though they are not aware of this divine guidance and judgment. Although the nations suppose that they are "known" by other gods, they are actually embraced within the sovereign control of the sole God, Yahweh. Israel, however, has been "known" by Yahweh in the context of a personal, covenantal relationship. Through crucial historical experiences indelibly imprinted upon their tradition, the people have come to know who God is and the lifestyle God demands. Therefore the Israelites cannot plead ignorance, but must stand under a more severe judgment than any other nation.

THE THREAT OF DOOM

Amos spoke in accents of doom. Scarcely a ray of light breaks through the dark clouds he saw on the horizon. Though he lived a generation before Assyria destroyed the

Northern Kingdom, he was so certain of impending catastrophe that he sang a funeral dirge over Israel. This little lamentation (Hebrew: *qinah*) appears in a special 3–2 meter, imitating the dirges that mourners wailed at the scene of a death:

> Fállen, no móre to ríse,
>> is Vírgin Iśrael;
> Forlórn upón her sóil,
>> nóne to líft her.
>
> —AMOS 5:2

Amos strikes the same theme in a series of five prophetic visions that transfigure everyday objects with religious significance. Four visions are introduced by the words, "Yahweh showed me." In the first, Amos is shown a locust plague about to consume the crop after the king has taken the first harvest for his tax (Amos 7:1–3). In the second, a supernatural fire has already licked up the subterranean waters that irrigate the earth and is about to consume the soil necessary for human livelihood (Amos 7:4–6). In both cases, Amos is sensitive to Israel's plight and intercedes on behalf of the people.

So far, there is still some hope for Israel. But not in the remaining visions: A plumb line, used by carpenters for construction, becomes the sign of the destruction that Yahweh will accomplish in the midst of "my people, Israel" (Amos 7:7–9). In a play on words, a basket of summer fruit (Hebrew: *qáyitz*) becomes a sign that "the end [*qētz*] has come upon my people Israel" (Amos 8:1–2). Finally, a vision of Yahweh destroying the worshipers in the Temple depicts the judgment of Yahweh from which there is no escape, either in the heights or the depths (Amos 9:1–4). The last clearly authentic word in the book of Amos is one of utter doom:

> Behold, the eyes of Lord Yahweh
>> are upon the sinful kingdom,
> and I will obliterate it from the
>> surface of the ground.
>
> —AMOS 9:8

This last prediction had nothing to do with political fatalism. True, from a purely military point of view, Israel had no chance of withstanding the Assyrian colossus. But Amos was not thinking of comparative military strength. Nor did his message of doom spring from social despair, for the age of Jeroboam II was one of great confidence. It rested solely on his conviction that Israel, though outwardly healthy, was inwardly diseased with a spreading cancer. Israel was guilty not merely of social crimes, but of unfaithfulness to its calling as the people of Yahweh. In the economy of God, such a society could not long endure.

SYMPTOMS OF SICKNESS

To Amos, Israel's unfaithfulness was shockingly evident in the evils of its flourishing urban society. Wealthy merchants, lusting for economic power, were ruthlessly trampling the poor and defenseless. Public leaders, reveling in luxury and corrupted by indulgence, reclined on beds of ease with no concern for "the ruin of Joseph" (Amos 6:1–7). Sophisticated ladies—whom Amos, the former herdsman, compared with the fat, sleek cows of Bashan—selfishly urged their husbands on (Amos 4:1–3). Law courts were exploited in the vested interests of the commercial class. Moreover, religion had no word of protest against the inhumanities perpetrated in the very shadow of the temples at Bethel, Gilgal, Dan, and Samaria. Amos saw all these things as symptoms of a deep "sickness unto death"—the estrangement of Israel from its God and its covenant calling.

Amos denounced the social injustices of his day with such severity that Amaziah regarded his message as high treason and insisted that "the land is not able to bear all his words" (Amos 7:10). Boldly, the prophet declared that Yahweh "hates," "despises," "abhors" the whole scene:

> Take away from me the noise of your songs;
>   I will not listen to the melody of your harps.
> But let justice roll down like waters,
>   and righteousness like an everflowing stream.
>   —AMOS 5:23–24 (NRSV)

This passage suggests that Amos opposed the forms in which people expressed their worship of God. Turning back to the Mosaic period, Amos asked a rhetorical question (seeming to call for a negative answer): "Did you bring to me sacrifices and offerings the forty years in the wilderness, O house of Israel?" (Amos 5:25). Moreover, Amos was merciless in his attack on the shrines, especially the royal shrine of Jeroboam II at Bethel (Amos 3:14; 7:7–9, 10–17; 9:1).

One doubts that Amos intended a wholesale abolition of the rituals of worship. He was probably demanding the purification of a cult so contaminated by pagan thought and practice that the people were indifferent to true worship and to Yahweh's ethical demands. The prophet's standard demanded that everything be swept away that did not conform to the proper worship of Yahweh, as revealed in the period of Moses. Thus divine surgery had to be applied radically at the source of Israel's sickness: the temples and their system of worship (Amos 9:1).

A CALL TO REPENTANCE

The divine purpose, however, was not one of mere destruction. Amos proclaims that Yahweh was in the people's midst, encouraging Israel to give up its evil ways and "return" to Yahweh. Repentance (Hebrew: *teshubah*) means a return to the One who is the source of Israel's life, a redirection of the will in response to Yahweh's jealous claim upon people's allegiance, and a corresponding change in lifestyle. Each of a striking series of oracles ends with the refrain "yet you did not return to me," affirming Amos' belief that repentance was the divine purpose behind the calamities that had befallen Israel (Amos 4:6–12). But Israel remained set in its rebellious ways, and the prophet warns that even more terrible events lie ahead:

> Assuredly,
> Because I am doing that to you,
> Even so will I act toward you, O Israel—
> Prepare to meet your God, O Israel!
>
> —AMOS 4:12 (TNK)

Amos does not specify when this rendezvous will take place, but he is certain it will take place in the historical arena—and soon. The end of Israel would be a great tragedy, but it would be a *meaningful* tragedy, and Israel would be completely responsible for it. People can choose whom or what they will serve, but they cannot escape the consequences of their choice.

The purpose of such prophecy was to give the people a chance to reform and reorient their lives while there was time. Amos proclaimed what Yahweh was about to do in order to show how urgent the need for change had become. Tomorrow, he said, might be too late; *today* is the time for decision, repentance, and change. The end is at hand! Therefore, "seek Yahweh and live." This was Amos' appeal as the approaching judgment thundered nearer and nearer.

There was little chance that the people of Israel, enslaved by habit and blinded by complacency, would listen to Amos and mend their ways. But the prophet was no fatalist. He admitted the slim possibility that a few (a remnant) might take his warnings to heart and "return" to Yahweh:

> Seek good, and not evil,
>   so that you may live,
> and that Yahweh, God of Hosts, may be with you,
>   as you maintain.
> Despise evil, and love good,
>   and establish justice in courts of law.
> It may be that Yahweh, God of Hosts, will be gracious
>   to the remnant of Joseph.
>
> —AMOS 5:14–15

The "may be," however, rested on the unpredictable response of the people and, above all, on the incalculable grace of God.

Tiglath-pileser III (745–727 B.C.E.) riding in his royal chariot, accompanied by his driver and an attendant who shades his head with an umbrella. The king apparently raises his hand in a salute. The inscription indicates that the scene is connected with the Assyrian deportation of inhabitants from Astartu, the fortified hilltop city (east of the Sea of Galilee) called Ashtaroth in the Bible (Deut. 1:4).

This passage hints that the message of doom was not Yahweh's last word, as later prophets would recognize more clearly. In his heavy emphasis upon doom, Amos leaned over backward to counteract the false optimism of his time. Later, when the desperate political situation drove people to fanaticism or despair, the prophets proclaimed a message of hope. In the age of Jeroboam II, however, the people did not need to hear the divine promise. Already believing that "God is with us" (Amos

5:14),[15] the people needed to hear a word of divine judgment that would shatter their complacency and false security. Then, perhaps, they would understand that the promise rests, not on political and economic fortunes, but on God's amazing grace.

THE PROPHECY OF HOSEA

We resume the history of the Northern Kingdom with the account in 2 Kings 15–17. Shortly after the death of Jeroboam II in 746 B.C.E., Tiglath-pileser III, whose official throne-name was Pulu ("Pul" in the biblical account), seized the Assyrian throne. Ending fifty years of Assyrian lethargy, he set in motion a military program that led ultimately to the conquest of Egypt.

Tiglath-pileser lost no time in setting out on the path of conquest. After conquering Babylonia he marched toward the Mediterranean, sending terror through all of Syria and Palestine. Especially frightening was his introduction of a new military policy, shrewdly calculated to crush nationalism and to hold captive countries firmly in control. This policy entailed uprooting conquered populations from their homeland and exiling them to remote parts of the Assyrian empire. The homeland was resettled with foreign colonists and incorporated into the system of Assyrian provinces. Israel, like other small nations, was destined to learn by bitter experience the meaning of the word "exile."

Neither the Northern Kingdom of Israel nor the Southern Kingdom of Judah could escape involvement in these political events, though Judah managed to maintain greater stability than Israel (see Chapter 10). Israel's political anxiety was reflected in the confused domestic events described briefly in 2 Kings 15 (with the usual Deuteronomistic flourishes). Zechariah, the last king of the Jehu dynasty, was murdered after only six months on the throne. His assassin, Shallum, was struck down by Menahem after one month's reign. Menahem died in his bed after ten years of rule purchased by appeasement of Assyria, but his son Pekahiah held on for only two years before he fell victim to the conspiracy of Pekah, the army commander. Pekah held the throne for a few precarious years, only to be knifed by Hoshea.[16] And Hoshea, the last king of Israel, died in chains (see Chronological Chart 6, p. 299). Never before in the history of the Northern Kingdom had there been such a tangle of murder and intrigue. Hosea vividly describes the situation:

---

[15]This is the literal meaning of "Immanuel," the name introduced later by the prophet Isaiah (see pp. 297–300).
[16]According to 2 Kings 15:27, Pekah reigned for twenty years. This figure is too high, however, for Samaria's fall occurred less than twenty years after the beginning of his reign. John Bright, in *History* [110], p. 273 (note 8), suggests that Pekah could have claimed that his rule began before he seized the throne, and that he might have exercised some authority in Gilead (2 Kings 15:25) from the time of Jeroboam's death.

On the day of our king the officials became sick
> with the heat of wine;
> he stretched out his hand with mockers.
For they are kindled like an oven, their heart
> burns within them;
> all night their anger smolders;
> in the morning it blazes like a flaming fire.
All of them are hot as an oven,
> and they devour their rulers.
All their kings have fallen;
> none of them calls upon me.

—HOSEA 7:5–7 (NRSV; see all of
6:11–7:7)

In the very year that Menahem (about 745–738 B.C.E.,) usurped the throne, Tiglath-pileser's armies began their invasion. Menahem had to surrender the northern part of his kingdom (Galilee), and in addition paid a heavy tribute to the Assyrian monarch, "that he might help him to confirm his hold of the royal power" (2 Kings 15:19). In his annals, Tiglath-pileser recorded that he received tribute from "Menahem of Samaria," along with gifts from numerous other peoples.[17] Menahem's policy of appeasement succeeded for the time being and the Assyrians marched away, allowing the Israelite king to keep his throne. But his capitulation, which resulted in heavy taxes on the wealthy class, was highly unpopular and fanned the fires of resentment and revolt.

HOSEA'S OPTIMISM OF GRACE

Hosea's prophetic career overlapped two eras: the last part of the age of Jeroboam II, and the succeeding period of political instability. Hosea's earliest prophecy (chapters 1–3 of the book of Hosea) was apparently delivered in the very year of Jeroboam's death (746 B.C.E.), since the dynasty of Jehu was reportedly still in existence (Hos. 1:4). The heading (Hos. 1:1), which in its present form comes from a later Judean editor, states that Hosea prophesied "in the days of Jeroboam," and adds that his career embraced the reigns of four Judean kings, the last being Hezekiah (about 715–687 B.C.E.). This is probably inaccurate, for it is doubtful whether Hosea was prophesying as late as the fall of the Northern Kingdom (721 B.C.E.). Nevertheless his career lasted at least ten years after Jeroboam's death, because the second section of the book (chapters 4–14) reflects the turbulent conditions of that period: the fall of the dynasty of Jehu; the rapid succession of kings as "the land devour[ed] its rulers;" and the people's confusion, demoralization, and anxiety as a result of international developments.

---

[17]See Pritchard, *Ancient Near Eastern Texts* [1], p. 283.

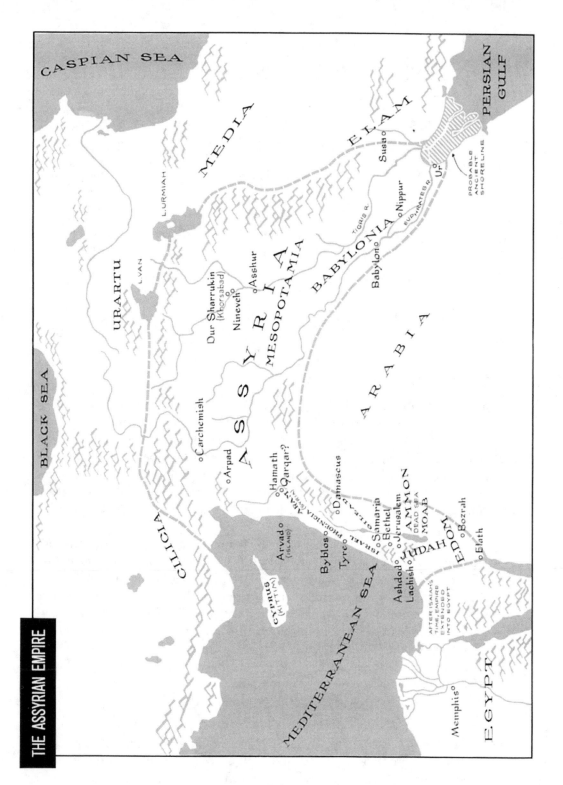

THE ASSYRIAN EMPIRE

CASPIAN SEA

BLACK SEA

MEDIA

URARTU

L.VAN

L.URMIAH

ELAM

Susa

PERSIAN GULF

Ur

PROBABLE ANCIENT SHORELINE

TIGRIS R.

EUPHRATES R.

Nippur

Babylon

BABYLONIA

MESOPOTAMIA

A S S Y R I A

Dur Sharrukin (Khorsabad)

Nineveh

Asshur

Carchemish

Arpad

Hamath

Qarqar?

ARABIA

CILICIA

Arvad (ISLAND)

CYPRUS (KITTIM)

Byblos

Tyre

Ashdod

Lachish

Damascus

Samaria

Bethel

Jerusalem

ISRAEL

PHOENICIA (SIDON)

ARAM

GILEAD (GALAAD)

AMMON

JUDAH

MOAB

DEAD SEA

EDOM

Bozrah

Elath

MEDITERRANEAN SEA

AFTER ISAIAH'S TIME, EMPIRE EXTENDED INTO EGYPT

Memphis

EGYPT

273

Chronological Chart 5

B.C.E.	Egypt	Palestine		Mesopotamia	
		THE DIVIDED MONARCHY			
		Judah	Israel	Syria	Assyria
850		Athaliah, c. 842–837	*Jehu Dynasty:*	Hazael, c. 842–806	Shalmaneser III, c. 859–825
	Decline	Joash, c. 837–800	Jehu, c. 843/2–815		(Jehu pays tribute, 841)
					Shamshi-Adad V, c. 824–812
			Joahaz, c. 815-801		Adad-nirari III, c. 811–784
		Amaziah, c. 800–783	Jehoash, c. 802–786		
		Uzziah (Azariah), c. 783–742	Jeroboam II, c. 786–746 (*Amos,* c. 750) (*Hosea,* c. 745)		*Decline*
c. 750			Zechariah (6 mos.) c. 746–745		Tiglath-pileser III, c. 745–727

Like the book of Amos, the book of Hosea is a compilation of brief oracles, delivered at different times and brought together in their present arrangement either by the prophet himself or by his disciples. Often the same prophetic themes are repeated, with variations, from situation to situation. The text of Hosea has not been preserved as well as that of Amos. Indeed, Hosea 4–14 is often so textually corrupt that the translator must turn to other ancient versions or resort to conjecture (see NSRV footnotes). Moreover, several additions have been made to Hosea's oracles, the most obvious being the concluding exhortation in Hosea 14:9.

Amos announced that the Day of Yahweh would be a day of pitch-darkness. Hosea balanced the word of divine judgment with the promise of restoration and renewal. He too saw the coming of the "Day of Darkness," but he proclaimed that, despite the total eclipse, the sun was still shining. Hosea's qualified optimism was not due to any improvement in the political or religious situation since the time of Amos, for affairs had gone from bad to worse in the Northern Kingdom. Rather, his "optimism of grace" was based on the belief that Israel's hope was grounded solely in the constancy of Yahweh's love for the people. In fact, Hosea's marriage experience became a "living parable" of the relation between Yahweh and Israel.

HOSEA'S MARRIAGE

The story of Hosea's marriage to Gomer is key to the interpretation of his prophetic message. But this story (Hos. 1–3) presents one of the most difficult problems in biblical studies. For one thing, Hosea was not interested in autobiography or in making a "true confession." As with Amos, Hosea the man recedes behind the prophetic word he proclaims. Hosea gives only enough details about his marriage to symbolize the story of Yahweh's relation to Israel, which occupies the center of his attention.

The facts behind Hosea's marriage are further obscured by the different types of material in Hosea 1-3: chapter 1 is written in the biographical third person, while chapter 3 is written in the autobiographical first person. Does the sequence of events in these chapters describe the prophet's experience with one woman, Gomer? The unnamed woman of Hosea 3 is not explicitly identified with Gomer, leading some scholars to believe that this chapter tells of Hosea's relationship with another woman. Most probably, however, these chapters recount Hosea's experience with one woman. Because Hosea 3:1–2 does not name the woman—as would be expected if she were different—we must presume that the woman is the previously mentioned Gomer. Moreover, the analogy with Israel (Hos. 3:1b) suggests that the prophet will be reconciled with the estranged Gomer, just as Yahweh takes back the alienated people. In Hosea 1 the theme is the faithlessness of Israel; in Hosea 3 it is the steadfastness of Yahweh's love in the face of infidelity. These themes suggest not one event, but a sequence of events in Hosea's relation with Gomer.

What was the marital experience on which the prophet based his parable? Forgetting for a moment the troublesome Hosea 1:2, we can reconstruct the events as follows: Hosea married a woman who bore him three children. Hosea gave these children significant names so that they might be "walking signs" of Yahweh's word to Israel, just as Isaiah gave symbolic names to his children (Isa. 7:3; 8:3). In recollection of the place where Jehu carried out his terrible blood purge (2 Kings 9) the first son was named Jezreel, signifying that "in a little while" Yahweh would punish the house of Jehu for those atrocities. The second child, a daughter, was named Lo-ruhamah ("Not-pitied"), a symbol that Yahweh's patience with Israel had been exhausted. And the third child, a son, was called Lo-ammi ("Not-my-people"), a sign that Yahweh had dissolved the covenant bond and rejected the people. Next the prophet's attention shifts from the children to their mother, who had proved unfaithful to the marriage bond (as suggested in Hos. 2:2). Reading between the lines—for at this point the biographical narrative is interrupted by the prophetic sermon in Hosea 2—we must assume that Hosea divorced Gomer because of her unfaithfulness (Hos. 2:2). Despite her disloyalty, however, Hosea was ready to go beyond the law and forgive. In Hosea 3 we read that Hosea ransomed her and, after a period of discipline, restored her as his wife.

Hosea 1:2, a kind of second introduction, might give Hosea's view in retrospect. When he married Gomer she was not yet a harlot, although she later became one. Since in the prophetic view a divine purpose is discernible in life's varied experiences, Hosea insists that all this has happened at Yahweh's command. He was ordered to take "a wife of harlotry and have children of harlotry," that is, children who would share the defect of their mother. Reflecting on Israel's relation to Yahweh, the meaning of his own marriage became clear: "for the land commits great harlotry by forsaking Yahweh."

Hosea's only reason for mentioning his private life was to make a real-life analogy to Yahweh's covenant. Consider then the story of the "marriage" between Yahweh and Israel.

THE BROKEN COVENANT

No prophet was more profoundly aware of the Mosaic past than Hosea. The memory of the Exodus, the sojourn in the wilderness, the covenant at Horeb, and the occupation of Canaan were always in his mind as he interpreted the events of his time. In fact, he understood himself to be a successor of Moses, the great interpreter and mediator of the covenant.[18] Since Hosea was a native of the Northern Kingdom, chances are he was nurtured in the northern (Ephraimitic) version of the Old Epic tradition, the so-called "Elohist" narrative (see Definition, pp. 261–262).

In the prophet's thinking, one epic theme stood out above the rest: Yahweh's gracious choice of Israel, manifested in the liberating experience of the Exodus. Israel's knowledge of God was based on that root experience: "I am Yahweh your God from the land of Egypt" (Hos. 12:9; 13:4–5). The Exodus was the sign of a special relation between God and people, on the analogy of a parent and child (compare the Old Epic passage in Exod. 4:22):

> When Israel was a youth I loved him;
>> Out of Egypt I called my son.
>>> —HOSEA 11:1 (NEB)

But Hosea was the first Israelite prophet who understood the covenant through analogy with the marriage relationship. In the setting of the Canaanite culture, this was a bold reinterpretation of Israel's faith. To be sure, the concept of sacred marriage was well-known in the ancient world, where mythological dramas portrayed the relations of gods and goddesses in the context of the cycles of nature. Using a completely new analogy, however, Hosea spoke of a *historical* marriage made in the wilderness between God and a people. The meaning of this marriage was disclosed to Hosea not by mythological drama, but by a deep understanding of his personal relationship to Gomer.

Just as Gomer betrayed her husband, so Israel had broken the covenant. The "wife" Yahweh had chosen had become a "harlot." This was the real historical tragedy, and the present troubles of Israel were its symptoms. A "spirit of harlotry" had inflamed the people, estranging them from their God (Hos. 4:12). Hosea's critique of Israel's society was more than a condemnation of social immorality, political confusion, or religious formalism. He was concerned with human motives, with the devotion of the heart, and with the values in which people place their trust. Echoing the criticism made by leaders of the old Tribal Confederacy (see pp. 187–189), Hosea condemned the monarchy as a symptom of a whorish spirit. Saul's hometown of Gibeah and his coronation at Gilgal were evidence of Israel's determination to reject Yahweh as king (Hos. 8:4; 9:15; 10:3, 9). The consequences of Israel's betrayal of the covenant were apparent

---

[18]See James Muilenburg, "The Office of the Prophet in Ancient Israel," in *The Bible in Modern Scholarship* [185], 94.

in the regicides (Hos. 7:3–7), the feverish foreign policy aimed at courting Egypt or Assyria (7:11), and the reliance upon arms and fortifications (8:14). Stubborn and determined, Israel had insisted on being "like the nations." As a result it was "swallowed up" among the nations (Hos. 8:8) and "strangers" consumed its strength (7:8–9).

This spirit of harlotry had led the people into a false and idolatrous religion. In Hosea's time popular religion provided a means of obtaining the bounty of nature and tethering God to human interests. Influenced by the fertility cult of Canaan, people thronged to the temples, not to acknowledge gratefully their dependence on the God who had brought them out of Egypt, but to "get something out of" religion: harmony, security, prosperity, and welfare. Exploiting the upsurge of religious interest, priests and prophets actually contributed to Israel's harlotry by "feeding on the sin" of Yahweh's people (Hos. 4:7–10). Israel's fidelity, then, was that of a fickle wife. It lacked the steadfastness, the trustworthiness of true covenant love. In Hosea's native language, Israel lacked *ḥésed* (see Definition, below).

This important term is applied especially to God. As the Sovereign who initiated the covenant relationship, Yahweh "abounds in *ḥésed* and faithfulness" (Exod. 34:6; compare Ps. 103:8). Yahweh's constancy in dealing with Israel is not based on law or necessity but solely on divine freedom and commitment. Hosea applies the term *ḥésed* to Israel's relationship to Yahweh, suggesting that the people should display a steadfast love like Yahweh's. But in the prophet's vivid figures, Israel's covenant faithfulness was like a transient morning cloud, or like the dew that evaporates quickly (Hos. 6:4). According to Hosea, Yahweh scorned existing forms of worship:

> For I desire steadfast love [*ḥésed*] and not sacrifice,
> the knowledge of God rather than burnt offerings.
> —HOSEA 6:6 (NRSV)

We should not take this to mean that Hosea was opposed to formal worship, though clearly he was opposed to forms devoid of the spirit of true faithfulness to the God of the covenant. The New Testament reports that Jesus, when accused of breaking the formal rules of orthodoxy, twice asked his hearers to go and reread Hosea 6:6 (Matt. 9:13 and 12:7).

DEFINITION: "ḤÉSED"

This word *ḥésed* is exceedingly difficult to render into English, as is evident in the various translations found in Hosea 6:6:

"mercy" (King James Version)
"steadfast love" (NRSV)
"goodness" (JPSV)
"loyalty" (REB), and so forth.

On a human level, *ḥésed* seems to apply to relationships in which one party is "superior" in the sense of having more power or influence by virtue of social position. A good illustration is the friendship between David and Jonathan. At one point David says to Jonathan: "Deal faithfully [show *ḥésed*] with your servant, since you have taken your servant into a covenant [of Yahweh] with you" (1 Sam. 20:8a, JPSV). As long as Jonathan had the superior position (son of the king), the sacred covenant of friendship obliged him to help David escape from Saul. But Jonathan asked David to promise that, when their roles were reversed and David came to power, David would manifest loyalty (*ḥésed*) to him (1 Sam. 20:12–17). David's obligation of friendship lasted even beyond Jonathan's death, for he was determined to "show *ḥésed*" to other members of Saul's family for the sake of Jonathan (2 Sam 9:1, 3, 7).

Ḥésed, then, is loyalty manifested by a stronger party toward someone who is in a weaker position (compare the suzerain-vassal treaty relationship, pp. 90–92). It is not an inherent virtue but something to be *done*, which accounts for the expressions "do *ḥésed*," "maintain *ḥésed*," "love *ḥésed* ." It is not, however, an act of *noblesse oblige*—as with people of high standing who behave nobly toward inferiors in a condescending manner or give alms to the poor. Loyalty arises not from any external legal obligation or social custom, but from the relationship itself. *Ḥésed* is an act of inner faithfulness and therefore of grace. Each participant is free to be loyal or unfaithful, although in a time of distress the weaker party in the relationship might have no other source of help.[19]

THE INNER FLAW

In Hosea 6:6, the prophet draws a poetic parallel between two important words: *ḥésed* (see Definition, pp. 277–278) and "the knowledge of God." Hosea insists that Israel did not *know* God (Hos. 4:1, 6, 11) and that this deficiency is the root of its problem. Hosea is speaking about a kind of knowledge that is intrinsic to the covenant relationship—a knowing of God that is the response to being known (chosen) by God (Amos 3:2). This meaning of the verb "know" is found in Hittite and Akkadian texts that describe the suzerainty treaty form (see pp. 90–92): The suzerain "recognizes" ("knows") his vassal, and the vassal "recognizes" his lord. In a related sense, the covenant party "recognizes" (acknowledges) that treaty stipulations are binding.[20] Thus it is not surprising that Hosea puts *ḥésed* (loyalty) and "knowledge of God" in poetic parallelism. The meaning of "know" for both parties of the covenant is brought out in this passage:

> Yet I am Yahweh your God
> > ever since the land of Egypt.
> You know no God but me,
> > and besides me there is no savior.
> I knew you in the wilderness,
> > in the land of drought.
>
> —HOSEA 13:4–5

---

[19]See Katherine D. Sakenfeld, *Faithfulness in Action* [165].
[20] See Delbert R. Hillers, *Covenant* [256], pp. 120–23.

On the human side such knowledge has two aspects. First is a *theological* knowledge that can be taught by parents in the home (Deut. 6:20–25) or by cultic officials at the sanctuaries, especially at covenant-renewal festivals. This is the knowledge of who God is (Hos. 13:4), what God has done for Israel, and what God requires of the people—in short, a knowledge of the covenant tradition. When this understanding is lacking, the people turn to strange gods and break the laws of the covenant epitomized in the Ten Commandments.[21] Hosea lays the blame for this state of affairs at the door of the priests and prophets, whose duty it was to instruct the people in the meaning of the covenant (Hos. 4:5–6).

The second aspect is a knowledge that includes the *will* as well as the mind. Hosea was talking about the knowledge of the heart[22]—that is, the response of the *whole person* to God's love. To know Yahweh means to respond to the claim Yahweh makes upon one's devotion, to obey Yahweh's will in society where the poor and needy cry for help (compare Jer. 22:16). In observing that Israel lacked knowledge of God, Hosea asserted that the people did not *acknowledge* God. The covenant was broken. Israel, the "wife," was estranged from her "husband":

> Their deeds do not allow them
> > to return to their God;
> For the spirit of harlotry is within them,
> > and they do not know Yahweh.
> > > —HOSEA 5:4

In the end, when God's purpose wins out, the covenant will be restored, and Israel will "know Yahweh" (Hos. 2:20).[23]

Hosea not only exposed the inner motives of Israel's contemporary life, but also saw clearly that behind Israel's infidelity lay a pattern of thought and action deeply ingrained in the people since their entrance into Canaan. In the wilderness, Hosea proclaimed, Yahweh had entered into covenant with a bride who was destined to prove unfaithful. Indeed, the "honeymoon" in the wilderness, when Israel was faithful, was all too brief. No sooner had the people set foot on the soil of Canaan than Israel began to deck itself alluringly in a harlot's attire, and to pursue its "lovers"—the nature gods of Canaan who promised the "harlot's hire" of prosperity and security. This is the theme of the prophetic sermon in Hosea 2. The people did not realize that the very gifts of fertility they sought from Baal had been mercifully provided by the God who brought Israel up from the land of Egypt! Indeed, Baal worship had infiltrated Israel so slowly and

---

[21]The Decalogue is specifically referred to in Hosea 4:2 (prohibitions against lying, killing, stealing, and adultery). The whole passage (4:1–10) is cast in the form of a legal controversy or lawsuit, in which one covenant partner accuses the other of violation of the covenant.

[22]In the anthropology of ancient Israel, the heart is the organ of thinking, willing, and feeling.

[23]In the last days, according to Jeremiah's prophecy of the "new covenant" (Jer. 31:31–34), knowledge of Yahweh will come from the heart, not from teaching (see pp. 381–382).

subtly through the years that in popular religion Yahweh had become identified with Baal (Hos. 2:16-17).

From the first, therefore, Israel's history was a sordid and shameful story of the betrayal of Yahweh's love. Now the people were caught in the coils of a sinful history from which they could not extricate themselves. "Their deeds," said Hosea, "do not permit them to return to their God" (Hos. 5:4). So enslaved were the people to false loyalties that it was almost useless to appeal to them: "Ephraim is joined to idols, let him alone" (Hos. 4:17). Every aspect of Israel's corporate life—politics, economics, religion—was tainted with the ideology of a false allegiance, a misdirected will, a vicious style of behavior. Enslaved by habitual ways of thinking and living, the people now lacked both the imagination and the willpower to change themselves. But, just as a great crisis in an individual's life sometimes makes possible a new beginning, so Hosea believed that the historical catastrophe about to befall the nation was intended by God as an opportunity for Israel to recover its health.

THE TRIUMPH OF LOVE

Like Amos, Hosea described the threat from Assyria in accents of doom. He gave his children born to Gomer names that signified Yahweh's judgment. The name of the youngest child, Lo-ammi, stood for Yahweh's termination of the covenant relationship: "You are not my people and I am not your God" (Hos. 1:9). Furthermore, the prophetic sermon in Hosea 2 begins with Yahweh's announcement of divorce from Israel, the harlotrous mother of harlotrous children: "She is not my wife, and I am not her husband" (Hos. 2:2). Elsewhere Hosea uses even stronger language: Yahweh is compared to a wild animal that pounces on human prey (Hos. 5:14; 13:7–8), and to moth or dry rot that destroys the social fabric (5:12). The people will seek Yahweh in vain (Hos. 5:6), for Yahweh will love them no more (9:15). A faithless people deserves rejection, just as Gomer did.

This is harsh language! With these metaphors, Hosea meant to create a kind of "future shock"—to awaken people to the urgency of the present in view of God's impending judgment. The eighth century prophets perceived that, in one sense, imminent calamity would result from the people's errant lifestyle and foreign policy. "They sow the wind," said Hosea, "and they shall reap the whirlwind" (Hos. 8:7). These prophets did not believe, however, that God merely ordained moral laws which, like the law of gravity, people break at their own risk. Rather, they announced that God *personally* was acting in the social sphere, using agents (like Assyria) to bring people to their senses. The absolute sovereignty of God in human affairs, on one side, and full human responsibility on the other, were equally important tenets of prophetic faith, though the paradox might be difficult for us to grasp.

The book of Hosea strikes its deepest note with the proclamation that God's "wrath" or judgment is redemptive. God's purpose is not to destroy, but to heal. Yahweh acts through historical crises to free people from their enslavement to false allegiances and to restore them to freedom in covenant loyalty. Just as Hosea's love was stronger than Gomer's infidelity, so Yahweh's love for Israel is truly steadfast, a divine love that will not let the people go, despite their fickleness and harlotry. Yahweh's "wrath" is not capricious, vindictive, or destructive. It expresses a love that seeks to break the chains of Israel's bondage and emancipate the people for a new life, a new covenant. In Hosea's view, this freedom would come only when God destroyed the false idols, so that the "wife" Israel could no longer pursue her "lovers" (Hos. 2:2–13). Then Israel would have the opportunity to *be Israel*, the people of the covenant, living in grateful dependence upon the God who redeemed them from Egypt and who continued to supply their needs in the land of Canaan.

PARENTAL DISCIPLINE

The holiness of Yahweh's love, which includes both judgment and mercy, is magnificently portrayed in Hosea 11, where the figure changes from the relationship between husband and wife to the relationship between parent and child. Here we read that the creative, nurturing love of Yahweh is behind and within Israel's history from the very first, giving meaning and purpose to its life. The first part of the poem (Hos. 11:1–4) announces that Israel, Yahweh's "son" (compare Exod. 4:22–23), was loved into being, and that Yahweh, like a parent, had gathered the child in a compassionate embrace and taught it how to walk. (In verse 4, the figure suddenly shifts to a farmer who gently leads and cares for an animal.) The next section (verses 5–7) states that Yahweh's patience is exhausted in dealing with this refractory child. Israel must be disciplined, and the punishment will come from Egypt or Assyria, the very nations to which they turned for political salvation.

Divine judgment is not the last word, however. Even in the hour of catastrophe Yahweh does not abandon the people, nor does divine love for them cease (verses 8-9). It is not Yahweh's will that Israel be destroyed, as Admah and Zeboim were leveled during the holocaust of Sodom and Gomorrah (Gen. 19:24–25; Deut. 29:23). Like a loving parent who disciplines a wayward child, the purpose behind Yahweh's judgment is love. These verses passionately describe a struggle, as it were, within the heart of God. But the love that will not let Israel go triumphs. In the last analysis, words cannot plumb the depths of this holy love:

> for I am God and no mortal,
>   the Holy One in your midst,
>   and I will not come in wrath.
>
> —HOSEA 11:9b (NRSV)

God's relationship with Israel has both the dark side of judgment and the bright side of promised renewal (Hos. 11:10–11). To us, the "wrath" and the "love" of God might seem contradictory. In the prophecy of Hosea, however, God's "pathos"—to use Abraham Heschel's expression—surpasses the logic of human understanding.[24]

THE RENEWAL OF THE COVENANT

Hosea understood his experience with Gomer (Hos. 3) as being analogous to the relation between Yahweh and Israel. Hosea continued to love his wife even though she proved unfaithful. Yahweh, too, steadfastly loved the people even though they turned to other gods (in Hos. 3:1, "raisin cakes" refers to food used in the Baal fertility cult). Hosea ransomed Gomer and restored her to relationship with him, though he disciplined her "for many days." Israel also had to endure a period of discipline and quarantine—"without king or prince, without sacrifice or pillar, without ephod or teraphim" (Hos. 3:4). The deprivation would be primarily political and religious, the very areas corroded by Canaanite culture. After "many days" of cleansing and purgation would come a new beginning, a new relationship. Israel would return (or "repent") and seek Yahweh, its God.[25]

Hosea develops this theme of discipline through suffering at great length in chapter 2. In vivid language he speaks of the exposure of Israel's harlotry and the frustration of all attempts to pursue "her lovers." However, Yahweh's purpose throughout is reconciliation:

> So, I am going to allure her,
> > and lead her into the wilderness,
> > and speak to her heart.
> From there I will give her her vineyards,
> > and the Valley of Achor as a gateway of hope.
> There she will respond as in the days of her youth,
> > as in the time when she came out of the land of Egypt.
> —HOSEA 2:14–15

The Valley of Achor was probably located in the wilderness of Judah, on a plateau overlooking the Dead Sea. At its eastern rim the brook Qumran plunges through a gorge and descends abruptly to the Jordan Valley, passing by a site where—centuries after Hosea's time—an Essene community was established (see pp. 575–576) and also spoke of a new covenant in the wilderness. Visitors to the valley, just above the cliffs of Qumran, are impressed with the stark contrast between the elemental simplicity of this barren place and the fertility of the hill country where great cities once stood as proud

---

[24]Abraham J. Heschel, *The Prophets* [352], chap. 3.

[25]In Hosea 3:5, the phrase "and David their king" is obviously a gloss by a later editor of the Southern Kingdom. Elsewhere the book has been touched up with Judean additions (Hos. 1:7; 4:15: 11:12b). Some scholars argue that all references to Judah are spurious. But Hosea, like Amos, probably applied his message to the kingdoms of both Israel and Judah.

symbols of human culture. Here, in the wilderness, the person of faith is reminded that life depends on God's mercies.

Significantly, Hosea saw the wilderness as the place of new beginning. Just as Israel was given life in the ancient wilderness, so in the present wilderness—away from all the temptations of culture—life will be renewed. Yahweh, he prophesied, personally would lure the people into the wilderness. To Israel, stripped of all false securities and purged of all cultural pretensions, Yahweh would "speak tenderly," or, as the Hebrew says, "speak to her heart." There Israel would regain the vineyards and learn that all the blessings of culture are gifts of God's grace. There the people would enter a door of hope, leading into a meaningful and secure future.

For Hosea, then, the wilderness would be the scene of the renewal of the covenant. Israel would *answer* Yahweh's overture of love, as the people had responded in trust and gratitude at the time of the Exodus. In the wilderness Yahweh would restore Israel to the marriage relationship forever, taking Israel as "wife" in righteousness and justice, in covenant faithfulness (*ḥésed*) and mercy. Israel's persistent infidelity would be conquered by love, and Israel would again *know* Yahweh (Hos. 2:19–20).

THE FALL OF SAMARIA

Hosea's hope rested on an "optimism of grace," not on political probabilities. To be sure, his message of doom was underscored by Israel's precarious position directly in the path of Assyria's advance across the Fertile Crescent toward Egypt. Politically, small Israel did not have a chance, especially when the leaders of the nation were pursuing suicidal foreign and domestic policies. But to Hosea the political crisis had another dimension. Within the events of the time he saw God's activity in judgment and renewal.

We are not sure how long Hosea's prophetic career continued. Some scholars believe he was active in 735–733 B.C.E., during the alliance between Syria and Israel (see Chapter 10), and suggest that Hosea 5:8–14 might reflect an invasion by the Southern Kingdom into Israel at that time.[26] In any case, Hosea's ministry extended into the turbulent period of the last days of the Northern Kingdom (as reflected in Hos. 4–14).

Events moved rapidly toward disaster. Tiglath-pileser's death in 727 B.C.E. gave Israel an opportunity to revolt (see Chronological Chart 6, p. 299). King Hoshea of Israel, foolishly relying on the "weak reed" of Egypt and hoping the new Assyrian emperor would be unable to control his far-flung empire, refused to pay tribute in about the year 724 B.C.E. But the new Assyrian king, Shalmaneser V (about 726–722 B.C.E.), quickly attacked Samaria. He died during the battle, and his successor Sargon II (about 721–705 B.C.E.) inherited the task of finishing the job. After a three-year siege, Samaria

---

[26]This view has been advanced by Albrecht Alt, "Hosea 5: 8–6: 6," in his *Kleine Schriften zur Geschichte des Volkes Israel,* II (Munich, 1953), pp. 163–87. See further James M. Ward, Hosea [390].

Sargon II (721–705 B.C.E.) was the conqueror of Samaria. Here he is shown wearing the royal headdress, long hair and curled beard, and a cruciform earring. The bust was found at Dur-Sharruken (Khorsabad), the city the ruler built as his residence a few miles east of Nineveh.

fell in the first months of the year 721 B.C.E.; and the land became an Assyrian province. According to his annals, Sargon deported 27,290 Israelites to the region of Persia (2 Kings 17:6) and repopulated Israel with colonists from Babylonia, Elam, and Syria.[27] The words of Amos' dirge had been translated into historical reality: "Fallen is the virgin Israel."

So far as we know, Hosea did not live through this final tragedy. But his prophecy was not forgotten. It was preserved in prophetic circles and eventually was edited in the Southern Kingdom of Judah, where it was contemporized and given new meaning.

[27]See Pritchard, *Ancient Near Eastern Texts* [1], pp. 284–87.

CHAPTER 10

JUDAH'S COVENANT WITH DEATH

All the great prophets we have considered up to this point—Elijah, Elisha, Micaiah, Amos, and Hosea—were active in the Northern Kingdom (Israel), which parted with the Davidic Southern Kingdom (Judah) after Solomon's death. Prophets were active in Judah during the same period, for the record speaks of obscure figures like Azariah (2 Chron. 15:1–7), Hanani (2 Chron. 16:7–10), and Jehu, son of Hanani (1 Kings 16:1–4; 2 Chron. 19:2). But none of these individuals held a candle to their northern counterparts, whose spiritual stature matched the great crises of their time. Even Amos, a southerner, chose to deliver his message in Bethel, the seat of the royal sanctuary of Jeroboam II.

In politics, as well as prophecy, the Northern Kingdom stayed in the lead after the division of the United Kingdom. Occasionally the Southern Kingdom achieved a position of equality, when Israel was temporarily weakened by domestic troubles or by the intervention of a foreign power. But on the whole Judah was overshadowed by its stronger and wealthier twin kingdom to the north. Whereas Judah was comparatively isolated in the hill country, off the main roads of the ancient world, Israel stood squarely in the path of history. Situated geographically astride the crossroads of com-

Biblical Readings: Of the prophetic literature dealt with in this chapter, read especially Isaiah 1–11 and 28–32, and Micah 1–3 and 6:1–8. The historical background is sketched in 2 Kings 15:32–20:21, with a parallel version in 2 Chronicles 26–32.

merce between Egypt and Mesopotamia, the Northern Kingdom inevitably played a leading role in Palestine. Providentially, a succession of great prophets appeared at the very time when this nation was recognized as a leader among the small nations.

When "the wide land of the house of Omri,"[1] as Sargon II called Israel, was swallowed up in the Assyrian empire, the prophetic succession was continued in Judah.[2] Here too the story of the prophets is intertwined with accounts of the nation's political fortunes, down to the time when it collapsed under the attack of the Babylonian armies. We will begin by considering the long and prosperous reign of Uzziah, or Azariah (about 783–742 B.C.E.), which paralleled the glorious era of Jeroboam II in the Northern Kingdom.

The Reign of Uzziah

In contrast to the political restlessness and economic discontent manifest during the history of the Northern Kingdom of Israel, the Southern Kingdom of Judah achieved a remarkable degree of political and economic stability. A single dynasty, that of David, remained on the throne of Jerusalem throughout the whole period, while the sequence of northern Israelite kings was punctuated by violence and intrigue. Unlike the Northern Kingdom, where swift economic changes led to an unstable social pyramid, the Southern Kingdom moved fairly smoothly from the relative simplicity of the old tribal system to the more advanced economy of town life. In the process, Judah preserved an astonishing degree of social equilibrium. True, the Northern Kingdom had no monopoly on evil. Judean prophets saw plenty of evidence that rapacious landlords were swallowing up the holdings of small farmers (Isa. 5:8–10; Mic. 2:1–2), that the rich were skinning the backs of the poor (Isa. 10:1–2; Mic. 3:1–4), and that flagrant social injustices were smoothed over with a veneer of religious piety (Isa. 1:10–17). Nevertheless, the relative stability of the social order, symbolized by the Davidic crown, must be kept in mind as we approach the book of Isaiah. This political stability was supported by the theological conviction that Yahweh had made a special covenant with David, promising to uphold his throne and to establish his descendants after him (see pp. 208–212).

Under Uzziah, Judah reached the peak of its economic and military power. The brief report in 2 Kings 15:1–7, supplemented by the longer account in 2 Chronicles 26, gives us a picture of Uzziah's extraordinary accomplishments: modernization of the army; conquests in the Philistine plain that put him in control of the main commercial

---

[1]This expression is used in Sargon's report of the conquest of Samaria (see Pritchard, *Ancient Near Eastern Texts* [1], pp. 284–85). It had been customary for Assyrians to name the Northern Kingdom of Israel in honor of Omri. Even Jehu was called "son of Omri" in Assyrian records.

[2]On prophecy in the Ephraimite and Judean traditions, see Robert R. Wilson, *Prophecy and Society* [371], chaps. 5 and 6.

highways; commercial expansion into Arabia; reconstruction of the trade-route seaport city of Elath (formerly Ezion-geber); and development of agriculture (we are told "he loved the soil").

To Judeans, the only disturbing event in Uzziah's reign occurred about 750 B.C.E., when their beloved king was stricken with leprosy and had to be confined to a separate house. His son, Jotham, appeared in public as regent. But not even this dread disease, which the Judean historians interpreted as a sign of Yahweh's disfavor, eclipsed the glory and fame of Uzziah. After his confinement Uzziah continued to be the recognized ruler, and his name remained a symbol of Judah's strength and stability (Isa. 6:1). While the Northern Kingdom of Israel swiftly declined after the death of Jeroboam II, Judah rose to a position of power and influence second only to that of the era of David and Solomon. The only cloud on the horizon was the threat of Assyrian imperialism.

The Assyrian threat was no new development. From the thirteenth century B.C.E. on, the dominant theme of international politics was the rise of Assyria and its ambition to establish an empire encompassing the whole Fertile Crescent. With the rise of Tiglath-pileser III, this threat became an ominous reality. Once the Assyrian war machine was rolling, it did not stop until, under one of Tiglath-pileser's successors, it reached the Nile valley (see map, p. 273).

In this time of political promise and international threat, Isaiah was called to be a prophet. The call came in 742 B.C.E.—the year King Uzziah died and Tiglath-pileser finished his siege of Arpad, the capital of a province in northern Syria. Isaiah's prophetic career lasted more than forty years, and during that time the political map of the world changed as crisis followed crisis. The first political upheaval occurred in 735 B.C.E., when the armies of Syria and the Northern Kingdom of Israel invaded Judean soil to force the Southern Kingdom into a coalition organized for the purpose of stopping the Assyrian advance. It was a futile enterprise, for in 733–732 B.C.E. Tiglath-pileser conquered Syria and swept down through Gilead, Galilee, and the Plain of Sharon.

The next major event of Isaiah's career occurred when Shalmaneser V, the successor of Tiglath-pileser, visited Palestine again—this time to lay siege to Samaria, capital of the Northern Kingdom (722–721 B.C.E.). Later, during the reign of the next Assyrian king, Sargon II, the Assyrian army marched down along the coastal highway of Palestine to put down another anti-Assyrian revolt, this time localized in the Philistine city of Ashdod (712 B.C.E.). Finally, toward the close of his ministry, Isaiah experienced Judah's foolish attempt to conspire against Assyria and lived through the terrible days of Sennacherib's invasion in 701 B.C.E. (see Chronological Chart 6, p. 299).

Through all these crises, the prophet maintained that an alliance against Assyria was a "covenant with death," as the Northern Kingdom had learned by bitter experience. But Isaiah was no mere political analyst. In the historical arena, where nations vied for power, he discerned the activity of Yahweh, Sovereign of Israel and the nations.

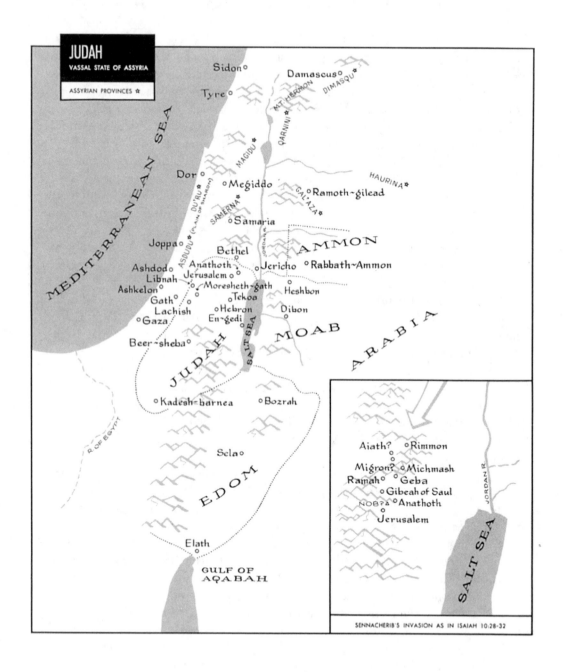

JUDAH
VASSAL STATE OF ASSYRIA

ASSYRIAN PROVINCES ✿

Sidon

Damascus
DIMASQU ✿

Tyre

MT. HERMON ✿

QARNINI ✿

MEDITERRANEAN SEA

MAGIDU

HAURINA ✿

Dor

Megiddo

Ramoth-gilead

GAL'AZA ✿

DU'RU ✿

SAMERNA ✿

Samaria

Joppa

AMMON

Bethel

Anathoth

Jericho

Rabbath-Ammon

ASDUDU (PLAIN OF SHARON)

JORDAN R.

Jerusalem

Ashdod

Libnah

Moresheth-gath

Heshbon

Ashkelon

Tekoa

Gath

Dibon

Lachish

Hebron

En-gedi

Gaza

SALT SEA

MOAB

Beer-sheba

ARABIA

JUDAH

Kadesh-barnea

Bozrah

R. OF EGYPT

Sela

EDOM

Aiath?

Rimmon

Migron?

Michmash

Ramah

Geba

Gibeah of Saul

NOB? ✿

Anathoth

Jerusalem

JORDAN R.

Elath

GULF OF
AQABAH

SALT SEA

SENNACHERIB'S INVASION AS IN ISAIAH 10:28-32

His task as prophet was to interpret what Yahweh was saying and doing in the tense political events of the time.

THE BOOK OF ISAIAH

Before turning to the message of Isaiah, we will first consider the book itself, which in its present form has sixty-six chapters. Most scholars agree that not all this material comes from the eighth-century prophet. A nucleus is undoubtedly from Isaiah, but a great deal of the material comes from others who were disciples and interpreters of the prophet. Keep in mind that our conception of "authorship" did not prevail in the biblical period. In a day when it was impossible to "publish" books for general circulation and when copyrights were unheard of, the only way to preserve prophetic material was to deposit it with a circle of followers who would faithfully remember the words of their leader and record the tradition for posterity.

Isaiah gives us a picture of how his message was handed on. Early in his ministry, when his message to Judah had fallen on deaf ears, Isaiah withdrew from public life in order to "bind up the testimony" and to "seal the teaching among [his] disciples" (Isa. 8:16–18; compare 30:8). If it was a time of "the eclipse of God," when Yahweh was "hiding his face from the house of Jacob," (Isa. 8:17), then he would wait for Yahweh to come in glory and to speak with power. Apparently he deposited his oracles for safe-keeping within the faithful prophetic community. There they were treasured, revised in the light of Isaiah's later teaching, and, after his death, handed on by his disciples. Thus the tradition was kept alive, and came to include not only Isaiah's original words, but also other accumulated materials that his followers believed were consistent with his teaching.

In the Hebrew Bible the writings of the prophets are contained in four major scrolls: "The Book of Isaiah," "The Book of Jeremiah," "The Book of Ezekiel," and "The Book of the Twelve." Together, these scrolls make up the so-called "Latter Prophets," as distinguished from the "Former Prophets" (see table, pp. 4–5). All four scrolls are approximately the same length. Apparently the size of a manageable scroll was one factor that determined the amount of material included. "The Book of the Twelve," for instance, contains twelve small prophetic books—Hosea, Joel, Amos, Obadiah, Jonah, Micah, Nahum, Habakkuk, Zephaniah, Haggai, Zechariah, and Malachi. These books are arranged in a single scroll, not because of chronology or relative importance, but because together they fill up the scroll. Like "The Book of the Twelve," the scrolls of Isaiah, Jeremiah, and Ezekiel are really prophetic collections, even though they are gathered under the name of a single prophet.

One of the primary tasks of biblical criticism is to understand these "books" in their final form. Usually the final text is the end result of a dynamic history of traditions, during which an original nucleus of material was interpreted and contemporized as it passed from generation to generation. Our understanding of a particular "book," such as the scroll of Isaiah, is enriched by discerning that the final text contains various levels of tradition. Each level—like the voices in a choir—contributes to the completed production.[3]

A BREAKDOWN OF THE MATERIAL IN ISAIAH

Consider the kinds of material included in the Isaiah scroll. To begin with, most scholars agree that chapters 40–66 do not belong to the Isaiah who prophesied in Jerusalem in the eighth century B.C.E. In particular, Isaiah 40–55 reflects a historical situation that existed about two centuries later—a time when Judah had fallen, the people were in exile, and Babylonia (the current world superpower) was about to fall to the rising Persian empire (see Chapter 14). Much of this material is usually attributed to the so-called "Second Isaiah." This scholarly epithet does not mean the writer was actually named Isaiah; only that this anonymous prophet's writings were included in the same scroll with those of the "First Isaiah" of Jerusalem.

The genuine writings of Isaiah, then, are found in the first thirty-nine chapters of the book of Isaiah. Even these chapters, however, contain a variety of material. Isaiah 36–39 has been lifted, with some modifications, from 2 Kings 18:13–20:19, and relates incidents from the latter part of Isaiah's ministry.[4] Isaiah 34 (a passage of doom) and 35 (a passage of hope) deal with the end-time and resemble the poems of Second Isaiah more than the preceding material. Scholars generally agree that these two chapters do not come from the eighth-century Isaiah. Isaiah 24–27 (often called "the little apocalypse") seems to reflect a later stage in the Isaiah tradition. By this process of elimination, three sections contain the prophecies of Isaiah of Jerusalem:

A. Isaiah 1–11, a series of prophetic oracles and prophetic narratives. A compiler added Isaiah 12, a hymn of praise (psalm), to round off this section.
B. Isaiah 13–23, a series of oracles against foreign nations. Many scholars believe that only a fraction of this material comes from Isaiah.
C. Isaiah 28–32, a series of prophetic oracles. Isaiah 33, a late prophetic liturgy, completes this section.

---

[3]The call to go beyond past biblical criticism and consider the book of Isaiah as a canonical unity was issued by Brevard Childs, *Introduction* [42], pp. 325–38. On "canonical criticism," see Definition, pp. 578–579.
    See further R. E. Clements, "The Unity of the Book of Isaiah," *Interpretation* 36 (1982), pp. 117–29, and "Beyond Tradition History: Deutero-Isaianic Development of First Isaiah's Themes," *Journal for the Study of the Old Testament* 31 (1985), pp. 95–113; also Walter Brueggemann, "Unity and Dynamic in the Isaiah Tradition," *Journal for the Study of the Old Testament* 29 (1984), pp. 89–107; Christopher R. Seitz, *Zion's Final Destiny: The Development of the Book of Isaiah* (Minneapolis: Fortress, 1991); Edgar Conrad, *Reading Isaiah* (Minneapolis: Fortress Press, 1991); Katheryn P. Darr, *Isaiah's Vision and the Family of God* (Louisville: Westminster, 1994).
[4]Christopher Seitz (cited in fn.3, above) argues that Isaiah 36–39 belongs essentially to "First" Isaiah, and serves to draw a contrast between the faithless King Ahaz (Isa. 7:10-14) and the faithful King Hezekiah (Isa. 38:5–6).

For our purposes, the section on the foreign nations (B) can be set aside temporarily, allowing us to narrow our focus to the eighteen chapters in sections A (Isa. 1–11) and B (Isa. 28–32). With this our study of the long career of Isaiah is greatly simplified, for each of these sections comes from a fairly well-defined period in the prophet's ministry. In general, Isaiah 1–11 reflects the early period of Isaiah, from the death of Uzziah to the time of the Syro-Israelite alliance—about ten years (about 742–732 B.C.E.). Isaiah 28–32 reflects the later period of the prophet's career, from the accession of King Hezekiah of Judah to the great crisis occasioned by Sennacherib's invasion of Judah (about 715–701 B.C.E.). These two major sections provide a convenient approach to the study of Isaiah. We will consider first the prophetic memoirs in Isaiah 6:1–8:18, then move on to the oracles of Isaiah's early career.

ISAIAH'S EARLY MINISTRY

Little is known about Isaiah's background. He was obviously a man of the city, judging from the number of urban metaphors he used. He might have grown up in the privileged circles of Jerusalem. Certainly Jerusalem—the place of Yahweh's Temple, the seat of David's throne, and the city hallowed with many sacred memories—had a deep place in his affection. Israel's wilderness tradition, which loomed so large in the message of prophets like Amos and Hosea, apparently had no great influence on Isaiah's prophecy. On the Exodus and the other great themes of Israel's sacred history he is virtually silent, even though he was obviously aware of these traditions. Isaiah seems to have been nurtured in circles that stressed the special relationship between Yahweh and the Davidic dynasty (2 Sam. 7). Given his absorbing interest in Davidic theology, it is not surprising that he is regarded as the chief exponent of the hope for a coming Messiah ("Anointed One") of David's lineage (see Definition, p. 211).

THE KINGSHIP OF YAHWEH

The account of Isaiah's prophetic call (Isa. 6) is one of the classic passages in prophetic literature. In a few verses of sublime poetic prose we are ushered into the worship experience that provided both the motive and content for his preaching. Written in retrospect, the account in its present form recalls a time when Isaiah was a very young man, yet it carries the overtones of his later experiences, especially his bewilderment over the people's dullness and blindness. This, in part, is why the prophetic commission is described in such bleak and unpromising terms (Isa. 6:9–13; see 29:9–12, an oracle from his later ministry). As a whole, however, the passage is a vivid portrayal of the great moment of decision in Isaiah's life, an experience that was to persist at the center of his message.

The reference to Uzziah's death signifies that this was a critical time, heavy with urgency and foreboding. Uzziah, a strong king, had remained a pillar of strength for the people even while his son Jotham was acting as regent. From the king's person blessing and strength went out through the whole nation, like life-giving sap through the branches of a tree. Hence Uzziah's death touched the life of the people, especially in view of the weakness of his son Jotham and the menacing shadow of Assyria. In such an hour, says the prophet, "I saw *the* King." His testimony implies that the people were ultimately dependent not on the Davidic king enthroned in Jerusalem, but on the cosmic King, Yahweh of hosts (heavenly armies; compare Judg. 5:20).

The setting of Isaiah's vision was the Temple of Solomon. Here the prophet envisioned Yahweh sitting on a heavenly throne, high and lifted up, while the chamber rang with the "holy, holy, holy" heard in worship services even today. The theme of Yahweh's enthronement as King over the earth and the whole universe was especially at home in the Jerusalem cult. The exclamation, "Yahweh is king!" sounded forth on the New Year's Day of the Autumn Festival, when worshipers sang hymns that portrayed Yahweh robed in majesty, exalted in "the beauty of holiness," and enthroned over the whole creation as Judge and Arbiter of the destinies of the peoples.[5]

THE PROPHET IN THE HEAVENLY COUNCIL

In Isaiah's vision the elements of priestly worship (antiphonal singing, the red-hot altar stones, the sanctuary filled with incense, the mysterious depths of the Holy of Holies) are transfigured. The Temple itself is suffused with celestial glory, for his vision presupposes the ancient view that the Jerusalem Temple was an earthly replica of the heavenly Temple. This view enabled people to believe that Yahweh was truly present in Mount Zion and at the same time the transcendent God, enthroned on high.[6] (See the reconstruction of the temple, p. 214.)

The earthly Temple suddenly enlarges and the prophet finds himself standing in a spacious heavenly Temple. He sees Yahweh seated upon a great throne, clothed in a majestic robe whose skirt fills the temple. A thrice-holy anthem resounds in the temple, and the visible radiance ("glory") of the King fills the whole earth. Yahweh is not only Israel's King, but the King upon whose sovereignty the destinies of all peoples depend. With appropriate reserve, Isaiah makes no attempt to describe Yahweh's appearance, but the imagery communicates the overpowering and awesome effect of divine power. Surrounding the throne are unearthly *seraphim*, like the strange figures (half-human and half-animal) portrayed in ancient times as attendants of the deity's sanctuary. Their three pairs of wings express symbolically the appropriate response to Yahweh's presence: With one pair they shield their faces from the King's blinding glory, with another they hide their nakedness from God's holy purity, and with the third they fly to do their appointed tasks.

---

[5]The so-called Enthronement Psalms (Ps. 47, 93, 96–99) will be discussed in Chapter 16. For an excellent discussion of Zion theology, see Bennie Ollenburger, "Zion, the City of the Great King" [400].
[6]See R. E. Clements, *God and Temple* [517], chap. 5.

The narrative suggests that the prophet, entering through the vestibule of Solomon's Temple, stands in Yahweh's celestial throne room, where the heavenly host surround the King.[7] Yahweh's speech employs the plural "us" (Isa. 6:8), a pronoun that includes the surrounding courtiers, the "heavenly host," to whom and for whom Yahweh speaks. Isaiah is drawn into Yahweh's Heavenly Council, where divine decrees are announced and where messengers are sent forth to execute them. In a visionary moment he beholds what is veiled to the sight of mortals (Exod. 33:20), for he exclaims that with his own eyes he has seen the celestial King.

CALLED TO BE THE KING'S MESSENGER

Isaiah's first response is to cry out that he is an "unclean" person and a member of an "unclean" people (Isa. 6:5). His response is evoked by an overwhelming sense of Yahweh's holiness, a fundamental aspect of Israel's experience of God's presence in the world (Exod. 19).

Yahweh's holiness means, first of all, that Yahweh is "God and not a human being" (Hos. 11:9)—One who completely transcends the human world and is therefore beyond all human analogies and categories. Although active within the human world, Yahweh cannot be domesticated within it or manipulated according to human purposes (recall the story of the Golden Calf, Exod. 32). Yahweh is God absolutely, before whom all beings stand under judgment and upon whom everything depends. Moreover, holiness is not limited to the sublimity of God as contrasted with human creatureliness; it also means the awful contrast between God's purity and human sinfulness. As "the Holy One of Israel"—a favorite expression of the prophet—Yahweh is exalted in righteousness (Isa. 5:16). In Yahweh's presence, nothing unclean, unrighteous, or idolatrous can survive. So when the threshold of the Temple shakes at the sound of the seraphim's anthem, Isaiah confesses that he belongs to a community in which there is no health (see Isa. 1:4–9). He links himself with his people in a woeful cry of dereliction: "Woe is me! For I am lost!"

One of the heavenly "priests" (a seraph) takes from the altar a glowing stone and purges Isaiah's unclean lips:

> Now that this has touched your lips,
> > your guilt has departed
> > and your sin is blotted out.
>
> —ISAIAH 6:7 (NRSV)

With this a new note is introduced into prophecy: The prophet himself needs purification before he can be God's messenger. Amos had prayed that Yahweh would forgive

---

[7]The Hebrew Bible contains many descriptions of the Heavenly Council, presided over by Yahweh. See 1 Kings 22:19, the prologue to the book of Job, and also various Psalms where the angelic hosts are summoned to praise Yahweh as "a great king above all gods" (Ps. 82:5–7; 95:3; 103:19–22; 148:2).

the people (Amos 7:1–6), but Isaiah begins his prophetic career as a person who has been forgiven. No sooner is he "consecrated"—that is, made holy or cleansed for God's service—than Yahweh, speaking in a manner that includes the whole Heavenly Council, says: "Whom shall I send, and who will go for us?" Isaiah volunteers, only to receive a commission so unbearable that he cries out, asking how long it must go on. The answer is that he is to proclaim Yahweh's word to a people whose heart[8] is fat (insensitive), whose ears are heavy (dull), and whose eyes are blind (Isa. 6:9–10).

This is a puzzling command. Isaiah's memory of his call seems to be colored by his later experiences of failure. But more is expressed in this language than later discouragement. Isaiah, like other prophets, believed that all events came from God's hand. Although we might explain the political developments of Isaiah's time in terms of human cause and effect, the prophet insisted that these experiences happened within the divine purpose. God was not taken by surprise, as it were. As excessive light can blind the eyes, or excessive sound can be deafening, so the words and signs of the prophet would increase the people's blindness to Yahweh's acts and their deafness to Yahweh's words— even though, strictly speaking, that was not the intention of the prophet's activity. If our interpretation is correct, however, the darkness of the ensuing passage of doom (Isa. 6:11–13) is illumined by a ray of light: After the fire of divine judgment has swept through the land, a "stump" will remain. And just as a new branch sprouts from a stump that stands in a burned forest, so new life will begin in a remnant of the people.

THE DAY OF YAHWEH

Before turning to the prophetic memoirs in Isaiah 7-8, it is appropriate to look back over the preceding chapters (Isa. 1-6), which elaborate the themes of Isaiah's vision.[9] In various situations the prophet reaffirmed that Yahweh is enthroned far above the tumult of history and the feverish strivings of the nations. As with Amos, the Day of Yahweh will not be light, but darkness: a day of judgment against all symbols of human pride and self-sufficiency—silver and gold, horses and chariots, fortified cities, and stately ships (Isa. 2:6–21). These cultural artifacts are not inherently bad. But when the people place their trust in them—when they are "lifted up" like the proud cedars of Lebanon—then they become objects of idolatry. The time will come, says the prophet, when people will cast their idols to the moles and the bats. The oracles of doom are punctuated with this refrain:

---

[8]"Heart" refers to the inward center of the person, not to mere feelings or emotions. In Hebrew a person thinks in the heart, and loves with the heart.

[9]Some scholars maintain that Isaiah 1 is a later editorial introduction, designed to introduce the themes announced in the entire Isaiah tradition (Isa. 1–66). See Brevard Childs, *Introduction* [42], p. 331 (referring to the view of G. Fohrer), and Katheryn P. Darr, *Isaiah's Vision and the Family of God* (cited in fn. 3, p. 290.)

Human haughtiness will be humbled,
    human pride will be abased,
And Yahweh alone will be exalted in that day.

            —ISAIAH 2:17

Yahweh's judgment is the theme of Isaiah's famous "Song of the Vineyard" (Isa. 5:1–7). The prophet begins by singing a vineyard song, like the popular ballads sung at the autumn vintage festivals. Perhaps Isaiah posed as a singer in order to catch the attention of the crowds on their way to the Temple to celebrate the harvest. He sings a song of disappointment. He did everything possible to insure a good harvest, only to find that his vineyard yielded wild grapes. What had gone wrong, what more could he have done? Then he announces that he will tear down the vines and let the vineyard become a briar patch. Suddenly, the unexpected point of the song is plunged into the people's heart: Yahweh is the speaker and the song is about Yahweh's chosen people, "the vineyard of Yahweh of hosts." With plays on words, the prophet announces Yahweh's indignant disappointment:

He looked for justice [*mishpaṭ*]
    but found bloodshed [*mispaḥ*];
for righteousness [*zedaqah*],
but heard cries of distress [*ze'aqah*].

           —ISAIAH 5:7 (REB)

No English translation can reproduce the Hebrew assonance with the same force (word-pairs like "justice"/"distress" and "right"/"riot" give a rough idea). The oracles that follow (Isa. 5:8–24) elaborate further the woes of a people guilty of the most flagrant injustice and exploitation.

Isaiah's earliest message, then, was one of doom, in keeping with the commission given to him in Isaiah 6. Yahweh announces a covenant lawsuit[10] against the people Israel, summoning them to stand trial before their Judge (Isa. 1:18–20; 3:13–15). Arraigned before Yahweh's holy presence, the prophet states on their behalf that they were "unclean"—indeed, that there was no health in them (Isa. 1:4–6). But Yahweh's purpose was not just destructive: It was to restore Israel to health, to make Israel a holy people fit to serve the King. Just as Isaiah was cleansed by forgiveness, so, in his interpretation, Yahweh was seeking to purify the people as by fire. Through the terrible sufferings of the time, Yahweh was purging the dross and alloy so that Jerusalem might become the New Jerusalem, city of righteousness (Isa. 1:24–26).

---

[10]See pp. 306–307 for the structure of the covenant lawsuit (Hebrew: *rîb*).

THE SYRO-ISRAELITE ALLIANCE

Now we return to the prophetic memoirs found in Isaiah 7–8.[11] A few years after Isaiah's call, his wife, the "prophetess" referred to in Isaiah 8:3, gave birth to a boy named Shear-yashub (Isa. 7:3). Like Hosea, Isaiah gave a symbolic name to his child, whom he considered to be a living sign from Yahweh and a visible confirmation of his message. The literal meaning of the name is "A remnant shall return" (that is, *turn to* God, *repent*, as in Isa. 6:10). Though in one sense negative ("*Only* a remnant shall return," see Isa. 10:22–23), in another sense the phrase concealed a promise ("A remnant *shall* return").

The sign-child figures prominently in a scene from the prophetic memoir in Isaiah 7, which deals with the Syro-Israelite crisis of 733–732 B.C.E. (touched on in connection with Hosea, pp. 283–284). Uzziah's regent, who had become king in his own right after his father's death, was succeeded on the throne of Judah by Ahaz (about 735–715 B.C.E.). The youthful king was no match for the political troubles he inherited. A plot was afoot among the small western states to stop the Assyrian advance. By pooling their efforts, these states apparently hoped to duplicate the feat of the western alliance more than a century earlier, when the Assyrian armies were temporarily turned back at Qarqar (see pp. 240–241). This international conspiracy made Israel (the Northern Kingdom) and Syria—one-time enemies—political bedfellows for a very short time. In 738 B.C.E. Menahem, king of Israel, joined with Rezin of Damascus to pay tribute to the Assyrian victor (2 Kings 15:19–20). This capitulation to Assyria enabled Menahem and his son Pekahiah to stay in power but was highly unpopular, especially since the tribute was raised by heavy taxes on the rich. The time was ripe for revolution. An army captain, Pekah, the son of Remaliah, murdered Pekahiah in 737 B.C.E. Shortly thereafter, while Tiglath-pileser was occupied in the north, Pekah conspired with Rezin of Damascus to form an anti-Assyrian coalition. The two kingdoms joined to attack Judah in an attempt to replace Ahaz with a non-Davidic puppet king (Isa. 7:6).

Ahaz was in a tight spot, for he had come to the throne during one of the gravest crises of Judean history. From a purely political standpoint he deserves our sympathy, even though as a leader he was weak and vacillating. The presence of the invading armies on his soil filled him with panic: "The heart of Ahaz and the heart of his people shook as the trees of the forest shake before the wind" (Isa. 7:2). Terror-stricken, he burned his son as an offering in the Valley of Hinnom just outside the city (2 Kings 16:3), hoping by this extreme rite to assuage the divine wrath that had come upon the

---

[11]These memoirs are found in the so-called "Book of Testimony" (Isa. 6:1–9:7), which Isaiah and his disciples might have composed after the described events (see Isa. 8:16). It includes the account of Isaiah's call (Isaiah. 6), his counsel to Ahaz (Isa. 7), the consequences of his spurned counsel (Isaiah. 8), and an oracle of promise to Judah (Isa. 9:1–7). When this "Book of Testimony" was inserted into the heart of chapters 2–11, the continuity of the material was disturbed. Thus the refrain in Isa. 5:25 continues in 9:12, 17, 21, and 10:4; and the sevenfold "woes" begin in Isa. 5:8 and are resumed in 10:1–19. See B. W. Anderson, "God With Us—in Judgment and in Mercy," in *Canon, Theology, and Old Testament Interpretation: Essays in Honor of Brevard S. Childs*, Gene M. Tucker et al., eds. (Philadelphia: Fortress, 1988), pp. 230–245.

city (compare the action of the Moabite king, 2 Kgs. 3:26–27). As a responsible political leader, Ahaz had to choose between accepting defeat at the hands of the invaders or appealing for outside help. Thoughts like these must have filled his mind as he went out to inspect the city's water supply, essential to Jerusalem's ability to survive a siege. At that moment Isaiah confronted Ahaz, accompanied by his little boy, Shear-yashub ("A remnant shall return").

The harassed Ahaz must have regarded Isaiah's counsel as an irrelevant interruption. But Isaiah's message was simple: "Trust in Yahweh; be quiet and keep calm." The appropriate response to the crisis, he said, was relaxed confidence, not feverish anxiety over the defenses of Jerusalem. Isaiah evidently was thinking of the weakness of the Syro-Israelite alliance, whose kings were "two smoldering stumps of firebrands," almost burned out. He probably realized that Judean involvement in the international rivalries of the time would be suicidal. But he viewed the crisis in a wider and deeper perspective than that of mere diplomacy and fortifications. Beyond the political schemes of nations was the sovereign activity of God, whose purpose shapes the course of events. The head of Ephraim is Pekah, and the head of Damascus is Rezin, *but these are men, not God.* Their plan to place a puppet king ("the son of Tabeel," probably an Aramean) on Judah's throne would fail, for Yahweh is bound in covenant loyalty (Hebrew: *ḥésed*) to David and David's descendants. Isaiah affirms that the greatest resource in time of trouble is faith—absolute trust in and dependence upon God (see Ps. 46:8–10). He underscores his message of faith with a play on words: "If your faith is not sure [Hebrew: *ta'aminu*], your throne will not be secure [Hebrew: *te'amenu*]" (Isa. 7:9b).[12] Abandon human "alliance," exclaims Isaiah, and place your "reliance" on Yahweh, whose sovereign will controls human affairs! Such faith demands a complete and firm commitment of one's whole being to God, in the confidence that Yahweh is the true King (see also Isa. 28:16; 30:15).[13]

Specifically, Isaiah's advice called for Ahaz to cancel his plan to ask for Assyrian intervention on behalf of besieged Judah. The prophet was convinced that Yahweh would overthrow the Syro-Israelite alliance by bringing Assyria against these foolish nations. The word of faith, then, was politically relevant in that situation. But Ahaz was not convinced. So later, when the king was mapping out a political strategy with his advisers, Isaiah came to him again with the offer of a "sign."

THE SIGN OF IMMANUEL

As elsewhere in the Bible, the "sign" in Isaiah 7 does not stand by itself (see Definition, p. 69). Its purpose is to make visible, to confirm dramatically, the truth and power of

---

[12]Both words are derived from the Hebrew verb *'amen* ("to be firm, to be sure"), from which comes the meaning "to trust, to believe."

[13]Martin Buber's term for Isaiah's attitude is "theopolitics"—that is, the attempt in a specific situation to bring Israel so completely under divine sovereignty that it accepts its historical task "to become the beginning of the kingdom of God"; *The Prophetic Faith* [313], p. 135.

Yahweh's word spoken by a prophet. The sign does not have to be a "miracle," in our sense of the word, for its significance is not so much its unusual character as its power to confirm a prophetic word spoken in threat or promise. In other instances, Isaiah's symbolic act of going about naked and barefoot (Isa. 20), or his children who were present with him (8:18), are called "signs." The ability to see signs points to a characteristic of Israel's faith: the people's vivid sense of divine activity in the realm of human affairs. God is not aloof from the scene of history, but *with the people*. Thus, not only can God's word be *heard* through the prophetic message, but also God's action can be *seen* in signs that the prophet points to or performs.

Remember that Isaiah was commissioned to speak to a people who could neither hear Yahweh's word nor see the signs of Yahweh's activity (Isa. 6:9). Ahaz had already failed to hear. So Isaiah told the king that Yahweh would confirm the prophetic word by any sign he might choose. Evidently Ahaz had already decided on another course of action, for he declined with a pretense of piety: He would "not put Yahweh to the test" (Isa. 7:11). Exasperated by the king's sacrifice of faith on the altar of political expedience, Isaiah tersely announced that Yahweh would nevertheless give "the house [dynasty] of David" a sign—one that would confirm the word of doom upon the Syro-Israelite alliance and at the same time confirm Yahweh's promises of grace to David.

The sign promised was the birth of a child whose name would be "God [is] with us" (Hebrew: *Immanuel*). The language presupposes that the mother is already, or soon will be, pregnant. Thus the child will be born in the near future:

> Look, the young woman is with child and about to give birth to a son.
> Let her name him Immanuel.
>
> —Isaiah 7:14 (JPSV)

Even before the child reaches the age of choosing between good and evil, the Syro-Israelite alliance will have broken up and the king of Assyria will have wrought havoc upon Judah. At that time Judah will be reduced to a primitive pastoral state in which the people live on curds and honey. Yahweh will "shave" Judah with an Assyrian razor. In other words, Isaiah promised Ahaz that Yahweh would bring immediate relief from the Syro-Israelite threat, but announced that the deliverance would be followed by even greater disaster for Judah (Isa. 7:15–24).

A great deal of interest has centered on the Immanuel prophecy of Isaiah 7:14. In the New Testament period some believed that the prophecy was fulfilled in Jesus, who was given the name "God is with us." Moreover, in certain circles the passage was appealed to in support of the Virgin Birth (Matt. 1:23). Our purpose here is not to consider the validity of such belief, but to understand the meaning of Isaiah's words in the concrete political situation we have been discussing.

First of all, the sign is the child himself—not the manner of his birth. To be sure, the prophet had explicitly said that Ahaz could ask for anything—"let it be deep as

Chronological Chart 6

B.C.E.	Egypt	Palestine — DIVIDED KINGDOM		Syria	Mesopotamia
		Judah	Israel		Assyria
750	Decline	Jotham (regent), c. 750–742	Shallum (1mo.), c. 745		Tiglath-pileser III, c. 745–727
		Jotham (king), c. 742–735 (*Isaiah*, c. 742–700)	Menahem, c. 745–737	Rezin, c. 740–732	EXPANSION OF ASSYRIAN EMPIRE
		Jehoahaz (Ahaz), c. 735–715 Invasion by Syro-Israelite Alliance, 735	Pekahiah, c. 737–736 Pekah, c. 736–732	SYRO-ISRAELITE ALLIANCE	
			Hoshea, c. 732–724	FALL OF SYRIA 732	Siege of Damascus, 732 Shalmaneser V, 726–722
		(*Micah*: before 722 to c. 701)	FALL OF SAMARIA 722–721		Siege of Samaria, 722/721
	XXV Dynasty (Ethiopian) c. 716–663	JUDAH Hezekiah, c. 715–687/6			Sargon II, 721–705 Siege of Ashdod, 712 Sennacherib, 704–681 Invasion of Palestine, 701
700					

Sheol or high as heaven" (Isa. 7:11)—on the assumption that all things are possible with God. Ahaz refused to ask, so Isaiah announced the *timely* birth of a child to a "young woman" of marriageable age (see NRSV).[14] The prophet, then, pointed to the advent of a child in the immediate future who would grow up among his people as a pledge that "God is with us."

THE DAVIDIC HEIR APPARENT

Isaiah apparently indicated, moreover, that the child would come from a particular family. In the Hebrew text he uses the definite article, saying, "*The* maiden is pregnant," as though he were referring to a particular woman already known to Ahaz. It has even been suggested that the woman was the queen and that the child was Hezekiah, Ahaz's son and successor. Whether or not this is true, it seems that Isaiah was thinking of a son of the house of David: The well-known poem in Isaiah 9:2–7 clearly says that the child will sit upon the throne of David.

How, then, does the imminent birth of the Davidic child relate to the Syro-Israelite alliance? In contrast to Ahaz, the king who shows no faith, Isaiah pictures the advent of a child-king who in due time will *faithfully* exercise the task of government. Initially, the Immanuel child will live in a time of great woe, for before he is very old, the Assyrian invasion will sweep through the land, converting it into a wilderness (Isa. 7:16–17).[15] But to those who have eyes to see, his presence will be a sign that God is leading the people through the fire of divine judgment to the dawn of a new day. The child will share his people's sufferings, live with them in the wilderness of destruction. As in Hosea's prophecy, however, "wilderness" will have a double meaning: It will be both the time of judgment and the opportunity for a new beginning. The fact that the child will eat milk and honey—the food of Paradise that tradition associated with the Promised Land ("the land flowing with milk and honey")—suggests that he will be a sign of the promised future lying on the other side of the dark days ahead. Yahweh's purpose is not to destroy, but to refine and cleanse a remnant of the people. Once the Assyrian yoke is removed, the child will ascend the throne as the agent of God's rule over the people. Then the meaning of the name, Immanuel, will be clearly understood.

Isaiah was not looking into the distant future. Still, it is difficult to resist the conclusion that he meant the child as a "Messianic" figure, although in Isaiah's time the

---

[14]Apparently this is the meaning of the Hebrew word *'almah*, which is used in the Hebrew Bible without prejudice as to a maiden's virginity (for example, Gen. 24:43; Exod. 2:8; Prov. 30:19). The usual Hebrew word for "virgin" is *bethulah*, for which the Greek translation of the Hebrew Bible (Septuagint) renders *parthenos* ("virgin") as its usual translation. But the Septuagint also uses *parthenos* for *'almah* here and in Gen. 24:43; compare Gen. 34:3. This simply shows that the Septuagint used the term *parthenos* freely, and did not necessarily imply literal virginity in Isa. 7:14. Other Greek versions render *neanis* ("maiden") here, which is more accurate.

[15]In Isa. 8:8 this devastated land is referred to as Immanuel's land. Here again the reference is to the child-king. See also the saying "God is with us" in 8:10.

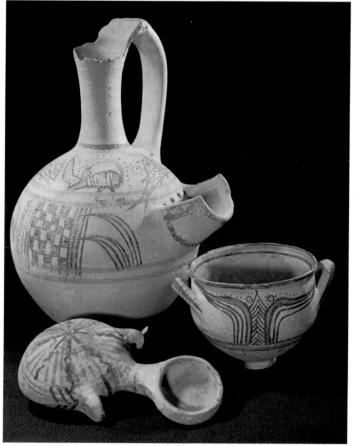

Insert 9-1 These groupings of Philistine pottery vessels reflect characteristic shapes and motifs. The large, two-handled bowl *(top, left)* is called a krater. The neck of the jug to its right is adorned with a lotus blossom, a sign of Egyptian influence. The upper band of the strainer-spout jug *(bottom, back)* is embellished with bird's head and fish designs. The "pilgrim flask" *(bottom, left)* dates from approximately 1100 B.C.E. The design on the small bowl to the right reflects Mycenaean influence.

Insert 10-1 Solomon's Gate at Gezer. Archaeologists debate whether this six-chambered gate to the city of Gezer was constructed during Solomon's reign. On either side of the entryway *(top of photograph)* are the ruins of a defensive tower.

Hebrew word *mashiah* ("messiah") referred to the reigning king (see Definition, p. 211). If so, the Messianic poem in Isaiah 9:2–7 fits in with the theme of his prophecy (see also Isa. 11:1–9). Like his initial words to Ahaz, this passage is introduced with a picture of doom and darkness, a reminiscence of the terrible destruction wrought by Tiglath-pileser in 733–732 B.C.E. in the territory of Zebulun and Naphtali (Galilee); (see Isa. 9:1). But the darkness is illumined by a great light:

> For a child has been born for us,
>   a son is given to us;
> authority rests upon his shoulders;
>   and he is named
> Wonderful Counselor, Mighty God,
>   Everlasting Father, Prince of Peace.
>   —ISAIAH 9:6 (NRSV)

THE WATERS OF SHILOAH THAT FLOW SOFTLY

At the outset of Isaiah 8, the prophet is still warning about the swift doom that will overtake the Syro-Israelite coalition. Some time after his encounter with Ahaz, Isaiah's wife gave birth to a second son, to whom was given the frightening name Maher-shalal-hash-baz ("The spoil speeds, the prey hastens"). Isaiah declared that before this sign-child spoke his first words, the Assyrian king would plunder Samaria and Damascus. This ominous message was written conspicuously on a tablet and properly "notarized," in order to remind people, when the anti-Assyrian coalition was finally overthrown, that God had given true words and signs to the prophet (Isa. 8:1–4).

But words and signs were of no avail, for Ahaz lacked the kind of faith the prophet called for. The king had to be "practical" in facing political realities, or so he would have said in self-defense. Taking advantage of Judah's plight, the king of Edom had already reclaimed the seaport of Elath (see 2 Kings 16:6). Ahaz had two alternatives, both undesirable: Either he could surrender to the forces of Syria and Israel, in which case he might lose his throne and would surely risk being on the wrong side in a showdown with Assyria; or he could throw in his lot with Assyria, in which case Judah would become a vassal state of the Assyrian empire. He chose the second. According to the record in 2 Kings 16, Ahaz appealed for help to the Assyrian king, emptying the treasuries of the Temple and his palace to court favor.

Tiglath-pileser was more than glad to come to the rescue. Damascus was overthrown, Rezin was killed, and Syria was subdivided into provinces of the Assyrian empire. A good part of the Northern Kingdom of Israel was annexed (2 Kings 15:29; compare Isa. 9:1), leaving only a strip of land from the plain of Jezreel to the border of the Southern Kingdom. Ahaz went to Damascus to pay homage to Tiglath-pileser and to congratulate him on his victories. While there, he obtained the blueprint for an Assyrian altar, which

King Hezekiah of Judah ordered the construction of a tunnel to divert fresh water to new reservoirs constructed within the fortifications of the city of Jerusalem.

he promptly ordered constructed in the Temple at Jerusalem (2 Kings 16:10–18). In a day when religion and politics were inseparable, there was no clearer way to demonstrate that the Southern Kingdom of Judah had become an Assyrian vassal.

To Isaiah, Ahaz's action was final proof of the lack of faith for which Judah would pay the consequences. In a vivid figure of speech, Isaiah denounced the people for rejecting "the waters of Shiloah that flow softly" (Isa. 8:5) to demonstrate their confidence in the mighty Euphrates of Assyria. Shiloah was a little aqueduct that carried water from the Spring of Gihon to a pool inside the city wall of Jerusalem—probably the very waterworks that Ahaz was examining when Isaiah went out to meet him (Isa. 7:3). This gentle stream was to Isaiah a symbol of quiet and confident faith in Yahweh, whose kingdom is more powerful and everlasting than the mightiest empires. The prophet had warned, "If you will not have faith, you shall surely not be established" (Isa. 7:9). The Assyrians, like a flood overflowing from the Euphrates, would sweep through the land, devastating not only Syria and Israel, but Judah as well.

BINDING UP THE TESTIMONY

Isaiah, then, met the stubborn resistance of a faithless generation. Words that should have awakened faith fell on deaf ears, and signs that should have made the truth visible were held up before blind eyes. But prophetic words and signs had not been given in vain. In the prophet's conviction, the future was controlled by "Yahweh of hosts," the heavenly Warrior-King. Just after Ahaz's overture to Assyria, Isaiah apparently separated himself from his unheeding fellow citizens and withdrew into the prophetic circle. According to Isaiah, "Yahweh spoke to me with his strong hand upon me and warned me not to walk in the way of this people" (Isa. 8:11). He told the prophetic community to "conspire" with God, not to join the political conspiracy, and to "fear" Yahweh of hosts, not to have the "fear" (panic) that drives a nation to political suicide.[16] The faithful community, the prophetic remnant, was to be separated from the rest of the nation by a different allegiance. They were to trust in God and wait expectantly for the fulfillment of the divine purpose in history.

Within this prophetic "community," the nucleus of the New Israel, Isaiah's *torah* (teaching) was sealed, entrusted to his disciples until a future day when Yahweh would make its truth plain. The prophet himself, as well as his children, were signs from Yahweh, and some day these signs would be understood. In a time of rebellion, a few people of faith turned to the future in patient hope: "I will wait for Yahweh, who is hiding his face from the house of Jacob, and I will hope in him" (Isa. 8:17). The command to "bind up the testimony" among Isaiah's disciples probably resulted in the composition of "The Book of Testimony" (Isa. 6:1–9:7), which included not only the prophet's early memoirs, but also the magnificent promise of the coming of a Davidic King and the dawning of a new day.

Isaiah evidently emerged from the prophetic circle, however, to address himself to the second great political crisis of his career: the imminent fall of the Northern Kingdom. As events rushed toward the final Assyrian blow against Samaria in 722–721 B.C.E., he spoke out against "the fading flower of Ephraim's glorious beauty" in oracles now scattered in various parts of the book (Isa. 5:26–30; 9:8–10:4; 17:1–11; 28:1–4). Of these the most forceful is the series in Isaiah 9:8–10:4 (and including Isa. 5:26–30). Blow after blow of divine judgment shatters the people, yet they do not learn the severe discipline of history. With ominous repetition, the ending refrain of each strophe discloses that Yahweh's hand is poised, ready to strike:

> For all this Yahweh's anger is not turned away,
> and his hand is stretched out still.
> —ISAIAH 9:12, 17, 21; 10:4

---

[16]The verbs of verses 12 and 13 are in the plural, indicating that they refer to the prophetic circle.

We know very little about Isaiah's activity during the remainder of the reign of Ahaz. This is an appropriate point, therefore, to turn to his great contemporary Micah, whose earliest oracles were delivered before the fall of Samaria.

MICAH, A RURAL PROPHET

We know little about Micah other than that his hometown was Moresheth-gath, a small village in the hills about twenty-five miles southwest of Jerusalem. Unlike the city-bred Isaiah, Micah was a country prophet who spoke for poor farmers suffering at the hands of powerful landlords. In many respects he reminds us of Amos, also a prophet of social justice. But Micah's message of divine judgment, evoked by the inexorable march of Assyria, is especially akin to the message of judgment and renewal proclaimed by Isaiah. Indeed, it has been suggested that Micah was one of Isaiah's disciples. Though doubtful, it is appropriate to link the two prophets in considering the fateful events that engulfed Judah toward the end of the eighth century B.C.E. Micah's career seems to have spanned events from the fall of Samaria in 721 B.C.E. to the arrival of the Assyrians at the gates of Jerusalem in 701 B.C.E.

In its present form the book of Micah, like Isaiah, comes from a prophetic school that preserved and expanded the prophet's poems. The book displays a two-beat rhythm of doom and hope, of judgment and renewal, characteristic of the message of the prophets. This rhythm is evident in the architecture of the book:[17]

    Part I: Oracles of judgment (Mic. 1–3)
              Oracles of salvation (Mic. 4–5)
    Part II: Oracles of judgment (Mic. 6:1–7:7)
              Oracles of salvation (Mic. 7:8–20)

The reference to exile in Babylonia (Mic. 4:8) is one of various indications that the original oracles of Micah, concentrated especially in Micah 1–3, were expanded and updated to speak to the situation after the fall of Jerusalem.

Micah's first oracle of judgment (Mic. 1:2–7) uses the imagery of a court trial (Hebrew: *rib*). The earth and all its inhabitants are summoned to hear the indictment and the verdict against both houses of Israel—the North (Samaria) and the South (Judah). Mountains melt and valleys divide as Yahweh, coming in awesome theophany from the cosmic temple, treads in gigantic steps upon the high places of the earth. The prophet insists that the capital cities are the source of the cancerous corruption that arouses Yahweh to come as Judge:

---

[17]On the structure of the book of Micah and the editing of Micah's oracles, see James L. Mays, *Micah* [406], pp. 2–12, 21–33.

All this is because of the transgression of Jacob
because of the sins of the house of Israel.
What is the transgression of Jacob?
Is it not Samaria?
And what is the sin of Judah?
Is it not Jerusalem?

—MICAH 1:5

The Assyrian devastation of Samaria in 721 B.C.E. is perceived as an expression of God's judgment in human affairs.

The ensuing poem, cast in the form of a dirge (Mic. 1:8–16), states further that Judah will suffer Samaria's fate. In a vivid passage containing Hebrew wordplays on the names of various cities and towns (Mic. 1:10–16), Micah portrays an Assyrian avalanche sweeping through Judah, causing suffering that "has reached to the gate of my people, to Jerusalem" (Mic. 1:9). The poem reflects the crisis of 701 B.C.E., when Sennacherib invaded Judah, engulfing both fortified cities like Lachish and villages like Micah's own home town of Moresheth near Gath (see p. 310.)

In contrast to the popular prophets who preached a message that buttered their bread (Mic. 3:5-8), this austere prophet was filled with the divine *charisma* (Mic. 3:9). Unlike Isaiah, Micah did not believe that Jerusalem would be spared, for it was "built with blood" (Mic. 3:10). The city was the scene of outrageous social injustice, a place where people lay awake at night devising wickedness (Mic. 2). Civil and religious leaders were to blame for the sad state of affairs, for they should have known what Yahweh demands (Mic. 3). What good is it, the prophet asks, to "lean upon Yahweh" and say that no evil will befall us because Yahweh is "in our midst" (referring to the "Immanuel" theme)? Yahweh issues an ominous indictment against Jerusalem:

Therefore, on account of your deeds,
Zion will be ploughed as a field.
Jerusalem will be a rubble heap,
and the Temple mount a wooded height.

—MICAH 3:12[18]

Micah's bold prophesy against Zion cannot be explained wholly by saying that, unlike the city-bred Isaiah, he came from the country and therefore could criticize the Davidic city with cool detachment. There must also have been profound *theological* differences between the two prophets, despite the fact that both books contain the famous

---

[18]This announcement was quoted a century later, when Jeremiah's life was in jeopardy because he made a similar prediction about Jerusalem and its Temple (Jer. 26:18–19). According to the Jeremiah passage, the oracle was first delivered in the time of King Hezekiah (about 715–687/6 B.C.E.), who succeeded Ahaz to the Judean throne.

prophecy concerning the elevation of Zion "in the last days."[19] In the indisputably original oracles of Micah there is no reference to Davidic covenant theology, which guaranteed the permanence of the Davidic dynasty and the security of the Davidic city. Even the "Messianic" passage in Micah 5:2–6 (compare Matt. 2:6) announces that the coming ruler will be born, not in the royal court of Jerusalem, but in Bethlehem among the humble clans of Judah, where David got his start.[20] Micah seems to have been nurtured in the Exodus tradition kept alive in the rural areas of the Southern Kingdom of Judah. Thus Micah 6:1–8, often hailed as the epitome of the message of the eighth-century prophets, turns to Israel's sacred history that centers in the Exodus.[21]

Like the book's opening oracle, Micah 6:1-8 employs the imagery of a controversy in a law court, a familiar theme of prophecy. Notice the dramatic structure of the "covenant lawsuit" (Hebrew: *rîb*):

A. SUMMONS (Mic. 6:1–2) The trial opens with a summons by the prophet who acts as Yahweh's prosecuting attorney. The mountains are witnesses: Before them Israel will present its case.

B. THE PLAINTIFF'S CHARGE (Mic. 6:3–5) Then Yahweh, through the prophetic attorney, raises a complaint. Significantly, Yahweh appeals to Israel's historical traditions, not to laws written in a statute book. The appeal is based on events that have manifested Yahweh's *ḥésed* or covenant grace toward the people, beginning with the Exodus from Egypt and culminating in the occupation of the promised land. These events are the foundation of the Covenant Community. The clear implication is that because the people Israel has forgotten Yahweh's great deeds on its behalf, it no longer knows what the Suzerain requires of the vassal. The prophet is appalled at the incongruity between Yahweh's benevolent actions and Israel's misconduct.

C. THE DEFENDANT'S PLEA (Mic. 6:6-7) At last the defendant, Israel, speaks. But before the cosmic Judge Israel has no case to plead, save to confess humbly that its actions are inconsistent with Yahweh's saving acts in history and a betrayal of the covenant. Burnt offerings, rivers of oil, even the most costly sacrifice of the firstborn—these things do not satisfy the

---

[19]This oracle is found in both Micah 4:1–4 and Isa. 2:2–4, with only slight variation. Isaiah clearly has the greater claim upon the oracle in view of his Zion-centered message. But it is possible that an independent oracle has been added to both prophetic books by compilers.

[20]The prophecies of a glorious future found in Micah 4:1–5:9 might reflect the message of Micah at points, but they were reworked by later prophetic circles, as evident from references to the Babylonian exile (for example, Mic. 4:10).

[21]Micah's prophecies are concentrated in Micah 1–3, though others of his oracles appear in 5:10–7:7. The arguments for denying Micah 6–8 to Micah are not decisive. The reference to child sacrifice (verse 7) was familiar from tradition, like that of Gen. 22, and perhaps was immediately based on the action of King Ahaz under stress (2 Kings 16:3). The evangelical appeal of these verses is similar to passages from Amos, who also spoke in accents of doom (for example, Amos 2:9–11).

covenant demands. In view of what Yahweh has done for Israel, such responses are empty mockery and wearisome offense.

D.   THE INDICTMENT (Mic. 6:8) The passage reaches a climax as the prophetic attorney proclaims that Yahweh has shown what is "good"—that is, the good relations of the covenant:

> What does the Lord require of you
> but to do justice, and to love kindness,[22]
> and to walk humbly with your God?
> —MICAH 6:8 (NRSV)

This single sentence expresses Amos' demand for justice, Hosea's appeal for the faithfulness that binds people in covenant with God and with one another, and Isaiah's plea for the quiet faith of the "humble walk" with God.

In this poetic unit, the Judge's verdict is not given. Appropriately, however, the covenant lawsuit is followed in the present arrangement by an oracle of divine judgment (Mic. 6:9–16), with the characteristic "therefore" (verse 13) announcing the consequences of human behavior. Micah pointedly likens Judah's sins to crimes committed by the dynasty of Omri, particularly the deeds of Ahab (Mic. 6:16).

ISAIAH'S LATER CAREER

Isaiah seems not to have been very active in public after the Syro-Israelite crisis. Perhaps, as has been suggested, he withdrew into the prophetic community for most of the remainder of the reign of Ahaz. The death of Ahaz, however, inaugurated a new period of Isaiah's prophetic activity. It must have seemed that the time had come to break the "seal" from his prophetic testimony, in the expectation that Hezekiah would give a more favorable hearing than had his father.

THE AGE OF HEZEKIAH

The accession of Hezekiah in 715 B.C.E. marked a turning point in Judean affairs. Ahaz had been a weak king, a servile and frightened vassal of Assyria. Hezekiah, however, was a wise and vigorous leader, whose policies instigated both a religious reformation and a stiffening of Judah's attitude toward Assyria. In 2 Kings 18, the Deuteronomistic historians give unqualified approval to Hezekiah's reign, comparing him to David and saying that "there was none like him among all the kings of Judah after him, nor among

---

[22]The word translated "kindness" is *ḥesed*, the same word we saw in our study of Hosea (see Definition, pp. 277–278). It refers to a covenant relationship that is steadfast and that finds expression in acts of mercy.

those who were before him." This tribute, of course, was based on the Deuteronomic premise that the true worship of Yahweh must be centralized in Jerusalem.

One of Hezekiah's accomplishments was his great religious reform. He suppressed local shrines ("high places"), centers of the Canaanized popular religion that had threatened Israel's faith from the very first. Not satisfied with destroying the sacred objects in these local sanctuaries (the altars, the sacred pillars, and the Asherah), Hezekiah carried his reform right into the Temple of Jerusalem. On his orders the copper serpent, Nehushtan—an object of veneration for centuries—was shattered (2 Kings 18:4). According to tradition, the serpent had been made by Moses himself (Num. 21:4–9). Hezekiah's aim was to purify Judah's worship and to concentrate it in the Jerusalem Temple. His sweeping reform prepared the way for the Deuteronomic Reform (see Chapter 11). Surprisingly, Isaiah makes no reference to Hezekiah's reform, although it might have been one factor that led the prophet to break his long silence and to reappear in public.

As in the case of other religious revivals in Israel, Hezekiah's religious reform had certain political implications. When he ascended the throne, Judah was growing restive under the Assyrian yoke. Ahaz's policy of appeasement, symbolized by the installation of an Assyrian altar in the Temple, had proved unpopular, especially among those who had to pay heavy taxes for Assyrian tribute. Hezekiah's purification of worship, including no doubt the removal of Assyrian cult objects from the Temple, was a stimulus to Judean nationalism. With his reforms the king virtually declared independence from Assyrian domination and threw his weight behind the revolutionary spirit of the day. He got away with this nationalistic policy for the time being because Sargon, the Assyrian king, was busy waging war in the mountains of northern Mesopotamia.

A symbol of Hezekiah's political energy was the construction of the Siloam tunnel at a time when political tensions were high (2 Kings 20:20; compare 2 Chron. 32:30). Ahaz had worried about Jerusalem's fresh water supply—one of the city's main defenses—during the Syro-Israelite crisis. As long as water had to be brought in through a conduit from the Spring of Gihon (Virgin's Spring) to the Pool of Siloam inside the wall, Jerusalem was vulnerable. Hezekiah overcame this problem with a remarkable engineering feat. A tunnel more than 1,700 feet long was cut through solid rock from the spring to the pool. Workers equipped with wedges, hammers, and picks started boring at both ends simultaneously, and after some winding met in the middle. At one time, visitors willing to wade knee-deep in cold spring water could walk through this tunnel and see the slanting pick marks where the workers met in the middle. The famous Siloam inscription, cut from the wall and taken to the museum at Istanbul, recounts the operation: "While there was yet three cubits to be bored through, there was heard the voice of one calling unto another."[23] Hezekiah also extended the walls and strengthened Jerusalem's fortifications (2 Chron. 32:5).

---

[23]See Pritchard, *Ancient Near Eastern Texts* [1], p. 321; also Simon B. Parker, "Siloam Inscription Memorializes Engineering Achievement," *Biblical Archaeology Review* 20 (1994), pp. 36–38.

The Siloam Tunnel was carved through 1,777 feet of solid rock for the purpose of bringing water from a spring outside Jerusalem to a pool inside the city wall. On the wall of the tunnel an inscription was found that described how the workers started at both ends and met in the middle after following a winding route.

Hezekiah was first tempted to join the rising rebellion against Assyria in 712 B.C.E. Instigated by the Egyptians, who were afraid of being overrun by Assyria, a revolution broke out in the Philistine city of Ashdod, a hotbed of unrest for several years (Isa. 14:28–32). At this time Isaiah performed a "sign" to dramatize Yahweh's judgment against the conspiracy (Isa. 20). The prophet was commanded to go barefoot through the streets of Jerusalem, clad only in the loincloth of a prisoner of war.[24] This was to signify that Assyria would lead Egypt and Ethiopia away into exile. As it turned out, Isaiah's prophecy did not apply to the Egyptians, who left the Philistines in the lurch at the last moment. Sargon's armies pointed up the folly of revolution by destroying Ashdod and two other Philistine cities, and by converting the Philistine coast into an Assyrian province. Sargon accused Judah of having a hand in the revolt, but evi-

[24]Ethiopia is mentioned because the new Egyptian dynasty was Ethiopian.

dently Hezekiah had avoided becoming too deeply involved, perhaps as a result of Isaiah's influence. In any case, Assyria did not invade Judah.[25]

LIVING IN REVOLUTIONARY TIMES

The death of Sargon in 705 B.C.E. set off a chain reaction of revolution throughout the Assyrian empire. To a political observer it must have seemed that the empire, founded by the power of the sword and upheld by the ruthless suppression of nationalism, was about to explode into fragments. This time the revolution centered in the eastern part of the empire, in the province of Babylonia. The leader was the king of Babylonia, Marduk-apal-iddina, referred to as Merodach-baladan (2 Kings 20:12 = Isa. 39:1). Something of a political genius, he might have established a Babylonian empire had the political situation been more favorable—but this dream was not realized until a century later.

Merodach-baladan, believing that the best way to win his political objectives was to stir up trouble for Sennacherib, kindled the fires of revolt throughout the Assyrian empire. He consolidated the revolutionary forces in his own area, and then sent embassies into Palestine. The story of the embassy to Hezekiah, and Isaiah's vehement protest against it, is given in 2 Kings 20:12–19 (= Isa. 39:1–8). Egypt, too, was experiencing a national revival at the time, under the leadership of an energetic Ethiopian king named Shabako, founder of the Twenty-fifth Dynasty. The oracle in Isaiah 18, apparently from this period, speaks about the coming of Shabako's ambassadors to secure Hezekiah's participation in the general revolt. Egypt wanted to recover its ancient imperial glory, and it hoped to bring about Assyria's collapse through diplomatic intrigue.

This time Hezekiah could not resist the temptation to join in. He went all out for the revolution, throwing his army against Philistia when several Philistine kings refused to join the conspiracy (2 Kings 18:8). Hezekiah even took Padi, king of the Philistine city of Ekron, back to Jerusalem as a prisoner (an act recorded in Sennacherib's annals).

Most of the prophetic oracles in Isaiah 28–33 reflect this period (the last five years of the eighth century B.C.E.). In this fateful hour of decision, Isaiah counseled the king of Judah to stay out of the revolution, just as he had counseled Ahaz. Isaiah's advice was not based merely on the shrewd political calculation that Assyria would eventually win. As a political observer, Isaiah was perhaps no wiser than others who might have come to a different conclusion. Because he was a great prophet, however, Isaiah brought a religious perspective to the international scene.

---

[25]Ashdod and Gath, two of the Philistine cities sacked by the Assyrians, were only a short distance from the prophet Micah's hometown. The distant sound of marching armies during this invasion prompted him to say that Moresheth-gath (near Gath) would fall to Assyria (Mic. 1:14–15).

IN QUIETNESS AND CONFIDENCE IS STRENGTH

Uppermost in Isaiah's mind was the conviction that Yahweh was in control and that Assyria was called to serve Yahweh's purpose. He elaborates this conviction in a magnificent oracle in Isaiah 10:5–19, which hails Assyria as "the rod of Yahweh's anger":

> Ah, Assyria, the rod of my anger—
> the club in their hands is my fury!
> Against a godless nation I send him,
> and against the people of my wrath
> I command him,
> to take spoil and seize plunder,
> and to tread them down like the
> mire of the streets.
>
> —ISAIAH 10:5–6 (NRSV)

Of course, the Assyrian dictator does not realize that he is an instrument in God's hand: He supposes he is pursuing his own political objectives. Nevertheless, behind the inexorable Assyrian advance is the overruling sovereignty of God. History is not governed by caprice or by the nation with the largest battalions. Seen in prophetic perspective, the terrible havoc wrought by the Assyrian invaders is the sign of God's judgment in human affairs, which even the people of Yahweh's choice cannot escape.

To be sure, when Yahweh's work on Mount Zion is finished, the king of Assyria will be punished for his "arrogant boasting" and his "haughty pride" (Isa. 10:12). It is folly for the axe to boast over the person who uses it, or for the saw to claim mastery over the one who wields it! In due time Yahweh "will trample the Assyrian underfoot" and the yoke of tyranny will be lifted from the people (see Isa. 14:24–27). Even the most powerful empire must learn that God is King, and that the tumultuous stream of history cannot break beyond the banks of God's purpose. Hence people of faith should willingly submit, not to the Assyrian yoke, but to the yoke of Yahweh's kingdom, accepting God's judgment as a call to purge flagrant wrongs from society, and waiting patiently for the time when Yahweh humbles the pride of the mighty.

Understanding that human power could not stay the Assyrian advance any more than it could prevent Yahweh's coming to judge and rebuke the people of Israel, Isaiah advises Hezekiah to shun the revolution against Assyria. Like Hosea, Isaiah condemns political alliances, calling them a "covenant with death" (Isa. 28:18). When the "overwhelming scourge" passes through the land, Judah will be inundated, for Yahweh will perform a "strange work," one that will utterly confound all human plans and hopes (Isa. 28:14–22). In particular Isaiah condemns the favorable reception given the Egyptian envoys (Isa. 18), just as he had denounced Hezekiah's secret negotiations with Merodach-baladan (2 Kings 20:12–19). He scorns those who go to Egypt for help, trusting in "chariots because they are many" and "horsemen because they are very strong" (Isa. 31:1–3):

> The Egyptians are human beings, and not God,
>   and their horses are flesh, and not spirit.
>   —ISAIAH 31:3

Such political efforts are clear evidence that people do not trust "the Holy One of Israel."

Isaiah 30:1-15 stresses the folly of taking refuge in "the shadow of Egypt." In a supreme summary of the meaning of faith, the prophet echoes his earlier advice to Ahaz (Isa. 7:9):

> In returning and rest you shall be saved;
>   in quietness and in trust shall be your strength.
>   —ISAIAH 30:15 (NRSV)

Judah's security lies not in politics but in returning to, and depending upon, Yahweh, in the confidence that deliverance will come in God's good time. But to the prophetic call for faith the people answer a flat "No!" (Isa. 30:16). They want to ride on horses. Indeed they will ride—but in flight from swift horsemen. And if they cannot hear the call to repentance in plain-spoken Hebrew, they will have to listen to Yahweh speaking to them in the strange babble of a barbarian tongue (Isa. 28:7–13).

From the beginning to the end of his ministry, Isaiah was baffled by the people's inability to hear what Yahweh was saying through the events of the time. Yahweh had spoken of "rest to the weary," the rest and repose of a steady and serene faith in a day of political anxiety and tumult, "yet they could not hear" (Isa. 28:12). More and more, however, Isaiah came to believe that a remnant of the faithful would hear and be saved from the impending destruction. In Jerusalem Yahweh would lay a foundation for "the faithful city" (see Isa. 1:26), a precious and well-tested cornerstone composed of a remnant whose strength is a quiet and patient trust in God:

> See, I lay stone in Zion,
>   a tested stone,
> a precious cornerstone for a sure foundation;
>   the one who trusts will never be dismayed.
> I will make justice the measuring line
>   and righteousness the plumb line.
>   —ISAIAH 28:16–17a (NIV)

This appeal for steady faith in Yahweh, the cosmic King of the world and the Holy One of Israel, was the prophet's central theme.

A reconstruction of the battle for Lachish. The fighting centers around the gate tower, which has three windows near its fortified top. Soldiers defend the battlement, while inhabitants of the city escape with their possessions through a doorway in the side of the tower. In the lower center, three naked victims have been impaled on pointed wooden stakes.

SHUT UP LIKE A BIRD IN A CAGE

Sennacherib moved quickly to crush the rebellion that threatened his empire. First he decisively defeated Merodach-baladan of Babylonia and all his allies. Then, having restored order throughout Mesopotamia, he launched a victorious campaign into the west in 703 B.C.E. He marched triumphantly through Phoenicia and into the Philistine plain, where he destroyed a large Egyptian army at the city of Ekron. Micah 1:10–16 reflects the inexorable Assyrian advance, before which all the cities in his neighborhood fell, including the fortress of Lachish. Evidently the Assyrian army moved inland through the hill country of Samaria and Judah, approaching Jerusalem from the north. The route of the Assyrian advance is reported in Isaiah 10:28–32, which gives us a vivid impression of the lightning speed with which cities were conquered. According to Sennacherib's annals, forty-six of Hezekiah's fortified cities were taken along with numer-

Sennacherib's Clay Prism announces his victory over Palestinian forces and their Egyptian allies. The hexagonal artifact tells how he overran Judah and shut up Hezekiah "like a caged bird" in his royal city, Jerusalem.

ous smaller cities, and 200,150 people were taken captive (see map, p. 288). The report in 2 Kings 18:13–16 agrees essentially with the Assyrian account.[26]

During the invasion of 701 B.C.E., Jerusalem was cut off from outside help.[27] "Like a caged bird," Sennacherib says, "I shut up [Hezekiah] in Jerusalem, his royal city." In even stronger terms, Isaiah compared the catastrophe to the destruction of Sodom and Gomorrah. Isaiah 1:4–9 apparently springs from this crisis. Why, he asks,

---

[26]See Pritchard, *Ancient Near Eastern Texts* [1], pp. 287–88.

[27]Difficulties in the biblical text have led some scholars to hypothesize that Sennacherib actually invaded Judah twice, once in 701 B.C.E. and again after 691 B.C.E., and that Jerusalem was miraculously spared on the latter occasion. John Bright, *History* [110], pp. 285–88, 298–309, favors this view, though he admits that Assyrian inscriptions do not mention the supposed second campaign. See the criticism of this view by Brevard S. Childs, *Isaiah and the Assyrian Crisis* [393], especially pp. 118–20. See also Christopher R. Seitz, *Zion's Final Destiny: The Development of the Book of Isaiah/A Reassessment of Isaiah 36–39* (Minneapolis: Fortress Press, 1991). Seitz gives a thorough analysis of Isaiah 36-39, including the Assyrian crisis, the original locus of these chapters, and their significance for the ongoing growth of the book of Isaiah.

does Judah continue to revolt? The country is stricken, like a sick person, from head to toe; aliens are devouring the land, and Zion is left isolated and alone, "like a booth in a vineyard, like a lodge in a cucumber field."

Jerusalem did not suffer the complete destruction of Sodom and Gomorrah, for Yahweh mercifully spared the city and left "a few survivors" (Isa. 1:9). The story of this unexpected, marvelous turn of events is related in 2 Kings 18 and 19 (= Isa. 36–37). During the siege of Lachish, Sennacherib sent a delegation, led by the Rabshakeh ("Chief Deputy"), to Jerusalem to demand unconditional surrender. The story is told so vividly that we can almost imagine ourselves on the walls with the city's defenders. We see the Rabshakeh standing off at some distance, with a detachment of the powerful Assyrian army behind him. Through the tensely silent air comes the shrewd propaganda speech of the Rabshakeh, threatening the stout morale of the city's defenders more than any Assyrian sword. In alarm, the Judean officials ask him to speak in Aramaic, the language of international diplomacy (see Definition, p. 453), lest his unanswerable challenge be heard by the civilian population. But this confession of weakness only incites the Rabshakeh to press his arguments with greater force. In effect, he says that the peo-

This portion of a relief from the palace of Sennacherib at Nineveh depicts Assyrian warriors with their spoils from the conquest of the Judean city of Lachish. The battle took place in 701 B.C.E.

ple are fighting for a lost cause. They have everything to gain and little to lose by discarding Hezekiah and surrendering unconditionally to the powerful army of Sennacherib.

ISAIAH'S MESSAGE DURING THE INVASION

Now comes a surprise: Isaiah counsels against capitulating to Assyria. This might seem to contradict his earlier message that Assyria was the rod of Yahweh's anger. But remember that Isaiah was not a politician who based his message on the relative strength of Assyria and the opposing powers. His perspective was *religious,* not political. Though firm in his belief that Assyria was an instrument in Yahweh's hand, Isaiah also believed that the instrument would be cast aside when Yahweh's "strange work" in Jerusalem was finished (compare Isa. 28:21). Because Assyria's power was given by God, that power could be checked or taken away when God chose to do so.

Isaiah and Micah proclaimed different messages during the crisis of Sennacherib's invasion. With unyielding conviction, Micah insisted that Zion would be "plowed like a field" (Mic. 3:12). Isaiah, on the other hand, declared that Zion could not fall. We must view Isaiah's claim within the total context of his prophetic ministry. He believed that Yahweh's saving purpose in history was linked in a special way with Jerusalem, the city Yahweh had founded and the place where the Ark rested in the Temple (Isa. 14:32). Mount Zion was "the place of the name of Yahweh of hosts" (Isa. 18:7). In the Temple Isaiah had seen the vision of Yahweh, the King. Moreover, Jerusalem was the City of David. And the Davidic dynasty, which had survived three troubled centuries of history, was a sign of the social stability that Yahweh had given.

All these convictions had their roots in a royal theology that developed in Jerusalem under the influence of Nathan's prophecy to David (2 Sam. 7). Nathan's oracle announced Yahweh's *unconditional* promise to maintain the Davidic throne, regardless of the merit or demerit of Israel's kings. In the Northern Kingdom, where the contingency of the Mosaic covenant was stressed, prophets like Amos or Hosea could announce that the people's disobedience was sufficient ground for Yahweh to bring Israel's history to an end. In the Southern Kingdom, however, Isaiah took his cue from Yahweh's promises of grace to David and, through the Davidic king, to the whole people. This did not mean soft-pedaling the call to repentance and reform: As we have seen, Isaiah was the equal of Amos in his radical criticism of society and his urgent demand for reform. Nevertheless, Isaiah believed that hope for the future rested not on the people's behavior or the greatness of their king, but solely on Yahweh's covenant commitment to David (see pp. 208–211).

Thus Isaiah insists that Yahweh's purpose is not to eradicate Jerusalem, but to build a new Jerusalem on the foundation of a righteous and faithful remnant. Remember that the doctrine of the remnant is in one sense positive: A remnant *will* return (repent) and "lean upon Yahweh" (Isa. 10:20–21). Yahweh would spare Zion "for my own sake and for the sake of my servant David" (Isa. 37:33–35), according to the tenets of the royal covenant theology.[28]

When we consider his message as a whole, Isaiah's stand during the invasion of Sennacherib turns out to be religiously consistent. We must be on guard against forcing the prophet's pronouncements into our own patterns of logic, or even assuming that all prophets said exactly the same thing about Jerusalem. *The prophets always addressed themselves to the situation at hand.* Isaiah, in 701 B.C.E., was called to speak to *that* situation, not to the earlier situation of the Syro-Israelite war or the later situation of Jeremiah's day. Experience had led him to realize that behind and within Yahweh's judgment was the divine will to deliver and renew. Hence the oracles from the stormy final years of Isaiah's ministry stressed Yahweh's saving power. On the completion of the *opus alienum*—God's "strange work" of purifying judgment on Mount Zion (Isa. 28:21)—the arrogant Assyrian empire will be punished. The Assyrians will fall "by a sword not of human making," for Yahweh "will come down to fight upon Mount Zion" and, like hovering birds, "will protect Jerusalem" (Isa. 31:4–9). A proud nation that fights against Mount Zion will be like a hungry man who dreams that he is eating, only to awake and find that his hunger is not satisfied (Isa. 28:1–8). Yahweh comes from afar to sift the nations with the sieve of destruction, and the Assyrians will be terror-stricken at Yahweh's mighty arm and furious voice (Isa. 30:27–33). This appearance will be the final reminder that Yahweh, and not Assyria or any other human power, is Ruler of History.

THE DELIVERANCE OF JERUSALEM

According to the narrative in 2 Kings 19 (paralleled in Isa. 37), when Hezekiah learned of the Rabshakeh's challenge, he was filled with despair. "This day is a day of distress, of rebuke, and disgrace; children have come to the birth, and there is no strength to bring them forth" (2 Kings 19:3).[29] Isaiah, following an urgent word from the king, delivered an oracle against the arrogance of the Assyrian king (2 Kings 19:20–28). To this prophetic word is linked another "sign," that a remnant will be saved and that after three years conditions in the land will return to normal (2 Kings 19:29–31).

The oracle against Assyria is in keeping with Isaiah's prophetic message in Isaiah 10:5–16, but the rest of the story in 2 Kings 19:32–37 teems with difficulties. True, the Assyrian armies departed without laying siege to Jerusalem—precisely as Isaiah predicted in 2 Kings 19:32–34. This "answer to prayer," however, was explained on the basis of a legend: Sennacherib's army was decimated by the Angel of Yahweh during the night, prompting Sennacherib to return to his capital, where he was assassinated by one

---

[28]The latter passage comes from the section of Isaiah (Isa. 36–39) excerpted from 2 Kings 18–19, which might give a slightly different view of Isaiah's stand in the crisis. See Brevard S. Childs, *Isaiah and the Assyrian Crisis* [393], pp. 69–103.

[29]See Katheryn P. Darr, *Israel's Vision and the Family of God* (cited in fn. 3, p. 290), pp. 205–17.

of his sons (2 Kings 19:35–37). This legend might refer to a disease or pestilence that spread through the Assyrian army, though Sennacherib's annals do not mention it. More likely, "a rumor" (as Isaiah is said to have predicted elsewhere; 2 Kings 19:7) concerning a new uprising in Babylonia led Sennacherib to withdraw hastily, in order to deal with a trouble spot potentially more dangerous than the little kingdom of Judah. Sennacherib had accomplished his objectives in Palestine: Egypt had been dealt a staggering blow, and the anti-Assyrian coalition inspired by Egypt had been broken up. Hezekiah, secure in his mountain fortress, had seen his land diminished and had yielded to Assyrian demands by paying a handsome tribute to the Assyrian king during his stay at Lachish. The payment of the tribute is described in detail in 2 Kings 18:14–16 and is corroborated by Sennacherib's own account of his western campaign. Why should Sennacherib waste time and manpower on a costly siege of Jerusalem when there were other, more pressing matters?

Whatever the explanation, Sennacherib's sudden withdrawal made a deep impression on Judean memory. In popular thought, the fact that Yahweh had spared Jerusalem in that crisis came to mean that Yahweh would spare Jerusalem under any circumstances. Zion would stand forever! One cannot imagine that Isaiah would have agreed. His message, like that of earlier prophets, included a condition:

> If you are willing and obedient,
>   you shall eat the good of the land;
> But if you refuse and rebel,
>   you shall be devoured by the sword.
>   —ISAIAH 1:19–20 (NRSV)

Isaiah 22:1–14 might come from the time when the Assyrian armies withdrew from Jerusalem. If so, it gives us a picture of the wild abandon of those who went up to the housetop "full of shoutings." In the midst of the victory celebration, Isaiah stood alone, weeping for "the destruction of the daughter of my people."

After the tumultuous events of the end of the eighth century B.C.E., Isaiah drops out of view. Whether he was active during the closing years of Hezekiah's reign (the king died in 687/6 B.C.E.) we do not know. Tradition has it that he was martyred during the reactionary reign of Hezekiah's successor, Manasseh. Perhaps Isaiah turned his attention to his disciples, giving fresh impetus to the extensive tradition associated with his name, and waited patiently within that prophetic community for God's purpose to be realized.

CHAPTER 11

THE
REDISCOVERY OF
MOSAIC TORAH

In times of insecurity, when the foundations of life are shaken, people often turn to the past to regain perspective, at the same time longing wistfully for "the good old days." This was the situation in the Southern Kingdom of Judah during the seventh century B.C.E. The literature of the period clearly shows a "nostalgic revival of interest in the past," reflecting a general tendency throughout the ancient Near East.[1] The prophet Jeremiah summed up the spirit of the times:

> Stand by the roads and consider,
> Inquire about ancient paths:
> Which is the road to happiness?
> Travel it, and find tranquility for yourselves.
> —JEREMIAH 6:16 (JPSV)

Biblical Readings: The historical background is presented in 2 Kings 21–23 (paralleled in 2 Chron. 33–35). A great deal of literature comes from this period. Read the "Mosaic" sermon in Deuteronomy 4:44 through Chapter 26 (especially Deut. 5–11); Zephaniah 1–3; Jeremiah 1:1–4:4 (his early prophecies); Nahum; and Habakkuk 1–2.

[1] W. F. Albright, *From the Stone Age* [127], pp. 240–44.

DIFFERING VIEWS OF THE COVENANT

We have already detected some of this nostalgia for the past in the prophet Isaiah, for whom the glorious reign of David was a golden age. Isaiah felt that the establishment of Jerusalem was the decisive time of the past, and that Yahweh's purpose in history was to restore Zion "as at the beginning" (Isa. 1:26). Isaiah's concern for Davidic tradition was a unique development in prophecy, for he apparently paid little attention to the great formative period of the Exodus and the Sinai covenant. In this respect he differed from prophets of the Northern Kingdom of Israel, such as Hosea and Elijah. Hosea traced Israel's beginning to the time of the Exodus and affirmed that the goal of Israel's history would be a renewal of the covenant made in the wilderness. Elijah's flight to Mount Horeb, the sacred mountain of the Mosaic covenant, was a symbol of the prophetic spirit in the Northern Kingdom.

In the Southern Kingdom of Judah a conception of the Covenant developed that was fundamentally different from the Northern Mosaic tradition. David, the architect of the United Kingdom, had tried to unify the twelve tribes under his rule by adopting the religious traditions and symbols of the old Tribal Confederacy. But in the circle of the Davidic court a new theology developed, based on the view that Yahweh made an absolute commitment to David, sealed by a solemn oath, and promised to preserve the Davidic line and spare the Davidic kingdom "for the sake of my servant David" (Isa. 37:35). The promises of grace to David in 2 Samuel 7 (see pp. 208–211) did not exempt corrupt administrations from punishment, but at least there was a guarantee of dynastic continuity. By contrast, the Mosaic covenant held out the possibility that the relationship between God and people could be dissolved (Hos. 1:9) and that the "end" could come upon the people Israel (Amos 8:2).[2]

We have seen that differences between the twin kingdoms were both political and theological. The theology of kingship, centered in Yahweh's covenant with David, provided the theological foundation for Judah's stability, with its unbroken succession of Davidic kings. In the Northern Kingdom, however, where traditions of the ancient Tribal Confederacy were kept alive, no single dynasty was able to maintain itself. There the remembrance of tribal independence contributed to revolutionary ferment, causing the downfall of kings. There also the accent fell upon the covenant made at Sinai, based on the great saving acts of Yahweh that placed a grateful people under obligation to serve their Covenant Suzerain. Recall our consideration of the "suzerainty" covenant or treaty (see pp. 90–92) with its emphasis upon the people's responsibility and the possible termination of the relationship in the event of infidelity.

---

[2]The theological differences between these two covenant traditions are set forth clearly by J. Coert Rylaarsdam, "The Two Covenants" [340]. The interaction of the two covenant traditions is considered by B. W. Anderson, "Exodus and Covenant in Second Isaiah and Prophetic Tradition," *Magnalia Dei* [179], 339–60.

In the seventh century B.C.E., however, the most significant development in the Southern Kingdom was "the rediscovery of Moses." The greatest literary monument to this revival of interest is the book of Deuteronomy. "Ask now of the days that are past," is a characteristic appeal. The context of this passage (Deut. 4:32–40)—one of the finest in Deuteronomistic literature—indicates that the decisive past history was not the golden age of David's rule, but the time of the Exodus. This was the time when Yahweh redeemed Israel "by trials, by signs, by wonders, and by war, by a mighty hand and an outstretched arm, and by great terrors, according to all that Yahweh your God did for you in Egypt before your eyes." The event of the Exodus, which fired the imagination and excited the wonder of the Deuteronomistic historians, provided the source of Israel's knowledge of God, the foundation of the covenant community, and the motivation for fulfilling the covenant obligations.

MANASSEH, THE VILLAIN OF JUDAH

The historical background of the rediscovery of the Mosaic Torah, or Teaching, is as follows.

In recounting events after the death of King Hezekiah, the Deuteronomistic historians portray Manasseh as the arch-villain of the whole gallery of Davidic kings. What Jeroboam I was to the Northern Kingdom of Israel, Manasseh was to the Southern Kingdom of Judah. He reversed the religious reforms made under Hezekiah and "seduced" the people into doing more evil than the surrounding nations (2 Kings 21:2–15). His long reign (about 687/6–642 B.C.E.) was painted as the darkest period of Judean history. Later historians, writing after the final fall of Jerusalem in the early sixth century B.C.E., held him responsible for provoking Yahweh into bringing judgment upon the nation (2 Kings 23:26–27; 24:3–4; compare Jer. 15:4).

The reign of Manasseh, however, was an important traditional link between the great eighth-century prophets and the revival of prophecy at the end of the seventh century B.C.E., and should be viewed in a larger and perhaps more sympathetic perspective. The critical report in 2 Kings 21 makes no allusion to the great political fact that overshadowed Manasseh's reign: Assyria's victorious advance toward Egypt and its almost undisputed sway over the whole Fertile Crescent. During this period Assyria reached the very pinnacle of its imperial power and glory. To be sure, even in the early part of the seventh century B.C.E., there were signs that the empire was built on shaky foundations. The murder of Sennacherib in 681 B.C.E. touched off yet another revolution in Mesopotamia; and for a while it seemed as if the staggering empire, held together by the power of the sword and a system of vassal provinces, would fall. But the next Assyrian monarch, Esarhaddon (about 680–669 B.C.E.), proved equal to the situation. After putting down all revolts, he marched into Egypt in 671 B.C.E., captured the city of

Memphis, and took captive Tirhakah, king of Egypt and Ethiopia. Esarhaddon's triumph is vividly portrayed on a stele that represents him standing before Assyrian religious symbols, while he holds two kneeling captives by ropes, one identified as Tirhakah.

DEFINITION: "DEUTERONOMISTIC HISTORY"

An earlier Definition (see p. 166) notes the distinction between two adjectives: "Deuteronomic," referring to the Torah ("Teaching") in Deuteronomy 5–28, and "Deuteronomistic," referring to the Deuteronomistic History that extends from Joshua through 2 Kings but also includes the framework to the book of Deuteronomy (Deut. 1–4 and 27–30). Indeed, Deuteronomy 1–4 serves as an introduction both to the book of Deuteronomy itself and to the whole Deuteronomistic History.

The last event reported in the Deuteronomistic History proper (Joshua through 2 Kings) is the release of the Davidic king Jehoiachin from Babylonian imprisonment in 561 B.C.E. (2 Kings 25:27–30). There is no mention of the rise of Cyrus of Persia or his conquest of Babylon (about 539 B.C.E.). This tells us that the Deuteronomistic History in its final form was finished after Jehoiachin's release, perhaps around 550 B.C.E. Some scholars maintain, however, that the Deuteronomistic History appeared in two versions: one composed during the late monarchy to express hopes for a national revival centering in King Josiah, the other written (or "overwritten") at a later date to make the narrative "relevant to exiles for whom the bright expectations of the Josianic era were hopelessly past."[3] If this hypothesis is correct, we have another instance of the updating or contemporizing of tradition that was characteristic of the Israelite community.

The Deuteronomistic History found in 1–2 Kings interweaves two theological themes. The dominant theme, set forth in Deuteronomy 1–4, is the call to be faithful to Yahweh's covenant with Israel, under the sanctions of blessing and curse. The consequences of failure in this responsibility are spelled out in passages such as the discourse on the fall of Samaria (2 Kings 17:1–23). A secondary theme is Yahweh's promises of grace to David (2 Sam. 7), which guarantee a future in spite of human failure "for the sake of David my servant and for the sake of Jerusalem which I have chosen"(1 Kings 11:13; compare 1 Kings 15:4, 2 Kings 8:19, 2 Kings 20:6, and elsewhere). With impressive counterpoint the Deuteronomistic historians interweave these two themes, one centering in Moses and the other in David, in an attempt to understand Israel's history of failure in the promised land and espouse hope in a king of the Davidic line.

The next Assyrian king, Ashurbanapal (about 668–627 B.C.E.), managed to hold his father's empire together during the first part of his reign. The city of Thebes in Upper Egypt was destroyed, and for a short while Egypt was held within the Assyrian

---

[3]See Frank M. Cross, "The Themes of the Book of Kings and the Structure of the Deuteronomistic History" [129], pp. 274–89. Note the references to "the First Deuteronomist" and "the Second Deuteronomist" in the New Oxford Annotated Bible [16].

orbit of power. Assyria had succeeded at last in building a great empire. But as time passed it became clear that this sprawling empire was slipping out of control. In 652, revolt broke out again in Babylonia, this time under the leadership of a brother of the Assyrian emperor who had been appointed ruler of that vassal kingdom. Ashurbanapal restored order, but not before the flames of revolution had spread throughout the Fertile Crescent. Other events conspired against Assyria. Egypt rose up under Psammetichus I (about 664–610 B.C.E.), founder of the Twenty-sixth Dynasty, and threw out the detested Assyrian army of occupation. To add to Assyria's troubles, hordes of invaders known as Scythians and Cimmerians poured into Mesopotamia from beyond the Caucasus mountains, and the Medes began to consolidate their position in the highlands of Iran. Assyria's days of imperial rule were numbered. The time was not far off when the Judean prophet Nahum would vent his people's spleen against Assyrian oppression, announcing that the Assyrian capital of Nineveh would be overtaken by the same destruction that Assyria had visited upon Thebes (Nah. 3:8).

Throughout the reign of Manasseh, however, the powerful Assyrian empire remained intact. Like Ahaz before him (see pp. 301–302), Manasseh believed that the best political policy was for Judah to play ball with Assyria as a faithful underling. There is some evidence that Manasseh was once taken captive to Babylon, presumably because of his part in an insurrection (2 Chron. 33:10–13).[4] If Manessah tried to revolt, however, he failed completely. Most scholars doubt the historicity of this account, which has no parallel in 2 Kings or Assyrian annals. Chances are that Manasseh bought peace and at the same time made his own throne secure by playing the part of an obsequious vassal. This expedient policy paid off, for while the Assyrian armies were marching up and down Palestine on their way to Egypt, Judah seems to have been left unmolested (see maps, pp. 273 and 288).

JUDAH'S DARK AGE

Manasseh's domestic policy reflected the religious and social consequences of his capitulation to Assyria. His acts infuriated the minority who still remembered the great wave of religious enthusiasm created by Hezekiah's reforms. 2 Kings 21 reports that "he rebuilt the high places that Hezekiah his father had destroyed"—that is, he reopened the local pagan shrines in communities outside Jerusalem. He brazenly sponsored a program to amalgamate the worship of Yahweh with Baal nature religion. Yahweh was worshiped at "altars of Baal" and an emblem of the mother-goddess, an Asherah, was made. Thus the paganization of Israel's worship, which had been a threat ever since the time of judges, was given free rein under royal sanction and patronage.

---

[4]The account in 2 Chronicles also states that while in exile the sinful king "humbled himself greatly before the God of his ancestors" and repented. The reference to his prayer (2 Chron. 33:19) prompted the composition, sometime during the last two centuries B.C.E., of "The Prayer of Manasseh." This is included in the Protestant Apocrypha; it is not contained in the Roman Catholic canon.

Moreover, the doors were thrown open to other pagan influences. The astral cult of Mesopotamia, referred to as "the worship of all the host of heaven" (the sun, moon, and stars were identified as deities) was introduced—clear evidence of the cultural influence that accompanied Assyrian political supremacy (see Insert 12–1). To make matters worse, these pagan practices crept into the Temple of Jerusalem, the central sanctuary Hezekiah had tried to purify of all alien defilement. Then, as if attempting to dredge up the foulest practices of the past, Manasseh revived the old cult of the dead (necromancy), which even Saul in his saner moments had suppressed and which Isaiah had vehemently condemned (Isa. 8:19). In this respect, too, Manasseh capitulated to Assyria's official sanction of astrology, magic, and divination. As a final concession to paganism, he resorted to the barbarous practice of human sacrifice. Following the precedent of Ahaz (2 Kings 16:3), he "burned his son as an offering," evidently in an attempt to court divine favor in an emergency (compare Jer. 7:31).

In 2 Kings, the Deuteronomistic historians compare Manasseh's reign with the time of Ahab and Jezebel, when paganism was sponsored and propagated by the crown. As in Ahab's time, pagan practices were probably welcomed by many of the people, who saw no difficulty in worshiping Yahweh while appropriating practices fashionable throughout the Assyrian empire. But there was one great difference between the time of Ahab and that of Manasseh: In Manasseh's day there was no Elijah to boldly rebuke the people for deviating from the Mosaic tradition and to summon them to a renewed loyalty to the jealous God of the Covenant. This weakness on the part of the prophets (mentioned anonymously in 2 Kings 21:10) might have resulted from Manasseh's police-state measures. We are told that he "shed very much innocent blood, till he had filled Jerusalem from one end to another" (2 Kings 21:16). Some have suggested that Manasseh tried to liquidate the prophets; indeed, according to tradition Isaiah was martyred at this time.[5] But this charge is only an inference, for which there is no real basis in the biblical record. It is hard to believe that, if an organized purge of the prophets had been carried out, all record of such events would have disappeared.

Quite possibly the historians exaggerated the account of Manasseh's reign somewhat, in order to contrast him with the reforming kings, Hezekiah and Josiah. Nevertheless, after due allowance is made for their Deuteronomistic bias, it is clear that the historians' verdict is substantially correct. Manasseh's desertion of Yahweh plunged Judah into a "dark age," for he bought peace at the terrible cost of surrendering Israel's distinctive religious heritage.

ANONYMOUS DEVOTEES OF YAHWEH

Under Manasseh's rule, however, the faithful devotees of Yahweh were far from inactive. Not many years after Manasseh's death, Jeremiah commended the Rechabites (see

---

[5]See the late apocryphal work, *The Martyrdom of Isaiah,* from about the first century C.E.

Chronological Chart 7

B.C.E.	Egypt	Palestine	Mesopotamia
		Judah	Assyria
700	XXV Dynasty, c. 716/15–663 (Ethiopian)	Manasseh, 687/6–642	Sennacherib, 704–681 Esarhaddon, 680–669 Invasion of Egypt, 671
	Tirhakah, c. 685–664	Amon, 642–640	
	Invasion by Assyria, 671	Josiah, 640–609	Ashurbanapal, 668–627
	Sack of Thebes, 663, by Ashurbanapal	First show of Judean independence, 629 (*Zephaniah,* c. 628–622) (*Jeremiah,* c. 626–587) Josiah's "Deuteronomic Reform," 621	RISE OF BABYLONIA Nabopolassar, 626–605
	XXVI Dynasty, c. 664–525 Psammetichus I c. 664–610		Fall of Ashur to Medes, 614
	Necho II, 610–593	Death of Josiah at Megiddo, 609	Fall of Nineveh to Medes and Babylonians, 612
		Jehoahaz II (Shallum), 609 (3 mos.)	Babylonian defeat of Assyrians and Egyptians at Haran, 609
		Jehoiakim (Eliakim), 609–598/7	Nebuchadrezzar, 605/4–562
600		(*Habakkuk,* c. 605)	Battle of Carchemish, 605
			FALL OF ASSYRIA

pp. 254–255) for fidelity to their religious vows in protest against the sellout of ancient Mosaic faith (Jer. 35). This group, and others like them, must have annoyed Manasseh's party no end. Moreover, Manasseh's submission to Assyria must have galled all patriotic Judeans. Undoubtedly the smoldering fires of nationalism were kept alive by prophets and priests who preserved and handed on the religious traditions of the past, especially by an order of teaching and preaching priests known as Levites, who were active in the towns and the country area.[6] The oracles of the northern prophet Hosea, preserved in Judah after the fall of Samaria, were updated to apply to the Southern Kingdom (evidenced by editorial touches such as Hos. 1:7; 4:15a). The Ephraimitic or Elohist version of the Old Epic tradition (see pp. 260–262) was inherited and at least partly preserved in Judah. Throughout the "dark age" of Manasseh, the all-Israelite Epic (JE) that included the traditions of the northern and southern kingdoms continued to thrive and expand (see Chapter 5).

---

[6]The role of the Levitical priests in the country outside Jerusalem has been stressed by Gerhard von Rad, *Studies in Deuteronomy* [cited under 418].

If we knew more about the period of Manasseh, we might find that many of the anonymous prophecies now mingled with the writings of the great prophets were composed at this time. Portions of the book of Isaiah, which apparently come from a time before Second Isaiah, were probably produced then, and might well have come from the circle of disciples among whom Isaiah deposited his original teaching. This was a reactionary period—a time when prophets went into retreat. Thus it would have been an appropriate time to cherish and reflect upon the prophetic tradition, waiting and hoping for the time when Yahweh's "face" would no longer be hidden from Israel (Isa. 8:16–17). Manasseh's time was perhaps an age of anonymous prophecy, when persons of faith trusted in Yahweh's promise to overthrow the proud oppressors and to renew and restore the people.

NEW OUTBURSTS OF PROPHECY

Manasseh's reign was not a time of complete decadence. Deep within the life of Judah a prophetic ferment was stirring as people turned to the past to rediscover the meaning of their Mosaic heritage. In anonymous circles, the way was being prepared for the na-

Ashurbanapal's horsemen battle camel-riding Arabs in this vivid action scene. Besides fighting wars on several fronts, Ashurbanapal was also a patron of culture, as shown by the excavations of this palace and royal library at Nineveh, where this artistic relief was found.

Ashurbanapal drinks a toast to a victory in war. The last great king of Assyria, reclining upon a high couch while banqueting in his royal garden, is joined in the quaffing by his queen, seated facing him on a throne. Attendants fan the couple and provide music and delicacies. From the tree just in front of the harpist (left) hangs a man's head, perhaps that of the Elamite king just conquered. This mixture of culture and brutality was characteristic of Ashurbanapal's reign.

tional and religious renaissance that took place in Judah in the last quarter of the seventh century B.C.E. This Judean revival was made possible by changes in the international situation after the death of Assyria's last great king, Ashurbanapal (about 627 B.C.E.).

Trouble was brewing for Assyria even before Ashurbanapal's death, as evidenced by the abortive revolt in Babylonia and the revival of Egyptian nationalism. With lightning speed, rumors of Assyria's weakness spread throughout the Fertile Crescent, exciting great restlessness among satellite nations. Manasseh's son, Amon, continued his father's pro-Assyrian policy, but after a brief reign of two years he was murdered during a patriotic revolt. He was succeeded by the boy-king, Josiah (about 640–600 B.C.E.), who came to the throne when he was eight years old. By the time Ashurbanapal died, Josiah was ready to take over the reins of government. And the time was ripe for a radical change in Judah's policy.

THE PROPHET ZEPHANIAH

Not long after the death of Ashurbanapal (about 627 B.C.E.), the long prophetic silence that had lasted for three-quarters of a century was broken by two prophets who raised their voices publicly against the apostasy and degeneracy of Judah. The first was Zephaniah, possibly a descendant of the reforming King Hezekiah (Zeph. 1:1). We cannot date Zephaniah's career exactly, although his attack upon corruptions in worship suggests a time before Josiah's great reform in 621 B.C.E. (see pp. 333–336). He must have been a citizen of Jerusalem, for he mentions the districts of the city by name (Zeph. 1:10–11). Indeed, he seems to have been part of the Jerusalem "establishment."[7]

Zephaniah's devastating message pierced the complacent atmosphere of Jerusalem like a trumpet blast. The central theme of his prophecy, the nearness of the Day of Yahweh, echoed a note struck earlier by Amos and Isaiah. Yahweh's Day would be "a day of wrath, a day of distress and anguish, a day of ruin and devastation, a day of darkness and gloom, a day of clouds and thick darkness, a day of trumpet blast and battle cry" (Zeph. 1:15–16). Isaiah had said that the Day of Yahweh would be ushered in by an Assyrian invasion; but by Zephaniah's time the whole political situation had changed. The proud capital of Nineveh was about to be turned into a wilderness (Zeph. 2:13–15); Assyria would soon taste the bitter suffering it had inflicted on others.

At first it might seem strange that these two prophets should change the *political* focus of their messages. But the prophets were not political forecasters, concerned only with tracing political developments. They viewed the historical scene from the perspective of faith in God, whose purpose is made known in, but is not identical with, political crises at definite moments of history. Since they were concerned with what Yahweh was saying and doing in the concrete situation at hand, the prophets did not think it inconsistent for the agent of divine judgment to vary from time to time. Notice that Zephaniah is rather vague about political details. Though he vividly describes an invasion that sweeps down out of the north, reducing the Assyrian capital of Nineveh to a dry waste (Zeph. 2:13–15) and approaching the Fish Gate of Jerusalem (1:10), he does not clearly identify the aggressor, the new "rod" of Yahweh's judgment. Some scholars think Zephaniah might have had in mind Scythian hordes who, along with other peoples, contributed to the ferment of the time.[8] In any case, behind and within the political upheaval that hastened the downfall of the Assyrian empire, Zephaniah saw Yahweh's judgment in the affairs of history.

Zephaniah spoke with a sense of urgency: "The great day of the Lord is near, near and hastening fast" (Zeph. 1:14). Events were hastening toward catastrophe; the clock was nearing midnight. Zephaniah summoned people to decision and repentance while they still had a chance. In scathing language he denounced the pagan practices that, under the influence of Manasseh, had defiled Judah and Jerusalem. He condemned Baal worship "in this place" (Jerusalem), the astral cult practiced on the roof of the Temple, and the linking together of Yahweh and Milcom (the god of Ammon; Zeph. 1:4–6). Even worse was the people's complacency, based on the preposterous notion that Yahweh had no sway over history and was impotent to do either good or evil (Zeph. 1:12). In one breath Zephaniah condemned the leadership of the nation: priests

---

[7]See Robert R. Wilson, *Prophecy and Society* [371], pp. 279–82, who maintains that Zephaniah stood within Jerusalem (Zion) traditions but was influenced by Josiah's "Deuteronomic" Reform.

[8]The theory of a Scythian invasion that swept as far as the border of Egypt is based on the report of the Greek historian Herodotus (*Persian Wars* I, 104 106). Recent historians, however, believe Herodotus' report must be taken with a grain of salt (see for example, John Bright, *History* [110], p. 315).

and prophets, politicians and judges (whom he likened to predatory "roaring lions" and "evening wolves"; Zeph. 3:3–4). Jerusalem was a "rebellious city," impervious to Yahweh's word and lacking in faith. Zephaniah's prophetic task was to interpret the world crisis as God's action in history.

The prophet held out no hope that "the shameless nation," deeply stained with paganism and firmly entrenched in rebellion, would reform. Rather, Judah along with the other nations of the world would be consumed by "the fire of Yahweh's jealous wrath." Like Isaiah, Zephaniah appealed for a remnant to repent and to seek refuge in Yahweh:

> Seek Yahweh,
> all you humble of the earth,
> who obey his commands.
> Seek uprightness,
> seek humility:
> you may perhaps find shelter
> on the Day of Yahweh's anger.
>
> —ZEPHANIAH 2:3 (NJB)

Since Yahweh's purpose was not utter destruction but cleansing and renewal, Zephaniah announced that a remnant would be saved from the catastrophe: "a people humble and lowly" who would live in sincerity and security (Zeph. 3:8–13; compare 1:7).

THE PROPHET JEREMIAH

The second prophetic voice heard early in Josiah's reign was that of Jeremiah. Postponing a full discussion of Jeremiah's long career to Chapter 12, we look briefly here at the early years of his ministry, which overlap that of his contemporary, Zephaniah. The heading of the book of Jeremiah (Jer. 1:1–3) states that he began to prophecy in the thirteenth year of Josiah's reign—that is, about 626 B.C.E.[9] Jeremiah was nurtured in the great traditions of Israel, for he is said to have come from a priestly family of Anathoth, a village about four miles northeast of Jerusalem. According to 1 Kings 2:26–27, Anathoth was the family residence of the priest Abiathar, a descendant of Eli whom Solomon had expelled because of his complicity in Adonijah's attempt to seize the crown. Possibly Jeremiah traced his priestly ancestry back to Eli, the custodian of the Ark in the old confederate sanctuary of Shiloh. The recollection of Shiloh's fall, an event that virtually brought the former Israelite Tribal Confederacy to an end (see pp. 185–186), made a deep impression on Jeremiah's thought.

---

[9]Some scholars, doubting that Jeremiah was active during Josiah's reform (621 B.C.E.), suggest changing "thirteenth year" to "twenty-third year." According to this improbable view, the prophet's call occurred in the year 617 B.C.E.

The materials in Jeremiah 1–3 have been revised and reinterpreted in the light of later events in the prophet's ministry. Even so, they give us important information about his career before the Deuteronomic Reformation of 621 B.C.E.

Evidently Jeremiah was a very young man at the time of his call (about 626 B.C.E.): He protested to Yahweh that he was a mere "lad" (Jer. 1:6). The interior struggle recorded in Jeremiah 1 is played out under the ominous shadow of international events that occurred in a restless, uncertain time, pregnant with the hope of national liberation. Not long before, Ashurbanapal's death had set off a chain reaction of events. Under Nabopolassar (about 626–605 B.C.E.), Babylonia had at last gained independence. Media had revolted under Cyaxares. Scythian hordes were on the move in the north. Egypt, like the famed phoenix bird, was rising from the ashes. Great nations were stirring, each watching for the opportune moment to strike the tottering Assyrian giant and become the new master of the world. The old world order, held together for over two centuries by Assyrian might, was crumbling. In this eventful hour of history "the word of Yahweh" came to Jeremiah.

THE POWER THAT DESTROYS REBUILDS

The story of Jeremiah's call, vividly presented in the form of a dialogue with Yahweh (Jer. 1:4–19), tells how irresistibly Yahweh's word came to him (see Jer. 5:14; 23:29). Throughout his career Jeremiah struggled with the power of Yahweh's word, but could not refrain from speaking it. In retrospect, he saw that his whole life, right back to the time when he was still in his mother's womb, was part of Yahweh's plan. This was the meaning of his life: to be "a prophet to the nations," consecrated for a "political office" in Yahweh's world government.

Like Moses (see Exod. 3–4) Jeremiah shrank from the great task, not only because he was too young—perhaps not yet twenty years old—but also because he felt he was the last man on earth to be chosen for such work. But attempts at evasion were in vain. His strength, after all, lay in the power of the One who spoke through him. He was to be the servant of Yahweh's word that "makes history," the word that was filled with the power to destroy and to rebuild (Jer. 1:10). In their feverish struggle to gain control of history, the nations had to learn that God controls human affairs. In vivid language the narrative portrays Yahweh touching the prophet's mouth, not to cleanse (as in Isaiah's vision), but to empower him to speak:

> Then Yahweh reached out his hand and touched my mouth,
>   saying to me:
>   "Look! I have put my words in your mouth.
>   You see, this day I have set you
>   over nations and over kingdoms,

> to tear up and to pull down,
> to demolish and to overthrow,
> to build and to plant."
>
> —JEREMIAH 1:9–10

Jeremiah's message conveys, more clearly and deeply than in the case of any other prophet, the message that Yahweh's word is sovereign not only over the nations but also over the interior life of the prophet himself.

The following passages (Jer. 1:11-13) relate two visions in a question-and-answer style reminiscent of Amos. The first, like Amos' vision of the basket of summer fruit (Amos 8:1-3), employs a favorite prophetic device, a play on words. In Hebrew there is close similarity between *shāqēd* ("almond") and the participle *shōqēd* ("watching"). According to one interpretation, the almond branch—called "waker" or "watcher" because it awakens (blossoms) in early spring—suggests to the prophet that God is the Waker or Watcher who "rises up early" to judge Israel. The emphasis probably falls more on the sound of the words, however, than on the association of ideas. The striking assonance of the Hebrew words was enough to evoke the conviction that Yahweh is "watching over his word"—that is, acting to bring the divine purpose to fruition (see Isa. 55:10–11). It was as if someone today, gazing intently at a watch, were to realize that God is "watching" (keeping alert) in order to bring a plan to fulfillment.

The second vision brings out what is implicit in the first: Yahweh's historical purpose is ominous for Judah, for judgment is at hand. The prophet sees an ordinary cooking pot. Although the details are not clear, the pot might be boiling in the north with its mouth tilted toward the south, pouring out an evil brew upon the land. The meaning is clear enough: An avalanche of evil will come upon the inhabitants of the land from the north. Some think the foe from the north in this passage and in the original version (Jer. 4:5–6:26) was the Scythians (but see the discussion of Zephaniah, pp. 327–329). Whatever the historical agency, Jeremiah was convinced that Yahweh was the real foe coming to execute judgment against the whole land. Yahweh's word, spoken by this prophet, was *against* the kings of Judah, its princes, its priests, and the people of the land (Jer. 1:18).

JEREMIAH'S EARLY PREACHING

The content of Jeremiah's message, delivered in the years between his call and the Deuteronomic Reformation, is set forth in a series of oracles now found in Jeremiah 2:1–4:4.[10] Here the Mosaic tradition is revived with a depth of understanding matched

---

[10]However, references to Egypt in 2:14–17 and 2:29–37 indicate that these passages were reworked in a time after the year 609 B.C.E., when the Egyptians were victorious over Josiah at Megiddo.

only by the prophet Hosea. Indeed, the striking affinities between Jeremiah 2 and the prophecy of Hosea suggest that Jeremiah knew and was influenced by Hosea's message, which by that time had become the possession of the Southern Kingdom of Judah. Jeremiah's memory goes back to the great formative period of Israel's past: the Exodus and the sojourn in the wilderness. This was the time of Israel's covenant faithfulness (Hebrew: ḥésed)[11] when the "bride" Israel was in love with her husband (Jer. 2:1–3). In the honeymoon of her "youth," Israel responded with her whole being to Yahweh's historical revelation. But things have changed. Using the form of the "covenant lawsuit" (Hebrew: rîb; see pp. 306–307), the prophet acts as Yahweh's prosecuting attorney (Jer. 2:4–13). After court is convened Yahweh the Plaintiff makes the charge: Israel's life in Canaan has been a history of unfaithfulness, with no sense of gratitude for Yahweh's past deeds of benevolence and continuing providence (Jer. 2:5–7). The leaders of the people—priests, rulers, prophets—have failed to acknowledge Yahweh's suzerainty (Jer. 2:8). The lawsuit reaches a resounding climax in the indictment against Israel (Jer. 2:9–13). To the prophetic attorney the whole thing seems fantastic: No other nation had ever repudiated its gods, even though they were really not gods at all, in order to follow after "emptiness" and thus become "hollow" people (see Jer. 2:5b). It is as appalling as if Jerusalem had rejected a supply of fresh water in order to store up water in cisterns that were no better than sieves! An appeal is made to the "jury"—the heavens:

> Stand aghast, you heavens, at this!
>   Be astounded—utterly appalled,
>   says Yahweh.
> For a double evil have my people committed:
>   Me they have rejected,
>   the fountain of living water,
>   only to hew out cisterns for themselves,
>   broken cisterns that cannot hold water.
>   —JEREMIAH 2:12–13

Further elaborating on this theme, Jeremiah likens Israel to a faithless wife who leaves her husband (Jer. 3:19–20). Indeed, Israel is no better than a common harlot driven by lusts as strong as those of an animal in heat (Jer. 2:20–25). The people's lifestyle has polluted the land, Yahweh's heritage, for Israel's harlotry is practiced "upon every high hill and every green tree" where Baal is worshipped at local sanctuaries. Like Lady Macbeth, Israel cannot wash away the stain of its guilt (Jer. 2:22). Therefore, a divorce must take place (Jer. 3:1–15). Judah has not learned the lesson of the history of the Northern Kingdom, which ended in a decree of divorce written in the visible language of tragic events: "Faithless Israel has shown herself less guilty than false Judah!" Judah

---

[11]In Jeremiah 2:2, NRSV translates ḥésed as "devotion." See the Definition, p. 277–278.

stands condemned for flagrant betrayal of the love that had called, redeemed, and sustained her throughout her history (Jer. 3:6–14). Nevertheless, says the prophet, there is still time for repentance (that is, for a change of lifestyle). In the current historical situation Yahweh is pleading with the faithless people to *return* ("repent"; see Definition, p. 362). Yahweh's purpose is to heal the broken relationship (Jer. 3:22) and to effect an inward transformation of the heart. Notice the conditional "if" of the Mosaic covenant that introduces the plea for repentance (Jer. 4:1–4). *If* Israel turns around and returns to the covenant relationship with Yahweh, *then* the ancient promise to Abraham will come into effect—that is, nations will bless themselves in the name of the God of Israel (Jer. 4:2).

Like Zephaniah, Jeremiah protested against the syncretism that had all but erased the distinctive elements of Israel's faith. He called for a reformation—not just a superficial reform of traditional rites and practices, but one that begins in the heart, the seat of human loyalties and affections. He called for a "circumcision of the heart,"[12] for a breaking up of the fallow ground that had encrusted the life of the people (Jer. 4:3–4). In a time when Israel's sacred past was neglected and forgotten, the message of Jeremiah revived the Mosaic faith of the ancient wilderness with new depth and power.

THE DEUTERONOMIC REFORMATION

The break-up of world order anticipated by Zephaniah and Jeremiah did not take place overnight. Instead, events in the decades after the death of Ashurbanapal seemed to favor a renaissance of Judean nationalism. The youthful Josiah, capitalizing on Assyria's impotence, took the initiative in removing every sign of Assyrian domination in Palestine. According to 2 Chronicles, which seems trustworthy in this instance, Josiah's first efforts at reform began in the twelfth year of his reign (629 B.C.E.), six years before the Deuteronomic Reformation (2 Chron. 34:3). At that time, Josiah expanded his influence into the territory of the former Northern Kingdom, which had become the Assyrian provinces of Megiddo and Samaria. The political situation evidently intensified Judah's aspiration to restore a United Kingdom under a Davidic king, and Josiah was eager to translate this nationalistic dream into reality.

THE DISCOVERY OF THE BOOK OF TORAH

With the rise to power of Nabopolassar (about 626–605 B.C.E.), who led the Babylonians to independence, Josiah probably stepped up his program of nationalistic reform. Just as Hezekiah expressed resistance toward Assyria by attempting to cleanse Judean

---

[12]This expression, found also in Deuteronomy 10:16 and 30:6 (compare Jer. 9:26), is a metaphor for opening the "heart," the center of one's being, so that it might be humbly submissive to the will of God.

worship of Assyrian and other alien elements, so Josiah's nationalism was accompanied by religious reform. His efforts were supported by the conservative landowners of Judah ("the people of the land"; 2 Kings 11:14, 20) who had been hostile to Manasseh's appeasement of Assyria and longed for national independence (see 2 Kings 21:23–24). Indeed, this reform was probably already underway when a remarkable discovery was made in the eighteenth year of Josiah's reign (621 B.C.E.). Taken outside its political context, the import of the account in 2 Kings 22 might be missed. We are told that a manuscript, "The Book of the Torah," was found when repairs were being made on the Temple of Jerusalem. Perhaps these were not routine repairs, but repairs designed to remove from the Temple all traces of Assyrian and other alien influences. In any case, when Josiah's secretary came to the Temple to supervise the payment of the workers' wages, he was informed of the "archaeological discovery" and immediately brought the matter to Josiah's attention.

When the document was read to him, Josiah tore his garments—a gesture of consternation or despair. Urgently he demanded that the High Priest verify the manuscript's authenticity. This was done, not by trying to determine its age and authorship (as modern archaeologists would do), but by consulting Huldah the prophetess. Her oracular response cut to the quick: Because of the violation of the words of the book, Yahweh would bring evil upon Jerusalem, making it "a desolation and a curse." At this point Josiah summoned the people to the Temple for a ceremony of covenant renewal, during which he read to them "The Book of the Torah" (here called "The Book of the Covenant"). Thereupon the people made a covenant before Yahweh to walk after Yahweh and to be obedient to the covenant commandments. The ceremony calls to mind the story in Joshua 24 about the convocation "before God" at Shechem, the ritual of covenant renewal, and "The Book of the Torah of God" in which the Shechem covenant was recorded. It also recalls the ancient covenant ceremony in Exodus 24:3–8, when Moses read to the people "The Book of the Covenant."

Josiah's covenant ceremony was followed by a great royal reform, similar to that of Hezekiah almost a century earlier but carried out with greater energy and thoroughness (2 Kings 23). The finding of "The Book of the Torah" at the opportune moment accelerated and gave direction to the reform initiated some years earlier. Behind Josiah's housecleaning was the desire to recover Judah's vitality and strength and to avoid the curse that the Torah invoked upon the nation when it disobeyed Yahweh's commandments (see Deut. 11:26–32; 28). The paganism against which Zephaniah had protested (Zeph. 1:4–6) was abolished, including Canaanite Baal worship, the Assyrian astral cult, and worship of other deities such as the Ammonite Milcom. Into the ash heap went all foreign objects found in the Temple: appurtenances of the male god Baal and mother goddess Asherah, the horses dedicated to the sun, and the astral altars on the roof. Pagan practices such as child sacrifice in the Valley of Hinnom and the consultation of mediums and wizards were discontinued. Moreover, Josiah's reform did not stop with the cleansing of the Jerusalem Temple. The outlying sanctuaries or "high places" that had been hotbeds of pagan religion were destroyed and defiled, and their idolatrous priests were deposed. Finally, Josiah's reform was carried into the former Northern Kingdom of Israel, then nominally under Assyrian control. The rival temple of Bethel was destroyed, along with other outlying high places. Josiah's declaration of independence from Assyria could hardly have been clearer!

One feature of Josiah's reform deserves special attention. According to 2 Kings 23:8–9, the Yahweh priests in the cities of Judah were put out of business when local shrines were abolished. We are told, however, that "the priests of the high places did not come up to the altar of Yahweh in Jerusalem, but they ate unleavened bread among their brethren" (2 Kings 23:9). Clearly, the most drastic aspect of the reform was the centralization of worship in the Jerusalem Temple, the central sanctuary for all Judah, where the official priesthood could keep rigorous watch. In this way the faith of Israel could be kept free from the defilement of pagan practices.

Josiah's reform, then, represented a break with Assyria, whose cultural influence had been deeply impressed upon Judah during the reign of Manasseh. Religiously, it involved a repudiation of what in those days might have been called "modernism": the attempt to conform to the religious fashions of the Assyrian empire and to blend Israel's religion with other religions. Josiah's reform was essentially conservative, for it sought to return to and conserve distinctive elements of Israel's faith, rather than capitulate to the cultural pressures of the world. The reform was based on the conviction that unless the people repudiated the syncretism that sapped their vitality, Judah would go the way of the Northern Kingdom of Israel. By means of the ancient ceremony of covenant renewal, Josiah made a serious effort to recover the past and restore its meaning in the present. In keeping with this effort, he ordered that the long-neglected feast of the Mosaic period, the Passover, be reinstituted (2 Kings 23:22–23).

THE DEUTERONOMIC BASIS OF JOSIAH'S REFORM

We now come to a major question: What document was discovered in the Temple and read in the ceremony of covenant renewal? Is "The Book of the Torah" still preserved somewhere in the Hebrew Bible? Scholars reason that it could not be the Pentateuch, for this was not completed until quite a bit later than Josiah's reform. Other legal collections within the Pentateuch, such as the so-called Covenant Code (Exod. 20:23–23:19) or the Holiness Code (Lev. 17–26), hardly fit the situation. If the Torah found in the Temple during Josiah's reign is still extant, it must be a book that strongly condemns the paganism of the Manasseh era, demands centralization of worship in Jerusalem, and solemnly warns that unswerving loyalty to Yahweh alone is the sole basis of the nation's existence.

These specifications are met by a body of law now found in Deuteronomy 12–26. Reading these chapters with the story of 2 Kings 22–23 in mind, one is immediately struck by the correspondence between the Deuteronomic Code and the reform measures of Josiah. Notice, for example, the demand that all local high places be abolished, and that worship of Yahweh be confined to the central sanctuary, "the place which Yahweh your God shall choose" (Deut. 12). The Deuteronomic Code also stipulates that while animals can be slaughtered for meat in any city, sacrifice to Yahweh is confined to the central sanctuary (Deut. 12:13–14; 16:5–6), and that the people must make pilgrimages to the central sanctuary to celebrate the great religious festivals (16:1–5). Deuteronomy 18:1–8 says that country priests, who would lose their jobs with the closing of the local sanctuaries, are entitled to minister in the central sanctuary (though the writer of 2 Kings 23:9, who evidently knew that it was impractical for all these priests to join the Jerusalem temple staff, states that they found their livelihood by sojourning in the midst of their own people). We cannot pursue all the parallels here. Suffice it to say that as early as the fourth century C.E. (for example, Jerome), and especially since the scholarly advances of the nineteenth century C.E., opinion has held that Josiah's reform was based on the Code of Deuteronomy in some form. We have already seen that the Deuteronomistic historians, who took the theological convictions of this so-called "Deuteronomic Reformation" seriously, produced a comprehensive history of Israel from the Mosaic period to the final fall of the nation (Deuteronomy through 2 Kings).

In both form and content the Deuteronomic Code shows dependence on an old legal tradition, although the tradition is recast and reinterpreted for the seventh century B.C.E.[13] Indeed, it is probable that the Deuteronomic Torah goes back ultimately to a northern covenant tradition preserved and interpreted by Levite teachers in the Northern Kingdom of Israel. In the Deuteronomic Code, Jerusalem is not explicitly identified as the site of the central sanctuary, though Josiah so identified it for his own reforming purposes. Originally, the Deuteronomic historians could have had in mind the city of Shechem, the scene of covenant renewal under Joshua and the city chosen by Jeroboam I as his first capital.

Thus the nucleus of Deuteronomy (Deut. 12–26) is quite old. It was kept in the Jerusalem Temple during the reactionary reign of Manasseh and later was "found" at the appropriate time during Josiah's reign. If it also contained Deuteronomy 28, as it probably did, we can understand why the reading of "the blessings and the curses" caused Josiah's consternation and contrition. Moreover, it is probable that other sermonic material was included in the book presented to Josiah. This question necessitates a brief consideration of the structure and contents of the whole book of Deuteronomy.

---

[13]The laws in Deuteronomy 12–26 show many similarities to the Covenant Code of Exodus 20:23–23:19. Moreover, many of the laws are cast in the "conditional" (casuistic) style of Near Eastern jurisprudence that influenced Israel during the settlement in Canaan. See pp. 86–87, 134–136.

THE BOOK OF DEUTERONOMY

The book of Deuteronomy merits special attention in view of its great importance in Judean faith and worship. Its publication under state sponsorship during Josiah's reign was the first serious step toward the creation of an official canon of sacred literature that would be binding upon the whole people in matters of faith and conduct. Later, the concept of an authoritative *Torah* ("Teaching") was extended to include not only Deuteronomy but also the Priestly edition of the Old Epic tradition (JE)—that is, the entire Pentateuch (see Chapter 13).

The book of Deuteronomy nourished and deepened faith in Yahweh during the critical period of the collapse of the Assyrian empire, as well as in subsequent generations. Significantly, it is one of the Old Testament books most frequently quoted in the New Testament. The First Great Commandment, which Jesus affirmed to be the fulfillment of the whole Torah, is a direct quotation from Deuteronomy 6:5 (Mk. 12:30 = Matt. 22:37 and Lk. 10:27). The Second Commandment, although quoted directly from Leviticus 19:18, is implicit in the Deuteronomic conception of neighborly love (see Deut. 10:19). Moreover, Jesus' answers to the Tempter, as recorded in the Gospels (Matt. 4:1–10 = Lk. 4:1–13), were couched in terms of Israel's trials of faith as recorded in Deuteronomy (see Deut. 6:13, 16; 8:3).

In its present form, the whole book of Deuteronomy purports to be a sermon given by Moses to the people in Moab, just before they crossed over the Jordan River to take possession of the Promised Land. As they stand on the threshold of a new life, with all its opportunities and dangers, Moses exhorts them to remember Yahweh's gracious acts revealed in the Exodus and the wilderness sojourn, and to hold firm to their covenant pledge when confronted with the temptations of Canaan. This sermon is all the more forceful and relevant because it actually reflects Israel's temptations to compromise its faith with Canaanite culture, from the earliest days of Israelite occupation to the heyday of paganism under Manasseh.[14]

Closer inspection of the book of Deuteronomy shows, however, that it is not in one piece. Around the nucleus of laws collected in chapters 12–26 cluster no less than three "Mosaic addresses." The book's structure can be outlined as follows:

A. The First Address (Deut. 1–4)
　　1. Introduction (Deut. 1:1–5)
　　2. Moses' summary of events since the departure from Mount Horeb (Deut. 1:6–3:29)
　　3. Moses' exhortation to Israel (Deut. 4:1–40)
　　4. Appendix (Deut. 4:41–43)

---

[14]Remember that the term "Israel" actually embraces the two kingdoms of Israel, Ephraim and Judah, making it possible to refer to them as "the two houses of Israel" (see Isa. 8:14). Thus, even after the Northern Kingdom had fallen, the term still applied to Judah. See Definition, pp. 6–7.

B. The Second Address (Deut. 5–26 and 28)
   1. Introduction (Deut. 4:44–49)
   2. Moses' exhortation to Israel (Deut. 5–11)
   3. The exposition of the Law (Deut. 12–26)
   4. Conclusion (Deut. 28)
C. The Third Address (Deut. 29–30)
D. Supplements
   1. The Shechem covenant ceremony (Deut. 27)
   2. Moses' last instructions (Deut. 31)
   3. Old poetry: "Song of Moses" (Deut. 32) and "Blessing of Moses" (Deut. 33)
   4. Narrative of Moses' death (Deut. 34)

The Second Address (B in the outline) is our focus here. Scholars generally agree that this is the oldest edition of Moses' "sermon" to Israel, though we cannot be sure whether the sermonic material that frames the law code (Deut. 12–26) was composed before or after Josiah's reform. Without exploring this critical question, we will assume that at least this section should be read as a unified whole, and that it was substantially the book presented to Josiah.[15]

MOSES' SERMON TO ISRAEL

Moses' farewell address is presented in a distinctive literary style. If we were to compare a Deuteronomic passage (such as Deut. 10:12–22) with a typical selection from either the Old Epic tradition or the Priestly Writing, the differences would be immediately apparent. Here we find not the chaste style of a narrator, or the formulaic prose of a priest concerned with cultic matters, but that of a preacher who uses skillful oratory to move a congregation to consider issues of life-and-death urgency. Very often the sentences are long flights of eloquent and impressive prose. As if to drive home the message, the preacher piles clause upon clause in a seemingly repetitious manner. Throughout the sermon are turns of speech characteristic of the Deuteronomistic History: "To go after [serve] other gods"; "to hearken to the voice of Yahweh"; "that you may prolong your days in the land"; "that it may be well with you"; "to do that which is evil (or good) in the eyes of Yahweh."[16]

---

[15]See the critical discussion by G. E. Wright, *Interpreter's Bible*, II [23], pp. 311–30, who argues that Josiah's lawbook could have included virtually the whole of 4:44–30:20 (that is, sections B and C) and that most of the material in section A was added later as a preface to the Deuteronomistic History of Israel, extending from Deuteronomy through 2 Kings.

[16]The closest affinities to Deuteronomic style are found in the Northern Elohist tradition (E)—as evidenced, for example, by the fact that Deuteronomy, like the Elohistic narrative, calls the sacred mountain Horeb instead of Sinai (J and P) and refers to the natives of the Promised Land as Amorites rather than as Canaanites. On the Elohistic narrative, see Definition, pp. 261–262.

This new literary style, found in the Deuteronomic literature and the prose sections of the book of Jeremiah, seems to have been characteristic of the late seventh and early sixth centuries B.C.E. The Lachish Letters, a series of inscribed potsherds found in 1935 and dating from the time just before the fall of Jerusalem, strengthen the impression that this "rhetorical prose" was the literary fashion of the period.[17] But if the *style* belongs to the Deuteronomic period, the *content* is much older. Several parts of the Mosaic sermon (especially Deut. 29–30) suggest that this material came out of a covenant-renewal ceremony initiated by Joshua at Shechem, one practiced at the old central sanctuary of Shiloh during the period of the Tribal Confederacy and later preserved in the Northern Kingdom. When the old covenant tradition was used as the basis of Josiah's reform, it was written down and expanded in the language of the time.

The authors of Deuteronomy remain anonymous, but placing the address in the mouth of Moses is not a complete literary fiction. The book of Deuteronomy is essentially a revival of Mosaic teaching as it was understood in the seventh century B.C.E. To be sure, it does not contain the verbatim utterances of Moses; but the atmosphere is that of Mosaic faith, charged with the religious and ethical insights of the prophetic movement. Like the prophets themselves, the Deuteronomic Torah does not pretend to lead Israel to new heights of religious development, but to recall the people to the original faith of the Mosaic period. This is a program of reform, not innovation. Hence the address appropriately is ascribed to Moses.

The title of the book evidently derives from the passage stipulating that the king must have at hand "a copy of this law" all the days of his life and must conduct himself in obedience to it (Deut. 17:14–20). The Hebrew title is simply "these are the words," the opening phrase of the book (Deut. 1:1). The Greek Septuagint, from which come our present names for the books of the Pentateuch, reproduces this phrase as "this second law" (Greek: *to deuteronomion touto*). Thus the Greek title designates the book according to its central theme: the "seconding" or repetition of the original law given by Moses. As the contents of Deuteronomy disclose, however, the English word "law" (from Greek *nomos* and Latin *lex*) inadequately covers the full meaning of the Hebrew word *torah*, which means "teaching," or perhaps even "revelation." Deuteronomy contains what we would call "law," but it is not narrowly confined to legal matters. Fundamentally the book contains a teaching or "exposition" (see Deut. 1:5) of the basis and demands of Israel's Covenant faith, and as such is directed not to professional administrators of law or to priests, but to the whole lay community of Israel. It is not a code of rules but "a preaching, a proclamation and exposition of the faith of the nation" that includes both the "good news" of Yahweh's liberating deeds and the requirements that are binding upon the people who have been liberated.[18] Therefore, the term *Torah* covers

---

[17]On the Lachish Letters, see Pritchard, *Ancient Near Eastern Texts* [1], pp. 321–22. On the style and theology of the book of Deuteronomy, see Moshe Weinfeld, *Deuteronomy* [420].

[18]See the excellent treatment of Deuteronomy by G. E. Wright, *Interpreter's Bible,* II [23], especially pp. 311–14.

not only the so-called "Code" in Deuteronomy 12–26 but also the whole Mosaic address.

The Renewal of the Covenant

Consider briefly the contents of Moses' address to Israel. It begins with an imperative that resounds like a trumpet call through the whole sermon: *"Hear, O Israel"* (Deut. 5:1). A message is being proclaimed with great urgency, and the community is called to listen. Moses is speaking at a time when the memory of the Exodus is still fresh and the people are faced with the hazards of entering Canaan. It becomes quite clear, however, that the message is not addressed to a generation long ago, but to "this day" when Israel stands before God. Moses is speaking *today.* The present generation was actually *there* when the covenant was made:

> Yahweh our God made a covenant with us at Horeb. It was not with our ancestors that Yahweh made this covenant but rather with us, all of us here, all of us who are living today.
>
> —DEUTERONOMY 5:2–3 (see also 29:10–15)

Every generation of Israel is involved in the covenant made at Mount Horeb. When the covenant is renewed, therefore, the decisive moment of the past is contemporized or "made present." The book of Deuteronomy does not advocate a retreat from the tumult of the present into a golden age of the past. Rather, it deals vigorously with the challenge of the present crisis, and with Israel's responsibilities and destiny in Yahweh's purpose. According to this sermon, the Mosaic past must come alive in the present if Israel is to have any future at all in the land that Yahweh has given. Hence the appeal for covenant renewal is made with life-and-death urgency. Another passage in the Third Address (Deut. 30:15–20), which might reflect a liturgy of covenant renewal, strikes the same urgent note:

> I call heaven and earth to witness against you this day, that I have set before you life and death, blessing and curse; therefore choose life. . . .
>
> —DEUTERONOMY 30:19

Here is a forceful restatement of Joshua's message before the ancient assembly at Shechem: "Choose this day whom you will serve" (Josh. 24:15).

The Fulfillment of the Law

Having sounded this keynote, the speaker immediately turns to the requirements binding upon the Covenant Community. These are summed up in the Ten Commandments (Hebrew: "the ten words"), given in Deuteronomy 5 with slight variation from the version in Exodus 20. The essence of the commandments, however, is given in Deuteronomy 6:4–5, where the first commandment of the Decalogue is presented in a positive, rather than a negative, form. This terse summary—known as "the Shema" from the opening Hebrew verb *shema'* ("hear")—was regarded by the rabbis and by Jesus as the core of the Torah. It states that Israel's first responsibility is to love God with its whole being—"with all your heart, and with all your soul [self], and with all your might."[19] This does not mean that one should love God in different ways, for the terms overlap in meaning. Israel is to love God with the unswerving, complete, steadfast loyalty that is the very foundation of the Covenant Community.

The emphasis on love is a characteristic theme of the book of Deuteronomy, one influenced in part by Hosea's message. In this respect Deuteronomy returns to and deepens the meaning of the original Mosaic covenant. Yahweh's gracious and undeserved love, manifested in deeds of benevolence on behalf of Israel (Deut. 6:20–23), should awaken Israel to respond with love of God and, as a corollary, love of neighbors. Deuteronomy actually revives the original Mosaic tradition in which Israel's "gospel"— the good news of what Yahweh had done on behalf of a people in bondage (Exod. 1–15)—provided the motive for accepting the obligations of the covenant (see pp. 83–84). Israel is to love God solely because God first loved them. According to Deuteronomy, love is "the fulfillment of the law." However, Israel's love of God must be combined with reverence ("fear," "obedience"), for Yahweh is a "jealous" God who will not tolerate a turning to other gods (Deut. 6:10–15). Divine love is a holy love, a wrathful love, that will become a consuming fire to those unfaithful to the covenant relationship.

THE CHOICE OF ISRAEL

In Deuteronomy 7–9, the speaker shows what Yahweh's choice of Israel means. Israel is a *holy* people, separated for a special relationship to Yahweh, the Holy God.[20] This is what makes Israel different from other nations:

> For you are a people holy to Yahweh, your God. Yahweh your God
> has chosen you to be his very own possession out of all the peoples that are
> on the surface of the earth.
>
> —DEUTERONOMY 7:6

---

[19]The New Testament quotation of this commandment adds "the mind" in order to bring out what is meant by the Hebrew word "heart." As we have noticed before, the word *néfesh*, often translated "soul," does not mean soul in the Greek sense, but refers to the whole person, the self.

[20]What is holy is withdrawn from the ordinary sphere and is drawn into relationship to the Holy God. In this sense, holiness implies separation.

Negatively, this means that Israel has been *separated from* the nations. Therefore, the people are not to intermarry with them or to adopt their cultural ways, lest the gods of the nations seduce them from loyalty to Yahweh. This is put so strongly that Israel is enjoined to practice the sacrificial ban (Hebrew: *ḥérem*) of "holy war" (see Definition, p. 128)—that is, to consign the inhabitants of Canaan to total destruction as a sacrifice to Yahweh (Deut. 7:1–6). Holiness demands purity; hence all alien elements must be removed from the covenant community.

Positively, Israel has been *separated for* special service to Yahweh. Here the speaker presents one of the finest treatments of Israel's special calling in the Hebrew Bible, although it lacks the universal breadth of the Old Epic tradition (Gen. 12:1–3). Israel did not first choose; Israel was chosen (compare Exod. 19:3–6). The initiative was Yahweh's. In marvelous grace Yahweh selected this people, not because they were stronger or more numerous than others, but solely because Yahweh fell in love with a small, insignificant band of slaves in Egypt (compare Hos. 11:1). Therefore, Israel has no reason to boast of its righteousness or superiority. Divine election is an act of grace that should evoke consecrated service, rather than pride (Deut. 7:6–11).

As the sermon continues, we realize that Moses is speaking about the "temptations of culture" that Israel experienced throughout its history as an independent nation. One temptation was a belief in *self-sufficiency:* "My power and the might of my hand have gotten me this wealth" (Deut. 8:17). The community is urged to remember the wilderness sojourn, when Yahweh graciously led them for forty years, feeding them with manna so that they might know that "one does not live by bread alone, but by every word that comes from the mouth of the Lord" (Deut. 8:3). In the spirit of Hosea, the speaker affirms that the sufferings of the wilderness period were a form of discipline, like the loving discipline that a parent gives to a child. The purpose was to "humble" Israel, to test the loyalty of its heart, and to awaken it to the realization that "life" is not subject to human control but is a gift received by those who acknowledge their constant dependence upon God.

The second cultural temptation was *self-righteousness:* the belief of a victorious people that "it is because of my righteousness that Yahweh has brought me in to possess this land" (Deut. 9:4). The speaker reminds Israel that victory in Canaan does not rest upon its righteousness, but upon the corruption of the peoples of the land, and especially upon Yahweh's faithfulness to the promise made to the ancestors (Deut. 9:5). Israel has no claim upon Yahweh because of moral virtue or special religious insight. Indeed, the wilderness sojourn, contrary to Hosea's idealized treatment, was not a honeymoon of covenant faithfulness, but a time of ingratitude and rebellion. Israel is "a stubborn people" by nature. Moses is represented as saying: "You have been rebellious against Yahweh from the day that I knew you" (Deut. 9:24)—a statement that applies not just to the generation of the wilderness but to the whole course of Israel's history. Had it not been for Moses' intercession on behalf of Israel, Yahweh would have destroyed the people in the wilderness and fashioned some better instrument. Israel's preservation, the speaker emphasizes, is due solely to Yahweh's freely bestowed grace and love (Deut. 9:6–10:11).[21]

ISRAEL'S SOCIAL RESPONSIBILITIES

The sermon reaches its climax in Deuteronomy 10:12–22. Here the speaker returns to the note on which the sermon began, one that also reverberates in Micah's great prophetic summary (Mic. 6:8). In answer to the question "What does the Lord require of you?" Israel is reminded that its calling is to be an obedient people, fearing Yahweh who is Sovereign of heaven and earth and loving the One who first loved them. Therefore, the basis for ethical responsibility is not dutiful obedience to a law code, but an inward, personal response to Yahweh's deeds of kindness and benevolence.

Furthermore, Yahweh's righteous activity on behalf of the weak and oppressed has shown the way in which Israel should walk. In Yahweh's sovereign rule, love and justice are perfectly combined. Israel's God, "God of gods and Lord of lords, the great, the mighty, and the terrible God," has not only demonstrated love for Israel but also has manifested divine love through the exercise of justice on behalf of oppressed slaves. Yahweh is the champion of the legally weak or helpless: the orphan, the widow, the alien resident. Yahweh shows no partiality: Everyone stands equal before the divine Judge. Israel must imitate this manner of dealing with people. This is the basis of the "humanitarianism" that infuses the laws in Deuteronomy 12–26. The justice of the weak members of society must be defended, for Israelites should remember that they were once slaves in Egypt (Deut. 15:1–18). Every member of the community—high or low, rich or poor, bond or free—must be accorded equality before the law (Deut. 16:18–20). This emphasis elevates Israelite legislation above other codes of the Near East, which favored the aristocratic class. Any exploitation of a fellow Israelite is ruled out, whether through murder, adultery, theft, dishonesty, false witness, or taking interest. The sanctities of the family are to be protected. Injustice in any form defiles the Covenant Community. The righteousness of God demands, negatively, the abolition of anything that defiles the community, even to the point of imposing the severest penalties, as in the case of idolatry (Deut. 13:1–18; 17:2–7) or sexual abuses (22:13–25). Positively, it means imitating God's ways so that a spirit of love and solidarity can pervade the community.

In Deuteronomy 11 and 28, separated from one another by the exposition of specific laws, Israel is reminded that its future depends on the response to Yahweh's requirements. The people confront a crucial decision, with the alternatives of blessing or curse. *If* Israel obeys faithfully, it will be strong in the land and will be blessed with fer-

---

[21]On the intercessory prayer of Israel's leaders, see Patrick Miller, *They Cried unto the Lord: The Form and Theology of Biblical Prayer* [534], chap. 7.

tility and welfare. But *if* Israel stubbornly turns aside to serve the gods of the land, Yahweh's anger will break forth, visiting the people with calamity.

The governing purpose of Deuteronomy is to summon Israel to a renewal of its covenant with Yahweh. Although this literature might reflect a tradition of covenant-renewal ritual, its immediate background is the cultural situation of the seventh century B.C.E., when Israel's faith was corroded by Canaanite cults and by Assyrian religious practices. The Deuteronomic writers demand exclusive loyalty to Yahweh as the condition for national welfare and survival.

INADEQUACIES OF THE REFORM

For a while, the Deuteronomic Reformation made a deep impression on the life and thought of Judah, as can be seen from the dominance of the Deuteronomic viewpoint in the Deuteronomistic History. The reform movement sincerely attempted to take prophetic teachings seriously and to return to the covenant faith of Moses. But alas, social reforms—even when sanctioned by the government and supported by popular demand—last only as long as the inward change in people's hearts. Josiah's reform reflected the political climate of the time. Inspired by the nationalistic spirit of rebellion against foreign rule, it could flourish only as long as the political situation that occasioned it.

THEOLOGICAL FLAWS

Jeremiah evidently supported the Deuteronomic Reformation for a time, although his attitude is not as clear as one might wish. An interest in reform would certainly have been in keeping with his concern for Mosaic tradition: In Jeremiah 11:1–13 we learn that the prophet went through the streets of Jerusalem appealing for acceptance of "this covenant." In the same chapter (Jer. 11:18–23), we are told that Jeremiah's kinsmen of Anathoth plotted to take his life. The reason might have been that this priestly family, associated with the local shrine, resented Jeremiah's support of a program that would centralize worship in Jerusalem, where the royal priesthood was in control.[22] Even in his later career, Jeremiah held Josiah in high esteem for his vigorous administration of justice (Jer. 22:15–16). In any case, if Jeremiah supported the reform movement at first, the resulting defiant nationalism and external piety must soon have turned him against it. Centralizing worship in Jerusalem made the people feel secure because Yahweh was present in their midst. Moreover, the *Torah* was being twisted into a way to "get something out of religion," to maintain the status quo. Jeremiah's prophecy of the "new

---

[22]Deuteronomy 18:6–8 specifies that village priests had a right to be included on the Jerusalem staff, but this proved impractical (2 Kings 23:9). The Jerusalem hierarchy would naturally oppose the intrusion of outside priests.

covenant" (see Chapter 12) must have been influenced partly by the failure of the Deuteronomic Reform.

A great defect of Deuteronomic theology was that it oversimplified God's ways in history. The Deuteronomic doctrine of divine justice is too neat: Obey Yahweh and all will go well, disobey and hardship will come. Perhaps the original version of Deuteronomy conveyed a more profound understanding of this truth, but in the Deuteronomistic History it sounds suspiciously like the "success philosophy" that forms the basis of much popular religion. Of course, the belief in divine reward (blessing) and divine punishment (judgment) was fundamental to Israel's faith from the very first. Isaiah and other great prophets added an important qualification: "*If* you are willing and obedient, you shall eat the good of the land" (Isa. l:19). But Deuteronomy added something new: the belief that obedience or disobedience could be measured by a code of rules set down in a book, "The Book of the Torah." Thus Joshua was promised success in the conquest of Canaan *if* he would study faithfully "this book of the law," the Deuteronomic Torah:

> Let not this Book of the Teaching cease from your lips, but recite it
> day and night, so that you may observe faithfully all that is written in it.
> Only then will you prosper in your undertakings and only then will you be
> successful.
>
> —JOSHUA 1:8 (JPSV)

In defense of Deuteronomy, the Mosaic address was not intended to encourage "bargain counter" religion. It was concerned primarily with personal relationship to Yahweh, not with personal profit gained by obeying religious rules. True, the people believed that the covenant relationship would result in concrete blessings. Indeed, the Hebrew Bible does not make a distinction between "material" and "spiritual" blessings—the latter confined to peace of mind, fortitude, patience, and so on. Deuteronomy sets forth a healthy "spiritual materialism": Just as the marriage covenant yields the blessings of home life, so Israel's covenant with Yahweh yielded the divine promise of tangible blessings such as security in the land, abundant crops, annual rainfall, and long life. The danger was that the people would renew the covenant *for the purpose of* obtaining these blessings ("in order that it may be well with you," or "in order that your days may be long upon the land which Yahweh your God gives you"). Because faith did not always bring people what they expected or wanted, a huge question arose with which later generations, influenced by the Deuteronomic view, had to struggle: If people obey the laws of God and are recompensed with suffering or hardship, how can God be just?

A PERIOD OF DISILLUSIONMENT

The easy moral logic of the Deuteronomic view was put to severe strain in the years following Josiah's reform. Josiah dreamed of restoring a United Kingdom under the single religious and political capital of Jerusalem. The Deuteronomic Reformation, viewed politically, was an attempt to consolidate and revitalize his expanded kingdom. Josiah evidently grew bolder and bolder as Assyria's star sank. The story of Assyria's final death throe is told on a Babylonian clay tablet now in the British Museum.[23] In 612 B.C.E. the Assyrian capital of Nineveh fell before a combined assault of Babylonians, Medes, and Scythians. The Assyrians tried to make a last-ditch stand at Haran, whence their capital had been moved, but this city too was captured by Scythian forces (see the prediction of Zeph. 2:13–15).

The prophecy of Nahum, dating from this period, powerfully expresses the pent-up feelings of bitterness and hatred that Assyrian occupation engendered in Judean hearts. Anticipating the fall of the capital city of Nineveh (612 B.C.E.), this "cultic" prophet used an acrostic (alphabetic) psalm to portray Yahweh's coming in a storm to rescue the faithful (Nah. 1). In this psalm he vividly describes an enemy attack upon the city as the battle rages through the streets (Nah. 2), and pronounces a terrible invective upon "the bloody city" (Nah. 3). With more patriotic zeal than prophetic insight into the tragic dimension of history, Nahum insists that Nineveh is about to get the same treatment that Assyrian kings once gave to Thebes, the capital of Egypt (Nah. 3:8). At last Assyria is going to taste the suffering it has inflicted upon other peoples, and no one will feel sorry:

> Your shepherds are asleep,
> > O king of Assyria;
> > your nobles slumber.
> Your people are scattered on the mountains
> > with no one to gather them.
> There is no assuaging your hurt,
> > your wound is mortal.
> All who hear the news about you
> > clap their hands over you.
> For who has ever escaped
> > your endless cruelty?

—NAHUM 3:18–19 (NRSV)

Then came a sudden turn of affairs, the result of a political somersault on the part of Egypt. Pharaoh Necho (about 610–594 B.C.E.), the son of Psammetichus I, decided belatedly to rescue Egypt's former enemy, Assyria—the same enemy that had sacked Thebes not many years before. From Egypt's standpoint, it was expedient to have a weak Assyria as a buffer against more dangerous foes in the north; moreover, Necho was eager to bring Syria and Palestine back under Egypt's sway. So in the year 609 B.C.E. Necho's army marched north to salvage the last remnants of the Assyrian empire. It was

---

[23]See J. B. Pritchard, *Ancient Near Eastern Texts* [1], pp. 303–5.

intercepted at the pass of Megiddo (see pp. 177–178) by Josiah, who gambled on achieving his goal of a United Kingdom by casting his lot with the Babylonians. In the ensuing battle Josiah was defeated, and evidently executed for his conspiracy with Babylonia. Judah became a vassal of Egypt (2 Kings 23:29–30), and Necho continued his march to the Euphrates to challenge Babylonia. The issue was decided in 605 B.C.E. at the battle of Carchemish, when Necho's army was decisively defeated by Babylonian forces under the command of the crown prince, Nebuchadrezzar II.[24] The Egyptian army, now in full retreat, was chased across Palestine to the borders of Egypt. Fleeing before its victorious enemies, Egypt made "a sound like a serpent gliding away" (Jer. 46). This was Egypt's last attempt to establish an empire in the Fertile Crescent. The fall of Nineveh and the victory at Carchemish made it clear that Babylonia was the new ruler of the world.

These developments must have profoundly shaken the morale of the people whose hopes had been kindled by Josiah's reform. Good king Josiah, not yet forty years old, was dead; and Jeremiah must have shared the general sorrow (Jer. 22:10; see 2 Chron. 35:23–25)[25] The dream of a Davidic kingdom that would include both Israel and Judah was shattered. After a brief interval of Egyptian rule, the temporary respite from Assyrian oppression was followed by the imposition of a Babylonian yoke not a bit lighter or more merciful. In the popular view, Yahweh's justice meant that good consequences would come from good actions, that obedience would result in security on the land, victory against foes, and abundant life. But the cruel facts of history contradicted this belief. No wonder that the first, fine rapture of the Deuteronomic Reform was soon spent! In the judgment of many scholars, the reformers' accomplishments were erased in a short time, just as Hezekiah's reform had been eclipsed during the reign of Manasseh.[26] As we learn from Jeremiah and Ezekiel, Mosaic faith was forgotten or compromised with pagan ways. Once again the people reverted to the easy tolerance of syncretism.

HABAKKUK'S WATCHTOWER OF FAITH

The strongest challenge to a simple view of God's justice in history was issued by the prophet Habakkuk. His prophecy, found essentially in Habakkuk 1–2, dates from a time just after the battle of Carchemish in 605 B.C.E., the event that established Neb-

---

[24]The name of the Babylonian prince is often spelled Nebuchad*n*ezzar, although Nebuchadezzar is perhaps the more proper spelling of the Akkadian name, *Nabu-kudurri-usur.* See the entry under this name in *Interpreter's Dictionary of the Bible* [31].

[25]Stanley B. Frost, in an article, "The Death of Josiah: A Conspiracy of Silence," *Journal of Biblical Literature* 87 (1968), 369–82, maintains that Josiah's death was not only a challenge to Davidic theology but also to Mosaic (Deuteronomic) theology and therefore could not be dealt with in the traditional manner of Israelite historiography.

[26]See, however, M. Weinfeld, *Deuteronomy* [420], who maintains that many of the reforms remained in effect.

uchadrezzar as world ruler.[27] In the form of a dialogue in two cycles between the prophet and Yahweh (Hab. 1:2–2:5), Habakkuk's poignant complaint, which echoes the anguished "How long?" of psalms of lament (see Chapter 16), is evoked by the social violence that seems to suggest that God has forsaken the people:

> How long, Yahweh, must I cry for help,
>> and you don't answer?
>> shall I cry to you "Violence!"
>> and you will not deliver?
> Why do you make me see evil,
>> make me look upon trouble?
> Destruction and violence are at hand,
>> controversy and contention arise.
> Therefore torah is feeble,
>> and justice does not achieve its end.
> Hence the wicked gang up around the righteous,
>> and on account of this justice is miscarried.
>> —HABAKKUK 1:2–4

The answer is that Yahweh is doing something almost unbelievable, namely, raising up the Chaldeans (the Babylonians): "that bitter and hasty nation" (Hab. 1:5–11). This hardly answers the question, however, for the new world power continues the monstrous, lawless evil that Assyria had unleashed. The prophet wonders whether history justifies the righteous, or whether brute power really determines human destiny. How is it that Yahweh rules history, yet the Chaldeans sweep like a wild avalanche over the world, destroying all patterns of meaning and defying the most elementary human justice? The ruthless invaders rule by defining justice in their own terms (Hab. 1:7); they are "guilty" and "their own might is their god" (1:11, NRSV). Not that Yahweh's people are guiltless! But at least they are "more righteous" than this nation. Divine judgment, which other prophets proclaimed in times of invasion, makes no sense if faith cannot discern some purpose in historical events.

A second time the prophet raises his complaint (Hab. 1:13–17):

> You whose eyes are too pure to look upon evil,
>> and who cannot countenance wrong,
> why do you countenance treacherous people,
>> and are silent when the wicked devour
>> those who are more righteous than they?
>> —HABAKKUK 1:13

---

[27]Most scholars believe that the psalm in Habakkuk 3, though appropriate there, comes from another hand. However, W. F. Albright, "The Psalm of Habakkuk," *Studies in Old Testament Prophecy* [419], pp. 1–18, regards the book as "substantially the work of a single author." See further J. J. M. Roberts, "Habakkuk," in *The Books of the Bible* [9], pp. 391–96.

Habakkuk's question becomes even more acute if, as some scholars maintain, he has in mind not only the enemy without but also the enemy within—namely, the wicked and worthless King Jehoiakim (Hab. 2:6-20; see Jer. 22:18–19). In any event, the prophet takes his stand on his "watchtower of faith" to await Yahweh's answer. No immediate answer is given. The answer that comes (Hab. 2:1–5) lifts his eyes to future horizons, when God's purpose ultimately will be realized. In the meantime, when God's presence in history is eclipsed, one must live in the courage of faith:

> Look at the proud!
>> Their spirit is not right in them,
>> but the righteous live by their faith.
>> —HABAKKUK 2:4 (NRSV)

According to this answer, the righteous person must face the enigmas of history in faith (or better, "faithfulness")—that is, by living and acting faithfully, confident that the issues are in God's hands and waiting patiently for the time when God's sovereignty will be made clear (compare Isa. 8:16–18).

FAITH AND NATIONALISM

One fact stands out in our study of the prophets of the seventh century B.C.E.: The rediscovery of the Mosaic heritage was accompanied by an upsurge of nationalism. Josiah's reform went far toward removing the religious influences of the Fertile Crescent that had weakened Israel's vitality. As in the period of the ancient Tribal Confederacy, Israel became strong when the people were loyal to their covenant pledge to Yahweh. But the centralization of worship in the Jerusalem Temple, though it purified the land of pagan religious practices, actually led to a confidence that God was on the side of the people and that no evil could befall them. Nationalistic pride died hard in the turbulent events that rolled over Judah toward the end of the seventh century B.C.E. (see Chapter 12). Ironically, it was the revival of the covenant faith in a time of nationalism that made it possible to understand the death of the nation. Israel was a Covenant Community before the rise of the nation; and the nation would have to be dissolved before people could understand again the meaning of the covenant.

CHAPTER 12

THE DOOM OF THE NATION

Josiah's reform was borne on a wave of nationalism that swept through the Southern Kingdom of Judah during the final days of the Assyrian empire. For a while it seemed that the people were standing on the threshold of a golden age, like the glorious era of David's empire. They were awakened from their patriotic daydream by a swift succession of events, beginning with Josiah's untimely death and culminating in the fall of the nation and the exile of part of its population. Nationalism died hard during those crowded years, for many prophets proclaimed a comfortable message of peace when there was no peace, promising that affairs would soon return to the good old days of national glory. Such prophets won great applause at the time, but in the long run the deepest impression was made by prophets whose sharp words punctured the illusions of the time and summoned people to face the realities of their history.

The Old Testament preserves for us the lengthy testimony of two great prophets who lived through this era of national cataclysm: Jeremiah and Ezekiel. Both men came from priestly families and, though differing greatly in temperament and outlook, complemented each other as had Amos and Hosea in an earlier time of national downfall. Their prophetic task was to speak to the crisis of their time by reflecting upon and reinterpreting the religious traditions in which they stood.

Biblical Readings: Read primarily the prophecies of Jeremiah's later career found in Jeremiah 4–25, supplemented with the biographical narratives of Jeremiah 26–45. For historical background read 2 Kings 24–25 (paralleled in 2 Chronicles 36) and, for a poignant expression of feeling in reaction to the fall of the nation, the book of Lamentations.

350

THE SUFFERING PROPHET

We turn first to Jeremiah, whose early career we traced in Chapter 11. Jeremiah's prophetic activity spanned forty years (about 626–587 B.C.E.), fateful years for the Southern Kingdom. Later tradition portrayed him as a "weeping prophet," a reputation that led to the invention of the word "jeremiad" for a doleful lament or complaint. Like his prophetic predecessors, Jeremiah announced that the Day of Yahweh would not be a day of victory and rejoicing, but a dark, bitter day of doom and gloom.

This portrait is overdrawn, but it is true that Jeremiah identified himself with his message and with his people in a more personal way than any other prophet. This helps to explain why we know more about Jeremiah *the man* than about any other Old Testament figure, with the possible exception of David. If Jeremiah was as staunch as "a fortified city, an iron pillar, and bronze walls" (Jer. 1:18), he was also as sensitive as a mother bereft of her children. His career was intimately tied to the tragedy of Jerusalem, a tragedy intensified by the very words he felt compelled to speak in the name of Yahweh. The wound of his people cut deeply into his heart, prompting him to mix his prophecies of doom with outcries of agony and grief (see Jer. 8:18–22). Though Jeremiah was not author of the elegies in the book of Lamentations, it is appropriate that these poems were attributed to him.[1]

THE BOOK OF JEREMIAH

First-time readers of the book of Jeremiah are apt to find themselves in a maze of confusion. A modern novelist would tell the story in a more orderly fashion, following a chronological time line throughout the prophet's career.[2] A modern theologian seeking to present the prophet's message would at least arrange the materials according to subject or topic. But there is no clear principle of organization or development in the book of Jeremiah. The compilers might have tried to group materials according to the early, middle, and later periods of Jeremiah's ministry; usually, however, they have not bothered to date materials in sequence or to give dates at all. And sometimes materials belonging to the same date are widely separated from each other: for example, Jeremiah's temple sermon (Jer. 7) and the account of the audience's response to it (Jer. 26). The picture is further complicated by the fact that the Greek Septuagint not only displays different readings and a different arrangement of the material, but also is about one-eighth shorter than the received Hebrew text.

---

[1]Apparently several writers were responsible for the book of Lamentations. Lamentations 2 and 4 might have been written by eyewitnesses to the fall of Jerusalem; 1 and 3 might have been inspired by the book of Jeremiah. With the exception of Lamentations 5, the poems are in the elegiac 3/2 meter (Hebrew: *qinah;* see p. 267) used by Jeremiah and Ezekiel.

[2]As Franz Werfel, *Hearken Unto the Voice* (New York: The Viking Press, 1938).

These difficulties indicate that the book of Jeremiah, like other prophetic literature, underwent a complicated history before reaching its present canonical form. Fortunately, we can provide a rough map to enable readers to find a way through the fifty-
two chapters of the book.

Section 1: Jeremiah 1–25

This section is a separate block of material consisting mainly of prophetic oracles,
with occasional biographical or autobiographical passages (for example, Jer.
1:4–19; 7:1–15; 11:1–17; 13:1–11).

Section 2: Jeremiah 26–45

By contrast, this section is composed largely of biographical narratives about Jeremiah, interspersed with prophetic sermons. It falls into two subdivisions:
a. Prophecies of judgment and hope (Jer. 26–35). Inserted into this material is
    "The Little Book of Comfort" (Jer. 30–33), partly poetic material.
b. Narratives that deal with the latest recorded events in Jeremiah's life (Jer.
    36–45).

Section 3: Jeremiah 46–51

This section consists of oracles against the nations. We are told that Jeremiah was
called to be "a prophet to the nations" (Jer. 1), but some of this material comes
from other writers.

Section 4: Jeremiah 52

The story of the fall of Jerusalem, extracted from 2 Kings 24:18–25:30, is placed
here as a fitting historical conclusion.

For this study Sections 1 and 2 are relevant (Section 1 is the more important for a first
reading).[3] Notice that, in general, the distinguishing feature of Section 1 is its poetic
form. On the other hand, Section 2 is largely prose. Thus we are immediately confronted with one of the major problems of the book: the relationship of poetry and
prose.

Literary critics have attacked this problem by singling out three basic types of material or "levels of tradition" in the book of Jeremiah.

A. *Poetry of Jeremiah,* found chiefly in Jeremiah 1–25 (Section 1). These re-
    ligious lyrics are frequently cast in a 3/2 meter (Hebrew: *qinah;* see Jer.
    9:20–21), the mournful cadence so appropriate for expressing sorrow (see
    Amos 5:2 and Lamentations). Some scholars insist that Jeremiah's genuine
    oracles are found only in the poetic sections, in which case the symbol A
    stands for "authentic."

---

[3]That these are separate units of the book is suggested by the fact that the Septuagint places section C between sections A and B (that is, after 25:13).

B.   *Biographical prose,* found chiefly in Jeremiah 26–45 (Section 2) but also interspersed among the poetic materials of Section 1. Many of these narratives seem to represent the memoirs of Baruch,[4] Jeremiah's faithful disciple and secretary, to whom a special oracle is directed at the very end of this prose section (Jer. 45). Thus the symbol B stands for "Baruch's biography."

C.   *Contributions by the Compilers (Redactors).* Frequently the prose sections of the book of Jeremiah resemble the language and literary style of Deuteronomy and the Deuteronomistic History: for example, the Temple Sermon (Jer. 7:1–15) or the passage about Jeremiah's support of Josiah's covenant reform (11:1–6). Indeed, Jeremiah is portrayed as a prophetic preacher of the type highlighted in Deuteronomic tradition (Deut. 18:15–22; compare 2 Kings 17:13–18). Passages of this kind may well preserve the substance of Jeremiah's message, but they also show that the book in its present form has been compiled by redactors of the Deuteronomistic school. Hence the symbol C stands for "compilers."

....

DEFINITION: "REDACTION   CRITICISM"

Franz Rosenzweig, a distinguished philosopher of Judaism, once observed that the sign "R" (for "Redactor") must not be underrated in critical scholarship. The sign, he said, should be construed to mean *"Rabbenu"* (Hebrew: "our master"), for we are dependent on the redactor who has given us the scriptures in their final form.

In recent years more and more attention has focused on the final shaping or redaction of biblical books. This so-called "redaction criticism" is concerned with two things. First, it seeks to understand how various literary units function in the present arrangement of the biblical text. In this view, a biblical book is not thrown together haphazardly, but displays an overall structure or "architecture." Hence it is important to see the parts in relation to the whole. Second, redaction criticism wants to understand, if possible, the social situation in which the text was given final shape and to which it was addressed. In this view, older traditions were brought together and updated for the purpose of speaking to new situations in the life of the people Israel.

In the case of Jeremiah, it is not enough to inquire for the historical individual, whose message is found in poetic materials and echoed in prose sections. We must also inquire into the theological message of the final redaction of the book. We must read particular literary units (such as the "confessions" of Jeremiah) in their given literary context. Further, we must inquire into the social situation of the (Deuteronomistic) redaction of the Jeremiah tradition preserved in poetic materials and refracted in prose narratives.

Redaction criticism has helped us to understand that the purpose of the final level of tradition in Jeremiah (often assigned to the Deuteronomistic compilers) was to relate

---

[4]The Book of Baruch is in both the Roman Catholic canon and the Protestant Apocrypha (see Chart, pp. 4–5). It purports to have been composed by Jeremiah's disciple in 582 B.C.E., five years after the fall of Jerusalem to the Babylonians. The book was written much later, however, and seems to reflect the destruction of Jerusalem by the Romans in 70 C.E.

Jeremiah's preaching to a new situation, that of the exile from Jerusalem in the catastrophic event of 587 B.C.E. In this view, the book of Jeremiah in its redacted and final form was not addressed just to the political realities of the final days of the Southern Kingdom of Judah. It became a new form of proclamation: a "preaching to the exiles." Uprooted from their homeland, the people needed to hear the "word of Yahweh," spoken through a prophet and addressed to them in their new situation.[5]

THE BURNING OF THE PROPHET'S SCROLL

An interesting account in Baruch's Memoirs (Jer. 36:4) throws light on a major development in Jeremiah's preaching career: the shift from preaching orally (reflected in poetic oracles) to a written form of proclamation.[6] The story is placed in the fourth year of King Jehoiakim (605 B.C.E.), the son of Josiah whom the Egyptians had elevated to the throne after Josiah was killed at Megiddo (see pp. 346–347). The battle of Carchemish had changed the political picture, and the time was ripe for Jeremiah to restate his message. Earlier the prophet had spoken vaguely of a threat from the north; now he could identify the northern foe as Babylonia. He hoped the publication of his oracles, which up to that time had been preserved only in memory, would awaken the people to the seriousness of their situation and encourage them to amend their ways. With this practical purpose in mind, Jeremiah dictated the oracles he had spoken during the twenty-three years since his call. Baruch took down the dictation, writing with ink on a scroll (compare Jer. 45).

Since Jeremiah was barred from the Temple, Baruch went in his place to read the scroll before all the people who had assembled for a fast day. Jeremiah's warning that Yahweh would display wrath against Judah by sending the Babylonian invader must have sounded like high treason. Alarmed, the royal officials advised Jeremiah and Baruch to go into hiding while the scroll was brought to the attention of King Jehoiakim. The haughty king's reaction was typical. We see him sitting in his luxurious winter palace, toasting himself before a fire burning in the brazier. As each few columns of the scroll were read, the king would reach over with his famous penknife, slash off the portion of the manuscript that had been read, and contemptuously toss it into the fire. And so it went, despite the protest of some of the princes, until the whole scroll had been shredded and burned. But this was not the end of the matter. Safe from arrest by the king, Jeremiah began his literary work again. This time, we are told, he not only dictated the contents of the original scroll but also produced an enlarged edition, for "many similar words were added" (Jer. 36:32).

This story helps us to understand how the book of Jeremiah took shape. The nucleus of the book is the enlarged scroll, written in the first person (as one might expect if the oracles were dictated). These oracles are dominated by the practical purpose of

[5]See E. W. Nicholson, *Preaching to the Exiles* [415].
[6]For further discussion of this transition, see Brevard Childs, *Introduction* [42], pp. 345–47.

awakening the people to the meaning of the Babylonian threat. To be sure, the scroll contains numerous oracles from Jeremiah's early period, such as the oracles in Jeremiah 1:1–4:4 (see pp. 330–333) and possibly the account of Jeremiah's support of the Deuteronomic Reformation (Jer. 11). These prophecies were reworked, however, in light of events that were fresh in Jeremiah's mind.[7] In addition, Jeremiah included many other oracles of more recent origin. One can only speculate as to the contents of the original scroll that was burned.

Of course, the process of building the tradition did not end once the second scroll had been dictated. We can imagine that Jeremiah paused from time to time to dictate more oracles, expanding the scroll still further. Other oracles and narratives now found in Section 1 were added by Baruch and later prophetic disciples. Then, toward the end of Jeremiah's career, Baruch composed his biography of Jeremiah, using the third rather than the first person. Most of these narratives are contained in Section 2, though some are found toward the end of Section 1 (beginning with Jer. 19). Finally, the redactors, probably of the Deuteronomistic school, gave the Jeremiah traditions their final shape during the period of the Exile.

IN THE REIGN OF JEHOIAKIM

The reading of Jeremiah's scroll before Jehoiakim gives us a convenient point from which to consider, first, his message during the early part of Jehoiakim's reign, and second, his career after he was driven into hiding by the king. To start with, we will consider the experiences that were still fresh in the prophet's memory as he revised and expanded his prophecies in 605 B.C.E. (see Chronological Chart, p. 325).

A new phase of Jeremiah's career had begun in 609 B.C.E., when Josiah was killed during his attempt to halt the Egyptian army at Megiddo. Josiah's immediate successor to the throne was his son Jehoahaz (called Shallum in Jer. 22:10–12), who was removed from the scene by the Egyptians after only three months. In his place the Egyptians elevated to the throne another son of Josiah, changing his name from Eliakim to Jehoiakim (2 Kings 23:31–36). Jehoiakim (about 609–598 B.C.E.) was a puppet of Pharaoh Necho. His first act in office was to impose a heavy tax upon the people of Judah in order to raise tribute for Egypt (2 Kings 23:35).

In almost every respect Jehoiakim was a different man from his father, Josiah. If his father wanted to model his reign after David, Jehoiakim's ambition was to be another Solomon. Jeremiah draws a sharp contrast between the two rulers (Jer. 22:13–19). Jehoiakim was a typical tyrant—cruel, selfish, and indulgent. Like Solomon, he subjected his people to forced labor to build his magnificent palaces (Jer.

---

[7]For instance, the references to Egypt in Jer. 2:14–19 and 2:36–37 reflect the situation during about 609–605 B.C.E., when the Southern Kingdom of Judah was temporarily a vassal of Pharaoh Necho (see pp. 346–347).

22:13)—to him, being a king meant living in luxurious style (22:15). Heedless of the prophetic reminder that to "know" ("recognize," "be loyal to") Yahweh is to do justice, he recklessly oppressed his people and shed innocent blood (Jer. 22:16–17). Those who opposed him courted death, for he feared neither God nor man. He was the only Judean king, so far as known, who dared to execute a prophet of Yahweh (Jer. 26:20–23). During the brief interlude of Egyptian control over Palestine (about 609–605 B.C.E., from the death of Josiah to the battle of Carchemish) Jehoiakim expediently followed a pro-Egyptian policy in order to stay in power.

THE TEMPLE AS A DEN OF ROBBERS

Jeremiah stepped into the public arena at the beginning of Jehoiakim's reign. He had been on the sidelines for several years, perhaps because of his growing disillusionment with Josiah's reform. Now he was at last "full of the wrath of Yahweh, weary of holding it in" (Jer. 6:11). In the first year of Jehoiakim's reign (see Jer. 26:1), Jeremiah made a bold public appeal in the Temple—the very shrine that had become the center of religious zeal as a result of the Deuteronomic Reformation. His Temple sermon is given to us in two versions. The first, found in Jeremiah's scroll (Jer. 7), gives a full account of what he said on the occasion. The second, found in Baruch's Memoirs (Jer. 26), briefly summarizes Jeremiah's message but concentrates on audience response. One must read both chapters to get the complete picture.

In addition to playing the tyrant, Jehoiakim revived the paganism that his father had tried to eliminate. Evidently the people, disillusioned with the Deuteronomic Reformation, were turning enthusiastically to their former ways. Every member of the family, we are told, had a part in making cakes for Ishtar, Queen of Heaven—the mother-goddess worshiped in Assyria and Babylonia (Jer. 7:18). The barbarous rite of child sacrifice was practiced in the Valley of Hinnom (Topheth), south of the city, and pagan abominations (idols) were set up in the Temple (Jer. 7:30–31; 19:5).[8] To make matters worse, social abominations were perpetrated in the very shadow of the Temple. The people supposed they could get away with these crimes as long as they went through the formalities of worship (Jer. 7:8–10).

All these things rankled Jeremiah's heart as he stood in the Temple court and watched the people entering to worship. He begins his message with a sharp summons: "Amend your ways and your doings!" Notice that, true to the Mosaic tradition, Jeremiah uses the conditional "If" (Jer. 7:5–7) and appeals to covenant law, the Decalogue (7:8–10). He challenges one of the premises of Davidic covenant theology: the Temple as the place of Yahweh's presence. There is no point in chanting glib words about the Temple being a sanctuary of refuge (compare Ps. 46) when it has become a den harboring thieves (see Mark 11:17). After all, what happened to Shiloh, the central sanctuary

---

[8]The same picture is presented in Ezek. 16:20–21; 20:26, 31; 23:29.

of the old Tribal Confederacy (see pp. 185–186)? The Temple is no bulwark of security, no guarantee that "God is with us" to see that no harm would come. Indeed, threatens the prophet, the Temple will fall and Judah will go into exile along with Israel (the Northern Kingdom). In another oracle, Jeremiah repudiates the practice of sacrifice. Yahweh, he says, did not command the people to offer sacrifices on the day Israel came out of Egypt, but rather asked for a loyal and obedient heart so that the covenant promise might be fulfilled: "I will be your God and you shall be my people" (Jer. 7:21–23).

According to Baruch's memoir (Jer. 26), Jeremiah's sermon created an uproar. The people must have been shocked by his challenge of royal covenant theology, with its divine guarantee of support for the Davidic king and its assurance of Yahweh's presence in the Jerusalem Temple. Like some of his prophetic predecessors, Jeremiah took his stand upon the covenant tradition rooted in the Exodus and the experiences of the wilderness. Had not some elders appealed to the precedent of Micah, who a century before had prophesied the fall of Jerusalem and the Temple, Jeremiah would have lost his life like the hapless prophet Uriah. Even more important was the support of Ahikam, son of Shaphan, a prince of great political influence (Jer. 26:24). More than once, a member of the family of Shaphan stood on Jeremiah's side in a time of need.

The comparison with Micah was apt, for Jeremiah also prophesied doom (see Jer. 28:8–9). The first effect of Yahweh's word—that is, the divine intention—was "to pluck up and to break down, to destroy and to overthrow" (1:10). To be sure, judgment was not the last word, for Yahweh's intention was also "to build and to plant." But the rebuilding would come only after the destruction. "Is not my word like fire, says Yahweh, and like a hammer that breaks the rock in pieces?" (Jer. 23:29).

THE BALM OF GILEAD

Jeremiah's word of doom seemed incredible both to the king and the people. They believed that reliance on Egypt was only a temporary device to protect them from the storm coming out of the north (see Jer. 2:16, 18, 36–37). Not surprisingly, Jeremiah's greatest adversaries were the popular prophets who promised a shortcut to divine restoration without going through the valley of judgment. Like spiritual quacks, these prophets cried "peace, peace" when there was no peace and tried to "heal the wound of the people lightly" by remedies that did not touch the root of the trouble (Jer. 6:13–15; compare 5:12–13, 30–31; 14:13–16; 23:9–40). Jeremiah accused them of lacking the proper credentials to speak, for they had not stood in "the Council of Yahweh" as had great prophets like Micaiah and Isaiah (see pp. 292–293). Moreover, they filled the people with vain hopes, deceiving their hearers with lies and stealing Yahweh's words from one another. Between them and the true circle of Yahweh's prophets there was no more similarity than between straw and wheat (Jer. 23:28). Yahweh's word brought not peace, but a sword—the sword that cuts like a surgeon's knife to the seat of a malignant cancer and makes possible a deep inward healing. To Jeremiah's poignant question, "Is there no balm in Gilead?" (Jer. 8:22)—a region famous for its healing ointments—came the answer that Yahweh's judgment was the beginning of restoration to health.

Jeremiah agonized over the incurable sickness of a people with "a stubborn and rebellious heart" (Jer. 5:23). Yahweh's discipline had failed. The word of the prophets had fallen on deaf ears; indeed, it had become an object of scorn (Jer. 6:10). With searching insight anticipated by Hosea, Jeremiah perceived that the problem lay *within*—in the heart. To be sure, Israel's "sickness unto death" showed itself outwardly in many ways. The people were putting their trust in institutions: the Ark (Jer. 3:16); the rite of circumcision (4:4); the Torah (8:8); sacrifice (7:21–26); the Temple itself (7:4). Moreover, the social bond of the covenant community was fractured. Every brother was another deceitful Jacob (Jer. 9:4–6). No one could be trusted; oppression was heaped up like a pyramid. The people were like "well-fed stallions," each neighing for his neighbor's wife (Jer. 5:8) and showing no concern for the defenseless victims of society (5:28). Blind nationalism, excited by deceitful prophets, was rampant. Idolatry was practiced not only in the Temple but also on every high hill and under every green tree.

These were only the outward symptoms of a problem rooted in the heart—the seat of human loyalties and devotion. Anticipating modern psychology, Jeremiah pointed out that the heart can cover up and justify ("rationalize") its real motives:

> The heart is devious above all else;
>> it is perverse—
>> who can understand it?
>>
>> —JEREMIAH 17:9 (NRSV)

Yet there is no hiding from the God who "probes the heart" in order to repay people with "the fruit of their deeds" (Jer. 17:10). The God whom Israel worships is not a god who is "at hand" (a value created by human need or a wishful fancy) but the God who is "far off," transcendent, and therefore the inescapable Judge of human motives and actions (Jer. 23:23–24; see the exquisite treatment of this theme in Ps. 139). In the awful exposure of divine scrutiny, the people's real condition comes to light. Yahweh's "eyes" look for truth (Jer. 5:3), for the inner integrity based on a true relationship to God and neighbors in the covenant. But instead, Yahweh finds an inner deceit evident throughout Israel's long history in Canaan. Shifting the figure of speech, Jeremiah stresses the deep-seated and elusive nature of the problem. If one were to run through the streets of Jerusalem seeking a single just individual, such a person could not be found (Jer. 5:1–3). Indeed, things are approaching a state of chaos; for every person recklessly follows a self-determined course, like a horse wildly plunging into battle (Jer. 8:6). Although the birds follow their homing instincts, Israel has no instinct for its covenant relationship (Jer. 8:7). Yahweh has set a bound for the restless waves of the sea, but

Israel's rebellion goes beyond all bounds (Jer. 5:20–29). Indeed, Israel's sin is deeply engraved upon the heart as though with a pen of iron or a diamond point (Jer. 17:1–4). Sin has become so "natural" that the people do not even know how to blush for it (Jer. 8:12).

Catharsis (to use the language of psychology) had to come through crisis and catastrophe that would shock the people to new awareness. In the past, Jeremiah says, Yahweh had shown forbearance. "Rising up early," to use the poetic expression for divine persistence, Yahweh had sent "his servants, the prophets." Moreover, Yahweh had tried the "shock treatment" of calamity with the purpose of bringing the people to their senses, but in vain. In Jeremiah's view, the people's hardness of heart was a puzzle to God. Ordinarily the person who falls gets up again, or the person who turns away comes back (Jer. 8:4–7). Not so in Israel's case, however. Despite all warnings and chastening experiences the people had *refused* to "return" (repent). At last Yahweh's patience was exhausted. "Weary of relenting" (Jer. 15:6), Yahweh had resolved to pour out divine wrath upon the people, destroying their idols and shaking the foundations of their existence.

Jeremiah perceived God at work in human history, dealing with the recalcitrant stuff of human nature. This conviction is vividly conveyed in the oracle Jeremiah received in the potter's house (Jer. 18)—an oracle that might have formed the pungent climax of Jeremiah's scroll dictated to Baruch, and, in any case, has a strategic position in the redaction of the materials.[9] Seeing a potter seated in his pit, his feet spinning the wheel and his hands deftly molding the clay, Jeremiah was reminded that Israel was like clay in the divine potter's hand. If the vessel was spoiled, owing to some imperfection or unmalleability of the material, it could be reworked into another vessel as the potter saw fit. And so it was with Israel. If a nation refused to be molded by the divine design, but instead insisted on following its own devices, then Yahweh would "repent" of the good planned for them and visit the nation with destruction.

Note that the threatened catastrophe results from human recalcitrance, not from the arbitrary, capricious wrath of the potter. Again and again the prophet reminds the people that the imminent tragedy will be the consequence of their own actions:

> Your ways and your doings
>   have brought this upon you.
> This is your doom; how bitter it is!
>   It has reached your very heart.
>   —JEREMIAH 4:18 (NRSV)

In one sense, the "wrath of God" is not so much God's intervention to punish as it is *withdrawal* from a rebellious people, leaving them to suffer the destructive consequences of their own actions and attitudes. God's sovereignty in human affairs means

---

[9]See Kathleen M. O'Connor, *The Confessions of Jeremiah* [438], chap. 8.

that people cannot live with impunity; but the punishment is only "the fruit of their devices" (Jer. 6:19). Thus in the very passage where Jeremiah proclaims the sovereignty of the potter over the clay, his word is accompanied by an urgent plea that the people amend their ways while there is still time. Divine sovereignty does not erase human responsibility.

DEFINITION: "REPENT"

A key word in Jeremiah's theological vocabulary is the Hebrew verb *shûb* ("turn"), found for instance in Jeremiah 8:4–5.

The people's "turning" can have two meanings that are, figuratively speaking, opposite sides of the same coin. One is a "turning away" from loyalty to the God of the covenant to some other loyalty or "God-story" (apostasy). This negative meaning is suggested in the NRSV translation of Jeremiah 8:5: "Why then has this people turned away in perpetual backsliding?"

The same passage suggests a second meaning: "They have held fast to deceit, they have refused to *return*" (Jer. 8:5; italics added). In a positive sense this is a "turning around" or "turning to" the covenant relationship with Yahweh. The return to Yahweh is also, therefore, "repentance"—a reorientation and change of lifestyle.

In the parable of the potter and the clay (Jer. 18) another verb (Hebrew: *niḥam*) is used for God's "repentance." In this case the idea is that God is not bound inflexibly to an announced course of action. If the people "turn from evil" or "repent" (Hebrew: *shûb*; see Jer. 18:8,11b) God will respond freely: Indeed, God will have a "change of mind" or will "relent" from bringing judgment upon them. Thus God's impending judgment is not to be identified with the inexorable Fate of Greek tragedies.

THE FOE FROM THE NORTH

During Jehoiakim's reign, Jeremiah saw the judgment of God taking political shape in international developments. At the time of his call, when he had a vision of a boiling cauldron pouring out evil upon Palestine, he spoke of an undefined foe from the north (Jer. 1:13–14). With the battle of Carchemish in 605 B.C.E., however, the northern foe came clearly into focus: The cauldron was boiling over from the land of Babylonia.

Scattered through Jeremiah 1–18 are a number of prophetic oracles occasioned by the advance of Babylonia, most from later in Jehoiakim's reign, after the battle of Carchemish. The cycle in Jeremiah 4 is an excellent example of the poems on "the foe from the north": As expressions of intense feeling, these lyrics are perhaps unsurpassed in the Old Testament. With urgent voice Jeremiah sounds the battle alarm, crying to the people to flee to the fortified cities for safety (Jer. 4:5–8). He sees the army approaching in chariots like the whirlwind and cries out to Jerusalem to repent while there is still time (Jer. 5:13–18). His heart beats wildly as he hears the enemy trumpet and sees disaster suddenly overwhelm the land (Jer. 5:19–22). He hears Jerusalem's death cry, like the piercing shriek of a woman in travail (Jer. 4:29–31); and like Jesus later weeps over the fate of Jerusalem (see 8:18–9:3). No other Old Testament prophet was more personally identified with the people or felt more keenly the "giant agony" of their tragedy.

Jeremiah 4 includes a powerful lyric portrayal of a scene of chaos. In a terrifying vision, Jeremiah sees the earth returning to the chaos that prevailed before Creation, the "waste and void" of Genesis 1:2:[10]

> I looked upon the earth, and lo, a chaotic waste,
>> and unto the heavens, and their light was gone.
> I looked on the mountains, and lo, they were quaking,
>> and all the hills were trembling.
> I looked, and lo, there was no human being,
>> and all the birds of the sky had vanished.
> I looked, and lo, the orchard land was wilderness,
>> before Yahweh, before his burning wrath.
>> —JEREMIAH 4:23–26

To Jeremiah, the catastrophe was of cosmic proportions, like the deluge of Noah's time that threatened to convert the world into pre-creation chaos. His deep sense of universal disorder is echoed in modern literature that speaks of the "wasteland," the threat of "nonbeing," "The Day After," the void.

SIGNS OF DOOM

Jeremiah's words of impending doom were accompanied by signs. One of the most enigmatic is described in Jeremiah 13:1–11, which tells how Jeremiah bought a linen waistcloth and wore it "to the Euphrates,"[11] where he hid it in a cleft of a rock. Later, when he found that the cloth was spoiled and good for nothing, he was told that Yahweh would spoil the pride of the people, even though they had clung to their God as closely as a garment. On another occasion, Jeremiah was commanded to buy a clay flask and to break it publicly in the Valley of Hinnom, the place where human sacrifice was practiced. This dramatically demonstrated that Jerusalem would be broken into fragments, with such great destruction that the accursed valley would have to be used for a burial place (Jer. 19). These signs or "enacted words" had an ominous significance, for Jeremiah portrayed *what Yahweh was about to do*. Understandably, when Jeremiah later

---

[10]The expression "waste and void" in Jeremiah 4:23 (Hebrew: *tohu wa-bohu*) is exactly the same as in the Priestly creation story (Gen. 1:2). See the interpretation of Jeremiah's poem on the return of chaos by a Japanese theologian, Kosuke Koyama, *Mount Fuji and Mount Sinai* (Maryknoll, N.Y.: Orbis Books, 1985), chaps. 3 and 5.

[11]It is difficult to understand this sign if it involves trips to the Euphrates (700 miles round trip). Probably Jeremiah went to Parah (modern 'Ain Farah), a short journey northeast from his home town of Anathoth. In Hebrew "to the Euphrates" and "to Parah" are spelled the same. See the commentary by John Bright [426], p. 96.

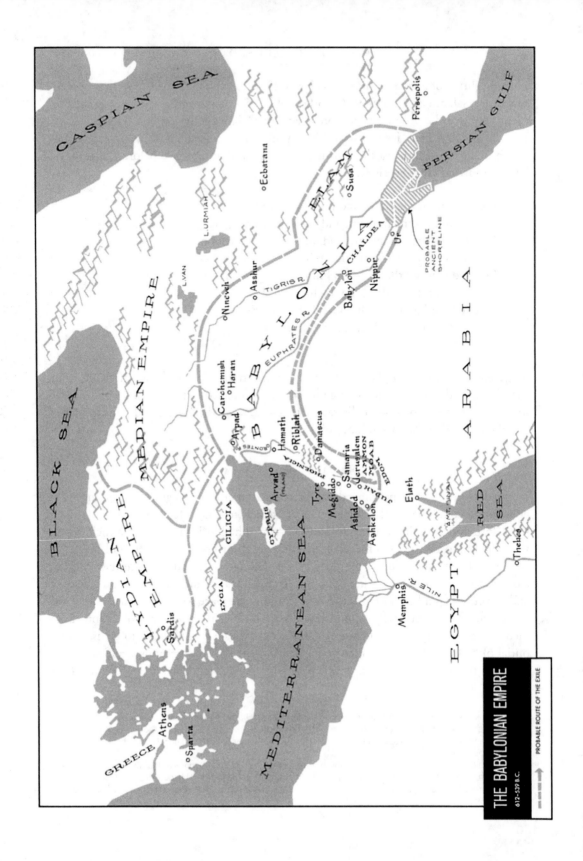

THE BABYLONIAN EMPIRE

612–539 B.C.

▷ ▷ ▷ ▷ ▷ PROBABLE ROUTE OF THE EXILE

repeated his message of doom against the Temple itself, Pashhur, the priest, seized him, flogged him, and put him in stocks for the night (Jer. 20:1–6).

Then came the battle of Carchemish, in which Egypt was decisively defeated and from which Babylonia emerged as the dominant world power.[12] From this fateful period comes the important prophecy of Jeremiah 25:1–14. In its present form, it is dated in the fourth year of Jehoiakim (605 B.C.E.), the same year the scroll was burned. Certain problems make it difficult to ascribe this passage to Jeremiah just as it stands, and the much shorter version in the Greek Septuagint might have a greater claim to authenticity. The Greek version makes no reference to Nebuchadrezzar or Babylonia, and concludes with the words: "I will bring upon that land [Judah] all the words that I have uttered against it, everything written in this book, which Jeremiah prophesied against all the nations" (Jer. 25:13). Moreover, the Greek version has the oracles against the foreign nations right after this sentence, where they appropriately belong, rather than after Baruch's Memoirs (Jer. 26–45) as in the Hebrew Bible.

Aside from these differences between the Hebrew and Greek texts, the story rings true to Jeremiah's message. In the shorter version, this story might have concluded the scroll that Jeremiah dictated to Baruch. Astonished at the people's refusal to heed the warnings of his twenty-three year ministry, the prophet announced that Yahweh would send "a family from the north" (Septuagint) to devastate the whole region and reduce the Southern Kingdom of Judah to utter ruin. The people would serve the conqueror for seventy years—a round number (the proverbial span of a human life) not intended to be taken literally. During this long period, the end of which would be seen by no person then living, the ordinary affairs of life would be interrupted. Yahweh would banish "the voice of mirth and the voice of gladness, the voice of the bridegroom and the bride, the grinding of the millstones and the light of the lamp" (Jer. 25:10).

Evidently this dire prophecy of Babylonian invasion, following closely in the wake of Babylonia's victory at Carchemish, infuriated Jehoiakim (Jer. 36:29). Certainly the king's feelings were not soothed by the announcement that he—an Egyptian vassal—would die a shameful death (Jer. 36:30–31) or that, as in another of Jeremiah's oracles, he would have "the burial of an ass" (22:18–19). This was more than a king could take.

JEREMIAH'S CONFESSIONS

We have turned in a circle back to where we began: the burning of Jeremiah's scroll by Jehoiakim. The sequence of events is:

609 B.C.E.   Death of Josiah at Megiddo
Jeremiah's Temple Sermon

---

[12]Probably Jeremiah's oracle against Egypt (Jer. 46:1–12) was delivered shortly after the battle of Carchemish.

605 B.C.E.   The Battle of Carchemish
              The burning of Jeremiah's scroll

Looking back over Jeremiah's ministry during these years, we have considered the content of his enlarged scroll of prophecy. Now we move ahead from the year 605 B.C.E. to the last decades of his career.

Hunted as a public enemy and traitor to the king, Jeremiah might have gone into seclusion for some time. From this "period of silence" might come a remarkable series of lyrics, usually called "The Confessions of Jeremiah." These intimate outpourings of the prophet's restless heart, similar in type to the *Confessions* of Augustine, actually come from several occasions in Jeremiah's career. Perhaps the prophet dictated them to Baruch while he was a fugitive from Jehoiakim's police. In any event, it is appropriate for us to consider them at this point.

These personal outcries are without parallel in the writings of early Israelite prophets or, for that matter, in other religious literature of antiquity. Earlier prophets were reticent about their personal conflicts. Even Hosea, who spoke out of the personal suffering of a broken marriage, receded behind the message he was called to proclaim. Amos, who expostulated with God about the heavy judgment that was about to fall upon Israel (Amos 7:1–6), did not explicitly identify with the sufferings of the people. With Jeremiah it is different. Not only does he proclaim "the word of Yahweh" but, like the people to whom it is addressed, he struggles against it. He complains about his lot, cries out for vindication, and even hurls defiance at God. He undergoes the trials of a faith shadowed by doubt, rebellion, self-pity, and despair. Indeed, he has "the courage to doubt."[13]

Applying the term "confessions" to these personal prayers can be misleading. The term could suggest a purely psychological view: the private confessions of a person's interior life with an honest-to-God frankness. Jeremiah's confessions, however, are expostulations with God that arise out of, and are essentially related to, his prophetic office. These prayers have been influenced by the genre of the "individual lament" found in the book of Psalms (see Chapter 16), in which a suppliant cries out of distress, expresses confidence in God, and pleads for vindication. Using language familiar in temple worship, Jeremiah prays to Yahweh out of the depths of the distress he experienced in the exercise of his prophetic role.

A MAN OF STRIFE AND CONTENTION

Dispersed through Jeremiah 11–20 are the following laments:

1. 11:18–12:6   "Like a gentle lamb led to the slaughter"
2. 15:10–21   "Will you be to me like a deceitful brook?"

---

[13]See Robert Davidson, *The Courage to Doubt* [152], chap. 7.

Insert 11-1 (Top) Woman at Window Ivory. This handsome ivory carving of the popular "woman at window" motif from Nimrud dates from the ninth or eighth century B.C.E. and is only 4" tall.

Insert 11-2 (Lower left) Nimrud Ivory. An eighth-century ivory griffin from Nimrud. The hybrid creature has a lion's body and the wings and beak of an eagle.

Insert 11-3 (Lower right) Ivory Cherub. A delicately carved, 5" tall ivory cherub dating from the ninth or eighth century B.C.E., probably from north Syria.

Insert 12-1   The Sun God, Shamash enthroned in his shrine *(right)* above the heavenly ocean represented by the wavy lines and four stars at the base of the picture. Above his head are the emblems of astral deities: the crescent (Sin), sun disc (Shamash), and eight-pointed star (Ishtar). The Babylonian king Nabuapaliddin *(middle figure in the trio, left)*, who endowed the sun temple at Sippar in the ninth century B.C.E. is escorted before an altar on which is a large sun disc. The altar is supported by ropes held by attendant deities on the roof. Astral motifs were characteristic of ancient Assyrian and Babylonian religion.

3. 17:14–18   "Heal me, O Yahweh!"
4. 18:18–23   "They have dug a pit for my life"
5. 20:7–13   "A burning fire shut up in my bones"
6. 20:14–18   "Cursed be the day on which I was born"

A key to understanding these poignant laments is given in the account of the prophet's call (Jer. 1:1–10), a passage that reverberates with overtones of the story of Moses' call (Exod. 3). The first literary unit (Jer. 1:4–8) discloses the tension between Jeremiah, the man, and his prophetic office. Shy and sensitive by nature, Jeremiah recoiled from the tremendous task to which he was predestined even before birth: to be "a prophet to the nations." The second literary unit (Jer. 1:9–10) also places Jeremiah squarely in the tradition of "the prophet like Moses," to whom it is said, "I [Yahweh] will put my words in his mouth" (Deut. 18:18; compare Jer. 1:9). The ensuing visions and their interpretation (Jer. 1:11–19) indicate that Jeremiah was to proclaim an ominous message—one certain to arouse people's hostility. He was to set himself *against* everyone, because God's judgment was against the whole land of Judah—its kings, princes, priests, and people. "They will fight against you," the prophet was warned. Yet he was to find a deeper resource than human approval: "They shall not prevail against you, for I am with you, says Yahweh, to deliver you" (Jer. 1:19, see 1:8).

Yahweh's commission went against Jeremiah's natural inclinations. He seemed to need the affection and acceptance of his family and friends, and probably would have been quite content to live peacefully on his ancestral estate in Anathoth. But his lot was to be that of a rejected man, "a man of strife and contention to the whole land" (Jer. 15:10), constantly surrounded by enemies, and "sitting alone" because "Yahweh's hand was laid upon him." Even marriage and children were denied him for, according to a dire passage in 16:1–13, Yahweh forbade him to take a wife and to have children, or even to take part in social gatherings. The prophet's isolation was to be a sign of the impending catastrophe that would disrupt family ties and silence the voice of mirth. Throughout his career he was torn on the one hand by his natural longing for peace and companionship, and on the other by the prophetic task that catapulted him into the arena of conflict. It is the Confessions, above all, that bear witness to the sufferings involved in being Yahweh's prophet, and to the prophet's passionate plea for vindication—a plea not for personal triumph but for the triumph of the cause that the prophet represents.

JEREMIAH'S VINDICATION

The first confession seems to hark back to Jeremiah's early career, possibly to the time of the Deuteronomic Reformation. It might reflect the fierce animosity of the people of Jeremiah's home town, Anathoth, perhaps aroused by his advocacy of a reform program that threatened to put local priests out of their jobs (see p. 344). The men of Anathoth plotted against his life, warning him not to prophesy in Yahweh's name lest he die by their hand (Jer. 11:21). Even members of Jeremiah's immediate family joined in the conspiracy (Jer. 12:6). This treachery evoked from the prophet a prayer for vengeance upon his persecutors and a passionate confession of his own innocence and integrity. To him it seemed inconceivable that Yahweh, who knows people's motives and judges their actions, would allow the wicked to prosper and even to get away with murder! Just as Habakkuk received an answer to his complaint (see above, pp. 347–349), so Yahweh responded to Jeremiah's lament. Vindication would come in Yahweh's good time, but in the meantime Jeremiah should realize that far greater ordeals lay ahead:

> If you race with the foot-runners and they exhaust you,
> How then can you compete with horses?
> If you are secure only in a tranquil land,
> How will you fare in the jungle of the Jordan?
> —JEREMIAH 12:5 (JPSV)

During the reign of Jehoiakim, plots against Jeremiah mounted in fury. After his Temple sermon he narrowly escaped with his life, and his later message in the Temple court prompted Pashhur to put him in jail for the night. Finally, Jeremiah was forced to hide from Jehoiakim's wrath. The fourth confession specifically refers to plots against his life occasioned by his alleged subversive activity against all the religious leaders—priests, prophets, and sages (Jer. 18:18). Incensed that they should treat him thus when he had interceded on their behalf before Yahweh, Jeremiah uttered a merciless prayer that Yahweh not forgive them and that they be destroyed in divine anger.

These are the fierce outbursts of a deeply wounded heart. In another confession (Jer. 15:10–21), Jeremiah vehemently protests his destiny, like Hamlet lamenting that the times were out of joint and that he was born to set them right. Jeremiah's faith had brought him to the very brink of despair, to serious doubt about Yahweh's righteous government of the world. He cries out that Yahweh has deceived him, like a deceitful Palestinian brook (Hebrew: *wadi*) that overflows with water during the heavy spring rains and then quickly dries up (Jer. 15:18). He accuses Yahweh of having overpowered him, making him a laughingstock all day long and filling him with an inward fire that would not allow him to be silent (Jer. 20:7–9). Finally, in the deepest midnight of his soul, he curses the day of his birth (Jer. 20:14–18) and castigates his mother for having borne him as "a man of strife and contention to the whole land" (Jer. 15:10).

We must not be too critical of the passionate queries and protests that Jeremiah hurled at God. His prayers—like so many human utterances—express the self-pity that often arises when a person's faith is put to the severest test. The question, "Why does this happen to *me?*" suggests that he had been badly treated after all the sacrifices he made for Yahweh's sake. He had not sat in the company of merrymakers, or committed an injustice in borrowing or lending. He was innocent, "like a gentle lamb led to the slaughter." Self-pity, moreover, is only the other side of self-righteousness. Hence Jeremiah pleads his case to the avenging God, hoping that his own righteousness would be vindicated and that the unrighteousness of his persecutors would be punished (Jer. 11:20; 12:1–3; 17:17–18; 18:19–23; 20:11–12).

Like the first, the second confession contains Yahweh's answer to Jeremiah's complaint. Yahweh rebukes the prophet for his self-centered attitude—the very attitude he had criticized in other people! The prophet who summoned the people to repent ("return" to Yahweh) stands in need of inward purification himself:

> At that Yahweh answered me as follows:
> "If you repent, I'll restore you
> to serve me once more.
> If you mix not the cheap and the precious,
> as my mouth you shall be.
> Let *them* come over to you;
> Don't *you* go over to them.
> Then before this people I'll make you
> An impregnable wall of bronze.
> Attack you they will—
> Overcome you they can't;
> For with you am I
> to help you and save you—Yahweh's word.
> From the grasp of the wicked I'll snatch you,
> From the clutch of the ruthless release you."
> —JEREMIAH 15:19–21[14]

After these first two confessions, no other answers come from Yahweh. The third confession ends with a plea for divine vengeance upon Jeremiah's persecutors; the fourth concludes by asking God not to forgive the enemies; and the fifth, after a similar prayer for vindication, seems to end with a song of thanksgiving for deliverance (Jer. 20:13). The final poem, if this is included in the sequence, ends dismally with Jeremiah, like Job, cursing the day of his birth. What are we to make of these confessions as a whole?

One way to deal with this question is to regard the confessions as a collection of prophetic prayers that once circulated independently. One interpreter points out that when these laments are read in succession, they seem to trace a *via dolorosa*—"a road that leads step by step into ever greater despair" and "threatens to end in some kind of metaphysical abyss."[15] Jeremiah's cross, so to speak, is eclipsed with darkness—the

---

[14]Translation by John Bright, *Jeremiah* [426], p. 107.
[15]Gerhard von Rad, *Theology*, II [163], 204. See the entire discussion of the Confessions, pp. 201–206.

unanswered question of his own prophetic suffering and the suffering of the people with whom he is identified.

Another interpretation swings to the opposite pole: "As a collection of poems, the confessions move toward greater praise of Yahweh and certainty about the triumph of the prophetic word."[16] This view is especially appealing when the confessions are read in the context given by the redactors of the Jeremiah traditions. During his career Jeremiah often must have wondered whether he really was a true prophet of Yahweh—especially when the popular prophets had the ear of the people. But the redactors who compiled the Jeremiah traditions during the period of the Exile knew that Jeremiah's word of doom against Jerusalem had been fulfilled, and hence viewed the confessions as testimony to the vindication of Yahweh's word and of Yahweh's prophet (compare 2 Chron. 36:20–21).

At whatever level of tradition the Confessions functioned, they brought Jeremiah's suffering into the center of the prophetic message. These poems were not private prayers or soliloquies. Rather, they served as a public witness to the prophet's commission as one who, in a special way, was called to walk through "the valley of deep darkness" (Ps. 23:4) with the divine assurance "I am with you" and the confidence that vindication lay ahead. Indeed, Yahweh was personally involved in the suffering of the people as typified by Jeremiah's anguished experience. A distinguished Jewish philosopher has said that "the fundamental experience of the prophets is a fellowship with the feelings of God, a sympathy with the divine pathos."[17] In a profound sense Jeremiah's suffering was a participation in God's suffering, so much so that God's concern became his concern and God's pathos, whether anger or love, flowed through his whole life and thought.

IN THE REIGN OF ZEDEKIAH

Jehoiakim could afford to display contempt for Jeremiah's scroll: There seemed to be no immediate threat to the security of his throne. The Babylonian king, Nabopolassar, had died shortly after the battle of Carchemish. Nebuchadrezzar, the crown prince who had led the army to victory, had returned to Babylon to assume the throne. About 601 B.C.E. his army swept through Palestine to the border of Egypt—an invasion that evoked some of Jeremiah's poems on the foe from the north. In the battle against Egypt, heavy casualties were suffered by both sides, and Nebuchadrezzar's crippled army had to return to Babylonia. The defeat of Babylonia and the weakness of Egypt

---

[16]Kathleen O'Connor, *The Confessions* [438], chap. 9, part ii. This view requires excluding the final poem, Jeremiah's curse of his birth, from the original collection.

[17]Abraham J. Heschel, *The Prophets* [352], p. 26. The theme of divine pathos is treated at various points in this important book.

This clay cuneiform tablet (only 3.25 inches by 2.5 inches), part of the Babylonian Chronicles, recounts events germane to Judah's history from 605–597 B.C.E., including Babylon's defeat of the Egyptians at Carchemish (605 B.C.E.) and Nebuchadrezzar's attack against Jerusalem in 597 B.C.E.

gave Jehoiakim the opportunity he had been waiting for. In 600 B.C.E. he made a reckless bid for independence by withholding tribute to Babylonia. This rebellion was an invitation to Nebuchadrezzar to strike (2 Kings 24:1–7; see Chronological Chart 8, p. 372).[18]

THE GOOD AND BAD FIGS

Because Nebuchadrezzar was unable to attend to Judah immediately, he incited raiders from neighboring peoples to devastate the land. During these disturbances Jehoiakim died, leaving his eighteen-year-old son, Jehoiachin, to pay the penalty for his father's political folly.[19] The Deuteronomistic historians, in typical fashion, charge Jehoiachin with doing evil as his father had done, despite the fact that his short reign hardly gave him a chance to do much of anything. In 598–597 B.C.E., Nebuchadrezzar mobilized his army for a full-scale invasion of Judah. Jehoiachin, after only three months on the

[18]For a discussion of historical developments during the last days of the Southern Kingdom of Judah, see David Noel Freedman, "The Babylonian Chronicle," *Biblical Archaeologist,* XIX (1956), 50–60. Reprinted in *The Biblical Archaeologist Reader,* I [119], 113–27.

[19]Jehoiachin is otherwise referred to as Jeconiah or Coniah. See Jeremiah's oracle in Jer. 22:24–28.

throne, was forced to capitulate. The Temple and royal treasuries were emptied, and the young king and his queen mother were taken prisoners to Babylonia. Into exile with the king went the leading figures of Judah, including, as we will see, a prophet named Ezekiel. Thus began the first chapter in the Babylonian Exile (2 Kings 24:10–17).

Nebuchadrezzar placed Josiah's youngest son, Mattaniah, on the throne of the Southern Kingdom of Judah, changing his name to Zedekiah. Under this king—the last member of the Davidic dynasty to rule in Judah—Jeremiah spent the rest of his prophetic career in Jerusalem. A good deal of the material in Jeremiah 1–25 (especially Jer. 21–24) reflects Zedekiah's reign (about 597–587 B.C.E.), as does most of the material in Baruch's Memoirs (Jer. 26–45).

In contrast to the despotic Jehoiakim, Zedekiah was mild and benevolent. He was a weak and vacillating ruler, however, easily swayed by the advice of those around him. This situation gave the princes a chance to control public policy in their own selfish in-

Chronological Chart 8

B.C.E.	Egypt	Palestine	Mesopotamia
		Judah	Babylonia
600		THE BABYLONIAN EMPIRE	
		Jehoiachin (Jeconiah), 3 mos., 598–597	Nebuchadrezzar, 605/4–562
		First Deportation to Babylonia, 597	
	Apries (Hophra), 589–570	Zedekiah (Mattaniah), 597–587	
		FALL OF JERUSALEM	
		SECOND DEPORTATION, 587	
		BABYLONIAN EXILE	
		Ezekiel, c. 593–573	
			Nabonidus, 556–539
			(his son: Belshazzar)
			RISE OF PERSIA
			Cyrus II, 550–530
			Defeat of Media, c. 550
			Invasion of Lydia, c. 546
		(*Second Isaiah*, c. 540)	Conquest of Babylon, c. 539
		Edict of Cyrus, 538	FALL OF BABYLON, 539
		THE EMPIRE OF PERSIA	
		THE RESTORATION	
		JUDAH	
	Conquest by Persia, 525	Return of exiles	Cambyses, 530–522
		Rebuilding of Temple, 520–515	Darius I, 522–486
		(*Haggai*)	
500		(*Zechariah*)	

terests. But it also presented Jeremiah with a golden opportunity. Now that the tyrant was dead and a more benevolent regime had been inaugurated, the prophet could appear in public with new prestige, for his oracles had been confirmed by history. On several occasions, Zedekiah sought the prophet's counsel behind closed doors, and evidently would have liked to follow it had he been more courageous. One might sympathize with Zedekiah and wish that he had appeared in a quieter period of Judah's history. Notice that Jeremiah's oracles against the royal house (Jer. 22:1–23:6) did not include Zedekiah. Perhaps, by a play on words, Jeremiah found in the name Zedekiah (Hebrew: "Yahweh is my righteousness") the suggestion that the Messianic king of the future would have a similar royal name: "Yahweh is our righteousness" (Jer. 33:16).[20]

Bereft of its first citizens, Judah was only a shadow of its former self. The cream of the leadership—the nobility, the artisans, the highest military ranks—had been shipped off to Babylonia. The nation was crippled—at the very time when the need for resourceful leadership and stable traditions was greatest. Into this vacuum moved a new nobility, ill-equipped for the heavy responsibilities of the hour and even less capable of perceiving the religious meaning of the crisis. Governed by a short-sighted nationalism and swayed by the emotional appeal of prophetic demagogues, these new leaders hastened the downfall of the nation (compare Ezekiel 11).

Jeremiah saw no hope in such people. In a vision he saw two baskets of figs placed before the Temple (Jer. 24). One basket, containing good figs, ripe and freshly picked, represented the exiles whom Nebuchadrezzar had carried away. According to Jeremiah, the future lay with them, for they would be restored to the land as Yahweh's covenant people. By contrast, the other basket, containing figs so bad they could not be eaten, represented Zedekiah, his nobles, and the remnant of people left in the land. Yahweh, said the prophet, would drive them out and make them a horror to all the kingdoms of the earth. Later, Jeremiah sent a letter to the Babylonian exiles (Jer. 29) advising them to settle down, build houses, raise families, and even pray for the hostile regime under which they were living:

> Seek the welfare of the city to which I have exiled you, and pray to
> Yahweh on its behalf, for in its welfare you will find your welfare.
>
> —JEREMIAH 29:7

Contrary to popular prophets who promised a quick return to the homeland, Jeremiah told the exiles to count on staying in the foreign land for a long time—until "seventy years are completed for Babylon" (Jer. 29:10; compare 25:11–12). Jeremiah saw the

---

[20]Passages that anticipate a coming Davidic "Messiah" (such as Jer. 23:5–6, 30:9; 33:14–26) are often regarded as later additions. But Jeremiah may well have looked forward to a future ruler, perhaps one of the Davidic line, who would arise from the people (Jer. 30:21).

Deportation of prisoners of war, a scene from the palace of Tiglath-pileser III (745–727 B.C.E.). As was customary in antiquity, the city was set on a hill and was fortified with double walls and turreted towers. The inscription identifies the city as Astartu, perhaps biblical Ashtaroth (Deut. 1:4). Scenes like this were duplicated by the Babylonians, who perpetuated the dread Assyrian policy of taking conquered people into exile.

hope of Israel in these displaced persons, for Yahweh had plans for them: "plans for welfare and not for evil, to give you a future and a hope" (29:11).

PLOTTING FOR REVOLUTION

Zedekiah was under terrific pressure to break with Babylon. The new nobility was pro-Egyptian. In Necho's successor, Psammetichus II—who came to the throne four years after Nebuchadrezzar's invasion (594 B.C.E.)—they saw the political potential for restoring a balance of power to the Fertile Crescent. Throughout this period Egypt, following its ancient foreign policy, was stirring up discontent among the small nations. Moreover, the popular prophets in Judah, like the ecstatics during Micaiah's time (see pp. 241–243), were beating the drums of nationalism. Not surprisingly, in the fourth year of Zedekiah's reign—the year of the accession of Psammetichus II—Egyptian agents encouraged the formation of an anti-Babylonian coalition consisting of Edom, Moab, Ammon, and Phoenicia. Envoys were sent to Zedekiah to persuade him to throw in his lot with the revolution (Jer. 27:3).

Speaking with an accent similar to Isaiah's in the Assyrian period (see pp. 310–312), Jeremiah condemned the conspiracy. His word to the envoys was accompanied by a sign. At the command of Yahweh, according to the narrative in Jeremiah 27, he made thongs and yoke bars and put them on his neck, thus dramatizing his prophecy that it was Yahweh's will for the nations to submit to Babylonia. He proclaimed to the conspirators that Yahweh, who created the earth and all that is in it, is sovereign in the affairs of history and therefore can give the earth into the temporary control of a chosen agent. For the time being, Nebuchadrezzar was Yahweh's "servant" (Jer. 27:6–7). Therefore, revolting against Babylonia was actually fighting against God. His message to Zedekiah and to the leaders of the people was this: "Serve the king of Babylon and live. Why should this city become a desolation?"

This was undoubtedly a wiser political policy than the reckless nationalism of the Judean leaders. Jeremiah, however, did not view the situation in terms of ordinary politics. He was not a collaborationist who wanted to see his country under foreign domination, nor was he a pacifist opposed to any kind of war on principle. Rather, he saw the crisis as God's sovereign activity in history for the purpose of overthrowing and rebuilding, of judgment and renewal. The people were not confronted with a choice between two political alternatives (whether to follow a pro-Egyptian or pro-Babylonian policy) but with a decision of faith that called for repentance and utter reliance upon God. But Jeremiah's message was either too subtle or too offensive for the people of Judah. Even when he had the ear of Zedekiah, he was misunderstood or repudiated. His advice that Judah surrender to Babylonia brought him into head-on conflict with the popular prophets, who claimed that Nebuchadrezzar's punitive measure of 597 B.C.E. was only a temporary setback, that the treasures taken from the Temple would soon be returned, and that life would return to normal (see Jer. 27:12–22). This easy optimism, said Jeremiah, was based on a lie. The popular prophets had not stood in "the Council of Yahweh." They were filling the people with vain hopes and speaking "visions of their own minds, not from the mouth of Yahweh" (see the oracles against the prophets, Jer. 23:9–32).

JEREMIAH'S CLASH WITH THE POPULAR PROPHETS

Baruch gives us a vivid account of the clash between Jeremiah and the popular prophets, who were evidently attached to the royal court (Jer. 28). In the very year in which foreign envoys came to talk Zedekiah into joining the anti-Babylonian movement, the prophet Hananiah challenged Jeremiah publicly in the Temple. An advocate of Davidic covenant theology, Hananiah announced that Yahweh would break the yoke of the king of Babylon, and that within two years the Temple treasures and the exiles, including Jehoiachin (Jeconiah), would be brought back. Evidently Hananiah and his prophetic colleagues still believed that the exiled Jehoiachin—instead of his uncle Zedekiah, whom Nebuchadrezzar had elevated to the throne—was Judah's legitimate king. They pinned their hopes for national revival on his return.

Jeremiah's sarcastic response was, in effect: Would that this were true! He reminded Hananiah and the assembled people that one thing had characterized Yahweh's prophets through the years:

> The prophets who preceded you and me from ancient times
> prophesied war, famine, and pestilence against many countries and great
> kingdoms.
>
> —JEREMIAH 28:8 (NRSV)

Any prophet who departed from this tradition by prophesying peace must accept the burden of proof. Incensed, Hananiah dramatically took the yoke bars, which Jeremiah was still wearing on his neck as a prophetic sign, and broke them before the people, repeating that in two years Yahweh would break the yoke of the king of Babylon from the neck of all the nations, and restore the exiled king to his rightful throne. Not to be outdone, Jeremiah proceeded to make a yoke of iron, for, he said, Yahweh had forged "an iron yoke of servitude to Nebuchadrezzar." The yoke could not be broken by human effort because the Babylonian king was the instrument of God's purpose. And it was futile to fight against God!

THE SIEGE OF JERUSALEM

For various reasons, including perhaps the influence of Jeremiah, Zedekiah did not join the conspiracy in 594 B.C.E. But political restlessness continued to mount, reaching its peak in 588 B.C.E., when a new Egyptian monarch, Apries (called Hophra in Jer. 44:30), came to the throne. Hophra's predecessor had confined himself to stirring up intrigue in Palestine, Phoenicia, and Transjordan, but Hophra revived the aggressive policy of Necho and began to organize an expedition into Asia. This turn of events gave new hope to nations chafing under the Babylonian yoke. Revolution broke out anew, this time in Ammon and Judah. Nebuchadrezzar moved swiftly to put down the revolt, establishing a military headquarters at Riblah in Syria, on the Orontes River. To decide whether first to attack Ammon or Judah, he resorted to divination (as vividly described in Ezekiel 21:18–23). In 588 B.C.E. Nebuchadrezzar's army laid siege to Jerusalem.

From this period come the Lachish Letters, found by archaeologists during expeditions between 1932 and 1938.[21] These inscribed fragments contain references to military activity, including the sending of fire signals, in the vicinity of Lachish and Azekah (see Jer. 34:6–7), and throw light on conditions in the country during the Babylonian invasion. An even more vivid picture of the suffering experienced during the siege of Jerusalem is given in the lyrical laments of the book of Lamentations (especially Lam. 2; 4).[22]

During the siege, Jeremiah never wavered in his conviction that the only course of action was surrender to Babylonia. This was the counsel Zedekiah received when he sent a messenger to Jeremiah (Jer. 21). The king hoped Yahweh would perform a miracle and make Nebuchadrezzar withdraw, as had happened during Sennacherib's siege in Isaiah's time (see pp. 317–318). But he received no comfort from the prophet. Jeremiah

---

[21]See Pritchard, *Ancient Near Eastern Texts* [1], pp. 321–22, for a translation of these letters.
[22]See the discussion by Claus Westermann, "Lamentations," in *The Books of the Bible* [9], pp. 303–18.

A reconstruction of Lachish, one of the largest cities of Judah, here shown from its west side. The flat summit of the mound, covering some 18 acres was surrounded by double walls, the higher one about 20 feet and the lower one about 13 feet thick. The fortified city was conquered and burned by Nebuchadrezzar in 589 B.C.E. The Lachish Letters, written to the commander of Lachish by an officer of a nearby garrison, were found in a guard room near the city's outer gate.

said that Yahweh, the Divine Warrior, would fight against the city "with outstretched hand and strong arm, in anger, and in fury, and in great wrath." Military resistance was futile. He even advised the citizens to desert to the Babylonians if they wanted to escape with their lives (Jer. 21:8–9).

Zedekiah was desperate. Hoping to gain Yahweh's favor, he tried to reinstate one feature of Deuteronomic law that had long been ignored: the prohibition against enslaving a fellow-Hebrew (see Deut. 15:12–18). According to Baruch's account in Jeremiah 34, the king made a covenant with the people in Jerusalem to release all slaves. The covenant was sealed by the ancient ceremony of cutting a calf in two and passing between the two halves (Jer. 34:18–19; compare Gen. 15:12–18). The upper class was undoubtedly motivated more by economic considerations than by religious conviction, for emancipation meant that slave-owners would not have to provide slaves with food when rations were short. When the political situation took a turn for the better with the advance of Pharaoh Hophra's forces and the temporary lifting of the Babylonian siege (Jer. 37:5), the slaves were promptly taken back. To Jeremiah this was final proof, if more proof were needed, of the people's violation of the covenant, a violation for which they would suffer the judgment of God.

JEREMIAH'S IMPRISONMENT

The withdrawal of the Babylonian army seemed a hopeful sign (Jer. 37). Again Zedekiah sent a messenger to Jeremiah, this time asking the prophet to pray to Yahweh on behalf of the people. But again, Jeremiah's response was infuriating. The Babylonian army, he said, would return, and even if the Babylonians were left with only wounded soldiers in their ranks, they would rise up and destroy Jerusalem! This was the last straw. Jeremiah was clearly too dangerous to be left at large. As the princes later said to the king (in words used also in one of the Lachish Letters), the prophet was "weakening the hands" of the soldiers and the people by advising capitulation and even desertion to Babylonia (Jer. 38:4–5).[23] As Jeremiah left the city on business he was arrested, beaten, and thrown into prison (Jer. 37:11–15). The pretext for the arrest was that Jeremiah himself intended to desert to the Babylonians.

The following scene (Jer. 37:16–21) is filled with pathos. The pitiful king, suspecting that Jeremiah might be right yet not daring to go against the princes, summoned the prophet from his prison cell. Instinctively one feels sorry not for Jeremiah but for Zedekiah, "a king, but much more bound than the prisoner who stands before him."[24] It was the king who was cowardly—a helpless puppet of his princes and a prisoner of circumstances. In the last hours, when darkness was falling upon Judah, he needed the help of the prophet. The meeting took place in secret. "Is there any word from Yahweh?" the king whispered, doubtless knowing that Jeremiah would give the same word he had been proclaiming day in and day out. This time Jeremiah spoke in a mild and friendly tone, tempered with the firm reminder that historical events had not vindicated the popular prophets. Zedekiah seems to have been almost persuaded. Yielding to the prophet's request to be moved to another jail, Zedekiah transferred him to the court of the guard.

Again the princes intervened: Fearful that Jeremiah's words would ruin the morale of soldiers and people, to say nothing of undermining their own position, they demanded that he be put to death (Jer. 38). Lacking moral courage, Zedekiah yielded with the pathetic words: "Behold, he is in your hands; for the king can do nothing against you." The princes let Jeremiah down by ropes into a cistern used to catch water during the rainy season, and left him to die in the mire. He was rescued, however, by an Ethiopian eunuch who at the king's orders, drew him out of the pit and restored him to the court of the guard.

Once more Zedekiah sent for Jeremiah and another secret conference took place, but with the same result (Jer. 38:14–28). So far as known, this was the last time the prisoner stood before the king. Shortly afterward, the Babylonian army breached the city wall and poured through to destroy the Temple, burn the city, and carry off much of the population into exile, leaving "some of the poorest of the land to be vinedressers

---

[23]See Lachish Ostracon No. VI; above, footnote 21.
[24]The words are those of Bernhard Duhm, quoted by J. P. Hyatt, *Interpreter's Bible*, V [23], 1072.

and plowmen" (2 Kings 25:12). The story of Zedekiah was tragic to the bitter end. Trying to flee Jerusalem, he was overtaken on the plain of Jericho and taken prisoner to Nebuchadrezzar's headquarters in Riblah. His sentence was terrible beyond words: His last sight was the execution of his own sons. Then his eyes were put out and he was carried in chains to Babylon. On orders from Nebuchadrezzar, Jeremiah was released from prison (Jer. 39).

BEYOND THE DAY OF DOOM

At the time of his call, Jeremiah realized that Yahweh's word had the double aspect of judgment and renewal, doom and promise. As the determining power in human affairs, the divine word was released through the prophet both "to wreck and to ruin" and "to build and to plant." Much of Jeremiah's preaching, especially in the days when people were seeking a false security, was devoted to announcing the day of doom. But the prophet never lost sight of the truth that God's purpose was not just to destroy and overthrow. Jeremiah understood that the ground had to be swept clean of false foundations so that God might build and plant anew (see Jer. 24:6; 42:10; 45:4). He would have been at odds with his deepest conviction and with the great prophets who preceded him had he not kept his eyes steadily on the vision of the New People and the New Age that lay beyond catastrophe. This theme of hope is prominent in a section of the book of Jeremiah often called "The Little Book of Comfort" (Jer. 30–33).[25]

JEREMIAH'S PURCHASE OF HIS FAMILY ESTATE

The key to Jeremiah's message stands out clearly in Jeremiah 32, an unassailably authentic episode that takes us back to the time when Jeremiah was imprisoned lest his words undercut the war effort. The Babylonian army was pounding at the walls of Jerusalem. Bread was so scarce that the people had resorted to cannibalism (Lam. 4:10). Death stalked the streets and came in at the windows (Jer. 9:21). It was only a matter of hours until sure doom would fall, "pitiless and dark." Clearly this was no time to think of the future, for most people despaired that there would be any tomorrow for Judah. Jeremiah did something at this point that must have seemed like sheer madness. Word was brought to him that as the next of kin, he had an opportunity to buy his cousin's field in the family city of Anathoth, which lay in territory under enemy control. While he was still in prison, he carried out the transaction according to the proper legal form and had the deeds put away in safekeeping. To Jeremiah, the invitation to acquire the land was a sign from Yahweh that the people Israel would be given a future in the Promised Land: that "houses and fields and vineyards shall be possessed again in the

---

[25]Some of the material in this section (such as the oracles in Jer. 33) comes from later Jeremianic tradition.

land." This was the same promise Jeremiah had given the exiles in his letter. Now, however, he expanded the promise to include others who would undergo a baptism by fire and suffering on the occasion of Jerusalem's destruction.

THE NEW COMMUNITY

Jeremiah is often called the prophet of individualism. This is a dubious tribute if one has in mind the "individualism" of American culture, which often glorifies the "rugged individualist" who acts and lives by private courage and personal faith. In this sense, Jeremiah was certainly *not* an individualist. True, he knew that in times of tragedy, when the social order was shattered, the individual might experience a deep sense of utter reliance upon God. This kind of personal faith is magnificently expressed in his Confessions. But Jeremiah did not advocate an individualism detached from the traditions of a people or separated from the covenant community. Even in his isolation, the prophet knew that individuals have access to God and experience "healing" or salvation only within a community. Hence when Jeremiah lifted his eyes to the horizon of God's future, he spoke of a New Community. The deepest rift in the people's history—the tragic separation of the "house of Israel" and the "house of Judah"—would be overcome. As in the ancient Tribal Confederacy, though on a higher plane, the people would become one in their one loyalty to the one God who had redeemed them (Jer. 31:27–30).

It is not surprising, then, that some of the oracles found in Jeremiah 30 and 31 are addressed to Ephraim, the "house of Israel" that had experienced defeat and exile in an earlier period. Through Jeremiah the people of the defunct Northern Kingdom of Israel were given this promise:

> A people that survived the sword
> > found grace in the wilderness.
> Israel marched to his rest;
> > Yahweh appeared to him from afar.
> I have loved you with an everlasting love,
> > therefore I extend loyalty [*ḥésed*] to you.
> Once more I will build you, and you will be rebuilt,
> > O Virgin Israel.
>
> —JEREMIAH 31:2–4a

Rachel, the ancestress of the Northern Kingdom who weeps bitterly for her children, is asked to stop crying, for "there is hope for your future" (Jer. 31:15–22):[26]

---

[26]On this intriguing passage, see B. W. Anderson, "'The Lord Has Created Something New': A Stylistic Study of Jer. 31:15–22," *Catholic Biblical Quarterly* 40 (1978), 463–78; reprinted in *From Creation to New Creation* [146], chap. 11. See also the illuminating essay by Phyllis Trible, "The Gift of a Poem: A Rhetorical Study of Jeremiah 31:15–22," *Andover Newton Quarterly* 71 (1977), 271–80.

> Isn't Ephraim my precious son,
>> a child in whom I delight,
> For as often as I speak against him,
>> I am still very much concerned for him.
> Therefore I yearn for him with my being,
>> I am filled with compassion for him,
>>> the oracle of Yahweh.
>
> —Jeremiah 31:20

These passages echo Hosea's message of divine love that would not let the people go (Hos. 11:8). Just as Hosea spoke near the end of the Northern Kingdom of Israel, so Jeremiah stood on the brink of the abyss into which the Southern Kingdom of Judah was to plunge. Jeremiah affirmed that Yahweh's love, working through the discipline of judgment, would make a new beginning for both Israel and Judah. It was a time of deep distress, the prophet said, and yet *out of it* the people would be saved (Jer. 30:7).

The New Covenant

This vision of the restored community of Israel is profoundly expressed in the prophecy of the new covenant (Jer. 31:31–34), which is stamped more indelibly on later prophetic tradition than anything else Jeremiah said. Eventually it gave the name to the canon of Christian writings ("New Testament" means "New Covenant"). Like a finely cut jewel, this prophecy reflects light from several facets. First, the new covenant, like the old, will be a result of God's initiative. Israel's faith will be a response to what God does, not a bilateral bargain between equal partners. This is the meaning of the words, "I will make. . . ."

Second, this covenant will not be like the Mosaic covenant, for the people's history has shown that to be a broken covenant. Even the attempt of the Deuteronomic Reformation to restore the Mosaic covenant had failed—a failure that must have been the background of Jeremiah's prophecy. History as it had been known—the history of the broken covenant—will come to an end and a new kind of history will be inaugurated.

Third—and this is the paradox—the new covenant will be new in the sense that it will fulfill the original intention of the Sinai covenant. The meaning of the original covenant had been eclipsed by religious ceremonies and written laws. In the new covenant, however, the Torah will be written upon the heart—the inward center of one's being. It will find expression in a personal response to the liberating God who says, "Obey my voice."

Fourth, the new covenant will create a new community, Yahweh's *people*: "I will be their God and they shall be my people" (Jer. 31:33). As we have seen repeatedly, this is the characteristic formula of the covenant (compare Jer. 24:7; 32:39–40; and so on). Verse 31 interprets this community as embracing "the house of Israel and the house of

Judah"—that is, the whole people that Yahweh brought out of Egypt. Individualism is far from Jeremiah's mind, for he stresses that this covenant formula will be *personally* true for each member of the community, from the least to the greatest. Because Yahweh will bring about a change of human nature by giving a new heart (will), there will be permanent harmony between Israel's will and Yahweh's will. Indeed, no longer will it be necessary to have religious instruction or covenant-renewal services that appeal for "the knowledge of God," for the whole community will "know" Yahweh in the trust and tryst of a loyalty that cannot be broken.[27]

Fifth, the new covenant will rest upon divine forgiveness. In the context of Jeremiah's whole message it is clear that pardon must be preceded by Yahweh's "discipline," which shatters human pride and self-sufficiency and destroys the idols in which people place their trust. When the people of Israel stand humbly before God, shamed by their sordid history and contrite about the betrayal of their covenant commitment, all things will be made new, "For I will forgive their iniquity, and I will remember their sin no more" (Jer. 31:34).

The sixth facet, though it appears first in the passage, has been left until last so that it can stand at the climax of our study. Jeremiah's new covenant prophecy pertains to "the last things," the consummation of the divine purpose in history. That is the significance of the opening formula, a characteristic preface to prophecies of the end-time: "Behold, the days are coming. . . ." The coming of the New Age cannot be dated on the calendar. It is the future for which Israel hopes, knowing that the time of its coming is measured by God's activity and purpose. Yet the hope is not for some never-never land, far removed from the concrete realities of Israel's history. As indicated by Jeremiah's symbolic purchase of a field, it is to be realized on the land to which the exiles would return, where they will once again join in "the dance of the merrymakers" and worship in Zion (Jer. 31:4–6).[28]

Since Jeremiah came from a priestly family, it is somewhat surprising that the Temple had no central place in his pictures of the future restoration. Perhaps this silence resulted from the prophet's reaction against false confidence in the Temple, encouraged by the Deuteronomic policy of centralizing worship in Jerusalem. Perhaps it resulted in part from his preoccupation with the present crisis. In any case, his attitude toward Israel's worship contrasts with that of his contemporary, Ezekiel, the prophet-priest with whom began a new phase of Israel's history.

---

[27]On "the knowledge of God," also a theme in the prophecy of Hosea, see pp. 278–280.

[28]Thomas A. Raitt, *A Theology of Exile* [471], effectively shows how the crisis of the fall of the nation and the exile of the people brought about a shift from oracles of judgment to oracles of salvation in the prophecies of Jeremiah and Ezekiel.

PART III

*Behold, the days are coming, says the Lord, when I will make a new
covenant with the house of Israel.*
—JEREMIAH 31:31

THE COVENANT
COMMUNITY
IS RENEWED

CHAPTER 13

BY THE WATERS
OF BABYLON

Although Jeremiah believed that the future lay with the exiles in Babylonia, he did not join them when Nebuchadrezzar's commanding officer gave him the chance. His decision to stay on in Jerusalem was clear proof to his accusers that he was not a deserter. The final phase of Jeremiah's career (as recorded by Baruch in Jer. 40–44) was interwoven with the troubles that beset the remnant left in the ruins of Judah. Gedaliah, whom the Babylonians had appointed governor of Judah, was assassinated by a certain Ishmael, an archpatriot whose Davidic blood was hot with the old nationalism. Ishmael's sword cut down many of Gedaliah's supporters, along with many of the Babylonian troops stationed at Mizpah. Fearing reprisals from Nebuchadrezzar, the Judean military chiefs, against Jeremiah's advice, fled to Egypt for refuge, taking the unwilling Jeremiah and Baruch with them.

We last hear of Jeremiah in Egypt, denouncing the colony of exiles for reverting to worship of the Queen of Heaven, Ishtar. The exiles justified themselves by recollecting that in the days before Jerusalem's fall, when they worshiped the mother-goddess in Judah, they had plenty of food, prospered, and experienced no evil. "But since we left off burning incense to the queen of heaven and pouring out libations to her, we have lacked everything and have been consumed by the sword and by famine" (Jer.

Biblical Readings: Read first the message of the priestly prophet, Ezekiel, in Ezekiel 1–24 and 33–39. Then read Priestly (P) writings in the Pentateuch such as Genesis 1:1–2:3, 9:1–17; Chaps. 17 and 23; and Exodus 6, 25–31, and 35–40.

44:17–18). Jeremiah, however, insisted to the very last that the "queen-of-heaven theology" was deceptive and that Yahweh's word would be vindicated, despite the ambiguities of historical experience.

THE JEWISH DISPERSION

Egypt became one of the major centers of the Jewish Dispersion. About a hundred years after the migration of Jeremiah and his fellow-Jews to Egypt, some of their descendants were settled at the first cataract of the Nile on the island of Elephantine (modern Aswan). We know this from the Elephantine papyri discovered there about the start of the twentieth century.[1] This Jewish colony included a temple where Yahweh (or Yahu) apparently was worshiped along with a goddess, Anath. Despite this strange departure from mainstream Mosaic tradition, these Jews recognized their allegiance to the Temple in Jerusalem, which at that time had been rebuilt. Later, important Jewish settlements sprang up in Alexandria and other Egyptian cities.

Nevertheless, Jeremiah was proven right: The future belonged not to the exiles in Egypt, but to those in Babylonia who preserved the traditions of their past and who eventually returned to Palestine to begin reconstruction. One of the leaders of the Jewish colonies in Babylonia was the prophet Ezekiel. To review Ezekiel's career, we must turn back to 597 B.C.E., the year of Nebuchadrezzar's first deportation, and retrace some of the story already followed in our study of Jeremiah (see map, p. 364 and Chronological Chart 8, p. 372).

EZEKIEL THE PRIEST

Of priestly descent, Ezekiel, son of Buzi, was one of the exiles who—along with Jehoiachin and other prominent citizens of Judah—was carried to Babylonia in the first captivity (Ezek. 1:2). The fact that he belonged to the first group of exiles is noteworthy, for Nebuchadrezzar's design was to take away only the cream of the population (2 Kings 24:14). We can assume, therefore, that Ezekiel belonged to Jerusalem's aristocracy, and perhaps that he was a member of the powerful priesthood claiming descent from Zadok, the High Priest installed by Solomon.

With his fellow-exiles Ezekiel settled by the banks of the river Chebar, a large canal that conducted water from the Euphrates through the city of Nippur, a short distance southeast of Babylon. In the village of Tel-abib, built on the edge of the canal, he received the call to prophesy five years after the deportation (about 593 B.C.E.). The date given for his last recorded prophecy is about 571 B.C.E. (Ezek. 29:17). Thus the

[1]See Pritchard, *Ancient Near Eastern Texts* [1], pp. 222–23.

twenty-year span of his ministry overlapped the periods before and after the fall of Jerusalem in 587 B.C.E.

Ezekiel's Babylonian environment undoubtedly influenced his thought and imagination. He probably visited the great city of Babylon, whose ancient glory is still dimly visible in the excavated ruins. Guarding the approach to the interior of the city was the magnificent Ishtar Gate, named in honor of Ishtar, mother-goddess and consort of Marduk. Through this gate one entered the processional street and advanced toward the ziggurat that rose above the city like a lofty mountain. Even today the beautiful brickwork, which throws into relief the figures of bulls and dragons, suggests the splendor that must have dazzled Jewish visitors of old.

This Babylonian influence, however, cannot account for the strange character of much of the book of Ezekiel. Ezekiel *himself* was an unusual person who might make a fascinating psychological study. We are told oracles often came to Ezekiel in an ecstasy or trance, when he was seized by "the hand of God" or transported by the Spirit. He was struck dumb, overwhelmed by cataleptic stupor, and seemingly gifted with second sight. One must emphasize, however, that these psychic peculiarities throw more light on the *form* of his message than upon its *content*. In the final analysis, the truth of what Ezekiel said cannot be measured by the manner in which his message came to him. Like many of the ancient prophets, Ezekiel was eccentric. His unusual temperament is perhaps reflected in some of the difficulties in the book of Ezekiel itself.

THE PROBLEM OF EZEKIEL

In the book of Jeremiah, the greatest difficulty for the reader is the shapeless, disordered character of the collected materials. At first glance, the book of Ezekiel presents no such difficulty. The oracles are precisely dated and arranged in relatively good order, as though the prophet had planned and executed the work himself.[2] Careful study of the book, however, has brought to light many difficulties lying beneath the surface.

One obvious problem is that in Ezekiel 1–24 the prophet, though represented as speaking to the exiles in Babylonia, focuses his attention on Jerusalem and seemingly has an intimate knowledge of what was going on there. For example, in Ezekiel 11 we are told that the prophet was "lifted up" by the Spirit and transported to the east gate of the Jerusalem Temple, where he saw twenty-five men plotting evil. Ezekiel was commanded by Yahweh to prophesy against them: "And it came to pass, while I was prophesying, that Pelatiah the son of Benaiah died" (Ezek. 11:13). This seems to mean that Pelatiah, one of the twenty-five men, died at the time Ezekiel was speaking, presumably in Jerusalem. If we take seriously the geographical distance separating Babylonia and Palestine, this passage is baffling. It strains credulity to say, in Ezekiel's language, that God took him by a lock of his hair and spirited him away to Jerusalem (Ezek. 8:1–3). It

---

[2]The *New Oxford Annotated Bible* [16] indicates that only three dates are out of order: Ezekiel 29:1 (January 7, 587 B.C.E.), 29:17 (April 26, 571 B.C.E.—the latest date given in the book), and 32:1 (March 3, 585 B.C.E.).

Ancient Babylon as depicted in a reconstruction. A procession is entering the beautiful Ishtar Gate, the entrance through the city's double wall to the palace, which supported on its roof the famous "Hanging Gardens"—one of the seven wonders of the world, according to the Greeks. Beyond the gardens can be seen the ziggurat, Etemenanki, which Nebuchadrezzar rebuilt.

has been suggested that Ezekiel never went to Babylonia at all, and that he really lived in Jerusalem during the final years of the Southern Kingdom of Judah.[3]

This view, however, is extreme. There is no convincing reason to doubt that Ezekiel was carried away from Jerusalem in the first deportation, and that his call to prophesy occurred in Babylonia. Perhaps some time after this experience he journeyed back to Jerusalem, believing that part of his prophetic commission was to warn Judah of impending doom. If so, this would explain how he had such good information about Jerusalem during its last days, and why he seems frequently to address his message to people in Palestine rather than Babylonia. On this hypothesis, he later returned to Babylonia and completed his career in the midst of the exiles. But this scenario raises other difficulties that cannot be dismissed lightly, the most obvious being that Ezekiel was specifically commissioned to preach to the exiles (Ezek. 3:10–11).

At least some of the problems connected with Ezekiel's mission to the exiles are resolved when we consider, first of all, that he had been brought up in Jerusalem and that he knew the city and its environs intimately, especially the Temple. There was probably frequent communication between the Jews in Babylonia and the residents of Jerusalem. Ezekiel's oracles against Judah and Jerusalem, if given in Babylonia, could have been sent by letter (compare Jer. 29). Exiles in Babylonia were undoubtedly kept posted on the latest developments in Jerusalem, and Ezekiel's lively religious imagination might readily have filled in many of the details. One must also keep in mind that the book of Ezekiel, like other prophetic collections, has been edited. It is conceivable that Ezekiel himself, like Jeremiah, revised his oracles during his career, and unquestionably the scroll was further revised and supplemented by later prophetic disciples (though by no means as extensively as some scholars have insisted).[4] All this adds up to the probability that Ezekiel's work was carried on among the Babylonian exiles.

In its present form, the book of Ezekiel is arranged according to a clear outline:

A. Prophecies given before the fall of Jerusalem (593–587 B.C.E.)
   1. Ezekiel's opening vision and commission (Ezek. 1–3)
   2. Oracles of doom against Judah and Jerusalem (Ezek. 4–24)
B. Oracles against the neighboring nations (Ezek. 25–32; the oracles against Tyre and Egypt are clearly from Ezekiel.)
C. Prophecies given after the fall of Jerusalem (587–573 B.C.E.)
   1. Oracles of promise (Ezek. 33–39)
   2. The New Jerusalem (Ezek. 40–48)

Our study will focus chiefly on Ezekiel 1–24 and 33–39 (sections A and C-1 of the outline).

---

[3]For a brief summary of various hypotheses proposed for the book of Ezekiel, see H. G. May, *Interpreter's Bible*, VI [23], 41–45. See also commentaries by Walther Eichrodt [460] and Walther Zimmerli [473].
[4]In his commentary [462], Moshe Greenberg maintains that nothing in the book of Ezekiel requires a historical setting later than the last date assigned to an oracle, that is, 571 B.C.E. (Ezek. 29:17).

EZEKIEL'S CALL

We turn first to the beginning of Ezekiel's prophetic career. The lot of the exiles, among whom Ezekiel lived for several years before his call, was not as bad as might have been feared. Many of the Jews deported in 597 B.C.E. were skilled artisans whose labor was evidently in great demand in Babylonia. Ezekiel, for example, had a private house (Ezek. 3:24) in which he was visited by the elders of the people from time to time. The Jews apparently were given a good bit of freedom to practice their religion, to live together in closely knit communities in the Babylonian cities, and to improve their economic status. Tablets from the reign of Nebuchadrezzar, discovered by archaeologists in the ruins of ancient Babylon, mention payments of rations in oil, barley, and so forth to foreign captives in exchange for skilled labor. Included in the list were Yaukin [Jehoiachin], king of Judah, five royal princes, and other Judeans.[5] It was probably easy enough for the exiles to accept Jeremiah's advice to build houses and plant gardens, to raise families, and to show interest in the welfare of the city in which they lived (Jer. 29:4–7). Life was fairly comfortable, even though many yearned to return to their homeland.

Ezekiel's prophetic call came in an extraordinary vision in the fifth year of the exile of Jehoiachin. On that day, he says, "the heavens were opened, and I saw visions of God" (Ezek. 1:1). This overpowering experience convinced him that "the hand of Yahweh was upon him there." At the time he was thirty years old, if that is the meaning of the mysterious opening words "in the thirtieth year."

It is said that ancient rabbis, disturbed by the possibility that strange doctrines might result from the account of Ezekiel's vision, ruled that the opening chapter was not to be read in the synagogue, and forbade persons under thirty years of age to read the book privately. Like Isaiah, Ezekiel saw Yahweh seated upon a heavenly throne in ineffable glory and transcendent majesty. To understand this vision recall that, according to Jerusalem theology, Yahweh was enthroned within the Holy of Holies of the Temple, and that the wings of the guardian cherubim stretched out protectively over the throne-seat (the Ark). This imagery (Ezek. 1) draws both from Israel's priestly tradition, with which Ezekiel was familiar through his experience as a priest in the Jerusalem Temple, and the Babylonian religious emblems that had influenced him in exile.

According to the narrative, Ezekiel saw Yahweh's heavenly chariot approaching from the north in a storm cloud flashing with lightning (compare Ps. 29). Looking more closely, he saw that the throne-chariot was borne by four strange creatures (see also Ezek. 10:9–22), part animal and part human, each moving in perfect coordination with the other because they were all animated by the divine Spirit. Alongside each cherub was a gleaming wheel—or rather, "a wheel within a wheel," as though set at

---

[5]Pritchard, *Ancient Near Eastern Texts* [1], p. 308. See also W. E. Albright, "King Joiachin [Jehoiachin] in Exile," *Biblical Archaeologist,* V (1942), 49–55. Reprinted in *The Biblical Archaeologist Reader* I [119], pp. 106–12.

A protective genius—one of a pair which once guarded the gateway to the palace of Ashurnasirpal II (884–860 B.C.E.) at Nimrud. These winged figures, a prominent feature of ancient art, help us to understand the imagery of Ezekiel's vision. The figure has the body of a lion, the wings and feathers of an eagle, and the head of a man.

right angles to each other to enable the chariot to move easily in any direction, as the Spirit directed. Above the creatures was something like a crystal platform or firmament (compare Exod. 24:10), carried on their wings with a roar like the sound of many waters. Looking still higher, the prophet saw above the firmament the likeness of a sapphire throne, and "seated above the likeness of a throne was a likeness as it were of a human form." In an ecstatic vision the prophet beheld Yahweh seated upon a lofty throne in dazzling radiance, or "glory." The holy God, whom Israel had once worshiped in the Temple at Jerusalem, had come to the people in exile!

Overwhelmed by the infinite distance separating the holy God from a mere mortal ("son of man"), the prophet fell prostrate. Raised to his feet when the Spirit entered him, he stood to receive his commission. He was to speak to "a nation of rebels," a people "impudent and stubborn" who had revolted against Yahweh's sovereignty from the very first. Like a sentry posted on the city wall, his duty as "watchman" was to give warning of Yahweh's approaching catastrophe, though there was little chance that a people with "a hard forehead and a stubborn heart" would respond (see also Ezek. 33:1–9). Whether the people heard or refused to hear, at least they would know that a prophet had been among them. In the prophet's vision a hand was stretched out to him, holding a scroll—the message that the messenger was to deliver to the people. Strangely, Yahweh offered him the scroll to eat and digest. When he did so, he found that it was "sweet as honey" (Ezek. 2:9–10; 3:1–3), indicating that he not only appropriated the message but also was in agreement with it, even though he would have to "sit upon scorpions."[6]

This vivid account of the prophet's commissioning (Ezek. 2; 3) recalls Isaiah's unpromising vocation (Isa. 6:9–13) and Jeremiah's unhappy lot of being set like a fortified city against the whole people (Jer. 1:17–19). Awestruck at the vision of Yahweh's unearthly glory and appalled by the fearsome task set before him, Ezekiel sat overwhelmed among the exiles for seven days.

✓ DEFINITION: "JEW," "JUDAISM"

The term "Jew(ish)" can be traced back through the Latin *iudaeus* and Greek *'joudaios* to the Hebrew *Yehudi*, which once referred to citizens of the Southern Kingdom of Judah who survived the fall of the Northern Kingdom of Israel (Ephraim) in 721 B.C.E. The term gained currency, however, during the period of the Exile and the period after the return. During the post-exilic period, the term "Jews" was used to refer to subjects of the Persian province of Judah (Neh. 1:2) and later to the state established by the Maccabean leaders (1 Mac. 8:20). The term was not geographically limited, however, for Jews who were "dispersed" or scattered in countries outside Judah, such as Babylonia or Egypt, continued to cherish their Judean background and ties. Those who did not share this "Jewish" identity were regarded as belonging to "the nations" (Acts 14:2)—that is, the gentiles.

Nationality is not the decisive factor in being a "Jew," as evident from the fact that many Jews today are not citizens of the state of Israel. In biblical times, the decisive factor was religion, specifically the conviction that God had entered into special relationship with the people and called them to be "separate" by virtue of their distinctive way of life.

The term "Judaism" is conventionally applied to the religion of the Judeans or "Jews," among whom the covenant faith came to new expression after the collapse of the na-

---

[6]Von Rad, *Theology*, II [163], 223–24, interprets the symbolism to mean that, unlike Jeremiah, there was agreement between the prophet and his message. Certainly the passage should not be construed to mean that Ezekiel found a sadistic satisfaction in pronouncing judgment against Israel.

tion in 587 B.C.E. This term is not found in the Hebrew Bible; it seems to have been coined in later Hellenistic circles of the Diaspora or "Dispersion" (see Gal. 1:13–14). In any case, the Exile marked the beginning of a completely new chapter in the history of Israel's faith. It is proper to reserve the terms "Jews" and "Judaism" for this new phase of Israel's life-story.

LAMENTATION, MOURNING, AND WOE

In the days before the fall of Jerusalem, Ezekiel's oracles were—like the writing in the scroll he was given to eat—"words of lamentation, mourning, and woe" (Ezek. 2:9–10). Like his great prophetic predecessors, he prophesied doom. While Jeremiah was prophesying in Jerusalem, Ezekiel was speaking about the imminent downfall of the state and the captivity of the people. The text explicitly states that he was to speak to "the house of Israel." Here "Israel" is used in its original sense of "the people of the covenant," and is applied to Jews, whether living in Judah or in Babylonian exile. At first glance, Ezekiel's message might seem more relevant to the people living in Judah. But granting that he spoke, at least during part of his ministry, to Jews in exile, what relevance did a message of divine judgment have for them? To deal with this question, we must consider the situation of the Jewish captives.

SMOLDERING NATIONALISM

We know from modern history that a legitimate ruler, even when living in exile, continues to be a symbol of nationalistic hope. This was true of Jehoiachin, who would have continued to rule in the succession of Josiah and Jehoiakim if not for the Babylonian intervention in the affairs of Jerusalem. To the exiles of 597 B.C.E., Jehoiachin was the legitimate Davidic king. Moreover, he was called "king of Judah" in Nebuchadrezzar's tablets, implying that his captors also recognized him as the legitimate ruler and Zedekiah as a regent. So long as the exiled king was free to move about, and even given an allowance by the Babylonian government, there was hope for a revival of the Jewish nation. We know that a party in Judah, suspicious of the Babylonian appointee Zedekiah, pinned their hopes on the exiled king, for the prophet Hananiah opposed Jeremiah by predicting that within the space of two years Jehoiachin and the other exiles would return (see pp. 375–376). Apparently the revolutionary intrigue that centered on the legitimate king, both in Judah and Babylonia, led to his subsequent imprisonment, though after the fall of Jerusalem he was freed from prison by Nebuchadrezzar's successor and given a regular allowance and special place at the king's table (2 Kings 25:27–30).

Ezekiel, then, faced a situation in which nationalism was still alive, even in the Exile. In Babylon popular prophets, of the same stripe as Hananiah, fanned the hope that Babylonian power would soon be shattered and the exiles would be able to return to the homeland. Every rumor from Jerusalem must have been followed with keen interest, especially news about the intervention of Pharaohs Psammetichus and Hophra. Jeremiah, as we have seen, wrote a letter to the exiles, rebuking them for being deceived by the lies of their prophets and advising them to plan on settling in Babylonia for a considerable time (Jer. 29). Two of these fanatical prophets were seized by Babylonian agents and burned alive (Jer. 29:20–23).

So long as Jerusalem was still standing Ezekiel's message—like Jeremiah's—was almost wholly one of doom. Convinced that Jerusalem's fall to Nebuchadrezzar was divinely ordained, and that rebellion against Babylonia was treason against God (Ezek. 17:20), Ezekiel saw in this imminent doom the coming of the Day of Yahweh, the day of judgment. As though the event had already occurred, he announced that the end had come:

> The word of Yahweh came to me:
> "You, O mortal man—this is what Lord Yahweh says
>   to the land of Israel.
> An end has come!
> The end has come upon the four corners of the land!
> Now is the end upon you [the land]!
> I am going to unleash my wrath against you
> I will judge you according to your ways,
>   and requite you according to your detestable practices.
> I will show no mercy to you, nor spare you at all.
> But I will requite you for your ways,
>   and the detestable practices among you.
> Then you will realize that I am Yahweh.
>   —EZEKIEL 7:1–4

THE PROPHETIC SIGNS

Ezekiel's prophetic word was accompanied by dramatic signs. Following divine instructions, he drew on a clay brick a diagram of Jerusalem under siege, showing the siege-mounds, camps, and battering rams (Ezek. 4:1–3). He was directed to lie for 390 days on his left side, then for 40 days on his right side, to indicate the number of years that Israel and Judah respectively would be punished (Ezek. 4:4–8). While lying on his side, he was to weigh out small rations of food and water to show the privations of the coming siege (Ezek. 4:9–11). He was told to cut off his hair with a sword and to separate it into three parts to portray the three kinds of fate that would befall the people of Jerusalem (Ezek. 5:1–12). He packed his baggage and at night dug through a wall, suggesting a person trying to flee from the city under cover of darkness (Ezek. 12:1–16). He ate his bread with quaking and drank his water with trembling to symbolize the nervous fear that people would experience during the coming siege (Ezek. 12:17–20). When his wife—the "delight" of his eyes—died, he refrained from mourning as a sign to the exiles that the news of Jerusalem's fall would fill them with sorrow too deep for tears (Ezek. 24:15–27).

Ezekiel's words and signs stirred up mild interest and curiosity, but did not evoke repentance or even provoke hostility. His signs were performed before those who had eyes to see but saw not, and ears to hear but heard not (Ezek. 12:2). The people even seemed to "enjoy" his sermons, for to them he was like one who sings with a beautiful voice or plays well on an instrument (Ezek. 33:30–33). The reaction was quite different from the one Jeremiah received, but it was no less indicative that Israel was a "rebellious house."

THE HISTORY OF REBELLION

According to Ezekiel, God's imminent judgment would be the harvest of a persistent apostasy reaching back to the very beginning of Israel's history. Hosea and Jeremiah had portrayed the time in the wilderness as the place of Israel's honeymoon, when the bride was faithful to the Groom (Hosea 2:15; Jer. 2:2). Not Ezekiel: He advocated what might be called a doctrine of "original sin" in historical terms, insisting that there never was a time in Israel's history when the people were sinless.

Recapitulating the "sacred history" with a new twist, Ezekiel traced Israel's unfaithfulness not only to the wilderness wanderings but also to the sojourn in Egypt, when its history began (Ezek 20:5–6). Israel's history was corrupted at the very beginning, for the people responded to Yahweh's choice and promise by rebelling against their liberating God and turning to the idols of Egypt. Had it not been for Yahweh's restraint "for his name's sake"—that is, for the sake of Yahweh's own honor and reputation—the people would have been blotted out on the spot. For God's holiness demanded a holy, faithful people, pure from the stain of idolatry. This fundamental theme runs through all of Ezekiel's discourses. His sense of the sublime majesty of God, vividly expressed in his opening vision, made him deeply aware of the infinite distance between sinful, mortal humanity and the holy, righteous God.

Ezekiel's somber summary of the sacred history from the Exodus to the settlement in Canaan is supplemented by allegories of the two chief cities: Jerusalem and Samaria. In two "extended metaphors" he portrayed Israel's history in the figure of harlotry (Ezek. 16; 23)—a figure that had been used effectively by Hosea and Jeremiah. Jerusalem's origin, the prophet said, was Canaanite: "Your father was an Amorite, and your mother a Hittite" (Ezek. 16:3; see 16:45). This statement has some historical accuracy, for Israel did come to birth in the welter of Canaanite culture (see pp. 29–38). In this context, however, Ezekiel is talking in theological, rather than historical terms. He affirms that Israel's perversity can be traced to the fact that she was the offspring of a lustful union, thus justifying the proverb "Like mother, like daughter" (Ezek. 16:44).

Yahweh took pity on this foundling whom others rejected, nurtured her to the beauty of maidenhood, and married her. The covenant was based on Yahweh's grace and initiative; but the maiden "trusted in her beauty," forgetting that she owed her life and beauty to God. Wantonly she lavished her harlotries on any passerby. Normally men pay to go to a harlot, but this passionate "lovesick" wife (Ezek. 16:30) was different—she actually bribed her lovers to come to her. According to Ezekiel, Jerusalem (the Southern Kingdom) had acted far worse than Samaria (the Northern Kingdom)—a point accented in the allegory of the twin harlots Oholah and Oholibah (Ezek. 23)—and had even outsinned Sodom, whose corruption was proverbial! Therefore, the harlot must bear the disgrace of judgment, becoming an object of reproach among the nations. Her history, the history of a broken covenant, must come to an end in order that Yahweh, remembering the covenant made "in the days of her youth," might establish an "everlasting covenant" (see Ezek. 16:59–63). Here Ezekiel's thought moves beyond the conditional Mosaic covenant to a covenant of grace, something like the Davidic covenant that would last in perpetuity.

KNOWLEDGE OF GOD

Before Israel could know Yahweh's forgiveness and enter into a new relationship in an "everlasting covenant," the people had to experience divine judgment. Ezekiel's oracles of doom are punctuated with the refrain: "Then they will know [realize] that I am Yahweh." Yahweh's sovereignty would be demonstrated in acts of judgment against a rebellious people, as with their ancestors in the land of Egypt (Ezek. 20:33–38). On the basis of these historical demonstrations, Israel would come to "know," that is, acknowledge or recognize, Yahweh as its God. Recall our earlier consideration of the meaning of "knowledge of God" in the context of the covenant (see pp. 90–92, 278–280).

Ezekiel's sense of divine holiness was accompanied by the realization that nothing unholy or profane could stand in God's presence. In the view of this priestly prophet, cultic and ethical sins were on the same level. In an extraordinary vision (Ezek. 8–11), Ezekiel was carried from Babylonia to the Jerusalem Temple, where he saw abominations being practiced: women weeping for Tammuz (the Babylonian name for the dying-rising god of fertility), men worshiping the sun with their faces toward the east, the secret chamber filled with murals depicting beasts and idols, and the princes—the very men who had persecuted Jeremiah—making their evil plans. Then the prophet saw the Glory of Yahweh—the divine presence that was believed to "tabernacle" in the Holy of Holies—depart from the defiled Temple, borne on the very throne-chariot he had seen in the vision by the River Chebar (Ezek. 10:18–22). So great was the idolatry of the people that even if three proverbially righteous men—Noah, Daniel, and Job—were found in the city, it would not escape destruction (Ezek. 14:12–20). The popular prophets came in for special censure, for they had misled the people by saying "peace" when there was no peace and had tried to whitewash the crumbling walls (Ezek. 13).

The indictment is made in terms of specific sins, including not only cultic abuses like the profanation of the Sabbath but also ethical crimes: bloodshed; adultery; extortion; dishonor of parents; and violation of the rights of the orphan, widow, and sojourner. Princes and prophets were linked in a conspiracy that had corrupted the whole people. No one was righteous:

> I sought for someone among them who should build up the wall and
> stand in the breach before me for the land, that I should not destroy it; but
> I did not find anyone.
>
> —EZEKIEL 22:30

THE DESTINY OF THE INDIVIDUAL

Ezekiel's message, like that of his predecessors, was addressed to the people as a whole— to the covenant community known as "the house of Israel." He declared that the community, from the beginning of its history down to his day, was so contaminated with evil that it could not endure. In the political event of national ruin he discerned God's judgment. But Ezekiel had to face the meaning of national calamity at another level: The community, though it deserved to suffer divine judgment, was made up of persons caught in the coils of tragedy. What about the destiny of the individual?

One must not suppose that before this Israel's faith had stressed only collective responsibility, without regard to individual members of the community. Israel's faith was not "totalitarian" in the sense that the individual was expendable in the interests of the whole. On the contrary, the covenant relationship, while binding the people together in communal solidarity, brought a sense of God's concern for each person. Within the community individuals had personal fellowship with God, and their rights were legally protected. In the biblical view, however, one is truly a person only when standing in a community, in relationship to God and neighbor. Isolated from the community (like the banished Cain), a person suffers the greatest loneliness and misery.

Nevertheless, in a time when individuals were torn from the old social context that had given meaning and support to their lives—when the community was temporarily shattered—the suffering of the innocent became a burning issue (compare Gen. 18:22–33). The question of individual destiny had to be faced more seriously than ever before. The popular complaint was expressed in a proverb: "The parents have eaten sour grapes, and the children's teeth are set on edge" (Jer. 31:29; Ezek. 18:1–4)—a cynical way of saying that people were victims of a situation inherited from their parents. Insisting that they were not responsible for the evil that evoked God's judgment, the people tried to shift the blame to earlier generations. Ezekiel was challenged to defend God's justice to those who were saying, "The way of Yahweh is not fair" (Ezek. 18:25, 29; see also 33:17–20).[7]

---

[7]See the discussion of theodicy by Thomas Raitt, *A Theology of Exile* [471], pp. 83–105.

Ezekiel sought to overcome the people's mood of fatalism (Ezek. 18:25–29). His generation was caught in a *fateful* situation, to be sure; but he insisted that individuals should not respond *fatalistically* by saying, "What's the use? God is not fair!" With some oversimplification, he argued that the acts of past generations do not determine the response of the present generation, for a good parent can have a bad child and a bad parent can have a good child. He emphasized that in each case persons are responsible for their own destiny—they are not the puppets of heredity, environment, or historical causation. Each individual must answer personally to God alone.

Had he been dealing with a case in a law court, Ezekiel would have denied the principle of "guilt by association" according to which, in ancient times, Achan's whole family was put to death with him for his sin (Joshua 7). This practice, rooted in ancient religious taboos, had been abandoned by Ezekiel's time. King Amaziah had refused to liquidate the children of the murderers who assassinated his father (2 Kings 14:6), and the Deuteronomic code made it illegal to punish children for the sins of their parents (Deut. 24:16). But Ezekiel had to deal with the question of divine justice, not in a law court, but in the historical arena where the deeds and decisions of one generation do affect later generations, and where retribution for past errors often falls not on the parents but on their children or grandchildren.

Ezekiel did not advocate extreme individualism, any more than did Jeremiah (see pp. 361–362, 380). As we have seen, he was deeply aware of the solidarity of the Israelite community, the oneness of the people past, present, and future, in the covenant. How, then, could he answer the people's question? He turned the question of God's justice back on the questioners themselves, reminding them that they were not as blameless as they supposed. They too were entangled in Israel's sins, and must accept full responsibility. Instead of trying to explain the problem of suffering, he insisted that suffering provided an occasion for repentance and faith (compare Luke 13:1–5). According to Ezekiel, God was puzzled that the imminent danger did not awaken Israel to repentance (see Definition, p. 362):

> Turn, turn from all your offences,
>   and your iniquity will not be your downfall!
> Get rid of all your offences
>   which you have committed against me,
>   and acquire a new heart and a new spirit!
> Why would you die, O house of Israel?
> For I take no pleasure in the death of anyone—
>   the oracle of Lord Yahweh—
> So, turn and live!
>
> —EZEKIEL 18:31–32 (compare
> 33:10–20)

Ezekiel's attempt to defend God's justice might strike us as unsatisfactory. For one thing, bad people do not always suffer and the good do not always prosper. But the prophet urged the exiles to hear in their crisis God's call to repentance, and to cast themselves in dependence upon divine mercy. His message touched only the edge of the mystery. In the following centuries, the problem of suffering was raised even more intensely as attempts were made to understand God's ways in history.[8]

THE PROMISE OF A NEW BEGINNING

Ezekiel's appeal was in vain, for the people were too enslaved by false loyalties to be moved even by the threat of catastrophe. The day of doom finally arrived. The prophet's oracles reflect the swift movement of those same events traced in our study of Jeremiah (see Chapter 12). In an allegory, Ezekiel tells of Zedekiah's revolt against the "great eagle" (Nebuchadrezzar) and his attempt to find refuge with "another great eagle," Egypt (Ezek. 17). He sees a sword polished and sharpened for slaughter (Ezek. 21:1–17), and portrays Nebuchadrezzar at the parting of the ways, waiting for an oracle's word on which rebel state he should attack first, Ammon or Judah (21:18–32). As long as Jerusalem still stood, however, the exiles refused to believe that the nation would fall. They chose to believe that Ezekiel was talking about the distant future, not about their own times: "The vision that he sees is for many days hence, and he prophesies of times far off" (Ezek. 12:27; see 12:22).

ISRAEL'S RESURRECTION

Then one day Ezekiel announced that Jerusalem was under siege (Ezek. 24:1–14). After an unexplained delay, a fugitive brought news that the city had fallen in 587 B.C.E. (Ezek. 33:21). From then on, the dominant tone of the prophet's message became one of hope. Earlier, when nationalistic feelings ran high, his task had been to shatter illusions with hard-hitting words of doom. Now, in a situation when the people were reduced to utter despair and remorse (Ezek. 33:1–11), his message was one of assurance. Apparently Ezekiel believed that God's sovereignty demands speaking against any form of human confidence, whether expressed positively in faith in the future, or negatively in despair about human possibilities. After disaster had struck, Ezekiel's recurring refrain, "You shall know that I am Yahweh," took on new meaning. The demonstrations that Yahweh is God to this people were to be found, not just in acts of judgment that expose human failure and sin, but also in divine action that initiates a new beginning in history.

[8]See the essays in J. L. Crenshaw, *Theodicy* [151].

This historical miracle is vividly portrayed in the famous vision of the valley of dry bones (Ezek. 37). Placed in the valley of death's shadow, Ezekiel was asked: "Can these bones live?" Then at Yahweh's command he prophesied to the bones, and suddenly they became living beings, clothed with sinews and animated by the divine Spirit. In the interpretation that follows, we learn that the bones symbolize Israel in despair. Israel as a community was dead, a historical nonentity. The cry was raised: "Our bones are dried up, and our hope is lost." Israel's extremity was God's opportunity, however. The prophet announced that Yahweh promised to resurrect the people from the grave (from exile), restore them to their homeland, and create new life by breathing the divine Spirit into their lifeless bodies. Yahweh would make Israel one people, embracing both Israel (Ephraim) and Judah, and would anoint one "prince" to rule over them. Then the unity of the people would be a historical fulfillment of the ancient covenant formula: "I will be their God, and they shall be my people."

THE GOOD SHEPHERD

Restoration is also portrayed in the image of a shepherd and his flock—an important image in both the Old Testament (Ps. 23; 100:3; Isa. 40:11) and the New (Luke 15:3–7; John 10:1–18). Unlike the false shepherds who feed themselves instead of their sheep, Yahweh is the Good Shepherd who seeks sheep that are lost, crippled, or strayed, in order to restore them to their home pasture (Ezek. 34). The initiative, according to Ezekiel, lies with Yahweh:

> Now I myself will ask after my sheep and go in search of them. As a shepherd goes in search of his sheep when his flock is dispersed all around him, so I will go in search of my sheep and rescue them, no matter where they were scattered in dark and cloudy days. I will bring them out from every nation, gather them from other lands, and lead them home to their own soil. I will graze them on the mountains of Israel, by her streams and in all her green fields.
>
> —EZEKIEL 34:11–13 (NEB)

After Yahweh has led the people back to their land, they will be given a good shepherd, a Davidic leader:

> Then I will set over them one shepherd, my servant David, and he shall lead them; he shall lead them, and he shall become their shepherd. And I, Yahweh, will be their God, and my servant David shall be a prince [*nasî'*] among them. I, Yahweh, have spoken.
>
> —EZEKIEL 34:23–24 (see 37:24–25)

Notice that the prophet does not refer to a coming Davidic "king," but rather to a prince (Hebrew: *nasî'*), a term once used for a leader of the old Tribal Confederacy.

Ezekiel seems to idealize the days before Israel became a nation, when Yahweh ruled as shepherd-king through a designated agent.

Ezekiel insisted that it was not because of Israel's goodness that Yahweh was about to act, but because other nations had inferred from Israel's tragedy that its God was powerless to save. This erroneous interpretation of Israel's defeat profaned God's honor, God's holy name. Therefore, Yahweh resolved to restore a helpless and hopeless people so that the nations might know who Yahweh is: the holy God who cannot be mocked. Like Jeremiah, however, Ezekiel insisted that Yahweh would have to effect a radical change in human nature if the people were to be a covenant people. Israel's "heart" ("mind," "will") must be transformed, so that a new lifestyle would be possible:

> A new heart I will give you, and a new spirit I will put within you. I will remove the heart of stone from your flesh and I will give you instead a heart of flesh. My spirit I will put within you, and I will cause you to walk in my statutes and faithfully observe my ordinances. You shall dwell in the land which I gave to your ancestors, and you shall be my people, and I will be your God.
>
> —EZEKIEL 36:26–28 (see 11:19–20)

Then Israel would have the will to obey God's voice, and the relationship between God and people would be that of an "everlasting covenant" (Ezek. 37:26). The affinities between Ezekiel 36 and Jeremiah's prophecy of the "new covenant" (Jer. 31:31–34) are so close that some scholars think Ezekiel must have seen or heard Jeremiah's oracle.

Ezekiel proclaimed the gracious action of the holy God in restoring a holy people to a holy land. In the time of the New Covenant, God would be in their midst, laving the land with "showers of blessing" (Ezek. 34:26) and multiplying the people in peace and security. In Ezekiel's vision, one feature of the restoration is especially prominent. Yahweh would "tabernacle" in the midst of the people:

> I will make a covenant of peace with them; it shall be an everlasting covenant with them; and I will bless them and multiply them, and will set my sanctuary among them forevermore. My dwelling place shall be with them; and I will be their God, and they shall be my people.
>
> —EZEKIEL 37:26–27 (NRSV)

The Temple would stand at the center of everything. Elaborating on this theme, Ezekiel portrays in detail a new Temple in a new Jerusalem (Ezek. 40–48). In a vision that recalls the one he saw at the beginning of his career, he beheld the "glory" of Yahweh returning to tabernacle in the sanctuary.[9] According to the prophet's lively imagination, the restoration of worship would have a transforming effect upon the land itself: From the temple mount a life-giving river, whose source is the fresh-water Deep beneath the

---

[9]For a discussion of the theology of Yahweh's "glory" (Hebrew: *kabôd*), see Tryggve N. D. Mettinger [160], chap. 3, especially pp. 97–103.

earth, will flow eastward in the wilderness and empty into the Salt Sea. Along its banks will grow trees that bear fresh fruit every month, and in the region of En-gedi fishermen will angle for fish, for the Dead Sea will become a fresh-water lake (Ezek. 47:1–12)! Ezekiel's vision of the New Jerusalem has profoundly influenced later portrayals of the end-time, such as the vision of "the holy city Jerusalem coming down out of heaven from God" in the last book of the New Testament (Rev. 21).

In Ezekiel's sketch of the new community, relations between "church" and "state" are to be carefully regulated. The priests of the line of Zadok, assisted by the Levites, are to have jurisdiction in all religious matters. The responsibility of the civil leader, the prince (Hebrew: *nasî*), is to support the religious community by providing sacrifices and upholding law and order (Ezek. 45:7–46:13). The land is reapportioned among the twelve tribes, unified through service of the central sanctuary in Jerusalem. Jerusalem will receive a new name, "Yahweh is there" (Ezek. 48:35). Thus Israel is to become a worshiping community, modeled on the pattern of the ancient Tribal Confederacy. As we will see, Ezekiel's priestly view was to have a profound influence on the Judaism that emerged out of the Exile.[10]

LIFE UNDER CAPTIVITY

Although Ezekiel had envisioned a reunion of the two houses of Israel—the tribes of the north and the south—this dream did not materialize. The remnant of the Northern Kingdom (later known as Samaritans) and the descendants of the Southern Kingdom (Judah) were eventually divided by such deep rivalry that in New Testament times it could be said that "Jews have no dealings with Samaritans" (John 4:9). Jews (Judeans) claimed that they were the true "Israel"—using Israel not in a political sense but in its ancient religious meaning of "the people of the covenant."

The Exile marked the beginning of a new movement in the unfolding drama of the people Israel, that of Judaism (see Definition, pp. 390–391). True to Jeremiah's prophecy, the future of the covenant people did not lie with the remnant left in Jerusalem. As a result of Nebuchadrezzar's blows, the city was so disorganized and crippled that its religious vitality was sapped. Even after the deportations of 597 and 587 B.C.E., Nebuchadrezzar had to intervene, probably because of disturbances in the wake of Gedaliah's assassination. In 582 B.C.E. another group of Jews was rounded up for exile to Babylonia. The total number of people taken into captivity is somewhat uncertain,[11] but the Exile did not involve a wholesale movement of the Jewish population to Babylonia, nor did the Babylonians follow the Assyrian policy of repopulating the land

---

[10]For discussions of Ezekiel's vision of restoration, see Jon D. Levenson, *Theology of the Program of Restoration of Ezekiel 40–48*, Harvard Semitic Monograph Series, 10 (Missoula: Scholars Press, 1976); and Moshe Greenberg, "The Design and Themes of Ezekiel's Program of Restoration," *Interpretation* 38 (1984) 181–208.

[11]Jeremiah 52:28–30, which is probably fairly accurate, mentions three deportations and gives the total for all three as 4,600, though this might refer only to the males. 2 Kings 24:14 (compare 24:16) states that 8,000 to 10,000 were taken away in the first deportation of 597 B.C.E. No count is given for the deportation of 587 B.C.E., and the third deportation is not mentioned.

The area of En-gedi—an oasis located on the western bank of the Dead Sea some 35 miles from Jerusalem. The climate in the depression of the Dead Sea—the lowest place on the earth's surface—is semitropical, and the terrain is ruggedly desolate. En-gedi, fed by a strong spring, was famous for its fertility (see Song of Solomon 1:14). Ezekiel's vision pictures the fertilization of the whole region and the transformation of the Dead Sea into a fresh water lake (Ezek. 47:1–12).

with foreign colonists. Only the cream of Jewish leadership was taken; poorer elements of the population were left behind to harvest the crops (see Jer. 29:10; 2 Kings 25:12). By paralyzing the country in this manner, Nebuchadrezzar effectively removed the threat of national revival. The land was left in such a wreck that even under favorable conditions it would have taken years to recover. Archaeological excavation indicates that the major fortified towns lay in ruins. The former state of Judah was partitioned, part going to the Babylonian province of Samaria and the rest absorbed by the Edomites (the later Idumeans), who moved out of their homeland southeast of the Dead Sea into the area around Hebron. Many Jews, finding economic and political conditions intolerable, migrated in a steadily increasing stream to Egypt to start life anew. Only a few Jews were left in the immediate environs of the ruins of Jerusalem.

ADJUSTMENT TO THE BABYLONIAN ENVIRONMENT

Things were not going too badly for the exiles in Babylonia. As already noted, the Jews were given a good bit of social freedom and economic opportunity. They proved so enterprising that a century later a Jewish family held the controlling interest in the business concern of Murashu and Sons in the city of Nippur.[12] Certainly their lot in Baby-

---

[12]A tax receipt (Late Babylonian) of Murashu and Sons is found in Pritchard, *Ancient Near Eastern Texts* [1], pp. 221–22.

lonia was a great deal better than that of modern Jews who have been crowded into dingy ghettos or concentration camps. In fact, "anti-Semitism" was unknown at that time. Babylonian Jews were permitted to move about freely, to live in their communities within or near the great cities, and to carry on their way of life.

The most serious adjustment for the Jews of Babylonia was a religious one. Their faith had been oriented to the land of Palestine, the inheritance Yahweh had given them, and to the Temple of Jerusalem, the place where Yahweh "tabernacled" in the midst of the worshiping people. The greatest danger was that in time the Jewish faith, torn from these historical moorings, would drown in the sea of Babylonian culture. In every respect, Babylonian culture was superior to the modest way of life the Jews had known in the land of Judah. In contrast to the farming and grazing land of Judah, the rich land of Babylonia was a scene of thriving agriculture and teeming industry. The proud Temple of Jerusalem, gutted by Babylonian soldiers, paled into insignificance before the marvelous temples of Babylonia. Many Jews must have wondered whether the high level of Babylonian culture might not be due to the superiority of Babylonian religion over their traditional faith.

The problem faced by the Jews in Babylonia was fundamentally the same as the one faced by early Israelites in their transition from the wilderness to the new land of Canaan. They believed that Yahweh's sovereignty had been manifested in Palestine, particularly in the Jerusalem Temple. But could Yahweh be worshiped in a strange land where other gods seemed to be in control? Even the most devout Jews, who remembered the joy they had once shared with worshipers in Jerusalem, raised this bewildering question. This mood is reflected in Psalm 137, which concludes with a terrible imprecation against the Babylonians who devastated Jerusalem and against the Edomites who gloated over its destruction.

WORSHIP WITHOUT A TEMPLE

It is a tribute to Israel's tenacity and vitality that the Mosaic faith not only survived this transition, but was immeasurably deepened and enriched. Though many Jews must have capitulated to the pressures of Babylonian culture and been absorbed into the general population, others were bound more closely to their Jewish tradition and community.

The great prophets had paved the way for the new expression of Israel's faith by proclaiming that Yahweh was not bound to the Temple of Jerusalem. In Jeremiah's letter to the exiles, he insisted that even in a place where there was no temple for Yahweh, the people could have access to God through prayer (Jer. 29:12–14). Ezekiel had a vision of Yahweh's "glory" going to the people in exile, just as the ancient ark had moved from place to place during Israel's wanderings. Similar assurance is given in a passage in Deuteronomy, written either in exile or shortly before:

> Yahweh will disperse you among the peoples, and you will be left few
> in number among the nations to which Yahweh will lead you. . . . But

from there you will seek Yahweh your God, and, if you search with all your heart and with all your being, you will find him.

—DEUTERONOMY 4:27, 29

In the Exile, then, the people realized that they could worship anywhere with the confidence that God would hear their prayers and be their sanctuary in a foreign land (see Ezek. 11:16). Undoubtedly a number of prayers in the book of Psalms were composed during the Exile by unknown individuals who, like Jeremiah in his Confessions, cried to Yahweh "out of the depths" (Ps. 130:1). Moreover, during this period Jews came together in small groups, like the elders who consulted Ezekiel in his house, to be instructed in their scriptural tradition and to worship informally. It has often been suggested that the synagogue (Greek *synagoge*, "gathering together") originated during the Exile. There is no evidence, however, of organized local assemblies: All one can safely say is that the later synagogues, which came to be scattered throughout the countries of the Dispersion, arose in response to a need first experienced during the Exile.

PRESERVATION OF THE TRADITION

Surprisingly, the sense of belonging to the covenant community was intensified, rather than weakened, by life under captivity. Even though the people were no longer held together by national allegiance, they had a common history and a received tradition. Like Isaiah in his time of discouragement (see Isa. 8:16–18), they devoted themselves to preserving the Torah until Yahweh's "face" (presence) would no longer be hidden from Israel. They studied and searched the tradition intensively for its meaning and carefully preserved their sacred lore in writing for future generations. Of course, not all the exiles were trained for this special task. But some, like Ezekiel, were priests who either knew the tradition by heart, as was common in the ancient Near East, or who had brought along with them from Jerusalem some of the sacred writings. The people looked to the priests for exposition of Israel's faith, relying especially on a class of priests known as Levites—descendants of Moses' tribe of Levi.[13] Before the Exile, these Levites had not always been priestly celebrants at the altar. Many of them, as we have seen (see p. 325), were "teaching priests" (2 Chron. 15:3; 17:9; 35:3). Their task was to give the people torah, or teaching, about how God was to be worshiped and served. Although the Levites lost some prestige as a result of Josiah's reform, which gave great power to the clergy of the Jerusalem Temple, priestly instruction continued in the Temple and later was resumed during the Exile.

---

[13]The book of Leviticus is named after these Levites in the Greek Septuagint; hence the name in the English Bible.

INTERPRETERS OF THE TRADITION

The Exile was thus a time of religious activity and of concentrated and consecrated attention to Israel's religious heritage. Some "editing" of the prophetic and historical literature was done in this period by redactors—anonymous interpreters of the tradition who believed that the sacred heritage was relevant to their time. To them the tradition was not just a museum-piece out of the past, but a living tradition through which God spoke to their contemporary situation (see Definition, pp. 355–356).

An illustration of the updating of prophecy is found at the end of the book of Amos.[14] In Amos 9:11–12, the reference to the rebuilding of "the fallen booth of David" points to a time when the Davidic dynasty had come to an end; and the prophecy that Israel would possess "the remnant of Edom" reflects resentment over Edom's grabbing a huge slice of Judah after the fall of Jerusalem. The prophetic literature was read and interpreted in light of what happened during the Exile. Increasingly the people realized that the prophetic message had been confirmed by historical events and was a basis for future hope.

During the Exile the Deuteronomistic History was brought into final shape. Most of the work had been completed in the years before Jerusalem's fall, perhaps around 600 B.C.E., slightly before the first captivity in 597 B.C.E. It is possible, however, that the first edition appeared around the year 610 B.C.E.—just before Josiah's death at Megiddo—and ended at about 2 Kings 23:25. Since the reforming king, measured by Deuteronomic standards, was a paragon of virtue, one doubts that the Deuteronomistic historians would have dealt with the king's untimely death, thereby presenting evidence to refute their central thesis that Yahweh rewards obedience. In any case, the first edition of the Deuteronomistic History could not have concluded with the last verses of the present book of Kings, which refer to the elevation of the exiled King Jehoiachin in 561 B.C.E. This means that the final chapters of 2 Kings were added during the Exile, perhaps around the year 550 B.C.E.[15]

The compilers of the Deuteronomistic History took for granted that the covenant community would be organized politically as a *kingdom*, ideally united under a Davidic king and centered in the Temple at Jerusalem. During the first years of the Exile, however, Ezekiel advocated a modified view of the covenant community. Although Ezekiel's picture of the future left room for a "prince" (Ezek. 44:3), he believed that fundamentally Israel would be a "kingdom of priests" (compare Exod. 19:6), an ecclesiastical community presided over by the priestly hierarchy of the "sons of Zadok"—that is, the Jerusalem clergy who had been in charge of the Temple since the time of Solomon, and who claimed direct descent from Aaron (Ezek. 44:13–15). This view was further devel-

---

[14]Some scholars defend Amos' authorship of some or all of the units found in the so-called "appendix" to the book of Amos (9:9–10, 11-12, 13–15). However, Amos 9:11–12 clearly comes from the exilic or early post-exilic period, and it is difficult to square the other two units with Amos' message.

[15]See Definition, p. 322, and Frank M. Cross [129], pp. 285–89.

oped by other members of the Zadok order who went into exile, especially in the second deportation of 587 B.C.E., when the Temple was destroyed and its treasures looted.

THE PRIESTLY TRADITION

The Priestly view of Israel's history is set forth in a large block of material found in the books of Genesis, Exodus, Leviticus, and Numbers. After we subtract from the Pentateuch the Old Epic tradition (J and E) and the book of Deuteronomy, the residue belongs to the Priestly tradition, usually designated by the letter P.

At one time it was believed that the Priestly material was the oldest part of the Pentateuch, and that all other literary sources were built on it. This view has been abandoned, however, because in style and theological outlook the Priestly Writing clearly reflects the worship and theology of the Jerusalem temple.[16] Yet the first impression of scholars was partially right. In the first place, the Priestly Writing preserves many ancient traditions. This does not mean that all of it is as old as the Mosaic period, for clearly one of the motives of this writing was to authorize the views and practices of Jerusalem priests by tracing their origins to Sinai. Still, much of the old tradition has been preserved. Remember that the date of literary composition does not necessarily provide an index to the age of the material itself. No longer do we think of the Pentateuch as being made up of "sources" that followed one another in chronological succession—J about 950 B.C.E., E around 750 B.C.E. or earlier, D after 700 B.C.E., and finally P in the period of the Exile. Rather, these are *parallel* traditions stemming from relatively ancient times.

In writing down their tradition, the Priestly writers drew on collections of priestly lore preserved in Temple circles. An illustration is the "Holiness Code" of Leviticus 17–26, so designated because the exhortation to Israel to be a holy people, even as Yahweh is holy, is the recurring theme of these ritual and ethical laws (Lev. 20:26). This block of Priestly teaching—really an exposition of Israel's faith—is best known for its high ethical fervor and especially for the law cited in the New Testament as the second great commandment (Mark 12:31):

> You must not exact vengeance or bear a grudge against the children of
> your people; but you must love your neighbor as yourself; I am Yahweh.
>
> —LEVITICUS 19:18

The date of the Holiness Code is uncertain. The theme suggests Ezekiel's influence, and the style at times resembles the exhortation of Deuteronomy. The Code might have been written in Jerusalem shortly before the fall of the nation, although it preserves older traditions as well.

---

[16]A major challenge to this scholarly consensus comes from the Jewish scholar Yehezkel Kaufmann, *The Religion of Israel* [134], who maintains that the whole Pentateuch is pre-exilic and specifically that P came before D. A more plausible view is that of M. Haran, *Temples and Temple Service* [463], who maintains that the Priestly Work was composed in and around the period of King Hezekiah (about 715–687 B.C.E.) and provided "the ideological conception" of Hezekiah's Reform. Later this work, preserved by priests, was promulgated as the basis of Ezra's Reform.

Thus the Priestly tradition did not originate in a single generation. Like the services of the Anglican Prayer Book, the Priestly Writing is the end product of many generations of temple usage. Study of the large mass of Priestly instruction concentrated in Exodus 25–31 and 35–40, along with all of the book of Leviticus and part of the book of Numbers, would show traces of a long history. This Priestly tradition was available to the exiled priests of the Temple of Jerusalem, some of it in oral and some in written form, some of it early and some recent in origin.

THE FORMATION OF THE PENTATEUCH

How, then, did the Priestly writers unify their religious traditions? To begin with, they did not have to create unity out of a mass of diverse materials. Already a fundamental unity was manifest in the Old Epic tradition received in expanded form, because after the fall of the Northern Kingdom, the northern (E) and southern (J) versions of this Epic were fused together (JE). The Priestly writers used the Old Epic material to enrich and supplement their own presentation, in the conviction that they were building upon and interpreting the received tradition. For example, the Priestly creation story (Gen. 1:1–2:3) was supplemented with Old Epic narratives about Paradise Lost (Gen. 2–3), and the Priestly version of the Flood was enriched with materials from the Old Epic account (Gen. 6–9). Similarly, the Priestly version of the covenant with Abraham (Gen. 17) was prefaced with Old Epic narratives about the call and covenant with Abram (Gen. 15). Thus Israel's history was presented in its final Priestly form as a comprehensive unity, moving from creation to the constitution of Israel as a worshiping community at Sinai—the presentation we now find in the books of Genesis through Numbers, the so-called "Tetrateuch." Later, the book of Deuteronomy (the preface to the Deuteronomistic History) was appended to the Priestly Writing, because it too dealt with the classical period that ended with Moses' death. The result was the Pentateuch as we have received it.

....

DEFINITION: "TETRATEUCH," "PENTATEUCH," "HEXATEUCH"

These terms, from the Greek *tetra* (four), *penta* (five), and *hexa* (six), frequently figure in discussions about the first four, five, or six books of the Bible.

One view maintains that the book of Joshua, which deals with the inheritance of the land, constitutes the climax and conclusion to the story found in the Pentateuch. Thus a "Hexateuch" gives us traditions that run continuously from Genesis through Joshua.[17]

Another view is that the old account of the occupation of the land has been lost, except for the fragmentary report of settlement in Transjordan (Num. 32). This gives us a "Tetrateuch" separate from Deuteronomy and the Deuteronomistic History in Joshua through Kings. Advocates of this view argue that Deuteronomistic influence is scarcely evident in the first four books of the Old Testament, while the Deuteronomistic style and viewpoint become dominant thereafter.[18]

---

[17]See Gerhard von Rad's seminal essay, "The Form-critical Problem of the Hexateuch" [191].
[18]This view is championed by Martin Noth in *The Deuteronomistic History* [278].

The importance of the argument for our study is that the Priestly Writing is essentially a "Tetrateuch" that extends from Genesis through Numbers, plus a passage at the end of Deuteronomy about Moses' death (Deut. 34; which resumes the story from the end of the book of Numbers). Apparently the Priestly writers felt that the climax of the story was the revelation at Sinai, not the story of the conquest of Canaan.

THE PRIESTLY POINT OF VIEW

With this background, we turn to the Priestly writing in the Pentateuch. First, notice that an atmosphere of worship pervades the whole work. To enter sympathetically into this part of the Pentateuch, one might imagine standing in an ancient cathedral, whose symmetrical design and religious symbolism, hallowed by centuries of worship, produce a solemn sense of God's holiness and majesty. To be sure, this might not be one's first impression when plowing through the prescriptions for various kinds of sacrifice, the elaborate specifications for the tabernacle and the altar, and the minute directions to priests and people. The book of Leviticus, to take one large example of Priestly teaching, seems far removed from modern forms of worship. Nevertheless, all the details bear witness to a long history of worship and to a vital experience of God's "tabernacling presence" in the sanctuary. Indeed, the purpose of the Priestly Writing is to show that the whole thrust of history, from the time of Creation, was the selection of Israel for the "service" of worship. Israel is conceived as a "congregation" (Hebrew: *'edah*), a religious community that not only bears witness to Yahweh's redemptive act of the Exodus, but also articulates the creation's praise of the Creator. Israel's whole life was to be a "liturgy," a service of God. Even today the solemnity of the Priestly blessing, entrusted to Aaron and his sons (the Zadokite Jerusalem clergy), brings a reverent hush over a worshiping congregation:

> Yahweh bless you and keep you:
> Yahweh deal kindly with you,
>   and be gracious to you:
> Yahweh look with favor upon you,
>   and give you peace.

> —NUMBERS 6:24–26

THE DIVINE PLAN IN HISTORY

The Priestly writers stand within the worshiping community of Israel, called into being by Yahweh's marvelous deeds in the time of the Exodus, and look backward to the very beginning, to Creation. From this perspective the divine purpose follows a prearranged, systematic plan that unfolds in three successive periods, each marked by an "everlasting covenant" (Hebrew: *berîth 'ôlam*) in which God makes an unconditional commitment. In the Priestly view, the succession of divine covenants represents a history of God's dealings with the world on the basis of pure grace (Latin: *sola gratia*), unconditioned by human performance. The first period reached a climax in God's unconditional covenant with Noah and through him with all creatures, human and nonhuman (Gen. 9:1–17). The high point of the second period was God's unconditional covenant with Abra[ha]m (and through him with all descendants of Israel's ancestors; Gen. 17:1–14). The third period culminated in the covenant of Sinai, regarded in priestly perspective as an "everlasting covenant" (Exod. 31:12–17) though at the same time a reaffirmation and ratification of the covenant with the ancestors (Exod. 2:24). The Priestly writers use the Old Epic tradition (JE) to enrich and fill out this "periodized history" of God's covenants, which extends from Genesis through Numbers (the Tetrateuch). Consider how the history unfolds in the final, Priestly version of the Torah:

1. FROM CREATION TO THE FLOOD. The first period began with the Creation and extended into the time of Noah. The Priestly writers set forth their understanding of the meaning of this era in the Priestly creation story (Gen. 1:1–2:3), supplemented with the Old Epic (J) story of Paradise.[19] Few passages in the Bible excel the majesty of style and sublimity of thought in this Priestly account. Its stately rhythms and sonorous refrains reflect years of usage in the Temple, where it was solemnly recited and gradually assumed its present form of liturgical prose. In other words, though the story now appears in the Priestly Torah, given final shape in the period of the Exile or even later, it reflects a long history of liturgical usage and bears the marks of intense theological reflection over many generations.[20] The majestic cadences of Priestly prose, verging on poetry, still evoke a sense of wonder before the mystery and marvel of the Creation. Appropriately, during the first human voyage around the moon, millions listened on Earth as the Apollo 8 commander, Frank Borman, read the first ten verses of Genesis (Christmas Eve, 1968).

Anyone looking for a scientific account of the origin of the world can find many discrepancies in the Priestly story. To the scientific mind it is odd to hear that the earth was created before the sun, or that light was created before the heavenly lights—sun, moon, and stars. It is fruitless to try to harmonize this account with modern science by saying, for instance, that the six creative days correspond to geological periods, or that the creation of living things followed a pattern of evolution. The cosmology, or picture of the universe, presupposed in the story was inherited from Israel's cultural environment. Unlike modern scientific cosmology, the universe was pictured as a three-storied

---

[19]For an exposition of the Priestly story, see Gerhard von Rad's *Genesis* [305] and "Notes on the Priestly Account of Creation," pp. 63–67. Von Rad rightly stresses that the two accounts supplement each other in order to provide a fuller picture.

[20]See B. W. Anderson, "A Stylistic Study of the Priestly Creation Story," *Canon and Authority* [178], pp. 148–62.

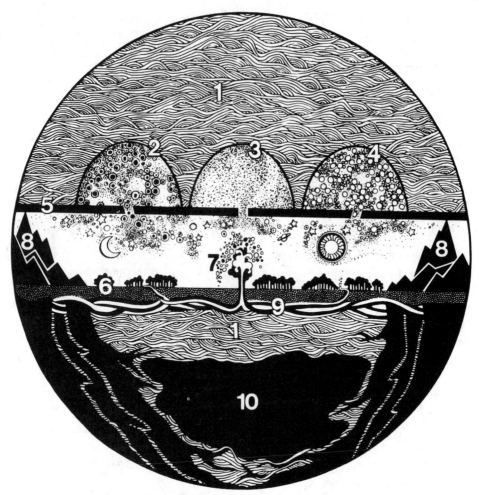

The ancient pictorial view of the universe: (1) The waters above and below the earth; (2,3,4) Chambers of hail, rain, snow; (5) The firmament with its "sluices"; (6) The surface of the earth; (7) The navel of the earth: "fountain of the Great Deep"; (8) The mountain-pillars supporting the firmament; (9) Sweet waters (rivers, lakes, seas) on which the earth floats; (10) Sheol, the realm of Death (the "Pit").

structure: "heaven above, the earth beneath, and the water under the earth," as an editorial expansion of the Ten Commandments puts it (Deut. 5:8). The earth was conceived as having been formed by dividing "the waters from the waters," by raising up a solid substance, or firmament, to hold back the primeval ocean (Gen. 1:6). Thus the habitable world was surrounded on every hand by chaotic waters that, unless checked by God's creative power, would destroy the earth (see the Flood story; Job 38:8–11; Ps. 104:5–9). In this respect, the story has affinities with the mythopoeic view of the uni-

verse presented in the Babylonian myth of *Enuma elish,* where the creation of the universe results from a fierce struggle between the god Marduk and Tiamat, the dragon of
watery chaos.[21]

But the Priestly account is not a treatise on scientific origins. Here the poetry of
faith speaks of something lying behind or beyond human experience: the origination
and ordering of all that exists by the sovereign, initiating will of the Creator (see Job
38:4–7). Unlike ancient polytheistic myths, which depicted the birth of the gods out of
the intermingling waters of chaos, this liturgy affirms the holy transcendence of the
Creator, upon whose sovereign will all creatures, terrestrial and celestial, depend for
their being. The heavens declare God's glory (Ps. 19:1), but the Creator is neither part
nor process of creation. Nothing is independent, self-created, self-sustaining. Indeed,
were it not for the Creator's power, the source and vitality of all that exists, the world
would revert to primeval, meaningless chaos.

The theme of God's sovereignty over all aspects of Creation reaches climactic expression in the account of the creation of humanity (Hebrew: *'adam*). By placing this
act last, the Priestly account indicates that human beings are the crown of God's creation and, as such, are commissioned with a special role in God's creation. This high
calling is emphasized by a solemn decision, announced in the Heavenly Council (see
the "us" and "our" of Gen. 1:26), to create *'adam*, consisting co-equally of "male and
female," in the image of God. Just as the image of a king, set up in various provinces of
an empire, was a visible token of his dominion, so human beings are to be living representatives of God's rule on earth.[22] Contrary to modern views of dominion, human beings are not given free license to exercise their power over nature and the environment.
Rather, they are to be God's image or representative on earth, administering God's
earthly estate wisely and benevolently. Inspired by the thought that human beings, so
tiny and ephemeral in the vast cosmos, have been given a special role in God's creation,
an ancient poet uses hymnic language with close affinities to the Genesis creation story:

> When I survey your heavens, your fingerworks,
>> the moon and the stars that you have established,
> what are human beings that you consider them,
>> human persons that you seek them out?
> Yet you have placed them slightly below heavenly beings,
>> and with honor and majesty have crowned them.

[21]The Babylonian myth is in Pritchard, *Ancient Near Eastern Texts* [1], pp. 60–72. See Hermann Gunkel, "The
Influence of Babylonian Mythology upon the Biblical Creation Story," in *Creation in the Old Testament*
[132], pp. 25–52; B. W. Anderson, ed., and "Mythological and Theological Dimensions of Biblical Creation Faith," pp. 1–24.

[22]This figure of speech comes from Gerhard von Rad, *Genesis* [305], pp. 57–61, who points out that the
"image" should not be restricted to the "spiritual" nature, but applies to the whole being—including the
human body, which is truly a work of divine art. Elsewhere the Hebrew word for "image" refers to very
concrete, visible things, like an idol (Num. 33:52) or a picture (Ezek. 23:14).

You have given them dominion over your handiwork,
> everything you have put in subjection to them:
sheep and oxen altogether, wild beasts also,
> birds of the air and fish of the sea,
everything that courses through the waterways.

—PSALMS 8:3–8

God's blessing

According to the Priestly scheme, the first period was inaugurated with God's (*Elohim's*) blessing, which empowered man and woman to "be fruitful and multiply, and fill the earth and subdue it" (Gen. 1:28). This blessing was accompanied by a divine restriction: Human beings were to be vegetarians rather than carnivores. Thus humans and animals were to live in a "peaceable kingdom."

The account reaches its conclusion with the "Sabbath rest," for after six days God "rested" (Hebrew: *shabath*) from all the work of creation (Gen. 2:2–3; compare Exod. 20:11; 31:17). Here we see that the story, though dealing with *'adam* (humanity), concerns Israel in a special way; for the Priestly writers anticipate the institution of the day of rest in the Mosaic period (Exod. 16). In this way they tie the beginning of the narrative to its climax, suggesting that the days of the week are not an empty cycle of "tomorrow and tomorrow and tomorrow," but times embraced within God's purpose for Israel and all humankind. God claims this one segment of time as holy, and thereby endows all times with ultimate meaning.

2. FROM NOAH TO ABRAHAM. According to the Priestly view, the Flood marked the end of the first period and the beginning of a new era. This great catastrophe, during which the earth almost reverted to pre-Creation chaos,[23] was motivated by the universal spread of "violence" (Gen. 6:11). The Priestly writers illustrate "violence" by incorporating episodes from the Old Epic tradition: the rebellion of the first human beings in the Garden (Gen. 3:1–24); murder in the first family (4:1–16); Lamech's measureless blood-revenge (4:17–26); and the strange story of the heavenly beings ("sons of God") who seized beautiful human maidens and had intercourse with them (6:1–4). At the end of the Flood, however, God made an "everlasting covenant" (Hebrew: *berîth 'ôlam*)—that is, an unconditional covenant, with Noah and all living creatures, promising never again to threaten the earth with a return to primeval chaos.

This unconditional commitment is prefaced by a renewal of the blessing given at the time of Creation to be fertile, multiply, and exercise dominion over the earth (Gen. 9:1–13). The Noachic covenant introduced a new privilege: Animal meat could be

---

[23]In the Flood Story (Gen. 6–9), the Priestly and Old Epic narratives are closely blended (see outline, p. 144). In the Old Epic tradition the Flood resulted from a heavy rain (Gen. 7:4, 12). According to the Priestly version, "the fountains of the great deep (Hebrew: *tehom*)" and "the windows of heaven" were opened (Gen. 7:11)—that is, the waters above and the waters below threatened a return to chaos.

eaten provided that it was properly slaughtered, for the blood, believed to contain the potency of life, was sacred to God. This principle of "reverence of life" was accompanied by a stringent prohibition: There shall be no wanton shedding of the blood of any creatures, especially the blood of a human being, for 'adam (humankind) is made "in the image of God" (Gen. 9:4–6). Since the Noachic covenant was a universal covenant with human and nonhuman creatures (including birds, beasts, and cattle) and even with earth itself, it was signified by a sign visible to all creatures on earth—namely, the rainbow. Every rainbow after a storm would be a token of God's ('Elohim's) gracious sovereignty over the whole creation (Gen. 9:8–17). In Jewish tradition the privileges and restrictions of the Noachic covenant are regarded as applicable to all peoples, for the covenant was made not only with Israel, but also with Noah, the father of Shem (Semites), Ham, and Japheth (see Acts 15:20; 21:25). According to the Priestly genealogy, all peoples sprang from these three sons (Gen. 10:32).   *ill peoples*

3. FROM ABRAHAM TO MOSES. The third period began with Abraham who, like Noah, was considered "blameless" in his generation (Gen. 17). Once again, a divine blessing is given, this time by 'El Shaddai ("God Almighty"), an ancient ancestral epithet for the deity, who promises that the patriarch will have a great posterity. At that time the older name Abram ("may the [divine] Father be exalted") was changed to *Name* Abraham (interpreted as "father of a multitude") to signify the new relationship.

The covenant with Abraham, like that with Noah, is an "everlasting covenant," unconditional in character. 'El Shaddai promises to give the land as an "everlasting possession" and to "be God" to Abraham and his descendants—an anticipation of the revelation at Sinai when God's personal name was given to the people (Exod. 6:2–9). Circumcision is not a condition of this covenant but a physical *sign* of membership in the covenant community. The Priestly writers state plainly that any male who has not kept this "covenant of flesh" is to be excluded from the Israelite community: Such a man breaks the covenant and has no claim upon the divine promises. The covenant relationship itself, however, is based solely on divine grace and initiative and cannot be annulled (compare Gal. 3:16–18). The Priestly writers prefaced this account with the Old Epic tradition of the Abrahamic covenant (Gen. 15:7–21), which also states that the covenant was based upon the deity's oath, not upon human performance (see pp. 41–42).

God's promise to Abraham is further emphasized in another Priestly narrative, the story of Abraham's purchase of a cave at Hebron for a burial place (Gen. 23). The burial of Abraham and Sarah in this place was to be an "earnest" or foretaste of the fulfillment of God's promise that Israel would some day inherit the land. Even though Abraham did not live to see that day, he entered into it through his death and burial in the promised land. The Cave of Machpelah, the traditional site of Abraham and Sarah's interment, also supposedly houses the remains of Isaac, Rebekah, Jacob, and Leah. (The traditional grave of Rachel is near Bethlehem.) Today a mosque, situated in the modern city of Hebron, rests upon what is claimed to be this cave; visitors can view the hallowed chamber through a small hole in the floor of the sacred religious center. The mosque of Hebron is called the *Haram el-Khalil* ("the sacred precinct of the friend [the Merciful One, God]") in recollection of Abraham's standing as "the friend of God" (2 Chron. 20:7; compare Isa. 41:8).

All these passages lead step by step to the supreme revelation in the Mosaic period, when the Abrahamic covenant was ratified. The Priestly covenantal history, as we have seen, begins with a canvas as wide as the whole Creation. The scope of vision is ecumenical, for the creation story, anticipating the covenant with Noah, embraces the entire human and nonhuman realm. From this wide scope the Priestly vision narrows until it concentrates on Abraham and Sarah, to whom are given covenant promises that anticipate the revelation at Sinai.

The Priestly Writing, in contrast to the Old Epic (JE) tradition, has no independent account of the covenant at Sinai. The reason for this seems to be that the Mosaic covenant, in Priestly perspective, is regarded as an extension and ratification of the Abrahamic covenant (Exod. 2:24; 6:4–5). On this assumption, the Priestly writers include the Old Epic tradition about the conditional Sinai covenant (Exod. 19–24, 32–34). When the ancient covenant tradition was incorporated into the Priestly context, however, the Sinai covenant received a new theological interpretation.

The Abrahamic covenant was an "everlasting covenant" that gave the assurance that *'El Shaddai* would be Israel's God and would give Abraham's descendants the land of Canaan as an "everlasting possession." In the Priestly view, the Mosaic covenant is of the same type: namely, a covenant in perpetuity (Hebrew: *berîth 'ôlam*, Exod. 31:16), the sign of which is the Sabbath (Exod. 31:12–17; compare 16:22–36). The key Priestly passage in Exodus 16:1–9 affirms that now a special relationship between God and people, symbolized by the giving of the sacred name Yahweh, is in effect. This new relationship, which constitutes Israel as a worshiping community, fulfills and ratifies the pledge made to Abraham and his descendants, "I will be your God" (Gen. 17:7–8).[24]

With this interpretation we begin to understand why the Tabernacle (Hebrew: *mishkan*) is the central Priestly institution, located in the center of the Israelite camp (Num. 2). The Priestly writers build on the ancient tradition of the Tent of Meeting (see p. 105), but they interpret the old shrine to mean that Yahweh has chosen to "tent" or tabernacle in the midst of the people:

> I will tabernacle in the midst of the Israelites, and I will be their God.
> And so they will know that I am Yahweh their God, who brought them out
> of the land of Egypt to tabernacle in their midst. I am Yahweh their God.
>
> —EXODUS 29:45–46

---

[24] See further B. W. Anderson, "Creation and the Noachic Covenant," in *From Creation to New Creation* [146], chap. 9.

The tabernacling presence is "the supreme benefit of the Sinai covenant," as one historian observes, for "Yahweh would not only become their god, he would become god in their midst."[25] Another Priestly passage strikes the same note: the holy God "walks about among them" (Lev. 26:11–13). Yahweh's sacramental presence in the center of the community requires that no ethical or ritual impurity be permitted to defile the people. The congregation (Hebrew: *'edah*) must be healthy and holy. Just as a doctor gives a patient a prescription to restore health, so the Priestly writers believed that God had revealed laws and institutions so that Israel could be a holy people. In the Priestly view, however, there was nothing burdensome in the Torah. Rather, it was a "means of grace" that God offered the people. Knowing that God's benevolence was behind all that was given, the Priestly writers move toward the climax of the Mosaic revelation as one would hasten to receive a great gift. In connection with the Old Epic account of the Sinai sojourn, for example, they introduce a large body of material dealing with the tabernacle and its furnishings, the Ark of the Testimony ("covenant"), various kinds of sacrifice, laws relating to "kosher" or permitted foods, regulations for the sacred calendar, and so on—all in the space between the Old Epic story of the making of the covenant (Exod. 24) and the departure from Sinai (Num. 10:11ff.).

This Priestly block of material particularly stresses the system of sacrifices. In Priestly tradition, sacrifice was not understood as a means of appeasing divine wrath or of cajoling God to show favors. Rather, the sacrifices described in Leviticus 1–7 are means of atonement, of healing a breach in the covenant relationship and reuniting the people in communion with God. Sacrifice was believed to be efficacious in restoring a broken relationship, not because blood had magical power in itself, but because God had provided the symbolic means of grace by which guilt was pardoned and the people could live in the presence of the holy God (Lev. 17:11; a key passage). Largely because of prophetic preaching concerning divine judgment, as well as the crisis of the Exile that prompted a profound sense of remorse and failure, Priestly tradition was deeply sensitive to the persistence of sin that threatened the holiness (wholeness) of the community. Thus the Day of Atonement (Lev. 16), one of the great holy days, provided an occasion for releasing the people from corporate guilt. Lest sacrifice become an end in itself, the Priestly tradition emphasized that no sacrificial rite was effective in the case of deliberate sin ("with a high hand"), which represented outright revolt against God and the revealed law (Num. 15:30). Sacrifice is effective only in the case of "hidden sins" inadvertently committed (see Ps. 19:12–13). Even then, sacrifice must be accompanied by confession and repentance.

---

[25]Frank M. Cross, "The Priestly Work" [129], pp. 298–300, points out that the Priestly Writer, in speaking of the "covenant presence" of Yahweh in the shrine, employed the archaizing technical term *škn* (*shaken, mishkan*) which in Canaanite meant "to tent" or "to lead the roving life of the tent dweller") and studiously avoided the verb *yšb* (*yashab*; "to dwell"), thereby repudiating the notion that the sanctuary is literally God's dwelling place. Our discussion of the Priestly "periodization" of history is influenced by this work.

The Priestly Periodization of History

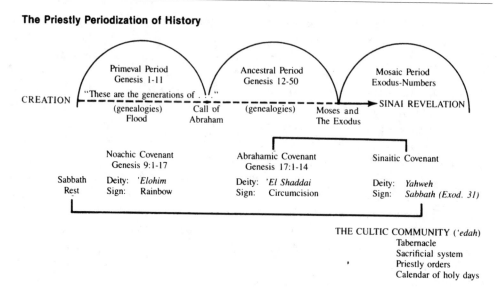

In the Priestly view, the successive periods of revelation were marked by a sequence of names for the deity. In the first era, with its ecumenical horizon, the deity was known as *'Elohim* (NRSV: "God"). In the second period, the deity was known to Abraham by the special name *'El Shaddai* (often translated "God Almighty"). Not until the third, Mosaic period was the cultic name (YHWH) introduced (Exod. 6:2–3)—a name so holy that it must not be taken in vain, so ineffable that no layperson could pronounce its sacred syllables. Thus the disclosure of the sacred name, at the very climax of God's historical design, inaugurated a new and special relationship between God and Israel. In this Priestly view the goal toward which everything moves is the constitution of Israel as a cultic community (Hebrew: *'edah*)—a community called to serve God by following the laws that order life and worship. In short, Israel is a holy people living in the presence of the holy God. The Priestly view of the historical movement from Creation through a succession of covenants to the realization of the divine purpose is illustrated in the diagram above, "The Priestly Periodization of History."

THE PRIESTLY VIEW OF HISTORY

One might say that the Priestly view is an "interpretation" that does not give us a realistic view of Israel's past. Admittedly, these writers viewed Israel's history through the tinted glasses of Priestly bias, giving a somewhat artificial picture of the Mosaic period. But is there *any* history without interpretation? Standing in the crisis of the Exile, the Priestly writers tried to understand why Israel had failed. Through their reconstruction of the Mosaic period they presented a program the people should follow, retelling the story in a way that might not have been appropriate in the time of Elijah or Jeremiah.[26] For our word "history" they would probably use "genealogy," as in Genesis 37:2 (NRSV: "This is the story of the family of Jacob"). Indeed, the Priestly writers punctuate the Primeval History (Gen. 2–11) and Ancestral History (Gen. 12–50)—received from the Old Epic tradition—with the recurring formula "These are the generations [genealogy] of . . ." (Gen. 2:4a; 5:1; 6:9; 10:1; 11:10; 11:27; and so on). In this way they set forth the history of God's covenants.

Like some of Israel's prophets, the Priestly writers combined belief in God's universal sway with belief in God's special revelation to Israel. They affirmed that God, the Creator and Sovereign of the nations, chose the people Israel out of all peoples, and separated them for a special blessing by giving them the Torah. We see this narrowing of attention in the genealogies or "family trees" that make up the skeleton of the Priestly Writing in the book of Genesis. With the exception of Jacob and Esau, the line is traced through the firstborn son, and other offspring are left aside .

Even in these dry genealogical tables (the "begats" of the King James Version of the Bible), we can see the theological purpose that governs the Priestly Writing. Just as—looking forward—the Creation sets the stage for the historical scheme that reaches its climax with the giving of the Torah to Moses, so—looking backward—Israel's line can be traced through the generations to the first man, Adam (Gen 5:1). The Creator has singled out Israel for special service in response to special revelation. The Priestly writers did not insist that Israel's special place in God's plan was based solely on birth, for Esau as firstborn should have been the rightful heir, not Jacob. Departing in this instance from tracing the line through the firstborn son, they recognized that Israel's election rests solely upon the grace of God who chooses freely. Nevertheless, when the Jews returned from the Exile it was considered very important to be born in a Jewish family that could trace its ancestry back through the generations.

A PRIESTLY THEOCRACY

During the Exile, as we have seen, the people sought a new understanding of the community that still bound them together despite national disaster. As they searched their scriptural tradition, they were reminded that the covenant community originated at a time when Israel was not a nation and had no king, except Yahweh. The priests sought to return to this ancient theocracy. Ezekiel, a member of the Zadokite clergy of the Temple, was influential in establishing the view that Israel was fundamentally a wor-

---

[26]See Walter Brueggemann, "The Kerygma of the Priestly Writers," *The Vitality of Old Testament Traditions* [70], pp. 101–30.

shiping community—a holy people, living in a holy city, and worshiping in a holy Temple. Indeed, Judaism had its major roots in the Exile. From Babylonia Ezra brought with him the Torah that priests compiled there, making it the basis of the post-exilic community (see Chapter 15). But before we consider these developments further, we turn to another figure of the Exile, one in whom Israel's prophetic movement reached its highest and deepest expression.

CHAPTER 14

THE DAWN

OF A

NEW AGE

According to the historian Charles A. Beard, one of the lessons of history can be summarized in the proverb: "The bee fertilizes the flower it robs." This is particularly true of the history of Israel during the Exile. Although the experience seemed bitter to many at the time, the people came to realize that God was working for good. Prophets like Hosea prophesied that Yahweh led the people of Israel into the wilderness—the "wasteland" of despair—in order to speak to their heart. Had it been possible to bypass this journey, a new pilgrimage "round about by way of the wilderness," Israel's political situation might have been better at the time, but its faith would have been immeasurably impoverished. Although the nation had been robbed and plundered by conquerors, Israel's experience of historical tragedy fertilized and deepened religious understanding.

NEW WORLD HORIZONS

As experiences in the twentieth century have shown, world-shaking events often have a double—and seemingly contradictory—effect on people's lives. Such crises can bring about both a renewal of national loyalties and a wider vision of "one world." This twofold perspective came to expression during the Exile. The collapse of the nation

Biblical Readings: The essential reading for this chapter is Isaiah 40–55. Supplement with the closely-related Isaiah 56–66, and Psalms 47, 93, and 96–99 (the "enthronement Psalms").

brought about an intense awareness of the uniqueness of Israel's calling, a point of view championed by Ezekiel and the Jerusalem priests who produced the Priestly edition of the Pentateuch. The surrounding culture was regarded as a threat to Israel's faith, as it had proved to be throughout Israelite history. Israel was called to be a holy people separated from the rest of the nations by the purity of its life and its complete submission to God's Torah. But the Exile also awakened a new world-consciousness. Israel's faith was enlarged by the vision of new horizons that had never been seen so clearly before, not even in the cosmopolitan age of Solomon. The people realized that they must look beyond their own circumscribed community to the whole civilized world if they would behold the glory and majesty of Yahweh's purpose in history. The time was ripe for a deeper understanding of the conviction, expressed in the narratives of the all-Israelite Old Epic tradition, that Israel was called to be Yahweh's agent in bringing blessing to "all the families of the earth" (Gen. 12:1–3; see pp. 153–156).

THE SECOND ISAIAH

A new understanding of Israel's special place in world history was magnificently expressed by an unknown prophetic interpreter whose writings are found in the latter part of the book of Isaiah, beginning with Isaiah 40. In contrast to Jeremiah, with whom this prophet had close affinities, or even Ezekiel, whose message also influenced him, we know absolutely nothing about his life or the events of his personal career. He is known to us only through the impact of his words. For want of a better title, this poet is usually called "Second Isaiah" (or "Deutero-Isaiah"), because his writings are included in the scroll of Isaiah of Jerusalem. In spite of his anonymity, many have acclaimed Second Isaiah as one of the greatest prophets of the Old Testament.

TROUBLES IN BABYLONIA

Before turning to the poems of so-called Second Isaiah, we must consider the sweeping historical changes that took place about the middle of the sixth century B.C.E. Keep in mind that for centuries the center of world civilization had been the Fertile Crescent. This area had been under the domination of Semitic empires since the time of Hammurabi in the eighteenth century B.C.E., with the exception of the interval of Hittite and Egyptian ascendancy in the middle of that millennium. The old Babylonian empire, which held sway about the time of Abraham, was succeeded eventually by the Assyrian empire in the time of Amos and Hosea. After more than a century of Semitic rule under the Assyrians, the Fertile Crescent next came under the sway of the Neo-Babylonian (or "Chaldean") empire. But this empire lasted not much longer than its first and greatest emperor, Nebuchadrezzar (605/4–562 B.C.E.), whose death set off a reaction of murder and intrigue. The throne changed three times in the space of seven years. One cause of the unrest was an attempt by the Babylonian priesthood, whom Nebuchadrezzar had sought to keep under the control of the crown, to regain power.

Rumors of these troubles spread throughout the vast empire, and to many it must have seemed that the end of Babylonian tyranny was near.

In spite of the Jew's tolerable conditions in exile, their hope for a return to Jerusalem (Zion) burned intensely. The Deuteronomistic History, completed after the fall of Jerusalem in 587 B.C.E., was dominated by the conviction that even the destruction of the Temple and the Exile could not eclipse Yahweh's promise to David: It concluded with the news that one of David's descendants, Jehoiachin, was still alive in exile. According to this history the successor of Nebuchadrezzar, Amel-Marduk (called "Evil-merodach" in the Hebrew Bible) did something that must have kindled the people's hopes of return. Jehoiachin, the legitimate claimant to the Davidic throne, was released from prison in the year 561 B.C.E. and given a position of prestige in the Babylonian court (2 Kings 25:27–30). The exiled Jewish king probably stood as a symbol to the nationalists who still dreamed of a restored Jewish state in Palestine under Davidic rule. Sheshbazzar, the man who later negotiated permission for the Jews to return to their homeland, might have been one of the sons of Jehoiachin.[1]

The favorable moment for Jewish "Zionism" came very soon. After seven years of instability, Nabonidus came to the throne of Babylon (556–539 B.C.E.). He was an unpopular king, especially with the priests of Marduk, who hated him for constructing a rival sanctuary to the moon god Sin. Nabonidus went off on a distant expedition to Tema in Arabia and, after conquering the city, established it as his royal residence. He shared rule over his empire with his son, Belshazzar (about whom we learn more in the book of Daniel). Political troubles started in the plateau of Iran (Airyana), the home of Aryan-speaking people. In the middle of the sixth century B.C.E. the Iranian highland was divided into three areas: Media, Persia, and Elam, although Elam was actually under the control of Persia. Thus the two peoples of the region were the Medes and the Persians. The Medes had earlier joined with the Babylonians to give the death-blow to the Assyrians, and the two allies had divided the spoils of the Assyrian empire between them.

THE RISE OF CYRUS OF PERSIA

Belshazzar must have seen the handwriting on the wall as he considered with envy and apprehension the growing Median kingdom stretching from central Asia Minor into the territory now known as Iran. When Cyrus, a Persian king from the Elamite city of Anshan, challenged the power of his Median overlord in the year 553 B.C.E., he was probably encouraged by the Babylonian ruler. After all, it was to Babylonia's advantage to cut down the power of its former ally. In the unpredictable game of politics, however, events took an unexpected turn. Within three years Cyrus had defeated Astyages,

[1]According to W. F. Albright, Sheshbazzar appears as a son of Jehoiachin under the name Shenazzar in the genealogy in 1 Chronicles 3:18. See *The Biblical Period from Abraham to Ezra* (Pittsburgh: Biblical Colloquium, 1950; New York: Harper & Row, 1963), pp. 48–49.

the Median king (550 B.C.E.). On the crest of this victory, he pressed on to further triumphs beyond the Median borders in Asia Minor. In 546 B.C.E., Cyrus conquered the kingdom of Lydia (now the western part of Turkey), ruled by Croesus, whose great wealth is still proverbial. As a result of these smashing victories, Cyrus controlled a vast empire extending from the Persian Gulf to the Aegean Sea. Finally Nabonidus, realizing the gravity of the situation, returned to Babylon to celebrate the New Year's festival. But it was too late to check the internal disorder within his empire and to halt the momentum of the Persian advance. In 539 B.C.E., the Persians and Babylonians fought a great battle at Opis on the Tigris River. The Persians won, and serious Babylonian resistance came to an end. A few weeks later, the city of Babylon capitulated to Cyrus without a struggle (see Chronological Chart 8, p. 372).

Cyrus' account of his Babylonian triumph is recorded on the famous Cyrus Cylinder—an inscription on a clay barrel.[2] The account begins with a condemnation of Nabonidus for ignoring the temple of Marduk and for subjecting the Babylonian people to slave labor. For this reason, "the lord of the gods [Marduk] became terribly angry" and, accompanied by his retinue of gods, withdrew from Babylon. Seeing the terrible ruin of the country, however, Marduk showed mercy on the Babylonians:

> He scanned and looked (through) all the countries, searching for a
> righteous ruler willing to lead him [Marduk] (in the annual procession on
> New Year's Day). (Then) he pronounced the name of Cyrus, king of
> Anshan, declared him the ruler of all the world.

The Persian account goes on to say that Marduk ordained Cyrus to march against Babylon, "going at his side like a real friend," for Marduk was pleased with the conqueror's kind treatment of his subjects. Cyrus was allowed to enter Babylon "without any battle," and the whole population of Marduk's city "greeted him as a master through whose help they had come (again) to life from death." Cyrus boasts of his efforts to obtain peace in Babylonia. He claims to have abolished forced labor, improved housing conditions, and enjoyed the affection of the people. The account concludes by referring to the renown of his name throughout the world, owing to his power and benevolence. The account explicitly states that he returned sacred images to the peoples from whom they had been taken, rebuilt their sanctuaries, gathered together foreign exiles and returned them to their former homes, and restored the idols of Sumer and Akkad that Nabonidus had displaced from their own chapels (see Insert 16–1).

This is the victor's own account, which undoubtedly contains a good bit of propaganda. Nevertheless, in contrast to other ancient Near Eastern conquerors—especially the Assyrians and the Babylonians—Cyrus was extraordinarily benevolent and humane. Instead of executing Astyages of Media and Croesus of Lydia, he permitted each to retain a royal retinue. He protected the treasures of Babylon, and respected traditional

[2]See Pritchard, *Ancient Near Eastern Texts* [1], pp. 315–16.

forms of religion. He discontinued the Assyro-Babylonian policy of deporting captive populations to foreign lands, even permitting exiles to return to their homelands. He has rightly been called one of the most enlightened rulers in human history.

So began the great Persian empire, which lasted for two hundred years until the rise of Alexander the Great. It is against the background of these momentous international developments, which sent a wave of expectancy throughout the ancient world and widened horizons of thought as never before, that we must understand the prophecy of Second Isaiah.

THE POEMS OF SECOND ISAIAH

FIRST ISAIAH AND SECOND ISAIAH

There is widespread agreement among biblical scholars that "First Isaiah" did not write Isaiah 40–66. The most obvious reason for this is the different historical circumstances presupposed in the two main sections of the book of Isaiah. In the writings of Isaiah of Jerusalem (Isa. 1–39), the people are still living in Judah under Davidic kings. Jerusalem is regarded as the holy City that Yahweh will not allow to fall, and the Temple—the scene of Isaiah's inaugural vision—is still standing. When we turn to the section beginning with Isaiah 40, however, a complete change in the historical situation is apparent. The cities of Judah are desolate, the Temple lies in ruins, and the people are in Babylonian exile. Clearly the Israelite monarchy is a thing of the past. These historical circumstances are not predicted for some time in the future, but are assumed to be existing in the *present* (see Isa. 44:26; 49:19, 51:3). Moreover, the Assyrians, whose advance across the Fertile Crescent Isaiah mentions specifically, are ignored. Instead, Babylonia rules the world (Isa. 47), though the end of its rule is at hand (48:14, 20; 52:11–12). Cyrus of Persia is mentioned twice (Isa. 44:28; 45:1): He is hailed as Yahweh's "shepherd" who will soon decree the rebuilding of Jerusalem and the Temple, and is called Yahweh's "Messiah" (Hebrew: *mashiah*)—that is, the one anointed to fulfill the divine purpose.[3]

Study of vocabulary, poetic structure, and meter further supports the view that the poems in Isaiah 40–66 were not written in the eighth century B.C.E. by Isaiah of Jerusalem. Literary style is always an important criterion of authorship. Even in English translation, literary differences between the two main sections of the book of Isaiah are noticeable. The oracles of Isaiah of Jerusalem are expressed in a balanced, stately, poetic form that was appropriate to his warnings of the impending day of disaster. In the last section of the book, however, we encounter poetry of great joy, beauty, and power. The poet breaks forth into lyrical strains of triumphant song. Prophecy and poetry merge in

---

[3]At that time "Messiah" was not a technical term for the future messianic king (see Definition, p. 211).

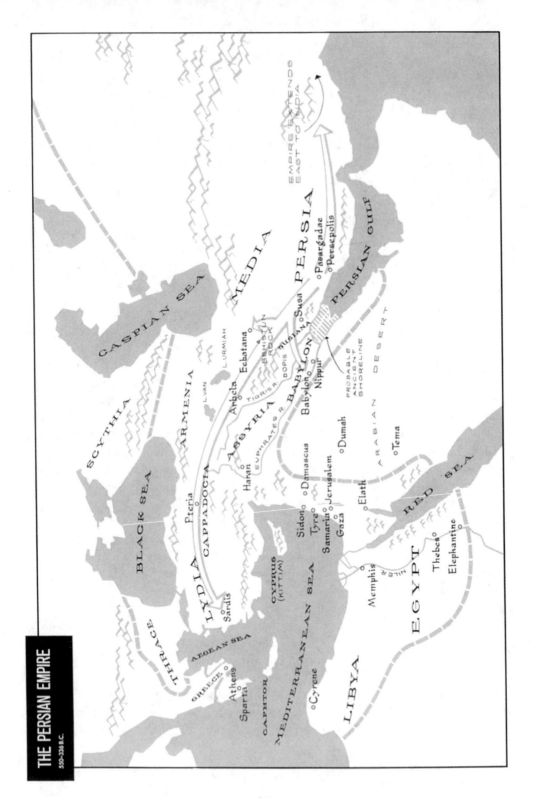

THE PERSIAN EMPIRE

550-330 B.C.

CASPIAN SEA

SCYTHIA

BLACK SEA

THRACE

AEGEAN SEA

GREECE
Athens
Sparta

CAPHTOR

MEDITERRANEAN SEA

CYPRUS
(KITTIM)

LYDIA
Sardis

CAPPADOCIA
Pteria

ARMENIA

MEDIA

PERSIA

EMPIRE EXTENDS EAST TO INDIA

Pasargadae
Persepolis

PERSIAN GULF

BEHISTUN ROCK

Ecbatana

Arbela

L.VAN

L.URMIAH

ASSYRIA

TIGRIS R.

EUPHRATES R.

Haran

Opis

Babylon
BABYLON

Susa

Nippur

PROBABLE ANCIENT SHORELINE

ARABIAN DESERT

Dumah

Tema

Damascus

Sidon
Tyre
Samaria
Jerusalem
Gaza

Elath

Dumah

RED SEA

NILE R.

Memphis

EGYPT

Thebes
Elephantine

LIBYA

Cyrene

such a matchless synthesis that we are justified in calling Second Isaiah one of the greatest poets of all time.

Accompanying this rhapsodic language is a new theological emphasis that gives the poems an entirely different tone from that found in the message of First Isaiah. While Jerusalem was still standing and the nation of Judah was involved in the political storm of the time, it was appropriate for Isaiah to speak words of warning and rebuke. To him the Day of Judgment was at hand, and he appealed to the people to repent while there was still time. But Second Isaiah strikes a different note. According to him, divine judgment had already taken place; Jerusalem had received from Yahweh's hand "double for all its sins" (Isa. 40:2). Second Isaiah's commission was to "speak tenderly" to Jerusalem, proclaiming to a despairing people that Yahweh was coming to release Israel from bondage and to restore the shattered foundations of the homeland. Pardon, deliverance, restoration, and grace are the characteristic notes of his message of comfort and hope.

These three lines of argument—historical setting, literary style, and theological perspective—lead to the conclusion that the author of much of the material found in Isaiah 40–66 was a prophet of the Exile who lived some 200 years after Isaiah of Jerusalem. His writings presuppose that Cyrus was already a prominent political figure, perhaps because of his victory over Croesus, king of Lydia, in 546 B.C.E., or because of his early triumphs in northern Babylonia shortly thereafter. Indeed, Cyrus' victorious campaign is actually described in Isaiah 41:2–3, 25. Since the fall of Babylon (539 B.C.E.) had not yet taken place, though it was expected at any moment, it is plausible to date the beginning of Second Isaiah's prophetic career at approximately 540 B.C.E.

It is important to read the book of Isaiah as a whole, remembering that "the whole is greater than the sum of its parts." But the message of Second Isaiah becomes much more meaningful when we *begin* to read it in the context of the stirring events of the mid-sixth century B.C.E. As we have seen, the word of the prophets was addressed to immediate, concrete historical circumstances; and their predictions about the future were oriented to Israel's present situation.

IN THE TRADITION OF ISAIAH

Nowhere in Isaiah 40–66 is it claimed that Isaiah of Jerusalem authored the poems, nor is his name mentioned even once. To be sure, the New Testament attributes quotations from this section to "the prophet Isaiah" (Matt. 3:3; Luke 3:4; 4:17), but this can hardly be used as evidence of authorship. In a day when scripture was not yet divided into chapter and verse, this was simply the way of indicating where the passage was to be found. Above all, the New Testament writers were concerned with the theological meaning and fulfillment of the prophecy, not with the critical question of authorship.

It is doubtful, however, that *all* of Isaiah 40–66 belongs to the "Second Isaiah." Isaiah 56–66 presupposes a historical setting different from that of Isaiah 40–55. Whereas the Isaiah of Isaiah 40–55 addressed the exiles in Babylonia, the Isaiah of Isaiah 56–66 presupposes that the people had returned to Jerusalem and were facing some of the difficulties of Restoration. True, Isaiah 56–66 is much more closely related to Isaiah 40–55 than the latter are to the oracles of Isaiah of Jerusalem. The prevailing view, however, is that Isaiah 56–66—often called "Third Isaiah" or "Trito-Isaiah"—was written by disciples of Second Isaiah soon after the return from Babylonia.

It seems strange that a prophet could write poems of such great literary charm and theological depth, without giving any inkling of personal identity. But remember that, by and large, the collections that make up the major prophetic scrolls are the end-result of a tradition that received its impetus from a great prophetic leader. This is particularly true of the book of Isaiah: Indeed, there is reason to believe a school of Isaiah extended over several generations. Recall that at one point in his career, Isaiah of Jerusalem gathered his disciples around him in order to "bind up" and "seal" the teaching for a future time when Yahweh's "face" would no longer be hidden from Israel (Isa. 8:16). One scholar suggests that the "Second Isaiah" believed himself to be one of Isaiah's later apprentices, whose task was to give a fresh exposition of his master's teachings in a time when Yahweh was doing "a new thing" (Isa. 43:19) in the people's history. This would explain why the poems of Second Isaiah are attached to Isaiah's teachings as an interpretive supplement. In this view, it was Second Isaiah who broke the seal of Isaiah's prophecy and gave the contemporary sense of his master's words, which had been preserved in the tradition and hearts of the disciples.[4]

If all this is so, we have here a classic example of the student surpassing the teacher. But Second Isaiah did not merely re-interpret Isaiah of Jerusalem. He was also heir to a larger prophetic tradition, including especially Jeremiah and Ezekiel. And he was not just an expositor of ancient prophecy. He was fresh and original in his prophetic insight. In him, prophecy reached a new height of poetic elevation, and plumbed a profounder depth of historical understanding than ever before.

A HERALD OF GOOD TIDINGS

From beginning to end, the prophecy of Second Isaiah is an exultant proclamation of good news. The people who dwell in darkness hear that a new day is dawning. Captives learn that deliverance is on the way. The brokenhearted are comforted. Every poem is filled with the excitement and expectancy of great events about to come to pass.

---

[4]Martin Buber, *The Prophetic Faith* [313], pp. 202–5.

IN THE HEAVENLY COUNCIL

The opening poem (Isa. 40:1–11) is apparently placed in heaven, where Yahweh's Council is assembled.[5] Several times before, we have noticed that prophetic authority rested upon a direct commission given to the prophet standing in this Council (see Jer. 23:18), as in the case of Isaiah's vision in the Temple (see pp. 292–294). Thus the prophecy of Second Isaiah begins with good news heard in the Heavenly Council, then moves poetically from heaven to earth. Since the first poem serves as a prologue to the poetic cycle, we will give it special attention.[6]

In the ancient view, decisions affecting human destiny were made in the Heavenly Council. According to the Babylonian creation myth, *Enuma elish* (see pp. 409–410), the council of the gods invested Marduk with supreme authority, acclaiming him with the shout: "Marduk has become king!" The New Year's celebration of Marduk's victory over the chaos monster Tiamat and her allies gave assurance that the world would be subject to the high god's sovereign decrees for another year. Perhaps Second Isaiah, who must have been familiar with Babylonian myth and ritual, was influenced by this religious background as he portrayed Yahweh's dominion over the world. He was influenced most, however, by the prophets who preceded him and the great convictions celebrated in Israel's worship in the context of "Zion theology."[7] The poems of Second Isaiah draw deeply on the hymns and liturgy of the pre-exilic worship services of the Jerusalem Temple, especially the services of the Fall festival when a number of psalms (Ps. 47, 93, 96–99) extolled Yahweh as King of the nations and of the whole universe (see pp. 208–212).

Second Isaiah, then, spoke primarily out of Israel's traditions in his portrayal of Yahweh, the King *par excellence*. The first poem begins with two imperatives, "comfort, comfort." In the Hebrew text these imperatives are in the plural, because God is speaking to members of the Heavenly Council, announcing the destiny of Israel and the nations.

THE COMING OF GOD'S KINGDOM

The opening words are arresting. When First Isaiah envisioned himself standing in the Heavenly Council, he was commissioned to proclaim a message of judgment upon an unresponsive people (Isa. 6:9–13). But in Isaiah 40:1–2, the declaration Yahweh makes to the Council is a message of consolation to weary and despairing exiles. Divine judgment is scarcely more than an echo from the past, for it is announced that Israel's "time

---

[5]See Frank M. Cross, "The Council of Yahweh in Second Isaiah," *Journal of Near Eastern Studies,* XII (1953), 274–77. In *The Formation of Isaiah 40–55* [481], pp. 83–86, Roy Melugin also argues that the text reflects the view of a prophetic commission in the Heavenly Council, on the analogy of the call of Isaiah of Jerusalem (Isa. 6), although he restricts the opening literary unit to Isa. 40:1–8.

[6]See the excellent discussion by James Muilenburg, *Interpreter's Bible,* V [23], 422ff.

[7]On Zion theology, see pp. 208–212, 316–317; see further Bennie C. Ollenburger, *Zion* [400].

of service" in exile—like a military "draft"—is completed. The people have suffered heavily under the hand of Yahweh's punishment (Isa. 42:24–25). But all that is past. Yahweh commissions the heavenly messengers to "speak tenderly to" (literally, "speak to the heart of") "my people" in the desolation of their bondage. Israel will be freed from a heavier thralldom than that of foreign captivity: The people will be released from the bondage of guilt. Yahweh's message is one of pardon and grace. Israel's past has been forgiven, not because sin and punishment have been balanced on the divine books, but because the free gift of God's forgiveness makes possible a wholly new beginning (Isa. 43:25; compare Jer. 31:34). Israel stands on the threshold of a new age. The decisive moment has come: The time is fulfilled and the kingdom of God is drawing near.

In First Isaiah's temple vision, seraphs antiphonally "called out" or "proclaimed" that Yahweh's glory fills the whole earth. Here, too, an unidentified speaker—evidently one of the Heavenly Council—responds to the divine decree announced in the first verses (Isa. 40:1–2). Many readers, especially those familiar with the New Testament (Mk. 1:3), are accustomed to the translation of a "voice crying in the wilderness" (derived from the Greek Septuagint). But more recent translations have restored the perfect poetic parallelism of the Hebrew:

> A voice cries out:
> "In the wilderness prepare the way of [Yahweh],
>   make straight in the desert a highway for our God."
>   —ISAIAH 40:3 [NRSV]

This first main strophe portrays Yahweh coming, like a conquering king, to lead the uprooted people from exile to their homeland. All obstacles are to be removed from the path. The people will be led through the wilderness along "the highway of God," in a manner reminiscent of Yahweh's deliverance of Israel from Egyptian bondage. This New Exodus, the speaker says, will disclose "the glory of Yahweh" unto "all flesh" (humanity). Ezekiel had said that the glory that had departed from the Temple would return to a New Jerusalem. Now it is announced that Yahweh's glory will be visible to all in the marvelous event that opens a new age.

THE WORD OF GOD STANDS FOREVER

In the next strophe (Isa. 40:6–8) a second speaker, presumably another member of the Heavenly Council, resumes the proclamation. But suddenly another voice breaks in, indicated by the words "and I said" (Isa. 40:6b).[8] Probably the "I" is none other than the

---

[8]The received Hebrew text of Isaiah 40:6 reads "and he said" (see the King James Version). Most modern translations (such as NRSV, NAB, NIV, JB) render "and I said" on the basis of the Greek Septuagint, the Vulgate, and a manuscript of the book of Isaiah found among the Dead Sea Scrolls.

prophet himself. If so, the passage suggests that the prophet stands within the Heavenly Council, where he receives his "call" from the King (compare Isa. 6). In response to his commission he asks, "What shall I proclaim?" The earlier announcement that "all flesh" will see Yahweh's glory awakens the melancholy thought that "all flesh" is transient. The span of human life is like the grass of the field or the wayside flower—green and lovely in its season, but withered when the hot desert wind blows over it. This cry of despair expresses the gloomy but realistic view that human beings are finite, their achievements evanescent, their existence merely temporal. But the prophet's despondent observation leads to a supreme affirmation of faith:

> The grass withers, the flower fades;
>> but the word of our God will stand forever.
>> —ISAIAH 40:8 (NRSV)

This is what it means for "all flesh" to behold the display of Yahweh's glorious power in the restoration of a captive people to their homeland. Though involved in the human world, Yahweh is transcendent, above history. Therefore Yahweh's "word" (expressed plan and intention) is not subject to the change and decay that can be seen all about but is the dynamic power within human history (see Isa. 55:8–11). Second Isaiah expresses one of the crucial tenets of Israelite faith: the revelation of the eternal God in time.

GOOD NEWS

In exultant language that has been set to music in Handel's *Messiah,* the poem sweeps toward its climax and conclusion (Isa. 40:9–11). The poet's thought moves from heaven to earth as he contemplates Yahweh's purpose in history. He sees that purpose concentrated in a particular City, representing the people of Israel. The language is significant, for according to Davidic theology Yahweh had elected the "mountain" of Zion as the divine dwelling-place in the midst of the people. Thus Jerusalem, although in ruins, is summoned to be a herald of "good news."[9] Ascending to a high mountain, she is to announce loudly and clearly to the stricken cities of Judah that Yahweh, the liberating God, is coming in might. Once again Yahweh will display the "mighty hand and outstretched arm" that, according to Israel's ancient confession of faith, delivered the people from Egyptian bondage. With consummate skill Second Isaiah fuses Israel's two major theological traditions—its liberation in the Exodus and the election of Zion (and David)—to announce the gospel of the Kingdom.

To the ordinary observer, the imminent collapse of Babylonia and the rise of Persia were political events with a political result: the release of exiles to return to their

---

[9]The meaning of the New Testament word for "gospel," *evangel* (Mark 1:15), is undoubtedly derived through the Septuagint from the verb used by Second Isaiah.

homeland. But these events, like the Exodus, are seen in a deeper dimension by Second Isaiah: The theological horizon of the event is the advent of Yahweh, the conquering King, who intends to make Zion the center of a kingdom of righteousness and peace that includes not only Israel but also the whole world. The poem ends on the same comforting note with which it began (Isa. 40:11). Blending the figure of the conquering Warrior-King with that of the Good Shepherd, the poet proclaims that Yahweh will gather and feed the "flock" (the community of Israel) with tender care. The range of Second Isaiah's thought spans the whole of heaven and earth, but its central focus on Israel's restoration is never lost.

THE CREATOR AND REDEEMER

Just as a Bach fugue introduces a major theme, then subjects it to complex contrapuntal development, the poems of Second Isaiah elaborate upon the major theme announced in the prologue: Yahweh's imminent coming to inaugurate the Kingdom of God on earth. In the remaining poems, this theme is artistically blended and enriched with other motifs as the work dramatically unfolds. There is no substitute for reading the literature itself, and we can only call attention to a few of the major movements in the poet's composition.

Of all the titles Second Isaiah ascribes to God, two of the most significant are "Creator" and "Redeemer." Creation and redemption are the supreme manifestations of Yahweh's dominion over Israel and the nations. Of course, the connection between Creation and Israel's sacred history was not original with this prophet. It already existed in the Israelite Old Epic, where the call of Abraham was seen against the spacious background of "the first things" (Genesis 2–11); and in the Priestly Writing, where Creation provides the foundation for Yahweh's special revelation to Israel. Second Isaiah was greatly influenced by Israel's Old Epic tradition, and was undoubtedly familiar with the creation story of Genesis 1. But this prophet grasped the connection between God's activity in the Creation and God's redeeming work in history more profoundly than any other in the Old Testament.

Like the Priestly writers of Genesis 1, Second Isaiah affirms that the heavens and earth originated through Yahweh's creative act "in the beginning."[10] In fact, the prophet emphasizes the special verb of the Genesis creation account that refers to effortless creation (Hebrew: *bara'*).[11] Yahweh created the heavenly host (Isa. 40:26), "the ends of the earth" (40:28), and humanity (45:12). Hence Yahweh alone is the sovereign of history, sharing the power and glory of Creator with no other deity. This truth is an-

---

[10]See Walther Eichrodt's "In the Beginning," in *Creation in the Old Testament* [132] pp. 65–73; also the introductory essay, "Creation as Origination," especially pp. 14–18.
[11]A theme later understood as "creation out of nothing" (*ex nihilo*; see 2 Macc. 7:28).

Insert 13-1 The Stele of Esarhaddon, standing 10.5' high, was erected in northern Syria to commemorate that ruler's conquest of Egypt. With his right hand the king offers a libation to deities pictured *(at top, riding on animals)* next to their respective symbols—the crescent, winged sun disc, star, and lance. In his left hand he grips a mace and holds ropes on which two prisoners are leashed. The one kneeling is doubtless Pharaoh Tirhakah, whose decisive defeat is described on the inscription written across the lower half of this stele, found at Zinjirli in North Syria.

Insert 14-1 Baruch's Bullah. "Belonging to Berekhyahu, son of Neriyahu, the Scribe" reads this bullah from the seventh or sixth centuries B.C.E. An astonishing discovery, this lump of clay bears the impression of a seal apparently belonging to Baruch (a shortened form of Berekhyahu, "Blessed of Yahweh"), son of Neriah (a shortened form of Neriyahu), Jeremiah's secretary (Jeremiah 36:4).

Insert 14-2 Galloping Horse Seal. This reddish limestone seal with its galloping horse reads, "Belonging to 'Asayahu, servant of the king." One-half inch long and dating to the seventh century B.C.E., it may have belonged to one of a number of persons called Asaiah (a shortened form of 'Asayahu) in the Bible (see, for example, 2 Kings 22:12; 2 Chronicles 34:20).

Insert 14-3 Shema Seal. A roaring lion appears on this seal, a replica of the original discovered at Megiddo. Dating from the tenth or eighth century B.C.E., it reads, "(belonging) to Shema, servant of Jeroboam." The king is either Jeroboam I (who ruled the Northern Kingdom of Israel from 922–901 B.C.E.) or Jeroboam II (who ruled from 786–746 B.C.E.).

nounced in the magnificent poem, bearing marks of the rhetoric of wisdom teachers, that follows the prologue (Isa. 40:12–21). In contrast to the God who has measured the waters "in the hollow of his hand" and has marked off the limits of the heavens with a handbreadth, the nations are "like a drop from a bucket." Their proud claim to control the affairs of history is absurd when contrasted with the sovereignty of the God whose hand holds the whole world in its grasp. Having seen idols made in Babylonia, the prophet pokes fun at the notion that these frail products of human craftsmanship influence human destiny. Enthroned above the vault of the heavens (Isa. 40:22), Yahweh is incomparable in power and majesty. No image or likeness can be made of Israel's God, as the Mosaic commandment had affirmed from ancient times. Yahweh, who is "God and not a human being" (Hosea 11:9) is "the Holy One of Israel"—an expression of First Isaiah to which Second Isaiah gave great emphasis.[12]

CREATION AS THE FOUNDATION OF HISTORY

The purpose of appealing to Yahweh's power as Creator was to comfort Israel, who in the desolation of Babylonian exile believed that Yahweh did not see or care about what happened to the people. Many Jews, observing the spectacular procession of idols in the great Babylonian festivals, must have all but conceded that Babylonian victory was historical proof that Marduk was the divine Warrior-King. Against this mood of despair Second Isaiah raised his voice:

> Haven't you known? Haven't you heard?
> Yahweh is the everlasting God,
> > Creator of the farthest reaches of the earth.
> He does not grow weary and get tired;
> > His understanding is unfathomable.
> To the weary he gives strength,
> > and for the powerless he increases vitality.
> Young people may weary and tire,
> > youths may stumble and fall,
> But those who wait for Yahweh will regain strength,
> > they will soar on wings like eagles,
> > they will run and not get weary,
> > they will walk and never become tired.
> > > —ISAIAH 40:28–31

The prophet's argument rests upon the conviction that the God of Israel is Creator and Sovereign; therefore, the weary exiles should "wait for God," eagerly straining toward

---

[12]See B. W. Anderson, "The Holy One of Israel," *Justice and the Holy: Essays in Honor of Walter Harrelson,* Douglas A. Knight and Peter J. Paris, eds. (Atlanta, Georgia: Scholars Press, 1989), pp. 3–19.

the future when Yahweh comes to liberate them from bondage and inaugurate a new age. Although caught in the grip of massive international forces, the people should hope in the God whose purpose overarches history from beginning to end, from creation to consummation.

Belief in Yahweh's wisdom and power as Creator undergirds the proclamation of Second Isaiah's good news of redemption. The prophet's thought reaches beyond Israel's sacred history, which had proved to be a history of failure, and grounds hope for the future in the sovereignty of God who is "the first" and "the last," the Alpha and the Omega (Isa. 41:4; 44:6; 48:12). Viewed within the ultimate horizons of beginning and end, human affairs are not governed by historical processes, human ambition, fate, or chance: They are controlled by "the everlasting God" who as Creator is Redeemer.

In this wide perspective Second Isaiah understands the events of his time. Vividly he describes the advance of "one from the east whom victory meets at every step of the way"—a reference to the far-flung victories of Cyrus in Media and as far west as the Aegean (Isa. 41:2–4, 25–29; 46:11). In a remarkable disputation that uses the language of a court trial (Isa. 41), the prophet challenges the nations to show evidence that their gods had been able to anticipate and bring about the rise of Cyrus, an event that aroused new hope for peoples living under the Babylonian yoke. Emphatically he affirms that it was Yahweh who summoned the victor from the east. The event did not catch Yahweh by surprise, so to speak, but was part of a prearranged divine plan. Yahweh, the liberating God, had been directing the course of history and working purposively for the day of release from bondage. Thus the trial between Yahweh and the nations demonstrates that Yahweh alone is God.[13]

From the perspective of Second Isaiah, this international event had special meaning for Israel. Israel might be pitifully weak and insignificant in the eyes of the powerful nations, but this "worm" is the object of Yahweh's love and concern (Isa. 41:14). More than that, Yahweh has chosen to become involved with this "family" and to act as Israel's "Redeemer" to secure their "justice" (Isa. 40:27)—that is, their rightful place in the larger assembly of the nations.

....

DEFINITION: "REDEEMER"

The special word for "Redeemer" (Hebrew: *go'el*) has many nuances in the Old Testament. The word came originally from the realm of family law. It was the duty of the *go'el* (next of kin) to vindicate a family member whose "justice" was threatened or violated. If the family member was forced to sell property for some reason, the *go'el*—the "redeemer"—was obligated to buy it and keep it in the family if at all possible. A good illustration is Jeremiah's purchase of the ancestral estate in Anathoth during the Babylonian siege (Jer. 32:6–12; see pp. 379–380). The story of Ruth presents another exam-

---

[13]On "Trial Speeches" in Second Isaiah, see Roy Melugin, *The Formation of Isaiah 40–55* [481], chap. IV (especially pp. 53–63).

ple of how property redemption worked out in practice (Ruth 4:3–9). In the case of murder, it was the obligation of the *go'el* to obtain justice for the deceased family member by taking revenge; in this case the "redeemer" was to be the "blood avenger" (Hebrew: *go'el haddam;* compare Num. 35:19). The practice of blood revenge was abandoned early in Israelite history, but the belief survived that, at a higher level, Yahweh is the "Redeemer" who vindicates the justice of the people. This in turn led to the larger question of *theodicy:* the question of whether God actually acts to vindicate the rights of the weak and oppressed. It was Job, above all, who appealed to God to be his *go'el* and to vindicate his justice (see Chapter 17).

Believing that Yahweh is Israel's Redeemer, Second Isaiah predicts the restoration of the people: Yahweh will gather the children of Israel from the east and west, north and south (Isa. 43:6–7), breaking the bars of their captivity and restoring them to their homeland (43:14–15; see 48:14, 20). After subjecting this theme to rich variation, the prophet mentions Cyrus by name (Isa. 44:28–45:6). In an earlier time, First Isaiah had said that the Assyrian conqueror was to be "the rod of Yahweh's anger." Second Isaiah, however, affirms that Cyrus, though unaware of it, is the historical agent by whom Yahweh will redeem Israel.

There are striking affinities between the language of the Cyrus Cylinder and Isaiah 45:1–6 (also 45:13), so much so that some scholars conjecture that Second Isaiah must have been acquainted with the Persian document. For example, the cylinder says that Marduk searched the countries for a righteous ruler, that he accompanied Cyrus as a friend, and that he called him by name. Second Isaiah, for whom Marduk is a powerless idol, ascribes these actions to Yahweh, who "anointed" the Persian to be the agent for liberating Israel.

THE NEW EXODUS

One of the central motifs in Second Isaiah's message is that of the "New Exodus."[14] For this prophet, the Exodus was the decisive event of Israel's past. Hence he portrays Israel's imminent liberation from the bondage and despair of exile in imagery drawn from the Exodus and wilderness traditions: the flight from Egypt, the deliverance at the Reed Sea, the march through the wilderness, the triumphant approach to the Promised Land.

Second Isaiah blends into this historical tradition imagery drawn from the Babylonian creation myth, according to which creation was the outcome of a fierce conflict between the Creator-god and the monster of chaos, Tiamat. We have seen that this myth, the *Enuma elish,* figured prominently in Babylonian religion and was transmitted to Israel through the Canaanites.[15] In Second Isaiah's poetic imagination these mythical

---

[14]See B. W. Anderson, "Exodus Typology in Second Isaiah," in *Israel's Prophetic Heritage* [174], pp. 177–95; and C. Stuhlmueller, *Creative Redemption* (Rome: Biblical Institute Press), pp. 59–98, 272.

[15]See Hermann Gunkel, "The Influence of Babylonian Mythology Upon the Biblical Creation Story," in *Creation in the Old Testament* [132], pp. 25–52; also B. W. Anderson, *Creation versus Chaos* [146], chap 4.

motifs are used to enhance the remembrance of Yahweh's deeds in *history:* The waters of the Reed Sea, through which Israel crossed long ago, become the waters of chaos, hostile to Yahweh's creative and redemptive act. Just as the arm of the Divine Warrior was victorious in that conflict, so in the present historical crisis Yahweh achieves victory on behalf of a people suffering under the powers of historical chaos. Yahweh commands the Deep, "Be dry," and prepares a way for the people to pass through the waters (Isa. 44:27). The poetry rises to a pitch of exultation as the prophet, contemplating the New Exodus, addresses the "arm" of the Divine Warrior:

> Awake, awake! Clothe yourself with strength,
> > O Arm of Yahweh!
> Awake as in days of old,
> > in ancient times.
> Was it not you [the Arm] that hacked Rahab in pieces,
> > that pierced the Dragon through?
> Was it not you that dried up Sea,
> > the waters of the great Abyss,
> and made the sea depths a roadbed
> > for the redeemed to pass over?
> So those whom Yahweh has liberated will come back,
> > they will enter Zion with singing.
> They will be crowned with unending rejoicing,
> > joy and gladness will come upon them,
> > sorrow and sighing will vanish.
> > > —ISAIAH 51:9–11

The approaching redemption is viewed as a new beginning, a New Creation. According to Second Isaiah, Creation was not just an event of the past. In the new age that the prophet heralds, God will make all things new. In God's creative work there is no boundary between "nature" and "history," for both human life and the natural setting will be marvelously transformed (Isa. 41:17–20). The wilderness, identified with the waste places of Judah, will be converted into a garden like Eden (Isa. 51:3; see also 41:17–20; 43:19–21). Above all, there will be a New Israel, bound to Yahweh in a new relationship (Isa. 54:4–10) and singing a "new song" (42:10–12).

....

DEFINITION: "RAHAB," "SEA"

Our study has frequently referred to the chaos monster or "dragon" that was slain by the Divine Warrior at the time of creation. This motif is found in the Babylonian creation myth, *Enuma elish*, which tells how the young warrior-god, Marduk, overcame the powers of chaos, headed by the goddess Tiamat. Marduk's victory, for which he was acclaimed King in the Heavenly Council, resulted in the separation of the upper and lower parts of Tiamat's body and thus the limitation of the spheres of heaven and earth. The mythical victory was not decisive, however. In the annual rotation of the seasons, the powers of chaos seemed to get the upper hand as springtime fertility was overtaken by winter barrenness. Hence the "myth of the eternal return"[16] was celebrated each New Year, when the Divine Warrior again won a victory over the powers of chaos.

This myth was known in various forms in the ancient world. The Western Semitic name for the chaos monster is Rahab (Isa. 51:9; see also Job 9:13; 26:12; Ps. 89:10) or Leviathan (Ps. 74:14; 104:26; Isa. 27:1). Sometimes the powers of chaos are described merely as Sea (Hebrew: *Yam*), or Abyss (Hebrew: *Tehom*), "mighty waters," or "floods." Similar language is found in ancient Canaanite (Ugaritic) mythology, where the sky-god Baal enters into conflict with Sea (*Yamm*) or subdues Leviathan (*L-t-n*), described as a fleeing, twisting serpent (compare Isa. 27:1).[17]

Celebrations of this myth portrayed the divine maintenance of the ordered cosmos against the powers of disorder. As the representative of the god, the king was empowered to maintain order in the mundane realm, and to put down enemies that threatened the social order. Israel also used this motif in various ways to express faith in the supreme Ruler, Yahweh, who is Creator and Liberator.

A LIGHT TO THE NATIONS

We have seen that Second Isaiah's perspective is as wide as Creation and as long as the whole sweep of history. This prophet's spacious horizons reflect the immense vistas opened to the Jewish people, who had been thrust out of the narrow corridor of Palestine into a larger world. Cyrus' conquests had carried him to the Aegean shores. Frequent references in the poems of Second Isaiah to the "coastlands" or the "isles" (the shores of the Mediterranean area) show that people were thinking of the world in wider terms than the Fertile Crescent.

There is broad universality in Second Isaiah's message, yet the prophet never surrenders his conviction that Israel occupies a special place in Yahweh's historical plan. The prologue begins by referring to Israel as "my people," and by announcing that Yahweh is Israel's God ("your God," Isa. 40:1). The ancient motif of the covenant faith, "I am your God and you are my people," runs through all the poems. The great poem about redemption (Isa. 51:1–16) concludes with Yahweh's assurance:

> I have put my words in your mouth,
>> and hidden you in the shadow of my hand,

---

[16]See Mircea Eliade, *Cosmos and History: The Myth of the Eternal Return* [138].
[17]See further B. W. Anderson, "The Slaying of the Fleeing, Twisting Serpent," in *From Creation to New Creation* [146], chap. 12.

> stretching out the heavens
>> and laying the foundations of the earth,
>> and saying to Zion, "You are my people."
>>> —ISAIAH 51:16 (NRSV)

In Second Isaiah's message the liberation of Israel was, in a profound sense, to be beneficial for all peoples. This theme had already been enunciated in the Israelite Old Epic where the call of Abraham (that is, Israel), viewed in the perspective of universal history, is to yield future blessing for all the families of the earth (Gen. 12:1–3). Second Isaiah appropriated this theme (echoed elsewhere; see Jer. 4:1–3) and gave it a new theological emphasis. In this view, God's choice of Israel was a commission to perform a special task in the Creator's far-reaching and world-embracing plan. It was Yahweh's intention that Israel should be "a light to the nations." Given by God as "a covenant to the nations," Israel was to demonstrate that the Gentiles—that is, the non-Jewish peoples—are also included within the divine promise (Isa. 42:5–9). Eventually every knee will bow before Yahweh, every tongue swear by the sacred name (Isa. 45:23).

THE CRITIQUE OF IDOLATRY

Scholars once tried to trace an ascending evolution from the presumed polytheism of the early period of Israel's history to the lofty heights of reflective monotheism in Second Isaiah. But this reconstruction, which reflects the perspective of Western rationalism, does not do justice to Israel's religious development. In the Old Testament the primary concern is not with the question of God's existence, but with the question of who God is and what God demands. From the very first, the Decalogue stipulated that Israel was to worship one God—the "sole Power" manifest in the "saving experience" of the Exodus and the "commanding experience" of Sinai. Later, Israel's prophets contended with the problem of polytheism in practical terms. They perceived that Israel was tempted to "forget" Yahweh (and the story in which the identity and purpose of Yahweh are known), yielding to the seductive allurements of other gods and their stories (myths).

The poems of Second Isaiah expand and deepen this prophetic teaching—found classically in Israel's Old Epic tradition, Amos, Isaiah, Deuteronomy, Jeremiah, and the Priestly Writing—making it relevant not just for Israel but for all nations. The prophet's fundamental criticism of the idols is that they are *powerless* in history, and therefore nothing. Again and again he issues the challenge to prove that the gods of the nations have been able to announce a plan in history and carry it through (Isa. 42:5–17; 43:8–13; 44:6–8, 21–23; 44:24–45:13; 48). Caricaturing Babylonian worship, he pokes fun at the idol-making industry (see Isa. 40:18–20; 44:9–20), arguing that these artifacts are mere expressions of human cleverness. They do not have the divine power to control history, nor can they sustain human life from birth to old age. With sharp satire he ridicules the Babylonian idols, Bel and Nebo (restored to their sacred cities by

Cyrus), who must be loaded on the backs of dumb animals, causing them to strain and stoop under the burden. These pathetic "gods" must be carried, but—says the prophet—Yahweh carries the people and lifts their burdens (Isa. 46).

A THEOLOGY OF WORLD HISTORY

Second Isaiah, then, advocates a "historical monotheism": He perceives that the whole course of history is under the control of Yahweh, who alone is Creator and Sovereign. This prophet has been called "the originator of a theology of world history."[18] This statement might seem a bit exaggerated when we consider the universal horizons of Israel's Old Epic tradition, which portrays the call of Abraham (Gen. 12:1–3) against the background of universal primeval history (Gen. 2–11). It is certainly true, however, in the sense that for the first time a vision of history's unity under the purpose of one God becomes the basis of an appeal to all humankind. Yahweh is Israel's Redeemer, but closely allied with Israel's liberation is the redemption of *all* peoples. Though the prophet first speaks comforting words to Israel in its despair and bondage, he addresses the same message to other nations who might see in the rise of Cyrus and the imminent return of the Jewish exiles the approach of a new age in which they too may participate. Since Yahweh is the Creator of the ends of the earth, all nations must also know that there is no other Savior. Yahweh's wisdom is the source and ground of the meaning of all history. Yahweh's power emancipates all peoples from their bondage (Isa. 42:7). Hence the prophet extends an invitation, in the name of the liberating God, to the farthest boundaries of the world of that time:

> Turn to me and be saved,
>   all the ends of the earth!
> For I am God, and there is no other.
>   —ISAIAH 45:22 (NRSV)

This universalism is reminiscent of a poem found in both Isaiah 2:2–4 and Micah 4:1–5, which announces that in the end-time the Temple hill will become the highest mountain, and "all the nations" will stream to it so that they might hear Yahweh's teaching. When the nations recognize the Temple of Zion as the spiritual center of the world, they will beat their swords into plowshares and their spears into pruning hooks. Second Isaiah's universalism runs even deeper than this: The prophet proclaims that Yahweh actively achieves world salvation through a chosen agent, Israel. Israel's redemption—which includes the forgiveness of past sins, the release from captivity, the return to Zion, and the beginning of a new age—is not an end in itself. Israel is to be a light to the nations. Through the witness of its life all the families of the earth will know divine blessing (compare Gen. 12:2–3). This is the deepest meaning of Israel's election.

---

[18]Martin Buber, *The Prophetic Faith* [313], pp. 208ff.

THE SERVANT OF YAHWEH

We come now to the most difficult, yet most important, problem in the interpretation of Second Isaiah's message. Several times a mysterious figure—designated "the Servant of Yahweh"—appears in the poems. In at least four passages the Servant is described, though not clearly identified:

Isaiah 42:1–4	"He will bring forth justice to the nations."
Isaiah 49:1–6	"Yahweh called me from the womb."[19]
Isaiah 50:4–9	"Morning by morning he wakens my ear."
	(Notice the reference to the Servant in vs. 10.)
Isaiah 52:13–53:12	"A man of sorrows, and acquainted with grief."

The last poem is best known in Christian circles, because it was appropriated as a portrayal of the Passion of Jesus, the Christ. From the Christian standpoint, this is the deepest meaning and fulfillment of the prophecy. But instead of putting the cart before **the horse by adopting a** "Messianic" interpretation, we will try to understand the "Servant" poems *within the context* of the poetry of Second Isaiah.

Admittedly, some scholars disagree with this approach. They argue that the Servant poems stand by themselves as originally independent pieces, displaying a conception of the Servant not found elsewhere in the writings of Second Isaiah. In this view, the poems were introduced into Second Isaiah's writings either by the prophet himself later in his career, or by prophetic editors. These arguments are not conclusive, however. The Servant poems are written in the style typical of Second Isaiah's poetry, and they fit well into their context. We will approach the question from the premise that the poems belong to Second Isaiah, and see where our investigation leads.

THE SERVANT AS ISRAEL

One of the Servant poems gives an important clue to the mystery. In Isaiah 49:3, the Servant is explicitly identified with Israel:

And [Yahweh] said to me, "You are my servant,
Israel in whom I will be glorified."

To be sure, the mystery does not vanish, for in the same poem it is stated, according to the usual interpretation of the Hebrew, that the Servant has a mission *to* Israel (Isa. 49:5–6). Nevertheless, this poem provides a bridge to another series of poems in which Israel is addressed as Yahweh's servant. In these poems the Servant's role is associated with Israel's task as Yahweh's chosen people, as is clear from the recurring parallelism

---

[19]The extent of the Servant poem in Isaiah 49 is disputed. It might end with verse 7, 9, or 13, according to various views.

"Israel, my servant—Jacob, whom I have chosen" (Isa. 41:8–10; 43:8–13; 44:1–2; 44:21; 45:4; compare 48:12). All these passages give the impression that in some sense Israel's task is that of the Servant.[20]

The figure of the Servant first appears in a disputation sometimes called "the trial of the nations" (Isa. 41:1–42:4).[21] The nations are arraigned before Yahweh, the Creator and Sovereign of history, and are asked to interpret the meaning of the rise of Cyrus (Isa. 41:1–4). When they can give no answer—save to encourage one another in their pitiful idol-making (Isa. 41:5–7)—Yahweh turns to Israel:

> But you, Israel, my servant,
>> Jacob, whom I have chosen,
>> the offspring of Abraham, my friend;
> you whom I took from the ends of the earth,
>> and called from its farthest corners,
> saying to you, "You are my servant,
>> I have chosen you and not cast you off";
> do not fear, for I am with you,
>> do not be afraid, for I am your God;
> I will strengthen you, I will help you,
>> I will uphold you with my victorious right hand.
>> —ISAIAH 41:8–10 (NRSV)

Here the prophet uses a traditional literary form ("the oracle of salvation"), with its characteristic command "do not fear" (compare Jer. 1:8), in order to encourage Israel to perform its God-given task.[22] Interestingly, the prophet traces Israel's election back from the time of the Exodus to the period of Israel's ancestors. It was then, at the beginning of Israel's history when the future people were still in Sarah's womb (Isa. 51:1–2), that Israel was called to be Yahweh's Servant.

In a later section of the poem, the nations are again summoned to present their case before Yahweh, and in particular to give evidence that their gods have been able to foretell the new age initiated by Cyrus' victories. Once more there is no answer (Isa. 41:21–29), so Yahweh turns to the Servant. This time the Servant is not explicitly identified with Israel, but in the context of the whole poem (Isa. 41:1–42:4) this view seems presupposed:

---

[20]See Tryggve N. D. Mettinger's discussion of the Servant Songs [482]. He argues that these poems are of one piece with the rest of Second Isaiah's poetry and that the Servant is Israel or "at least the exiled minority."

[21]James Muilenburg, *Interpreter's Bible* V [23], pp. 406–14, 447–66, maintains that the Servant poem in Isaiah 42:1–4 is the climax of the last strophes of 41:1–42:4, a passage he treats as "The Trial of the Nations." However, Roy F. Melugin, *The Formation of Isaiah 40–55* [481], pp. 8–10, 53–63, questions whether the passage actually reflects the language of a "court trial" and prefers to regard it as a disputation, the purpose being "to convince doubters that Yahweh is God."

[22]On the oracle of salvation, see Patrick D. Miller, Jr., *They Cried Unto the Lord* [534], chap. 7.

Here is my servant, whom I uphold,
    my chosen, in whom my soul delights;
I have put my spirit upon him;
    he will bring forth justice to the nations.
He will not cry or lift up his voice,
    or make it heard in the street;
a bruised reed he will not break,
    and a dimly burning wick he will not quench;
    he will faithfully bring forth justice.
He will not grow faint or be crushed
    until he has established justice in the earth;
    and the coastlands wait for his teaching [torah].
                  —ISAIAH 42:1–4 (NRSV)

Notice that something is added to the portrait of the Servant in the previous poem. Not only does Yahweh "uphold" or "hold" the Servant (Isa. 41:10; 42:1), but also the Servant is Yahweh's agent—endowed with divine charisma—who in a quiet way will bring justice to the nations. Israel's election is for responsibility. Like Cyrus, the Servant is the agent of Yahweh's historical purpose. As described in this poem, however, the Servant's victory contrasts sharply with the methods of a military conqueror, even one as benevolent as Cyrus.

So far, it would seem that Second Isaiah identifies the Servant with the covenant community of Israel. Plumbing the meaning of the intense suffering occasioned by the fall of the nation, he affirms that Yahweh has refined the people in "the furnace of affliction" (Isa. 48:10; compare Isa. 1:25) for greater service. In one sense, the national catastrophe was God's judgment upon Israel's foolishness and disobedience, just as prophets of the past had prophesied (see 42:18–25). But Israel has paid the penalty for the past, and is now accepted and renewed by Yahweh's freely-offered forgiveness (Isa. 40:1–2; 43:22–44:5). As iron is tempered by fire and shaped on the anvil, so Yahweh re-creates the people through sufferings so that they might be a more effective instrument of the divine purpose in history.

THE SERVANT AS AN INDIVIDUAL

There are difficulties with this interpretation. The poems also suggest that the Servant is an individual. The second poem (Isa. 49:1–6) is crucial: Although it emphatically states that the Servant is Israel (Isa. 49:3), it also claims that he has a mission *to* Israel, implying a distinction from the covenant community. The Servant affirms that Yahweh has called him from the womb (compare Jer. 1:5) to gather Israel to Yahweh. And, lest this task appear "too light," he is also given the mission of being "as a light" to the nations, so Yahweh's salvation can reach to the ends of the earth (Isa. 49:5–6). In this poem one is struck by similarities between the Servant's testimony (Isa. 49:1–4) and the Confessions of Jeremiah. The "I" who speaks appears to be an individual, an impression strengthened by the concrete and personal description of "the man of sorrows" in Isaiah 53. We are confronted with a singular problem: In many cases, there are such close similarities between Israel and the Servant that they seem to be the same; yet there are also sharp differences that seem to indicate Israel is not the Servant (see table below).

Some interpreters believe the differences outweigh the similarities. They maintain that if the Servant is interpreted in a corporate sense—either as the covenant community of Israel or as a faithful remnant—this does not account for the fact that the Servant has a role to perform on behalf of Israel, as well as on behalf of the nations. Nor does it do justice to the concrete detail of the Servant's portrait, modeled after that of an individual (especially Isa. 53). Hence a long list of candidates for the Servant has been

The Servant of the Lord

The Servant Israel	The Anonymous Servant
Likenesses:	
1. Chosen by Yahweh 41:8–9; 45:4; 43:10; 44:1; 49:7	1. Chosen by Yahweh 42:1
2. Formed by Yahweh in the womb 44:2; 44:21, 24	2. Formed by Yahweh in the womb 49:1, 5
3. Upheld and comforted by Yahweh 41:10; cf. 42:6	3. Upheld and comforted by Yahweh 42:1
4. Hid in the shadow of Yahweh's hand 51:16	4. Hid in the shadow of Yahweh's hand 49:2
5. Endowed with Yahweh's spirit 44:3	5. Spirit-endowed 42:1
6. Honored by Yahweh 43:4	6. Honored by Yahweh 49:5
7. A light to the nations 42:6; cf. 51:4	7. A light to the nations 49:6
8. Gives torah and justice to the nations 51:4–8; cf. 42:21, 24	8. Gives torah to the nations, establishes justice 42:4
9. Yahweh glorified in Israel 44:23	9. Yahweh glorified in the Servant 53:10c; cf. 49:3
Differences:	
1. Israel despairs 40:27; 41:8–10; 49:14, etc.	1. The Servant is undiscouraged 42:4; 50:7–9 (*But see 49:4*)
2. Israel is rebellious, sinful 48:4; cf. 43:27	2. The Servant is not rebellious but faithful 50:5; 53:4–6, 12
3. Israel is blind and deaf 42:18–25	3. The Servant is attentive, responsive 50:4–5
4. Israel suffers unwillingly, seeks vindication 51:21–23, etc.	4. The Servant suffers patiently, willingly 50:6; 53:4–9 (*Notice 50:7–9*)
5. Israel suffers for her own sins 42:24–25; 43:22–28; 47:6, 50:1	5. The Servant innocently suffers for the sins of others chap. 53
6. Israel is to be redeemed 43:1–7, etc.	6. The Servant's mission is to redeem Israel 49:5

proposed, beginning with Moses and ending with Second Isaiah himself. Other interpreters, believing that no historic person of ancient Israel fits the picture, propose that the Servant is one who appears on the horizon of God's future. Still others, aware of the Babylonian background of Second Isaiah's thought, believe the portrait of the Servant was influenced by the role of the king as representative of the people in the Tammuz cult (Babylonian fertility religion), suffering ritual humiliation for them and taking upon himself their sins.[23]

THE ONE AND THE MANY

Two questions emerge from our discussion: Did Second Isaiah understand the Servant in a corporate or in an individual sense? Did he understand the work of the Servant was to take place in his time or in the future (the "last days")? Our study of Isaiah 40–55 suggests that there is no real basis for distinguishing these sharp alternatives in the prophet's message.

A great deal of light is thrown on the first question by considering how the relationship between the individual and the community is understood in Israel's scriptures. We have seen that an individual might incarnate the whole community of Israel or, vice versa, that the community might be addressed as an individual who stands in direct, personal relation to God. Modern interpreters make a sharp contrast between "collectivism" and "individualism," but in Israel's covenant faith the issue was not an either-or. Take the case of Israel's ancestors—Abraham, Sarah, and the others. They are certainly portrayed as individuals. But the various stories about them also depict the life of the community they represent. The individual and the community are one. When Yahweh speaks to Abraham, for instance, Israel in every age is involved in the call and the promises. In this individual ancestor, Israel sees its whole life mirrored and condensed, just as the parent lives on in the child. The "one" includes the "many" in a spiritual unity binding all generations together. Therefore Second Isaiah exhorts Israel to turn to its ancestors, in whom the contemporary meaning of its history is represented:

> Look to the rock from which you were cut,
>> to the quarry from which you were mined,
> Look to Abraham your father
>> and to Sarah who gave birth to you.
> For when he was but one I called him,
>> I blessed him and made him many.
>
> —ISAIAH 51:1–2

---

[23]For a review of various theories on the identity of the Servant, see C. R. North, *The Suffering Servant* [484]; H. H. Rowley, *The Servant of the Lord* [485], pp. 3–60; and John L. McKenzie, *Second Isaiah* [480], pp. xxxviii–lv.

On the other hand, the community of Israel is often personalized or regarded as a "corporate personality."[24] Yahweh does not deal with a collection of individuals but with a *people,* bound so closely by their common history and single covenant obligation that Israel is addressed in the dialogue of "I and Thou." Moreover, the most personal and intimate images are applied to the relation between Yahweh and Israel: a mother carrying a child in her womb (Isa. 46:3); a widow restored to her husband (54:4–8); children who are returned to a parent (49:19–21). In other words, the community is depicted as an individual. This throws light on something confusing to the modern mind—the fluctuating use of singular and plural verbs and pronouns. In Hosea 11, for example, Yahweh begins by addressing Israel in the singular: "I loved him . . . I called my son." But in the very next line (Hos. 11:2) the language suddenly shifts to the plural: "The more I called them, the more they went from me."

There is no need to choose between an individual and a corporate interpretation of the Servant of Yahweh, for both are true to the Israelite sense of community. The conception oscillates between the servant Israel and the personal servant who would perfectly fulfill Israel's mission. The portrait of the Servant is painted with colors drawn from many sources in Israel's history. Some scholars emphasize that the prototype of the Servant is Moses. Especially in Deuteronomistic tradition, Moses was portrayed as the true prophet: the covenant mediator who interceded for his people and who finally died vicariously for their sins (Deut. 3:23–27; 4:23 and so on). Thus Second Isaiah, whose message is dominated by the theme of the New Exodus, envisions the rise of a prophet *like Moses* to lead Israel into the new age.[25] Doubtless this influenced Second Isaiah's thought. In shaping the portrait of the Servant, however, the prophet also drew on other traditions, especially the Confessions of Jeremiah. The Servant is a person, but no single person—past or contemporary—corresponds completely to the type.

THE SERVANT WHO IS TO COME

The second question—whether the Servant's work was thought of as present or future—must be considered from the standpoint of Second Isaiah's proclamation that a new age was beginning. The prophet was not looking into the distant future, envisaging the coming of a Servant not yet visible on the horizon. His prophetic task was to interpret the *contemporary* political situation occasioned by the rise of Cyrus and the imminent collapse of the Babylonian empire. In the political ferment of the time he saw a sign of Yahweh's coming to liberate captive people and to inaugurate the kingdom of

---

[24]See the classic study by H. Wheeler Robinson, "The Hebrew Conception of Corporate Personality," in *Corporate Personality in Ancient Israel* (Philadelphia: Fortress Press, 1964), pp. 1–20.

[25]See von Rad, *Theology,* II [163], pp. 260–62, 273–77, who calls attention to the expectation of a prophet like Moses in Deut. 18:15–19, and to the "suffering prophet" tradition that developed especially in the time of Jeremiah and Ezekiel.

God. With Yahweh's advent the Servant would appear on the world stage, born out of the travail of Israel's history, to be Yahweh's agent for bringing salvation to the ends of the earth. In the past, Yahweh had called the Servant, had tested and refined his life by suffering, and had hidden him like an arrow in his quiver. But now the time was fulfilled. The work of the Servant was about to begin.

In a sense, the Servant was a future figure, but he was also a figure of the present. He stood in the dawn—when the darkness of the old order was lingering and the light of the new day was breaking on the horizon. This seems paradoxical now, for we insist on measuring time as a chronological progression from present to future: The work of the Servant must be *either* present or future, *either* today or tomorrow. In prophetic literature, however, historical time is measured not by the calendar, but by God's activity and purpose. From this perspective the future *can* enter the present, and the power of the coming Kingdom *can* be felt in the old order. The task of the Servant, therefore, must be considered in relation to Second Isaiah's message concerning the "last things" or the consummation of history. Within this theological perspective, the prophet perceived the meaning of Israel's suffering and the role of the "suffering Servant" depicted in the Servant poems.

VICTORY THROUGH SUFFERING

Throughout the poems of Second Isaiah runs the theme of Israel's vindication. On this exultant note the prophet's message begins in Isaiah 40, and ends in Isaiah 55. God did not disregard Israel's "justice" (Hebrew: *mishpat;* Isa. 40:27)—rather, the people of God were invited to walk along a royal highway leading from bondage into the glorious freedom of a new life. Had Second Isaiah's message been stated only in the language of deliverance from captivity, it would have been no more than a lofty nationalism inspired by stirring international developments of the time. But the prophet proclaimed that through Israel's witness the good news of the dominion of Yahweh would reach to the ends of the earth.

Second Isaiah also affirmed that Israel would be exalted through suffering. This was the deepest mystery of its calling. The mystery is illumined by the figure of the Servant who, unlike Cyrus or any great nation, would tread a path leading through defeat to victory.

The four Servant poems depict the unusual character of the Servant's task. His method is extraordinary: "A bruised reed he will not break, and a dimly burning wick he will not quench"—but quietly, gently, he will persist until he has established *mishpat* ("justice") in all the earth (Isa. 42:1–4). Despite his discouragement he believes that Yahweh has hidden him like an arrow in a quiver until the appointed time when he will be sent forth victoriously to accomplish a mission that will have an effect far beyond the confines of Israel (Isa. 49:1–6). His close fellowship with God enables him to bear affliction: the lash of the smiters, the disgrace of the plucking of the beard and of being spat upon (Isa. 50:4–9). In all his suffering he knows that Yahweh has chosen him to walk this *via dolorosa,* at the end of which will be vindication and exaltation. *It is through the suffering of the Servant that Yahweh inaugurates the kingdom of God,* when the nations will share with Israel the heralded good news: "Your God reigns"—Yahweh is King (see Isa. 52:7).

THE MAN OF SORROWS

The theme of the exaltation of the Servant rises to a great climax in the fourth Servant poem, which portrays "the man of sorrows" (Isa. 52:13–53:12). The poem is divided into five poetic units. At the beginning and end Yahweh is the speaker; when Yahweh speaks, the nations learn that the Servant will be exalted through suffering.

In the first strophe (Isa. 52:13–15) Yahweh introduces the Servant and announces his triumph and elevation. Although the promise is spoken primarily to Israel, for whom the prophet's words are meant most immediately, attention centers on the nations. The Servant has an international role, as indicated in two other Servant poems where we read that "the coastlands wait for his *torah* [teaching]" (Isa. 42:4) and where the Servant addresses himself to peoples from afar (49:1). The mystery of the Servant's suffering will finally be understood: His garb of humiliation will be removed, and the peoples will come to know who he really is. The contrast between the Servant's ultimate triumph and his present form—"marred beyond human semblance"—will be so overwhelming that the nations will be astonished and kings will bow in reverent silence before him. This motif runs through the entire message of Second Isaiah: the reversal of Israel's position of distress and humiliation and the recognition of its *mishpaṭ* ("justice")—its proper and just place in Yahweh's world order.

The new understanding of the nations is elaborated in the second strophe (Isa. 53:1–3), in which the rulers of the nations are represented as speaking for their peoples. The kings express their astonishment at what they finally see and hear. To them the whole thing is fantastic and unbelievable. The Servant had grown up before Yahweh (or perhaps "before us"—the nations) like a young sapling, like a root in dry, unpromising ground. Some interpreters find here an allusion to the Messiah, who elsewhere is called a "branch" or a root from the stock of Jesse (see Isa. 11:1, 10; Jer. 23:5), but more likely the kings are describing Israel's unpromising career. Possibly with the figure of leprosy in mind, the poet portrays the Servant's "form" (Isa. 52:14) as so marred that people hide their faces from him (compare Lev. 13:45). The kings are utterly amazed that such an unlovely, despised, and revolting figure is actually the one to whom "the arm of Yahweh"—the victorious power of the Divine Warrior—has been revealed. They had not recognized the Servant in his humiliation.

The world's rulers continue to speak in the next strophe (Isa. 53:4–6). Although they formerly had no esteem for the Servant, their eyes are suddenly opened to the true meaning of his suffering. In their previous understanding, the Servant was stricken, smitten, and afflicted by God for his own sins. Actually, he had been suffering in their stead—taking upon himself the consequences of their transgressions and restoring them to "wholeness" (Hebrew: *shalom;* "peace" or "well-being"). Astonishingly, the one who seemed diseased was the source of their health and healing! It was not Israel's sins that the Servant was bearing, for according to the initial proclamation of the prophet Israel had suffered more than enough for its sin. The "overplus" of Israel's suffering was vicarious—for the nations. The nations confess that the Servant's sacrifice was Yahweh's redemptive act for their welfare, their salvation:

> All of us like sheep have gone astray,
>> we have each turned to our own way,
> and Yahweh has imposed on him
>> the guilt of us all.
>
> —ISAIAH 53:6

Here is a profound insight into the meaning of suffering, for which there is no parallel elsewhere in the Old Testament.

The nations are still speaking in the fourth strophe (Isa. 53:7–9), which emphasizes the way the Servant endured his suffering (compare Isa. 42:1–4; 50:4–9). Unlike most sufferers—even Jeremiah, according to his Confessions—the Servant did not cry out in bitterness or self-pity when he was afflicted. He bore his burden silently, without any complaint or vindictiveness, "like a lamb that is led to the slaughter, and like a sheep that before its shearers is dumb" (Isa. 53:7; see Jer. 11:19, where the same figure appears with a slightly different meaning). The speaker goes on to describe the character of the Servant's affliction, although the details are not too clear. Evidently the Servant was imprisoned, brought to trial, and led away to death (Isa. 53:8a). He died in complete loneliness, for no one gave a thought to his "generation"—that is, his posterity.[26] He was "cut off from the land of the living" for the sake of other peoples (each king speaks of his nation as "my people"; Isa. 53:8b). Adding insult to injury, he was buried in a criminal's grave. The strophe ends by repeating the theme of the sacrificial lamb: The Servant was meek and innocent through the whole ordeal.

THE EXALTATION OF THE SERVANT

In the concluding strophe (Isa. 53:10–12), as in the opening one, Yahweh speaks. The tones of all the preceding strophes are blended together in this great climax, in which Yahweh announces that the outcome of the Servant's mission will be victory and exalta-

---

[26]The translation "generation" is advocated by a number of scholars. Others translate the Hebrew word (*dor*) as "fate" that is, "who gave a thought to his fate. . . ." (New English Bible), or "who would have thought any more of his destiny?" (New American Bible).

tion. The power of God is manifest in the Servant's sacrifice. The Servant is not a victim, but a victor, for Yahweh will reverse the Servant's position of humiliation and disgrace, establishing his "justice" before the whole world. In Yahweh's determination the Servant will have a posterity and a long life (Isa. 53:10)—both of which, to the Israelite mind, were signs of divine favor. God's purpose will prosper in the career of the Servant, and the Servant will look with satisfaction upon the successful result of his travail.

At first glance, it seems that the prophet had in mind an individual Servant, whose resurrection from the grave is implied in this passage. But the doctrine of the resurrection of the individual appeared only later in Israelite tradition (see Chapter 18). Up to this point, the only instance of resurrection in the Hebrew Bible is Ezekiel's vision in the valley of dry bones, and Ezekiel was speaking metaphorically of the resurrection of Israel of the Dispersion from the grave of exile (Ezek. 37). Probably this is also the meaning in Isaiah 53. The prophet portrays the victorious destiny of Israel in language that oscillates between the conception of the Servant as an individual and the conception of the Servant as the community.

The poem ends by referring back to the beginning. Just as the opening claimed that great kings and many nations would be astonished at the Servant, so the conclusion announces that Yahweh will make him great. His greatness is described in the concrete terms characteristic of Israelite tradition. The Servant will receive a portion with the great and will divide the spoil of conquest, for he is the true conqueror who advances along the royal road of God's kingdom.

In Second Isaiah's portrait of the Suffering Servant, theology of sacrifice attains its highest expression in the Old Testament.[27] The conception of vicarious sacrifice was well-known in the ancient world. The belief was widespread that animal sacrifice was a means of sustaining life and assuring good relations with the deity: Recall Abraham's sacrifice of a ram caught in the thicket (Gen 22:13), or the famous Israelite ceremony of the scapegoat driven into the wilderness after the sins of the community had been put upon it (Lev. 16:8–26). Some of the language of the Servant poems suggests the ritual drama of the Babylonian Tammuz cult in which the king, on behalf of his people, subjected himself to humiliation and pain.

The poet echoes ancient views, but transforms them by putting them into a new theological context. To be sure, the Servant is led like a lamb to the sacrificial slaughter, but he is not a scapegoat upon whom people may cast their sins, thereby escaping responsibility for their actions. Rather, his is a willing self-sacrifice—a voluntary "offering for sin."[28] This moves the nations to confess that, like sheep, they have pursued the devices and desires of their own hearts, when all the while the Servant suffered on their behalf. Above all, the poet stresses that the Servant's suffering is the result of God's ini-

[27]See R. de Vaux, *Studies in Old Testament Sacrifice* [498].

[28]In Isaiah 53:10 the word translated "offering for sin" (Hebrew: *'asham*) is a priestly term for the "guilt offering" (Lev. 5:14–6:7)—one of the sacrifices that effects "atonement" (restores communion or "at-one-ment" with God).

tiative and pathos. Through this humble agent God overcomes broken relations and effects reconciliation. The people are led to confess that through the Servant's sacrifice they are restored to health (Isa. 53:5) and that many are "justified," that is, brought into a new relation with God (Isa. 53:11).

THE SERVANT AND THE MESSIAH

Belief in Israel's election is a basic conviction of Second Isaiah, who with profound insight expounds its universal implications for the whole of human history. But the prophet never wavers from his central premise that Yahweh has chosen Israel for a special task in a world-embracing plan. Second Isaiah's message begins with the "good news" of Yahweh's comfort and grace to Israel and, after many variations on this theme, the poems reach a mighty climax on the same note (Isa. 54 and 55):

> For a brief instant I forsook you,
>> but with tremendous compassion I will gather you.
> In bursting wrath for a moment
>> I hid my face from you,
> but with everlasting loyalty I'll have compassion on you,
>> says Yahweh, your Redeemer.
>
>> —ISAIAH 54:7–8

Nowhere does Second Isaiah include the Davidic king in his portrayals of the coming Kingdom of God. This is surprising when one considers the resurgence of messianic hope among the Jews who returned from exile to Jerusalem. Although the prophet frequently extols Zion's role in Yahweh's unfolding worldwide plan, he mentions the Davidic covenant only once, in connection with Yahweh's invitation to an eschatological banquet (Isa. 55:1–5). In this instance, however, the "everlasting covenant" (Hebrew: *berîth 'ôlam*) is made not with the Davidic king but with all Israelites who respond to the call (Isa. 55:3–5).[29] Yahweh's promises of grace (Hebrew: *ḥésed*) to David do not guarantee the continuance of a dynasty but rather support the community of Israel, whose suffering will bring divine blessing to the world.

Jewish thought did not usually identify the suffering Servant with a future Messiah. This revolutionary identification was carried out mainly by Christians, although the way had been prepared in some Jewish circles such as the Essene community that occupied Qumran on the northwestern shore of the Dead Sea at the beginning of the

---

[29]See Otto Eissfeldt, "The Promises of Grace to David in Isaiah 55:1–5," in *Israel's Prophetic Heritage* [174], pp. 196–207. Eissfeldt contrasts the motif of the Davidic covenant in Psalm 89 with the use of the same motif by Second Isaiah. *See also* E. W. Conrad, "The Community as King in Second Isaiah" [176], pp. 99–111.

Common Era (see pp. 575–576). Martin Buber, the distinguished Jewish interpreter, affirms that "in the essential point" a messianic interpretation "approximates closely" the intention of Second Isaiah. The Servant represents true Israel, for whenever the humble worshiper lives in such close fellowship with God that suffering is borne willingly, Israel is fulfilling its task. Then "God's purpose for Israel has put on skin and flesh."[30]

THE CONTINUING ISAIAH TRADITION

Our study has been based on the widely held view that Isaiah 40–55 constitutes a separate body of literature composed by an inspired poet living in Babylonian exile. The unity of this collection is evident in its structure: It begins with the keynote of the New Exodus (Isa. 40:3–5), and ends resounding the same theme (Isa. 55:12–13). Here we find a carefully wrought literary whole that reflects the situation of the Exile and announces a message of consolation to a captive people.

THE DISCIPLES OF SECOND ISAIAH

The remaining chapters of the book of Isaiah (Isa. 56–66), often put under the rubric of "Third Isaiah," seem to reflect the post-exilic period (see Chapter 15). At this time disciples of Second Isaiah handed on and reinterpreted their master's message in a new situation that included the building of the second Temple (about 520–515 B.C.E.). Reading the poems of "Third Isaiah" with this struggling Palestinian community in mind, the shift of emphasis from the message of Second Isaiah becomes clear. Second Isaiah's poetry pulses with the excitement of an imminent return to Jerusalem—a New Exodus and a new entry into the Promised Land. Isaiah 56–66, on the other hand, reflects bitter disillusionment and acrimonious controversy in the Palestinian community. Second Isaiah had announced that Israel's vocation was to be Yahweh's Servant, who mediates the blessing of God to all peoples. Isaiah 56–66 speaks of Yahweh's "servants" (plural)—a repentant and righteous remnant who, though oppressed by rebellious elements within the Jewish community itself, faithfully awaits the fulfillment of Yahweh's plan for Israel and the nations (Isa. 65:8–12, 13–16).

On the whole the poems of "Third Isaiah" lack the lyrical quality and theological depth of Isaiah 40–55. Yet there are clear echoes of the poetry of Second Isaiah, both in form and content, especially in Isaiah 60–62 but also in passages such as 57:14–21, which recapitulates the motif of preparing a "way" for the people into the future (Isa. 57:14; compare 40:1–4). Here Israel's consolation is based on the grace of the holy

---

[30]Martin Buber, *The Prophetic Faith* [313], pp. 218–32.

God, who is both transcendent in celestial majesty and redemptively present in human history:

> Thus says the high and exalted One,
>> who inhabits eternity, whose name is Holy:
> "I dwell in a lofty and holy place,
>> but also with the crushed and humble in spirit,
> to give the humble in spirit new life,
>> and to revive the heart of the crushed."
>> —ISAIAH 57:15

No finer interpretation of the demands of the covenant can be found in the scriptures of Israel than Isaiah 58:1–12, which interprets the meaning of the cultic rite of fasting:

> Is not this the sort of fast that pleases me:
>> to break unjust fetters,
>> to undo the thongs of the yoke,
>> to let the oppressed go free,
>> and to break all yokes?
> Is it not sharing your food with the hungry,
>> and sheltering the homeless poor;
> If you see someone lacking clothes, to clothe him
>> and not to turn away from your own kin?
> Then your light will blaze out like the dawn
>> and your wound be quickly healed over.
> Saving justice for you will go ahead,
>> and Yahweh's glory come behind you.
>> —ISAIAH 58:6–8 (NJB)

The collection of poems in Isaiah 56–66, however, transposes the message of Second Isaiah into a new key. Whereas Second Isaiah portrayed the saving activity of Yahweh within the context of the political realities attending the rise of Cyrus and the beginning of the Persian empire, the poetry of his disciples tends to move away from the plane of history into a suprahistorical realm of religious imagination. Here the Divine Warrior is portrayed as coming to conquer the powers of evil and chaos that corrupt the world and to introduce a new age, one that is discontinuous with all previous history. We hear about a New Jerusalem, indeed a cosmic "New Creation:"

> For I am about to create new heavens
>> and a new earth;
> and the former things shall not be remembered
>> or come to mind.

But be glad and rejoice forever
> in what I am creating;
For I am about to create Jerusalem as a joy,
> and her people as a delight.
I will rejoice in Jerusalem,
> and delight in my people;
No more shall the sound of weeping be heard in it,
> or the cry of distress.

—ISAIAH 65:17–19 (NRSV)

Poems like these bring us into "the dawn of apocalyptic" and thus to the new theological horizons of the post-exilic community (see Chapter 18).[31]

THE BOOK OF ISAIAH AS A WHOLE

We have seen that the large scroll of Isaiah—sixty-six chapters in all—actually falls into three parts: Isaiah 1–39, reflecting the Assyrian period when Isaiah of Jerusalem was active (about 740–700 B.C.E.); Isaiah 40–55, reflecting the transition from the Babylonian to the Persian periods when Second Isaiah flourished (about 538 B.C.E.); and Isaiah 56–66, reflecting conditions of the early post-exilic period under Persian rule (about 520–500 B.C.E.). Our critical study has discerned no fewer than three "Isaiahs." Yet before modern biblical criticism, the book of Isaiah was regarded as a literary unity and as such entered the canon of the Bible. Without sacrificing our gains in historical understanding, is it possible to move from analysis back to synthesis?

At this stage of study, one can make only a beginning in this difficult task.[32] Notice, first of all, that the sections we have labeled "Second Isaiah" and "Third Isaiah" were never intended to stand by themselves. Unlike other prophetic collections (including that of Isaiah of Jerusalem, or "First Isaiah"), there is no superscription associating the materials with a particular prophet or a particular historical time (see Isa. 1:1; Jer. 1:1–3; Hag. 1:1; Zech. 1:1). Apparently, so-called "Second Isaiah" and "Third Isaiah" were meant to be subsumed under the seminal work of the eighth-century prophet, Isaiah of Jerusalem.

Moreover, both blocks of material (Isa. 40–55, 56–66) serve as supplements to, and even commentaries on, previous prophetic tradition. Second Isaiah—a theological

---

[31]See Paul D. Hanson, *The Dawn of Apocalyptic* [502], chap. 2, whose important work has influenced this discussion.

[32]On the question of the unity of the book of Isaiah, see Brevard Childs, *Introduction* [42], pp. 325–38, whose canonical approach opens the question in a new way. For further discussion see the articles listed in the Bibliography [101–103].

supplement to the message of First Isaiah—was composed in a later time for the purpose of contemporizing the original message. This disciple elaborated on the message of his predecessor, who proclaimed that Yahweh, the exalted King of the cosmos, is "the Holy One of Israel" whose earthly rule is manifest through the Davidic king and the Temple of Zion. But the student also enriched, and even went beyond, the thought of his teacher. Whereas Isaiah of Jerusalem had ignored the Exodus tradition, Second Isaiah drew deeply on the Israelite Old Epic: the promises to the ancestors, the deliverance from Egypt, the wanderings in the wilderness; and the entrance into the land. As we have seen, he combined the Exodus and Zion traditions in the exuberant proclamation that Yahweh, the cosmic Creator and King, was leading an uprooted people in a New Exodus through the wilderness to Zion, Yahweh's holy hill (compare Exod. 15:1–18). Moreover, he "democratized" the unconditional promises of grace to David by loosing them from the fallen Davidic dynasty and applying them to the people (Isa. 55:3–5).

Similarly, the collection known as Third Isaiah is actually a supplement to Second Isaiah, as evidenced by the reworking of received poetic forms and theological motifs. In Isaiah 56–66, as one scholar observes, "we are dealing with a living, ongoing tradition, restlessly seeking new applications as the situation changes."[33]

In the last analysis, however, we are not just dealing with a series of supplements to an original Isaianic prophecy, but with a new work in which "the whole is greater than the sum of its parts." The question of the unity of Isaiah leads to a consideration of the "canonical shape" of the book as it was used scripturally in the synagogue.[34] At the very least the question leads to "redaction criticism"—that is, an examination of how the final redactors organized and interpreted various levels of the Isaiah tradition so that, as a whole, it spoke to the situation of their time (see Definition, pp. 355–356).

We have noted that redactors, probably members of the Deuteronomistic school, were responsible for shaping the materials of the book of Jeremiah so that the prophet's message would speak to people in exile (see Chapter 12). Can anything be said about the redaction of the book of Isaiah? Though shrouded in mists of uncertainty, one important clue might be found in the later chapters, where prophecy moves into the idiom of apocalyptic. In the words of one scholar, this transition entailed "a growing indifference to the concrete events of plain history" and "a flight into the timeless repose of myth."[35] The message of Second Isaiah is detached from its historical moorings in the political realities of the mid-sixth century B.C.E. and lifted into the symbolic world-view of apocalyptic. No longer is the scene restricted to Israel's history. Rather, it enlarges into a universal drama, in which the Kingdom of God stands in opposition to the powers of evil that afflict and crush people.

---

[33]See Paul D. Hanson, *Dawn of Apocalyptic* [502], p. 45.

[34]Brevard Childs, *Introduction* [42]. For further discussion of this canonical approach, see Definition, pp. 578–579.

[35]See Paul D. Hanson's illuminating discussion of myth and history, *The Dawn of Apocalyptic* [502], pp. 126–34.

It is not enough, however, to note the transition from Second Isaiah to the disciples designated as "Third Isaiah." The apocalyptic interpreters of Isaiah not only called for a new reading of Second Isaiah, but also for a new reading of the whole Isaiah tradition. This would explain the presence of the so-called "Little Apocalypse of Isaiah" (Isa. 24–27), usually regarded as having no relation to its context. It also helps us understand why the book of Isaiah is punctuated at other points with passages akin to the apocalyptic idiom (such as Isa. 34, 35). Viewed in this total context, the thread that binds all the Isaianic traditions together is the City of Zion, regarded as the earthly locus of the Kingdom of God and, in apocalyptic thinking, the symbol of the new age introduced through Yahweh's decisive triumph over the powers of chaos.[36] Thus an apocalyptic passage, found in the very heart of the book of Isaiah, describes the ultimate victory of the Divine Warrior:

> In that day Yahweh will punish with his heavy, great, and mighty
> sword Leviathan the fleeing serpent, Leviathan the twisting serpent, and he
> will slay the Dragon that is in the Sea.
>
> —ISAIAH 27:1

Much more could be said on this subject. Already, however, we have anticipated developments that lie ahead.

---

[36]See B. W. Anderson, "The Apocalyptic Rendering of the Isaiah Tradition," *The Social World of Formative Christianity and Judaism,* Jacob Neusner *et al.,* eds. (Philadelphia: Fortress, 1988), pp. 17–38, and "The Slaying of the Fleeing, Twisting Serpent," in *From Creation to New Creation* [146], chap. 12.

CHAPTER 15

A KINGDOM
OF PRIESTS

Modern history provides memorable images of people who, having been crowded into concentration camps or subjected to military occupation, become wild with joy at the sight of a liberating army. Similarly, the Cyrus Cylinder (see pp. 419–421, Insert 16–1) is a firsthand historical witness to the jubilation evoked by the advance of the Persian army in the middle of the sixth century B.C.E. Cyrus' benevolent policy was a welcome relief from Babylonian tyranny, both to the Babylonians, who in high anticipation opened the doors of their cities and their hearts to him, and to the many captive peoples then under his rule. Apparently Cyrus sensed the futility of trying to lash people of diverse backgrounds and national traditions into subservient unity—a policy that had been the foundation of the empires whose lands he inherited. To be sure, he did not relax his political power. The Persian army had proved a powerful fighting force, and the Persian government soon developed a swift system of communications—a forerunner of the American "pony express"—that made it possible to supervise his far-flung empire, efficiently divided into "satrapies" (provinces). But Cyrus must have understood the limitations of power, or perhaps he realized that the emperor who inspires honor and loyalty from his people also enjoys an increase in power.

Biblical Readings: For historical background on the period of the return from Babylonian captivity, read the books of Ezra and Nehemiah; also the small prophetic collections of Haggai, Zechariah 1–8, Malachi, Obadiah, and Joel. For the meaning of the Torah for Judaism, read Psalms 1, 19:7–14, and 119.

During the post-exilic period, the Aramaic language gradually became the common tongue of the Jewish people. Keep in mind, however, that Aramaic was at least as old as Hebrew, and both belonged to a common family of Semitic languages. The differences and similarities between them were like those between such modern Romance languages as Spanish and Italian. This kinship of language might help to explain the close relations that existed between the Aramean (Syrian) and Hebrew people, as reflected in the ancestral stories of Jacob and Laban.

In the ancient Mediterranean world, Aramaic commanded great international prestige. When the Rabshakeh came to demand the surrender of Jerusalem in the time of Isaiah (Isa 36:11; 2 Kings 18:26), he was asked to speak in Aramaic rather than in the native tongue of the Judeans. During and after the Exile, the Persian authorities used Aramaic as an international language in addressing their satrapies, thereby enhancing its importance.

Gradually, the Jews came to think of Hebrew as a literary or classical language. But in Palestine and throughout the Dispersion (for instance, at Elephantine) their spoken language was Aramaic. Thus, well before the Common Era, Hebrew scripture had to be accompanied by a *targum*—a free translation into Aramaic—to enable ordinary Jews to understand it. Moreover, the Babylonian Talmud, a voluminous collection of writings that set forth Jewish religious and civil law, was written in an eastern branch of the Aramaic language.

CYRUS' EDICT OF LIBERATION

In a part of the Cyrus Cylinder that speaks of the various regions he has conquered, Cyrus reports: "I returned to (these) sacred cities on the other side of the Tigris, the sanctuaries of which have been in ruins for a long time, the images which (used) to live therein and established for them permanent sanctuaries. I (also) gathered all their (former) inhabitants and returned[1] (to them) their habitations."[1] Clearly, Cyrus chose to abandon the "scorched-earth" tactics of the Assyrians and Babylonians, who had destroyed cities and temples, looted sacred treasuries, and transported idols and people into captivity. With a political about-face, he permitted his subject peoples to carry on their customs, to worship their gods, and to resettle in their homelands (see Chronological Chart 8, p. 372).

It is against this background that we should read the account of the edict of liberation that Cyrus proclaimed to the Jewish exiles in the first year after Babylon's fall (538 B.C.E.). This edict is preserved in two versions: one in Hebrew, the traditional language of Israel (Ezra 1:2–4), and the other in Aramaic (6:3–5).

---

[1]Pritchard, *Ancient Near Eastern Texts* [1], p. 316.

The very fact that Cyrus' edict is preserved in two versions speaks in favor of its authenticity. Though some scholars believe the Aramaic version is the original account, there are no fundamental discrepancies between the two. According to the Hebrew version, Cyrus claimed that "Yahweh, the God of heaven" had given him all the kingdoms of the earth and had charged him to build Yahweh a temple in Jerusalem. This claim reminds us of Second Isaiah, who regarded Cyrus as Yahweh's agent by whom Jerusalem would be rebuilt (Isa. 44:28; 45:1–3, 13). Undoubtedly the Jewish historian has touched up the edict theologically, for in his Cylinder, Cyrus claimed that Marduk gave him world dominion. Still, the Hebrew report is not inconsistent with Cyrus' policy, for he regarded himself as the patron of the gods of conquered peoples. Both versions of the edict say that he permitted the Jews to return to their homeland, ordered the Temple of Jerusalem to be rebuilt with support from the Persian treasury (Ezra 6:4), and commanded that the vessels taken by Nebuchadrezzar from the Temple be returned (Ezra 1:7–11).

The tomb of Cyrus at Pasargadae, his royal residence. According to Plutarch, a Roman writer of the early common era, it bore this inscription: "O man, whosoever thou art and whencesoever thou comest, for I know that thou wilt come, I am Cyrus and I won for the Persians their empire. Do not, therefore, begrudge me this little earth which covers my body." Alexander visited Cyrus' tomb on his return from India and, Plutarch reports, was deeply moved by the inscription.

THE RETURN UNDER A DAVIDIC PRINCE

To head the first contingent of Jews returning from exile, Cyrus appointed "a prince of Judah" who carried a Babylonian name, *Sin-ab-uṣur* (Sheshbazzar). Sheshbazzar might have been of Davidic lineage; if so, his appointment accorded with the Persian practice of turning now and then to a member of a royal house for leadership of a local state. Not much is known about Sheshbazzar's term as governor, although Ezra 5:16 reports that he was responsible for laying the foundations of the Temple. He was succeeded by a better known figure who also bore a Babylonian name: *Zer-babili* (Zerubbabel), a descendant of Jehoiachin (1 Chron. 3:19), the exiled king whom many had regarded as Judah's legitimate ruler. Clearly the Persian administration was following a conciliatory policy, for not only was the observance of Jewish customs encouraged but also, to a limited degree, a national revival was permitted. These developments must have stirred the hearts and kindled the hopes of many Jews, to whom it appeared that the new age, in the dawn of which Second Isaiah stood, was about to break into the full light of day.

Second Isaiah's picture of the new age, however, was so elevated in grandeur, so transfigured in the light of eternity, that no ordinary historical era—least of all the post-exilic period of Judaism—could measure up to his vision. He spoke not of a Davidic king, but of the Servant exalted through suffering. He pictured no ordinary Jerusalem, but a New Jerusalem that would be a sign to all nations that Yahweh is King. He described a marvelous transformation that would begin in people's hearts and be mirrored in the whole drama of history and the vast scenery of nature. His message had to do with "last things," the consummation of all history in the redemptive purpose of God. But the exiles who chose to return to Jerusalem under the protection of Cyrus experienced not the poetry of Second Isaiah, but the prose of a grim and bitter struggle.

To tell the story of the return as briefly as possible, our study will concentrate on three figures and three events: (1) Zerubbabel and the rebuilding of the Temple; (2) Ezra and the renewal of the covenant; and (3) Nehemiah and the rebuilding of the walls of Jerusalem. We will also look briefly at prophets like Haggai and Zechariah, Joel and Malachi, and try to understand the character of the Judaism that emerged with Ezra.

THE WORK OF THE CHRONICLERS

Before turning to the period of post-exilic Judaism, we will consider the major historical source for our knowledge of Jewish life in Palestine during the Persian period that extends from the rise of Cyrus to the coming of Alexander the Great (333 B.C.E.). The source is two seldom-read books of the Old Testament: Ezra and Nehemiah. These books provide the only biblical history of the Persian period, and even this history covers no more than half the period. Admittedly, the books of Ezra and Nehemiah might seem anticlimactic after the stirring poems of Second Isaiah. Yet this period of Judaism is an important chapter in Israel's life-story, far more important than is often realized. Without it Jews and Christians would not have received the religious heritage that has so profoundly influenced Western civilization.

THE BOOKS OF EZRA AND NEHEMIAH

Ezra and Nehemiah tell the story of Israel's history from the first return to Jerusalem to the end of Nehemiah's second term as governor of Judah (538 to shortly before 400 B.C.E.). Apparently the material was first split into two books by Jerome, who in the fourth century C.E. produced the Latin translation—known as the Vulgate—that came to be the authoritative translation of the Roman Catholic Church. Before Jerome, the account was treated as one book in the earliest Hebrew and Greek manuscripts.[2] During the early centuries of the Common Era, the standard Hebrew text (called the *Masora*, or "tradition") was meticulously preserved by Jewish scholars known as Masoretes, who counted all the words to be sure that no one would ever add or take away a single one. Based on their count, they established that the exact middle of the account of Ezra and Nehemiah fell at what is designated in the Old Testament as Nehemiah 3:32. This, of course, is not the middle of the present book of Nehemiah, but of the single book Ezra-Nehemiah, which was one scroll when the rabbis did their counting. Thus the story of Ezra is found partly in the book of Ezra and partly in Nehemiah (Neh. 7:73b–10:39).

In the original Hebrew the scroll Ezra-Nehemiah was part of a large historical work. Because of its distinct overall unity, this work is generally attributed to "the Chroniclers"—a term applied to a school of historical interpreters active in the post-exilic period. The nucleus of the work is 1–2 Chronicles (one book in the Hebrew Bible), possibly composed in the early post-exilic period around the time of the building of the Second Temple (520–515 B.C.E.). The work was probably enlarged in various stages until it attained its final form (1–2 Chronicles, Ezra and Nehemiah) sometime after the year 400 B.C.E.[3] Some interpreters, including the philosopher Spinoza, have surmised that Ezra was the final editor.

Curiously, in the Hebrew Bible the book called *Dibrē Hayyim* ("Events of [Past] Times"; corresponds to 1–2 Chronicles in the Old Testament) is in most manuscripts placed at the very end of the third part, the Writings, and immediately after Ezra-Nehemiah. This puts the cart before the horse, for clearly the proper chronological order is just the reverse. The concluding verses of 2 Chronicles, which deal with the rise of Cyrus, are identical with the opening verses of Ezra—an ancient scribe's way of connecting the narratives in their proper sequence.

---

[2]In the Greek Septuagint the single work is known as "Ezra" ("Esdras B"). There is also an apocryphal work called "I Esdras" that includes 2 Chron. 35–36, Ezra, and Neh. 8:1–12, plus other material.
[3]See David Noel Freedman and Bruce E. Willoughby, "I and II Chronicles, Ezra, Nehemiah," in *The Books of the Bible* [9].

The Chroniclers' Work adds one more major historical work to those we have already investigated. Leaving out the Old Epic tradition (J and E), which belongs in the category of historical epic, the list includes:

1. The Deuteronomistic History (Joshua through 2 Kings with Deuteronomy as introduction)
2. The Priestly Writing (Genesis through Numbers, and the end of Deuteronomy)
3. The Chroniclers' Work (1 and 2 Chronicles, Ezra-Nehemiah).

The list should probably be reduced by one, for the Priestly Writing is actually an expanded version of the Israelite Old Epic. We are left, then, with two major works that recount Israel's history. The Deuteronomistic History begins with the last days of Moses and, in its final form, concludes with the fall of the nation and the exile of the people. The Chroniclers' Work begins essentially with the rise of David and carries the story into the post-exilic period to about 400 B.C.E.

THE CHRONICLERS' PRIESTLY PERSPECTIVE

It is interesting to compare the Deuteronomistic History and 1–2 Chronicles where they run in parallel.[4] For example, a comparison of the David story—found in both 1 Samuel 15–1 Kings 2 and in 1 Chronicles 10–29—reveals how the past is reviewed in the Chroniclers' Work. Sometimes these historians excerpt entire passages from the books of Samuel and Kings word for word—another reminder that our conceptions of authorship (and plagiarism!) did not apply in antiquity. At other times they ignored or changed the tradition according to their interests. This seems a cavalier way of writing history. But these historians were primarily *interpreters* of the past, who selected the materials that would emphasize aspects of the tradition relevant to their own time. Of course, when historians deal with 600 years (a much longer span than the whole of American history) they cannot avoid selecting and weighting their materials. This is especially true in a manuscript of 100 pages—approximately the extent of the Chroniclers' Work. We can see the Chroniclers' theological bias clearly when we observe how, in dealing with the tradition of Samuel-Kings, they select, omit, add, and modify. This is propaganda—not in the derogatory sense that the word has acquired in modern history, but in its primary meaning of an effort to spread particular doctrines.

It would be wrong, however, to suppose that because this work was written in a late period and from a priestly point of view, it is mere fiction. The Chroniclers' Work relied not only on Samuel and Kings, but also on source material that was either not in-

---

[4]Ezra and Nehemiah, which make up the remainder of the Chroniclers' Work, are not paralleled in the Deuteronomistic History, which concludes with the Exile.

cluded in the Deuteronomistic History or not available at the time it was written. An example of the Chroniclers' use of reliable historical sources is found in Ezra-Nehemiah, where the historians excerpt almost verbatim the autobiographical "Memoirs of Nehemiah." The "Memoirs of Ezra" are also a very important historical witness. These two sources are found in the following places:

1. Memoirs of Nehemiah: Nehemiah 1:1–7:73a; 11:1–2; 12:27–43; 13:4–31.
2. Memoirs of Ezra: Ezra 7:27–9:15.[5]

The Chroniclers' Work represents a fundamental revision—or reinterpretation—of Israel's history. It is important to understand the overall purpose of this history, for the story of Ezra-Nehemiah is the final phase of the unfolding history that begins with David. The Chroniclers were dominated by one central conviction: Israel was called to be a worshiping community. In a broad sense, Israel was to be "a kingdom of priests and a holy nation"—that is, a people whose whole life was to be a "liturgy" or divine service (compare Exod. 19:6). But in a special sense the community was to have its center in the Temple, where priests and especially Levites had an indispensable place in the conduct of worship. This liturgical interest is one of the major motifs of the Chroniclers' Work, which is essentially a history of Israel's worship centering in Zion, the Holy City.[6]

DAVID AND THE CULT

In the Samuel-Kings tradition, David is presented as a political leader, a man with strengths and weaknesses that endeared him to his people as the first and greatest king of all Israel. The Chroniclers, however, were not particularly interested in David's *political* genius. By the time they wrote, Israel had ceased to be a nation. To be sure, they gloried in David's military accomplishments and the splendor of his kingdom. Further, they emphasized the covenant with David (1 Chron. 17; compare 2 Sam. 7), which guaranteed the continuation of the Davidic house. Indeed, there is something "messianic" in their depiction of David, for he is the ideal king, the prototype of the "Messiah" or "Anointed One."

For these historians, however, David was primarily the one who organized Israel as a worshiping community. It was David who had made Jerusalem, the Holy City, his religious capital; who had conceived the building of the Temple according to a plan alleged to have come directly from Yahweh (see 1 Chron. 29:19); who had organized the

---

[5]It is difficult to determine how much of the Ezra narrative (Ezra 7:11–10:24; Neh. 7:73b–9:5) belongs to the Memoirs of Ezra. One problem is that sometimes Ezra speaks in the first person, and sometimes he is spoken of in the third person.

[6]See Jacob M. Myers' *I and II Chronicles*, [505], especially "The Intention of the Chronicler," pp. xviii–xl, where he deals with the continuity of true worship in Jerusalem.

music of the Temple and had assigned the Levites their duties. The ecclesiastical robes with which the Chroniclers invested David tend to cover up the man.

The Chroniclers' Work ignores aspects of the tradition that might detract from David's messianic stature, such as the story of his earlier career as an outlaw, his adultery with Bathsheba, Absalom's rebellion, and much of the material in the Court History. Most striking, it glorifies David's last words. Suppressing David's deathbed instructions to liquidate Joab and Shimei (1 Kings 2:5–9), it affirms that David's mind was engrossed to the very last with the dream of the future Temple (1 Chron. 28–29) and places on his lips one of the finest prayers found in the Old Testament (1 Chron. 29:10–19). No one tried more earnestly than the authors of the Chroniclers' Work to encircle David's head with a halo.

The Chroniclers did not make all this up out of whole cloth, so to speak. There is considerable basis in the tradition for David's liturgical interest. After all, David had brought the Ark to Jerusalem, had purchased Araunah's threshing floor to build an altar (2 Sam. 24), and had set in motion plans for building a temple. Moreover, David's interest in temple music was well established in Israelite tradition. He was "a skillful player on the lyre" (1 Sam. 16:14–23; compare Amos 6:5) and a noted composer of songs and laments, like the exquisite lament over Saul and Jonathan (2 Sam. 1:17–27). Surely it is mistaken to regard David as the author of the whole book of Psalms, which contains hymns, laments, and supplication from many times and poets.[7] But in view of David's reputation as a poet-musician, one can understand how later generations attributed the Psalter to him. Also, there is probably some element of truth in the Chroniclers' claim that David instituted changes in Israel's worship service, especially in instrumental music (1 Chron. 23–27). Nevertheless, the Chroniclers' ecclesiastical portrait of David was colored by the interests of post-exilic, priestly Judaism.

ISRAEL'S ECCLESIASTICAL HISTORY

Starting with the account of the origin of the worshiping community under David, the Chroniclers proceed to tell the history of Israel in ecclesiastical terms. Agreeing with the author of 2 Samuel 7, they affirm that Yahweh's blessing rested upon the Davidic dynasty. (Since there was only one legitimate kingship, they even pass over the tradition about the anointing of Saul.) The Northern Kingdom fell because, owing to the sins of Jeroboam I, it had separated itself from the true community of worship. The Southern Kingdom, too, eventually proved so corrupt that Yahweh brought severe judgment upon it: The Holy City of Jerusalem fell; the Temple that David had planned to be "exceedingly magnificent, of fame and glory throughout all lands" (1 Chron. 22:5) was destroyed; and the priests and people were taken into exile.

---

[7]Less than half of the psalms are attributed to David in the headings. The Davidic Psalter is discussed further in Chapter 16.

At this point the Chroniclers begin the story found in Ezra-Nehemiah. The historians tell how Cyrus' edict enabled faithful Jews to return to Jerusalem, where they immediately built an altar on which to offer burnt offerings to the God of Israel and, some years afterward, rebuilt the Temple. The Jewish community was threatened, however, by the paganism that had precipitated the destruction of the first Temple. Next, according to the Chroniclers' scheme, Ezra the priest came from Babylonia with the Torah of Moses in his hand, and initiated a great religious reform aimed at maintaining the identity of the community. Shortly after, if we follow the present order of the narratives, Nehemiah came from Babylonia to Jerusalem. Vested with the authority of governor of the Persian district of Judah, he supervised the rebuilding of Jerusalem's walls and instituted various social and religious reforms.

Thus Israel came back from exile not as a nation, but as a religious community. **This account is in keeping with the historical situation** of the post-exilic period. The Chroniclers' intention, however, is to show that **the profound change in Israel's life was** not just a response to the political vicissitudes of the period. Rather, it was a return to the charter of Judaism handed down from David.

ZERUBBABEL, THE BRANCH

Having established the place of the books of Ezra and Nehemiah in the Chroniclers' Work, we turn attention to the pioneers who responded to Cyrus' edict and returned to the homeland. One must not suppose there was a mass exodus from Babylonia. The list in Ezra 2 (compare Neh. 7) puts the number at about 50,000. This could be an expanded census list from the time of Nehemiah several generations later, for Nehemiah 7:5 explicitly states that Nehemiah published the list. The number of those "whose spirit God had stirred to go up to rebuild the house of Yahweh in Jerusalem" (Ezra 1:5) was unquestionably much smaller, and the immigration took place over a period of several generations. Many Jews were comfortably settled in Babylon and were doing well in business: Josephus (37 to after 100 C.E.), the famous Jewish historian, was correct in saying that many were loath to leave their possessions.[8] To many Jews it must have seemed sheer recklessness to start out on a long, hazardous, and costly journey that could end only in uncertainty and insecurity in the impoverished environs of Jerusalem.

TENSIONS WITHIN THE PALESTINIAN COMMUNITY

Some time later, however, we find a small community of people in Jerusalem under the leadership of the High Priest Jeshua (or Joshua) and Zerubbabel, who as successor to Sheshbazzar was the recognized civil authority. Among the first acts of this community,

---

[8]*Antiquities of the Jews,* xi, 1, 3.

Insert 15-1a (Top) A reconstructed temple stands in back of the ruins of the famous Ishtar Gate at the site of ancient Babylon. *Insert 15-1b (Bottom)* The processional street of Babylon, which led through the Ishtar Gate to the great "Tower of Babel" ziggurat, was adorned with sacred dragons and bulls of Hadad.

Insert 16-1 The famous Cyrus Cylinder tells of Cyrus' conquest of Babylon "without any battle" and of his policy of allowing captives to return to their homelands and rebuild their temples. Although Second Isaiah claims that Cyrus was Yahweh's agent, this inscription affirms that Marduk, the god of Babylon, selected Cyrus to become "the ruler of the world" and then went by his side "like a real friend."

Insert 16-2 This exquisite gold bowl from Persian, sixth–fifth century B.C.E., stands 4.5" high.

according to the Chroniclers' account in Ezra 3, were the building of an altar, the installation of the Levites, and the laying of the foundation of a new Temple. Worship was carried out "according to the directions of King David of Israel" (Ezra 3:10), which, of course, shows the Chroniclers' interest in the Davidic charter for Judaism.

During the remaining years of Cyrus' reign the work of restoration was hampered by controversies and conflicts within the Palestinian community. For one thing, "the people of the land"—that is, those who did not take part in the Babylonian captivity (Hebrew: *golah*) but stayed in Palestine—caused trouble. The Chroniclers' Work is based on the assumption that the true "Israel" was represented by the exiles (the "good figs" of Jeremiah's vision; Jer. 24) and that they had the God-given authority to rebuild the foundations of the Jewish community. One can be sure, however, that the people who had been living in the land for several generations did not welcome wholeheartedly the influx of thousands of refugees, nor did they accept unquestioningly the view that leadership belonged to the newcomers. Indeed, the literature of the period, when studied carefully, shows evidence of bitter controversy between the priestly establishment in Jerusalem—that is, the priests in the line of Zadok who returned from exile—and others who felt oppressed by their claims of power and authority.[9]

Neighboring people to the north, living in the former Assyrian province of Samaria, also stirred up trouble—the first signs of tension between Samaritans and Jews that eventually led to outright hostility and the building of a rival Samaritan temple on Mount Gerizim overlooking Shechem. From the Jewish standpoint, the Samaritans had been corrupted by mixing with the foreign people whom the Assyrians had settled in that area (see Ezra 4:2). The Samaritans themselves felt they were faithful adherents to the Mosaic tradition, and shared the Jewish interest in rebuilding the Temple at Jerusalem. On the other hand, they looked with apprehension and resentment upon the possible revival of a Jewish state on their very doorstep.

The Samaritans offered to cooperate with the Jews in rebuilding the Temple, but their offer was spurned by Zerubbabel. The hand extended in friendship curled into a fist. Of course, Samaritan hostility was not prompted by the Jewish rebuff alone, for there was undoubtedly economic and political rivalry between the two peoples. But the Samaritans did everything in their power to stop the building of the Temple, which they regarded as a symbol of revived Jewish nationalism. These political troubles led to suspension of work on the Temple for the remainder of the reign of Cyrus (who died in 530 B.C.E.), the entire reign of his successor, Cambyses II (about 530–522), and on into the reign of Darius I, the Great (Ezra 4:4–5:24; see Chronological Chart 8, p. 372).[10]

---

[9]Paul Hanson, *The Dawn of Apocalyptic* [502], sets forth this interpretation persuasively in connection with his study of "Third Isaiah" and other prophetic literature of the time.

[10]Ezra 4:6–23 obviously is out of place, for the passage deals with the reigns of Xerxes (Ahasuerus) and Artaxerxes I, kings who succeeded Darius. For historical details, see the classic history by A. T. Olmstead, *History of the Persian Empire* (University of Chicago Press, 1948).

THE TIME OF HAGGAI AND ZECHARIAH

After a lapse of about eighteen years, in 520 B.C.E. (the second year of the reign of Darius I, 522–486 B.C.E.),[11] the work of rebuilding the Temple was resumed. Zerubbabel's leadership at that time must be seen in the context of events that shook the Persian empire to its foundation. Darius' predecessor, Cambyses, under whose military leadership Egypt was conquered and incorporated into the Persian empire, went insane and committed suicide. His death was followed by murder and intrigue within the court and by nationalistic uprisings in the Persian provinces.

After a time, Darius managed to quell the far-flung revolution, celebrating his triumph by carving a huge relief and trilingual inscription high on the Behistun Rock.[12] It portrays Darius, followed by two attendants, putting his foot on the prostrate rebel chief and pointing to the winged disc, symbol of the Zoroastrian god Ahura Mazda. Before him stand nine rebel leaders, their necks tied together by a rope and their hands manacled behind their backs. The accompanying cuneiform inscription was written in three languages—Old Persian, Elamite, and Akkadian (see Insert 17–1b). This amazing achievement has opened up new vistas of knowledge in modern research, for by deciphering the Old Persian, scholars were able to translate the other two languages.

In the second year of Darius' reign, revolt broke out in Babylonia under the leadership of Nebuchadrezzar, a namesake of the ruler we met previously in our study of Jeremiah. Scarcely a month after the Babylonian uprising, the Jews began rebuilding the Temple under the Davidic leadership of Zerubbabel and the High Priest Joshua.

According to Ezra 5:1, the work was inspired by two prophets, Haggai and Zechariah, whose brief writings are preserved in the Old Testament.[13] Encouraged by the apparent success of the Babylonian revolution in 520 B.C.E., Haggai preached with nationalistic fervor. He proclaimed to the people that economic conditions in the land were precarious because they had left Yahweh's house lying in ruins while they lived in fine, paneled houses. His very first oracle aroused the Jews to action. Hoping that Yahweh would favor them if they put first things first, the people fell in behind the leadership of Joshua the priest and Zerubbabel the governor (Hag. 1). A month later, when the people became downcast over the contrast between their inferior structure and the splendor of Solomon's Temple, Haggai fired their imaginations with the dream of an edifice whose glory would outshine the former Temple. He announced that divine intervention would soon come, and prophesied that Yahweh would shake the heavens and the earth, as well as all nations (Hag. 2:1–9), so that the treasures of the nations would be brought into the new Temple. Evidently, Haggai was looking forward to the down-

---

[11]The Chroniclers have mistakenly dated the laying of the foundation of the Temple in the second year of Cyrus (Ezra 3:6–13) rather than the second year of Darius (Hag. 1:1–6).

[12]The inaccessibility of this relief challenged the acrobatic ability of archaeologists for many years before a platform and stairs were finally installed.

[13]The authentic prophecies of Zechariah are found in Zechariah 1–8; the rest of the book comes from a later time.

Darius on his throne holds a scepter in one hand and a lotus blossom in the other. Behind him stands the crown prince, Xerxes—the Ahasuerus mentioned in Ezra 4:6 and in the book of Esther. The king is receiving a foreign dignitary, whose hand is raised to his mouth in a gesture of respect. This relief was found at Persepolis.

fall of the Persian empire. His final oracle, addressed to Zerubbabel, struck the same nationalistic note, announcing in veiled language that the Jewish governor—a descendant of Jehoiachin—was Yahweh's Anointed One, the Davidic Messiah (Hag. 2:20–23).

The prophecy of Zechariah, dated slightly later, expresses the same hope for a restoration of the Jewish state under the co-leadership of the High Priest and the Davidic prince. The oracles are cast in a bizarre apocalyptic form popular in Judaism in the late post-exilic period. Like the prophecy of Second Isaiah, this new type of prophecy deals with the end-time, the consummation of history in Yahweh's sovereign purpose. Unlike the earlier prophecy it is couched in cryptic language, abounds with marvelous visions of the future, and foresees the coming of a dramatic finale when Yahweh's foes will be shattered and the dominion of God will be established.[14] Convinced that the might of the nations will be broken by Yahweh miraculously (see Zech. 4:6–10), the prophet Zechariah names Zerubbabel as the Davidic Messiah. Speaking to the High Priest Joshua, who was given charge over the Temple, Yahweh says through the prophet: "Behold, I will bring my servant the Branch" (Zech. 3:8). The word "Messiah" ("Anointed One") is not used here, for it was only in the later period of Judaism that the term took on the special meaning of *the* Anointed One, *the* Messiah (Greek: *Christos*).[15] With Zechariah, the word "branch" refers to the messianic king, the descendant of David's line (compare Isa. 11:1). According to the prophet, the sign of Zerubbabel's messianic authority is that he will complete the building of the Temple:

[14]This type of prophecy is known as an "apocalypse," a Greek term meaning "revelation"—that is, revelation of the shape of things to come. Since the book of Daniel is the best Old Testament example of apocalyptic literature, discussion of this kind of thinking will be postponed until Chapter 18.

[15]See definition, p. 211. In the earlier tradition of messianic prophecy, the future Davidic king is referred to as "a shoot from the stump of Jesse," "the branch" that will "grow out of his roots" (Isa. 11:1).

Thus says Yahweh of Hosts:

"Behold, a man whose name is The Branch. He will sprout up [literally "branch out"] where he is, and will build the temple of Yahweh. It is he who will build the temple of Yahweh, and he will bear royal majesty. He will sit upon his throne and rule, and a priest will be at his right hand [Septuagint translation], and between both of them there will be peaceful agreement."

—ZECHARIAH 6:12–13; compare 4:6–10

Possibly the name Zerubbabel once stood in this context (Zech. 6:9–15), but for some unknown reason was deleted. In any case, the prophecy of Zechariah leaves no doubt that the symbol of the Branch referred to Zerubbabel. Apparently the first part of the Chroniclers' Work (1–2 Chronicles) was composed to support hope for reestablishing the Davidic dynasty.[16]

THE SECOND TEMPLE

In spite of attempts by Tattenai, the satrap of Syria, and the leaders of Samaria to obstruct the project, the Temple was finished in the year 515 B.C.E. When the project is viewed in light of the troubles of the Persian empire in the first years of Darius' reign, it is apparent that the Jews were motivated by hope for the revival of the Jewish state. Zerubbabel mysteriously vanished from the scene at this point. There is no record of what happened to him, leading to the conjecture that the Persians spirited him away in fear that the messianic movement associated with him was a symptom of revolution. More likely, his appointment, like that of other governors, was limited and was not extended owing to unknown political circumstances in the Persian administration. In any event, we hear no more of attempts to revive the Davidic state during the Persian period. Leadership of the community was now vested in the High Priest, Joshua, and his successors. Henceforth Israel was to be a Temple-centered community, a kingdom of priests, patterned after the instructions that (according to the Chroniclers) were given by David.

It was, however, "a day of small things" (Zech. 4:10). The second Temple did not compare in splendor to the Temple of Solomon, a product of the artistry of Phoenician architects. We are told that when the old men who remembered the former Temple saw the foundations of the new Temple laid, they wept with a loud voice (Ezra 3:12–13). Yet the modest new Temple served as the center and bulwark of Israel's life in the postexilic period. What was lacking in architectural beauty was covered over by the great devotion lavished upon it, and above all by the conviction that it was the place where Yahweh tabernacled in the people's midst.

---

[16]See the essay by David Noel Freedman [501], who maintains that Ezra's final hand in the Chroniclers' Work is evident in the de-emphasis of the Davidic dynasty and emphasis upon the role of Moses as the mediator of Covenant Law.

The Chroniclers were right to speak of the importance of music and praise in Israel's history. To be sure, the writing of these historians reflects the interests of the post-exilic Temple, but fundamentally they were correct in believing that continuity of worship extended back to David. In a profound sense, the foundation of the second Temple was the people's religious devotion. As a worshiping community Israel was a singing people; instrumental and choral music had an important place in its life. Both the Chroniclers' Work and the headings of the Psalms name leaders of musical guilds—choristers like Heman, Asaph, and Ethan or Jeduthun—who played a special role in the worship service. According to the Chroniclers, the main function of the Levites was to lead the worshiping congregation in praise and prayer.

Israel's life and thought were nourished in the Temple until its final destruction in the Roman period (70 C.E.). Because it was not always possible, however, for Jews living outside Jerusalem to attend Temple services, synagogues began to dot the Palestinian countryside during the post-exilic period and eventually were found throughout the Dispersion. The synagogue made a deep impression upon Israel's life and thought, and in the long run outlived the Temple. During the post-exilic period, however, there was no real substitute for the Temple. Devout Jews made pilgrimages to Jerusalem to participate in the drama of priestly sacrifice and congregational praise. We can sense from the book of Psalms—sometimes called the "Hymnbook of the Second Temple"—that in these worship services they found comfort in their sorrow, forgiveness in their guilt, and hope in times of trouble. A day in Yahweh's courts, said a psalmist, was better than a thousand spent elsewhere:

> How lovely is your tabernacle,[17]
> > O Yahweh of hosts!
> My whole being longs and yearns
> > for Yahweh's [Temple] courts.
> My heart and my flesh sing for joy
> > to the living God.
>
> —PSALM 84:1–2

RECONSTRUCTION AND REFORM

The period from the completion of the second Temple (515 B.C.E.) to the appearance of Nehemiah in Jerusalem (445 B.C.E.) spans about three generations. In this period, Persian culture reached its greatest height, as evidenced by the impressive ruins standing at Persepolis, the main capital of the Persian empire (see Insert 17–1a). Both Darius I

---

[17]The word translated "tabernacle" (the Hebrew word is plural: *mishkanôth*) reflects the ancient view that Yahweh "tents" or "goes about" among the people. The Temple is Yahweh's dwelling place, not in the sense that Yahweh resides there but in the sense that it is the place of divine visitation from time to time.

The remains of the Apadana or Audience Hall, at Persepolis, the place to which Darius I moved to the main Persian capital from Pasargadae. The structure was begun by Darius and completed by Xerxes. Thirteen of the 72 columns that once supported the wood roof of the spacious room (about 195 square feet) still stand. The monumental stairways leading to the royal terrace were adorned with exquisite reliefs. This capital, which represented the height of Persian art and architecture, was destroyed by Alexander the Great in 331 B.C.E.

and Xerxes, builders of this magnificent capital, waged campaigns against Greece, only to be defeated at the famous battles of Marathon (490 B.C.E.), Thermopylae, and Salamis (480 B.C.E.).

Since the Chroniclers leap over this period in order to get to the great cultic reform of Ezra, modern historians must rely on other sources for information about Jewish affairs. The Elephantine papyri (see p. 384) come from the fifth century B.C.E., but are chiefly important for an understanding of Judaism in the Egyptian Dispersion. There are, however, several minor prophecies that throw some light on conditions in Palestine during this period, in addition to the writings of so-called "Third Isaiah" (Isa. 56–66; see pp. 447–450).

OBADIAH'S DENUNCIATION OF EDOM

The prophecy of Obadiah is a bitter outcry against Edom, the nation that had seized part of Judah's territory after the fall of Jerusalem (see Mal. 1:2–5; compare Ps. 137:7). Obadiah denounced the pride and treachery of Edom, traditionally related to Israel in the story of the twin brothers, Jacob and Esau. Yahweh, said the prophet, was about to summon the nations to destroy Edom for the violence done to "Jacob." The date of Obadiah's prophecy cannot be determined exactly. The reference to Edom's malicious actions on the day of Judah's ruin (Obad. 1: 11–14) dates it after the fall of Jerusalem in 587 B.C.E. Yet because the destruction of Edom is presented as a future threat (Obad. 1: 1–10), it must have been written before the fifth century B.C.E., when Arab tribes began pressing into Edomite territory from the Arabian Desert. By the fourth century B.C.E. these invaders, known as Nabateans, had claimed the Edomite mountain acropolis of Sela (compare Obad. 1: 3). In time they carved into the red limestone cliffs their splendid capital, the "rose city" of Petra—today one of the archaeological attractions on the eastern side of the Jordan (see Insert 19–1).

MALACHI'S PLEA FOR SINCERE WORSHIP

Other evidence of conditions in the Jewish community is provided by the book of Malachi, probably written a generation or so before Nehemiah's arrival in Jerusalem. At this time the Jewish community was ruled by a Persian governor (see Mal. 1:8). The second Temple had been completed, but the people's heart was no longer in their worship (Mal. 1:13). Echoing Obadiah's outcry against Edom, this prophet began by giving a bitter twist to the ancestral story of the twin brothers: "I have loved Jacob, but I have hated Esau"—in this way stressing Yahweh's favor for Israel (Mal. 1:2–5). This divine favor, said the prophet, only throws into sharp relief the people's faithless and ungrateful actions. He accused them of dishonoring Yahweh by placing polluted food on the altar and by offering sacrifices of blind, lame, and sickly animals not even acceptable to the governor. It would be better, the prophet said, to close the doors of the Temple, for Yahweh deserved nothing but the best gifts and the most sincere worship. With a note of universalism, Malachi pointed out that even the Gentiles magnified Yahweh's name (Mal. 1:11; see 2:10), whereas Israel was profaning it by inadequate and insincere worship. The priests were not guarding the true torah, men were divorcing their Jewish wives to marry foreign women, and social injustices abounded. To make matters worse, the people were complaining that serving God did not pay, since evildoers came out on top. "Where is the God of justice?" they asked (Mal. 2:17). Why serve God if religion yields no tangible benefits (Mal. 3:13–15)?

Malachi does not measure up to his predecessors, but his prophetic critique is vigorous. He suggests that if the people would only present a tenth (tithe) of their income, and stop "robbing God" of what was due, then Yahweh would pour upon them a great blessing and Israel would be great among the nations (Mal. 3:6–12). In a vivid passage he announces that the Messenger[18] will appear to prepare the way for the coming of Yahweh. Suddenly Yahweh will come to the holy Temple, and on "the day of his coming" people will shrink back in fear, "for he is like a refiner's fire." Yahweh's purpose is first of all to refine the priests, purifying them until they present "right offerings" to Yahweh. Then divine judgment will fall on sorcerers, adulterers, false witnesses, and those who oppress the poor and defenseless (Mal. 3:1–5). Even now, the prophet says, segregation of the righteous from the wicked is beginning, for a "Book of Remembrance" records the names of those who fear Yahweh and they will be spared on the day of judgment (Mal. 3:16–18). The writing ends with the prophecy that Yahweh will send Elijah, the prophet *par excellence*, to summon Israel to repentance and to prepare the people for "the great and terrible day of Yahweh" (Mal. 4:5).

JOEL AND THE ARMY OF LOCUSTS

The prophecy of Joel might come from this same period, though it is difficult to assign a precise date (between 500 and 350 B.C.E.). Whatever the date, the occasion of Joel's preaching was a plague of desert locusts that devastated the country, not an uncommon scourge in ancient Palestine. The event precipitated "an ecological crisis of national proportions."[19] In Joel's vivid imagination, the locusts were an invading "army," symbolizing the impending Day of Yahweh. Urgently the prophet summoned the people to a great fast for repentance and lament, perhaps in connection with the festival of the New Year:

> "But now—declares Yahweh—
>   come back to me with all your heart
>   fasting, weeping, mourning."
> Tear your hearts
>   and not your clothes,
> and come back to Yahweh your God,
>   for he is gracious and compassionate,
>   slow to anger, rich in faithful love,
>   and he relents about inflicting disaster.
>   —JOEL 2:12–13 (NJB)

Then, with a sudden shift from warning to promise, Joel announces that beyond the judgment Yahweh will restore "the years which the swarming locust has eaten" (Joel 2:25) and will pour out the divine spirit upon young and old (2:28–29; compare Acts 2). Joel's prophecy is reminiscent of pre-exilic preaching concerning the Day of Yah-

---

[18]The Hebrew expression *mal'aki* ("my messenger") in Mal. 3:1 is also given as the prophet's name in Malachi 1:1, and is probably the source of the name attributed to the prophet. Actually, we know nothing about the author of the book.

[19]See Theodore Hiebert's perceptive discussion, "Joel," in *Books of the Bible* [9], pp. 391–96.

weh, but it also contains descriptions of cosmic upheavals like those found in post-exilic apocalyptic literature (Joel 2:30–32).

Thus the books of Obadiah, Malachi, and Joel depict a struggling Jewish community, threatened from the outside by neighboring peoples and the pressures of foreign culture, and weakened from within by poverty, discontentment, and religious apathy. This was the situation when Ezra and Nehemiah appeared on the scene.

THE DATE OF EZRA'S MISSION

Here one must consider a major conundrum in biblical studies: Who came to Jerusalem first—Ezra or Nehemiah? There is no doubt about the date of Nehemiah's arrival. The beginning of his first term as governor is definitely fixed as the twentieth year of the reign of Artaxerxes (Neh. 1:1; 2:1). By general agreement, this is a date during the reign of Artaxerxes I Longimanus, not one of the later Artaxerxes (see Chronological Chart 9, p. 475). This establishes the date of Nehemiah's arrival as 445 B.C.E. Beyond that point, however, the historical picture becomes blurred.[20]

The Chroniclers believed that Ezra came first and dated his appearance in Jerusalem in the seventh year of Artaxerxes I, 458 B.C.E. (Ezra 7:7–8). Hence in the Chroniclers' scheme the next event after the completion of the Temple in the year 515 B.C.E. (Ezra 6) is the account of Ezra's return with a band of Zionists in the mid-fifth century B.C.E.—a leap of more than half a century (Ezra 7–8). Some time after his arrival, Ezra gathered the people before the Water Gate of Jerusalem for a reading of "The Book of the Torah of Moses" (Neh. 8–10). Before and after this event the Chroniclers placed Nehemiah's Memoirs (Neh. 1–7, 11–13), on the assumption that the careers of the two men overlapped.

Problems arise when one reads the Chroniclers' account in its final form. For one thing, the insertion of Nehemiah's Memoirs has the effect of postponing Ezra's reading of the Torah from the seventh year of Artaxerxes—the year of his arrival—to the twentieth year (Neh. 2:1). This editorial arrangement allows thirteen years to elapse before Ezra initiated the reform based on the Mosaic Torah. It seems a bit strange that Ezra waited so long to carry out the task for which he was commissioned by the Persian king. Moreover, if Ezra's reform was carried out first, as the present text indicates, he must have failed, for Nehemiah had to redo much of the work during his second term as governor (Neh. 13). Finally, if the two leaders collaborated, Nehemiah implementing the reform of Ezra, it is curious that Nehemiah's Memoirs do not refer to Ezra except, pos-

---

[20]Archaeological evidence fixes the date of Nehemiah's mission as 445 B.C.E. One of the Elephantine letters from the year 407 B.C.E. mentions "the sons of Sanballat, the governor of Samaria" (Pritchard, *Ancient Near Eastern Texts* [1], "Petition for Authorization to Rebuild the Temple of Yaho," p. 491). The face that Governor Sanballat was Nehemiah's contemporary precludes dating the prophet under a later Persian king bearing the name Artaxerxes.

sibly, in one place (Neh. 12:36) where Ezra heads a procession at a dedication cere-mony. Ezra's Memoirs do not pay much attention to Nehemiah, either.[21]

These and other problems have led to vigorous disagreement among historians. There are three possibilities for the date of Ezra's arrival in Jerusalem:

1. 458 B.C.E.   This is the Chroniclers' view, and there is much to be said for it.[22]

2. 428 B.C.E.   This requires changing the notation in Ezra 7:7 from the seventh to the thirty-seventh year of Artaxerxes, as-suming that the word "thirty" was omitted by scribal error.[23]

3. 398 B.C.E.   This view assumes that the Persian ruler referred to in Ezra 7:7 is not Artaxerxes I (about 465–414 B.C.E.) but Artaxerxes II (about 404–358 B.C.E.).[24]

This problem arises partly because the book of Ezra-Nehemiah went through several stages of redaction before receiving its final form.[25] The final editor was interested in emphasizing the great reform of Ezra, not in harmonizing previous accounts to keep the historical record straight.

Though this question might never be settled, the testimony of the final editor—who probably wrote within a reasonably short time after the Judean restoration—de-serves the benefit of doubt. In this view, Ezra preceded Nehemiah, although the two men worked contemporaneously, at least during part of their careers. Ezra's reform was not very successful at first; he needed the administrative power and organizational abil-ity of Nehemiah to institute changes and make them stick.[26] After all, even the great "Deuteronomic" Reform, authorized and supported by the power of King Josiah, proved short-lived (see p. 347). For the purposes of our study, we will assume that the Ezra-Nehemiah sequence is the proper one.

---

[21]The reference to Ezra's presence at the dedication of the wall of Jerusalem in Nehemiah's Memoirs (Neh. 12:36) could be a harmonizing addition. In the first-person sections of the Ezra Memoirs, Nehemiah is not mentioned at all. In the third-person sections he is referred to twice: at the ceremony of the reading of the law (Neh 8:9) and as one of the signers of the covenant document (Neh. 10:1).

[22]This view is defended by Frank M. Cross, Jr., "A Reconstruction of the Judean Restoration" [497]; also Freed-man and Willoughby, *Books of the Bible* [9], pp. 157–59.

[23]A champion of this view is John Bright, *History* [110], pp. 374ff.

[24]Peter Ackroyd, "The History of Israel in the Exilic and Post-Exilic Periods," in *Tradition and Interpretation* [175], observes that "The late date of 398 B.C.E. (Artaxerxes II) remains possible, even probable, but un-proven" (p. 134).

[25]Freedman and Willoughby [9], pp. 155–56, trace four stages of redaction, suggesting that Nehemiah might have been the final Chronicler.

[26]So argues Siegfried Hermann, *A History of Israel in Old Testament Times,* trans. by John Bowden (Philadel-phia: Westminster, 1977), p. 315. See the whole discussion, pp. 307–19.

EZRA, THE ARCHITECT OF JUDAISM

In the year 458 B.C.E., if our chronology is correct, Ezra conducted a second caravan of exiles from Babylonia to Palestine. Ezra was not sent to Palestine by the Persian king as a political authority. Rather, he went with Persian authorization to investigate and regulate religious matters in Jerusalem and Judah, which belonged to the fifth Persian satrapy (the province "Beyond the River"). Ezra was entitled to institute judicial arrangements in accord with "the law of your God and the law of the [Persian] king" (Ezra 7:26), and is pictured as "a scribe skilled in the law of Moses, which Yahweh, the God of Israel, had given" (Ezra 7:6). Elsewhere, he is referred to as "Ezra the priest, the scribe of the law of the God of heaven" (Ezra 7:12, 21).

On arriving in Jerusalem, Ezra's first task was to insure the strength of the family, an institution fundamentally important for maintaining a sense of Jewish identity and for preserving the traditions of Israel. Accordingly, he took stern measures against intermarriage with foreigners, especially mixed marriages involving non-Jewish women. His authority for executing this unpopular policy derived from two sources. First, he had the backing of the Persian government in the appointment of judges and magistrates who enforced the decree. Second, and more importantly, he appealed to tradition going back to Moses and specifically to Israel's obligations as a people of the covenant.

A CEREMONY OF COVENANT RENEWAL

One of the important items that Ezra brought from Babylonia was a copy of "The Book of the Torah of Moses" (Neh. 8:1). In the month of the autumn harvest festival, known as the Feast of Tabernacles, the people gathered "as one person" into the square before the Water Gate of Jerusalem to listen to Ezra's book of the Torah (Neh. 8:1–8). Ezra climbed up to a specially constructed wooden pulpit and, while the people stood in rapt attention, read to them from early morning until noon. Levites stood at his side to give "the sense" in order that the people could "understand the reading." The next day the people began the celebration of the Feast of Tabernacles according to directions in the Torah (see Lev. 23:42–43). They cut branches and built booths ("tabernacles") to live in during the seven-day festival, and readings from the Torah continued during this whole time (Neh. 8:13–18). The climax of the ceremonies came in a solemn act of covenant renewal (Neh. 9) when the people confessed their sins and Ezra, as a covenant mediator, offered a prayer on their behalf, ending with the words of covenant renewal (Neh. 9:38). The covenant document was officially signed by representatives of the people, and all the rest of the people joined with them, taking an oath under penalty of a curse "to walk in God's Torah which was given by Moses the servant of God" (Neh. 10). According to the present text of the Chroniclers' Work, "Nehemiah the governor" was a signatory to the covenant (Neh. 10:1).

This is strikingly similar to the covenant ceremony of Josiah's time as related in 2 Kings 23:1–3. The same features are present: public reading of the Torah; confession of sin; cultic and social reform; and the solemn covenant to follow the divine commandments under penalty of a curse. The covenant ceremony under Ezra, as well as that under Josiah, was based on an ancient tradition of periodic covenant renewal at the sanctuary. At such times the Levites acted as interpreters of the Torah, for the Torah was not just special direction to the priests but teaching for the whole community. Thus the distinction arose between the "priest" and the "Levite" (compare Luke 10:30–37). The priests who claimed descent from Aaron were in charge of sacrifices at the altar; the Levites who claimed Moses as an ancestor (Exod. 2:1) had the task of explaining the meaning of Israel's faith (2 Chron. 15:3; 17:8–9; 30:22; 35:3).

EZRA'S BOOK OF THE LAW

What was "The Book of the Torah of Moses" that Ezra read to the people? Suggestions include the Holiness Code, the Priestly Code, Ezekiel's plan of restoration (Ezek. 40–48), Deuteronomy, and the Pentateuch. Some have tried to answer this question by figuring out how long it took Ezra to finish his reading—a difficult task, since the Levites used an unknown amount of time giving their interpretations. Moreover, the text does not explicitly state that Ezra read the whole book of the Torah from beginning to end. Perhaps he selected certain key passages as a prelude to the covenant-renewal ceremony. In this case, the Deuteronomic Torah is a good possibility—especially in view of the place given to the Levites in Deuteronomic tradition—but Ezra's reform seems to presuppose instruction in matters of a more priestly character. Some suggest the Priestly "source" of the Pentateuch, but this view assumes that the Priestly Writing had an independent existence, which is dubious (see pp. 405–406). So we come to the view evidently held by the final redactor, namely, that "The Book of the Torah of Moses" Ezra read was the Pentateuch itself, that is, the Priestly Writing (Tetrateuch) plus Deuteronomy.

If this is true, Ezra's greatest contribution was to establish the Pentateuch as the authoritative canon for Jewish faith and practice. The word "canon" (from the Sumerian) refers in its primary sense to any measurement or yardstick—a carpenter's rule, for example. In a metaphorical sense, the Greeks referred to their classics as *kanones*—that is, standards of excellence. As applied to the Pentateuch, however, this term establishes the claim that the literature is *sacred* scripture and as such constitutes the community's rule for faith and conduct. In the time of Ezra and later, the authority of the Pentateuch was underscored by the dogma that this was none other than "The Book of the Torah of Moses," delivered by God to Moses on Mount Sinai. Ezra probably introduced the Pentateuch as the officially recognized Mosaic tradition and, by his cultic reforms, brought Israel's life into conformity with this norm. He is truly "the architect of Judaism," for under his influence the life and religion of the Jews were molded by the sacred Torah.

THE SAMARITAN PENTATEUCH

The Jews had no monopoly on the Pentateuch. It was also the scripture of the Samaritan community, who likewise followed Mosaic tradition. The tension that developed between Jew and Samaritan was not over the authority of the Torah (Pentateuch), but over the interpretation of its meaning, and particularly over the issue of who the true people of the Torah were. Occasioned originally by political and economic factors in the early post-exilic period, the split between the Jews and the Samaritans gradually widened until eventually, perhaps in the middle of the fourth century B.C.E., the Samaritans built their own temple on Mount Gerizim.[27] A story in the New Testament relates that, when Jesus paused at Jacob's well while passing through Samaria, a Samaritan woman reminded him that the Jews had no dealings with the Samaritans, for they worshiped God in separate places (John 4:4–29). Even today a colony of Samaritans lives

---

[27]The Gerizim temple was destroyed by the Jewish leader John Hyrcanus in 128 B.C.E., 200 years after it was built, according to Josephus (*Antiquities*, xiii, 9, 1; *Jewish Wars*, i, 2, 6). If Josephus' reckoning is correct, the temple must have been built about the middle of the fourth century B.C.E.

near Mount Gerizim. Their priests proudly display to visitors their scrolls of the Pentateuch, the sole scriptural basis of their religion.

NEHEMIAH'S TERMS AS GOVERNOR

We turn now to the leadership of Nehemiah who, according to the Chroniclers, was Ezra's contemporary. With the exception of Nehemiah 8–10 (materials dealing with Ezra), the book of Nehemiah is based largely on Nehemiah's Memoirs, written by his own hand.[28] It is the only example in the Old Testament of the continuous story of a person's career—that is, autobiography—and as such is a historical record of great importance. It is also a narrative written in a fresh and interesting manner. The story tells how Nehemiah, a cupbearer to Artaxerxes I in the court at Susa, the Persian winter capital (see picture, p. 549), heard of the dismal conditions within Jerusalem; how he prevailed upon the king to send him there with the authority of a governor; how, after an inspection tour of the walls at night, he roused the people to undertake the rebuilding of the city's defenses; how the project was completed in fifty-two days, even though some of the workers had to carry a tool in one hand and a weapon in the other because of the hostility of neighboring peoples; and how at last, amid scenes of singing and thanksgiving, the walls were dedicated.

NEHEMIAH'S REFORMS

Throughout his first term as governor, as well as during the second term that began in 432 B.C.E. (Neh. 13:6–7), Nehemiah introduced various reforms to bind the Jews into a closely knit community—reforms inspired by powerful pressures that threatened to erase Israel's identity. During the days when the walls were being rebuilt, Sanballat, the governor of Samaria, and his allies did everything in their power to frustrate the project. Sanballat claimed the Jewish territory, which had been assigned to the province of Samaria by the Babylonians after the destruction of Jerusalem. Moreover, the Ammonites of Transjordan and the Edomites to the south of Jerusalem looked with a jealous eye on the Jews' activities. At first, these enemies accused the Jews of plotting a revolution against Persia; then they ridiculed the feeble strength of the walls; and finally they threatened to attack. Clearly their design was to break the workers' morale. Some of the Jews themselves, especially members of the wealthier class, took an easygoing attitude toward their neighbors, even to the point of mingling and intermarrying with them. To meet these circumstances, Nehemiah enforced a stiff policy of exclusivism, thereby sharpening the division between Jew and Gentile, and between Jew and Samaritan.

---

[28]Nehemiah's Memoirs, found in the passages listed on p. 458, have been supplemented by lists and other material added by the Chroniclers.

Chronological Chart 9

B.C.E.	Egypt	Palestine	Mesopotamia
		Judah	Persia
500	Egypt under Persian rule, 525–401	(*Malachi,* c. 500–450)	Xerxes I (Ahasuerus), 486–465
		Ezra's mission, 458(?)	Artaxerxes I (Longimanus), 465–424
		Nehemiah arrives, 445	
		Ezra's mission, c. 428(?)	Xerxes II, 423
			Darius II, 423–404
400			
		Ezra's mission, c. 398(?)	Artaxerxes II (Mnemon), 404–358

Membership in the Jewish community, according to Nehemiah, was determined by two standards. The first was birth. We are told that when the walls were built God put it into Nehemiah's head to enroll all the citizens according to genealogy (Neh. 7:5–69; see also Ezra 2). In the context of the rest of Nehemiah's work, this can mean only one thing: It was important to be born into the right family and to be able to trace one's ancestry to a Jewish parent, grandparent, and so on. During his second term, Nehemiah strictly prohibited intermarriage on the basis of Deuteronomic legislation (Neh. 13; see Deut. 23:3ff.). He banished a priest from office when it was discovered that he was married to a daughter of Sanballat, the Samaritan governor. Ezra carried these measures to an extreme by not only denouncing mixed marriages, but also forcibly breaking up those already in existence (Ezra 10:2–5).

THE CRISIS OF IDENTITY

Another qualification for being a Jew, according to Nehemiah's policy, was loyalty to the Torah and faithful support of the Temple. The purity of the people demanded strict observance of the Sabbath. When Nehemiah found that work and commercial activity were going on during the holy day, he threatened that divine wrath would fall upon the people if the abuse were not stopped. He organized a regular service of worship in the Temple and demanded that the people support the Temple staff with their tithes. Thus a strong wall was built around the Jewish community—not just the wall of Jerusalem but the wall of an exclusivity based on birth and religious loyalty.

What was the real motive behind these severe measures? Political considerations were undoubtedly a factor, but more was involved than the question of Jewish survival or restoring prestige to Jerusalem. The desire to maintain Jewish purity was fundamentally a struggle to preserve Israel's identity and distinctive faith in the face of tremendous cultural pressures. With some justification, Nehemiah reminded the people of the folly of Solomon's cosmopolitanism, especially the influence of his foreign wives. The work of Ezra and Nehemiah did not rest on nationalism or racialism, but on a passionate loyalty to Israel's religious heritage, for "they feared that the faintly burning flame of Judaism might be quenched altogether."[29]

The problem of syncretism had haunted Israel from the time of its occupation of Canaan. The threat of cultural assimilation persisted and intensified in the post-exilic period, especially after the rise to power of Alexander the Great, who made a conscious effort to absorb all religious and cultural differences into the synthesis known as Hellenism. The mystery is that Israel resisted assimilation, instead creatively transforming what was borrowed from others into a vehicle for expressing its own faith. Israel's calling was not to be "like the nations," but to be a "peculiar" people set apart from the nations. It is easy to criticize the narrow theological focus of Judaism under Nehemiah and Ezra with its all too intense concentration upon membership in the holy community through family descent and obedience to the stipulations of the Torah. The line was sharply drawn between "us" and "them," insiders and outsiders. But this circumscribed community preserved the spiritual heritage that eventually burst with transforming power upon nations and cultures, turning the course of Western civilization into a new channel.

THE LAW AND THE PROPHETS

Strict conformity to Torah stipulations became one of the major characteristics of post-exilic Judaism. Christianity reacted to such "legalism," largely in protest of the view that one's relation to God, one's "justification" or rightness with God, is based on righteous deeds in obedience to the Law (see the parable of the Publican and the Pharisee in Luke 18:9–14, and Paul's discussions of justification by faith, Gal. 2:16; 3:11). In time, a sharp antithesis developed between grace and law in Christian circles. In fairness to post-exilic Judaism, however, our study will attempt to correct certain one-sided views about the place of Torah in Jewish faith.[30]

....

DEFINITION: "HALAKA," "HAGGADA"

The Hebrew word *Torah* cannot be translated adequately by the English word "law." Torah, we found, has two dimensions: salvation and obligation, story and stipulation. The people who have been liberated are under obligation to walk in the way that is consonant with the action and will of their redeeming God.

In later rabbinical discussions, found in the comprehensive work known as the Talmud, these two dimensions were designated by the terms *haggada* (from a Hebrew word meaning "tell, relate") and *halaka* (from a verb meaning, "to walk, go").

[29]H. H. Rowley, *The Rediscovery of the Old Testament* (Philadelphia: Westminster, 1946), p. 164; see also chap. 7 for an excellent treatment of the ethos of Judaism.
[30]See Jon Levenson, *Sinai and Zion* [159].

The post-exilic period witnessed a great concentration on the *halakic* or legal dimension of Torah. The books of Chronicles omit the whole Exodus tradition, concentrating instead on the royal (messianic) theology with its twin pillars of kingship and Temple. The "Torah of Yahweh" or the "Torah of Moses" refers primarily to "commandments" and "statutes" that guide the people in their cultic and social life (such as 1 Chron. 22:12–13; 2 Chron. 14:4; 23:18). In later phases of the Chroniclers' Work found in Ezra-Nehemiah, the Mosaic revelation receives greater emphasis, but the accent continues to fall on this aspect of Torah.

Such a shift in emphasis is understandable in insecure times, when people needed guidance in the way that they should "walk" and the lifestyle that distinguished them as a community. Nevertheless, it is wrong to regard Judaism as a "religion of law" in the narrowly *halakic* or legal sense for, as shown by the book of Ezra-Nehemiah, the narrative or *haggadic* side of Israel's faith was never forgotten.

First, Ezra did not invent the emphasis on Torah obedience. As we have seen time and again, the commandments had an indispensable place in Israel's covenant faith from the very first. A person's relation to God, according to Israelite faith, imposed obligations in worship and social relations within the covenant community. The Ten Commandments, probably dating back to the Mosaic period, are witness to the divine demands. The ancient legal tradition was expanded and refined as Israel responded in new historical situations to the question: "What does Yahweh require of you?" (Mic. 6:8). Thus the prescriptions in the Pentateuch are the end result of a legal development that had its source in the ancient covenant of Sinai.

GRACE AND LAW

Second, there is no basis for the notion that the Torah sets forth a law code to be obeyed as dutifully as the laws of a city or a state. Behind specific laws stands the Lawgiver, who is none other than the God who graciously redeemed the people and guided them in their historical pilgrimage. The preface to the Ten Commandments, "I am Yahweh your God who brought you out of the land of Egypt, out of the house of bondage," introduces all the laws of Israel. As we have seen, prior divine initiative, manifest in deeds of benevolence, stirred the people to respond with heart, being, and strength. The book of Deuteronomy, which accompanied a great social reform, is one of the most eloquent expressions of Israel's understanding that grace has priority over law. In Israel's faith, the good news of what God has done precedes the exposition of what the people must do.

The relationship between salvation and obligation is clearly expressed in the covenant renewal ceremony of Ezra's time. According to Nehemiah 9, the making of the covenant was preceded by a long prayer, essentially a confession of Israel's faith. This public prayer is unique in that it recites the whole history of Israel—or, better, the history of Yahweh's dealings with the people. It articulates the community's remembrance of its shared history, its unique life story. The salient aspects of the prayer can be outlined as follows:

1. Yahweh, the sole God, is creator and sustainer of all that is (Neh. 9:6).
2. Having called Abraham out of Ur of Babylonia, Yahweh promised to give his descendants an inheritance in Canaan (Neh. 9:7–8).
3. When Israel was oppressed in Egypt, Yahweh kept that promise. Yahweh's gracious presence in the midst of the people was demonstrated by various signs and wonders, and by the giving of commandments to Moses on Mount Sinai (Neh. 9:9–15).
4. In spite of Israel's incapacity for faith, Yahweh proved to be "a God ready to forgive, gracious and merciful, slow to anger and abounding in ḥésed [faithfulness]" (see Exod. 34:6–7). Rebellious Israel was sustained in the wilderness by divine grace (Neh. 9:16–21).
5. Yahweh gave Israel kingdoms and peoples, and brought them victoriously into Canaan. Thus the people prospered and increased (Neh. 9:22–25).
6. Nevertheless, Israel continued to be rebellious. So Yahweh disciplined the people, raising up prophets to warn them and giving them into the hand of enemies when they refused to listen. However, Yahweh graciously spared a remnant (Neh. 9:26–31).
7. Especially since the time of the kings of Assyria, the hardships have been grievous. Yet Yahweh has been just in all these events. Indeed it is Yahweh who has been faithful; the people have been unfaithful (Neh. 9:32–34).
8. Because of their sins the people are now slaves (that is, vassals of Persia) in the very land that Yahweh gave them, and its rich yield is taken away by heavy taxation (Neh. 9:35–37).

This prayer is a stirring recital of past events in which, according to the confession of faith, Yahweh had been active in Israel's history. It resounds with Yahweh's gracious initiative and redemptive activity. On the basis of this declaration the people renewed the covenant and dedicated themselves to serving Yahweh according to "the Torah which was given by Moses." Among other things, this pledge required refusing to engage in marriage with foreigners, as stipulated in Deuteronomy 7:1–4.

REJOICING IN THE TORAH

Third, we must not get the idea that the Torah, conceived of as a gift from God, was regarded as burdensome. Later, it is true, the canonical laws were hedged about by so many casuistic rules—for instance, on the subject of what constitutes work on the Sabbath—that the common people must have had difficulty in keeping them. According to rabbinical count, the Torah contained 613 laws that had to be followed! In the period of the Hebrew Bible, however, and even more so in the rabbinic period that followed, the Jewish attitude was that of "rejoicing in the Torah" (Hebrew: *simḥath hat-torah*). To obey the Torah was to take upon one's self "the yoke of the Kingdom"—that is, to surrender to God's sovereignty. But, as many Psalms testify, the yoke was easy and the burden was light. The devout Jew took great delight in the study of the Torah, for it was the source of life and blessing (see Ps. 1). Its precepts, "rejoicing the heart," were "more to be desired . . . than gold" (Ps. 19:7–14). The longest psalm in the Psalter is devoted to praise of the Torah (Ps. 119).

Fourth, one must not suppose there was a sharp antithesis between the Torah and prophetic tradition. To be sure, the corpus called the Prophets—the second division of the present Hebrew Bible (see Chart, pp. 4–5) was not canonized until considerably later. But it was preserved, read, and interpreted during the post-exilic period. Rather than oppose prophecy, the post-exilic priests wanted to take prophetic demands seriously, as can be seen by careful study of Ezra's prayer. They realized that the prophetic message of divine judgment had been confirmed in their history. The remnant, whom Yahweh had spared from national destruction and exile, took to heart the lessons of history as interpreted by prophets. Far from repudiating the ethical demands of the prophets, the priests of Judaism attempted to "put teeth" into prophetic teaching. As H. H. Rowley observes:

> It is very doubtful if Ezra thought of this religion [Judaism] as in any way the antithesis of prophetic religion. He doubtless thought he was serving the ideals of the prophets, and embodying them in the Law, that they might achieve more than the preaching of the prophets had hitherto achieved.[31]

THE CESSATION OF PROPHECY

Nevertheless, prophecy almost ceased in the post-exilic period. There were a few prophets—such as "Third Isaiah," Haggai, Zechariah, Obadiah, Malachi, and Joel—but they were second-rate in comparison with the great prophets who had gone before. The spirit of prophecy seemed stifled by preoccupation with the Torah. This is understandable, for if the basis of the holy community was the Torah—regarded as directly revealed to Moses and written in a book—the greatest need was for scribes (like Ezra) who could study it, expound its meaning, and preserve it carefully. In the Chroniclers' Work the prophets are, for the most part, good churchmen. Instead of viewing their role as interpreters of the events of the time, as was true of all the major prophets, the Chroniclers insisted that the prophets' chief function was in the worship service. Like their predecessors, prophets of the post-exilic period were "cultic prophets" who "prophesied" by leading the congregation in music (1 Chron. 25:1). In addition, they

---

[31]H. H. Rowley, *Rediscovery of the Old Testament* (Philadelphia: Westminster, 1964), p. 166, and the whole discussion, pp. 161–86. See further Peter Ackroyd, *Exile and Restoration* [494], pp. 254–56.

might have taken part in the liturgical recitation of some psalms. After Ezra's time the belief emerged that the age of charismatic prophecy was over until the coming of the Messianic Age (Joel 2:28–29]).

In one sense prophecy did continue within Judaism. The writings of the prophets were preserved and eventually canonized, which shows the great importance that the exponents of Judaism attached to the prophetic message. The Pentateuch—the charter of Judaism—contains many "prophetic" elements, from the Old Epic tradition of the oral period down to its final literary formulation in the time of the Exile.

In the post-exilic period prophecy found a new form of expression in the literature known as "apocalyptic." Although this type of literature was anticipated by Ezekiel, Third Isaiah, and Zechariah, it flourished in the later years of Judaism, beginning with the Maccabean period. The chief example in the Old Testament is the book of Daniel. Before turning to this new expression of prophecy, however, our study will focus on two other matters: Israel's worship as reflected in the book of Psalms (see Chapter 16), and the reflections of the sages of Israel (see Chapter 17).

CHAPTER 16

THE PRAISES OF ISRAEL

Israel understood its history to be a life of "co-existence with God"—that is, a "partnership with God" in a historical drama.[1] In the time of the Exodus Yahweh created a people out of nothing and entered into a covenant relationship with them. Later, Yahweh initiated a new phase of the drama by raising up David to be king, opening up to Israel wider horizons than the people had ever seen. Prophetic interpreters declared that Yahweh was active in the secular sphere of politics, punctuating Israel's life-story with historical events that manifested God's active presence in the midst of the people. Even the most catastrophic event—the end of Israel as a nation—was interpreted as Yahweh's coming to judge and to renew the people and to mediate, through Israel's suffering, blessing for all nations. This view of history as the dramatic narrative of God's deeds was a significant breakthrough in the history of religions. "It may be said with truth," writes an authority on comparative religions, "that the Hebrews were the first to discover the meaning of history as the epiphany of God."[2]

Biblical Readings: Read selected psalms such as the following: Laments (psalms of supplication): 3, 7, 10, 22, 25, 27:7–14, 31, 38, 44, 51, 77, 88, 130, 137, 143; Songs of Thanksgiving: 92, 116, 118, 138; Jonah 2; Hymns (psalms of praise): 8, 19:1–6, 33, 93, 95–100, 103, 105, 135, 136, 145–150.

[1]The phrase is Abraham Heschel's; see B. W. Anderson, "Coexistence with God: Heschel's Exposition of Biblical Theology," in *Abraham Joshua Heschel: Exploring His Life and Thought* (New York: Macmillan, 1985).
[2]Mircea Eliade, *Cosmos and History* [138], p.104.

Israel was called to be a partner with God in this historical drama, and to respond to divine presence and activity. In the Old Testament the accent appropriately falls on Yahweh's actions. But, as Gerhard von Rad has observed, when these "mighty acts" of Yahweh occurred, "Israel did not keep silent." Not only did the people recall Yahweh's actions in narrative and written traditions, but also they "addressed Yahweh in a wholly personal way." The people raised hymns of praise, boldly asked questions, and complained in the depths of distress; for Israel was chosen "for converse with Yahweh"—not to be "a mere dumb object" of the divine will.[3] The finest examples of Israel's "converse" with Yahweh are found in the book of Psalms, often called the Psalter.

WORSHIP IN THE TEMPLE OF ZION

Throughout its history in the biblical period, Israel's primary bond of unity was worship of Yahweh. According to the Exodus story, the people were liberated from Egyptian bondage so that they might "serve" (worship) God at Sinai (Exod. 3:12). The Tribal Confederacy, instituted by Joshua, had its focal point in the central sanctuary to which the people gathered for the great annual festivals. During the time of David, Jerusalem became the cultic center of the nation. Solomon contributed further to Zion's centrality by building an impressive Temple for Yahweh. So strong was the pull to Jerusalem for worship that, after the disruption of the monarchy, Jeroboam I found it necessary to establish pilgrimage shrines in his own territory, especially at Bethel. When the exiles returned from Babylon, their first thought was to rebuild the Jerusalem Temple. Throughout its history, Israel was a *worshiping* community.

For this reason the book of Psalms lies at the very heart of the Hebrew Bible. The Chroniclers' Work (see Chapter 15) refers to the singing of songs of praise, some of them drawn from the book of Psalms.[4] When, in the chronicler's view, the Ark was brought into the Temple (2 Chron. 5:2–6:11), there was a great liturgical celebration to the accompaniment of cymbals, harps, lyres, and trumpets. Singers chanted a refrain heard in many of the Psalms (such as Ps. 136):

[Yahweh] is good,
　　His faithfulness endures forever.

—2 CHRONICLES 5:13

And the people responded at appropriate points with "Amen."

---

[3]A paraphrase of Gerhard von Rad, *Theology*, 1 [163], 354. His discussion of the Psalter is placed under the rubric, "Israel Before Yahweh (Israel's Answer)."

[4]For example, 1 Chron. 16:7–36 quotes portions of Pss. 105, 96, and 106.

THE BOOK OF PSALMS

Just as the hymnbooks of church or synagogue unite the voices of many generations, so the Psalter reflects the whole drama of Israel's history with Yahweh. It is almost impossible, however, to locate most psalms in their proper historical periods or life-situations. Unlike modern hymnbooks, no reliable indication of the date or occasion of a particular psalm is given in a superscript or postscript.[5] Moreover, with the exception of Psalm 137, which clearly presupposes the Babylonian Exile, the content of a particular psalm tells us little about the situation in which it was composed. This great poetry transcends specific time and circumstance, and hence provides the language of prayer and praise for people in all generations.

....

DEFINITION: "PSALMS," "PSALTER"

The title "the book of Psalms" actually comes from the New Testament (Luke 20:42; Acts 1:20). The early Christian community read Israel's scriptures in the Greek translation of the Hebrew Bible, the Septuagint. There the prevailing title was *psalmoi*, referring to "songs" sung to the accompaniment of stringed instruments. Another title, *psalterion*, found in one codex of the Greek Bible, refers primarily to a zither-like instrument, and secondarily to songs sung to stringed accompaniment. From this title comes the term "Psalter."

Whereas the Greek terms *psalmoi* and *psalterion* emphasize the musical dimension of the psalms, the Hebrew title *Tehillim* ("praises") stresses their content. Indeed, in whatever mood or mode, these songs are praises to God.

Although there is some variation in the numbering of the psalms included in the book of Psalms, the traditional total of the collection is 150. The Greek Bible contains an additional Psalm 151, associated with David's single-handed combat with Goliath, though the superscription explicitly states that it is "outside the number." Interestingly, a scroll discovered at the site of the ancient monastery of Qumran contains other psalms not found in the Hebrew Bible. This is further evidence of the flexibility in number.

....

ENTHRONED ON THE PRAISES OF ISRAEL

The title found in the Hebrew Bible, "Praises" (Hebrew: *Tehillim*), is most appropriate for these songs of supplication, thanksgiving, and praise. Whether the mood was sorrow or joy, bewilderment or confidence, these songs were intended as anthems to the glory of God. They ushered worshipers into the sanctuary where, as one psalmist put it, Yahweh was "enthroned on the praises of Israel" (Ps. 22:3, NRSV).

---

[5]It is generally recognized that the few superscriptions or headings that associate psalms with particular events in David's career were added later. Such superscriptions are found at the head of thirteen psalms: 3, 7, 18, 34, 51, 52, 54, 56, 57, 59, 60, 63, 142.

There is increasing awareness among biblical scholars that the religion of the Psalms is "cultic"—that is, it expresses the faith of the community at worship, especially on occasions of temple festivals. True, many laments, thanksgivings, and hymns were composed by individuals who spoke out of concrete life-situations. Still, one must not suppose that in every case these psalms were composed as private meditations. Some were probably intended for use in connection with a liturgical act or for recitation at a temple festival. In any case, the treasury of Psalms was appropriated by the worshiping community, just as songs of various origins are incorporated into modern hymnbooks. When the pronouns "I" and "my" are used, as in the well-known Shepherd's Psalm (Ps. 23), one must think of the whole community joining to express its faith.

Modern people often assume that worship is a private affair between a person and God, and that God is accessible apart from the established means of public worship. This premise creates serious difficulties in a study of the Psalter. Starting from this view-

The blind harper of Leiden is one of a group of musicians portrayed on a tomb in a temple of Hatshepsut at Karnak, dating from the Amarna period (c. 1400–1350 B.C.E.). In Israel the "harp" and "lyre" were used to accompany religious songs (Pss. 92:3, 150:3), but we have to turn to the art of Egypt to visualize what these stringed instruments were like.

point, the first step would be to divide the psalms into those that reflect public worship and those that reflect personal piety. But this contrast is completely alien to Israel's covenant faith, according to which the individual is related to God as a member of a community. God is free to meet a person at any time or place (invariably to the surprise of the one who receives the theophany). For access to God, however, the worshiper must come to the designated rendezvous and seek God at the appointed times. Only as a member of the community does the individual share in the promises and blessings of the covenant. To be a solitary person, cut off from the established means of grace and therefore, as fugitive David said, having "no heritage of Yahweh" (1 Sam. 26:19), was the greatest calamity imaginable. According to Israel's faith, Yahweh is present—enthroned on the praises of the people—when the congregation worships together at the sanctuary on holy days or festivals.[6] The individual praises God *with* the worshiping community:

> O magnify Yahweh with me,
>   and let us exalt his name together!
>   —PSALM 34:3

THE HYMNBOOK OF THE SECOND TEMPLE

The book of Psalms in its present form is the product of post-exilic Judaism. Insofar as the Psalter reflects the liturgical practice of this period, one can speak of it as the "Hymnbook of the Second Temple." The Temple staff arranged the hymns and supplications of the ages in suitable form, providing them with musical and liturgical notes that puzzle modern readers. Although their notations clearly suggest that the psalms were sung in public worship, we cannot be sure of the details. For example, the Hebrew term *selah*, which occurs repeatedly in some psalms (such as Ps. 46), apparently signaled a musical interlude and the singing of a refrain. In other instances, a note at the beginning indicates the type of musical accompaniment, whether stringed instruments or flutes (as in Ps. 5). Some of the superscriptions might indicate the tune to which the psalm was to be sung.[7]

The Psalter, however, did not receive its final form in a single edition. The process of completion took place in stages, extending from about the fifth to the second centuries B.C.E. It is composed of five collections or "books," each of which concludes with

---

[6]Claus Westermann, *The Praise of God in the Psalms* [539], is critical of excessive emphasis on the cultic character of the psalms of Israel, though he is equally critical of reading into them individualistic piety. He prefers to speak of the "forensic character of the praise of God" (p. 10)—that is, praise occurs "in public" and makes the individual conscious of being "a member of a congregation" (see especially pp. 15–25).

[7]For example, "The Hind of the Dawn" (Ps. 22:1) might refer to a well-known tune. Perhaps the Israelite community appropriated secular tunes for its hymnody, as modern churches and synagogues have sometimes done.

an appended doxology that is not part of the psalm itself. Psalm 1, extolling the Torah, and Psalm 2, portraying the installation of Yahweh's "Anointed" (the Davidic king) on Mount Zion, serve as an introduction to the present collection. Psalm 150 is the concluding doxology. The organization is as follows:

> Introduction to the whole book: Psalms 1 and 2
> Book I: Psalms 3–41
>   (concluding doxology: Ps. 41:13)
> Book II: Psalms 42–72
>   (concluding doxology: Ps. 72:18–19)
> Book III: Psalms 73–89
>   (concluding doxology: Ps. 89:52)
> Book IV: Psalms 90–106
>   (concluding doxology: Ps. 106:48)
> Book V: Psalms 107–150
>   (concluding doxology for the whole Psalter: Ps. 150)

According to an early *Midrash* (Hebrew: "commentary") on the Psalms, this fivefold arrangement is analogous to the five books of the Torah.

An important clue to the origin of the Psalter is found in the postscript following Book II: "The prayers of David, the son of Jesse, are ended" (Ps. 72:20). This passage indicates that at one stage in the formation of the Psalter the "Davidic" collection ended here. In this first book almost all of the psalms are prefixed with the word *leDawid* (Hebrew: "to David" or "belonging to David"). This collection is undoubtedly the oldest, and probably goes back to liturgical usage in the pre-exilic Temple in Jerusalem. To this old nucleus other collections gravitated, until eventually the fivefold arrangement of the Psalter came into being. Only 73 out of the 150 psalms are attributed explicitly to David; some are assigned to Moses (Ps. 90), Solomon (Ps. 72, 127), or others. Yet all the successive editions were issued under the aegis of David, who was popularly held to be the author of the entire Psalter. This view undoubtedly reflects the community's conviction, highlighted in 1–2 Chronicles, that David was the ideal king with whom the people identified as they came before God in worship,[8] and the prototype of the "Messiah" (Yahweh's Anointed One; Ps. 2) who would fulfill the hopes of Israel. The ascription of the Psalms to David is not entirely inappropriate, for apparently he gave leadership in music and composed some songs (Amos 6:5; 2 Sam. 23:1). Thus the relation of David to the Psalter is analogous to the relation of Moses to the Pentateuch.

---

[8]Christoph Barth, *Introduction to the Psalms* [527], points out that David was a "typical" or representative figure for the Israelite people; therefore, in worship they remembered "the king, pursued and abandoned in innocence and guilt, but always delivered and restored to power by the faithfulness of God, in whom their own existence as the People of God had found an expression that was valid for all time" (pp. 64–65).

THE WORSHIP OF PRE-EXILIC ISRAEL

It is one thing to speak of the present book of Psalms as the "Hymnbook of the Second Temple," but quite another thing to deal with the origin and use of particular psalms. At one time scholars dated most of the psalms in the post-exilic period or even in the Maccabean period, near the dawn of the Common Era. However, increasing knowledge of Israel's worship during the period of the monarchy, as well as wider understanding of the psalmody of the ancient Near East, suggest that a great number of psalms were composed and used liturgically during the pre-exilic period.[9] Although the Psalter received its final shape at the hands of the staff of the second Temple, many of the psalms reflect Israel's pre-exilic worship.

The origin and earliest use of many psalms are beyond recovery, just as the authors of many hymns in modern hymnbooks are unknown. Through the method of study known as "form criticism," however, we can gain a clearer understanding of Israel's pre-exilic worship as reflected in the book of Psalms.[10]

When analyzed in terms of literary form, the psalms generally fall into three major categories. The first genre is the *lament* (or petition), which presupposes a problematic situation in which God's sovereignty seems temporarily eclipsed. The second is the *song of thanksgiving*, which expresses praise for divine deliverance from trouble. The third is the *hymn*, in which the worshiping community celebrates God's majesty and faithfulness.[11] Our study will consider these literary types briefly, then turn attention to the temple festivals in which various psalms were used liturgically.

....

DEFINITION: "FORM CRITICISM"

The literary approach known as "form criticism" includes three types of study.

First, one determines the bounds of a particular literary unit or *pericopē* (Greek: "a cutting all around"). This suggests that a passage, when cut out of its context, has its own literary integrity: a definite beginning and end, internal structure and dynamic, and a self-contained meaning (a parable would be a good example).

Second, one attempts to understand the function of the literary unit in its setting in life (German: *Sitz im Leben*), perhaps in everyday affairs (a wedding song or funeral dirge) or, as in the case of the Psalms, in community worship.

---

[9]For the Babylonian hymns, see Pritchard, *Ancient Near Eastern Texts* [1], pp. 383–92; for Egyptian literature, pp. 365–81.

[10]The pioneer in form-critical study of the Psalms was Hermann Gunkel; see his *The Psalms: A Form-Critical Introduction* [530]. Gunkel's work was advanced by Sigmund Mowinckel; see *The Psalms in Israel's Worship, I–II* [535]. Whereas Gunkel stressed the classification of psalms according to literary type (such as hymn, lament, thanksgiving), Mowinckel concentrated on the function of the psalms in the setting of the temple festivals, especially the New Year's festival.

[11]An excellent discussion of these literary types appears in Patrick D. Miller, *They Cried Unto the Lord* [534]. See also B. W. Anderson's study guide, *Out of the Depths* [526], which uses a form-critical approach.

This terracotta figurine of a female musician depicts a woman holding a hand drum in her left hand and striking it with the palm of her right hand. Her hand-modeled head and arms were attached to a base formed on a potter's wheel. Biblical references suggest that Israelite women were associated with musical instruments, singing, and dancing.

Third, one assumes that these literary units, which reflect general human experiences, display formulaic patterns and literary conventions evident elsewhere in the Hebrew Bible or in other literature of the ancient Near East. Therefore, a study of analogous literary forms can be illuminating.

Closely related to form criticism is the method known as "rhetorical criticism," which concentrates on the stylistic features and literary patterns of a text rather than on social setting or historical context.[12]

ISRAEL AT WORSHIP

Worship inevitably expresses a conviction about who God is and how God relates to the world. When gods are regarded as part of nature's cycle of decay and renewal, worshipers seek to leave the profane sphere of everyday life and enter a sacred realm where divine re-

[12]See James Muilenburg, "Form Criticism and Beyond" [90].

newal takes place.[13] When God is regarded as a numinous Reality existing beyond the phenomena of the human world, as in mystical religions, worshipers withdraw from the realm of change and illusion to achieve ineffable communion with the unknown "It."

Israel's faith avoids both of these extremes. The holy God, who transcends earthly phenomena, enters the human world, establishes an "I-thou" relationship with the people, and intervenes to deliver the oppressed and to humble the proud and mighty. Therefore the beginning of praise is meditation upon what God has done, is doing, and will do:

> One generation shall laud your works to another,
>   and shall declare your mighty acts.
> On the glorious splendor of your majesty,
>   and on your wondrous works, I will meditate.
>   —PSALM 145:4–5 (NRSV)

These "mighty acts" that evoke praise undoubtedly include what the psalmist has personally experienced. But reference is primarily to great events of the past, going back to the creation of the world, in which Yahweh's greatness and goodness were displayed. As we have seen, a major characteristic of Israel's worship is remembrance of the tradition—not just the recollection of what happened once upon a time, but a "cultic remembrance" that makes the past present. Through worship the worshipers become contemporary with historic events crucial for the community of faith (see pp. 74–75, 378–379).

One must not suppose that ancient Israel had exclusive rights on the view of divine activity in history. In the religions of other peoples, such as the Babylonians, deities were believed to be active in historical affairs.[14] One of the distinctive traits of Israel, however, was that in the cult the people turned primarily to their *historical experiences* to confess faith in God:

> Yahweh achieves vindication
>   and justice for all the oppressed.
> He manifested his ways to Moses,
>   his actions to the Israelites.
>   —PSALM 103:6–7

LAMENTS IN DISTRESS

Remembrance of Yahweh's deeds can have the effect of plunging an individual or the whole Israelite community into bewilderment about the present situation of suffering and distress. Although the modern conception of "atheism" was unknown in the bibli-

---

[13]On this archaic view see especially M. Eliade, *The Sacred and the Profane* [139].
[14]See Bertil Albrektson, *History and the Gods* [22]. At the end of his study, Albrektson notes the peculiar way that Yahweh's acts in history were remembered and celebrated in the Israelite cult.

Supplicants appealing to a royal servant are depicted on a tomb relief of Hor-em-heb at Memphis (c. 1349–1319 B.C.E.). Such gestures of prostration were also appropriate to express humble and fearful adoration of God (see Psalm 95:6).

cal period, Israel was afflicted from time to time with the feeling that Yahweh had abandoned the people. These were times of the "eclipse of God."[15]

When one considers that Israel, situated in a storm-center of world politics, so often suffered deeply, it is not surprising that about two fifths of the Psalter consists of laments in which a suppliant cries to God "out of the depths" (Ps. 130:1). What is surprising is that psalms of this type display so little bitterness or self-pity. The praise of God reverberates through all human sorrows. "Lament" might not be the best description of this literary form. Form critics distinguish between a *lamentation* (dirge), suitable in a situation that cannot be changed (such as a person's death), and a *lament*, which presupposes that a situation of distress can be changed if and when Yahweh intervenes in answer to prayer.

The lament has a characteristic literary form, although it varies in details.[16]

A. *Invocation:* Address to God, a brief cry that can be expanded into an ascription of praise to the God addressed.

B. *Complaint:* In community laments, the distress can be some great crisis such as enemy attack, famine, or plague. Individual laments can be occasioned by such problems as sickness, persecution, or acute awareness of guilt.

[15]Martin Buber, *Eclipse of God: Studies in the Relationship between Religion and Philosophy* (New York, NY: Harper, 1952).
[16]See Claus Westermann [453], pp. 52, 81; also B. W. Anderson, *Out of the Depths* [526], chap. 3.

C. *Confession of Trust:* In spite of the problematic situation, the suppliant relies on God's faithfulness.

D. *Petition:* The suppliant appeals to God to intervene and change the situation.

E. *Vow of Thanksgiving:* In the confidence that God hears and answers prayer, the suppliant vows to testify before the community about what God has done. (This element is usually lacking in community laments.)

Psalm 44 is a good example of a community lament. In the *Invocation* (A) the community, in a time of crisis, recalls the faith of ancestors who told the story of Yahweh's marvelous acts (Ps. 44:1–8). The community raises its *Complaint* (B), contrasting former days with the present, when Yahweh has "cast us off" and "made us like sheep for slaughter" (Ps. 44:9–16). Then comes the community's *Confession* (C) of its steadfast trust in Yahweh:[17]

> All this has come upon us,
>> yet we have not forgotten you,
>> or been false to your covenant.
> Our heart has not turned back,
>> nor have our steps departed from your way,
> yet you have broken us in the haunt of jackals,
>> and covered us with deep darkness.
>> —PSALM 44:17–19 (NRSV)

The lament concludes with the community's fervent *Petition* (D) to Yahweh to act once again and bring to an end the eclipse of God's presence (Ps. 44:13–16). Other examples of community laments are found in Psalms 10, 74, 79, 106, and 137.

Many laments are cries of individuals in distress. In these cases the suppliant's suffering is veiled in traditional imagery, making it almost impossible to determine the concrete situation out of which the lament is raised. The heart of the complaint is that the suppliant feels abandoned by God and about to be overwhelmed by the powers of death (often described as Sheol or the subterranean waters surrounding it). Psalm 22 is an example of an individual lament. The suppliant begins with a poignant cry:

> My God, my God, why have you forsaken me?
>> and are distant from my cry for help,
>>> my groaning words?
> O my God, I call out by day, and you don't answer,
>> by night and find no repose.
>> —PSALM 22:1–2[18]

---

[17]In his great work *The Prophets* [352], Abraham J. Heschel quoted part of this psalm in a dedication to "the martyrs of 1940–45," the victims of the Nazi holocaust in which about six million Jews were consumed in a "burnt offering."

[18]These opening words, according to Christian tradition, became Jesus' cry of dereliction from the cross (Mark 15:34).

As a member of the worshiping community, the suppliant falls back on the faith of the ancestors, which lives on in spite of fire and sword:

> But you are holy,
>> enthroned on the praises of Israel.
> In you our ancestors trusted,
>> they trusted and you rescued them.
> To you they cried, and they were delivered,
>> in you they trusted and were not disconcerted.
>
> —PSALM 22:3–5 (also vs. 9–10)

Recollection of the past, when Yahweh's mighty acts were made known to the ancestors, is only "an island of comfort in the midst of the ocean" of suffering (Artur Weiser). In ever-shifting figures of speech, the suppliant complains to God:

> Many bulls surround me,
>> mighty bulls of Bashan encircle me.
> Open-mouthed to swallow me
>> are ravenous and roaring lions
> I am drained away like water,
>> and all my bones are out of joint.
> My heart has become like wax,
>> it melts inside me.
> My palate is dry like earthenware,
>> and my tongue sticks to the roof of my mouth;
> You have brought me to the point of death.
>
> —PSALM 22:12–15

In subsequent verses the crisis is described in different imagery: The suppliant is attacked by a pack of dogs, or by brigands who take away everything—including garments—and divide the spoil (Ps. 22:16–18). The suppliant's complaint reaches a climax in a cry for help:

> But you, O Yahweh, do not be distant!
>> O my Strength, hurry to my aid!
> Rescue my life from the sword,
>> my solitary self from the power of the dog!
> Save me from the mouth of the lion
>> from the horns of the wild ox!
>
> —PSALM 22:19–21

Insert 17-1a (Above) Gate of Xerxes. The eastern portal of the Gate of Xerxes at Persepolis, the main Persian capital, was guarded by colossal human-headed "bulls." An inscription on the gate reads: "King Xerxes says: By the grace of Ahura Mazda, I constructed this gateway called All-Countries." This splendid piece of architecture was a casualty of Alexander's conquest.

Insert 17-1b (Left) Carving on Behistun. A relief carved on Behistun Rock commemorated Darius I's victory over rebels who seized the Persian throne.

Insert 18-1 Qumram Settlement. The excavated ruins of Qumram, located at the northwest end of the Dead Sea.

Then, following the Hebrew text,[19] the suppliant breaks out into an exclamation, "You have answered me!" (Ps. 22:21c). The mood modulates from the minor mode of lament to strains of praise in a major key (Ps. 22:23–31). The suppliant's prayer has been heard; no longer is Yahweh's "face" (presence) hidden (Ps. 22:24). The psalm ends with a jubilant testimony before the congregation to Yahweh's demonstration of grace, which opens up a new possibility of life.

How can one account for this abrupt shift, here and elsewhere in laments (as in Ps. 28:6)? Many scholars believe that in the interval between the final parts of the psalm a minister of the Temple, perhaps a priest or temple prophet, uttered "words of assurance" (an "oracle of salvation") to the effect that God had heard the suppliant's prayer and promised deliverance.[20] Perhaps one of these "oracles of salvation," spoken in the name of the liberating God, is preserved in Psalm 12:5. The response to this liturgical act (Ps. 22:22–28) was a vow of praise before the worshiping community:

> You are the source of my praise in the great community,
> I will fulfill my vows before those who fear Yahweh.
> Let humble ones eat and be satisfied!
> Let those who seek Yahweh praise him,
> their hearts ever full of vitality.
>
> —PSALM 22:25–26

This interpretation helps clarify the place of individual laments within the Israelite cult. It also shows that lament does not stand by itself but, like the second movement of a symphony, moves through the minor strain to the major key of the final movement, from petition out of distress to joyful praise of God. Other individual laments are found in Psalms 3, 13, 31, 54, 56, and 102.

In a number of laments suppliants cry out to God for vindication, even praying for divine vengeance against an enemy: unidentified persons or powers that threaten people's welfare and security. There are several so-called "imprecatory psalms" (Pss. 35, 59, 69, 70, 109, 137, 140), in which the psalmist's passion for vindication finds expression in imprecations or curses against hostile powers. A conspicuous example is Psalm 137 (see p. 402), a folk song that cries out for vengeance against both the Babylonians who destroyed Jerusalem in 587 B.C.E., and the Edomites who assisted in its destruction (compare Ob. 10–14). These psalms, like the rest of the laments, presuppose that God has entered into covenant relationship with the people Israel and can be appealed to as the Judge who defends the weak and upholds justice. "Vengeance," that is, vindication,

---

[19]Most translations change the Hebrew text here. This literal translation of the Hebrew follows the interpretation of H. J. Kraus in his commentary on the Psalms [532].

[20]On the "oracle of salvation," see Patrick D. Miller, *They Cried Unto the Lord* [534].

is the prerogative of God, not the right of those who take justice into their own hands (Deut. 32:35; compare Rom. 12:19).

At the opposite extreme to the imprecatory psalms are a number of psalms called "penitential psalms" (Pss. 6, 32, 38, 51, 102, 130, 143). In these cries *de profundis* (see Ps. 130:1), the human problem is not located "out there" in political and social structures, but within, in the heart. Conscious of human fallibility and failure, suppliants cast themselves upon God's mercy and forgiveness. Psalm 51, composed in the typical pattern of the lament, is an exquisite illustration. The suppliant begins with an appeal to God:

> Have mercy on me, O God, according to your steadfast love [*ḥésed*];
> > according to your abundant mercy blot out my transgressions.
> Wash me thoroughly from my iniquity,
> > and cleanse me from my sin.
> > > —PSALM 51:1–2 (NRSV)

Then follows an expression of distress (Ps. 51:3-5)—a profound sense of being in the wrong:

> Against you, you alone, have I sinned,
> > and done what is evil in your sight.
> > > —PSALM 51:4 (NRSV)

The suppliant petitions for purification, forgiveness, and inner renewal:

> Create in me a clean heart, O God,
> > and put a new and right spirit within me.
> Do not cast me away from your presence,
> > and do not take your holy spirit from me.
> > > —PSALM 51:10–11 (NRSV)

Finally the suppliant vows to help other troubled people know God's grace and to offer a sacrifice acceptable to God: "a broken and contrite heart" (Ps. 51:13–17). Scholars generally agree that the final verses (Ps. 51:18–19) were added in the early post-exilic period by editors who believed that when the Temple was rebuilt, Yahweh would delight in animal sacrifices.

SONGS OF THANKSGIVING

The main characteristic of the individual song of thanksgiving is its retrospective character: It looks back to the time when a suppliant, in a situation of lament, cried to Yahweh for help. That former situation, however, no longer exists. The time of the eclipse of God has ended. In response to a cry for help, Yahweh has heard and has acted with liberating power, with the result that the suppliant now sings "a new song":

I waited and waited for Yahweh
>and he turned to me,
>>and heard my cry.
He raised me out of the pit of despair,
>out of the miry clay,
and set my feet on a rock,
>securing my steps.
He has put on my lips a new song,
>praise to our God.
Many will observe and fear,
>and will put their trust in Yahweh.

—PSALM 40:1–3

The individual song of thanksgiving has a distinctive literary form that is subject to poetic variation. An excellent illustration is Psalm 116, which can be outlined as follows:

A. *Introduction* (Ps. 116:1–2)
   The individual begins by offering praise to Yahweh and, as in the case of hymns, gives the motive for praise.
B. Main Section: *Narration of the Psalmist's Experience in the Past* (Ps. 116:3–9)
   1. Portrayal of the distress the psalmist once experienced when the power of death almost prevailed (verse 3).
   2. Recollection of the cry for help (verse 4).
   3. Recognition of Yahweh's response to the prayer:

      For you have delivered my soul from death,
      >my eyes from tears,
      >my feet from stumbling.
      I walk before [Yahweh] in the land of the living.

      —PSALM 116:8–9 (NRSV)

C. Conclusion: *Praise to Yahweh for Deliverance* (Ps. 116:10–19)
   In gratitude for Yahweh's gracious deliverance, the suppliant testifies to the divine grace that supports all the people:

   What shall I give back to Yahweh
   >for all his bounty to me?
   The cup of salvation I'll lift,
   >and call on the name of Yahweh.
   My vows to Yahweh I will complete
   >here in the presence of all his people.

   —PSALM 116:12–14

Other individual psalms of thanksgiving are Psalms 92, 118, 138, and the psalm found in Jonah 2:1–9.

Fewer in number are community songs of thanksgiving used at the major festivals in the Temple, such as Psalms 107 and 124.

HYMNS OF PRAISE

The hymn is a song that extols God's greatness and goodness, manifest in history and creation. Psalms of this type generally begin with an imperative call to worship. Then comes a section that gives the ground for praise, often introduced by "for" (Hebrew: *kî*). Sometimes they conclude with a renewed summons to praise, thus echoing the note sounded at the first. The structure of a hymn can be seen plainly in Psalm 117, the shortest psalm of the Psalter:

A.   Introduction: *Invocation to worship*
Praise Yahweh, all nations!
    Extol God, all peoples!

B.   Main section: *Motive for praise*
For (*kî*) great is God's steadfast love (*ḥésed*) toward us,
and the faithfulness of Yahweh endures forever.

C.   Conclusion: *Recapitulation*
Praise Yahweh!

This structure is found with various modifications in a number of hymns, such as Psalms 33, 95, 100, 145, 148, 149, and 150.

Israel characteristically confessed its faith by telling the story of how Yahweh acted with liberating power. The poetic couplet composed by Miriam to celebrate the crossing of the Reed Sea ("Miriam's Song"; Exod. 15:21) is a brief example of a cry of praise to Yahweh: The first line is a summons to praise, and the second grounds praise in Yahweh's deed at the Sea. In line with this ancient tradition, a number of psalms extol Yahweh by reciting and elaborating major themes of the story: the Exodus, deliverance at the Reed Sea, wandering through the wilderness, and the occupation of the land. In these storytelling psalms, or psalms of sacred history (such as Ps. 78, 105, 106, 135, 136), the psalmists re-present Israel's history as the story of Yahweh's actions centered in the deliverance from Egypt.

Psalm 136 illustrates how Israel's praise (or thanksgiving) is evoked by the recitation of what Yahweh has done.[21] The invocation, in the same form at beginning and end, echoes the language of the ancient proclamation of God's name (Exod. 34:6-7):

---

[21]This psalm, though it seems to begin with a call to thanksgiving, is actually a hymn (as Weiser correctly recognizes [538], p. 53), giving further evidence that there is no sharp distinction between praising God and thanking God.

> *Sentence:*   O give thanks to Yahweh, for he is good,
> *Response:*   for [Hebrew: *kî*] his faithfulness [*ḥésed*] endures for ever.

The pattern of call to praise followed by liturgical response runs through the whole psalm, sentence by sentence. The first three verses represent the invitation to worship. The concluding verse (Ps. 136:26) rounds off the whole by recapitulating the theme struck at the beginning. The remaining portion of the psalm gives the ground for this praise by reciting Yahweh's marvelous acts. In Hebrew, each of these ascriptions usually begins with a participle. For example:

> "to the One who smote the first-born of Egypt,"
>> *response*
> "and brought Israel out from among them,"
>> *response*
> "with a strong hand and an outstretched arm,"
>> *response*
> "to the One who divided the Reed Sea in two,"
>> *response*
> "and made Israel pass through the midst of it,"
>> *response*
>
> . . .

....

DEFINITION: "ASCRIPTION"

An "ascription" is a grammatical form in which a narrative clause follows—or even takes the place of—the divine Name, for the purpose of identifying who God is as known through divine actions. In the Bible, ascriptions are usually formulated grammatically either by using the relative pronoun ("who") or a participle referring to the actor (or action), as in Psalm 136 (translated "the One who"). Other examples are found in Psalm 103:3–5 and in hymnic passages of Second Isaiah (such as Isa. 44:24–28).

Ascriptions often belong to hymnic style because the hymn praises God by telling what God has done, is doing, or will do. A story that identifies who God is can be reduced to a single sentence, as in the prologue to the Decalogue: "I am Yahweh your God, who brought you out of the land of Egypt."[22]

....

In this section of the psalm (Ps. 136:10–22), the psalmist elaborates on the ancient Israelite story. It is striking, however, that the psalmist begins the recitation of Yahweh's mighty acts with the Creation (Ps 136:4–9):

---

[22]See further James T. Clemons. "God, Ascriptions to" in *International Standard Bible Encyclopedia*, II., rev. ed. G. W. Bromily, ed. (Grand Rapids, MI: Eerdmans, 1979), pp. 503–04.

> "to the One who alone does great wonders,"
>> *response*
> "to the One who by understanding made the heavens,"
>> *response*
> "to the One who spread out the earth upon the waters,"
>> *response*
> "to the One who made the great lights,"
>> *response*
> "the sun to rule over the day"
>> *response*
> "the moon and stars to rule over the night,"
>> *response*

Here Creation is not an independent article of faith but the *beginning of history*—that is, the first of a series of divine acts that unfold into the story of God's dealings with Israel. Israel expanded its own sacred history by tracing Yahweh's actions back to the very beginning. Thus the worshiping community confessed that Yahweh's "faithfulness" (Hebrew: *ḥésed*), revealed in Israel's history, underlies all historical times and embraces all humankind, a theme also found in Israel's Old Epic tradition (see pp. 154–156).

In other psalms, however, praise of God the Creator is not linked directly with the sweep of sacred history centered in the Exodus, but is prompted by awe of the marvelous order of creation. An excellent example is Psalm 104, influenced by the Egyptian "Hymn to the Aton"—the deity symbolized by the sun disc whom the reforming Pharaoh Akhnaton worshiped in the fourteenth century B.C.E.[23] In its present form the hymn follows the general order of the Priestly creation story in Genesis 1, emphasizing that all creatures, human and animal, are radically dependent upon the Creator at every moment for existence. In fact, if the Creator's upholding power ("spirit") were withdrawn, everything would collapse. The Hebrew verbs, translated in the present tense, indicate God's *continuing* creative activity:

> All of them [animals and humans] look to you
>> to give them their food in its season.
> When you give to them, they gather up,
>> when you open your hand, they are satisfied to the full.
> When you hide your face, they are disturbed,
>> when you take away their breath, they expire
>>> and return to their dust.
> When you send forth your spirit, they are [re]created,
>> and you renew the surface of the soil.
>
>> —PSALM 104:27–30

---

[23]The text of this magnificent Egyptian hymn is found in Pritchard, *Ancient Near Eastern Texts* [1], pp. 369–71. See further B. W. Anderson, *Creation versus Chaos* [146], chap. 2.

ISRAEL'S PILGRIMAGE FESTIVALS

From the time when Israel was organized as a Tribal Confederacy, it was customary to make pilgrimages to the central sanctuary (see 1 Sam. 1:3ff.). Three times a year, according to the covenant law, representatives of the people were to "appear before Yahweh, God of Israel" (Exod. 23:14; 34:23). These three pilgrimage feasts, adopted from the old Canaanite calendar, were the feasts of Unleavened Bread, of Weeks, and of Tabernacles.[24] In the course of time these agricultural feasts were historicized—reinterpreted in terms of Israel's sacred history. The spring feast of Unleavened Bread, held at the beginning of the barley harvest, was connected with the Passover, and both became commemorations of the Exodus. The feast of Weeks, held seven weeks later at the time of wheat harvest, might have been observed in a special way at Gilgal, the threshold of the Promised Land, where it commemorated Yahweh's gift of the land to Israel.[25] The fall festival, known as the feast of Ingathering or Tabernacles and held at the turn of the year (New Year), became a time for renewal of the covenant with Yahweh.

The ancient custom of making pilgrimages to the central sanctuary was perpetuated throughout the period of the Monarchy and was revived after the completion of the second Temple. The little collection of psalms in Psalms 120–134, each titled "A Song of Ascents," seems to have been a handbook used by pilgrims who went up to Jerusalem for the great festivals. One of these songs expresses the joy of going to Jerusalem, the city decreed as the pilgrimage shrine for the tribes of Israel:

> I rejoiced that they said to me,
> > "Let us go to the house of Yahweh."
> At last our feet are standing
> > at your gate, Jerusalem!
>
> —PSALM 122:1–2 (NJB)

Do the Psalms tell us anything, directly or indirectly, about worship during these great festivals?

COVENANT RENEWAL FESTIVALS

Although our knowledge of the history of Israelite worship is very limited, there is reason to suppose that the ancient covenant renewal festival, first held at Shechem during the time of the Tribal Confederacy, was revived in the Northern Kingdom. We are told that Jeroboam I, the first king of North Israel, instituted a Fall festival in his domain "like the feast that was in Jerusalem" (1 Kings 12:32–33), in order to counteract the custom of making pilgrimages to the Jerusalem Temple. Apparently the Jerusalem festi-

[24]For a discussion of the festivals, see R. de Vaux, *Ancient Israel* [130], pp. 484–506.
[25]This theory, first advanced by Gerhard von Rad, has been developed by H. J. Kraus, *Worship in Israel* [523], pp. 152–61.

val had acquired important features of Davidic theology (see below). The northern festival, however, must have been very like the old covenant renewal festival observed during the days of the Tribal Confederacy. In both cases the festival in question is the great annual festival (the Feast of Tabernacles) held in the fall at the turn of the year.

Form-critical studies of the Psalter have connected various psalms to this festival.[26] For example, scholars believe Psalm 81 has close affinities with the classic account of covenant renewal in Joshua 24, telling of the gathering of the tribes to Shechem, the recitation of Yahweh's saving acts, the challenge to give undivided allegiance to Yahweh, and the promulgation of covenant law in connection with the covenant pledge (see pp. 152–154). Psalm 81:1–5 presents a summons to worship "the God of Jacob" at the sanctuary "on our feast day." The next section (Ps. 81:6–10) is a recitation of Yahweh's deeds of benevolence. (Notice that the announcement "I am Yahweh" is associated with the first commandment, precisely as in the Decalogue.) The psalm reaches its climax with an appeal to the community to hear Yahweh's voice and receive divine blessings (Ps. 81:11–16). Cultic prophets might have taken part in the service, particularly at the point where the challenge to renew loyalty to the God of the covenant was presented.

Psalm 81 possibly originated with the northern covenant renewal festival. Doubtless a number of northern psalms, once used in the sanctuary at Bethel, found their way into the south after the fall of the Northern Kingdom, and were adapted for use in Zion festivals. Psalm 50 is another illustration of a covenant psalm, though in this case the old Sinai theophany has become a theophany on Mount Zion (Ps. 50:2). This psalm presupposes the form of the "covenant lawsuit" (see pp. 306–307). In the first part (Ps. 50:1–6) Yahweh is described as coming to judge the people, with heaven and earth as witnesses. The charge that Israel has failed to live up to the requirements of the covenant in daily life (Ps. 50:7–21) invalidates ritual and sacrifices—a note the prophets had struck. The conclusion (Ps. 50:22–23) reminds those who "forget God" that God shows salvation only to those who order their way aright.

THE FESTIVAL AT JERUSALEM

In some respects the covenant renewal celebrated in the Southern Kingdom of Judah was unique, owing to profound changes brought about by the Davidic monarchy. Recall that David, in order to support his regime with the religious sanctions of the Tribal Confederacy, brought the Ark to his capital and planned to install it in a temple. David's plan, realized by Solomon, called for a reinterpretation of Yahweh's covenant

---

[26]Weiser, *The Psalms* [538], pp. 35–52, classifies a great number of psalms in this category. Walter Harrelson, *Interpreting the Old Testament* [11], pp. 421–24, more conservatively lists as covenant renewal psalms: 50, 76, 78, 81, 82, 89, 105, 111, 114.

with Israel. The royal court of Jerusalem advanced a new theology of king and Temple,[27] proclaiming that Yahweh had elected the Davidic king to be "the son of God" and had chosen Zion as the central sanctuary, the place of Yahweh's sacramental presence (see pp. 208–211). The effect of the new theology, especially under Solomon's influence, was to modify Israel's worship. The covenant renewal festivals of the former Tribal Confederacy were transformed into fall New Year celebrations of the foundation of the Temple and the election of the Davidic house. It was not until the great reformation of Josiah that the Mosaic covenant tradition was "rediscovered."

In view of this southern theology, reflected in the oracles of Isaiah of Jerusalem, it would be natural for the Jerusalem fall festival to take on a character of its own. From various psalms one can glean fragmentary references to cultic activities. An "entrance liturgy" (Ps. 24) includes the command to the gates of Jerusalem to lift up their arches so that Yahweh, the King of Glory (presumably enthroned invisibly on the Ark), can come in. There are festal processions into the sanctuary, led by singers and musicians (Ps. 68:24–25; 118:27), dancing and making melody to Yahweh (Ps. 149:3), the blowing of trumpets and raising of "the festal shout" (Ps. 89:15). Much remains obscure, even when these psalms are compared with extrabiblical texts dealing with New Year celebrations of other peoples in the ancient Near East.[28] Undoubtedly, however, a major aspect of the festival was the processional bearing of the Ark into the Jerusalem Temple, where Yahweh was acclaimed as King of the universe and where Yahweh's covenant with the house of David was reaffirmed.

Psalm 78, which seems to reflect pre-exilic worship in Jerusalem, is an interesting example of how the Exodus-Sinai tradition and the Davidic-Zion tradition were related in the Southern Kingdom. Most of the psalm is a long summary of Yahweh's historical acts, beginning with the Exodus (Ps. 78:1–66). The purpose is to show how Yahweh's people, especially the Northern Israelites, did not keep the covenant. Then the psalmist shifts to the Davidic covenant tradition:

> [Yahweh] rejected the tent of Joseph,
> >   He did not choose the tribe of Ephraim;
> but he chose the tribe of Judah,
> >   Mount Zion, which he loves.
> He built his sanctuary like the high heavens,
> >   like the earth, which he has founded forever.
> He chose his servant David,
> >   and took him from the sheepfolds;

[27]See Frank M. Cross, "Ideologies of Kingship" [129], 238f. See also H. J. Kraus, *Worship in Israel* [523], pp. 179–236.
[28]For a study of the bearing of Babylonian and other Near Eastern cultic ceremonies upon the Israelite cult, see Sigmund Mowinckel, *The Psalms in Israel's Worship*, I–II [535].

from tending the nursing ewes he brought him
　　to be the shepherd of his people Jacob,
　　of Israel, his inheritance.
With upright heart he tended them,
　　and guided them with skillful hand.
　　　　　　　　　　—PSALM 78:67–72 (NRSV)

The psalmist affirms that the old sacred history, centered in the Exodus and the inheritance of the land, has reached its dramatic climax in events that occurred in Judah: the founding of Zion and the establishment of the Davidic dynasty. In this slanted view, Yahweh's rejection of Ephraim has made Judah the bearer of the sacred tradition.[29]

The festival of Zion is clearly reflected in a liturgical hymn, Psalm 132, which refers to the processional of the Ark to Zion (2 Sam. 6) and the promises of grace to David (2 Sam. 7; 23:1–7). The psalm tells of David's oath to provide a shrine for Yahweh (Ps. 132:1–5) and of the discovery of the Ark in Kiriath-jearim (verses 6–7; see 1 Sam. 7:1–2). In words recalling the ancient "Song to the Ark" (Num. 10:35–36), Yahweh, enthroned invisibly on the Ark, is summoned to go triumphantly to a new abode:

Arise, O Yahweh, and go to your resting place,
　　you and the ark of your power!
Let your priests be vested in righteousness
　　and let your devotees sing for joy.
　　　　　　　　　　—PSALM 132:8–9

The second part of the psalm recalls Nathan's oracle to David:

Yahweh swore to David
　　an oath faithful and irrevocable:

　　"One of your own offspring
　　I will put on your throne.
　　If your descendants keep my covenant,
　　　　and my testimonies that I teach them,
　　then their descendants too in perpetuity
　　will sit upon your throne."
For Yahweh has chosen Zion,
　　coveted it for his dwelling-place:

---

[29]Some scholars interpret this psalm to mean that the old sacred history had been superseded, for Yahweh made a new beginning by raising up David and selecting Mount Zion as the central sanctuary. Katheryn P. Darr holds, however, that it is Ephraim's participation in the sacred history that has come to an end, not the sacred history of Exodus and Conquest—events that Judah celebrates in the context of the climactic events of the Davidic period.

"This is my resting-place for all time,
Here I will dwell for that is what I desire."
—PSALM 132:11–14;
see 2 Sam. 7:11–16

A similar view is expressed in Psalm 89.[30] The first part (Ps. 89:1–37) is a hymn to Yahweh, who showed covenant faithfulness (Hebrew: *ḥésed*) to David by choosing the dynasty of David. The second part (Ps. 89:38–52) is a lament in which the psalmist complains that Yahweh's oath has been violated by the defeat of the Davidic king. The suppliant appeals to Yahweh to remove the national distress and thereby to reaffirm the promises of grace once made to David.[31]

TEMPLE AND KING

The twofold emphasis on the election of Zion and the election of the Davidic king helps us understand the theological significance of two other groups of psalms in the Psalter.

One group is the so-called Zion psalms (Ps. 46, 48, 76, 84, 87, 122) based on the conviction that Zion, the city of the Temple, is the place of Yahweh's presence in the midst of the people. One of the best known Zion psalms is Psalm 46, which provided the keynote for Martin Luther's hymn, "A Mighty Fortress is our God." In three strophes, each concluding with a choral refrain on the theme of Immanuel ("God is with us"),[32] the psalm announces that human confidence is grounded in the transcendent sovereignty of the cosmic Creator and King whose rule on earth is announced and celebrated in Zion. The liturgy reaches a resounding climax in the proclamation of the "word of Yahweh":

Yield, and acknowledge that I am God!
I am exalted among the nations,
exalted in the earth!
—PSALM 46:10

The Hebrew imperative, often translated "Be still. . . . ," is not a call to quiet meditation, but rather a stentorian command ("Be quiet!") to the nations to cease and desist from their wars and military buildup and to recognize the deity of Yahweh, whose will is for peace (Hebrew: *shalom*; "welfare," "wholeness").

---

[30]Note that in Ps. 132:12 and Ps. 89:30–32 a conditional "if" qualifies Yahweh's *berîth 'ôlam* with David, without cancelling the unconditional promises of grace. Apparently the Davidic covenant was influenced by the conditional Mosaic covenant.

[31]See the discussion of Psalm 89 in Otto Eissfeldt, "The Promises of Grace to David," in *Israel's Prophetic Heritage* [174], pp. 196–207.

[32]The Immanuel theme (compare Isa. 7:14) is heard in Psalm 46: 7, 11, and probably should resound at the end of verse 3 at the point marked by *selah* (perhaps referring to a musical interlude), as in the NJB translation.

The other group, often called "royal" psalms, consists of prayers on behalf of the reigning king, Yahweh's "Messiah" or "Anointed One" (Ps. 2, 20, 21, 45, 72, 110). Israel shared with other peoples the view that the task of the king was to mediate the order and righteousness of the cosmic order to human society, thus acting as God's agent in bringing blessing to the nation. But unlike other nations (such as Egypt) who absolutized monarchy or deified kings, Israel affirmed that the reigning king was only the *chosen* agent or the *adopted* "son of God" (Ps. 2:7). The monarch does not have autonomous power but rules in dependence upon God:

> For the king trusts in Yahweh,
>> and through the faithfulness [*ḥésed*] of the Most High
>> will never be made to totter.
>
> —PSALM 21:7

THE COSMIC KING

Thus worshipers in the Jerusalem Temple were aware of both the transcendence and imminence, the distance and presence of God. Recalling Isaiah's vision, the God whose glory fills the Holy of Holies in the Temple is enthroned "high and lifted up" as cosmic King and Creator (see pp. 291–292). A distinct group of psalms celebrate this theme of Yahweh's dominion (kingdom) on earth (Ps. 47, 93, 96, 97, 98, 99). The place of these hymns in the pre-exilic cult is an intriguing question in the study of the history of Israelite worship.

Scholars influenced by the creative work of Sigmund Mowinckel have described these hymns as "enthronement psalms."[33] Under the assumption that a common pattern of "myth and ritual" prevailed in the ancient Near East, they argue that these psalms belonged in the cultic setting of a New Year "throne-ascension festival," when Yahweh's sovereignty over Israel, the nations, and the cosmos was celebrated in song, ritual, and pageant. Every year, when the cycle of the seasons returned to its beginning, the worshipers reexperienced and reactualized the victory of the powers of life over the powers of death. The creation myth of *Enuma elish* depicted the victory of the Babylonian god Marduk over the dragon of chaos, Tiamat.[34] During the festival, worshipers not only recited the myth, but also reenacted the battle. At the climax of the celebration worshipers joined in the acclamation, "Marduk has become king!"—interpreted to mean that the deity had reascended his throne for another year.

At first glance one is tempted to understand the biblical psalms in light of this mythological drama and to suppose that at the New Year festival in Jerusalem, Israelites sang hymns to celebrate Yahweh's victory over hostile powers and ascension to the

---

[33]Sigmund Mowinckel, *Psalms* [535]. See further J. H. Eaton, *Kingship and the Psalms* [520].
[34]See Pritchard, *Ancient Near Eastern Texts* [1], pp. 60–72.

throne. Psalm 93, for example, begins with the festal shout *Yahweh malak*, which some interpreters translate "Yahweh has become king!" One might translate:

> Yahweh is King!
>   —robed in majesty.
> Yahweh is robed!
>   —girded with strength.
> Indeed, you have established the world,
>   it will never be moved.
> Your throne is from primordial time,
>   you are from everlasting.
>
> —PSALM 93:1–2

Though grammatically possible to translate the opening cultic exclamation as either "Yahweh has become king" or "Yahweh is king [reigns]," one doubts whether Israelite poets adopted wholesale the mythical views of the ancient world, even in the cosmopolitan atmosphere of Jerusalem. The notion that Yahweh is caught up in the cycles of the seasons and must fight anew to win dominion over the powers of chaos is incongruent with Israel's faith. The so-called "enthronement" psalms explicitly say that Yahweh's throne is established "from of old," that Yahweh's kingship is "from everlasting." Yahweh does not need to reclaim the heavenly throne at every turn of the new year. Properly, then, modern versions render "Yahweh reigns" or "Yahweh is king."

Nevertheless, scholars rightly suspect that mythical views influenced Israel's hymns of worship. What the people borrowed from the cultural environment, however, they transmuted in the alchemy of Israel's faith to enrich the praise of Yahweh as King. The ancient myth of a divine victory over "Flood" or "Sea" (the rebellious "waters of chaos" that threaten the security of the world) was employed to express the faith that Yahweh triumphs over all powers, especially historical enemies who threaten to convert the world into dark and meaningless chaos:[35]

> The floods lift up, Yahweh,
>   the floods lift up their sound,
>   the floods lift up their pounding,
> More majestic than the thunders of many waters,
>   more majestic than the breakers of the sea,
>   on high Yahweh is majestic!
>
> —PSALM 93:3–4

---

[35]Recall that in Isaiah 51:9–10 the victory over the chaos-dragon Rahab is reinterpreted as a historical event: Yahweh's victory at the Reed Sea. See B. W. Anderson, *Creation versus Chaos* [146], chap. 3.

Not surprisingly Jerusalem, which came to be a metropolitan center under David and especially Solomon, was hospitable to cultural influences of this sort. Indeed, the Israelite theologians who developed royal covenant theology seem to have capitalized on the doctrine of Creation to buttress the stability of Yahweh's sanctuary in Zion (Ps. 78:69) and the permanence of the Davidic dynasty (Ps. 89:36–37). Psalm 89 is completely consistent with Davidic theology when, to emphasize the firmness of the covenant with David, the poet praises Yahweh's power as Creator and even portrays Yahweh's victory over the primeval chaos-dragon, Rahab (Ps. 89:5–14).

This suggests that the hymns to Yahweh as King belonged to the New Year's festival celebrated in Jerusalem during the pre-exilic period.[36] Impressive testimony to the ancient cultic celebration is found in Psalm 24, which probably goes back to the time of David when the ceremonial bringing of the Ark into Jerusalem was reenacted in the cult. The psalm opens with an ascription of praise to the Creator:

> To Yahweh belongs the earth and everything in it,
> > the world and those who inhabit it.
> For Yahweh has founded it upon seas,
> > and established it upon floods.
>
> —PSALM 24:1

The remaining verses reflect a temple liturgy, reaching a climax as the procession, with priests bearing the Ark, reaches the gates of Zion. There voices sing responsively:

> Lift up your arches, you gates,
> > lift yourselves up, you venerable doors,
> so that the King of glory may enter.
>
> Who is this King of glory?
>
> > Yahweh strong and mighty,
> > > Yahweh mighty in battle!
> >
> > —PSALM 24:7–8

Enthroned beyond and above the earthly king is the mighty Yahweh—Creator of the universe and Ruler of history (Isa. 6:1). The Davidic king is Yahweh's chosen agent, through whom the divine rule on earth is manifest. The cosmic King, whose palace is a bulwark against threatening foes (Ps. 8:2), has promised to maintain the Davidic throne in the face of all foes (Ps. 2:4–6). Hence the Zion festival was a time when the people Israel not only acclaimed Yahweh as the "King of glory" but also heard anew Yahweh's promises of grace to David.

---

[36]This view is also held by J. H. Eaton, "The Psalms and Israelite Worship," in *Tradition and Interpretation* [175], pp. 238–73. But H. J. Kraus, *Worship* [523], pp. 205–8, maintains that the so-called "enthronement psalms" come from the post-exilic period and show dependence on Second Isaiah (see Isa. 52:7–8). Claus Westermann's form-critical studies, [539], pp. 145–51, led him to the same conclusion.

THE BOOK OF PSALMS AS A WHOLE

Up to this point we have considered the Psalter as a collection of literary types (laments, thanksgivings, hymns, festival liturgies, and so on) for use in Temple worship. During the period of the Monarchy, many people longed to go to the Jerusalem Temple, where, it was believed, Yahweh was present:

> One thing I ask of Yahweh,
>   that I seek:
> To dwell in the house of Yahweh
>   all the days of my life,
> To contemplate the beauty of Yahweh,
>   and to inquire in his temple.
>
> —PSALM 27:4

This situation changed when the Temple was destroyed and people had to learn to pray to God away from Jerusalem. Even after the second Temple was built in 515 B.C.E., many people read the psalms in a non-liturgical setting, perhaps in the synagogue or at home. The book of Psalms in its final form was regarded as scripture, to be read and studied.

Given this important development, it is appropriate to turn attention from discrete psalms to the book of Psalms as a whole. The final form of the Psalter is divided into five parts on the analogy of the Pentateuch. One immediately notices that Psalms 1 and 2 serve as an introduction to the collection: Unlike most of the psalms that follow in Book I, they lack superscriptions identifying them with a Davidic collection. The compilers must have placed them here to sound basic themes of Judaism—namely, God's revelation in the Torah (Ps. 1) and hope centering in a Davidic king, Yahweh's "Anointed One" (Ps. 2). Furthermore, the Psalter is rounded off with hymns of praise, especially Psalm 150, a doxology beginning and ending with the exclamation *hallelujah* ("praise Yahweh").

Since the final editors, in contrast to editors of modern hymnbooks, have not divulged their editorial plan, one must deduce it from the structure of the book. Some suggest that the editors' purpose was to cope with the failure of royal covenant theology based on God's promises of grace to David (2 Sam. 7).[37] The evidence is found in the "seams" of the five-book whole—that is, where one book is joined to another. Book I begins with a royal psalm (Ps. 2) and perhaps ends with a royal psalm (Ps. 42); a royal psalm appears at the end of Book II (Ps. 72); and another royal psalm is placed at the end of Book III (Ps. 89). Psalm 89 is particularly significant, because it begins with hymnic praise to God for promises of grace to David (referring to Nathan's oracle in 2

---

[37]Gerald B. Wilson, *The Editing of the Hebrew Psalter* [540]. See also "The Psalms as a Book" by Patrick D. Miller, *Books of the Bible* [9], pp. 214–20.

Sam. 7) and ends with a powerful lament over the eclipse of those divine promises (Ps. 89:38–51). In this interpretation, the problem of the breakdown of Davidic theology is overcome in Book IV, "the editorial center of the final form of the Hebrew Psalter." At this climactic point editors have placed the marvelous hymns celebrating God's rule over all the powers of chaos (Ps. 93, 95–99). Thus the arrangement of the book of Psalms has the effect of lifting sovereignty from the human level of kings and princes to the cosmic level of God's eternal kingship.

This attractive hypothesis might illumine the spiritual crisis the people faced after the fall of Jerusalem in 587 B.C.E. Its validity is called into question by Psalm 132—a powerful reaffirmation of the tenets of Davidic theology (see pp. 500–501) placed well after the psalms of Yahweh's kingship (see pp. 504–506). Nevertheless, it is true that the general movement of the book of Psalms is from laments, which abound in the first part, to hymns of praise to God the Creator and King in the last part.

A more commendable proposal is that the book of Psalms is arranged to concentrate on God's *Torah* ("teaching"), the revelation of God's will. Significantly, the first psalm in the present Psalter emphasizes the benefits of meditating on God's Torah (a theme picked up in Ps. 19:7–14). Moreover, the Psalter seems to reach its climax with Psalm 119, the longest in the Psalter. This Torah psalm is organized according to an "acrostic" or alphabetical pattern, consisting of as many eight-line stanzas as there are letters in the Hebrew alphabet (see the arrangement in JPSV). Indeed, it is possible that at one stage of editing the Psalter ended with Psalm 119, in which case the book concluded on the same note as it began: God's revelation in the Torah.[38] In any case, a major purpose of the book of Psalms was to provide religious education for faithful members of the Jewish community.[39]

Torah psalms do not presuppose the worship of Yahweh in the Temple, and in this sense might be called "noncultic." One of the striking things about these psalms is the theme that study of the Torah makes one wise and happy ("blessed"). Psalm 1 is an especially good example. The psalmist divides people into two types, a customary practice in wisdom schools. The righteous individual, who meditates on God's law day and night, is likened to a tree planted by running water, which yields fruit in season and whose foliage "never fades." The wicked, on the other hand, are like "the chaff that the wind scatters," for their success is evanescent and their way "leads to naught."[40]

The Torah psalms probably have their setting in the post-exilic period—a time when the synagogue came to have increasing influence. The synagogue did not replace the Temple, at least not until the Temple was finally destroyed by the Romans in 70

---

[38]So Claus Westermann, "The Formation of the Psalter," in *Praise and Lament in the Psalms* [539].

[39]J. Clinton McCann, Jr. observes: "Although [the Psalms] may have originated primarily within the liturgical life of ancient Israel and Judah, [they] were finally appropriated, preserved, and transmitted as instruction to the faithful," "The Psalms as Instruction," *Interpretation* 46 (April, 1992), pp. 117–28. Quotation appears on p. 117.

[40]For further discussion of the Torah psalms, see "Meditations on the Good Life," in B. W. Anderson, *Out of the Depths* [526], pp. 215–33.

C.E. In the synagogue, however, Jews developed a distinctive pattern of worship centered on the reading and study of the Torah.

The sharp contrast in the Torah psalms between the righteous and the wicked, the wise and the foolish, is too neat and simple. In the next chapter we shall see that Israel's wisdom movement probed to a much deeper level of understanding, in order to deal adequately with the problem of life's imbalances.

CHAPTER 17

THE BEGINNING
OF WISDOM

Philosophy literally means "the love of wisdom" (Greek: *philo-sophia*). Among ancient Greeks the search for wisdom reached its greatest maturity and refinement, especially with Socrates in the age of Pericles (460–429 B.C.E.) and, in succeeding generations, with Plato and Aristotle. But the Greeks knew that love of wisdom is not bounded by culture, nation, or race. Wisdom is a fundamentally human concern: Greek or Jew, Babylonian or Egyptian, male or female, monarch or slave. The search for wisdom is the quest for the meaning of life. And this quest is the basic interest of every human being.

THE WISDOM OF THE EAST

Long before the meeting of East and West in the Hellenistic empire founded by Alexander the Great (333 B.C.E.), the search for wisdom was carried on in the Fertile Crescent, especially in Egypt and Babylonia.[1] Situated at the cultural crossroads of the

Biblical Readings: Of the extensive wisdom literature, read at least Proverbs 1–9, Ecclesiastes, and Job (omitting Job 32–37); also Psalms 1, 32, 34, 37, 49, 112, and 128. "The Wisdom of Ben Sira" ("Ecclesiasticus") and "The Wisdom of Solomon" are good sources outside the Hebrew Bible.

[1]For Egyptian and Babylonian literature, see Pritchard, *Ancient Near Eastern Texts* [1], pp. 405–40. A brief introduction is R. B. Y. Scott, "International Wisdom and its Literature," in *Proverbs and Ecclesiastes* [557], pp. xl–lii; see further James L. Crenshaw, *Old Testament Wisdom* [543], pp. 212–35.

ancient world, Israel was influenced from an early time by Eastern wisdom writings. These writings, which circulated far beyond the country of their origin, dated back to the Egyptian Pyramid Age (about 2600–2175 B.C.E.) and to the Sumerian era in Mesopotamia. But wisdom had a timeless quality, transcending time and culture. Though ancient sages reflected on problems of society as they knew them, these were human problems found in varying forms in all societies. Thus the wisdom movement was fundamentally international.

THE SAGE'S INDIVIDUALISM

Wisdom literature focuses on the individual. The sages were interested in the human person: more concerned with human being (Hebrew: 'adam; Gen. 2–3) than with peoples identified by particular histories and societies. They brought history to a standstill, so to speak, in order to analyze in depth the problem of human existence. Not concerned with the unrepeatable events and dynamic movement of a people's unique history, they focused on recurring experiences and the fixed moral order in which every individual participates.

Wisdom literature falls into two classes. The first consists of practical advice to the young on how to attain a successful and good life. This "prudential literature" is illustrated by the Egyptian *Teaching of Amen-em-opet*, the Babylonian *Counsels of Wisdom*, and maxims found in the biblical book of Proverbs. The second consists of reflective probing into the depth of human anguish about the meaning of life, often in a skeptical mood. This "reflective literature" is illustrated by the Egyptian *Dispute over Suicide*, the Babylonian composition *I will Praise the Lord of Wisdom*, and the biblical books of Ecclesiastes and Job. Both types of wisdom literature isolate the human problem from the particulars of history, and in this respect they stand in contrast to most of the biblical literature.

Although the Jewish-Christian faith has given Western civilization a dynamic sense of history, reflected in the doctrine of "progress" or the Marxist view of history, modern people are profoundly indebted to the "love of wisdom" inherited from Greeks, Egyptians, Babylonians, and others. Indeed, it is more natural for us to think of a human being as a "citizen of the world" than in the context of a particular history, especially the history in the Hebrew Bible that begins with Abraham and Sarah. Modern sages insist that the way to solve the problem of world unity is to concentrate on the human person, whose needs and aspirations are fundamentally the same in all situations, and to discount the memories, loyalties, and cultural peculiarities that make for human diversity and conflict.

ISRAEL'S WISDOM LITERATURE

A certain amount of wisdom literature was included in the Hebrew Bible, and with it comes the tension that exists between these two ways of viewing humankind—as individuals or groups within a particular historical context, or simply as human beings. The

An Egyptian scribe from the Fifth Dynasty (c. 2500–2350 B.C.E.) holding a partly opened papyrus roll on his lap. After the invention of writing in the early third millennium B.C.E., the scribe came to be regarded as a person having special skill and intellectual power, and often held an influential post at a royal court. From the Pyramid Age come several wisdom writings, such as the instruction of Ptah-hotep (c. 2250 B.C.E.), principal minister of a king of the Fifth Dynasty.

three wisdom writings included in the Old Testament are Proverbs, Ecclesiastes, and Job.[2] In addition, there are a number of poems, now included in the Psalter or the prophetic collections, that apparently came from the circle of Israel's sages.

All the literature we have considered so far is marked by Israel's awareness of its unique history. This historical sense is at the very heart of Israel's faith, summed up in the confession that Yahweh is the God of Israel, and Israel the people of Yahweh. To be sure, within the covenant community there were different ways of viewing this history; but there was general agreement that of all the peoples of earth Yahweh had "known" Israel in a unique way (Amos 3:2). In Israel's wisdom literature, however, the distinctive features of Israel's faith are lacking. The prophetic themes that dominate the Pentateuch and the prophetic writings—Israel's election, the Day of Yahweh, covenant and Law, priesthood and Temple, prophecy and the messianic hope—are dealt with hardly at all.

---

[2]Outside the Hebrew Bible, but included in the Roman Catholic and Orthodox canons, are the important wisdom books called "Ecclesiasticus," or "The Wisdom of Ben Sira" (dating from the early second century B.C.E.) and "The Wisdom of Solomon" (from the first century B.C.E.). Both books are included in the Protestant Apocrypha (see Chart, pp. 4–5).

Although much of the wisdom literature was produced in the post-exilic period, when Israel was deeply conscious of being a worshiping community, references to acts of worship are strikingly few. These references, moreover, say little about the centrality of worship (Prov. 3:9–10; Eccl. 5:4–5; Job 12:19 [compare 1:5; 42:8–9]). The personal name Yahweh is not used in Ecclesiastes or with few exceptions notably Chaps. 38–42 in the poetry of Job. Even when the name is used, as in Proverbs, nothing is made of the special relationship between Yahweh and Israel. Yahweh is not identified as the One who brought Israel out of Egypt or who acted repeatedly in the people's long history. Indeed, there are no explicit allusions to Israelite history or to outstanding Israelite personalities, with the single exception of Solomon (Eccl. 1:1, 13–14). The form of address, "my son" (as in Prov. 1–7), follows the ancient tradition of the wisdom schools in which sages counseled their pupils in this fashion.

Israel's wisdom literature, then, stands by itself—so much so that some theologians have great difficulty understanding how it relates to the mainstream of Israel's faith. Yet these books were not dragged into the Hebrew canon "by the heels." From a very early period Israel had its own wisdom movement that exerted a pervasive influence on all types of Israelite literature: historical, prophetic, and poetic.[3] Eventually Israel's wisdom literature was fully integrated into Israel's historical faith, as evidenced by the identification of Torah and Wisdom.[4] The book of Psalms contains psalms that celebrate the wisdom of meditating upon the Torah, as well as a group of "wisdom psalms" (Ps. 32, 34, 37, 49, 112, 128). Finally, in the apocalypse of Daniel, Daniel's wisdom—exceeding that of the Babylonian sages—was based on fidelity to the Torah (see Chapter 18).

The beginnings of an indigenous wisdom movement can be seen in the period of the early monarchy, beginning especially with the Age of Solomon. This movement eventually culminated in the full assimilation of wisdom literature into Israel's sacred heritage. Although Israel borrowed wisdom materials from its cultural environment, these materials were stamped with its distinctive faith and experience.

What was the place of the sage in Israel's life? And how did the wisdom literature of the Bible, which drew deeply on the wisdom of the East, ultimately come under the sway of Israel's distinctive religious tradition?

THE COUNSEL OF THE WISE

Jeremiah refers obliquely to the three important classes of religious leaders in Israelite society. We are told that the conspiracy against Jeremiah sprang from the conviction that "the *torah* shall not perish from the priest, nor counsel from the wise, nor the word

[3]See J. A. Emerton, "Wisdom," in *Tradition and Interpretation* [175], especially 221–27 and the literature cited there. A helpful discussion of the criteria for determining the presence of "wisdom" is given by J. L. Crenshaw, "Method in Determining Wisdom Influence upon 'Historical' Literature," *Journal of Biblical Literature* 88 (1969), 129–42.

[4]J. C. Rylaarsdam, *Revelation in Jewish Wisdom Literature* [553].

from the prophet" (Jer. 18:18; see also 8:8–9; Ezek. 7:26). This passage clearly implies that all three leaders spoke with authority derived from Yahweh—an authority that Jeremiah allegedly was trying to subvert. The passage also indicates that each leader had a different spiritual gift. The prophet, who claimed to have stood in the Heavenly Council, spoke the "word of Yahweh" for concrete situations. The priest gave the people *torah* or instruction, based on the Mosaic tradition. The sage's counsel, however, derived from a keen observation of life, from years of experience, and from wide acquaintance with the fund of ancient wisdom.

From a modern standpoint, the sage's counsel was based on "rational" or "empirical" observation, as distinct from the priest and the prophet who relied on "supernatural" sources of insight. But the distinction between "reason" and "faith" was not made in ancient Israel. Wisdom was regarded as a divine gift, not just a human ability based on superior intelligence, serious study, or long years of experience. This charismatic gift was bestowed on the elders who sat at the gate (compare Prov. 1:21), skilled artisans (Exod. 31:1–5), counselors, and above all the ruler of the people. According to Israelite tradition, the gift of wisdom was bestowed in greatest measure upon Solomon, a wise ruler whose reputation for wisdom spread far beyond the boundaries of his empire.

From time to time the prophets were critical of "wisdom" (see Isa. 29:14, Jer. 8:9), indicating that the wisdom movement was strong enough to warrant their attack.[5] In fact, in Israel the wisdom tradition preceded and outlasted the prophetic movement, reaching its peak only after prophecy had declined. The origin of Israel's wisdom movement is unknown. A vigorous Canaanite wisdom movement might have been assimilated by Israel in the period before the monarchy, as suggested by various affinities between the book of Proverbs and the Ras Shamra literature. Balaam, the Babylonian diviner (Num. 22–24), was related to Israel's early wisdom movement. From the earliest period of Israel's oral tradition come the proverb, the riddle (see Judg. 14:14), and the fable (Judg. 9:8–15)—ancient types of Near Eastern wisdom. Moreover, Egyptian wisdom motifs have been detected in the Joseph novella (Gen. 37–50).

In any case, by the time of the early monarchy sages were well-known and respected leaders in Israelite society. We are told that the counsel of Ahithophel, one of David's court advisers, was "as if one consulted the word of God" (2 Sam. 16:23). During Absalom's rebellion a wise woman from Tekoa, the home town of Amos, was summoned to use her influence on David (2 Sam. 14:1–21); later during the same crisis another wise woman negotiated with Joab (2 Sam. 20:14–22). The remark that the wise woman went to the people "in her wisdom" indicates that she was a recognized leader with professional standing, perhaps like the "wise women" found in the Canaanite court in the "Song of Deborah" (Judg. 5:29). Certainly women were included among Israel's sages, just as they were sometimes found among the prophets (Judg. 4:4; 2 Kings 22:14).

---

[5]See William McKane, *Prophets and Wise Men* [356].

SOLOMON, ISRAEL'S PATRON SAGE

Israel regarded Solomon as the fountainhead of its wisdom. Just as the Pentateuch was ascribed to Moses and the Psalms to David, so Israelites attributed much of their wisdom literature to Solomon: the books of Proverbs, Ecclesiastes, the "Song of Songs," and Psalms 72 and 127. Outside the Hebrew Bible, "The Wisdom of Solomon," "The Psalms of Solomon," and "The Odes of Solomon" are attributed to Solomon. Though extravagant, these claims nevertheless reflect Solomon's lively interest in wisdom and education in the royal court (see Chapter 7).

We are told that Solomon uttered three thousand proverbs and one thousand and five songs (1 Kings 4:32). According to later tradition, the "sweetest" of Solomon's songs—about twenty-five of them—are found in the "Song of Songs." The lovers in these songs are allegedly King Solomon himself and the famed Shulammite or Shunammite beauty who, according to 1 Kings 1:1–4, was brought to David to minister to him and keep him warm during his declining days. There is no clear evidence that Solomon took Abishag as his wife (compare 1 Kings 2:13–25), and still less for the claim that Solomon composed these sensuous love lyrics. Nevertheless, their association with Solomon and their popularity at wedding festivities established them firmly in Israelite life. Eventually the songs were admitted to the rank of sacred scripture, on the ground that they presented an allegory of the covenant love between Yahweh and Israel. Quite apart from this rather strained interpretation, the songs accent truths basic to Israel's faith: that a human being should live before God as a total personality; that man and woman should find fulfillment in their union with each other; and that sexual love should partake of the goodness of God's creation. Hellenistic notions of a dualism of "body" and "soul" are not supported in the Hebrew Bible, certainly not in the "Song of Songs"![6]

Solomon's proverbs, on the other hand, became the basis for the claim that Solomon was the author of the book of Proverbs. The English word "proverb" refers to a maxim or aphorism (such as "A word to the wise is sufficient"). The Hebrew word *mashal* can have this meaning, but can also refer to a longer unit like the "parable" of the New Testament. Solomon might have spoken some of the proverbs found in the oldest sections of the book of Proverbs (Prov. 10–29), but we cannot be sure. Undoubtedly much of the treasury of Solomonic wisdom was absorbed into the reservoir of Israel's wisdom tradition.

Solomon's cosmopolitan interests admirably qualified him to be the patron of wisdom. When the Queen of Sheba came on a visit from far-off Arabia, Solomon displayed his wisdom by propounding and solving riddles (1 Kings 10:1–10). It is said that God gave Solomon "largeness of mind like the sand of the sea-shore" (1 Kings 4:29). This claim is confirmed by the historical record, which shows that Solomon was ex-

---

[6]See Jack M. Sasson, "Unlocking the Poetry of Love in the Song of Songs," *Bible Review* I (1985), 11–19.

tremely hospitable to the cultural influences of the Fertile Crescent, in particular fostering close relations with Phoenicia and Egypt. It was in the Age of Solomon that Israel
broke out of the confines of the former Tribal Confederacy, with its limiting religious
institutions and perspectives, and enlarged its horizons of faith beyond the boundaries
of the Mosaic covenant heritage (see Chapter 7). The spirit of the time was one of "sec-
ularization" (though one must use this word cautiously) in that there was a disposition
in some circles to concentrate upon the *human* element in social experience. Such a
trend is manifest in the Court History of David (2 Sam. 9–20; 1 Kings 1–2), which
portrays the chain reaction of action and consequence in the royal court with a surprising lack of divine intervention. It can be seen also in the wisdom tradition found in the
oldest section of the book of Proverbs, which discerns a seemingly self-operating law of
cause and effect in human experience and cherishes the worldly benefits of long life,
honor, family welfare, and possessions.[7]

Egyptian wisdom made a deep impression on Israel's thought from at least the
time of Solomon. Close parallels between the *Instruction of Amen-em-opet* and Proverbs
22:17–24:22 indicate that this section of Proverbs depended heavily on its Egyptian
source: Only a few verses have no counterpart in the Egyptian text (dated during the
period 1000–600 B.C.E.).[8] The subject matter, form of presentation, and the telescoping of the thirty chapters of the Egyptian work into thirty sayings in the book of
Proverbs (compare Prov. 22:20) are eloquent proof of Israel's contact with the wisdom
of Egypt.[9]

AN ANTHOLOGY OF PROVERBS

The history of Israel's wisdom movement is condensed in the book of Proverbs. Scholars generally agree that in its final form the book comes from the period of Judaism—
probably after Ezra's time—when wisdom schools were flourishing. Like the Pentateuch, the book of Proverbs represents the final stage of a tradition that stretches back at
least to the time of Solomon, who might have composed or collected the original nucleus. Several wisdom collections are contained in the book:

1. "The proverbs of Solomon" (Prov. 1–9)
2. "The proverbs of Solomon" (Prov. 10:1–22:16)
3. "The words of the Wise" (Prov. 22:17–24:22)
   "These also are sayings of the Wise" (Prov. 24:23–34)

[7]See Gerhard von Rad, *Wisdom in Israel* [552], pp. 57–65, who maintains that in the Solomonic age the "experience of reality" took a completely new form.
[8]See Pritchard, *Ancient Near Eastern Texts* [1], pp. 421–24.
[9]On the interrelation between the two wisdom movements, see Glendon E. Bryce, *A Legacy of Wisdom* [542].

4. "The proverbs of Solomon collected by the men of King Hezekiah" (Prov. 25–29)
5. "The words of Agur the son of Jakeh" (Prov. 30)
6. "The words of Lemuel king of Massa" (Prov. 31:1–9)
7. Alphabetic poem on the accomplished woman (Prov. 31:10–31).

Notice the diversity of the material. In general, the first four collections belong to the tradition of Solomon, while the remainder of the book is of foreign origin. Many scholars regard the second collection as the oldest portion of the book of Proverbs. The first collection is often regarded as the latest, though Canaanite elements suggest that at least part of it belongs to the pre-exilic tradition. What is certain is that the book of Proverbs represents a complex tradition, extending throughout almost the entire period of the Hebrew Bible.

COMMON-SENSE PROVERBS

The wisdom sayings of this anthology are often short, crisp, two-line sentences dealing with some aspect of experience. In some instances, the second line of the proverb runs parallel to the thought of the first.[10] An example of this symmetrical or "synonymous parallelism" is found in Proverbs 22:1 (NRSV):

A good name is to be chosen rather than great riches,
    and favor is better than silver and gold.

Often the lines are a balanced pair of opposites. This "antithetic parallelism" is found in Proverbs 10:1 (NRSV):

A wise child makes a glad father,
    but a foolish child is a mother's grief.

Sometimes the second line of the pair completes the thought of the first, in a kind of "ascending parallelism." Thus Prov. 4:18 (NRSV):

But the path of the righteous is like the light of dawn,
    which shines brighter and brighter until full day.

In addition to the short "two-liners" are a number of proverbs that expatiate on a theme for the purpose of instruction. These units, belonging to an "instruction genre," are in the imperative rather than the indicative, and adduce reasons for following the advice.[11] In one passage the industry of the ant provides a lesson in planning for the future:

---

[10]For discussions of biblical poetry, see James L. Kugel, *The Idea of Biblical Poetry: Parallelism and Its History* (New Haven, CT: Yale University Press, 1981) and Patrick D. Miller, Jr., *Interpreting the Psalms* [99]. See Miller's summary, "The Poetic Character of the Psalms," in *Books of the Bible* [9], pp. 204–6.
[11]See W. McKane, *Proverbs* [556].

> Go to the ant, you lazybones,
>> consider its ways, and be wise.
> Without having any chief
>> or officer or ruler,
> it prepares its food in summer,
>> and gathers its sustenance in harvest.
> How long will you lie there,
>> O lazybones?
> When will you rise from your sleep?
> A little sleep, a little slumber,
>> a little folding of the hands to rest,
> and poverty will come upon you like a robber,
>> and want, like an armed warrior.
>> —PROVERBS 6:6–11 (NRSV)

Another characteristic rhetorical device is the numerical saying, based on the scheme *x + 1*, as in the collection found in Proverbs 30 and 31:10–31.

> Three things are too wonderful for me;
>> four I do not understand:
> the way of an eagle in the sky,
>> the way of a snake on a rock,
> the way of a ship on the high seas,
>> and the way of a man with a girl.
>> —PROVERBS 30:18–19 (NRSV)

Many proverbs give the impression of being "secular," though this modern term might not adequately describe them. In any case, the oldest proverbs show a positive, healthy view toward worldly affairs. Reflecting on various courses of human conduct, the sages suggest that the good life can be achieved through diligence, sobriety, and prudence; and that the marks of the good life are success, well-being, and a long and fruitful life. In this respect the proverbs are similar to the prudential advice given by sages in Babylonia, Egypt, and elsewhere. Many of the biblical proverbs deal with ordinary problems that hinder one from attaining fullness of life: laziness (Prov. 6:6–11; 24:30–34), drunkenness (23:20–21, 29–35), relations with harlots (5:9–10), unwise business dealings (6:1–5), and so on.

But this seemingly secular advice is infused with a religious spirit. Recall that the Deuteronomistic historians based their scheme of rewards and punishments on the Mosaic covenant, with its curses and blessings. Likewise, Israel's sages believed that written into the very nature of things is a divine order that can be found through human search and reflection. Living in harmony with this order brings the good life; going against it results in personal disaster. The convergence of these two points of view, based on divine initiative and human initiative respectively, eventually prompted the identification of Torah and Wisdom in Israel's history of traditions.

THE FEAR OF THE LORD

A poetic couplet in Proverbs sums up the characteristic teaching of Israel's sages:

> The fear of Yahweh is the beginning of wisdom,
>   and the knowledge of the Holy One is insight.
>   —PROVERBS 9:10

This formulation, which occurs several times in the Old Testament with some variation, also appears at the beginning of the first collection (Prov. 1:7) and at the conclusion of the second (15:33; see also Job 28:28 and Ps. 111:10). True wisdom, according to Israel's sages, comes only to the person who acknowledges Yahweh's sovereignty, who "fears" or lives in reverence before the Holy One (see Prov. 1:29; 2:5). Faith in Yahweh is the "beginning"—that is, the foundation or starting point from which one seeks understanding:

> Trust in the Lord with all your heart,
>   and do not rely on your own insight.
> In all your ways acknowledge him,
>   and he will make straight your paths.
> Do not be wise in your own eyes;
>   fear the Lord, and turn away from evil.
> It will be a healing for your flesh
>   and a refreshment for your body.
>   —PROVERBS 3:5–8

"Fools" grope in confusion and "evil persons" lack an understanding of justice (Prov. 28:5) precisely because they fail at the starting point. Reason is not an obstacle to faith, as many people suppose; rather, faith is the precondition for understanding.[12]

This theme, unique to Israel's wisdom tradition, shows a direct contact between wisdom teachers on the one hand, and Israel's exposition of the covenant traditions on the other. Recall that the same theme was emphasized by Israel's prophets. Hosea insisted that Israel's lack of "the knowledge of God" (see pp. 278–280) was the fundamental flaw in its history. Jeremiah contrasted true wisdom with folly:

> Thus says Yahweh:
>   Let not the wise boast in their wisdom,
>   let not the strong boast in their strength,
>   let not the rich boast in their riches;

---

[12]See Gerhard von Rad, *Wisdom in Israel* [552], pp. 65–73, who observes that this wisdom formulation contains in a nutshell "Israel's entire theory of knowledge," or epistemology.

> rather, let those who boast boast in this,
>> that they understand and know me,
> For I am Yahweh who practices faithfulness *[ḥésed]*,
>> justice, and righteousness in the earth,
>> for in these things I delight,
>>> says Yahweh.
>
> —JEREMIAH 9:23–24

The motif of "the fear of Yahweh," central to the biblical wisdom literature, was deeply ingrained in Israel's religious traditions (see Gen. 22:12). One must not minimize the profound differences between the wisdom perspective and Israel's traditional covenant faith. Clearly, however, wisdom teachers in their own way developed theological interests that also belonged to Israel's covenant traditions.

Basic to the covenant perspective was the theme of divine retribution—the notion that Yahweh brings upon people the fruit of their own deeds. In ancient Near Eastern wisdom, the pattern of action and consequence was perceived to be written into creation itself.[13] One could not violate the moral order of the universe, any more than one could defy gravity by driving horses up cliffs or plowing the sea with oxen (compare Amos 6:12). Israel's sages agreed with this teaching, but apparently did not go so far as to say that the moral order operates independently of Yahweh's control, or that Yahweh is bound by the fixed order of creation. As the holy and transcendent God, Yahweh retained the initiative (compare Exod. 33:19: "I will be gracious unto whom I will be gracious"):[14]

> No wisdom, no understanding, no counsel
>> can prevail against Yahweh.
> A horse is made ready for the day of battle,
>> but to Yahweh belongs the victory.
>
> —PROVERBS 21:30, 31

THEOLOGICAL WISDOM

Under the influence of Israel's faith in Yahweh, a change took place in the traditional conception of wisdom. Some scholars maintain that Israel's wisdom tradition went from robust "secularity" to theological sophistication and maturity.[15] Initially the sage,

---

[13]H. H. Schmid, "Creation, Righteousness, and Salvation," in *Creation in the Old Testament* [132], pp. 102–17, maintains (somewhat extremely) that wisdom's creation theology is the "broad horizon" of biblical theology.

[14]Thus J. A. Emerton, "Wisdom," in *Tradition and Interpretation* [175], p. 288, observes that "the scheme is sometimes shattered by the free (and, it must be said, somewhat irrational) grace of God." See his entire discussion of divine retribution, pp. 215–21.

[15]This view of the increasing theological maturity of the wisdom movement is advocated by Gerhard von Rad, *Wisdom* [552], pp. 53–73.

while recognizing wisdom to be a divine gift, was not particularly interested in reflecting upon its divine Source. Rather than attempting to explore divine mysteries, wisdom helped people to harmonize their conduct with the order of things, thus to achieve happiness and reap practical benefits. Only later, in this view, did wisdom become theologically conscious, as evident in the late section of the book of Proverbs (Prov. 1–9), where wisdom is not just the key to proper ethical behavior (Prov. 4:10–19), but seeks to grasp the divine secret of the whole creation:

> By wisdom Yahweh founded the earth,
>> by understanding established the heavens;
> by his knowledge the deeps broke forth,
>> and the clouds rain down dew.
>
> —PROVERBS 3:19–20

This view of direct development from secular to theological might oversimplify the matter. For one thing, it is not certain that all of Proverbs 1–9 comes from the post-exilic period. During the period of the monarchy, moreover, royal theologians of the Jerusalem court resorted to a high conception of wisdom to justify the foundation of the Davidic throne upon the cosmic order.[16] Even in Israel's early wisdom tradition the line between the worldly and the sacred was not sharply drawn; and wisdom reflection, at least in some circles, probably ventured beyond mundane concerns to the cosmic realm. Clearly, there was great interest in theological wisdom in the period of Judaism, but the later sages built upon and elaborated religious dimensions of wisdom present from the first. Thus the affirmation that "the fear of Yahweh" is the beginning of wisdom came to have, on the basis of theological reflection, a wider and deeper meaning than ever before. Israel's sages, reflecting on the mystery of God's creation, reached the very limits of human thought:

> These are indeed but the outskirts of [God's] ways;
>> and how small a whisper do we hear of him!
> But the thunder of his power who can understand?
>
> —JOB 26:14 (NRSV)

WOMAN WISDOM

In the first part of the book of Proverbs, those who seek wisdom are invited to choose between two women. On the one side is the Strange Woman, a harlot who calls seductively to passers-by to follow her foolish and destructive ways (Prov. 9:13–18). On the

---

[16]See B. W. Anderson, *Creation versus Chaos* [146], pp. 60–74; and *Creation in the Old Testament* [132], pp. 7–11.

other side is the Wisdom Woman, who entices people to pursue ways leading to peace and joy. Wisdom, a prophetess like Miriam (Exod. 15:20), Deborah (Judg. 4:4), and Huldah (2 Kings 22:14), stands in the marketplace and summons people to mend their ways or face the consequences (see Prov. 1:20–33).[17] Elsewhere Wisdom appeals to young men to "seek and find her" (Prov. 8:17), to "love" and "embrace" her (Prov. 4:6–9). These appeals are couched in erotic language, like the love poetry in the "Song of Songs."[18]

The most profound personification of Wisdom (Hebrew: *Hohmah;* Greek: *Sophia*) is found in Proverbs 8:22–36, where as a prophetess she encourages people to follow her ways. Here her appeal takes on great urgency and power because she is preexistent, God's agent at the time of Creation. The poem has its own literary structure:

Thematic Statement (Prov. 8:22–23)
God created Wisdom "at the beginning of his work, the first of his acts of long ago" (NRSV). The verb translated "created" is the same used of Eve's creative labor when giving birth to Cain and Abel (Gen. 4:1), and of God's fashioning the fetus in the womb (Ps. 139:13).

Negative Assertions (Prov. 8:24–26)
The maternal imagery continues. The poet speaks negatively of the situation before Creation: There were "no depths," "no springs abounding with water." In this period, before there were mountains and hills, Wisdom was brought forth or "birthed."

Positive Assertions (Prov. 8:27–29)
The language shifts from negations to positive creative actions, using verbs of ordering: God "established the heavens," "made firm the skies above," "assigned to the sea its limits." The imagery shifts from the creativity of birth to construction and building, the architectural imagery used by the Voice from the Whirlwind in Job 38:8–11 (see pp. 540–541).

Recapitulation, Elaboration of Theme (Prov. 8:30–31)
The poet returns to the opening theme in an envelope construction (Latin: *inclusio*). Wisdom says that in the beginning she was "beside God, like a master worker" (NRSV) or "with Him as a confidant" (JPSV). In another translation:

---

[17]For an exquisite study of this passage, see Phyllis Trible, "Wisdom Builds a Poem: The Architecture of Proverbs 1:20-33," *Journal of Biblical Literature* 94 (1975), 509–18.

[18]Richard J. Clifford, S. J., makes this point in his essay, "Woman Wisdom in the Book of Proverbs," *Biblische Theologie und Gesellschaftlicher Wandel*, ed. by George Braulik, OSB, Walter Gross, and Sean McEvenue (Herder, 1993), p. 61.

> Then I was at his side each day,
>   his darling and delight,
> playing in his presence continually,
>   playing over his whole world,
> while my delight was in mankind.
>
> —PROVERBS 8:30–31 (REB)

The meaning of Proverbs 8:30 is not clear because of uncertainty about how to translate the Hebrew *'amon*. Some favor "little child, darling" (REB), which goes well with the maternal imagery at the beginning of the poem. Most translators opt for "craftsperson, master craftsman" (NRSV, NIV). Depending on the translation, Wisdom is portrayed as a child playing before God at the time of creation, or as an artisan assisting God in the planning and execution of the work of creation.

Several things should be said about this wonderful poem. First, the bold use of maternal imagery: Wisdom is not explicitly called God's daughter, but the poem verges on that meaning. Second, Wisdom is portrayed as close to God, indeed, with God in the beginning, but not as co-eternal with God, or as a "goddess." She is subordinate to God, "the first of God's works" who preexists all else in creation.[19] Third, the language is metaphorical, as is all God-language.[20] The holy God is beyond all human categories, including gender distinctions of masculine or feminine. This poem breaks out of masculine metaphors that dominate much of Scripture and creatively makes use of feminine imagery.[21]

THE WISE AND THE FOOLISH

Despite this refinement of the conception of wisdom, the book of Proverbs sets forth a "pat" doctrine of rewards and punishments. The search for wisdom, according to the sages, divides people into two classes: the wise and the foolish. This classification, admittedly, is the result of a decision made in freedom, having nothing to do with native intelligence, social position, or right doctrine. The "fool" is not deficient in intelligence, but is one who through pride and passion decides against the course of wisdom and must accept the consequences of that decision.[22] Thus there are two types of people: those who follow the way of life and those who pursue the way of death.

---

[19]The language approaches the view of the Logos (Word) in John 1:1–18. The Logos, however, is masculine and described as being fully divine, indeed co-eternal with God.

[20]For a discussion of the nature and limitations of metaphor, see Gale Yee, "The Theology of Creation in Proverbs 8:22–31," in *Creation in the Biblical Traditions*, eds. Richard J. Clifford and John J. Collins (CBQ Monograph Series 24, 1992), p. 85.

[21]See further B. W. Anderson, "Moving Beyond Masculine Metaphors," *Bible Review*, X, 5 (Oct. 1994), 22ff.

[22]Several terms are used to describe the fool: "the evil one," "the self-confident one," "the empty person," and "the thick-headed one."

The Deuteronomic portrayal of the Two Ways (Deut. 11:26–28; 30:15–20) was a forceful and urgent appeal for covenant renewal in a time of national crisis. Psalm 1, which has affinities with wisdom thinking, also points to the Two Ways. But the inadequacy of this doctrine, whether expressed in terms of wisdom or *torah* ("teaching"), became apparent to some sages who wrestled profoundly with the riddle of life's meaning.

THE SKEPTICISM OF ECCLESIASTES

The distinctive teaching of Israel's sages was that wisdom is a gift of Yahweh, not a human achievement:

> To human beings belong the plans of the mind,
>> but from Yahweh comes the answer of the tongue.
>> —PROVERBS 16:1

Though the sages were aware of the limits of the human quest, they firmly believed that wisdom, when based upon "the fear of Yahweh," could not only show the right course of action but also lead to some understanding of the divine secret underlying the Creation.

This confidence was challenged, however, by the author of the book of Ecclesiastes. Unlike the book of Proverbs, a "collection of collections" covering a long history of wisdom tradition, Ecclesiastes is fundamentally the work of one sage who wrote during the late post-exilic period, perhaps between 250 and 200 B.C.E. Ecclesiastes' bold challenge to Judaism, with its simple "Deuteronomic" doctrine of rewards and punishments, offended the religious sensibilities of the orthodox. Consequently, editors touched up the book here and there to make it more palatable.[23] Two conclusions were added. The author of the appendix in Ecclesiastes 12:9–11 praises the sage for the genius displayed in weighing, studying, and arranging proverbs. But the author of Ecclesiastes 12:12–14 cautioned readers to take the teaching with a grain of salt, for "of making many books there is no end, and much study is a weariness of the flesh." According to the second editor, the fundamental tenet of Judaism stands unscathed in spite of the book's teaching: *fear God and keep God's commandments.*

Had it not been for these pious revisions and the tradition that ascribed authorship to Solomon, the book of Ecclesiastes might not have found its way into the Hebrew canon. In fact, it was one of three books whose right to be included was seriously questioned by the rabbis during the Tannaitic period (first century B.C.E. to third century C.E.).[24] Today Jews read Ecclesiastes on the third day of the Feast of Tabernacles,

---

[23]See Michael V. Fox, *Qoheleth and his Contradictions* (Sheffield: Almond Press, 1989).
[24]The other two questionable books were Esther and the "Song of Songs."

Insert 19-1 The Rose City of Petra.

Insert 19–1a (Top left) The only access to the Nabatean capital was through the Siq, a narrow ravine nearly a mile long running between sheer walls of rock over 260' high in some places.

Insert 19–1b (Lower left) The Treasury (Khazneh, meaning "the Rock" in Greek), one of the many buildings carved out of the rose-red sandstone by the ancient Nabateans.

Insert 19–1c (Lower right) The hills surrounding Petra, the "rose-red" city that was the capital of the Nabateans and probably the former city of the Edomites, Sela (II Kings 14:7). In the background is the facade of a tomb cut into a cliff.

Insert 20-1   In the background the magnificent Mosque of Omar, a Byzantine structure built over the sacred rock which was once the site of Solomon's temple. Some maintain that the Holy of Holies, the most sacred part of the temple, was once located on bedrock beneath the cupola seen in the foreground.

to add a serious note to the festivity by reminding the congregation that the joys of life are transient and that we should number our days in the hope of acquiring wisdom (see Ps. 90:12).

THE MELANCHOLY TEACHER

The word "Ecclesiastes" comes to us from the Greek Septuagint by way of Jerome's translation, the Latin Vulgate. The Greek translator used the word *ekklesiastes* to render the Hebrew *qohéleth,* a participle related to the noun meaning "assembly, congregation" (Hebrew: *qahal;* Greek: *ekklesia*). Apparently the Hebrew word refers to "one who speaks to an assembly"—that is, a lecturer or teacher. Thus *qohéleth* is not a proper name, but a description of a function. The belief was that this function was performed by Solomon, who "assembled" the leaders of Israel in Jerusalem (compare 1 Kings 8:1) and showed himself to be the Teacher *par excellence* (see Eccl. 1:1). "When king over Israel in Jerusalem," Solomon says, "I applied my mind to seek and to search out by wisdom all that is done under heaven" (Eccl. 1:12–13; compare 2:4–11).

With no particular pattern or scheme of development, the book of Ecclesiastes is a rambling lecture on the meaning of life by a professional wisdom teacher. One gets the impression that the main point of the discourse is made by the end of the second chapter. The thesis of the lecture, announced at the beginning and again at the end, is that all human activity is vanity and a striving after the wind:

> Vanity of vanities, says the Teacher,
>   vanity of vanities! All is vanity.
> —ECCLESIASTES 1:2; 12:8

Writing in the melancholy vein of Omar Khayyam's *Rubáiyát,* the Teacher announces that human wisdom cannot "grasp the sorry scheme entire." Admittedly, Wisdom has some value, for it enables one to walk circumspectly, aware of the limitations of mortal life. "The sage has his eyes in his head, but the fool walks in darkness" (Eccl. 2:14). Indeed, wisdom is the source of strength greater than ten rulers (Eccl. 7:19). But the advantage won through practical wisdom is doubtful (Eccl. 2:12–23; 7:7–8), for with wisdom comes increase of sorrow (1:18), and in the end death comes alike to the sage and the fool (2:14–17). The Teacher advises his pupils to make the best of life while they can, enjoying the present and not trying to probe into the future (Eccl. 2:24–25; 3:12–15; 7:14). The grim truth is that, despite its practical value, wisdom cannot penetrate the mystery of life and deal with the ultimate questions—though the very existence of a person hangs on the answers to these questions. Unable to gain access to the divine wisdom underlying the Creation, the sage is thrown back upon personal insight and experience to find meaning in life. He despairs over life's emptiness, even developing a hatred of life (Eccl. 2:17) that suggests the "nausea" of modern existentialists.

GOD'S HIDDEN PURPOSE

Some scholars believe that Ecclesiastes' author, living in the Hellenistic period inaugurated by Alexander the Great, was influenced by Greek philosophy and by the sense of fate (Greek: *moira*) that obsessed Greek culture. There is a superficial resemblance to the philosophy of Epicureanism, for the sage advises "seizing the day" and enjoying momentary pleasures while they last (Eccl. 8:15–9:9; compare 1 Cor. 15:32). Moreover, there is a kind of determinism in his outlook—a realization that whatever happens has been foreordained long ago. Qoheleth (Teacher) accepts the joys and sufferings of life with an inner serenity, undisturbed by the ebb and flow of fortune (Eccl. 6:10–11; 9:1). This teaching is reminiscent of the philosophy of Stoicism; indeed, some have suggested that several words used by Qoheleth are taken from a Greek context. For instance, the word translated "chance, accident" (Eccl. 2:14; 3:19; 9:2–3) is said to be the philosophical equivalent of Greek *tyche* ("chance").

Clearly Qoheleth was influenced in some degree by the spirit of Greek culture, whose atmosphere he breathed.[25] He could no more escape the Hellenistic spirit than a modern writer could avoid the influence of twentieth-century science. In spite of his "tragic sense of life," however, Qoheleth never surrenders the conviction that God is sovereign over human affairs. The tragedy of life is not that the inexorable power of fate governs both human beings and the gods, as in Greek culture, but that divine wisdom is so inscrutable that human beings cannot know God's ways. Qoheleth affirms that everything is "in the hand of God" (Eccl. 9:1). The trouble is that God's sovereignty is so completely hidden that one is left in the dark about the divine plan. Therefore, to human wisdom events appear to be ultimately meaningless. "There is nothing new under the sun": The days turn in a circle, rather than moving toward the fulfillment of purpose (Eccl. 1:4–11).

THE TIMES OF OUR LIVES

Qoheleth's outlook is disclosed in an important discussion of the nature of time (Eccl. 3), in which the sage expresses a poignant awareness of the transience of life. One is reminded of the words of the nineteenth-century hymn:

> Time, like an ever-rolling stream,
>   Bears all its sons away;
> They fly forgotten, as a dream
>   Fades at the break of day.

Time is not an inexorable process, however, that mechanically grinds out the days and years. Rather than speaking of time abstractly, Qoheleth writes of concrete "times"—

---

[25]In a paper "Is Qoheleth a Pyrrhonist?" presented to the Society of Biblical Literature (New Orleans, Nov. 1996), Steve Bishop maintained that there are significant parallels between Qoheleth's view of wisdom and the speculative philosophy of the Greek philosopher, Pyrrho of Elis.

that is, times that have a specific content or purpose. "For everything there is a season and a time for every matter under heaven" (Eccl. 3:1). Among others, there is:

> A time to be born, and a time to die;
> a time to plant, and a time to pluck up
>   what is planted;
> a time to weep, and a time to laugh;
> a time to embrace, and a time to refrain
>   from embracing;
> a time to keep silence, and a time to speak;
> a time for war, and a time for peace.
>
> (See ECCLESIASTES 3:2–8)

A "time" is an opportunity that invites a particular action, just as we say "now the time is ripe" or describe an action as "timely." Qoheleth speaks of times in the plural—the times of human life. Moreover, these times are somehow in God's hand (compare Ps. 31:13). Each time is a heaven-sent opportunity, for God "has appointed a time for every matter, and for every work" (Eccl. 3:17).[26]

The problem is that human beings, with their limited wisdom, cannot discern an overall purpose running consistently through life's experiences. The times just come one after another, and everything seems to turn in a circle of futility. Qoheleth acknowledges that God, with suprahuman wisdom, can see the whole drama from beginning to end or, to change to a musical figure, can hear the successive notes as a melody. Human beings are not God. Humans are like animals in that they must die; but they are more miserable than animals for they long to "see life steadily and see it whole" (Matthew Arnold). Qoheleth testifies that God has given humans "a sense of past and future, but no comprehension of God's work from beginning to end" (Eccl. 3:11, REB).[27] Mortals cannot peer beyond the veil that hides God's purpose from human understanding; consequently, they are overwhelmed with the meaninglessness of human experience. If one cannot discern the thread that binds the times together purposefully, the verdict of futility must be pronounced on all human thought and activity.

THE PROBLEM OF DEATH

For Qoheleth the tragedy of life is heightened by the intense realization that the problem of existence must be answered within the brief span between birth and death (see Eccl. 8:6–8). The problem of death—the most universally human experience—casts a

---

[26]The Hebrew word is equivalent in meaning to the New Testament word *kairos*, as found, for instance, in Mark 1:15.

[27]The Hebrew *'ôlam* (RSV: "eternity"; NAB: "the timeless") is difficult to understand here. The NEB translation, "a sense of time past and future," seems appropriate to the context. In any case, *'ôlam* does not refer to eternity in a philosophical sense.

dark shadow over the whole book. The death of the individual had not loomed as a serious problem in the early period of Israel, for it was believed that the individual's life was given meaning through participation in the covenant community. The parent lived on in the child, and all generations were bound together in the psychic solidarity of Israel.

Apparently Qoheleth was not governed by the covenant thinking of Israel's priests and prophets.[28] Separated from a historical community that bears life's meaning, the destiny of the individual becomes an acute problem. Qoheleth does not evade the problem by affirming the survival of the individual beyond death, for he knows too well the limitations of human nature. Human beings are mortal. There is nothing in them that is immortal or "deathless." In this respect, humans are no better than the animals (Eccl. 3:18–22), for at death "all go to one place" (3:20). Only in this life is there hope, for "a living dog is better than a dead lion" (see Eccl. 9:5–6). Because Qoheleth takes death seriously, he takes life seriously.

This sage, then, looks upon the world with a pessimistic eye. Unable to see God's handiwork in nature, he complains that the sun, wind, and sea follow an aimless course, for "all things are full of weariness" (Eccl. 1:5–8). According to him, the doctrine of the Two Ways does not ring true to experience, for the righteous are rewarded with suffering and the wicked are chastened with success. Ironically, a person who has toiled with wisdom has to leave everything to someone who did not work for what was received (Eccl. 2:18–23). The dead are more fortunate than the living, but better than both is not to be born at all (Eccl. 4:1–3; see 6:3–6). Qoheleth advises discreet reverence in the house of God, "for God is in heaven, and you upon earth; therefore let your words be few" (Eccl. 5:1–7). He recommends moderation in both wisdom and folly, for too much of either could lead to disaster (Eccl. 7:15–18). He counsels enjoying marital bliss and finding satisfaction in work, for all too soon one must go to Sheol, the land of the dead, where there is "no work or thought or knowledge or wisdom" (Eccl. 9:9–10). He broods over the accidents of life that make planning for the future absurd:

> Again I saw that under the sun the race is not to the swift, nor the
> battle to the strong, nor bread to the wise, nor riches to the intelligent, nor
> favor to the skillful; but time and chance happen to them all.
> —ECCLESIASTES 9:11 (NRSV)

A person's "time"—that is, the time of one's death—is unknown; like a bird caught in a snare, it suddenly "falls upon" one. Ecclesiastes concludes with the exhortation to enjoy life while one is young, before the infirmities of age, or the bludgeonings of death, take their toll (Eccl. 11:9–12:8).

---

[28]The word "Israel" appears only once (Eccl. 1:12), referring to the people over whom Solomon ruled.

THE SHADOW OF DESPAIR

This skepticism, however, is fundamentally religious. To be sure, Qoheleth does not pretend to give divine teaching, after the manner of prophets or priests. He sets forth the lessons derived from experience and reflection (see Eccl. 1:13; 7:23; 9:1). Yet his conception of God is fundamental to his world outlook, even though he uses the general name *'Elohim* instead of the special Israelite name, Yahweh. The basic tenet of his theology is that God is hidden, transcendent, completely other—separated from the human world by an infinite gulf (see Eccl. 5:2). No other writer puts more emphasis on divine sovereignty. God orders and controls all events, but God's sovereignty is completely hidden to human understanding (Eccl. 8:17; 11:5). Even though human wisdom cannot probe the divine mystery, one has no ground for questioning God, for "who can make straight what God has made crooked?" (Eccl. 7:13). A human being "is not able to dispute with one stronger than he" (Eccl. 6:10). Qoheleth makes such statements from the standpoint of "the fear of the Lord"—that is, in faith:

> I know that whatever God does endures forever; nothing can be added
> to it, nor anything taken from it; God has done this, so that all should stand
> in awe before him.
> —ECCLESIASTES 3:14 (NRSV)

The book of Ecclesiastes vigorously repudiates the claim that traditional wisdom can discern God's purpose. The sages of the book of Proverbs had claimed confidently that wisdom, beginning with "the fear of Yahweh," could chart the Two Ways and even identify the travelers along each road. But Qoheleth insisted that wisdom can do none of this, for the human mind cannot fathom God's wisdom (Eccl. 8:16–17).

Since religious people are prone to settle comfortably in their faith, supposing that they possess the answer to life's questions, it is fortunate the rabbis finally decided to include the book of Ecclesiastes in the canon. As one of the editors of Ecclesiastes wrote, "the sayings of the wise are like goads" (Eccl. 12:11). Like the prophets, they awaken people from complacent orthodoxy and stimulate the struggle for faith that can stand all the tests of doubt and despair.[29]

THE BOOK OF JOB

We turn now to the greatest monument of wisdom literature in the Old Testament, the book of Job. Through the centuries, this book has received the highest praise. Luther extravagantly said that Job is "magnificent and sublime as no other book of Scripture." Tennyson called it "the greatest poem of ancient and modern times," and Carlyle de-

---

[29]See the excellent treatment of Ecclesiastes in Robert Davidson, *The Courage to Doubt* [152], chap. 10.

clared that "there is nothing written, I think, in the Bible or out of it of equal merit." Philosophers, supposing that the book is concerned with the problem of evil or theodicy, have manifested a great interest in Job, and the playwright and poet Archibald MacLeish has attempted a modern interpretation of Job in his drama, *J.B.*[30] Indeed, the author of Job has been acclaimed as "the Shakespeare of the Old Testament."

THE IMPATIENCE OF JOB

Strangely, many who celebrate Job have only a faint understanding of what the book is about. This ignorance is clearest among those who refer to the "proverbial patience" of Job (see James 5:11). In popular thinking Job is a model of piety—a man who patiently and serenely suffered without losing his faith. But this portrait holds true only in the prologue (Job 1:1–2:13) and the epilogue (42:7–17), both of which are written in prose. The main part of the book is in poetic form, and here Job is anything but a paragon of patience. He begins by cursing the day of his birth, and his spirit gathers the fury of a tempest as he hurls his protests to God. Only at the very end, after Yahweh has rebuked him, does he repent of his wild and impatient charges, lapsing into something like the lull that follows a storm.

Before considering the relation between the prose and poetic sections of Job, we will summarize the contents of the prologue and epilogue. The narrative tells the story of Job, a man renowned for his piety and blessed with the divine favor that accompanied his righteousness. Job's sincerity, however, was suspect to one member of the Heavenly Council—"the satan." Notice that the definite article is used with *satan*, a Hebrew word that literally means "adversary." In the prologue, the satan is not represented as God's archenemy, as in later Jewish and Christian thought (where "Satan" becomes a proper name). Rather, the satan is an angel in good standing in the Heavenly Council (see Zech. 3:1ff.), whose special function is to investigate affairs on earth.

When Yahweh boasts to the Council about "my servant Job," the prosecuting angel, suspecting that Job's service is motivated by self-interest, cynically asks: "Does Job fear God for nought?" Thereupon the angel makes a wager with Yahweh that if Job's prosperity and family were taken away his faith would be destroyed. These losses do not shake Job's faith, however, for in his sorrow he patiently murmurs: "Yahweh gave, and Yahweh has taken away; blessed be the name of Yahweh." So the satan proposes a more severe test. Job is stricken with loathsome sores from head to foot, making it necessary for him to sit alone in the city refuse ground. Ignoring his wife's advice, he refuses to "sin with his lips" by cursing God. Then his three friends—Eliphaz, Bildad, and Zophar—come to comfort him in his plight. In the end, according to the epilogue, Yahweh accepts Job's prayer and restores to him twice as much as he had before. And, as in all good folktales, Job lives happily ever after.

---

[30]Archibald MacLeish, *J. B. A Play in Verse* (Cambridge, Massachusetts: Riverside Press, Sentry Edition, 1961).

THE RELATION BETWEEN THE PROSE AND POETRY

Scholars generally agree that the author of the poetic sections did not create the story that appears in the prologue and epilogue. Not only is there the difference between prose and poetry, but also the portrait of Job himself differs, as already noted. Moreover, the author of the narrative uses the name Yahweh, whereas the author of the poems uses general Hebrew terms for deity, such as *'Eloah* ("God") or *Shaddai* ("The Almighty").[31] Finally, the prose parts are written in the charming manner of a folktale, whereas the poetic sections resemble the wisdom literature in Proverbs and Ecclesiastes. It follows, then, that if we are to understand the viewpoint of the author of Job we must rely primarily on the poems rather than on the prologue and epilogue.

This does not mean, however, that the prose narrative is unrelated to the poetic meditations. In fact, the effectiveness of the poems is due largely to their being framed within the folk story. Since the story is located in Edom, the area southeast of the Dead Sea on the border of the Arabian desert, it is possible that the Job legend originated in Edomitic territory around Teman (Job 1:1; 2:11; compare Hab. 3:3). In any case, the author of the poems appropriated the old story as a literary framework within which to place the poetry. The story provides the life-situation that occasions the poetic meditations. Intending to speak to the deepest problem of every human being, the poet wisely bases this meditation upon the experience of one man whose legendary righteousness was well known in antiquity. Ezekiel mentions Job and Daniel together as legendary wise and righteous men (Ezek. 14:14, 20). Daniel (or *Dan'el*) was celebrated in Canaanite legend appearing in the Ras Shamra literature. The story of Job must have circulated orally for many years before it was written down. In short, the author took a well-known story and inserted the poetic meditation between the first part and the conclusion, substituting the poetic dialogue for the conversation between Job and his three friends. As a result, the prose and poetic sections constitute *a unified literary whole* that elaborates a single theme.

It is worth repeating that the author's distinctive theological viewpoint is found within the poetic section of the book (Job 3:1–42:6). The uniting of the prose story with the poetic cycle has created both harmony and dissonance, demanding that one reread the old story critically. Clearly the author must not be held accountable for some theological problems in the narrative, such as the satan's gamble with Yahweh over a man's life. On the other hand, some of the narrative elements, such as the restoration in the end, might be understood more deeply when seen through the courageous sufferings of Job.[32]

---

[31]Outside the prologue the name Yahweh occurs only in the headings in Job 38–42. It also occurs in Job 28:28, which many scholars regard as a later addition, and in 12:9 where the text is uncertain.

[32]In his commentary on Job [568], Norman Habel defends the unity of the book of Job on structural grounds.

THE POETIC PATTERN

Unlike other wisdom literature such as Proverbs and Ecclesiastes, the poetry in Job is devoted to a single theme, developed in the exchange between Job and his friends. Job speaks first, uttering a terrible lament over the day of his birth (Job 3). Then Eliphaz responds (Job 4–5), and Job gives his rebuttal (6–7). Next, Bildad joins the discussion (Job 8), and Job replies (9–10). The third friend, Zophar, adds his advice (Job 11), to which Job again responds (12–14). Here we have a complete cycle, during which Job has answered each of his friends. The discussion then goes back and forth in the same manner until three full rounds are completed. After a final monologue by Job (Job 29–31), Yahweh answers him out of the whirlwind and Job repents (38:1–42:6).

Clearly this is a carefully planned literary scheme. The third cycle (Job 22–27), however, has been thrown out of order by editors who tried to tone down Job's heretical utterances. Furthermore the poem on wisdom (Job 28) has been inserted into its present context by later editors. Another irregularity is the presence of a long poetic rebuke of Job by Elihu (Job 32–37), definitely an intrusion into the literary scheme. Elihu is not mentioned as one of Job's friends in either the prologue or epilogue. He has nothing to say during the three rounds of discussion, and his advice comes as an afterthought, following the statement that "the words of Job are ended" (Job 31:40). The Elihu speech was probably added by a later writer who sought to uphold orthodox Judaism even more vigorously than the three friends.

To summarize, the book of Job falls naturally into the following outline:

1.   The prose prologue (Job 1:1–2:13)
2.   Three cycles of discussion
    a.   Job's lament (Job 3)
    b.   First cycle:
        Eliphaz (Job 4–5)
          Job's answer (Job 6–7)
        Bildad (Job 8)
          Job's answer (Job 9–10)
        Zophar (Job 11)
          Job's answer (Job 12–14)
    c.   Second cycle:
        Eliphaz (Job 15)
          Job's answer (Job 16–17)
        Bildad (Job 18)
          Job's answer (Job 19)
        Zophar (Job 20)
          Job's answer (Job 21)

      d. Third cycle:[33]
         Eliphaz (Job 22)
           Job's answer (Job 23:1–24:17, 25)
         Bildad (Job 25:1–6; 26:5–14)
           Job's answer (Job 26:1–4; 27:1–12)
         Zophar (Job 24:18–24?; 27:13–23?)
           Job's answer is displaced by the chapter on wisdom (Job 28)
      e. Job's final defense (Job 29–31)
  3. Yahweh's answer from the whirlwind
      a. The first speech (Job 38–39), followed by Job's submission (40:1–5)
      b. The second speech (Job 40:6–41:34), followed by Job's repentance (42:1–6)[34]
  4. The prose epilogue (Job 42:7–17).

THE AUTHOR OF JOB

The date and authorship of the poem of Job are almost impossible to determine, for the writer gives us no hint about circumstances at the time of composition. Like Ecclesiastes, the author displays no interest in traditional motifs of Israel's faith, such as Yahweh's activity in history or the election of Israel. The hero of the book is not an Israelite, but an Edomite sheik from the land of Uz, evidently located in the southeastern part of Palestine around Edom (compare Jer. 25:19–24; Lam. 4:21), the area from which Job's friends came (Job 2:11). The locale of the book is not the city of Jerusalem, but the edge of the desert. All these facts, together with certain peculiarities of language, lead to the conjecture that the author was not an Israelite at all, but perhaps an Edomite. This hypothesis has yet to be proved, and it is equally plausible that the author was an Israelite sage who lived on the outskirts of Palestine.

    The fact that the Edomites are pictured in a favorable light seems to indicate that the oral version of the Job folktale arose in the pre-exilic period. Beginning with the sixth century B.C.E., when the Edomites encroached upon Judean territory, the Jews viewed their southern neighbors with bitter hatred (compare Obad. 1:10–14), making it hard to believe that the old story would have circulated during this period. As to the poetic section of Job, there is no general agreement on whether it should be assigned to

---

[33]Various reconstructions of the third cycle have been attempted. This outline follows the proposal of Samuel Terrien, *Interpreter's Bible*, III [23], p. 888. Notice that according to the confused state of the received text the speech of Zophar is missing, that of Bildad is curiously short, and Job inconsistently seems to endorse the view of his friends (see Job 24:18–24; 26:5–14; 27:13–23). Evidently, editors have tried to correct Job's statements by rearranging the text.

[34]The Yahweh speeches apparently have been expanded, perhaps by the addition of the poem on the ostrich (Job 39:13–18) and some of the description of Leviathan (41:12–34). Some scholars regard the descriptions of Behemoth (hippopotamus) and the Leviathan passage (Job 40:15–41:34) as later additions.

the period of the Exile or to some time in the post-exilic period. A possible clue is the relationship of the poems of Job to Second Isaiah, for there are numerous parallels of thought and language between the two writings. Did Second Isaiah depend on Job or vice versa? Scholars have tentatively concluded that Job preceded Second Isaiah, and that the book was written sometime between the time of Jeremiah and Second Isaiah.[35]

The date of Job is not critical for our interpretation of the poem: Like wisdom literature in general, it deals with a human situation that cannot be confined to any particular time. Even the Edomite locale of the story is incidental, for the writer deals with human existence as such, regardless of nationality. Not that the author is unconcerned with historical existence. The concrete portrayal of the man Job is evidence enough that the poetry deals with the stuff of daily experience, with human life as it is lived in history. Yet the author raises the historical question in a way that has universal relevance. In the last analysis, the historical question is the religious question: What is the meaning of *my* life—this solitary person who thinks and loves, remembers and hopes, lives and dies? The poet, looking into the depths of one person's existence, has exposed the *human* question. The dramatic quality of the book of Job arises from its intense concentration. And as with any great drama, the reader knows that the hero is undergoing one's own interior struggles. Job is the existing one, hence everyone.

JOB AND OTHER WISDOM LITERATURE

The author of the poetry of Job might have been acquainted with a Babylonian writing often referred to as the "Babylonian *Job*."[36] In that narrative, a man who was originally rich and influential is suddenly stricken with great illness and trouble. Bitterly he complains that his prayers and sacrifices have been in vain. Like Job, he protests his innocence, insisting that the will of the god was beyond human understanding:

> Oh that I only knew that these things are well pleasing to a god!
> What is good in one's sight is evil for a god.
> What is bad in one's own mind is good for his god.
> Who can understand the counsel of the gods in the midst of heaven?
> The plan of a god is deep waters, who can comprehend it?
> Where has befuddled mankind ever learned what a god's conduct is?

> —I WILL PRAISE THE LORD OF WISDOM,
> lines 33–38;
> compare JOB 9:1–12

[35]See Marvin H. Pope, *Job* [573], who judiciously discusses the problem and inclines to a date in the late pre-exilic period, namely, the seventh century B.C.E. Terrien, *Interpreter's Bible*, III [23], pp. 888–90, proposes a date between 580 and 540 B.C.E. Other scholars favor a later date in the fifth or fourth century B.C.E.

[36]Entitled *I Will Praise the Lord of Wisdom*, after its opening words. See Pritchard, *Ancient Near Eastern Texts* [1], pp. 434–37.

Finally, as the man verges on death, the god Marduk rewards him for his virtue and restores him to health.

Even more interesting is the Babylonian *Dialogue about Human Misery*[37] between a skeptic who, having known nothing but suffering, questions the justice of the gods, and a pious friend who advocates humble surrender to the divine will and faithful performance of religious obligations. As in the book of Job, the conversers speak in turn, beginning with the skeptic. This dialogue resembles the book of Job so strikingly, both in form and content, that one is tempted to suppose one directly influenced the other.

From Egypt come other examples of the literary form used in the book of Job. For instance, in the *Protests of the Eloquent Peasant*, the poetic discussion is framed between a prose prologue and epilogue.[38] Also, Egyptian pessimism is illustrated by the *Dispute with His Soul of One Who Is Tired of Life*, otherwise known as the *Dispute over Suicide*.[39]

There is no way to prove that the author of the book of Job was directly dependent on these and other writings of antiquity. Clearly the poet was a person of broad vision and education, influenced by currents of thought from Mesopotamia, Egypt, Arabia, Edom, and elsewhere. Certainly the writer did not borrow indiscriminately, for the poetry is stamped with the impression of a highly original mind and a creative genius. One must assume, moreover, that the poet's interpretation of human existence was influenced by the Israelite heritage, even though no special interest is shown in the traditional themes of Israel's faith.

FROM DESPAIR TO FAITH

People often assume that the purpose of the book of Job is to treat the problem of suffering (evil), or to raise the philosophical question of how absolute goodness and absolute power are reconciled in the nature of God (theodicy). But the reader who expects to find answers to these questions will be disappointed. Indeed, it is doubtful whether the author had any intention of trying to answer them. To be sure, the poet wrestles with an inescapable problem of human life: the suffering of the innocent. But the problem of suffering—and its counterpart, the question of divine justice—provides the occasion for probing a much deeper question: *What is a person's relationship to God?* This issue is first introduced in the prologue, where the satan insinuates that Job's relation to God is not one of unqualified trust "for better or for worse," but a fair-weather service in order to obtain the blessings of health, reputation, family, and long life. In the poetic sections, the nature of Job's faith is explored at a much deeper level. Finally, after the discussion has ranged through the whole realm of experience, Yahweh answers out of

---

[37]Pritchard, *op. cit.* [1], pp. 438–40.
[38]Pritchard, *op. cit.*, pp. 407–10.
[39]Pritchard, *op. cit.*, pp. 405–7.

the whirlwind. Job then submits in silence and *repents,* whereupon his life is put on a new axis. In order to understand the book of Job, one must view the poetic meditations in light of the whole composition, which reaches its climax when Yahweh speaks and Job humbly repents.

THE DIALOGUE BETWEEN JOB AND HIS FRIENDS

Underlying the friends' argument is the well-known doctrine of rewards and punishments. According to this view, virtue is rewarded with prosperity, health, and long life; conversely, wickedness is punished by poverty, sickness, and untimely death. This doctrine was applied both to Israel's national history, by the Deuteronomistic historians, and to the individual, by the book of Proverbs and later "The Wisdom of Ben Sira." The three friends claim to understand the meaning of life in terms of this doctrine of retribution.

The dialogue begins with Job's lament, one of the most poignant passages in the Bible. Like one of Jeremiah's confessions (Jer. 20:14–18), it expresses the aching misery of human existence in language of rare imaginative power. Notice that Job's death wish springs from his sense of the emptiness of life when estranged from a meaningful relation to God. He does not question God's sovereignty; rather, he laments that divine sovereignty is so completely eclipsed that life has no meaning (Job 9:11; 13:24). Job's outcry expresses the anxiety of meaningless suffering. Such suffering, more terrible than the torment of physical pain, can be assuaged only by death, "the king of terrors" (Job 18:14)—or better, by not coming through birth to consciousness. With fine poetry Job wishes that the light had never dawned upon his natal day, and that the night of his conception had never seen "the eyelids of the morning" (Job 3:9–10).

Eliphaz tries to give comfort by suggesting that the flaw lies in Job himself. At first, Eliphaz is courteous in offering his advice. All human beings have sinned, he points out; therefore Job should humbly confess his sin rather than hurl his protest at God. Since the fault really lies within Job, as the friends agree, the remedy also is within his power (see Job 11:13ff.; 22:21). When Job stubbornly insists on his innocence, the friends become vehement in their accusations. Attempting to defend God's majesty, they use every argument available to demonstrate the justice of God's ways according to the orthodox formula of rewards and punishments. They accuse Job of pride for not accepting the finite limitations of humankind. They say that if he were really honest he would admit that God had punished him more lightly than he actually deserved. Again and again they entreat him to surrender his haughty defense of his righteousness and to make supplication to the Almighty.

The poet portrays the three friends in a way that makes them more pitiable than Job, the sufferer. Though they are sincere in their stand, and at times speak eloquently of the meaning of faith, they cling desperately to their orthodoxy, sensing in Job's dangerous words a threat to their own security. Orthodoxy invariably fears the heretic, as the history of Western civilization has shown. But the author of Job champions the creative power of heresy, suggesting that faith is often most vigorous when it dares to break with theological dogmas and move to the "cutting edge" of thought or practice. The three friends were too smug in their orthodoxy, too sure of the answers to life's enigmas, too confident that God was bound by their logic. Eventually their rigidity prevented them from having real sympathy for Job. They supposed they had grasped God's wisdom. "It is not God they defend," observes a modern interpreter, "but rather their own security. Indeed, it is their pride which they uphold when they condemn Job, and it is their sin which they reveal when they pay tribute to divine sovereignty."[40]

JOB'S PROMETHEAN DEFIANCE

Job retorts that the friends speak only "windy words" that bring poor comfort in the search for life's meaning. Despite their claim that they have diagnosed his malady, they are "worthless physicians." Annoyed by their pious taunts, Job maintains his innocence and integrity with increasing passion. He admits that he might have sinned, as all people do, but insists that he is comparatively righteous and, in any case, that the punishment does not fit the crime (Job 14:1–6). At first he contents himself with cursing his miserable existence, or wishing that God would crush him instantly instead of prolonging his torture (Job 6:8–9). But soon his words break beyond all restraint. The flaw, Job cries, is not in himself but in God, who is responsible for his misery. He accuses God of appearing as a sinister enemy. Instead of caring for a mortal creature, God is like a capricious tyrant (Job 9:13–24), a savage beast (16:7, 9), a treacherous assailant (16:12–14). In a display of wild imagination, he likens himself to the mythical sea monster (Tiamat or Rahab), God's archenemy, over whom God has set a watch (Job 7:11–12). He wishes that God would let him alone long enough to swallow his saliva:

> What is man, that You make much of him,
> That You fix Your attention upon him?
> You inspect him every morning,
> Examine him every minute.
> Will You not look away from me for a while,
> Let me be, till I swallow my spittle?
>
> —JOB 7:17–19 (JPSV)

These words reflect a mood opposite to that of the psalmist who raised the same question (Ps. 8:4). If he could only escape God, Job cries, his spiritual agony would end.

In the prologue Job is a submissive man who, despite the enormity of his misfortune, does not "sin with his lips." But in the poems Job is a different person altogether. His accusations are so wildly defiant that they must have appeared heretical to any or-

---

[40]Samuel Terrien, *op. cit.* [574], p. 900. Terrien's insight have influenced this study.

thodox Jew, which undoubtedly explains why the third cycle of poems was rearranged and the Elihu speeches added. Jeremiah in his Confessions had hurled bold questions to God; but Job goes even further in challenging the Almighty. Clinging adamantly to his own integrity (Job 27:6; 31:36), Job virtually sets himself up as the judge of God. In one mood he wishes he could escape God's clutches; in another he wishes he could meet God in a fair debate—even as an equal—in order to vindicate his integrity (Job 31:37). Like Prometheus, Job is a titanic figure who doubts, rebels, and shouts defiance at God.

JOB'S PLEA FOR VINDICATION

Throughout his spiritual struggle, Job is tortured by the remoteness and hiddenness of God—the God who "hides his face" (Job 13:24). If only there were some point of contact, some common meeting ground, then Job could present his case to God and receive a fair hearing:

> Oh, that I knew where I might find him,
>   that I might come even to his dwelling!
> I would lay my case before him,
>   and fill my mouth with arguments.
> I would learn what he would answer me,
>   and understand what he would say to me.
> Would he contend with me in the greatness of his power?
>   No; but he would give heed to me.
> There an upright person could reason with him,
>   and I should be acquitted forever by my judge.
>   —JOB 23:3–7 (NRSV)

With increasing clarity Job perceives a great gulf between the Creator and the creature; indeed, one is foolish to try to span the chasm (Job 9:32–33). The wisdom of God completely surpasses the reach of human wisdom: God is the wholly Other, the transcendent One, the absolute Sovereign. By contrast a human being is an earthbound creature, subject both to the power of sin that taints human nature (Job 4:17–21; 14:4; 15:14–16; 25:4–6) and to the dominion of death (4:19; 7:6).

Although Job finds no access to God from the human side, he dares to hope that one day a reconciliation will take place. The impassable gulf will be bridged, the contradiction between divine goodness and divine power overcome. Now and then Job speaks of a mediator: an "umpire" between him and God (Job 9:33–35) or a "heavenly witness" who would speak for him even after his death (16:18–21). This might be the meaning of the well-known passage (included in the libretto to Handel's *Messiah*) in which Job affirms that his Vindicator (Hebrew: *go'el*) will defend his case and restore him to wholesome relationship with God:[41]

> But I know that my Vindicator lives,
> In the end He will testify on earth—
> This, after my skin will have been peeled off.
> But I would behold God while still in my flesh,
> I myself, not another, would behold Him;
> Would see with my own eyes:
> My heart pines within me.
>
> —JOB 19:25–27 (JPSV)

Unfortunately the Hebrew text is uncertain, especially in Job 19:26. Interpreters differ on whether the text refers to a vindication before, or after, death. What is absolutely clear is that Job rejects a post-mortem solution to his problem. To him, death is a tormenting issue precisely because it appears to be the end, beyond which there can be no satisfactory answer to the enigma of life (Job 14:7–15). Whatever lies beyond that final barrier, the existential problem is whether a person can find, in the midst of the brief interim of existence, an ultimate meaning that sanctifies birth and glorifies death.

Job's search for the meaning of life carries him to the very limit of human thought, where momentarily his vision is enlarged. His stance is not changed, however: He remains concerned primarily with his own self-vindication. His questions betray a stubborn self-sufficiency, a determination to find the meaning of life on his own terms. To the very end Job asserts his integrity. In answer to his friends' accusations, he is convinced that his life's record is unblemished:

> Far be it from me to say that you are right;
>   until I die I will not put away my integrity from me.
> I hold fast my righteousness, and will not let it go;
>   my heart does not reproach me for any of my days.
>
> —JOB 27:5–6 (NRSV)

Job's concluding defense is a long declaration of the high ethical standards by which he has lived, and a vivid portrayal of a righteous person (Job 29; 31). His final word is a ringing challenge: "Let the Almighty answer me!" (Job 31:35).

---

[41]See Definition, p. 430–431. Marvin Pope [573], pp. 134–35, compares Job's *go'el* to the personal god in Sumerian tradition who acts as a defender in the Council of the gods.

THE VOICE FROM THE WHIRLWIND

Now Yahweh—notice the shift to the personal divine name—answers Job out of the whirlwind. But what a response! One wonders whether God even heard Job. As Martin Buber remarks, "What God says does not answer the charge; it does not even touch upon it."[42] Indeed, Job is told that he is not the one to raise questions but the one to be questioned by God:

> Who is this that obscures divine plans
> > with words of ignorance?
> Gird up your loins, now, like a man;
> > I will question you, and you tell me the answers!
> > > —JOB 38:2–3 (NAB)

A series of ironical questions follow, intended to make Job's questions irrelevant. The effect is to overwhelm Job with the realization that he is a creature whose finite standards are completely inadequate for judging the Creator.

In the two divine discourses (Job 38:1–40:5 and 40:6–41:34) Yahweh's response to Job is twofold. First, God is the Creator who originated the whole cosmos in the beginning, when no human being was present. It is presumptuous, then, for a creature like Job to challenge God:

> Where were you when I founded the earth?
> > Tell me, if you have understanding.
> Who determined its size; do you know?
> > Who stretched out the measuring line for it?
> Into what were its pedestals sunk,
> > and who laid the cornerstone,
> While the morning stars sang in chorus,
> > and all the sons of God shouted for joy?
> > > —JOB 38:4–7 (NAB)

Second, God the Creator upholds the cosmos with uncontested divine power. In contrast to other Israelite traditions such as the poetry of Second Isaiah, there is no attempt to demonstrate Yahweh's sole power by appealing to a discernible plan or purpose in history. Rather the argument, strictly cosmological, is intended to show that the cosmos would return to chaos were it not for God's upholding power.

Job talks as if he could advise God on how to run the world. His sense of integrity is the basis of a presumptuous claim that God should have treated *him* better. Outraged that he cannot square his innocence with his fate, Job dares to challenge and judge his Creator. Therefore, Yahweh's answer comes in the form of a rebuke—an overwhelming

---

[42]Martin Buber, *At the Turning: Three Addresses on Judaism* (New York: Farrar, Straus, & Young, 1952), p. 61.

reminder that the first religious obligation of the creature is to acknowledge and glorify the Creator. The beginning of true wisdom is "the fear [awe] of God."

JOB'S REPENTANCE

Yahweh's speeches raise questions that Job cannot answer. He has presumed to know too much, to be more than he is. Silenced, he admits that he has no ground for arguing with God (Job 40:1–3). As his final word, he retracts his rash charges and casts himself humbly and repentantly before God:

> Therefore I have uttered what I did not understand,
>> things too wonderful for me, which I did not know . . .
> I had heard of you by the hearing of the ear,
>> but now my eye sees you;
> therefore I despise myself,
>> and repent in dust and ashes.
>> —JOB 42:3, 5–6 (NRSV)

Along with Job's confession of his sin of self-sufficiency goes a new consciousness of relationship with God—not the God of traditional religion, but "the Living God." This in itself is a form of "vindication," but not the kind that Job has asked for. The prose epilogue is appropriately placed just after Job's words of repentance, with the implication of Job's restoration to a new and meaningful relationship to God. Indeed, the epilogue now functions to endorse Job's honest-to-God struggles to have a faith that seeks understanding. Yahweh's final word is that Job should intercede for his three friends, for they "have not spoken of me what is right, as my servant Job has" (Job 42:8).

It might seem disconcerting that the book of Job does not end with a resolution of the problem of suffering. However, that expects too much of a work that grapples with the problem of evil so radically and courageously. The poet has clearly made major contributions to Israel's theological understanding. For one thing, the book of Job is a powerful challenge to any notion that calamity is to be understood as deserved punishment for human sin. That doctrine, whether stated in terms of Israel's covenant faith or in terms of wisdom's perception of the unbreakable connection between action and consequence, is inadequate in the face of the enormous suffering that too often falls, like rain, upon both the just and the unjust.

Moreover, the book of Job challenges any attempt to provide a rational theodicy (see Definition, p. 542). The mystery of suffering is left rationally unanswered, as it is finally unanswered in the Hebrew Bible as a whole. The crux of the human problem, in the perspective of Israelite faith, is not the fact of suffering, for Israel was born in suffering and was bred in affliction. Rather, the basic issue is relationship with God. Outside the "I-thou" relationship for which human beings were created, suffering can drive people to despair or to the easy solutions of popular religion. Within the relationship of faith—the relationship that finally defined Job's existence—suffering can be faced in the confidence that the times of a person's life "are in God's hand" (Ps. 31:15) and that God in a surprising manner brings good out of evil (Gen. 50:20; compare Rom. 8:28). Thus the climax of the Job poetry occurs at the very end, when a false relationship based on a conception of God received from tradition ("I had heard of you by the hearing of the ear") is converted into a relationship of personal trust and surrender—"but now my eye sees you" (Job 42:5).

DEFINITION: "THEODICY"

Theodicy—the philosophical explanation of God's ways—is an important issue in dealing with the problem of suffering and evil. Coined by the German philosopher Leibniz (1646–1716), the term is composed of the Greek words *theos* ("God") and *dike* ("justice, righteousness"). It refers to attempts to give a rational explanation of God's justice in allowing evil to exist in a world under divine control.

Beginning with ancient Greek philosophy, human reason has attempted to justify or vindicate the ways of God. If, as in Aristotle's philosophy, God is the summit of being (imagine a triangle representing "being," with God at the apex), then reason, which human beings share with the divine, should be able to achieve an intelligible and comprehensive view of the whole. The philosopher Immanuel Kant (1724–1804) stood within this tradition but, in *On the Failure of All Philosophical Attempts in Theodicy*, attempted to show the limitations of reason. Not surprisingly, this work devotes considerable space to interpreting the book of Job.

The book of Job presents a challenge to rational theodicy from the perspective of Israelite wisdom. God is neither the summit of being nor a process or entity within the phenomenal world. Rather, God is the Creator who transcends the whole creation—the One who originated and sustains all being (Aristotle's "triangle"). In this perspective, the sense of mystery is not capable of rational explanation, but is a fundamental datum of faith that responds in amazement and wonder to the holiness of God.

LATER REFLECTIONS ON WISDOM

There is more to be said about the cosmic significance of the wisdom of God that lies beyond human grasp. We have noticed that passages in the book of Proverbs portray wisdom as a distinct personality, a prophetess, a "child," or a "confidant" present with Yahweh from the foundation of the earth. In these cases, something more is involved than the mere description of abstract concepts in the concrete terms of Hebraic thought. Wisdom is, or is becoming, a distinct entity or "person" (Greek: *hypostasis*)—to use the language of later Christian metaphysical discussion of the Godhead.

This lofty conception of wisdom was not original with Israel, but it was subjected to special development in Israelite tradition. The magnificent "Hymn to Wisdom" in

Job 28 affirms that wisdom, the design of the universe, is hidden from human beings.[43] Search as one will, wisdom cannot be found in the sky, the earth, or the deep. God alone knows the path to wisdom, having established it at the time of Creation:

> God understands the way to [wisdom],
>> and he knows its place.
> For he looks to the ends of the earth,
>> and sees everything under the heavens.
> When he gave to the wind its weight,
>> and apportioned out the waters by measure;
> When he made a decree for the rain,
>> and a way for the thunderbolt;
> Then he saw it and declared it;
>> he established it, and searched it out.
>> —JOB 28:23–27 (NRSV)

Beyond the boundaries of the Hebrew Bible the cosmic significance of wisdom received even greater attention. In "The Wisdom of Ben Sira" ("Ecclesiasticus"), a deuterocanonical writing from about 50 B.C.E., wisdom is compared to the breath issuing from God's mouth—an emanation that penetrates all things:

> I came forth from the mouth of the Most High,
>> and covered the earth like a mist.
> I dwelt in the highest heavens,
>> and my throne was in a pillar of cloud.
>> —WISDOM OF BEN SIRA (ECCLESIASTICUS)
>> 24:3–4

Here too wisdom is said to have been created before all things and poured out upon all that God made (Ben Sira 1:1–20). However, wisdom found rest only in Israel, where she was associated with the Temple of Jerusalem and the Law of Moses (Ben Sira 24).

Influenced by Hellenistic views, the author of "The Wisdom of Ben Sira" takes a step beyond the personification of Wisdom found in the book of Proverbs (see pp. 521–523). Wisdom, a feminine agency (Sophia), is regarded as an intermediary, close to and almost identified with God. She provides the bridge between the Creator who transcends Creation and the God immanent within Creation, who maintains its order and renews all things:

---

[43]The poem has obviously been inserted into its present context, for it places words in Job's mouth that presuppose Yahweh's later speech reminding him of the limitations of human understanding. It might have been written by the author of Job and placed here by later editors.

For Wisdom is mobile beyond all motion,
> and she penetrates and pervades all things
> by reason of her purity.
For she is an aura of the might of God
> and a pure effusion of the glory of the Almighty;
> therefore nought that is sullied enters into her.
For she is the refulgence of eternal light,
> the spotless mirror of the power of God,
> the image of his goodness.
And she, who is one, can do all things,
> and renews everything while herself perduring.

—WISDOM OF SOLOMON 7:24–27 (NAB)

Here wisdom is regarded as a semi-independent power—the agent of God's Creation and the intermediary between God and the world. Israel's sages sensed the chasm between the world and God, between human wisdom and the wisdom of God. But their reflection also led them to understand that the gulf is spanned from God's side through the agency of the divine wisdom that dwells in the world of human experience.

CHAPTER 18

THE UNFINISHED STORY

At times the river of history flows quietly, smoothly, like the wide waters of the St. Lawrence, and at other times cascades with a thunderous roar, like Niagara Falls. This figure of speech applies to Israel's history in the period inaugurated by Cyrus' liberation of the exiles in Babylonia. Despite the troubles faced by the struggling Jewish community during the Reconstruction, the Jews of Palestine presumably enjoyed security throughout most of the period. To be sure, this inference is drawn from silence. The story of the Jewish community breaks off with the Chroniclers' account of the Reconstruction under Ezra and Nehemiah and does not resume until 1 Maccabees, a book outside the Hebrew Bible that covers events of the second century (175–132 B.C.E.).[1] Much of the interim, especially the fourth century B.C.E., is obscure or totally blank, perhaps indicating that Judah was relatively secure for a century or more after Ezra and Nehemiah. But the times were destined to change. Before the biblical period closed, the stream of Israel's history plunged and swirled along a turbulent course.

Biblical Readings: Scan the books of Jonah and Esther, then focus on the book of Daniel. For the historical background of Daniel, read the book of 1 Maccabees. Also belonging to this genre are the "little apocalypse" of Isa. 24–27 and so-called "Second Zechariah" (Zech. 9–14).

[1]See Robert Doran, "I and II Maccabees," *Books of the Bible*, II, [9] pp. 93–114; also George W. E. Nickelsburg's introduction to the same volume, "The Apocrypha: A Window into the Ancient World," pp. 3–11.

TENSIONS WITHIN JUDAISM

While the remarkable stability of the Persian empire persisted (539–333 B.C.E.), the Jewish community in Palestine was not molested by external political threats. At the height of its power, Cyrus' empire included the whole Fertile Crescent, extending beyond to the Aegean on the west, the Indus Valley on the east, the steppes beyond the Caspian Sea on the north, and Egypt on the south (see map, p. 422). Long before the rise of Alexander the Great, the Persians created a far-flung political regime that encouraged citizens to widen their horizons, to lengthen their trade arteries, and to jostle with people and ideas from other lands. Although no attempt was made to superimpose Persian religion on the nations, one can be sure that the influence of Zoroastrianism was widely felt in Judah.

Judah's problem was no longer that of being caught in the rip tide of rivalry between Mesopotamia and Egypt. More pressing was the local problem of increasing tension between Jews and Samaritans (pp. 460–461)—a situation that led to the building of the rival Samaritan temple on Mount Gerizim, probably in the middle of the fourth century B.C.E.[2]

There were also tensions within Judaism itself. Judaism was not a monolithic structure, fashioned by the great reforms of Ezra and Nehemiah. True, the reconstruction along the lines of an exclusive community, with the Temple as its center and the Torah as its constitution, was carried out with great vigor. Nehemiah's position as a Persian governor gave great prestige to his leadership, and Ezra too enjoyed the blessing of the Persian government. But other currents flowed within Judaism, reflected in the book of Psalms and other anonymous literature composed in this period. At the very time Jewish exclusivism was developing, wisdom teachers were reflecting on the meaning of life in an atmosphere of thought more international than Israelite.

THE STORY OF JONAH

The book of Jonah, part of the "The Book of the Twelve" (see chart, pp. 4–5), expresses a prophetic universalism reminiscent of Second Isaiah.[3] As is typical of literature of the post-exilic period, the author is not identified. Instead, the author's message is presented in the story of a prophet who lived in the classical period of Israelite prophecy, the days of Jeroboam II (see 2 Kings 14:25). The story is not a biographical account of what actually happened, but is told to drive home a prophetic message to the writer's generation. In the judgment of some scholars, it was written in the post-exilic period,

---

[2]See Ephraim Stern, *Material Culture of the Land of the Bible in the Persian Period 538–332 B.C.* (Jerusalem, Israel: Israel Exploration Society/Warminster, England: Aris and Phillips, 1982). In the future, one can expect more light from archaeology on these local affairs of the post–exilic community.
[3]See Katheryn P. Darr, "Jonah," in *Books of the Bible*, I [9], pp. 381–84.

no earlier than the fifth century B.C.E., and perhaps toward the end of the Persian period in the fourth century B.C.E.

The story tells how Yahweh commissioned Jonah, son of Amittai, to go to the Assyrian capital of Nineveh and proclaim that the city would be destroyed if it did not repent. No task could have been more distasteful, for the Assyrians had oppressed Israel cruelly and were bitterly detested (see Nah. 1–3). Jonah ran as fast as he could—in the opposite direction. From Joppa, he took a ship bound for Tarshish (somewhere in the western Mediterranean), whereupon Yahweh hurled a great wind upon the sea. The panic-stricken sailors cried out to their gods to find the cause of the divine anger threatening to destroy the ship. The lot fell on Jonah, who was sleeping peacefully in the hold, and he was arraigned before the captain. After some discussion, it was agreed to throw Jonah overboard. Suddenly the sea became calm, and Yahweh prepared a great fish (the narrative says nothing about a whale) to swallow Jonah. After three days and nights in the fish's belly, he was vomited onto the land.[4]

Once again Yahweh commissions Jonah to preach to Nineveh—a city so expansive, according to the writer's exaggerated description, that it took three days to walk through it. This time Jonah proclaimed God's word of judgment to the wicked city, and was shocked to find that his preaching was successful. The whole city was converted and Yahweh "repented" of the evil planned against Nineveh. Jonah was so discouraged and angry about this turn of events that he wished to die. He made a booth for himself on the outskirts of the city and sat down beneath its protective shade to observe what would happen. Yahweh commanded a gourd to grow up as an umbrella over Jonah's head, but the next day sent a worm to wilt it, exposing Jonah to the sun's merciless heat. When Jonah expressed pity for the gourd, he was rebuked for not understanding that Yahweh would show at least as much pity toward the city of Nineveh, with its many inhabitants.

Is the story intended to be humorous? Surely the author did not keep a straight face when telling how a big fish belched Jonah back in the direction from which he had come, how the Assyrian king immediately believed Jonah's preaching and commanded everyone—including livestock—to put on sackcloth, and how no sooner had Jonah settled down comfortably in the shade of a plant than Yahweh, the jokester, sent a small worm and a withering desert wind (sirocco) to undermine his comfort.

The storyteller's humor and satire, however, point directly to the theological truth of the story.[5] Jonah was troubled by a Mosaic teaching echoed in various parts of the Hebrew Bible—namely, that Yahweh is "gracious and merciful, slow to anger and

---

[4]The psalm in Jonah 2:2–9, which ostensibly Jonah recited in the fish's belly, was probably inserted by an editor. For a discussion of the function of the psalm in the final redaction, see George M. Landis, "The Kerygma of the Book of Jonah," *Interpretation*, 21 (1967), 3–31.

[5]See E. M. Good, *Irony in the Old Testament* (Philadelphia: Westminster, 1965). Millar Burrows judiciously discusses various scholarly views and gives a perceptive interpretation in "The Literary Category of the Book of Jonah," in *Translating and Understanding the Old Testament* [181], pp. 80–107.

abounding in faithfulness [Hebrew: *ḥésed*]" (Jon. 4:2; see Exod. 34:6–7). Jonah's message was based on the conviction that God's word of doom upon Assyria was inexorable, and that God would not go back on the threat. But he learned there is a wideness to God's mercy that extends beyond the bounds of what people expect or deserve. Abraham Heschel has put the matter incisively:[6]

> God's answer to Jonah, stressing the supremacy of compassion, upsets the possibility of looking for a rational coherence of God's ways with the world. History would be more intelligible if God's word were the last word, final and unambiguous like a dogma or an unconditional decree. It would be easier if God's anger became effective automatically: once wickedness had reached its full measure, punishment would destroy it. Yet beyond justice and anger lies the mystery of compassion.

At the very time when the policies of Ezra and Nehemiah were fostering narrow nationalism and doctrinaire exclusivism, the unknown prophetic author of the book of Jonah proclaimed "the mystery of [God's] compassion." Yahweh's grace cannot be programmed theologically or circumscribed by exclusive boundaries, for Yahweh is free to "be gracious unto whom I will be gracious" and "to show mercy upon whom I will show mercy" (Exod. 33:19)—even to the enemies of the people of God.

THE BOOK OF ESTHER

The story in the book of Esther reflects quite a different spirit. Part of the third section of the Hebrew Bible (the Writings; see chart, pp. 4–5), Esther is one of five festal scrolls still read on important Jewish festival days. Though it contains not a single explicit reference to God or the religious practices of Judaism, the Esther scroll came to be regarded, in later Jewish tradition, as second only to the Torah.[7] Its seemingly nonreligious character, and the fear that its nationalistic spirit would be misunderstood, led various rabbis of the Tannaitic period (first century B.C.E. to third century C.E.) to question its inclusion in the canon. But the popularity of the Feast of Purim, with which the book was associated, eventually caused such doubts to fade away.

Esther's story is placed during the reign of Ahasuerus, or Xerxes I (486–465 B.C.E.). The scene opens in Xerxes' winter palace at Susa, whose remains—once comparable with the beautiful architecture of Persepolis—have been excavated. On the seventh day of a lavish wine banquet, the king commands Queen Vashti to come and parade her well-known beauty before the assembled guests—but she refuses. Determined

---

[6]Abraham Heschel, *The Prophets* [352], pp. 486–87.

[7]The Greek Septuagint contains several additions to the Hebrew scroll that give the story a more religious tone. The translator of the Vulgate, Jerome, placed these extra passages at the very end of the story (after Esth. 10:3); in the Protestant Apocrypha they are included as "The Additions to the Book of Esther." See Katheryn P. Darr, "Esther and Additions to Esther," *Books of the Bible*, I [9], pp. 173–79.

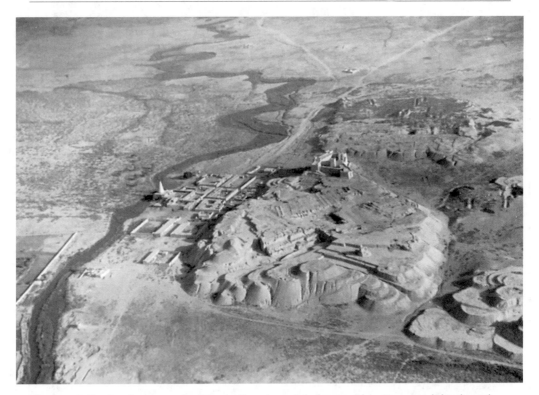

The mound of ancient Susa as seen from the air. Once the capital of ancient Elam, Susa was inhabited as early as the fourth millennium B.C.E. Under Cyrus, the city was one of several capitals of the Persian empire (see Neh. 1:1; Esth. 1:2); it later served as a winter residence for Persian kings. The mound is situated on roads leading to the sites of other former Persian capitals: Ecbatana (a summer capital) and Persepolis (the main capital). The chateau visible in the center of the picture was built by archaeologists whose work in the nineteenth century uncovered the Code of Hammurabi and the Stele of Naram-Sin. The cone-like building to the left is a mosque which, according to Moslem tradition, covers the tomb of Daniel.

to make the point that "every man should be master in his own house," the king deposes her. The vain king then commissions a search throughout the empire for the most beautiful young women, from among whom he will select a new queen. One of the candidates entered in this "beauty contest" is Esther (her Jewish name is Hadassah), the adopted daughter of Mordecai, a Jew living in Susa. Esther's loveliness is so natural that, without going through the year of beauty treatments required by other young women, she captures the king's affections. Her position as queen of Persia subsequently enables her to avert a plot to liquidate the Jewish people.

The writer subtly constructs the story of Esther around the ancient hostility between Israel and the Amalekites, which began in Moses' time (Exod. 17:16; compare Num. 24:20; Deut. 25:17–19) and was exacerbated when Saul, at Yahweh's command, subjected king Agag and his Amalekite tribesmen to the sacrificial ban (see Definition,

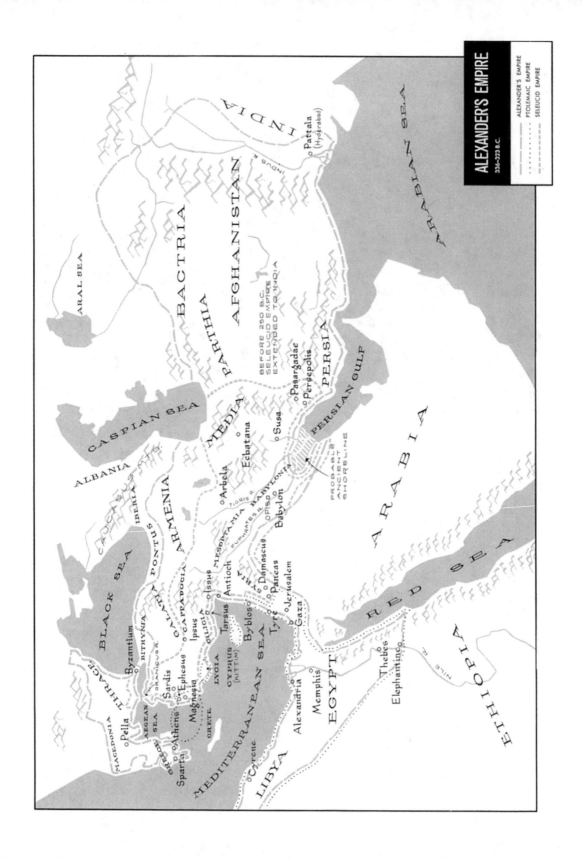

ALEXANDER'S EMPIRE
336–323 B.C.

ALEXANDER'S EMPIRE
PTOLEMAIC EMPIRE
SELEUCID EMPIRE

INDIA

ARABIAN SEA

ARAL SEA

BACTRIA

AFGHANISTAN

PARTHIA

Pattala
(Hydraotes)

INDUS R.

BEFORE 250 B.C.
SELEUCID EMPIRE
EXTENDED TO INDIA

MEDIA

PERSIA

Pasargadae

Persepolis

CASPIAN SEA

Ecbatana

Susa

PERSIAN GULF

ALBANIA

Arbela

TIGRIS R.

MESOPOTAMIA

EUPHRATES R.

Opis

Babylon

PROBABLE
ANCIENT
SHORELINE

ARABIA

CAUCASUS MTS.

IBERIA

ARMENIA

PONTUS

CAPPADOCIA

GALATIA

BITHYNIA

BLACK SEA

THRACE

Byzantium

Damascus

Antioch

Panças

ISSUS

CILICIA

Tarsus

Ipsus

LYCIA

Byblos

Tyre

Jerusalem

Gaza

RED SEA

ETHIOPIA

Sardis

Ephesus

Magnesia

AEGEAN SEA

CYPRUS
(KITTIM)

GREECE

CRETE

MEDITERRANEAN SEA

MACEDONIA

Pella

Athens

Sparta

LIBYA

Cyrene

EGYPT

Alexandria

Memphis

Thebes

Elephantine

NILE R.

p. 128). Two of the story's principal characters embody this hostility: Mordecai the Jew, regarded as a Benjaminite descendant of Kish, the father of Saul (1 Sam. 9:1), and the grand vizier Haman, identified as the son of Hammedatha "the Agagite"—a descendant of the Amalekite king defeated by Saul. Because Mordecai refused to pay him the proper courtesies, Haman plans to liquidate the Jews scattered throughout the empire. When Haman tells Xerxes that the Jews refuse to be assimilated, choosing instead to live by their own laws (Esth. 3:8), the king grants him permission to issue an edict for a wholesale massacre of Jews on the thirteenth day of the month Adar (February-March).

Mordecai persuades Esther to risk her life on behalf of her people by going to the king, even though an unsummoned visit was punishable by death. Through a remarkable series of coincidences, the tables are turned on the enemies of the Jews. The sacrificial ban (Hebrew: *ḥérem*) is executed on Haman, who ironically is hanged on the towering gallows (83 feet high) he had constructed for Mordecai. Haman's ten sons are also executed—bringing the last of the "Amalekites" to an end. Moreover, by royal decree the thirteenth of Adar was made a day on which the Jews were permitted to slaughter their persecutors throughout the empire; and on the next day—the fourteenth of Adar—the Jews in Susa got extra time to continue the bloodshed. At the end of the *ḥérem* a festival of rejoicing was to be held. This festival came to be known as Purim in

This lot (puru), four of its small sides covered with cuneiform writing, belonged to Iahali, a prominent official in the courts of two Assyrian kings, Shalmaneser III and Shamshi-Adad V.

remembrance of the lot (Hebrew: *pur*) that Haman had cast to determine the day of vengeance. The story purports not only to explain the origin of this popular festival, but also to account for its celebration on two days.

Undoubtedly there are many elements of fiction in the story—like the irrevocable royal decree that a husband should be the boss in his own house (Esth. 1:21–22) and the fabulous bribe that Haman promised to raise—the equivalent of tens of millions of United States dollars (3:9). The episodes describing how Haman was duped into proposing that Mordecai should be honored by the king (Esth. 6), and how he was trapped in an absurd situation leading to his own execution (Esth. 7), were designed to tickle Jewish humor. Nevertheless, the book of Esther might recall the event of a real threat to Jews of the Dispersion. If so, this historical novella dates from late in the Persian period, when memories of Xerxes' reign were dim and Jews were subject to persecution for refusing to be assimilated.[8] Certainly the story of the origin of Purim became popular during the later Maccabean period, when the separation of Jews from Gentiles occasioned violent persecution. And through subsequent Jewish history, Haman has symbolized the persecution of leaders who, like Hitler, carried out vicious anti-Semitic policies.

Esther is unique among the books of the Hebrew Bible in that it studiously avoids religious matters. The author makes a point of avoiding direct mention of God, as for instance in Esther 4:14, where the reference to deliverance coming "from another place" might or might not be a veiled allusion to God. This theological reticence was probably motivated by fear that the Name of God would be profaned in connection with the carefree festival of Purim when, as we learn from the Talmud (*Megillah* 7b), it was permissible to drink wine to the point of confusion. Beneath the heady worldliness of the book of Esther, however, lies the conviction that God has called this people to be separate from the world (see Esth. 3:8) and to demonstrate exclusive covenant loyalty.[9]

The vindictive spirit of the book of Esther is closer to the prophecy of Nahum than to the wide vistas of Second Isaiah or Jonah. When the vitality of its tradition was threatened by foreign domination and aggressive cultural influence, however, Israel felt compelled to narrow its loyalty. In its own way, the book of Esther expresses Elijah's prophetic words: "I have been very jealous for Yahweh God of hosts" (1 Kings 19:10). The same kind of religious jealousy, or "zealousy," is articulated in another writing composed under foreign domination: the book of Daniel. Before turning to Daniel, however, we must consider the political changes brought about by the rise of Alexander the Great.

---

[8]Some scholars believe the book of Esther reflects the persecution of Jews during the Maccabean period; for further discussion, see B. W. Anderson, *Interpreter's Bible*, III [23], pp. 825–28. For a literary approach, see Sandra B. Berg, *The Book of Esther* [609]; also Sidnie Ann White, "Esther," in *The Women's Bible Commentary* [13], pp. 124–29.

[9]The Greek translation (Septuagint) supports this interpretation.

THE HELLENISTIC ERA

The westward expansion of the Persian empire resulted in a series of clashes between Greeks and Persians in such famous battles as Marathon, Thermopylae, and Salamis. Then, toward the end of the fourth century B.C.E., the political tide was turned with the rise of one of the greatest military leaders in the history of civilization, Alexander of

Alexander the Great presents an offering to the Egyptian god Amon in this relief on a wall of the Temple of Karnak. Although Alexander himself (left, holding tray of objects) never visited Thebes, he had no difficulty appropriating the ancient Egyptian belief that a king is the son of a god. The blending of occidental and oriental culture in Hellenism is also symbolized by the Greek inscription underneath the Egyptian hieroglyphic.

Macedon (336–323 B.C.E.). Twenty years of age when his father, Philip of Macedon, was assassinated, Alexander set out on a dramatic military career in which victory followed victory—at the Granicus in Asia Minor (334 B.C.E.), Issus in upper Syria (333), Tyre and Gaza (332), and Arbela in Mesopotamia (331). From these triumphs his armies swept on through Persia and Afghanistan, and by 326 B.C.E. had reached the Indus River in present-day Pakistan. Never before had a military leader achieved such dazzling victories. It is said Alexander stood weeping on the banks of the Indus River because there were no more worlds to conquer (See Chronological Chart 10, p. 564).

A student of the philosopher Aristotle, Alexander was interested not only in military conquest, but also in spreading the fruits of Greek culture. Believing that Greek learning was superior to all other, he considered it his divine mission (for he was honored as a god) to leaven ancient civilization with Greek scholarship, art, and manners. His namesake city of Alexandria, Egypt, became a monument to the Greek way of life.

Alexander did not live to see his dream of "one world" fulfilled. He died in the year 323 B.C.E. before reaching his thirty-third birthday. His vast empire was partitioned among his generals, with Mesopotamia and Syria going to Seleucus, whose capital was Antioch, and Egypt to Ptolemy, whose capital was Alexandria. Once again, Palestine was caught in a struggle between the powers of the Fertile Crescent. Despite the rivalry between Alexander's successors, however, his policy of spreading Greek culture through the world was continued.

THE STRUGGLE FOR CULTURAL UNITY

The term "Hellenism" (from *Hellas*, the ancient name for Greece) refers to the perpetuation of the Greek ethos or culture within the countries of the Alexandrian empire. Just as visitors to the Middle East today see signs of the spread of American culture, such as "fast-food" outlets and movie houses, so in the Hellenistic period a visitor to the same area would find Greek-inspired gymnasiums and outdoor theaters. Greek dress became fashionable, especially among the well-to-do. The Hellenistic vernacular known as *koiné* Greek became the spoken language of international business and political affairs, as distinct from the classical Greek of the Age of Pericles. Hellenism represented a synthesis of "Occident" and "Orient."

The rivalry between Seleucids and Ptolemies was not just military. Both Antioch and Alexandria vied to become cultural capitals as great as Athens had been. Surpassing the "School of Antioch," the Ptolemies, patrons of the arts and sciences, built a famous museum with a huge library at Alexandria that would compare favorably with the best modern libraries. Under their sponsorship, research was carried on by a band of notable scholars, including the mathematician Euclid and the physicist Archimedes. The cultural ascendancy of Alexandria was enhanced by the city's strategic commercial relations with the Mediterranean world on the one hand, and with Arabia and the Fertile Crescent on the other.

At first, the Jews apparently did not regard Hellenism as a serious threat to their faith, for since the days of the founding of the Elephantine colony (see p. 384) Egyptian Jews had been receptive to foreign influences. Under the aegis of Ptolemy II (285–246 B.C.E.) scholars began translating Jewish scripture into *koiné* Greek, eventually producing the Septuagint version of the Hebrew Bible. Since language inevitably conditions the way one thinks about the world, it is not surprising that Greek-speaking Jews produced a number of books, such as "The Wisdom of Solomon," that reflect a Hellenistic world view.[10]

Shortly after the partition of Alexander's empire, Palestine came within the orbit of the Ptolemies. These Egyptian rulers, rather easygoing in contrast to the aggressive Seleucids, made no attempt to coerce Jews into cultural conformity. On a visit to Jerusalem, Ptolemy III (246–221 B.C.E.) is said to have deferred to Jewish custom and presented a thank-offering at the Temple. Under the mild, patronizing rule of the Ptolemies many Jews—particularly those whose education or business interests exposed them to international influence—probably welcomed Hellenism, seeing no contradiction between the new cultural fashion and their traditional faith.

THE RESISTANCE MOVEMENT

The spread of Hellenism thus inevitably revived the problem Israel had wrestled with ever since its entrance into Canaan: the relation between faith and culture. Again and again, when Israel's faith was on the verge of being sold out in the world's markets, individuals had rigorously protested in the name of the jealous God of the covenant. Like Elijah, these champions zealously upheld the covenant faith and brought about its renewal in times of degeneration. Such protests were often accompanied by the revival of Israelite nationalism, as in the case of the Deuteronomic Reform. In the Hellenistic era, the stage was set for another such revival, kindled by both conservative religious loyalty and nationalistic hope for the re-establishment of a Davidic state. The revival caught fire in a sect known as the *Hasidim* (the "loyal, or pious ones")—forerunners of the later Pharisees. While Hellenizers generally belonged to the Jewish upper classes, the Hasidim in many (but certainly not all) instances came from rural areas, where they were more or less isolated from the allurements of the outside world. Filled with great zeal for the Torah, they frowned upon fellow Jews who welcomed Hellenistic styles of thought and behavior, and they clung conservatively to the faith of their ancestors. Although this resistance movement must have started early in the Hellenistic period, it did not appear on the historical scene until a dramatic turn in political affairs ended the rule of the Ptolemies in Palestine.[11]

[10]See John J. Collins, "Wisdom of Solomon," in *Books of the Bible*, I [9], pp. 51–63.
[11]The ancient source for the history of the Maccabean period, 1–2 Maccabees, is not part of the Hebrew Bible; however, these books are included in the Roman Catholic canon and the Protestant Apocrypha (see chart, pp. 4–5). Additional material is found in important works by the first-century C.E. Jewish historian, Josephus.

THE OUTBREAK OF JEWISH PERSECUTION

Although the Seleucids of Syria repeatedly tried to gain control of the Mediterranean coastland, Palestine remained under Egypt's control during the third century B.C.E. Then, in 223 B.C.E., Antiochus III (the Great) assumed the throne in Antioch. After more than two decades of war with Egypt, he won a decisive victory over Ptolemy V in 198 B.C.E. at Panias (or Paneas), near the source of the Jordan River, thereby bringing Palestine into his political orbit.

Antiochus the Great was a vigorous apostle of Hellenism. His policies were fanatically upheld by one of his successors, Antiochus IV (175–163), known as Antiochus Epiphanes because he claimed to be god (Zeus) manifest (Greek: *theos epiphanes*). Coins bearing his image were inscribed with *theos* ("god"). His pretensions to divinity, although in line with the claims of Alexander and others, prompted him to rule with absolute authority and to stop at nothing in imposing Hellenistic culture upon his realm. People were allowed to have other gods and follow local religious customs, but the test of political loyalty was worship of Zeus—that is, submission to the absolute authority of the king or "god manifest." No policy could have been better calculated to stir up trouble in Palestine. From the very first Israel's prophets had proclaimed the "jealousy of Yahweh," who absolutely refused to have a place beside any other god and would not tolerate idolatry in any form.

Antiochus' enthusiasm for Hellenism was not the only reason for his intervention in Jewish affairs. He needed money badly, for protracted wars with the Ptolemies and the staggering expense of keeping the sprawling Seleucid kingdom under control had drained his treasury. Jewish resentment against Antiochus was first felt at the economic level, in the form of stepped-up taxes. But it rose to a riotous pitch when the most sacred office, that of the High Priest, was auctioned off to the highest bidder. This scandal involved two Jewish "Hellenizers," Jason and Menelaus (both had Greek names). Jason handsomely bribed Antiochus to depose his brother, Onias III, and to give him the high priesthood. In addition he offered to build a Greek-style gymnasium in Jerusalem in honor of Antiochus (1 Macc. 1:11–15). While Jason was attending the Greek games held at Tyre in honor of Heracles, however, Menelaus outbid his rival and was given the office. In the ensuing riots, Jason returned and banished Menelaus who, naturally enough, appealed to Antiochus for help. So Antiochus came to Jerusalem with his army, reinstated Menelaus, and punished the populace by plundering the Temple and shedding Jewish blood (2 Macc. 4–5).

This action only made matters worse. Infuriated over the Jews' stubborn defiance, and smarting under his army's defeat in an Egyptian campaign, Antiochus determined to "get tough" with the rebels. He outlawed Jewish religion and issued orders intended to "Hellenize" Jewish life: for example, mothers who circumcised their children were to be put to death, copies of the Torah were to be burned, and both observance of the Sabbath and possession of a copy of the Torah were made capital offenses. To carry out his plan to exterminate Judaism, he marched his troops into Jerusalem in 168 B.C.E. He desecrated the Temple by erecting "an abomination of desolation" (the Jewish description of an altar to Zeus) over the altar for burnt offerings, and then sacrificed swine—the most unclean animal according to Jewish law (1 Macc. 1:54; see Dan. 9:27; 11:31; 12:11; Mk. 13:14)—in the Temple court. Pagan altars were built in the land; Jews were forced to make sacrifices to Zeus and to eat swine's flesh. Moreover, Antiochus' troops policed the country to see that the royal edict was obeyed.

MACCABEAN PALESTINE

THE MACCABEAN REVOLT

During this reign of terror many Jews yielded to the king's decree. Others, refusing to surrender their faith at any cost, went to their deaths or fled into hiding. The tinder for revolution needed only a spark to ignite it.

The spark was struck one day in Modein, a town in the hill country a few miles northwest of Jerusalem. Mattathias, a local priest, flatly refused when a Syrian officer demanded that local citizens make a pagan sacrifice. Then, seeing another Jew come forward to make sacrifice, Mattathias flew into a rage and killed both the Jew and the Syrian officer. He and his five sons fled to the hills, where they gathered around themselves a band of loyal Jews. What they lacked in numbers and weapons they hoped to make up for by guerrilla tactics, and, above all, by their zeal. Mattathias' battle cry was the shout: "Let everybody who is zealous for the Torah and stands by the covenant come out after me" (1 Macc. 2:27).

On his deathbed in 166 B.C.E., the aged Mattathias commissioned his oldest son, Judas, to carry on. An exceedingly vigorous fighter, Judas was given the title "Maccabeus," often translated "Hammer" to refer to his hard-hitting blows against the enemy, both Jewish assimilationists and Syrians. Despite overwhelming odds, Judas and his band of recruits soon won a surprising victory over Antiochus' general and demanded a peace treaty. On the twenty-fifth day of Kislev (December) in 165 B.C.E. he rebuilt the altar of the Temple and restored the service of Jewish worship, thereby inaugurating the celebration of the Feast of Lights or Hanukkah ("Rededication") that Jews still celebrate today.

What began as a resistance movement eventually exploded into the Maccabean wars, carried on successively by the brothers Judas, Jonathan, and Simon. Favored by international developments, especially Rome's increasing interference in Near Eastern affairs, the zealous Maccabees achieved a century of independence, ending only when the Roman ruler, Pompey, came to Jerusalem in 63 B.C.E.

THE APOCALYPSE OF DANIEL

Shortly after the outbreak of the Maccabean wars an unknown writer composed the book of Daniel. Undoubtedly the author was one of the Hasidim, who felt revulsion for Hellenistic ways and the tyranny by which it was imposed. The book was intended to rekindle Israel's faith, in danger of being extinguished by the aggressive and severe policies of the Seleucids, and to summon the Jewish people to unyielding loyalty to the Torah. Affirming that the course of history was completely under Yahweh's control, the author summoned the Jewish people to a courageous faith that would allow them to act without fear of consequences. The book of Daniel sets forth the theology of the Maccabean revolution, and is rightly called "the Manifesto of the Hasidim."

The author's portrayal of incidents and visions supposedly experienced by Daniel during the Babylonian Exile are sometimes regarded as a prophetic preview of the centuries to come and, indeed, of the unfolding divine program. Thus the book has become a happy hunting ground for those who look for some mysterious and hidden "blueprint" of the future. Our study has already questioned this view of prophecy (see pp. 223–225). Although the Israelite prophets looked to the future, they were concerned primarily with the meaning of the present. This observation holds true for the book of Daniel even though, properly speaking, it is not classed with the Prophets in the Hebrew Bible but with the Sacred Writings, or Hagiographa (see chart, pp. 4–5). The author of Daniel spoke to people of the day in the guise of a writing predated to the Babylonian period, as though one were looking forward into the future rather than backward from the present. The release of writings under the name of some figure of ancient Jewish tradition was common practice in the late post-exilic period, when prophecy was believed to have ceased.[12] In this case, the author chose the name of Daniel—known as a traditional, pious Israelite (Ezek. 14:14, 20, 28:3) but also a legendary hero of the Ras Shamra literature.

PROPHECY AND APOCALYPTIC

The book of Daniel belongs to a special class of literature known as "apocalyptic" (from the Greek *apokalyptein,* "uncover," "reveal") of which there are many examples in the late post-exilic and early Common Era.[13] One example is the book of Revelation (Apocalypse of John) in the Christian New Testament, written in an idiom strikingly similar to—even dependent on—the book of Daniel. Apocalyptic literature abounds with bizarre visions, strange symbolism, and supernatural happenings. Written in times of persecution, it employs a kind of spiritual code that makes it a "sealed book" (Dan. 12:4) to those outside the circle of faith.

The central theme of apocalyptic literature is God's revelation concerning the end-time, the coming of the kingdom of God. Though written at a time when prophecy supposedly had ceased, the literature continues and gives new expression to the prophetic message. From the very first, Israel's faith had been oriented toward the future. History did not spin in circles, like the cycles of the seasons, nor was it governed by bind fate or chance. Rather, the story of "the people of God" was part of a great drama which, in the purpose of God, was moving toward the divine goal for Israel and the nations.

---

[12]A collection of late writings called the Pseudepigrapha (spurious writings) contains works issued under the names of various biblical characters, such as "The Assumption of Moses," "The Testament of the Twelve Patriarchs," and so on. See R. H. Charles, *Apocrypha and Pseudepigrapha of the Old Testament* [5] and James H. Charlesworth, *The Old Testament Pseudepigrapha* [7].

[13]See John J. Collins, *Daniel with an Introduction to Apocalyptic Literature* [601]; also Klaus Koch, *The Rediscovery of Apocalyptic* [597].

In the pre-exilic period, hope for the future was expressed in the popular doctrine about the "Day of Yahweh," when Yahweh would vindicate Israel by humbling its foes and raising the people to a position of prestige among the nations. The great prophets challenged this popular view. Standing in the market place, before the Temple, or in the presence of kings, they rebuked the people for their unfaithfulness to the covenant and urged them to change their lifestyle or face the consequences. They interpreted the meaning of current events—such as the rise of Assyria or the destruction of Jerusalem—in light of God's stern discipline and surprising grace. Convinced that Yahweh was about to act in the historical arena, using some historical agency, they preached to the people with great urgency to mend their ways while there was still time.

To be sure, Israel's prophets were also concerned about the end-time—the divine consummation of history. Beyond the darkness of the Day of Yahweh (compare Amos 5:20), they saw the dawn of God's new day. They proclaimed that God's kingdom was near at hand, for the King was coming both to judge and renew the people. Sometimes they portrayed the New Age in glorious colors, as a time when the political schism of the Israelite monarchy would be healed, the blessings of fertility would be poured out abundantly, nations would beat their swords into plowshares, and the wilderness would blossom like a rose. But in general the great prophets did not speculate about the New Age, for their concern was with the future as it impinged upon the present.

PROPHECY IN A NEW IDIOM

Beginning with the Exile, a gradual shift in prophetic emphasis took place. One sees this change in the prophet Ezekiel, who stood on the boundary between the old national era and emerging Judaism. Although he spoke in accents of doom and hope like his prophetic predecessors, Ezekiel's message was cast in a new style of bizarre visions and unusual symbolism. Looking beyond the Day of Judgment, he produced a diagram of the New Age, drawn according to the pattern of a priestly utopia. If the oracles found in Ezekiel 38–39 come from Ezekiel himself, he believed that this New Age would be preceded by a final assault on Jerusalem by Gog from the land of Magog. In that day, Yahweh would intervene decisively, shaking nature itself with cataclysmic power and destroying the mysterious hosts of Gog. Thus the earlier prophets' vision of the coming of a foe from the north (as in Jeremiah) was transformed into the prophecy of the final battle of history that would usher in the Kingdom of God.

The overthrow of Gog, a symbolic foe, illustrates how apocalyptic literature shifts the burden of responsibility from Israel's covenant failure to the uncanny sway of the mythical powers of chaos. Earlier prophets tried to account for suffering in the context of a covenant with Yahweh, and called Israel to repent. But apocalyptic writers realize that the sufferings of Israel, or any people, could not be explained simply on the basis of "sin." Rather, Israel is the victim of a monstrous power of evil that sweeps like an avalanche over the righteous and the wicked (see Hab. 1:6–11). Too often in history the "punishment" seems out of all proportion to the "crime," as we know from holocausts such as Hiroshima and Auschwitz. Therefore apocalyptic writers, grappling with the mystery of evil, are profoundly pessimistic about the present sorry scheme. "The present age," dominated by sinister evil powers symbolized by *satan*, the archenemy of God, is separated by a deep qualitative gulf from "the age to come," a time of freedom from moral corruption, evil oppression, and death. There is no continuity between these two ages; humanly speaking, nothing can be done to change things as they are. God must intervene to destroy the present system and, as in the Apocalypse of the New Testament, overthrow the kingdom of Satan. In the apocalyptic vision, history moves with inexorable momentum and predetermined divine plan toward the final showdown and the ultimate victory of God's Kingdom.

Outside the book of Daniel, a number of passages in the Old Testament are written in the apocalyptic idiom. One example is Zechariah 12–14.[14] Here an unknown apocalyptist portrays the last great conflict, when all nations will gather to Jerusalem for battle (compare Joel 3:9–21) and Yahweh, overthrowing resisting forces, will become Ruler over all the earth. From about the same time comes the so-called "Little Apocalypse" of Isaiah (Isa. 24–27). The writer portrays the Last Judgment, when Yahweh will judge all the nations by bringing about a cosmic catastrophe. The earth will be turned upside down and will reel to and fro like a drunkard, the sun and moon will be eclipsed, and universal chaos will reign. But in the midst of this catastrophe, Israel—"the righteous nation that keeps the truth" (Isa. 26:2)—will remain secure, its mind fixed on Yahweh. The righteous of earlier generations will be raised from the dead in order that they too can participate in the consummation of history (Isa. 26:19). Here, apparently, is the first reference in the Hebrew Bible to the resurrection of the individual. Ezekiel had spoken of the resurrection of the people (Ezek. 37), but now the doctrine is extended to a general resurrection at the end-time, in order that the wicked might not escape the final judgment and the righteous might be rewarded for their faithfulness.[15]

The apocalyptic literature, then, is prophecy in a new idiom.[16] Though with a shift in emphasis, it expresses the prophetic convictions that Yahweh is King, that the Kingdom of God is near at hand, and that individuals are called to be faithful under all circumstances. In our time, when it seems history is controlled by political, social, and

---

[14]Zechariah 9–14, often called Deutero-Zechariah, consists of prophecies usually assigned to a period much later than that of the prophet Zechariah, perhaps in the late third century B.C.E.

[15]In the Hebrew Bible, hope for the individual beyond the grave is expressed in terms of the resurrection of the body—that is, the self. The doctrine of the immortality or deathlessness of the "soul," a deathless substance imprisoned within the body, rests upon an extrabiblical view of human nature. See Oscar Cullmann, *Immortality of the Soul or Resurrection of the Dead?* London: Epworth Press, 1958.

[16]Among others Paul Hanson, *The Dawn of Apocalyptic* [502], argues that apocalyptic belongs in the prophetic tradition. Gerhard von Rad, *Theology*, II [163], pp. 301–15, *Wisdom* [552], pp. 263–83, maintains that apocalyptic is primarily related to wisdom.

environmental forces beyond our control, the message of apocalyptic writing like Daniel has spoken with new relevance.

THE KINGDOM THAT IS GOD'S

The book of Daniel is in two sections: stories about Daniel and his companions (Dan. 1–6), and Daniel's visions (Dan. 7–12).[17] Part of the book is written in Aramaic rather than Hebrew; oddly enough, the Aramaic portion overlaps the two main sections (Dan. 2:4b–7:28). Probably, the author has drawn upon and adapted earlier materials. In any case, the book in its present form is fundamentally a unity, issued during Antiochus Epiphanes' persecution (probably about 165 B.C.E.).

In placing the narratives at the time of the Babylonian Exile, the author makes several historical blunders. The book begins with a glaring historical error, for Nebuchadnezzar[18] did not take Jerusalem in the third year of King Jehoiakim (606 B.C.E.), and it was Jehoiakim's son—Jehoiachin—who was borne away to captivity (see 2 Kings 24). The author did not have the history of the Persian empire straight, as shown by confusion about the sequence of kings (see Dan. 5:31; 9:1) and telescoping of historical periods (11:2). These and other inaccuracies indicate that the writer was looking back over four centuries of history from a time when memories were blurred or distorted by popular views. After all, his purpose was not to give a correct history, after the manner of Thucydides or Herodotus, but to proclaim a religious message to embattled fellow Jews. Writing in a cryptic code that the enemy could not understand, the author cleverly disguised references to contemporary historical events and personalities in narratives and visions that allegedly originated long ago.

LOYALTY TO THE TORAH

The author of Daniel belonged to the Hasidim, whose religious faith demanded loyalty to the Torah at any cost. As you read the stories in Daniel 1–6, keep in mind that this apocalyptic tract was released at a time when even the possession of a copy of the Torah was a capital offense. One can easily guess the actual identity of the tyrants of the past—rulers who did everything in their power to destroy the faith of Daniel and his friends.

---

[17]See W. Sibley Towner, *Daniel* [607]; also "Daniel and Additions to Daniel," *Books of the Bible*, I [9]. The Greek Septuagint version of the book of Daniel is longer than the Hebrew-Aramaic text. It contains at the beginning "The Story of Susanna" and at the end "The Story of Bel and the Dragon," as well as "The Song of the Three Children" (see footnote 19). This surplus material is included in the Roman Catholic canon and in the Protestant Apocrypha as "Additions to Daniel" (see Chart pp. 4–5).

[18]This is the spelling of the Babylonian king's name in the book of Daniel; the more authentic spelling is Nebuchad*r*ezzar (see [31]).

The book tells how Daniel and his friends were brought to Nebuchadnezzar's court in Babylon and trained for royal service (Dan. 1). Even in foreign surroundings, where they were under great pressure to eat the king's sumptuous fare, the friends were faithful to the dietary regulations of the Jewish Torah. Although they ate nothing more than vegetables and water, they proved stronger than anyone else in the training program. Moreover, God gave them wisdom that put to shame all the magicians and enchanters of Babylon—indicating that in the period of Judaism "wisdom" was identified with understanding and obeying the Torah.

Daniel's wisdom far surpassed that of all the sages of Babylonia. He performed an impossible task set by the king: not just to interpret his dream, but to tell him its contents (Dan. 2). Nebuchadnezzar was so impressed by Daniel's feat that he confessed faith in Daniel's God, "a revealer of mysteries" (Dan. 2:47; here we see the meaning of apocalypse)—that is, of the ultimate divine purpose. Daniel was elevated to governor of the province of Babylon and leader of all the Babylonian sages.

The next stories treat the theme of faithfulness to Yahweh in severe circumstances. When Nebuchadnezzar commands that all his subjects must either bow down and worship a huge golden idol or be thrown into a fiery furnace (a veiled reference to the forced worship of Zeus), everyone complies except Daniel's three friends (Dan. 3). Their courageous faith reflects the spirit of the Hasidim of the Maccabean Revolution:

> If our God whom we serve is able to deliver us from the furnace of
> blazing fire and out of your hand, O king, let him deliver us. But if not, be
> it known to you, O king, that we will not serve your gods and we will not
> worship the golden statue that you have set up.
> —DANIEL 3:17–18 (NRSV)

In a fit of rage, Nebuchadnezzar (Maccabean readers would read "Antiochus Epiphanes") orders that the furnace be heated seven times hotter than usual. Once again, the astonished king is moved to faith in Israel's God when he sees the three men, joined by an angel, walking around in the furnace unsinged by the roaring fire.[19] In response, the king promotes the three Jews to a higher rank.

Another story (Dan. 4) describes Nebuchadnezzar on his palace roof, bragging about his imperial glory as he surveys the new Babylon that was—as archaeologists have confirmed—his very own creation. But even as he speaks, a voice comes from heaven to remind him who really controls history. Just as Daniel had predicted in his interpreta-

---

[19]The Greek Septuagint includes an account (after Dan. 3:23) of how Azariah (Abednego) prays to God for deliverance from the fiery furnace; when deliverance comes, the three friends sing a song of praise. This addition to the Hebrew Bible ("The Song of the Three Children," with the accompanying prayer of Azariah) is also found in the Vulgate, and in the Protestant Apocrypha under "Additions to Daniel."

Chronological Chart 10

B.C.E.	Egypt	Palestine	Mesopotamia Persia
			Artaxeres III, 358–338
			Arses, 338–336
			Darius III, 336–331
400 to 300		EMPIRE OF ALEXANDER THE GREAT, 336–323	
	Ptolemaic Kingdom	Egyptian Control	*Seleucid Kingdom* (Mesopotamia and Syria)
	Ptolemy I, 323–285		Seleucus I, 312/11–280
300 to 200	Ptolemy II, 285–246		Antiochus I, 280–261
	Ptolemy III, 246–221		Antiochus II, 261–246
		Egyptian Control	Seleucus II, 246–226
			Seleucus III, 226–223
	Ptolemy IV, 221–203		Antiochus III, 223–187
	Ptolemy V, 203–181	Syrian Conquest, 200–198	
	Ptolemy VI, 181–146		Seleucus IV, 187–175
			Antiochus IV (Epiphanes), 175–163
		MACCABEAN REVOLT, 168 (167)	Antiochus V, 163–162
200 to 100			Demetrius I, 162–150
		Judas, 166–160	Alexander Balas, 150–145
	Ptolemy VII, 146–116	Jonathan, 160–143	Demetrius II, 145–138
		Simon, 143–134	Antiochus VI, 145–141
		John Hyrcanus, 134–104	Antiochus VII, 138–129
		Conquest of Shechem, 128	
100 to C.E.	Roman Conquest, 30	Pompey captures Jerusalem, 63	Roman occupation of Syria, 63
		THE EMPIRE OF ROME	

tion of the king's dream, in which an angel chopped down a huge tree (Dan. 4:4–27), the proud king has a great fall. He goes to live with wild animals, eating grass like an ox. After seven years of such humiliation his sanity is restored, and in a hymn of praise he confesses that the kingdom, power, and glory belong to the God of Israel alone.

Next we learn that Belshazzar, supposedly Nebuchadnezzar's successor to the Babylonian throne, is holding a great banquet for a thousand nobles of his kingdom

(Dan. 5).[20] While carousing, the guests decide to drink wine out of the sacred vessels that Nebuchadnezzar had taken from the Temple in Jerusalem. But a great hush falls when "the fingers of a human hand" appear and write "on the plaster of the wall of the king's palace." When the king sees the ghostly hand write MENE, MENE, TEKEL, and PARSIN, he is overcome with fright and summons the wise men of the realm to interpret the mysterious message. When they fail, Daniel is called. He interprets the words as a message of doom upon Belshazzar's kingdom: The king has been "weighed in the balances and found wanting." Daniel is given the highest honors for his success in decoding the message, but that very night Belshazzar is slain and the kingdom passed to "Darius the Mede." (Notice that Cyrus and Cambyses actually followed Nabonidus/Belshazzar.)[21]

Darius is so pleased with Daniel that he makes him one of three presidents over the 120 satraps of his empire (Dan. 6). Fearing that Daniel will soon become the chief administrative officer of the realm, the jealous presidents and satraps persuade the king to sign an irrevocable decree that anyone, except the king himself, who petitions a god or human being during a thirty-day period will be thrown to the lions. When Daniel is found praying to his God in his upper chamber, the king reluctantly commands that he be cast into the den of lions, although he hopes that Daniel's God will deliver him because of his faithful obedience to the Torah. To the king's great joy, Daniel is found unharmed the next morning, and his accusers are thrown to the lions. Orders are issued for everyone in the empire to reverence the God of Daniel. Daniel prospers during the reign of Darius' presumed successor, Cyrus the Persian (see Chronological Chart 8, p. 372).

In all these stories, the faith of the Hasidim during the trials of the Maccabean period finds magnificent expression. Individuals must be loyal to the Torah at all costs, for God is able to deliver the faithful. God's dominion is an everlasting kingdom—in contrast to the kingdoms of the world, symbolized in a dream by a colossal statue with a head of gold (the Babylonian kingdom), chest and arms of silver (Median kingdom),

---

[20]Actually Belshazzar never reigned as king of Babylon, nor was he the son of Nebuchadnezzar (Dan. 5:2, 11). It is true, however, that when Belshazzar's father, Nabonidus, went off to Arabia to spend his final years at Teman, the empire was left temporarily in Belshazzar's control (see p. 419 and Chronological Chart 8, p. 372).

Note, however, that in a fragmentary document from Qumran, designated as "The Prayer of Nabonidus," a story similar to that of Daniel 4 is told of Nabonidus, rather than Nebuchadnezzar. This suggests an older tradition in which Nabonidus was regarded as the father of Belshazzar (see Dan. 5:2). See Frank M. Cross, *The Ancient Library of Qumran* [613], pp. 166–68.

[21]Strictly speaking, the idea of a Median kingdom *between* the Babylonian and Persian regimes is a historical inaccuracy. It is true that in the Babylonian period the Medes were a formidable power; indeed, they joined with Babylonia to overthrow Assyria (see pp. 345–346). But they never established themselves as imperial successors to the Babylonians. Rather, their leader, Astyages, was vanquished by Cyrus, who established the Persian empire as the successor to Babylonia.

abdomen of brass (Persian kingdom), legs of iron (Alexander's kingdom), and feet of iron mixed with potsherds (the Hellenistic kingdoms of Syria and Egypt); (Dan. 2:31–36). Though tyrants strut and boast, their days are numbered; their power is nothing when measured against the Ruler of history. Like "the stone cut without hands" that shattered the statue and became a great mountain, God's kingdom—with its center in the holy community of Judaism—will vanquish all earthly kingdoms and endure forever.

VISIONS OF THE END-TIME

Daniel 7–12 consists of four visions that portray the dramatic movement of historical events toward the final consummation, when God will overthrow the tyrannical rule of world powers and establish the kingdom of God on earth, as in heaven. Four successive empires are pictured—the Babylonian, Median, Persian, and Greek—each surpassing the preceding one in evil and violence. In this view, the accumulated evil of history is finally concentrated in one kingdom (the Seleucid) and in one depraved king (Antiochus Epiphanes). The increase in evil means that history was hastening toward the final showdown.

In the first vision (Dan. 7), Daniel sees four beasts arising out of the "great sea"— that is, the watery chaos, the mythical source of powers hostile to God's creation. The last of these beasts is the worst: "terrible and dreadful and exceeding strong," and with ten horns. An "interpretive angel" explains that these beasts are four successive empires (Dan. 7:15–17): the Babylonian (a lion with eagle's wings), the Median (a bear with three ribs in its mouth), the Persian (a leopard with four wings and four heads), and the Hellenistic or Seleucid (the ten horns refer to Seleucid kings, and the little horn "speaking great things" is Antiochus Epiphanes).[22] "The Ancient of Days," presiding over the Heavenly Council at the Last Judgment, sentences the fourth kingdom to destruction; the other three, whose rule has not been so monstrously evil, are deprived of their dominion and permitted to survive for a time. Then, with the clouds of heaven, in contrast to the beasts' origin from the depths of the sea, comes "one like a human being"— that is, a figure with a human rather than a beastly countenance. The angel interprets this heavenly figure to symbolize the holy community of Israel—"the saints of the Most High." Instead of a transient kingdom, they will be given an everlasting and universal dominion that is to be inaugurated after "a time, two times, and a half a time" of the little horn—a cryptic reference to the three and a half years when Antiochus Epiphanes persecuted the Jews (168–165 B.C.E.).

---

[22] In a passage from the Sibylline Oracles (3:381–400), written about 140 B.C.E., the expression "ten horns" refers to the ten kings who preceded Antiochus Epiphanes. As a matter of historical fact, Antiochus was the seventh in the series of Seleucid kings after Alexander's death.

Daniel 7 introduces an important motif of apocalyptic literature. The original Aramaic, *bar 'anash*, literally means "a son of man." Elsewhere in the Old Testament a comparable expression is sometimes used to refer to "a human being." For example, the King James Version translates Psalm 8:4: "What is man, that thou art mindful of him, and the son of man, that thou visitest him?"

The Hebrew expression *ben 'adam*, translated "son of man," really means a mortal person, for "son" is an idiomatic way of referring to a member of a class. Examples of this idiomatic usage are "sons of the prophets," or a prophetic company (Hebrew: *bené han-nebe 'im*); and "sons of God," or the angels in Yahweh's Heavenly Council (Hebrew: *bené ha-'elohim*; see Job 1:6). The book of Ezekiel frequently uses the same expression, with special emphasis, to highlight the mortal weakness and finite humanity of the prophet in contrast to the holy, majestic deity of Yahweh.

The expression has a special linguistic function in the context of Daniel's apocalyptic vision. First, we are dealing with a similitude: "one like" a human being, in contrast to the oppressive empires that are like beasts. Second, this human-like figure is a heavenly being, one who comes transcendently "with the clouds of heaven," in contrast to the beasts who emerge from the sea, the locus of the powers of chaos. It would be erroneous to literalize the symbolism and think of the offspring ("son") of a man or even a "human one."

In an apocalyptic writing known as "The Book of Enoch," based on a tradition reaching back into a time before the Common Era (first century B.C.E.), there are references to a figure of the end-time, "the Son of Man," who comes to establish God's kingdom (Enoch 46:1; 48:2–10). In the Jewish apocalypse called II Esdras (or Fourth Ezra/Fourth Esdras), found in the Apocrypha and dating from the close of the first century B.C.E., a vision is described in which Ezra sees emerging out of the sea "as it were the likeness of a man [human being]" who flies on the clouds of heaven (Esdras 13). This figure is understood to be the heavenly agent of God's judgment in the last days. "Son of Man" or "The Heavenly Being" is often used in this messianic sense in the gospels of the New Testament (as Mark 8:31).[23]

The same theme is developed in the second vision (Dan. 8), interpreted by Gabriel, patron angel of the Jewish people (compare Dan. 12:1). A two-horned ram (the Medo-Persian empire) is charging to the west, north, and south. He holds undisputed sway until a he-goat (the Greek empire), with a conspicuous horn between his eyes (Alexander the Great), engages him in battle and decisively defeats him. But when the he-goat is strong, the "great horn" is broken (the death of Alexander), and in its place come up four horns (the partition of Alexander's empire into four kingdoms). Out of one of these horns (the Seleucid kingdom) sprouts "a little horn" (Antiochus

---

[23]For the Enoch literature, see the Apocrypha and Pseudepigrapha editions by R. H. Charles [5] and James Charlesworth [7].

Epiphanes), whose power extends southward and eastward. In his pride, this horn exalts himself against the heavenly host, and challenges the authority of the Prince of the host (God) by defiling the Temple, casting truth to the ground, and interrupting the daily sacrifice. The celestial being announces that the power of the boastful tyrant will be broken, although "by no human hand." The daily sacrifice will be resumed after 2,300 evenings and mornings—that is, the three years and two months from Antiochus' proscription of Jewish worship in 168 B.C.E. to Judas' rededication of the Temple in 165 B.C.E. Daniel is reminded that "the vision was for the time of the end," for it would be fulfilled "many days hence."

In the third vision, however, Daniel comes to see that the "many days" are not too far away, for according to the divine timetable, the Kingdom of God is at hand (Dan. 9). Daniel is puzzled by Jeremiah's prophecy that seventy years must pass before the desolation of Jerusalem will end (Jer. 25:11–12; 29:10), and he prays to God for light on this mystery. His prayer, like that of Ezra (Neh. 9), gratefully acknowledges Yahweh's great deeds of mercy, beginning with the deliverance from Egypt, and humbly confesses Israel's persistent covenant disloyalty for which great calamity has fallen on the people. His petition for speedy relief is not based on Israel's faithfulness to the covenant, but solely on Yahweh's steadfast and gracious goodness:

> We do not present our supplications before you on the ground of righteousness, but on the ground of your great mercies. O Lord, hear; O Lord, forgive; O Lord, listen and act and do not delay!
> —DANIEL 9:18–19 (NRSV)

Thus Judaism, even when it concentrated on obedience to the Torah, affirmed that in the last analysis Israel had no ground for boasting—except God's incalculable mercy.

While Daniel is praying, confessing his sin and the sin of his people Israel, the angel Gabriel comes to interpret the seventy years (Dan. 9:20–27). In the prophecy of Jeremiah the figure seventy apparently referred to the full span of a human life; but here it comes to mean "seventy weeks of years" (490 years), at the end of which the Jews will have atoned for their sins and the desolation of Jerusalem will have ended. This period falls into three parts: seven weeks, sixty-two weeks, and one week. The first seven weeks (49 years) apparently extended from King Zedekiah to Joshua the High Priest (587–538 B.C.E.), who was in office in the days of Cyrus; the sixty-two weeks (435 years) extended from the return from Exile to the assassination of the High Priest Onias III (538–171 B.C.E.); and the last week covers the reign of Antiochus Epiphanes. During the first half of this week (171–168 B.C.E.), Antiochus showed some lenience toward the Jews; but during the last half (168–164 B.C.E.), in which the author of Daniel lived, Antiochus attempted to abolish Jewish religion and desecrated the Temple by installing an altar to Zeus of Olympus. In Hebrew, this altar was ascribed to the "Lord of heaven" (Hebrew: *Baal shamáyim*), which came to be, by a malicious pun, "the abomination of desolation" (Hebrew: *shiqqutz shomem*; see Dan. 11:31; 12:11).

According to this view, history follows a prearranged timetable in which the length of each period is set by divine decree. Once we realize that the author was not really looking forward from the time of the Babylonian Exile, but looking backward over the ages from the Maccabean period, this mathematical calculation, though mechanical, takes on religious meaning. The writer believed that people were living in the "last days," in the final moments of the second half of the last week of years. The days of Antiochus were numbered, for he had insulted God. The clock was beginning to strike midnight. The time was near when God, through a mighty act, would win the decisive victory, ending Israel's long years of desolation and introducing the Messianic Age.[24]

The author's backward glance from the Maccabean period also explains why historical knowledge about the period before the rise of Alexander is blurred, and why historical information becomes more exact as one approaches the time of writing. An example is the final vision (Dan. 10–12): Though dated in the third year of Cyrus of Persia (Dan. 10:1), it sketches the Persian period in just one verse (Dan. 11:2)— enough space, however, to make a major historical blunder, for ten Persian kings (not the stated three) succeeded Cyrus. The author knows of Alexander's triumph over Persia (Dan. 11:3; compare 8:6–8, 18–21; 10:20), and that because he had no heir his empire was divided (11:4; compare 8:8, 22).

From this point on, the author's historical memory improves. Ptolemy I (323–285), the king of the south, will establish a strong kingdom, but even stronger will be that of Seleucus I (312/11–280 B.C.E.), the king of the north, whose kingdom will include Syria and Mesopotamia (Dan. 11:5). Ptolemy II (285–246 B.C.E.) will make an alliance with the Seleucid kingdom by marrying his daughter, Bernice, to Antiochus II (247 B.C.E.). This will anger Laodice, Antiochus' former wife, and she will conspire to have the couple and their son murdered (Dan. 11:6). To avenge his sister Bernice, Ptolemy III (246–221 B.C.E.) will march triumphantly against Seleucus II (246–226 B.C.E.), the son of Laodice; but after a few years the latter will counterattack and a truce will be declared (Dan. 11:7–9).

The seer's vision then focuses on the shift in the balance of power under two sons of Seleucus II—Seleucus III (226–223 B.C.E.) and especially Antiochus III, the Great (223–187 B.C.E.). The latter will be successful at first in a war against Egypt (Dan. 11:10), but the king of the south, Ptolemy IV (221–203 B.C.E.), will successfully counterattack at Raphia in 217 (Dan. 11:11–12). Then, in the seesaw struggle, Antiochus will overrun Palestine by defeating the Egyptians at Gaza in 201 B.C.E. (Dan. 11:13–15) and Panias in 198 (Dan. 11:16). Hoping to secure his grip on Egypt, Antiochus will marry his daughter Cleopatra to Ptolemy V, but this move will not work to

---

[24]This chronological calculation has led to many attempts, ancient and modern, to predict the date of the coming of God's kingdom (compare Acts 1:7).

his political advantage (Dan. 11:17). When he attempts to conquer "the coastlands" (Asia Minor and Greece), he will be defeated by a Roman general at Magnesia in 190 B.C.E., and on his return to his own country will die as a result of his plunder of a temple (Dan. 11:18–19). Seleucus IV (187–175 B.C.E.) will be assassinated by the very tax collector he has appointed to raise money for the reparations owed to the Romans after the battle of Magnesia (Dan. 11:20).

The rest of Daniel 11 deals with prophecies concerning Antiochus IV Epiphanes, "a contemptible person." Pushing aside his brother, who legally had title to the throne (Dan. 11:21), he will plot the assassination of "the prince of the covenant," the High Priest Onias III, in 171 B.C.E. (Dan. 11:22), and plunder the riches of the provinces (11:23–24). After his first campaign against Egypt in 170 B.C.E., he will return in triumph to Palestine and set his heart against "the holy covenant," thus initiating his anti-Jewish pogrom (Dan. 11:25–28). His second campaign against Egypt (168 B.C.E.) will be frustrated by the interference of "ships of Kittim" (the Romans), and on his return he will vent his spleen on the Jews, sparing only those who desert their faith (Dan. 11:29–30). At this time, the lines will be drawn between the Jews who betray the covenant, and the Hasidim who stand firm under persecution, receiving "a little help" through the brave leadership of Judas Maccabeus (Dan. 11:32–35). Antiochus will magnify himself above every god by taking the title Epiphanes, and will honor the Olympian Zeus, a Greek deity strange even to his own Syrian countrymen (Dan. 11:36–39). Finally, "at the time of the end," Antiochus will attack the king of Egypt and win a great victory, but on his way home will die "by no human hand" while encamped in Palestine between Jerusalem and the Mediterranean Sea (Dan. 11:40–45; compare 8:25).

Antiochus IV in profile according to a coin bearing his image. The reverse side carries the Greek words: Basileos Antiochou, Theou Epiphanous, Nikephorou—"(coinage) of King Antiochus, God Manifest, Bearer of Victory." The king represents himself as Zeus, seated on a throne, holding in his left hand a royal staff and in his right the figure of the goddess of victory, Nike, who holds the laurel wreath in her hand, the symbol of victory.

Although Daniel's historical summary is cast in the form of a vision of events to come, written down in God's "book of truth" (Dan. 10:21), very little of it is prediction. Rather, it is a resumé of past events. The only example of pure prediction is the prophecy concerning the death of Antiochus (Dan. 11:40–45), an event that had not yet transpired in the author's time. As it turned out, moreover, Antiochus did not die near Jerusalem (the setting of the final apocalyptic battle), but in Persia in 163 B.C.E.[25] The author's haziness about this event supports the view that the book of Daniel was written before the death of Antiochus in the East, yet after the outbreak of the Maccabean revolution—between 168 and 164 B.C.E.

Thus the story of the past is told so that persecuted Jews can see their sufferings in the perspective of God's historical purpose. The author insists that none of these events happened by accident. Like a master chess player, God knew in advance every play that would be made and let the game run its course. Even the tyranny of Antiochus was part of God's preordained plan: "He shall prosper until the period of wrath is completed, for what is determined shall be done" (Dan. 11:36). This extreme emphasis on God's absolute sway in human affairs was not intended to encourage complacency, any more than the Marxist vision of the inevitable movement of history toward the classless utopia is meant to discourage revolutionary activity. On the contrary, the confidence that history moves inevitably and by prearranged plan toward the Kingdom of God fired the zeal of a small band of Jews, enabling them to act and hope when everything seemed against them. "The people who are loyal to their God shall stand firm and take action" (Dan. 11:32). If God was for them, what did it matter how many battalions were against them? And who cared how many battles were lost, so long as God would soon give the final victory? Daniel expresses the dynamic faith of a courageous group who lived and died for the glory of God, confident that their martyrdom would "cleanse" and "refine" the community and somehow prepare for the coming of God's Kingdom (Dan. 11:35).[26]

THE MESSIANIC HOPE

The book of Daniel contains no mention of the Messiah ("Anointed One") who, in the last days, would appear as God's agent, either to execute judgment on Israel's oppressors or to rule over God's people in righteousness. To be sure, the expression "one like a human being [son of man]" would soon be interpreted to mean a heavenly ruler whom God would send to shatter the powers of evil and to inaugurate the kingdom.[27] In

---

[25]1 Maccabees 6:1–16; Josephus, *Antiquities*, xii, 9, 1.

[26]This view of martyrdom, which came to have great importance in Jewish circles and in later Christian history, is stressed in 2 Maccabees 6–7, a book later than 1 Maccabees, probably dating from about the dawn of the Common Era. See Robert Doran, "I and II Maccabees," [9], II, pp. 104–14.

[27]See Definition, p. 567. For further discussion, see Sigmund Mowinckel, *He That Cometh*, trans. by G. W. Anderson (New York: Abingdon, 1956), chap. 10.

Daniel 7, however, the heavenly figure symbolizes the covenant community, "the people of the holy ones of the Most High," as the dream interpretation makes clear. Still, in a broad sense this is a messianic passage, for the Hasidim are the standard-bearers for God's Kingdom. They live and die in anticipation of the Messianic Age, which God will inaugurate with power and glory at the end of the times. Indeed, one passage anticipates the dawn of the new age in three and a half years (Dan. 12:7), the time of the cessation of the regular sacrifices in the Temple (Dan. 9:27; compare 7:25).[28]

According to one tradition found in the Hebrew Bible and later literature, the Messiah would be of David's lineage and would restore David's kingdom (see Isa. 9:1–7; 11:1–9). This political messianism filled the air during Jesus' lifetime, and is expressed in a psalm from the late Maccabean period:[29]

> Behold, O Lord, and raise up unto them their king, the son of David,
> At the time in which thou seest, O God, that he may reign over Israel, thy
> servant.
> And gird him with strength, that he may shatter unrighteous rulers,
> And that he may purge Jerusalem from nations that trample her down to
> destruction.
>
> —PSALMS OF SOLOMON 15:21–25

In the book of Daniel, however, the coming Kingdom is not portrayed in terms of political realities such as inspired the Messianic movement in Zerubbabel's time (see pp. 460–461). Rather, the consummation is a divine victory, transcending and transfiguring the ordinary realities of history. Daniel's last vision leaves the sphere of politics, where the Seleucids and the Ptolemies vie for power, and moves to a higher plane (Dan. 12). The goal of history is *God's* Kingdom—not a human kingdom of any kind. It will come solely by God's miraculous power and in God's good time. According to Daniel, the Kingdom will be preceded by "a time of trouble"—the birth pangs of the Messianic Age (Dan. 12:1). But the faithful whose names are written in "the book" will be rescued, and many who have already died will be raised up in order that they too can share in the grand fulfillment of the historical drama:

> Many of those who sleep in the dust of the earth shall awake, some to
> everlasting life, and some to shame and everlasting contempt. Those who
> are wise [the Hasidim] shall shine like the brightness of the sky, and those
> who lead many to righteousness, like the stars forever and ever.
>
> —DANIEL 12:2–3 (NRSV)

This doctrine of the future life, one of the great contributions of apocalyptic literature, was late in coming. Unlike the Greek doctrine of the immortality of the soul, it is

---

[28]Later editors extended this time to 1,290 days (Dan. 12:11) and to 1,335 days (12:12).
[29]The Psalms of Solomon, found in a body of literature known as the Pseudepigrapha, date from about 50 B.C.E.

infused with the Israelite sense of history. According to Israel's portrayal of the eschatological future, the individual cannot experience the fullness of life without participating in the redeemed community, the Kingdom of God. Therefore the resurrection of the body (that is, the self) is portrayed as occurring in the end-time, at the very consummation of the historical drama, when God's victory over the powers of evil is complete. In one sense, the apocalyptic literature is other-worldly, for it proclaims that the historical drama points beyond the tragic strife of this world to God's ultimate kingdom. But in another equally important sense, it is profoundly this-worldly, for the sufferings of this world are to be overcome in history's grand finale. Unlike some forms of Eastern mysticism, it does not encourage a repudiation of this world, but appeals to the faithful to face present suffering in the confidence that the whole historical drama, from beginning to end, is embraced within God's sovereign purpose.

BEYOND THE OLD TESTAMENT

With the book of Daniel (about 168 B.C.E.) the biblical period comes to a close chronologically—if we limit attention to books included in the Hebrew Bible.[30] In the Old Testament, Israel's life-story ends on a note of intense expectation that soon the time will come of which the prophets have spoken: the dawning of God's Kingdom.[31] But the apocalyptic vision of the speedy arrival of the Messianic Age—a vision that stirred faithful Jews to resist the tyranny of Antiochus Epiphanes—did not become a historical reality in the years that followed. Contrary to Daniel's dating of the time of the Kingdom, history moved on in its usual course. To be sure, the Maccabean revolution was successful for a time. But the Maccabees' successors lost the religious zeal for revolution, turning to political games of intrigue and deceit that rewarded the successful schemer with the office of high priesthood. Finally, after about a century of Jewish independence, the Jews were subjected to a world power not envisioned in Daniel's scheme: the Roman empire. This phase of Israel's story lies beyond our purview.

PARTY MOVEMENTS WITHIN JUDAISM

In the period between the outbreak of the Maccabean revolution and the dawn of the Common Era, the religious struggle continued. There were external sources of conflict, such as the rivalry with the Samaritans that exploded in 128 B.C.E. when one of the Maccabees, John Hyrcanus, conquered Shechem. But the struggle also went on in the

---

[30]Other books outside the Hebrew Bible, such as 1–2 Maccabees and "The Wisdom of Solomon," come from a slightly later period.

[31]Canonically, the Hebrew Bible ends with 1–2 Chronicles, the last book in the Writings. The Christian Old Testament ends on a note of prophetic expectation with the books of Haggai, Zechariah, and Malachi. See chart, pp. 4–5.

very heart of Judaism. All devout Jews subscribed to what is central in the book of Daniel: the authority of the Torah, the sacrificial services of the Temple, and the promise that God's Kingdom would have its center in the Holy Land. Party differences arose, however, over how devout Jews should interpret these tenets of faith in daily life.

One group, known as the Sadducees, advocated a policy of tolerance and compromise—an understandable attitude, since they came from families of priestly prestige and political influence. They claimed to be strict devotees of the written Torah (the Pentateuch)—so strict that they would not accept the body of oral Torah that gathered around it. They rejected the doctrine of the resurrection because they found no support for it in the Torah (see Mk. 12:18). For the same reason they opposed other aspects of apocalyptic thought, such as the belief in angels and demons, and predictions about the end-time. Their view of history was essentially that of the Priestly version of the Pentateuch (pp. 407–416), according to which the divine plan was realized in the establishment of a theocratic community, designed according to the pattern revealed to Moses. Instead of looking to the future, the Sadducees sought to maintain this holy community by strict fidelity to the written Torah, especially the regulations dealing with sacrifice and priestly prerogative. Since they were interested in the priestly status quo, they advocated a policy of collaboration with foreign rulers and even a certain degree of compromise with Hellenism, provided the Temple services were permitted to continue.

On the other side were various religious groups who stood in the tradition of the Hasidim, those whose zeal for the Torah brought them into conflict with Hellenistic culture and with all Jews who wanted to collaborate with foreign rulers. Like the author of the book of Daniel, they believed that the present age was under the dominion of wicked powers and anticipated the time when God would intervene and establish the Kingdom of God on earth, thus restoring the Holy Land to the Jewish people. Out of the circles of the Hasidim there eventually arose a party known as the Pharisees. Like Daniel and his friends, they practiced strict devotion to the customs that separated Jews from Gentiles: dietary rules; circumcision; fasting; and prayer. Though in one sense stricter than the Sadducees, in another sense the Pharisees were more liberal, for they accepted the teachings found in books outside the Torah, such as the Prophets. Moreover, they believed that Moses had not only promulgated the written Torah but also a body of oral Torah that interpreted the meaning of what was written. This oral Torah, called "The Tradition of the Elders," was eventually codified in the Mishnah (about 200 C.E.) and finally came out in an expanded edition known as the Talmud.[32]

The Pharisees, then, were able to adapt the rules and teachings of the written Torah to the changing conditions of life, and even to accept doctrines not found in it, like the resurrection of the body and the apocalyptic Kingdom. Most Pharisees opposed

---

[32]See H. Danby, *The Mishnah,* translated from the Hebrew with introduction and brief explanatory notes (Oxford: Clarendon Press, 1954). The Talmud is a large library; see Jacob Neusner, *Invitation to the Talmud* [587].

fanatical revolt against foreign rulers. They preferred to maintain the strictest separation from the contaminations of the world, waiting for the time when God would establish the Kingdom. Closely related to the Pharisees was another group, known as the Zealots, whose views on political action were more in line with the Maccabean revolutionaries.

With the discovery of the "Dead Sea Scrolls" in the mid-twentieth century, attention was focused on an ancient community of Essenes (or a closely related sect), whose headquarters were located toward the northwest end of the Dead Sea near the mouth of the Wadi Qumran (see Insert 18-1). The fascinating story of this community would carry our study far afield. Suffice it to say that this group, regarding itself as the community of "the new covenant," separated itself from the world in order to practice monastic devotion to the Torah and to await the end of the historical drama, when God would overthrow the powers of evil and inaugurate the divine Kingdom. In many respects these "covenanters" resembled the Hasidim of the early Maccabean period. Their zeal for the Torah and their hope for the apocalyptic Kingdom led them to revive the ancient conception of "holy war," including the sacrificial ban (Hebrew: *ḥérem*) by

Cave Number Four is located in a cliff overlooking the Wadi Qumran. In this cave many fragments of manuscripts that belonged to the library of the monastic community of the ancient Essenes were found. Some eleven caves in the area have yielded materials, including the famous Isaiah Scroll.

which the land would be purified of the contaminations of pagan culture in "the war of the sons of light against the sons of darkness." There are close affinities, and at the same time significant differences, between the eschatological beliefs of this Jewish sect and those of the early Christian community.[33]

It is evident, then, that many currents were moving through Judaism in the two centuries preceding the Common Era. The book of Daniel is only one sample of the great amount of religious literature produced in this creative period. Some of this literature is well known, such as the writings found in the Apocrypha and the Pseudepigrapha. The manuscripts of Qumran include not only portions of the Hebrew Bible and manuals for the sect, but also a whole library whose fragmentary remains were found in caves near the community center.[34]

But of all the literature coming from this period—wisdom literature, history, novellas, psalms, interpretation of Torah—the most popular was the apocalypse. In troubled times, when faith was severely tested, devout Jews hoped for the coming Kingdom. And since it came to be believed that "the exact succession of the prophets" ended in the time of Ezra,[35] and even that prophecy had ceased altogether (see 1 Macc. 9:27), anonymous writers couched their prophecy in the form of a revelation ("apocalypse") given to a figure of ancient times, like Adam, Enoch, Noah, or Moses, or to a figure who lived in the centuries just before the cessation of prophecy, like Jeremiah, Baruch, Daniel, or Ezra. The apocalyptic hope for the Kingdom was one of the major influences on the early Jewish sect known as "Christians."

THE CANON OF ISRAEL'S SCRIPTURES

Devotion to the Torah was clearly the unifying force of Judaism, yet within this community was great richness and diversity. Studies of the Qumran community show that "the tree whose trunk was the Old Testament had then many branches which later were lopped off or withered away."[36] This occurred during the terrible ordeals of Judaism in the Roman period, especially the smashing blow struck against Jewish nationalism by the war of 66–70 C.E., when the Temple was destroyed, never to stand again, and Jews were scattered or reduced to an insignificant remnant in Palestine. The Sadducees, whose religion was inseparably bound to the Temple, were shorn of their *raison d'être* by this catastrophe. Many of the covenanters of Qumran perished in the conflict, and their headquarters was destroyed. Only the Pharisees, with their flexible interpretation

---

[33]See Frank M. Cross, Jr., *The Ancient Library of Qumran* [613], pp. 216–30; also "The Early History of the Apocalyptic Community at Qumran," *Canaanite Myth and Hebrew Epic* [129], pp. 326–42.

[34]Thanks to this archaeological discovery, we now have extensive manuscripts of the Hebrew Bible, such as the famous Isaiah Scroll. Before this discovery, with the exception of the small Nash Papyrus (first century C.E.) which contains a few verses of Exodus 20 and Deuteronomy 5–6, the oldest manuscripts of the Hebrew Bible came from the ninth century C.E. and later. Every book of the Hebrew Bible except Esther is represented, at least in fragmentary form, in the Qumran library.

[35]Josephus, *Against Apion*, i, 8.

[36]Millar Burrows, *The Dead Sea Scrolls* (New York: Viking Press, 1955), p. 345.

of the written Torah and their support of synagogue worship, were able to survive and place their stamp on subsequent Judaism.

The crisis of Judaism resulting from the fall of Jerusalem and the destruction of the second Temple raised in a new way the question of the identity of the people Israel. As our study makes clear, this question had persisted since the formation of the community out of the historical oblivion of slavery in Egypt. In times of social change the question became inescapable; indeed, much of the prophetic message should be understood as response in various theological accents to new situations. In times of political catastrophe, especially the first fall of Jerusalem in 587 B.C.E. and the uprooting of

Jewish catacombs at Beth She'arim (Sheikh Ibreiq), located not far from modern Haifa. After the fall of Jerusalem in 70 C.E., and especially from the second to the fourth centuries, a loyal group of Jews lived here. Tombs were cut into solid rock and arranged in stories. Of all the symbols carved in the interior, the menorah, or seven-branched candlestick, was the most important and apparently had a significance to Jews comparable to the cross in Christian catacombs.

many of the people from their homeland, the "identity crisis" was met by priests who demonstrated the deep continuity of the divine purpose, by prophets who announced the "new thing" (Isa. 43:19) that Yahweh was about to perform, and by sages who perceived the congruity between Wisdom and Torah.

Our study has also shown that these crises, which called into question both the identity and vocation of Israel and the identity and faithfulness of Yahweh, were not faced in a vacuum. The present was understood by appealing to, and reinterpreting, the heritage received from the past. God spoke to the people "in many and various ways" (Heb. 1:1) as inspired spokespersons kept alive and contemporized the sacred tradition, whether in oral or written form, or both.

The new crisis that came upon Judaism in the centuries just before and after the dawn of the Common Era provided great impetus for the "stabilization" and "fixation" of the whole tradition. The loss of Judaism's vital center—the Temple in the Holy Land—posed the threat that the tradition would be distorted or weakened by various cultural influences and that the scattered Jews would lose their sense of identity and vocation. The result was an increasing concern for "scripture" (what is written) and "canon" (the writings that are normative for faith and practice).

DEFINITION: "CANONICAL CRITICISM"

In connection with the discussion of Ezra as the architect of Judaism (see Chapter 15), we touched briefly on the question of *canon* (literally "measuring line" or "rule"), referring to sacred writings that conform to the "rule" of a community's faith and practice. This narrow definition, however, hardly does justice to the biblical canon, or to recent discussions about "canonical criticism" in scholarly circles.

Two views of "canonical criticism" have emerged. The first, championed by Brevard Childs,[37] emphasizes the final form of a biblical book or canonical unit (such as the Pentateuch). By "final form" Childs does not mean the form given to a writing by redactors who revised given materials for a new situation in the life of the people. That kind of study, or other historical criticism (such as source, form, stylistic/rhetorical) might have value in helping us to understand the prehistory of the final text. But Childs contends that to read a book in "canonical context" is to read it as it was shaped by the community of faith through use in worship and teaching—that is, as "scripture" in which God's word is mediated through the *given* written form. Thus, for example, the Pentateuch (Torah) is to be read "holistically" as a work in which the parts are related to one another, and hence as a work in which the whole is greater than the sum of the parts.

The second view, advocated by James Sanders,[38] emphasizes "the canonical process": the whole sweep of Israel's history of traditions in which the word of God comes to the community of faith as their heritage is reappropriated and contemporized in ever-new

-----

[37]Brevard Childs, *Introduction to the Old Testament as Scripture* [42].
[38]James A. Sanders, *Torah and Canon* [102] and *Canon and Community* [103].

situations in history. To be sure, "canonical criticism is very interested in what a believing community had in mind at that passing moment when the final form was achieved." But once the text is fixed in its final form, the community finds ways "to break it down to reapply to their purposes and needs." There were "periods of intense canonical process," such as the period after the first fall of Jerusalem in the sixth century B.C.E. and especially the period around the second fall of Jerusalem in the first century C.E. But *tradition,* even when fixed in scripture, always proved to be "adaptable for life" and hence was able to answer for the believing community "the two essential and existential questions of *identity* and *lifestyle.*"[39]

Notice that the story/history approach of our study leans more toward so-called "canonical process" than to a hermeneutical stance that places excessive weight upon the final "scriptural" or "canonical" shape given the traditions in the late period of biblical Judaism.

At one time, great emphasis was placed on the rabbinical discussions held in an academy established at Jabneh, or Jamnia (the name used in Christian circles), on the coast of Palestine. The school was founded by a certain Rabbi Johannan ben Zakkai, who had escaped from Jerusalem during the bitter siege of the city. By attracting to it some of the ablest and most learned Jewish leaders, Jamnia became an important center of Pharisaic Judaism. Scholars formerly referred to the "Council of Jamnia" held about 90 C.E.

Scholars increasingly recognize, however, that the question of "canonicity" was not decided in conciliar debate in a fashion analogous to early Christian councils that dealt with theological and christological matters (such as Nicea). One Jewish scholar warns against the notion that Jamnia was a kind of modern convention during which rabbis debated an agenda and reached binding decisions by vote. "Canon," he says, "was a matter of the evolution of opinions which converged over a period of decades, 90 being a likely terminal date, but far from a definite one."[40]

Undoubtedly rabbinical discussions at Jamnia were influential, but not decisive. Long before this, the main contours of the scriptural "canon" were being determined. The Torah (Pentateuch) was promulgated by Ezra as the authoritative basis of the postexilic covenant community, and from then on it had a unique place in Jewish life. Moreover, shortly after 200 B.C.E. the collection known as the Prophets (Former and Latter) was regarded as sacred scripture—for instance, in the prologue to Ecclesiasticus (about 130 B.C.E.). By the time of the New Testament, "the Law and the Prophets" was a standing expression for Jewish Scripture (Matt. 22:40; Luke 24:27). In addition, a third collection of miscellaneous literature, called the Writings (Hagiographa), was gradually taking shape. One of these books, the Psalms, gained a place of scriptural im-

[39]Sanders, [103], pp. 28ff.
[40]Samuel Sandmel, *The Hebrew Scriptures* [48], p. 14, footnote 6. See also Jack P. Lewis, "What Do We Mean by Jabneh?" in *Journal of Bible and Religion* 32 (1964), 125–32.

portance owing to the use of the psalms in worship (see Luke 24:44). Thus well before Jamnia, the community of faith was registering its verdict on the authority of certain books by making them central in its life and worship.

There was considerable fluidity in the boundaries of Jewish scripture, however, especially beyond the authoritative nucleus of the Torah. Striking evidence of this fluidity has come from the library of the Essene community at Qumran, founded during the life of the Maccabean brothers. This archive contained not only "biblical" books such as the famous Isaiah manuscript and numerous commentaries on biblical books such as Psalms, Hosea, Habakkuk, and Nahum, but also a rich variety of apocryphal and pseudepigraphical writings, some of which were scarcely known before.[41] This diversity has prompted one scholar to observe that "pluralism is a part of responsible perception of the concept of canon."[42]

Further evidence of fluidity in the understanding of "scripture" appears in the Greek translation of the Hebrew Bible (Septuagint) produced by Hellenistic Jews in Alexandria. At the basic level, the student confronts the problem of trying to establish the scriptural text itself (so-called text criticism). The many differences between the received Hebrew text and the Greek version have been explained in various ways. According to one hypothesis, there were several textual traditions in the period of biblical Judaism:

A)   an Egyptian text that was the basis of the Greek Septuagint;

B)   a Palestinian text that included the Samaritan version of the Pentateuch; and

C)   a Babylonian text that eventually was adopted as the standard (Masoretic) text, still studied by students of biblical Hebrew.

According to another view, there was a "central stream" of textual tradition, with variant rivulets running alongside.[43]

Further, the Greek translation indicates that there was flexibility in regard to the number of books considered as scripture. The Egyptian Jews translated a larger number of books than we find in the received Hebrew Bible (see chart, pp. 4–5). The differing scriptural usage of Jews in Palestine and Jews in Alexandria points to an uncertainty about the extent of the sacred writings. Thus, not surprisingly, theologians of the early Christian church were not clear about the extent of the Old Testament. Jerome (about 342–419 C.E.), the great scholar who translated the Latin Vulgate, was inclined to follow the "Babylonian" tradition and to relegate the "extra" writings found in the Greek Septuagint to a secondary place. But his contemporary, Augustine (354–430 C.E.), in-

---

[41]See Frank M. Cross, Jr., *The Ancient Library of Qumran* [613], pp. 30–47.
[42]J. A. Sanders, *Canon and Community* [103], p. 15.
[43]For further discussion, see J. A. Sanders, "Text and Canon: Concepts and Method," *Journal of Biblical Literature*, 98 (1979), 5–29.

sisted that the catalog of Old Testament writings also included books found in the Septuagint that had been established in Christian church usage. Uncertainty about the extent of the so-called "Old Testament" continued in the Christian community for a long time.[44]

In the Jewish community, however, the canonical issue was more or less settled by around 100 C.E., with the academy of Jamnia providing the leadership in rabbinical discussions. To be sure, the rabbinical opinions expressed were "unofficial," that is, not "conciliar"; but in the light of further discussion and the needs of the Jewish community, they were accepted as valid.[45] The major uncertainty was over which books belonged to the Writings. There was no question about the authority of the Torah, and by this time there was general agreement on the number of books belonging in the category of Prophets. But since a basic criterion was harmony with the scriptural Torah, the book of Esther posed difficulties: Besides its seemingly secular character, it explains a festival (Purim) for which there is no explicit provision in the Torah. Even the book of Ezekiel was questioned by some rabbis, for at points it seems to conflict with prescriptions of the Torah (compare Ezek. 46:6 with Num. 28:11). According to the Talmud, one rabbi filled three hundred jars of oil and literally "burned the midnight oil" until he solved the problems. The Pharisaic freedom of interpretation, based on the oral law, meant that the principle of harmony with the scriptural Torah could be applied flexibly.

Another rabbinical principle was a doctrine of prophetic inspiration that assumed the cessation of prophecy in the post-exilic period, just after the time of Ezra. According to this view, Haggai, Zechariah, and Malachi were the last of the prophets, for with their death "the Holy Spirit departed from Israel." Therefore, only writings coming from the period before the cessation of prophetic inspiration were regarded as having religious authority. This criterion might have been adopted because the rabbis believed that the more recent prophetic (apocalyptic) movement, closely associated with the Maccabean revolt and the war of 66–70 C.E., had finally been proved false by Palestine's tragic history. In any case, it automatically excluded books known to have arisen in the Hellenistic period, like "The Wisdom of Ben Sira" or 1–2 Maccabees. The rabbis had serious questions about the "Song of Songs" and Ecclesiastes, but these books were admitted on the supposition that Solomon had written them. Finally, the rabbis rejected books written in Greek, since that language was not employed in the period of prophetic inspiration. On this basis, writings like the Wisdom of Solomon were re-

---

[44]The issue came to the fore in the sixteenth century C.E. The Protestant Reformers, insisting on a return to the Bible, called for the elimination of the extra books not found in the Hebrew Bible. The disputed writings were put in a separate section, "Apocrypha," either at the end of the Old Testament or of the entire Bible, with the note that they deserved to be read but were not equal with canonical books. The Roman Catholic Church at the Council of Trent (1545–1563 C.E.) officially adopted a larger canon, which included both protocanonical and deuterocanonical books (see chart, pp. 4–5). The acceptance of deuterocanonical books was based on long use of these books in Christian liturgy.

[45]See Alfred C. Sundberg, Jr., *The Old Testament of the Early Church* [623], chap. 8.

jected, even though they had been published under the name of great figures of Israel's tradition.

These criteria might seem arbitrary. It would certainly not have detracted from Jewish scripture if, for instance, some reason had been found to include the Wisdom of Ben Sira or some of the psalms from the Qumran community. Keep in mind, however, that the question of the authority of most of the writings now found in the Hebrew Bible had been answered before the closure of the canon, especially in the worship practice of the community. Those writings that were preserved and used devotionally spoke authoritatively to the community of faith.

ISRAEL'S PILGRIMAGE

Pausing to survey the ground we have covered, one point stands out clearly: The Old Testament represents the memories and interpretations of the historical experiences of Israel, from the formation of the community to the time of its great test of faith in the Maccabean period. It is Israel's life-story—a story that cannot be told adequately apart from the conviction that God had entered into covenant relationship with a people, separated them from the nations for a special responsibility, and commissioned them with the task of being servants of, and witnesses to, the One who is Creator of the Universe and Ruler of human history. Remembering its sacred past and preserving its traditions, the "pilgrim people" were able to live in the present with their face set toward the future—the time of the New Covenant, the New Creation, the Kingdom of God. The scriptures of Israel end as an unfinished story. According to the Jewish community, Israel's pilgrimage leads through the Jewish Bible (Torah, Prophets, Writings) to the Talmud and a continued life of Messianic hope. According to the early Christian community, the pilgrimage of the people of God leads through the Old Testament to Jesus Christ, who came not to destroy but to fulfill the Torah and the Prophets. Both communities, however, read essentially the same Bible and are bound together inseparably in witnessing to the God who is Creator of the cosmos and Ruler of history.

COMPREHENSIVE CHRONOLOGICAL CHART

B.C.E.		Egypt	Palestine and Syria	Mesopotamia (and Asia Minor)
2000 to 1900	(Middle Bronze Age)	XII Dynasty	Egyptian Control	Third Dynasty of Ur (c. 2060–1950) Hurrian Movement Amorite Invasion
1900 to 1800		XII Dynasty		First Babylonian Dynasty (c. 1830–1530)
1800 to 1700		Hyksos Invasion (c. 1720)	Abraham	The Mari Age Hammurabi (c. 1728–1686)
1700 to 1600		Hyksos Rule (XV to XVI Dynasties) XVII (Theban Dynasty)	Hyksos Control Descent of Jacob family into Egypt	Decline of Babylonia
1600 to 1500		XVIII Dynasty Ahmose (c. 1552–1527) Expulsion of Hyksos	Egyptian Control	Old Hittite Empire (c. 1600–1500)
1500 to 1400	(Late Bronze Age)	Thutmose III (c. 1490–1436)		Kingdom of Mitanni (c. 1500–1370)
1400 to 1300		Amenhotep III (c. 1403–1364) Amenhotep IV or Akhnaton (c. 1364–1347)	Amarna Age (c. 1400–1350) Egyptian Weakness	New Hittite Empire (c. 1375–1200) Rise of Assyria (c. 1356–1197)
1300 to 1200		XIX Dynasty: Seti I (c. 1305–1290) Rameses II (c. 1290–1224) Merneptah (c. 1224–1211)	Egyptian Revival (The Exodus, c. 1280) Israelite Conquest (c. 1250–1200) Merneptah's Victory (c. 1220)	
1200 to 1100	(Iron Age)	XX Dynasty (c. 1185–1069) Sea Peoples defeated by Rameses III (c. 1175) Egyptian decline	Period of the Judges (c. 1200–1020) Philistines settle in Canaan Battle of Megiddo (c. 1125)	Assyrian Dominance; Collapse of Hittite Empire Assyrian decline
1100 to 1000		XXI Dynasty (c. 1069–935) Egyptian decline	Philistine ascendancy Fall of Shiloh (c. 1050) Samuel and Saul (c. 1020–1000)	Brief Assyrian revival Tiglath-pileser I (c. 1116–1078)

584

B.C.E.	Egypt	Palestine		Phoenicia	Mesopotamia
(Iron Age) 1000 to 900	Decline XXII Dynasty Shishak I (c. 935–914) Shishak invades Judah c. 918	THE UNITED KINGDOM David, c. 1000–961 Solomon, c. 961–922 Division of the kingdom at death of Solomon, c. 922 THE DIVIDED KINGDOM JUDAH DAVIDIC DYNASTY: Rehoboam, c. 922–915 Abijah (Abijam), c. 915–913 Asa, c. 913–873	ISRAEL Jeroboam I, c. 922–901 Nadab, c. 901–900	Hiram I, c. 969–936	Assyrian Decline Assyrian Revival
900 to 850	Egyptian Weakness	Jehoshaphat, c. 873–849 Jehoram, c. 849–843 Ahaziah, c. 843/2	Baasha, c. 900–877 Elah, c. 877–876 Zimri, c. 876 (7 days) *Omri Dynasty:* Omri, c. 876–869 Ahab, c. 869–850 (*Elijah,* c. 850) Ahaziah, c. 850–849 Jehoram, c. 849–843/2	SYRIA Ben-hadad I, c. 885–870 Ben-hadad II, c. 870–842 Hazael, c. 842–806	Adad-nirari II, c. 912–892 Ashur-nasir-apal II, c. 884–860 Shalmaneser III, c. 859–825 Battle of Qarqar, 853
850 to 750	Decline	Athaliah, c. 842–837 Joash, c. 837–800 Amaziah, c. 800–783 Uzziah (Azariah), c. 783–742	*Jehu Dynasty:* Jehu, c. 843/2–815 Joahaz, c. 815–801 J(eh)oash, c. 802–786 Jeroboam II, c. 786–746 (*Amos,* c. 750) (*Hosea,* c. 745) Zechariah (6 mos.), c. 746–745		(Jehu pays tribute, 841) Shamshi-Adad V, c. 824–812 Adad-nirari III, c. 811–784 Decline

B.C.E.	Egypt	Palestine			Mesopotamia
		DIVIDED KINGDOM			
		JUDAH	ISRAEL	Syria	Assyria
750 *to* 700	Decline	Jotham (regent), c. 750–742 Jotham (king), c. 742–735 (*Isaiah,* c. 742–700) Jehoahaz (Ahaz), c. 735–715 Invasion by Syro-Israelite Alliance, 735	Shallum (1 mo.), c. 745 Menahem, c. 745–737 Pekahiah, c. 737–736 Pekah, c. 736–732	Rezin, c. 740–732	Tiglath-pileser III, c. 745–727 EXPANSION OF ASSYRIAN EMPIRE
			SYRO-ISRAELITE ALLIANCE	SYRO-ISRAELITE ALLIANCE	
		(*Micah:* before 722 to c. 701)	Hoshea, c. 732–724 FALL OF SAMARIA 722–721	FALL OF SYRIA, 732	Siege of Damascus, 732 Shalmaneser V, 726–722 Siege of Samaria, 722/721
	XXV Dynasty (Ethiopian) c. 716/15–663	JUDAH Hezekiah, c. 715–687/6			Sargon II, 721–705 Siege of Ashdod, 712 Sennacherib, 704–681 Invasion of Palestine, 701

	Egypt	Judah	Assyria / Babylonia
		Manasseh, 687/6–642	Esarhaddon, 680–669
	Tirhakah, c. 685/4–664	Amon, 642–640	Invasion of Egypt, 671
	Invasion by Assyria, 671		
	Sack of Thebes, 663, by Ashurbanapal	Josiah, 640–609	Ashurbanapal, 668–627
		First show of Judean independence, 629	RISE OF BABYLONIA
	XXVI Dynasty, c. 664–525	(Zephaniah, c. 628–622)	
	Psammetichus I c. 664–610	(Jeremiah, c. 626–587)	Nabopolassar, 626–605
700 to 600		Josiah's "Deuteronomic Reform," 621	
	Necho II, 610–593	Death of Josiah at Megiddo, 609	Fall of Ashur to Medes, 614
			Fall of Nineveh to Medes and Babylonians, 612
		Jehoahaz II (Shallum), 609 (3 mos.)	Babylonian defeat of Assyrians and Egyptians at Haran, 609
		Jehoiakim (Eliakim), 609–598/7	Battle of Carchemish, 605
		(Habakkuk, c. 605)	FALL OF ASSYRIA

B.C.E.	Egypt	Palestine	Mesopotamia
		THE BABYLONIAN EMPIRE	**BABYLONIA** Nebuchadrezzar, 605/4–562
	Apries (Hophra), 589–570	Jehoiachin (Jeconiah), 3 mos., 598–597 First Deportation to Babylonia, 597 Zedekiah (Mattaniah), 597–587 FALL OF JERUSALEM SECOND DEPORTATION, 587	
600 to 500		**BABYLONIAN EXILE** *Ezekiel, c. 593–573*	
		(*Second Isaiah*, c. 540) Edict of Cyrus, 538	Nabonidus, 556–539 (his son: Belshazzar) RISE OF PERSIA Cyrus II, 550–530 Defeat of Media, c. 550 Invasion of Lydia, c. 546 FALL OF BABYLON, 539
	Conquest by Persia, 525	**THE EMPIRE OF PERSIA** **THE RESTORATION** JUDAH Return of exiles Rebuilding of Temple, 520–515 (*Haggai*) (*Zechariah*)	Cambyses, 530–522 Darius I, 522–486
500 to 400	Egypt under Persian rule, 525–401	(*Malachi*, c. 500–450) Ezra's mission, 458(?) Nehemiah arrives, 445 Ezra's mission, c. 428(?)	PERSIA Xerxes I (Ahasuerus), 486–465 Artaxerxes I (Longimanus), 465–424 Xerxes II, 423 Darius II, 423–404
		Ezra's mission, c. 398(?)	Artaxerxes II (Memnon), 404–358 Artaxerxes III, 358–338 Arses, 338–336 Darius III, 336–331

B.C.E.	Egypt	Palestine	Mesopotamia
		EMPIRE OF ALEXANDER THE GREAT, 336–323	
400 to 300	*Ptolemaic Kingdom* Ptolemy I, 323–285	Egyptian Control	*Seleucid Kingdom* (Mesopotamia and Syria) Seleucus I, 312/11–280
300 to 200	Ptolemy II, 285–246 Ptolemy III, 246–221 Ptolemy IV, 221–203	Egyptian Control	Antiochus I, 280–261 Antiochus II, 261–246 Seleucus II, 246–226 Seleucus III, 226–223 Antiochus III, 223–187
200 to 100	Ptolemy V, 203–181 Ptolemy VI, 181–146 Ptolemy VII, 146–116	Seleucid (Syrian) Conquest, 200–198 MACCABEAN REVOLT, 168 (167) Judas, 166–160 Jonathan, 160–143 Simon, 143–134 John Hyrcanus, 134–104 Conquest of Shechem, 128	Seleucus IV, 187–175 Antiochus IV (Epiphanes), 175–163 Antiochus V, 163–162 Demetrius I, 162–150 Alexander Balas, 150–145 Demetrius II, 145–138 Antiochus VI, 145–141 Antiochus VII, 138–129
100 to C.E.	Roman Conquest, 30	Pompey captures Jerusalem, 63 THE EMPIRE OF ROME	Roman occupation of Syria, 63

SELECTED

BIBLIOGRAPHY

No attempt has been made to mention all important books on Old Testament subjects or even to include everything referred to in footnotes. Rather, the list includes selected basic works which will be valuable to the student who for the most part is confined to what is available in English. To facilitate footnote references, the various items are listed by number.

TOOLS FOR BIBLE STUDY

TRANSLATIONS: When a student is unable to read the Old Testament in the original language, it is important to consult more than one recent translation. Among the best are:

[RSV] The Revised Standard Version (Division of Christian Education, 1973). This translation,

endorsed by Protestant, Roman Catholic, and Eastern Orthodox representatives, was issued as the *Common Bible* (New York: Collins, 1973).

[NRSV] The New Revised Standard Version (Division of Christian Education of the National Council of Churches of Christ, 1989).

[NAB] The New American Bible (New York: P. J. Kenedy & Sons, 1970). A translation by members of the Catholic Biblical Association of America.

[REB] Revised English Bible (New York: Oxford University, 1989; revision of *The New English Bible,* 1970). A vivid, idiomatic translation by British scholars.

[OSB] The Oxford Study Bible: Revised English Bible with Apocrypha. M. Jack Suggs, Katharine Doob Sakenfeld, and James R. Mueller, eds. (Oxford: Oxford Univ., 1992).

[NIV] The New International Version (Grand Rapids, MI: Zondervan, 1978). A fresh translation by a team of "evangelical" scholars.

[NJB] *The New Jerusalem Bible* (Garden City, NY: Doubleday, 1985; revision of *The Jerusalem Bible*, 1966). Another translation by Roman Catholic scholars.

[JPSV] *Tanakh: The Torah, The Prophets, The Writings. A new translation of the Holy Scriptures according to the Masoretic text* (Philadelphia: Jewish Publication Society of America, 1985). A revised translation by Jewish scholars.

Extra-biblical Sources

1. [ANET] *Ancient Near Eastern Texts Relating to the Old Testament*, 3rd ed. with supplement, ed. by J. B. Pritchard (Princeton: Princeton University, 1969). A basic tool for the study of the Old Testament period.

2. *The Ancient Near East in Pictures Relating to the Old Testament*, 2nd ed. by J. B. Pritchard (Princeton: Princeton University, 1969).

3. *The Ancient Near East: An Anthology of Texts and Pictures*, ed. by J. B. Pritchard (Princeton: Princeton University, 1965). Contains selections from nos. 1 and 2.

4. *Near Eastern Texts Relating to the Old Testament*, ed. by W. Beyerlin, Old Testament Library (Philadelphia: Westminster, 1978).

5. *Apocrypha and Pseudepigrapha of the Old Testament*, 2 vols., ed. by R. H. Charles (Oxford: Clarendon, 1912). A classic work.

6. *Old Testament Parallels: Laws and Stories from the Ancient Near East*, ed. by Victor H. Matthews and Don C. Benjamin, Jr. (New York: Paulist, 1991).

7. *The Old Testament Pseudepigrapha*, ed. by James H. Charlesworth (Garden City, NY: Doubleday), I: Apocalyptic Literature and Testaments (1983); II: Expansions of the "Old Testament" and Legends, Wisdom and Philosophical Literature, Prayers, Psalms, and Odes, Fragments of Lost Judeo-Hellenistic Works (1985).

8. *Writings from the Ancient World: Society of Biblical Literature*, ed. by Simon B. Parker (Atlanta: Scholars, 1990 and on).

Single-volume Commentaries

9. *The Books of the Bible*, ed. by Bernhard W. Anderson (New York: Scribner's, 1989). Basic treatments of biblical books; I: The Old Testament/Hebrew Bible; II: Apocrypha and New Testament.

10. *The Interpreter's One Volume Commentary on the Bible*, ed. by Charles M. Laymon (New York: Abingdon, 1971).

11. *Interpreting the Old Testament*, by Walter J. Harrelson (New York: Holt, Rinehart & Winston, 1964). Commentary based on the structure of the Hebrew Bible.

12. *The Cambridge Annotated Study Bible: New Revised Standard Version*. Notes and references by Howard Clark Kee (New York: Cambridge University, 1993).

13. *The Women's Bible Commentary*, ed. by Carol A. Newsom and Sharon H. Ringe (Louisville: Westminster/John Knox, 1992).

14. *The HarperCollins Study Bible* (New York: HarperCollins, 1993). Based on the NRSV, with illustrations and rather extensive annotations.

15. *The New Jerome Biblical Commentary*, ed. by Raymond E. Brown, J. A. Fitzmeyer, and Roland E. Murphy (Englewood Cliffs, NJ: Prentice Hall, 1990). An excellent commentary by Roman Catholic scholars.

16. *The New Oxford Annotated Bible with Apocrypha*, ed. by Herbert G. May and Bruce M. Metzger (New York: Oxford University, 1991). Based on the New Revised Standard Version and provided with brief articles, notes, maps, and other aids.

17. *The New English Bible with the Apocrypha*, Oxford Study Edition, ed. by Samuel Sandmel (New York: Oxford University, 1976). Provided with introductions, annotations, maps, and other aids.

18. *The NIV Study Bible* (Grand Rapids, MI: Zondervan, revised 1983). Fairly detailed commentary, with introductions, maps, and other aids.

Commentary Sets

19. *The Anchor Bible*, ed. by W. F. Albright and D. N. Freedman (Garden City, NY: Doubleday). This series contains fresh translations and commentary.

20. *The Cambridge Bible Commentary on the New English Bible*, ed. by P. R. Ackroyd et al. (Cambridge: Cambridge University). A series of brief commentaries begun in 1972.

21. *Hermeneia: A Critical and Historical Commentary*, ed. by Frank M. Cross et al. (Philadelphia: Fortress). Volumes of this important series appear from time to time.

22. *Interpretation: A Bible Commentary for Teaching and Preaching*, ed. James L. Mays, Patrick D. Miller, and Paul J. Achtemeier. (Atlanta, GA: John Knox). A promising series begun in 1980.

23. *The Interpreter's Bible*, ed. by G. A. Buttrick (New York: Abingdon, 1952–57). Some of the commentaries, by a previous generation of scholars, still deserve attention.

24. *The New Interpreter's Bible*, ed. by Leander E. Keck et al. (Nashville: Abingdon). The successor to No. 23; started appearing in 1994.

25. *The New Century Bible Commentary*, ed. by Ronald E. Clements and Matthew Black (Grand Rapids, MI: Eerdmans).

26. *The Old Testament Library*, ed. by Peter Ackroyd et al. (Philadelphia: Westminster). An outstanding series.

Bible Dictionaries and Reference Works

27. *The Anchor Bible Dictionary*, ed. by D. N. Freedman (New York: Doubleday, 1992). Gathers some of the best of 20th-century scholarship.

28. *Dictionary of the Bible*, ed. by James Hastings, rev. by F. C. Grant and H. H. Rowley (New York: Scribner's, 1963). A classic reference work.

29. *Harper's Bible Dictionary*, ed. by Paul J. Achtemeier (San Francisco: Harper & Row, 1985). A basic reference work.

30. *International Standard Bible Encyclopedia*, rev. ed., 4 vols., ed. by B. W. Bromiley et al. (Grand Rapids, MI: Eerdmans, 1979 and on). A work by a team of "evangelical" scholars.

31. *The Interpreter's Dictionary of the Bible*, 4 vols., ed. by G. A. Buttrick et al. (New York: Abingdon, 1962). Dated but still useful.

32. *The Interpreter's Dictionary of the Bible*, Supplementary Volume, ed. by Keith Crim et al. (New York: Abingdon, 1976). Updating of some of the entries in the work listed above.

33. *The Oxford Companion to the Bible*, ed. by Bruce M. Metzger and Michael D. Coogan (New York: Oxford University, 1993).

34. *Theological Dictionary of the Old Testament*, in several volumes, ed. by G. J. Botterweck and Helmer Ringgren, trans. by J. T. Willis et al. (Grand Rapids, MI: Eerdmans, 1974 and on).

Bible Atlases and Geography

35. Aharoni, Y., and M. Avi-Yonah, *The Macmillan Bible Atlas* (London and New York: Macmillan, 1968). An excellent atlas by two leading Israeli scholars. See also Y. Aharoni, *The Land of the Bible*, trans. by A. F. Rainey (Philadelphia: Westminster, 1967).

36. Baly, Denis, and A. D. Tushingham, *The Atlas of the Biblical World* (New York: World, 1971). Detailed topographical and historical maps; an excellent work. See also Denis Baly, *The Geography of the Bible*, 2nd ed. (New York: Harper & Row, 1974).

37. Grollenberg, L. H., *Atlas of the Bible*, trans. and ed. by J. Reid and H. H. Rowley (New York: Nelson, 1956). An unusually impressive work.

38. May, Herbert G., *Oxford Bible Atlas*, 3rd ed., revised by John Day (New York: Oxford University, 1984). Brief and useful.

39. Pritchard, James. B., *The Harper Atlas of the Bible* (New York: Harper & Row, 1987).

40. Smith, G. A., *Historical Geography of the Holy Land,* 25th ed. (New York: A. C. Armstrong & Son, 1931). Dated but still regarded as one of the best biblical geographies.

41. *The Westminster Historical Atlas to the Bible,* ed. by G. Ernest Wright and Floyd V. Filson (Philadelphia: Westminster, revised 1956). The first major atlas that set the standard; many archaeological views must now be updated.

Journals

The best way to keep abreast of biblical research is to read the journals. A good, nontechnical journal is *Interpretation,* published quarterly (Richmond, VA); also *The Expository Times,* published monthly (Edinburgh). Other important quarterly journals, to mention a few, are:

[CBQ] The Catholic Biblical Quarterly

[JBL] The Journal of Biblical Literature

[JSOT] Journal for the Study of the Old Testament

[VT] Vetus Testamentum

In the field of archaeology, see especially:

[BA] The Biblical Archaeologist

[BAR] The Biblical Archaeology Review

[BR] Bible Review, a magazine for the general reader, published by *BAR.*

For research purposes, consult *The BAR/BR 20-Year Index,* covering discussions about archaeology and biblical interpretation during the years 1975–94.

Introductions to the Old Testament

In recent years many general introductions have appeared, many of them based on a book-by-book approach to the Old Testament. For the most part the following selected list is limited to more technical works.

42. Childs, Brevard S., *Introduction to the Old Testament as Scripture* (Philadelphia: Fortress, 1979). Not an "Introduction" in the technical sense, so much as a foundation for a canonical approach. Note the excellent bibliographies.

43. Driver, S. R., *Introduction to the Literature of the Old Testament,* rev. ed. (New York: Scribner's, 1913; Merdian, 1956). A classic work, helpful for understanding the literary criticism of an older generation.

44. Fohrer, Georg, *Introduction to the Old Testament,* trans. by David F. Green (Nashville: Abingdon, 1968). A thorough revision of Ernst Sellin's *Introduction* (1910), stressing a form-critical approach.

45. Gottwald, Norman K., *The Hebrew Bible: A Socio-Literary Introduction* (Philadelphia: Fortress, 1985). A comprehensive approach based on the sociological premises of his previous work, *The Tribes of Yahweh* [271].

46. La Sor, W. S., D. A. Hubbard, and F. W. Bush, *Old Testament Survey: The Message, Form, and Background of the Old Testament* (Grand Rapids, MI: Eerdmans, 1982). An "evangelical" approach, based on "verbal inspiration," although open to critical biblical scholarship.

47. Rendtorff, Rolf, *The Old Testament: An Introduction* (Philadelphia: Fortress, 1986). Compared with most Introductions, this represents a new venture.

48. Sandmel, Samuel, *The Hebrew Scriptures: An Introduction to Their Literature and Religious Ideas* (New York: Knopf, 1963). A presentation by an eminent Jewish scholar.

BIBLICAL CRITICISM

History of Biblical Criticism

49. *The Cambridge History of the Bible,* I: From the Beginnings to Jerome, ed. by P. R. Ackroyd and C. F. Evans; II: The West from the Fathers to the Reformation, ed. by G. W. B. Lampe; III: The West from the Reformation to the Present Day, ed. by S. L. Greenslade (London: Cambridge University, 1970).

50. Clements, R. E., *One Hundred Years of Old Testament Interpretation* (Philadelphia: Westminster, 1976).

51. Fishbane, Michael, "Jewish Biblical Exegesis: Presuppositions and Principles," *Scripture in the Jewish and Christian Traditions: Authority, Interpretation, Relevance,* ed. by Frederick F. Greenspahn (Nashville: Abingdon, 1982), 91–110.

52. Frei, Hans, *The Eclipse of Biblical Narrative* (New Haven: Yale University, 1974). A penetrating discussion of biblical interpretation since the Enlightenment.

53. Froehlich, Karlfried, *Biblical Interpretation in the Early Church* (Philadelphia: Fortress, 1984). A valuable translation and introduction to major sources for understanding biblical interpretation in the "patristic" period. Note the bibliography.

54. Grant, R. M., *A Short History of the Interpretation of the Bible* (Philadelphia: Fortress, 1963, 1984), a revised and updated version of *The Bible in the Church* (Philadelphia: Fortress, 1983), with a special word from David Tracy on the modern use of the Bible.

55. Hahn, H. F., *The Old Testament in Modern Research,* 3rd ed. with a bibliographical survey by Horace D. Hummel (Philadelphia: Fortress, 1966).

56. Knight, Douglas A., and Gene M. Tucker, *The Hebrew Bible and Its Modern Interpreters* (Philadelphia: Fortress, 1985). Deals with the history of biblical interpretation in the period after World War II.

57. Kraeling, Emil G., *The Old Testament Since the Reformation* (New York: Harper & Row, 1955; Schocken Books, 1969). A helpful survey of the history of historical criticism.

58. Kugel, James L., and Rowan A. Greer, *Early Biblical Interpretation,* ed. by Wayne A. Meeks (Philadelphia: Westminster, 1986).

59. Levenson, Jon D., *The Hebrew Bible, the Old Testament, and Historical Criticism* (Louisville: Westminster, 1993). See chaps. 1 and 5 on historical criticism.

60. Reventlow, H. G., *The Authority of the Bible and the Rise of the Modern World,* 1st Fortress ed. (Philadelphia: Fortress, 1985).

61. Rogerson, J. W., *Old Testament Criticism in the Nineteenth Century,* 1st Fortress ed. (Philadelphia: Fortress, 1985).

62. Smalley, B., *The Study of the Bible in the Middle Ages,* 2nd ed. (Oxford: Basil Blackwell, 1952).

63. Stuhlmacher, P., *Historical Criticism and Theological Interpretation of Scripture,* trans. and with an introduction by Roy A. Harrisville (Philadelphia: Fortress, 1977).

Methods of Biblical Criticism

Depending on the nature of the material under study, biblical texts may be approached from various angles.

64. Amerding, Carl E., *The Old Testament and Criticism* (Grand Rapids, MI: Eerdmans, 1983). A general introduction to methods of biblical criticism, written particularly for "evangelicals."

65. Barton, John, *Reading the Old Testament: Method in Biblical Study* (Philadelphia: Westminster, 1984). A judicious discussion of various approaches to the Bible, including the "canonical" approach advocated by Brevard Childs [42].

66. Buss, Martin, ed., *Encounter with the Text: Form and History in the Hebrew Bible* (Philadelphia: Fortress, 1979). Consideration of principles of interpretation, using various methods of biblical criticism.

See also discussions in general Introductions, e.g., *New Jerome* [15], 1113–29.

1. Source Criticism

This method is advocated in older Introductions, e.g., S. R. Driver [43]; see the summary by Walter Harrelson [11], pp. 28–40, and his source analysis of the Pentateuch, pp. 28–40; see also the appendix to Martin Noth's *Pentateuchal Traditions* [76].

67. Cassuto, U., *The Documentary Hypothesis and the Composition of the Pentateuch*, trans. by Israel Abrahams (Jerusalem: Magnes, 1961). Criticism of the source hypothesis by a Jewish scholar.

68. Clements, R. E., "Pentateuchal Problems," *Tradition and Interpretation* [175], 96–124. A judicious discussion which upholds, in general, the results of literary criticism, although welcoming subsequent developments in scholarly research.

69. Habel, Norman C., *Literary Criticism of the Old Testament* (Philadelphia: Fortress, 1971).

70. Wolff, H. W., and Walter Brueggemann, *The Vitality of Old Testament Traditions*, 2nd ed. (Atlanta: John Knox, 1982). Essays on the "kerygma" or message of various literary traditions: the Yahwist (J), the Elohist (E), the Deuteronomistic Historian, (DtH), and the Priestly Writer (P).

2. Form Criticism
(see Definition, p. 487)

71. Hayes, John, ed., *Old Testament Form Criticism* (San Antonio: Trinity University Press, 1974). Essays dealing with various types of Old Testament literature.

72. Koch, Klaus, *The Growth of the Biblical Tradition: the Form-critical Method*, trans. by S. M. Cupitt (New York: Scribner's, 1969). A basic work.

73. Tucker, Gene M., *Form Criticism of the Old Testament* (Philadelphia: Fortress, 1971). A helpful, brief introduction.

Interpretation 27, 4(1973) is devoted to this method of biblical interpretation. For an example, see George W. Coats' study on Genesis [302].

3. History of Traditions

This method, based on a form-critical analysis of the genres of oral tradition, studies the history of the transmission of the tradition through various stages of composition until the end result of canonical scripture.

74. Coats, G. W., "Tradition Criticism, O. T." in Supplement to *The Interpreter's Dictionary of the Bible* [32], 912–14.

75. Knight, Douglas, *Rediscovering the Traditions of Israel* (Missoula: Scholars, 1975). See the review of *Tradition and Theology in the Old Testament* (Philadelphia: Fortress, 1977) by B. W. Anderson, *Religious Studies Review*, 6, 2 [1980], 104–10, where this method is evaluated.

76. Noth, Martin, *A History of Pentateuchal Traditions*, trans. with introduction by Bernhard W. Anderson (Chico, CA: Scholars, 1981; original German edition, 1948). A fundamental work in the field of traditio-historical investigation.

77. McKenzie, Steven L., and M. Patrick Graham, eds., *The History of Israel's Traditions: The Heritage of Martin Noth*, JSOT Supplement 182 (Sheffield: JSOT, 1994). Essays evaluating the application of Noth's traditio-historical method to the Pentateuch and the Deuteronomistic History.

78. Rast, Walter E., *Tradition History and the Old Testament* (Philadelphia: Fortress, 1972).

79. Rendtorff, Rolf, *The Problem of the Process of Transmission in the Pentateuch*, trans. by John J. Scullion, JSOT Supplement 89 (Sheffield: JSOT, 1977). A student of Noth treats traditio-historical and more recent approaches to the Pentateuch. See also *Noth Heritage* [77], pp. 91–100.

80. Whybray, R. N., *The Making of the Pentateuch: A Methodological Study,* JSOT Supplement 53 (Sheffield: JSOT, 1987). Reviews source-critical and traditio-historical studies of the Pentateuch with an eye to new approaches.

The so-called Scandinavian School rejects source criticism and emphasizes the oral history of traditions. See:

81. Anderson, G. W., "Some Aspects of the Uppsala School of Old Testament Study," in *Harvard Theological Review,* XLIII (1950), 239–56.

82. Engnell, Ivan, *A Rigid Scrutiny: Critical Essays on the Old Testament,* trans. and ed. by John T. Willis (Nashville: Vanderbilt University, 1969). One of the leaders of the Uppsala School.

83. Lemaire, Andre, and B. Otzen, *History and Traditions of Early Israel: Studies Presented to Eduard Nielsen* (Leiden: E. J. Brill, 1993).

84. Nielsen, Eduard, *Oral Tradition,* Studies in Biblical Theology 11 (Naperville: Alec R. Allenson, 1954).

4. Redaction Criticism
   (see Definition, pp. 355–356)

85. Perrin, Norman C., *What is Redaction Criticism?* (Philadelphia: Fortress, 1969). Although this book deals with the New Testament, the method is also pertinent to the Old Testament.

For examples of the use of this method, see Bernhard W. Anderson, "From Analysis to Synthesis: The Interpretation of Genesis 1–11," *Journal of Biblical Literature,* 97 (1978), (23–39); Hans Walter Wolff's "The Kerygma of the Deuteronomic Historical Work (*The Vitality of the Old Testament Traditions* [70]) is essentially a study in redaction criticism.

5. Rhetorical (Stylistic) Criticism

This method attempts to move "beyond form criticism" (see Muilenburg [90]) into a study of the literary and structural features of a particular text of scripture. See also the section on "Analysis of Hebrew Poetry" [97–100].

86. Alter, Robert, and Frank Kermode, eds., *The Literary Guide to the Bible* (Cambridge, MA: Belknap, 1987).

87. Gabel, John B., and Charles B. Wheeler, *The Bible as Literature: An Introduction,* 3rd ed. (New York: Oxford University, 1995).

88. Jackson, Jared J., and Martin Kessler, eds., *Rhetorical Criticism: Essays in Honor of James Muilenburg* (Pittsburgh: Pickwick, 1974). See the introductory essay by B. W. Anderson, "The New Frontier of Rhetorical Criticism."

89. McEvenue, Sean, *Interpretation and Bible: Essays on Truth in Literature* (Collegeville, MN: Liturgical, 1984).

90. Muilenburg, James, "Form Criticism and Beyond," *Journal of Biblical Literature,* 88 (1969), 1–18. A pioneering venture in rhetorical criticism.

Studies in rhetorical criticism appear in Phyllis Trible, *God and the Rhetoric of Sexuality* [167]; see, for example, chap. 4, "A Love Story Gone Awry." See also B. W. Anderson, "'The Lord Has Created Something New': A Stylistic Study of Jer. 31:15–22," *Catholic Biblical Quarterly,* 40 (1978), 463–78; reprinted in *From Creation to New Creation* [146], chap. 11.

6. Narrative Criticism and Structuralism

91. Alter, Robert, *The Art of Biblical Narrative* (Philadelphia: Fortress, 1976).

92. Crenshaw, James L., *Samson: A Secret Betrayed, A Vow Ignored* (Atlanta: John

Knox, 1978). The author describes his approach as "aesthetic criticism."

93. Culley, R. C., *Studies in the Structure of Hebrew Narrative* (New York: Basic Books, 1981).

94. Fishbane, Michael, *Text and Texture: Close Readings of Selected Biblical Texts* (New York: Schocken Books, 1979).

95. Patte, Daniel, *What is Structural Exegesis?* (Philadelphia: Fortress, 1976). Deals with the New Testament, but is relevant to biblical studies in general. Note the bibliography.

96. Polzin, Robert M., *Biblical Structuralism: Method and Subjectivity in the Study of Ancient Texts* (Philadelphia: Fortress, 1977).

7. Analysis of Hebrew Poetry

97. Alter, Robert, *The Art of Biblical Poetry* (New York: Basic Books, 1985).

98. Berlin, Adele, *The Dynamics of Biblical Parallelism* (Bloomington, IN: Indiana University, 1985).

99. Miller, Patrick D., Jr., *Interpreting the Psalms* (Philadelphia: Fortress, 1986). On the poetry of the Psalms. See also Robert Alter, "Psalms: Beauty and Poetic Structure," *Approaches to the Bible* [104], 237–52.

100. Petersen, David L., and Kent H. Richards, *Interpreting Hebrew Poetry* (Minneapolis, MN: Fortress, 1992).

8. Canonical Criticism
   (see Definition, pp. 578–579)

This method aims to go beyond tradition-history and redaction criticism to deal with the final form of biblical literature.

101. Mann, Thomas, *The Book of the Torah* (Atlanta, GA: John Knox, 1988). A very good introductory study that treats the Pentateuch as a canonical whole.

102. Sanders, J. A., *Torah and Canon* (Philadelphia: Fortress, 1972). See also his essay "Adaptable for Life: The Nature and Function of Canon," in *Magnalia Dei* [179], 531–60.

103. Sanders, J. A., *Canon and Community: A Guide to Canonical Criticism* (Philadelphia: Fortress, 1984).

Brevard Childs champions a canonical approach which cannot be easily categorized; certainly it is different from the canonical criticism mentioned above. See his *Introduction* [42]; also the critical responses of James Barr, *Holy Scripture: Canon, Authority, Criticism* [147], and John Barton, *Reading the Old Testament* [65]. See the review by M. O'Connor, "How the Text is Heard: The Biblical Theology of Brevard Childs" (*Religious Studies Review*, 21, 2 [April, 1995], pp. 91–96).

9. Sociological Approach

A relatively new horizon in biblical studies, and yet not so new (cf. earlier studies by Max Weber).

104. *Approaches to the Bible: The Best of Bible Review*, ed. by Harvey Minkoff (Washington, DC: Biblical Archaeology Society, 1995), Part II, "Sociology and the Bible," including evaluation of Gottwald's socio-literary approach [45].

105. Clements, R. E., *The World of Ancient Israel: Sociological, Anthropological, and Political Perspectives* (New York: Cambridge University, 1989).

106. Gottwald, Norman, "Sociological Method in the Study of Ancient Israel," *Encounter with the Text* [66], 69–82. This approach is spelled out in his *Tribes of Yahweh* [271] and *Introduction* [45].

107. Matthews, Victor H., and Don C. Benjamin, *The Social World of Ancient Israel, 1250–587 B.C.E.* (Peabody, MA: Hendrickson, 1993). Excellent study which shows the impact of social sciences; note

especially chap. 2 on the role of mothers in ancient Israel.

108. Wilson, Robert R., *Sociological Approaches to the Old Testament* (Philadelphia: Fortress, 1984). An excellent introduction to the method.

HISTORY OF ISRAEL

109. Ahlström, Gösta W., *The History of Ancient Palestine from the Paleolithic Period to Alexander's Conquest*, ed. by D. V. Edelman, JSOT Supplement, 146 (Sheffield: JSOT, 1993). The history of ancient Palestine, including Syria, Israel, and Jordan, in light of current knowledge in archaeology, history, and textual studies. A major work.

110. Bright, John, *A History of Israel*, 3rd ed. (Philadelphia: Westminster, 1981). Highly recommended.

111. De Vaux, Roland, *The Early History of Israel*, trans. by David Smith (Philadelphia: Westminster, 1978). An important work, left incomplete at the time of the author's death. The discussion extends from Israel's origins to the settlement in Canaan.

112. Hayes, John H., and J. Maxwell Miller, eds., *Israelite and Judaean History*, Old Testament Library [26], 1977. The various essays include thorough bibliographies.

113. Hermann, Siegfried, *A History of Israel in Old Testament Times*, trans. by John Bowden (Philadelphia: Fortress, 1975). Excellent brief history.

114. Kitchen, K. A., *Ancient Orient and Old Testament* (London: Tynsdale, 1966). See also *The Bible in Its World* [123].

115. Noth, Martin, *The History of Israel*, 2nd ed., trans. by Stanley Godman from 2nd German ed. and revised by P. R. Ackroyd (London: Adam and Charles Black, 1960). One of the major works in the field, by a leader of the German school of tradition-history.

116. Ramsey, George W., *The Quest for the Historical Israel* (Atlanta: John Knox,

1981). A valuable discussion which updates the student to the time of writing.

117. Shanks, Hershel, *Ancient Israel: A Short History from Abraham to the Roman Destruction of the Temple* (Washington, DC: Biblical Archaeological Society, 1988). Each chapter is written by a specialist in the historical period discussed.

118. Van Seters, John, *In Search of History: Historiography in the Ancient World and the Origin of Biblical History* (New Haven: Yale University, 1983).

ARCHAEOLOGY

A good way to keep up with current archaeology is to read *The Biblical Archaeologist (BA),* published by the American School of Oriental Research, or *The Biblical Archaeology Review (BAR).*

119. *The Biblical Archaeologist Reader*, I (1961), II (1964), III (1970), IV (1983), ed. by G. E. Wright, E. F. Campbell, and D. N. Freedman (Garden City, NY: Doubleday Anchor). Selected articles from past issues of *The Biblical Archaeologist.*

120. Ben-Tor, Amnon, ed., *The Archaeology of Ancient Israel*, trans. by R. Greenberg (New Haven: Yale University, 1992).

121. Dever, William G., *Recent Archaeological Discoveries and Biblical Research* (Seattle: University of Washington, 1990); "The Contribution of Archaeology to the Study of Canaanite and Early Israelite Religion," *Ancient Israelite Religion: Essays in Honor of Frank Moore Cross*, ed. by P. D. Miller, Jr., et al. (Philadelphia: Fortress, 1987), pp. 209–48; also "Archaeology and the Bible: Understanding Their Special Relationship," *BAR* 16:3 (May/June, 1990), 52ff.

122. Kenyon, Kathleen, *Archaeology in the Holy Land* (New York: Praeger, 1960). A basic work by a distinguished archaeologist.

123. Kitchen, K. A., *The Bible in Its World: Archaeology and the Bible Today* (Downers Grove: InterVarsity, 1978; c1977); see also *Ancient Orient* [114].

124. Mazar, Amihai, *Archaeology of the Land of the Bible, 10,000 to 586 B.C.E.* (New York: Doubleday, 1990). Rated as one of the best books on archaeology.

125. Wright, G. Ernest, *Biblical Archaeology*, 2nd ed. (Philadelphia: Westminster, 1962). A valuable book by an eminent authority.

RELIGION OF ISRAEL

126. Ackermann, Susan, *Under Every Green Tree: Popular Religion in Sixth-Century Judah.* HSMS 46 (Atlanta: Scholars, 1992).

127. Albright, W. F., *From the Stone Age to Christianity* (Baltimore: Johns Hopkins, 1940; New York: Doubleday Anchor, rev. ed., 1957). A classic in modern scholarship. See also his *Archaeology and the Religion of Israel,* 2nd ed. (Baltimore: Johns Hopkins, 1946; Doubleday, 1969).

128. Alt, Albrecht, *Essays on Old Testament History and Religion,* trans. by R. A. Wilson (Garden City, NY: Doubleday, 1967). Important essays by a leading German scholar of a former generation.

129. Cross, Frank, M., *Canaanite Myth and Hebrew Epic: Essays in the History of the Religion of Israel* (Cambridge, MA: Harvard University, 1973). Creative essays covering the whole Old Testament period. See also "The Development of Israelite Religion," *Bible Review,* 8, 5 (October, 1992), pp. 18–29, 50.

130. De Vaux, Roland, *Ancient Israel: Its Life and Institutions,* trans. by John McHugh (London: Barton, Longman and Todd, 1961). A monumental study by the one-time director of the Dominican École Biblique in Jerusalem.

131. Frymer-Kensky, Tikva, *In the Wake of the Goddesses: Women, Culture, and the Biblical Transformation of Pagan Myth* (New York: Free, 1992).

132. Gunkel, Hermann, "The Influence of Babylonian Mythology upon the Biblical Creation Story," in B. W. Anderson, *Creation in the Old Testament* (Philadelphia: Fortress, 1984). Translation of part of Gunkel's classic *Schöpfung und Chaos in Urzeit und Endzeit* (Göttingen: Vandenhoeck und Ruprecht, 1985).

133. Hanson, Paul, "Israelite Religion in the Early Postexilic Period," *Ancient Israelite Religion* [135], pp. 485–508.

134. Kaufmann, Yehezkel, *The Religion of Israel,* trans. and abridged by Moshe Greenberg (Chicago: University of Chicago, 1960; Schocken, 1972). A provocative study by a highly original Jewish scholar who departs from many of the accepted tenets of historical criticism.

135. Miller, P. D., Jr., et al., eds., *Ancient Israelite Religion: Essays in Honor of Frank Moore Cross* (Philadelphia: Fortress, 1987). Valuable essays in tribute to a great scholar in the field of Israelite religion.

136. Pedersen, Johannes, *Israel: Its Life and Culture* I–II, 1926; III–IV, 1940 (New York: Oxford). A major study of the socio-psychological characteristics of ancient Israel.

137. Ringgren, Helmer, *The Religion of Israel* (Philadelphia: Fortress, 1966). One of the best works in this field.

ANCIENT RELIGION IN GENERAL

138. Eliade, Mircea, *Cosmos and History: The Myth of the Eternal Return* (New York: Harper Torchbook, 1954). This work, and the one listed next, are indispensable studies of the religious outlook of so-called archaic societies.

139. Eliade, Mircea, *The Sacred and the Profane: The Nature of Religion* (New York: Harper Torchbook, 1961).

140. Frankfurt, H. and H. A., et al., *The Intellectual Adventure of Ancient Man* (Chicago: University of Chicago, 1946). Reprinted as *Before Philosophy* (New

York: Penguin, 1949). See especially the chapters on Egypt and Babylonia.

141. Gaster, T. H., *Thespis: Ritual, Myth and Drama in the Ancient Near East* (New York: Henry Schuman, 1950; New York: Doubleday Anchor, 2nd ed., 1961). See also his compendium, *Myth, Legend, and Custom in the Old Testament* (New York: Harper & Row, 1969).

142. Kramer, S. N., ed., *Mythologies of the Ancient World* (Chicago: Quadrangle Books, 1961; New York: Doubleday Anchor, 1961).

143. Otto, Rudolf, *The Idea of the Holy*, 2nd ed., trans. by John W. Harvey (London: Oxford University, 1950). See also *Rudolf Otto: An Introduction to his Philosophical Theology* by Philip C. Almond (Chapel Hill, NC: University of North Carolina, 1984).

144. Ringgren, Helmer, *Religions of the Ancient Near East*, trans. by John Sturdy (Philadelphia: Westminster, 1973).

145. Van der Leeuw, G., *Religion in Essence and Manifestation*, trans. by J. E. Turner (London: Allen & Unwin, 1938; New York: Harper Torchbook, incorporating the additions of the 2nd German edition by Hans H. Penner, ed., 1963).

Old Testament Theology and Hermeneutics

146. Anderson, Bernhard, W., *Creation versus Chaos: The Reinterpretation of Mythical Symbolism in the Bible* (New York: Association Press, 1967). See also *From Creation to New Creation: Old Testament Perspectives* (Minneapolis: Fortress, 1994).

147. Barr, James, *The Bible in the Modern World* (New York: Harper & Row, 1973). A stimulating treatment of the authority and relevance of the Bible. See also *Holy Scripture: Canon, Authority, Criticism* (Philadelphia: Westminster, 1983).

148. Birch, Bruce, *What Does the Lord Require?: The Old Testament Call to Social Witness* (Philadelphia: Westminster, 1985).

149. Brueggemann, Walter, *Old Testament Theology: Essays on Structure, Theme, and Text*, ed. by Patrick D. Miller, Jr. (Minneapolis: Fortress, 1992). See his forthcoming Old Testament theology.

150. Childs, Brevard, *Old Testament Theology in a Canonical Context* (Philadelphia: Fortress, 1986).

151. Crenshaw, James L., ed., *Theodicy in the Old Testament* (Philadelphia: Fortress, 1983).

152. Davidson, Robert, *The Courage to Doubt: Exploring an Old Testament Theme* (London: SCM, 1983). An invigorating study of the faith that boldly seeks understanding.

153. Eichrodt, Walther, *Theology of the Old Testament*, 2 vols., trans. by J. A. Baker from the 6th German ed. (Philadelphia: Westminster, 1961, 1967). One of the best theological works of our time, to be compared with the work by Gerhard von Rad listed below [163].

154. Fretheim, Terence E., *The Suffering of God: An Old Testament Perspective* (Philadelphia: Fortress, 1984).

155. Gammie, John, *Holiness in Israel*, Overtures to Biblical Theology (Minneapolis, MN: Fortress, 1989). An important study of the mystery and majesty of God according to various circles in ancient Israel.

156. Hayes, John H., and Frederick Prussner, *Old Testament Theology: Its History and Development* (Atlanta: John Knox, 1985).

157. Janzen, Waldemar, *Old Testament Ethics: A Paradigmatic Approach* (Louisville: Westminster/John Knox, 1994).

158. Knight, Douglas A., ed., *Tradition and Theology in the Old Testament* (Philadelphia: Fortress, 1977). Theological essays based on a traditio-historical approach; see the review essay by B. W. Anderson (*Religious Studies Review*, 6, 2 [1980], pp. 104–10).

159. Levenson, Jon D., *Sinai and Zion: An Entry into the Jewish Bible* (Minneapolis, MN: Winston-Seabury, 1985). A Jewish perspective on the relationship between two major theological trajectories in Hebrew scripture.

160. Mettinger, Tryggve N. D., *The Dethronement of Sabaoth: Studies in the Shem and Kabod Theologies,* trans. by Frederick H. Cryer (Lund, Sweden: Gleerup, 1982).

161. Oden, Robert A., "The Place of Covenant in the Religion of Israel," *Ancient Israelite Religion* [135], pp. 429–48. See also Nicholson [263].

162. Perdue, Leo, *The Collapse of History: Reconstructing Old Testament Theology,* Overtures to Biblical Theology (Minneapolis, MN: Fortress, 1994).

163. Rad, Gerhard von, *Old Testament Theology,* 2 vols; I: The Theology of Israel's Historical Traditions; II: The Theology of Israel's Prophetic Traditions, trans. by D. M. G. Stalker (New York: Harper & Row, 1962, 1965). A major work based on the history of Israel's traditions; compare the work by Eichrodt listed above [153].

164. Rendtorff, Rolf, *Canon and Theology: Overtures to an Old Testament Theology.* Overtures to Biblical Theology (Minneapolis, MN: Fortress, 1993). See his forthcoming Old Testament theology.

165. Sakenfeld, Katharine D., *Faithfulness in Action: Loyalty in Biblical Perspective,* Overtures to Biblical Theology (Philadelphia: Fortress, 1985).

166. Terrien, Samuel, *The Elusive Presence: Toward a New Biblical Theology* (New York: Harper & Row, 1978).

167. Trible, Phyllis, *God and the Rhetoric of Sexuality,* Overtures to Biblical Theology 1 (Philadelphia: Fortress, 1978). A brilliant example of how rhetorical criticism (see above under Methods of Biblical Criticism, Rhetorical Criticism) illuminates biblical interpretation. See further her studies of troublesome Old Testament stories, *Texts of Terror: Literary-Feminist Readings of Biblical Narratives,* Overtures to Biblical Theology 13 (Philadelphia: Fortress, 1984).

168. Voegelin, Eric, *Israel and Revelation* (Baton Rouge: Louisiana State University, 1956). A monumental work by a political philosopher. See the review essay by B. W. Anderson, "Politics and the Transcendent," in *Eric Voegelin's Search for Order in History,* ed. by Stephen A. McKnight (Baton Rouge: Louisiana State University, 1978), 62–100.

169. Weinfeld, Moshe, *Social Justice in Ancient Israel and in the Ancient Near East* (Minneapolis, MN: Fortress, 1995).

170. Westermann, Claus, *Elements of Old Testament Theology,* trans. by Douglas W. Scott (Atlanta: GA: John Knox, 1982). A central aspect of his theological exposition is developed in *Blessing in the Bible and in the Life of the Church,* Overtures to Biblical Theology, trans. by Keith Crim (Philadelphia: Fortress, 1978).

171. Wright, G. Ernest, *The Old Testament and Theology* (New York: Harper & Row, 1969). A vigorous theological discussion by an exponent of "theology of recitation" (see *God Who Acts* [200]).

172. Zimmerli, Walther, *Old Testament Theology in Outline,* trans. by D. E. Green (Atlanta: John Knox, 1978).

Collected Essays (not listed in another category)

173. Alt, Albrecht, *Essays on Old Testament History and Religion,* trans. by R. A. Wilson (Garden City, NY: Doubleday, 1967). Important essays by a leading German scholar of a former generation.

174. Anderson, Bernhard W., and Walter Harrelson, eds., *Israel's Prophetic Heritage: Essays in Honor of James Muilenburg* (New York: Harper & Row, 1962).

175. Anderson, G. W., ed., *Tradition and Interpretation* (Oxford: Clarendon, 1979). Essays on major aspects of Old Testament studies by members of the British Society for Old Testament Study.

176. Butler, James, Edgar Conrad, and Ben C. Ollenburger, eds., *Understanding the Word, Essays in Honor of Bernhard W. Anderson,* JSOT Supplement 37 (Sheffield: JSOT, 1985).

177. Buss, Martin, ed., *Encounter with the Text* [66]. A consideration of the central principles of interpretation, using various critical methods.

178. Coats, George, and Burke O. Long, eds., *Canon and Authority* (Philadelphia: Fortress, 1977). Essays dedicated to Walther Zimmerli.

179. Cross, Frank M., Werner E. Lemke, and Patrick D. Miller, eds., *Magnalia Dei: The Mighty Acts of God* (Garden City, NY: Doubleday, 1976). Essays in memory of G. Ernest Wright.

180. Durham, John I., and J. R. Porter, eds., *Proclamation and Presence* (Richmond: John Knox, 1970). Essays in honor of G. H. Davies.

181. Frank, H. T., and W. L. Reeds, eds., *Translating and Understanding the Old Testament* (New York: Abingdon, 1970). Essays in honor of Herbert G. May.

182. Halpern, Baruch, and Jon D. Levenson, eds., *Traditions in Transformation: Turning Points in Biblical Faith* (Winona Lake, IN: Eisenbrauns, 1984). Essays in honor of Frank M. Cross.

183. Hopfe, Lewis M., *Uncovering Ancient Stones: Essays in Memory of H. Neil Richardson* (Winona Lake, IN: Eisenbrauns, 1994).

184. Huffmon, H. B., et al., *The Quest for the Kingdom of God: Studies in Honor of George E. Mendenhall* (Winona Lake, IN: Eisenbrauns, 1984).

185. Hyatt, J. Phillip, ed., *The Bible in Modern Scholarship* (New York: Abingdon, 1963).

186. Jackson, Jared J., and Martin Kessler, eds. *Rhetorical Criticism: Essays in Honor of James Muilenburg* (Pittsburgh: Pickwick, 1974).

187. Mays, James Luther, et al., eds., *Old Testament Interpretation: Past, Present, and Future* (Nashville: Abingdon, 1995). Essays in honor of Gene M. Tucker.

188. Mendenhall, George E., *The Tenth Generation: The Origins of the Biblical Tradition* (Baltimore: Johns Hopkins University, 1973). Creative essays on the period of Israel's origins, supplementing his seminal study on "The Hebrew Conquest of Canaan" [276].

189. Meyers, Carol L., and M. O'Connor, eds., *The Word of the Lord Shall Go Forth: Essays in Honor of David Noel Freedman* (Winona Lake, IN: Eisenbrauns, 1983).

190. Noth, Martin, *The Laws in the Pentateuch and Other Studies* (Philadelphia: Fortress, 1967).

191. Rad, Gerhard von, *The Problem of the Hexateuch and Other Essays* (New York: McGraw-Hill, 1966). The lead essay is especially important for understanding form criticism and the traditio-historical method.

192. Rowley, H. H., *From Moses to Qumran: Studies in the Old Testament* (London: Lutterworth, 1963).

193. Westermann, Claus, ed., *Essays on Old Testament Hermeneutics,* trans. and ed. by J. L. Mays (Richmond, VA: John Knox, 1971).

194. Zimmerli, Walther, *The Law and the Prophets,* trans. by R. E. Clements (Oxford, England: Blackwell, 1965).

READINGS CHAPTER BY CHAPTER

Introduction: The Old Testament as the Story of a People

195. Anderson, Bernhard W., "The Bible as the Shared 'Story of a People,'" in *The Old and New Testaments: Their Relationship and the "Intertestamental" Literature,* ed. by James H. Charlesworth and Walter P. Weaver (Valley Forge, PA: Trinity Press International, 1993), 19–37.

196. Brueggemann, Walter, *The Creative Word: Canon as a Model for Biblical Education* (Philadelphia: Fortress, 1982).

197. Gese, Hartmut, "The Idea of History in the Ancient Near East and the Old Testament," *Journal for Theology and Church,* 1 (1965), 49–64.

198. Herberg, Will, "Biblical Faith as *Heilsgeschichte:* The Meaning of Redemptive History in Human Existence," in *Faith Enacted as History: Essays in Biblical Theology,* ed. by Bernhard W. Anderson (Philadelphia: Westminster, 1976), 32–42. In the same volume see the essay on "Five Meanings of the Word 'Historical,'" 132–37.

199. Niebuhr, H. Richard, *The Meaning of Revelation* (New York: Macmillan, 1941). Chap. 2, on "The Story of Our Life," is especially valuable in this connection.

200. Wright, G. Ernest, *God Who Acts,* Studies in Biblical Theology 8 (Naperville, IL: Alec R. Allenson, 1952). An exposition of Israel's historically oriented faith. For a challenge to this understanding of biblical theology, see Brevard Childs, *Biblical Theology in Crisis* (Philadelphia: Westminster, 1970).

CHAPTER 1:
CREATION OF A PEOPLE

The Nature of the Tradition

Today it is recognized that the refined analysis of putative literary "sources," as found, for instance, in S. R. Driver's *Introduction* [43], is inadequate. Attention has turned to a study of the oral formation and transmission of the traditions (form criticism, history of traditions, canonical criticism) or the formulation of the traditions in final, written form (rhetorical criticism, redaction criticism, structuralism) [See Nos. 85–96]. Also, attention has turned to the narrative character of Israel's history and the limitations of historical methods.

201. Barr, James, "Story and History in Biblical Theology," *Journal of Religion,* 56 (1976), 1–17.

202. Bright, John, *Early Israel in Recent History Writing,* Studies in Biblical Theology 19 (London: SCM, 1965). A vigorous criticism of the historical approach of Martin Noth [115].

203. De Vaux, Roland, "Method in the Study of Early Hebrew History," *The Bible in Modern Scholarship* [185], 15–29. See also the responses to this article by George E. Mendenhall and Moshe Greenberg in the same volume.

204. Harvey, Van A., *The Historian and the Believer* (New York: Macmillan, 1966). An important study of the relation between religious faith and a "scientific" approach to history. See further George W. Ramsey, *The Quest* [116], chap. 1, "The Historian's Craft."

205. Miller, J. M., *The Old Testament and the Historian* (Philadelphia: Fortress, 1976).

206. Noth, Martin, "Analysis of the Elements of the Traditions," in *Pentateuchal Traditions* [76], 52ff. See also the translator's introductory essay on Noth's "traditio-historical approach."

207. Rad, Gerhard von, "The Form-critical Problem of the Hexateuch," in *Essays* [191], 1–78. His position is summarized in his commentary on Genesis [305], pp. 1–23.

Historical and Religious Background— Period of Israel's Ancestors

208. Alt, Albrecht, "The God of the Fathers," in *Essays* [128], 1–100. A fundamental essay on "patriarchal" religion; compare Cross's essay listed next.

209. Cross, Frank M., "The Religion of Canaan and the God of Israel," *Canaanite Myth and Hebrew Epic* [129], 1–75. An important and illuminating discussion based on his earlier essay, "Yahweh and the God of the Patriarchs," *Harvard Theological Review* LV (1962), 225–59.

210. De Vaux, Roland, "The Hebrew Patriarchs and History," *The Bible and the Ancient Near East: Essays in Honor of W. F. Albright,* ed. by G. Ernest Wright (Garden City, NY: Doubleday, 1965), 111–21.

211. Greenberg, Moshe, *The Hab/piru* (New Haven: American Oriental Society, 1955). A basic work on the subject.

212. Holt, John, *The Patriarchs of Israel* (Nashville: Vanderbilt University, 1964). Emphasizes a core of historicity in patriarchal traditions; compare this view with the chapter on "The Patriarchal Period" in George W. Ramsey, *The Quest* [116], chap. 2.

213. Luke, J. T., "Abraham and the Iron Age: Reflections on the New Patriarchal Studies," *Journal for the Study of the Old Testament,* 4 (1977), 35–47. See other essays in this journal.

214. Mazar, B., "The Historical Background of the Book of Genesis," *Journal of Near Eastern Studies,* 28 (1969), 78–83.

215. McKane, W., *Studies in the Patriarchal Narratives* (Edinburgh: Handsel, 1979).

216. Moberly, R. W. L., *The Old Testament of the Old Testament: Patriarchal Narratives and Mosaic Yahwism,* Overtures to Biblical Theology (Minneapolis, Fortress, 1992).

217. Thompson, T. L., *The Historicity of the Patriarchal Narratives,* Beiheft zur Zeitschrift für die alttestamentliche Wissenschaft 133 (Berlin; New York: W. de Gruyter, 1974). This monograph, and the book by Van Seters listed next, are at the center of current controversy.

218. Van Seters, J., *Abraham in History and Tradition* (New Haven: Yale University, 1975). Argues that Israel's Epic traditions date from the post-exilic period. Summarized in "Patriarchs," Supplement to *Interpreter's Dictionary of the Bible* [32], 645–48.

219. Van Seters, J., *Prologue to History: The Yahwist as Historian in Genesis* (Louisville: Westminster/John Knox, 1992).

220. Wright, G. E., "History and the Patriarchs," in *Expository Times* LXXI (1960), 292–96. See also the response by Gerhard von Rad, "History and the Patriarchs," in *Expository Times* LXXII (1961), 213–16.

Neighboring Peoples

221. Albrektson, Bertil, *History and the Gods: An Essay on the Idea of Historical Events as Divine Manifestations in the Ancient Near East and in Israel* (Lund, Sweden: C. W. K. Gleerup, 1967). A challenge to the notion that the theme of divine acts in history was unique with Israel. See the review of this important book by W. G. Lambert, *Orientalia,* 39 (1970), 170–77.

222. Dever, W. G., "The Peoples of Palestine in the Middle Bronze I Period," *Harvard Theological Review,* 64 (1971), 197–226.

223. Gurney, O. R., *The Hittites,* 2nd ed. (New York: Pelican, 1954). An authoritative discussion.

224. Kramer, S. N., *The Sumerians: Their History, Culture, and Character* (Chicago: University of Chicago, 1963). One of the definitive works in this field.

225. Lichtheim, M., *Ancient Egyptian Literature,* I–II (Berkeley CA: University of California, 1973–76).

226. Morenz, Siegfried, *Egyptian Religion,* trans. by Ann E. Keep (Ithaca, NY: Cornell University, 1973).

227. Moscati, Sabatino, *The World of the Phoenicians,* trans. by Alastair Hamilton (New York: F. A. Praeger, 1968).

228. Oppenheim, A. Leo, *Ancient Mesopotamia: Portrait of a Dead Civilization* (Chicago: University of Chicago, 1964). Emphasizes the complexity and variety of Mesopotamian religion.

229. Pitard, Wayne T., *Ancient Damascus: A Historical Study of the Syrian City-State from Earliest Times Until Its Fall to the Assyrians in 732 B.C.E.* (Winona Lake, IN: Eisenbrauns, 1987).

230. Saggs, H. W. F., *The Greatness that Was Babylon* (New York: Hawthorne Books, 1962).

231. Steindorff, George, and Keith C. Seele, *When Egypt Ruled the East*, 2nd ed. (Chicago: University of Chicago, 1957; Phoenix, 1963). Reliable, interestingly written, beautifully illustrated.

232. Toorn, K. van der, *From Her Cradle to Her Grave: The Role of Religion in the Life of the Israelite and the Babylonian Women*, trans. by Sara J. Denning-Bolle (Sheffield: JSOT, 1994).

233. Wilson, John A., *The Burden of Egypt* (Chicago: University of Chicago, 1951); also *The Culture of Ancient Egypt* (Chicago: University of Chicago, 1971, copyright 1956). An illuminating exposition of Egyptian history and culture. See especially chaps. 7–10.

CHAPTER 2: LIBERATION FROM BONDAGE

234. Beegle, Dewey M., *Moses, Servant of Yahweh* (Grand Rapids, MI: Eerdmans, 1972). Advocates the essential historicity of the Moses story on the basis of literary criticism and archaeology.

235. Buber, Martin, *Moses* (London: East & West Library, 1946; Harper Torchbook, 1968). Selections from this study by the great Jewish philosopher appear in *The Writings of Martin Buber*, II, ed. by Will Herberg (New York: Meridian, 1956).

236. Campbell, Edward F., "Moses and the Foundations of Israel," *Interpretation* 29 (1975), 141–54.

237. Cassuto, U., *A Commentary on the Book of Exodus*, trans. by Israel Abrahams (Jerusalem: Magnes, 1967). An important work by a Jewish scholar who rejects the conclusions of source criticism.

238. Childs, Brevard S., *The Book of Exodus*, The Old Testament Library [26], 1974. A fresh study which stresses the place of the book of Exodus in the biblical canon.

239. Clements, Ronald E., *Exodus*, Cambridge Bible [20], 1972.

240. Croatto, J. Severino, *Exodus: A Hermeneutics of Freedom*, trans. by Salvator Attanasio (Maryknoll, NY: Orbis Books, 1981). A superb example of Latin American "liberation theology." See also the works of Gustavo Gutierrez, e.g., *A Theology of Liberation* (Maryknoll, NY: Orbis Books, 1973) and *The Power of the Poor in History* (Maryknoll, NY: Orbis Books, 1983).

241. Fackenheim, Emil L., *God's Presence in History: Jewish Affirmations and Philosophical Reflections* (New York: Harper & Row, 1970). A profound philosophical discussion of Exodus and Sinai in Jewish tradition.

242. Fretheim, Terence E., *Exodus,* Interpretation [22], 1991.

243. Gowan, Donald E., *Theology in Exodus: Biblical Theology in the Form of a Commentary* (Louisville: Westminster/John Knox, 1994).

244. Greenberg, Moshe, *Understanding Exodus* (New York: Melton Research Center of the Jewish Theological Seminary of America, 1969). A very helpful commentary.

245. Miller, Patrick D., *The Divine Warrior in Early Israel* (Cambridge, MA: Harvard University, 1973).

246. Nicholson, E. W., *Exodus and Sinai in History and Tradition* (Richmond. VA: John Knox, 1973).

247. Noth, Martin, *Exodus*, trans. by J. S. Bowden, The Old Testament Library [26], 1962. This commentary is too brief to do justice to Noth's work.

248. Olson, Dennis, *The Death of the Old and the Birth of the New: The Framework of the Book of Numbers and the Pentateuch*, Brown Judaic Studies 71 (Chico, CA: Scholars, 1985).

249. Rad, Gerhard von, *Moses*, World Christian Books (London: Lutterworth, 1960). A profound little book, simply written.

250. Widengren, G., "What Do We Know About Moses?" in *Proclamation and Presence* [180], 21–47.

CHAPTER 3: COVENANT IN THE WILDERNESS

251. Alt, Albrecht, "The Origins of Israelite Law," *Essays* [128], 101–71. A basic form-critical study of types of law in the Pentateuch.

252. Baltzer, Klaus, *The Covenant Formulary in the Old Testament, Jewish and Early Christian Writings*, trans. by David E. Green (Philadelphia: Fortress, 1971). One of the basic studies of the treaty or covenant form.

253. Beyerlin, Walter, *Origins and History of the Oldest Sinaitic Traditions*, trans. by Stanley Rudman (Oxford: Blackwell, 1965). Argues that Exodus and Sinai traditions have a common origin. See also E. W. Nicholson [246].

254. Coats, George W., *Rebellion in the Wilderness* (New York: Abingdon, 1968).

255. Harrelson, Walter, *The Ten Commandments and Human Rights,* Overtures to Biblical Theology (Philadelphia: Fortress, 1980).

256. Hillers, Delbert R., *Covenant: The History of a Biblical Idea* (Baltimore: Johns Hopkins, 1969), Clearly written, illuminating discussion of covenant language and motifs in the Old Testament. See further the work of Mendenhall listed below [260].

257. Huffmon, Herbert B., "The Exodus, Sinai and the Credo," *Catholic Biblical Quarterly* XXVII (1965), 101–13.

258. McCarthy, Dennis J., *Treaty and Covenant, A Study in Form in the Ancient Oriental Documents and in the Old Testament,* Analecta Biblica 21 (Rome: Pontifical Biblical Institute, 1963). Another important investigation of the relation between Israel's covenant form and the treaty form of Hittite (also pre-Hittite and non-Hittite) documents.

259. McCarthy, Dennis J., *Old Testament Covenant* (Richmond: John Knox, 1972). A summary of discussions on the subject.

260. Mendenhall, George F., *Law and Covenant in Israel and the Ancient Near East* (Pittsburgh: Biblical Colloquium, 1955), reprinted from *The Biblical Archaeologist,* XVII, 2 (May 1954), 26–46; and no. 3 (Sept. 1954), 49–76. A seminal discussion of Israel's covenant tradition, seen in the light of Hittite parallels. See also his later article, "Covenant," *The Interpreter's Dictionary of the Bible* [31], and his book, *The Tenth Generation* [188].

261. Muilenburg, James, "The Form and Structure of the Covenantal Formulations," *Vetus Testamentum,* IX (1959), 347–65.

262. Newman, Murray Lee, *The People of the Covenant: A Study of Israel from Moses to the Monarchy* (New York: Abingdon, 1962). An analysis of two major covenant traditions, showing their bearing upon Israel's history.

263. Nicholson, Ernest N. *God and His People: Covenant and Theology in the Old Testament* (Oxford: Clarendon Press, 1986). Excellent study of a familiar theme which brings to expression a distinctive understanding of the relationship between God, the chosen people, and the world.

264. Noth, Martin, "The Laws in the Pentateuch: Their Assumptions and Meaning," *Laws in the Pentateuch* [190], 1–107.

265. Stamm, J. J., and M. E. Andrew, *The Ten Commandments in Recent Research,* Studies in Biblical Theology, 2nd series, 2 (Naperville, IL: Alec R. Allenson, 1967). See also the discussion of the Decalogue in Brevard Childs' commentary [238], pp. 385–439.

CHAPTER 4: THE PROMISED LAND

On the geography of Canaan see especially Nos. 35–41.

266. Alt, Albrecht, "The Settlement of the Israelites in Palestine," *Essays* [128], 133–69.

267. Bright, John, "Introduction and Exegesis to the Book of Joshua," *The Interpreter's Bible,* II [23]. See further his *History* [110], chap. 3.

268. Brueggemann, Walter, *The Land,* Overtures to Biblical Theology (Philadelphia: Fortress, 1977).

269. Conrad, Edgar W., *Fear Not Warrior. A Study of 'al tîra' Pericopes in the Hebrew Scriptures,* Brown Judaic Studies (Chico, CA: Scholars, 1985).

270. Freedman, D. N., and D. F. Graf, *Palestine in Transition: The Emergence of Ancient Israel* (Sheffield: Almond, 1983). Important essays dealing with the origins of Israel, especially in the light of the sociological approach advocated by Gottwald [271].

271. Gottwald, Norman, *The Tribes of Yahweh: A Sociology of the Religion of Liberated Israel, 1250–1050 B.C.E.* (Maryknoll, NY: Orbis Books, 1979). A monumental study which builds on Mendenhall's thesis of a "peasant revolt" [188] and uses a sociological method for interpreting Israel's early history.

272. Kenyon, Kathleen, *Digging Up Jericho* (New York: Praeger, 1957). By the distinguished archaeologist who excavated the ancient city.

273. Lapp, Paul, "The Conquest of Palestine in the Light of Archaeology," *Concordia Theological Monthly,* 38 (1967), 283–300.

274. Lind, Millard C., *Yahweh is a Warrior: The Theology of Warfare in Ancient Israel* (Scottdale, PA: Herald, 1980). A fresh and illuminating treatment of the subject.

275. Mayes, A. D. H., *The Story of Israel between Settlement and Exile: A Redactional Study of the Deuteronomistic History* (London: SCM, 1983).

276. Mendenhall, George E., "The Hebrew Conquest of Canaan." *The Biblical Archaeologist,* XXV (1962), 66–87; reprinted in *Biblical Archaeologist Reader,* III [119], 100–20. See further *The Tenth Generation* [188]. A seminal and influential theory that the conquest was a revolution within Canaan.

277. Miller, J. M., and G. M. Tucker, *The Book of Joshua,* Cambridge Bible Commentary [20], 1974.

278. Noth, Martin, *The Deuteronomistic History,* JSOT Supplement 15 (Sheffield: JSOT, 1981). A fundamental work on the Deuteronomistic History; the section on the Chronicler's Work is not translated. See McKenzie and Graham, *Heritage of Martin Noth* [77].

279. Peckham, Brian, *The Composition of the Deuteronomistic History,* Harvard Semitic Monographs 35 (Atlanta: Scholars, 1985).

280. Rad, Gerhard von, *Holy War in Ancient Israel,* trans. and ed. by Marna J. Dawn, intro. by Ben C. Ollenburger (Grand Rapids, MI: Eerdmans, 1991).

281. Soggin, J. A., *Joshua,* trans. by R. A. Wilson, Old Testament Library [26], 1972. Advocates essentially the view of Noth.

282. Weippert, Manfred, *The Settlement of the Israelite Tribes in Palestine,* Studies in Biblical Theology, 2nd series, 21 (Naperville, IL: Alec R. Allenson, 1971). An important study which advocates the "peaceful entry" hypothesis.

283. Wright, G. Ernest, "The Literary and Historical Problems of Joshua 10 and Judges 1," *Journal of Near Eastern Studies,* 5 (1946), 105–14. Argues that the two accounts reflect different phases of Israel's incursion into Canaan.

284. Wright, G. Ernest, *Shechem: The Biography of a Biblical City* (New York: McGraw-Hill, 1965). A vivid account of the results of excavation at the former center of the Tribal Confederacy.

285. Yadin, Yigael, *Hazor: The Rediscovery of a Great Citadel of the Bible* (London: Weidenfeld & Nicolson, 1975). See also the works cited under "History" and "Archaeology."

Chapter 5: The Formation of an All-Israelite Epic

On Myth and Legend

286. Anderson, Bernhard W., "Mythopoeic and Theological Dimensions of Biblical

Creation Faith," in *Creation in the Old Testament* [132], 1–24.

287. Batto, Bernard Frank, *Slaying the Dragon: Mythmaking in the Biblical Tradition* (Louisville: Westminster/John Knox, 1992).

288. Brandon, S. G. F., *Creation Legends of the Ancient Near East* (London: Hodder & Stoughton, 1963).

289. Buber, Martin, "Saga and History," *The Writings of Martin Buber,* ed. by Will Herberg (New York: Meridian Books, 1956), 149–56. A valuable aid to understanding the character of biblical narratives.

290. Gunkel, Hermann, "The Influence of Babylonian Mythology Upon the Biblical Creation Story," in *Creation in the Old Testament* [132], 25–52. Excerpted from his seminal work, *Schöpfung und Chaos* [132].

291. Gunkel, Hermann, *The Legends of Genesis: The Biblical Saga and History* (New York: Schocken, 1964). This little book, which carries a preface by W. F. Albright, is a reprint of the introduction to Gunkel's monumental commentary on Genesis, dating to the year 1901, which provided the foundation for modern form-critical studies. See also *The Folktale in the Old Testament,* Historic Texts & Interpreters in Biblical Scholarship (Sheffield: Almond, 1987), a translation of Gunkel's work by Michael D. Rutter.

292. Heidel, Alexander, *The Babylonian Genesis,* 2nd ed. (Chicago: University of Chicago, 1951; Phoenix Books, 1963). Also *The Gilgamesh Epic and Old Testament Parallels* (Chicago: University of Chicago, 1946; Phoenix Books, 1963).

293. Hooke, S. H., *Middle Eastern Mythology* (Baltimore: Penguin Books, 1963).

294. Lord, Albert, *The Singer of Tales* (Cambridge, MA: Harvard University, 1964; Atheneum, 1973). A treatment of the transmission of Homeric poetry which may throw light on the history of Israelite storytelling.

295. Otzen, Benedikt, et al., *Myths in the Old Testament,* trans. by Frederick Cryer (London: SCM, 1980). This book, which is impressively introduced by Thorkild Jacobsen, carries on the important Scandinavian contribution to biblical studies. See Nos. 81–84.

296. Rogerson, J. W., *Myth in Old Testament Interpretation,* Beiheft zur Zeitschrift für die alttestamentliche Wissenschaft 134 (Berlin and New York: W. de Gruyter, 1974).

On mythology, see also Nos. 138–45.

On the Israelite Epic Tradition

See above all the essays by Gerhard von Rad on the formation of the Israelite epic [191].

297. Clements, R. E., "Pentateuchal Problems" in *Tradition and Interpretation* [175], 66–124. A valuable discussion of trends in the understanding of the Torah.

298. Clines, David J. A., *The Theme of the Pentateuch,* JSOT Supplement 10 (Sheffield: JSOT, 1978). A study of the overall thematic unity of the Pentateuch in its final form, which does not ignore the history of traditions.

299. Ellis, Peter, *The Yahwist: The Bible's First Theologian* (Notre Dame, IN: Fides Publishers, 1968).

See also works by J. A. Sanders, especially *Torah and Canon* [102], which stress the dynamic character of the "Torah Story."

On the Book of Genesis

300. Brueggemann, Walter, *Genesis,* Interpretation [22], 1982. A fresh and illuminating commentary.

301. Cassuto, U., *A Commentary on the Book of Genesis,* 2 vols., trans. by Israel Abrahams (Jerusalem: Magnes, 1961, 1964). A valuable commentary by a conservative Jewish scholar. It extends only to Gen. 13:5, for it was cut short by the author's death.

302. Coats, George W., *Genesis, with an Introduction to Narrative Literature,* I: The Forms of the Old Testament Literature (Grand Rapids, MI: Eerdmans, 1983). The first in a form-critical series designed to cover the whole Old Testament.

303. Davidson, Robert, *Genesis,* 2 vols., Cambridge Bible Commentary [20], 1973, 1979.

304. Jacob, B., *The First Book of the Bible: Genesis,* trans. and ed. by Ernest I. Jacob and Walter Jacob (New York: KTAV, 1974). A condensation of a major work in German.

305. Rad, Gerhard von, *Genesis,* trans. by John Marks, rev. ed., Old Testament Library [26], 1972. A masterful, perceptive interpretation in light of form-critical studies.

306. Sarna, Nahum M., *Understanding Genesis,* The Heritage of Biblical Israel 1 (New York: McGraw Hill, 1966; Schocken, 1970). An excellent study by a Jewish scholar.

307. Speiser, E. A., *Genesis,* Anchor Bible [19], 1964). A fresh translation with helpful notes, many of which deal with alleged Near Eastern parallels.

308. Vawter, Bruce, *On Genesis: A New Reading* (Garden City, NY: Doubleday, 1977). A valuable work by a leading Roman Catholic scholar.

309. Westermann, Claus, *Genesis,* 3 vols., Biblischer Kommentar (Neukirchen: Neukirchener, 1970–1982). Genesis 1–11, trans. by John J. Scullion (Minneapolis, MN: Augsburg, 1984). A monumental work based on a form-critical approach.

See also the study of the legends of Genesis by Gunkel [291] and some of the studies listed under "Methods of Biblical Criticism" [64–108].

CHAPTER 6: THE STRUGGLE BETWEEN FAITH AND CULTURE

310. Albright, W. F., *Yahweh and the Gods of Canaan* (Garden City, NY: Doubleday Anchor Books, 1969). Israel's faith is compared and contrasted with surrounding Canaanite culture. See also his *Archaeology and the Religion of Israel* [127], chap. 4.

311. Anderson, G. W., "Israel: Amphictyony: 'Am; Kahal; 'Edah," in *Translating and Understanding the Old Testament* [181], 135–51.

312. Boling, Robert G., *Judges,* Anchor Bible [19], 1975.

313. Buber, Martin, *The Prophetic Faith* [348], especially the discussion of the Song of Deborah and the clash between Israel's faith and Canaanite religion, pp. 8–12 and 70–80.

314. Cross, Frank M., "The Cultus of the Israelite League," *Canaanite Myth and Hebrew Epic* [129], chaps. 4, 5, 6.

315. Dothan, Trude, *The Philistines and Their Material Culture* (New Haven: Yale University, 1982).

316. Driver, G. R., *Canaanite Myths and Legends* (Edinburgh: T. & T. Clark, 1956).

317. Gray, John, *The Legacy of Canaan,* 2nd ed. (Leiden: Brill, 1965). A popular study of the Ras Shamra texts and their bearing on the Old Testament by the author of *The Canaanites* (London: Thames Hudson, 1964).

318. Gray, John, *Judges,* New Century Bible [25], 1967.

319. Maier, Walter A., III., *Asherah: Extrabiblical Evidence* (Atlanta: Scholars, 1986).

320. Martin, J. D., *The Book of Judges,* Cambridge Bible Commentary [20], 1975.

321. Morton, James D., *Judges,* Cambridge Bible Commentary [20], 1975.

322. Noth, Martin, *Das System der Zwölf Stämme Israels* (1930; reprinted, Darmstadt: Wissenschaftliche Buchgesellschaft, 1966). A seminal essay arguing that Israel was constituted as a twelve-tribe amphictyony. For one critical response, see the essay by G. W. Anderson listed above [311].

323. Smend, R., *Yahweh War and Tribal Confederation: Reflections Upon Israel's Earliest History,* trans. from the 2nd ed. by Max G. Rogers (Nashville: Abingdon, 1970).

324. Smith, Mark S., *The Ugaritic Baal Cycle* (Leiden; New York: E. J. Brill, 1994).

325. Wright, G. Ernest, *The Old Testament Against Its Environment,* Studies in Biblical Theology 2 (Naperville, IL: Alec R. Allenson, 1950).

See also works on the Religion of Israel, Nos. 126–37; and works dealing with the History of Israel, 109–18.

CHAPTER 7: THE THRONE OF DAVID

326. Ackroyd, P. R., *The First Book of Samuel* (1971), *The Second Book of Samuel* (1977), Cambridge Bible Commentary [20].

327. Alt, Albrecht, "The Formation of the Israelite State in Palestine," *Essays* [128], 223–309.

328. Birch, Bruce C., *The Rise of the Israelite Monarchy: The Growth and Development of I Samuel 7–15* (Missoula: Scholars, 1976). See also his essay on "The Development of the Tradition on the Anointing of Saul in I Sam 9:1–10:16," *Journal of Biblical Literature* 90 (1971), 55–68.

329. Clements, R. E., *Abraham and David,* Studies in Biblical Theology, 2nd series, 5 (Naperville, IL: Alec R. Allenson, 1967).

330. Cross, Frank M., "The Ideologies of Kingship in the Era of the Empire: Conditional Covenant and Eternal Decree," in *Canaanite Myth and Hebrew Epic* [129], chap. 9.

331. Gray, John, *I and II Kings,* 2nd ed., Old Testament Library [26], 1970.

332. Hertzberg, H. W., *The Books of Samuel,* trans. by J. S. Bowden, Old Testament Library [26], 1964.

333. Long, Burke, *I Kings, with an Introduction to Historical Literature,* The Forms of the Old Testament Literature IX (Grand Rapids, MI: Eerdmans, 1984).

334. McCarter, P. K., *I–II Samuel,* Anchor Bible [19], 1980.

335. Mendenhall, G. E., "The Monarchy," *Interpretation* 29 (1975), 155–70. Suggests that Israelite society was corrupted by alien political and social models.

336. Mettinger, Tryggve N. D., *King and Messiah: The Civil and Sacral Legitimation of the Israelite Kings* (Lund, Sweden: Gleerup, 1976). A study that brings one to the frontier of research in this area.

337. Porter, J. R., "Old Testament Historiography," *Tradition and Interpretation* [175], 125–62. Discussion of recent research on the Deuteronomistic History (as well as the Chronicler's Work).

338. Roberts, J. J. M., "The Davidic Origins of the Zion Tradition," *Journal of Biblical Literature,* 92 (1973), 329–44.

339. Robinson, J., *I Kings* (1972), *II Kings* (1976), Cambridge Bible Commentary [20].

340. Rylaarsdam, J. C., "Jewish-Christian Relationship: The Two Covenants and the Dilemmas of Christology," *Journal of Ecumenical Studies,* 9 (1972), 249–70; reprinted in *Grace Upon Grace: Essays in Honor of L. J. Kuyper* (Grand Rapids, MI: Eerdmans, 1975), 70–84. This essay contains a clear and illuminating comparison of the Mosaic and Davidic covenant traditions. See also the work by Jon D. Levenson [159].

Literature of the Period

341. Campbell, E. F., *Ruth,* Anchor Bible [19], 1975. Persuasively places this short story in the context of the literature of the early monarchy.

342. Gunn, David, *The Story of David: Genre and Interpretation,* JSOT Supplement 6 (Sheffield: JSOT, 1978).

343. Miller, P. D., and J. J. M. Roberts, *The Hand of the Lord* (Baltimore: Johns Hopkins, 1977). A study of the ark narratives in I Samuel.

344. Rost, Leonard, *The Succession to the Throne of David,* trans. by M. D. Ritter and D. M. Gunn, Historic Texts and Interpreters in Biblical Scholarship 1 (Sheffield: Almond, 1982). A basic study of the Court History.

345. Whybray, R. N., *The Succession Narrative: A Study of II Samuel 9–20; I Kings 1 and 2,* Studies in Biblical Theology, 2nd series, 9 (Naperville, IL: Alec R. Allenson, 1968). Contrary to Rost [344], he questions the historical reliability of this narrative.

On the Yahwist, see Peter Ellis [299], Wolff and Brueggemann [70].

CHAPTER 8: PROPHETIC TROUBLERS OF ISRAEL

General Works on Prophecy in Israel

346. Barton, John, *Oracles of God: Perceptions of Ancient Prophecy in Israel after the Exile* (New York: Oxford University, 1988, copyright 1986).

347. Blenkinsopp, Joseph, *A History of Prophecy in Israel* (Philadelphia: Westminster, 1983).

348. Buber, Martin, *The Prophetic Faith,* trans. by C. Witton-Davies (New York: Macmillan, 1949; Harper Torchbook, 1960). A subtle, sensitive interpretation of the prophetic tradition.

349. Clements, R. E., *Prophecy and Covenant,* Studies in Biblical Theology, 43 (Naperville, IL: Alec R. Allenson, 1965).

350. Crenshaw, James L., *Prophetic Conflict: Its Effect upon Israelite Religion,* Beiheft zur Zeitschrift für die alttestamentliche Wissenschaft 124 (Berlin: Walter de Gruyter, 1971).

351. DeVries, Simon, *Prophet Against Prophet* (Grand Rapids, MI: Eerdmans, 1978). A discussion of the role of the Micaiah Narrative (I Kings 22) in early prophetic tradition.

352. Heschel, Abraham J., *The Prophets* (New York: Harper & Row, 1963). A discerning work by a Jewish philosopher; one of the best books on prophecy.

353. Jemielity, Thomas, *Satire and the Hebrew Prophets* (Louisville: Westminster/John Knox, 1992).

354. Johnson, Aubrey R., *The Cultic Prophet in Ancient Israel,* 2nd ed. (Cardiff: University of Wales, 1962). This valuable study traces the connection of many early prophets with the cult.

355. Lindblom, Johannes, *Prophecy in Ancient Israel* (Philadelphia: Muhlenberg, 1963). A fundamental work by a Swedish scholar.

356. McKane, William, *Prophets and Wise Men,* Studies in Biblical Theology 44 (Naperville, IL: Alec R. Allenson, 1965).

357. Miller, P. D., Jr., *Sin and Judgment in the Prophets: A Stylistic and Theological Analysis* (Chico, CA: Scholars, 1982).

358. Mowinckel, Sigmund, *Prophecy and Tradition,* Avhandlinger utgitt av Det Norske Videnskaps-Akademi (Oslo, Norway: Jacob Dybwad, 1946). A traditio-historical approach to the study of Israelite prophecy.

359. Newsome, James D., Jr., *The Hebrew Prophets* (Atlanta: John Knox, 1984).

360. Niditch, Susan, *The Symbolic Vision in Biblical Tradition* (Chico, CA: Scholars, 1983, copyright 1980).

361. Noth, Martin, "History and Word of God in the Old Testament," in his *Laws in the Pentateuch* [190], 179–93. Prophecy at Mari compared with Israelite prophecy.

362. Overholt, Thomas W., *Channels of Prophecy: The Social Dynamics of Prophetic Activity* (Minneapolis, MN: Fortress, 1989).

363. Parker, S. B., "Jezebel's Reception of Jehu," *Maarav* I (1978–79), 67–78. A reconsideration of Jezebel's motives in the story found in II Kings 9:30–37.

364. Rad, Gerhard von, *The Prophetic Message,* trans. by D. M. G. Stalker (London: SCM, 1968). Based on his *Old Testament Theology,* II [163].

365. Rofé, Alexander, *The Prophetical Stories* (Jerusalem: Magnes, Hebrew University, 1988).

366. Ross, James, "Prophecy in Hamath, Israel, and Mari," *Harvard Theological Review,* LXIII (1970), 1–28. See also his essay, "The Prophet as Yahweh's Messenger," *Israel's Prophetic Heritage* [174], 98–107.

367. Rowley, H. H., "Elijah on Mount Carmel," in *Bulletin of the John Rylands Library,* XLIII (1960–61), 190–210.

368. Scott, R. B. Y., *The Relevance of the Prophets,* rev. ed. (New York: Macmillan, 1968). This book continues to have great value.

369. Ward, James M., *Thus Says the Lord: The Message of the Prophets* (Nashville: Abingdon, 1991).

370. Westermann, Claus, *Basic Forms of Prophetic Speech,* trans. by Hugh K. White (Philadelphia: Westminster, 1967). A form-critical study of the genres used in prophetic speech.

371. Wilson, Robert R., *Prophecy and Society in Ancient Israel* (Philadelphia: Fortress, 1980). An important sociological approach to the types of prophecy in ancient Israel. See also the essays on Israelite prophecy in *Interpretation,* 32, 1 (1978).

CHAPTER 9: FALLEN IS THE VIRGIN ISRAEL

See the general books listed under the preceding chapter. For an introduction to eighth-century prophecy, see the following:

372. Anderson, Bernhard W., *The Eighth Century Prophets* (Philadelphia: Fortress, 1978).

373. Davies, Philip R., and David J. A. Clines, eds., *Among the Prophets: Language, Image and Structure in the Prophetic Writings,* JSOT Supplement 144 (Sheffield: JSOT, 1993).

374. Koch, Klaus, *The Prophets,* I: The Assyrian Period, trans. by Margaret Kohl (Philadelphia: Fortress, 1983).

On Amos

375. Barton, J., *Amos' Oracles Against the Nations* (London and New York: Cambridge University, 1980).

376. Coote, R. B., *Amos Among the Prophets: Composition and Theology* (Philadelphia: Fortress, 1981).

377. Kapelrud, Arvid S., *Central Ideas in Amos* (Oslo, Norway: Oslo University, 1961; first printed 1956). See also "New Ideas in Amos," Supplements to Vetus Testamentum XV (1965), 193–206.

378. King, Philip J., *Amos, Hosea, Micah: An Archaeological Commentary* (Philadelphia: Westminster, 1988).

379. Mays, James L., *Amos,* The Old Testament Library [26], 1969. Highly recommended.

380. Smith, George Adam, *The Book of the Twelve Prophets,* I, rev. ed. (New York: Harper & Row, 1940). This is a great classic. Smith's treatments of Amos and Hosea deserve special attention.

381. Ward, James M., *Amos and Isaiah: Prophets of the Word of God* (New York: Abingdon, 1969).

382. Wolff, H. W., *Amos, the Prophet: The Man and His Background,* trans. by Foster R. McCurley, ed. by John Reumann (Philadelphia: Fortress, 1973). Argues that Amos' native environment was that of clan wisdom.

383. Wolff, H. W., *Joel and Amos,* trans. by W. Janzen et al., Hermeneia [21], 1977.

On Hosea

384. Anderson, F. I., and D. N. Freedman, *Hosea,* Anchor Bible [19] 1980.

385. Brueggemann, Walter, *Tradition for Crisis: A Study in Hosea* (Richmond, VA: John Knox, 1968).

386. Emmerson, Grace I., *Hosea: An Israelite Prophet in Judean Perspective,* JSOT Supplement 28 (Sheffield: JSOT, 1984).

387. Mays, James L., *Hosea,* Old Testament Library [26], 1969. Highly recommended.

388. Rowley, H. H., "The Marriage of Hosea," *Bulletin of the John Rylands Library,* XXXIX (1956), 203–33. A good survey of a major problem in the book of Hosea.

389. Snaith, Norman H., *Mercy and Sacrifice: A Study of the Book of Hosea* (London: SCM, 1953).

390. Ward, James M., *Hosea: A Theological Commentary* (New York: Harper & Row, 1966).

391. Wolff, H. W., *Hosea,* Hermeneia [21], 1977. One of the best commentaries.

392. Yee, Gale A., *Composition and Tradition in the Book of Hosea: A Redaction-Critical Investigation,* SBL Dissertation Series 102 (Atlanta, GA: Scholars, 1987).

CHAPTER 10: JUDAH'S COVENANT WITH DEATH

On Isaiah of Jerusalem

393. Childs, Brevard, *Isaiah and the Assyrian Crisis,* Studies in Biblical Theology, 2nd series, 3 (Naperville, IL: Alec R. Allenson, 1967).

394. Clements, R. E., *Isaiah 1–39,* New Century Bible [25], 1981. See also *Isaiah and the Deliverance of Jerusalem: A Study of the Interpretation of Prophecy in the Old Testament,* JSOT Supplement 13 (Sheffield: JSOT, 1980).

395. Hayes, John H., *Isaiah, the Eighth-Century Prophet: His Times and His Preaching* (Nashville: Abingdon, 1987).

396. Irvine, Stuart A., *Isaiah, Ahaz, and the Syro-Ephraimitic Crisis* (Atlanta, GA: Scholars, 1990).

397. Jensen, Joseph, *Isaiah 1–39,* Old Testament Message 8 (Wilmington, DE: Michael Glazier, 1984). A compact, illuminating commentary by a leading Roman Catholic scholar.

398. Kaiser, Otto, *Isaiah 1–12,* trans. by R. A. Wilson, Old Testament Library [26], 1972; also *Isaiah 13–39,* trans. by R. A. Wilson, Old Testament Library [26], 1974.

399. Kissane, Edward J., *The Book of Isaiah,* 2nd ed., 2 vols. (Dublin: Browne & Nolan, 1960).

400. Ollenburger, Bennie C., "Zion, the City of the Great King: A Theological Investigation of Zion Symbolism in the Tradition of the Jerusalem Cult." Diss., Princeton Theological Seminary (Ann Arbor: University Microfilms International, 1983). Excellent introduction to Zion theology.

401. Scott, R. B. Y., "Introduction and Exegesis to Isaiah 1–39," *The Interpreter's Bible,* V [23], 1956.

402. Seitz, Christopher R., *Isaiah 1–39,* Interpretation [22], 1989.

403. Vriezen, Th. C., "Essentials of the Theology of Isaiah," *Israel's Prophetic Heritage* [174], 128–46.

See also J. M. Ward [381].

On Micah

404. Hagstrom, David Gerald, *The Coherence of the Book of Micah: A Literary Analysis* (Atlanta, GA: Scholars, 1988).

405. Hillers, Delbert, *A Commentary on the Book of the Prophet Micah,* Hermeneia [21], 1984.

406. Mays, James L., *Micah,* Old Testament Library [26], 1976. An important commentary, concerned with redaction criticism.

407. Wolff, H. W., *Micah the Prophet,* trans. by R. D. Gehrke (Philadelphia: Fortress, 1981).

CHAPTER 11: THE REDISCOVERY OF MOSAIC TORAH

408. Bright, John, "The Date of the Prose Sermons of Jeremiah," *Journal of Biblical Literature,* LXX (1951), 15–35. Opposes the view maintained, for instance, by Hyatt [434], that the book of Jeremiah has been radically reworked by Deuteron-

omistic editors; reprinted in *Prophet to the Nations* [439], 193–212.

409. Clements, R. E., *God's Chosen People: A Theological Interpretation of the Book of Deuteronomy* (London: SCM, 1968).

410. Craige, P. C., *The Book of Deuteronomy,* New International Commentary on the Old Testament (Grand Rapids, MI: Eerdmans, 1976). Represents a conservative position on date and unity.

411. Cross, Frank M., "The Themes of the Book of Kings and the Structure of the Deuteronomistic History," in *Canaanite Myth and Hebrew Epic* [129], chap. 10.

412. McConville, J. G., *Law and Theology in Deuteronomy,* JSOT Supplement 33 (Sheffield: JSOT, 1984).

413. Miller, Patrick D., Jr., *Deuteronomy,* Interpretation [22], 1990.

414. Nicholson, E. W., *Deuteronomy and Tradition* (Philadelphia: Fortress, 1967).

415. Nicholson, E. W., *Preaching to the Exiles: A Study of the Prose Tradition in the Book of Jeremiah* (Oxford: Blackwell, 1970). Holds that the "Deuteronomic" prose sermons of the book of Jeremiah were addressed to the situation of the Exile.

416. Philips, Anthony, *Deuteronomy,* Cambridge Bible Commentary [20], 1973.

417. Pressler, Carolyn, *The View of Women Found in the Deuteronomic Family Laws* (Berlin; New York: W. de Gruyter, 1993).

418. Rad, Gerhard von, *Deuteronomy,* trans. by Dorothea Barton, Old Testament Library [26], 1966. See also his *Studies in Deuteronomy,* Studies in Biblical Theology 9 (London: SCM Press, 1953).

419. Rowley, H. H., "The Prophet Jeremiah and the Book of Deuteronomy," in the book edited by the same author, *Studies in Old Testament Prophecy* (Edinburgh: T. & T. Clark, 1950), 157–74. Also in Rowley's *From Moses to Qumran* (London: Lutterworth, 1963), 187–208.

420. Weinfeld, M., *Deuteronomy and the Deuteronomic School* (Oxford: Clarendon, 1972). Shows the affinity of Deuteronomic theology to Wisdom.

421. Weinfeld, M., *Deuteronomy 1–11: A New Translation with Introduction and Commentary* (New York: Doubleday, 1991).

422. Wright, G. Ernest, "Introduction and Exegesis to Deuteronomy," *The Interpreter's Bible,* II [23], 1953. An excellent treatment.

See also essays on Jeremiah's call, his relation to the Deuteronomic Reform, and the "Foe from the North" in Perdue and Kovacs, eds., *A Prophet to the Nations* [439]. Works on the Deuteronomistic History are listed above under chap. 4.

CHAPTER 12: THE DOOM OF THE NATION

423. Anderson, Bernhard W., "The New Covenant and the Old," *The Old Testament and Christian Faith* (New York: Herder and Herder, 1969), 225–42. A discussion of a crucial passage in Jer. 31:31–34.

424. Berridge, John M., *Prophet, People, and the Word of Yahweh: An Examination of Form and Content in the Proclamation of the Prophet Jeremiah* (Zurich: EVZ, 1970).

425. Blank, Sheldon, *Jeremiah: Man and Prophet* (Cincinnati: Hebrew Union College, 1961).

426. Bright, John, *Jeremiah,* Anchor Bible [19], 1965. A fresh translation with helpful interpretation. See also his essay listed above [408].

427. Brueggemann, Walter, *To Pluck Up, to Tear Down: A Commentary on the Book of Jeremiah 1–25* (Grand Rapids, MI: Eerdmans; Edinburgh: Handsel, 1988).

428. Carroll, R. P., *From Chaos to Covenant: Prophecy in the Book of Jeremiah* (New York: Crossroad, 1981). A revolutionary work which maintains that Jeremiah is known only through the community that produced the book of Jeremiah. See also his essay, "Prophecy, Dissonance, and Jer. 26," in Perdue and Kovacs, eds., *A Prophet to the Nations* [439], 381–91.

429. Carroll, R. P., *Jeremiah: A Commentary,* Old Testament Library [26], 1986.

430. Clements, R. E., *Jeremiah* (Atlanta: John Knox, 1988).

431. Habel, Norman, *Jeremiah, Lamentations,* Concordia Commentary (St. Louis: Concordia, 1968).

432. Holladay, William A., *The Architecture of Jeremiah 1–20* (Lewisburg, PA: Bucknell University, 1975). See also his brief introduction, *Jeremiah: Spokesman Out of Time* (Philadelphia: United Church, 1974).

433. Holladay, William A., *Jeremiah 1: A Commentary on the Book of the Prophet Jeremiah, Chapters 1–25,* Hermeneia [21], 1986; *Jeremiah 2: A Commentary on the Book of the Prophet Jeremiah, Chapters 26–52,* Hermeneia [21], 1989.

434. Hyatt, J. P., *Jeremiah, Prophet of Courage and Hope* (New York: Abingdon, 1958). See also his "Introduction and Exegesis to Jeremiah," *The Interpreter's Bible,* VI [23], 1956.

435. King, Philip J., *Jeremiah: An Archaeological Companion* (Louisville: Westminster/ John Knox, 1993).

436. Lundbom, Jack R., *Jeremiah: A Study in Ancient Hebrew Rhetoric,* SBL Dissertation Series 18 (Missoula, MT: Scholars, 1975).

437. McKane, William, *A Critical and Exegetical Commentary on Jeremiah* (Edinburgh: T. & T. Clark, 1986–).

438. O'Connor, Kathleen, *The Confessions of Jeremiah,* SBL Dissertation Series 94 (Chico, CA: Scholars, 1985).

439. Perdue, Leo G., and Brian Kovacs, eds., *A Prophet to the Nations: Essays in Jeremiah Studies* (Winona Lake, IN: Eisenbrauns, 1984). Notice Perdue's introductory essay, "Jeremiah in Modern Research: Approaches and Issues."

440. Rowley, H. H., "The Early Prophecies of Jeremiah in their Setting," *Bulletin of the John Rylands Library,* XLV (1962), 198–234. Reprinted in Perdue and Kovacs, eds., *A Prophet to the Nations* [439], 33–61.

441. Seitz, Christopher R., *Theology in Conflict: Reactions to the Exile in the Book of Jeremiah* (Berlin; New York: De Gruyter, 1989).

442. Skinner, John, *Prophecy and Religion* (New York: Cambridge, 1922). This has long been a standard book on Jeremiah.

On Zephaniah

443. Berlin, Adele, *Zephaniah: A New Translation with Introduction and Commentary,* Anchor Bible [19], 1994.

444. Kapelrud, A. S., *The Message of the Prophet Zephaniah* (Oslo, Norway: Universitetsforlaget, 1975).

On Habakkuk

445. Albright, W. F., "The Psalm of Habakkuk," in *Studies in Old Testament Prophecy: Essays in Honor of T. H. Robinson,* ed. by H. H. Rowley (New York: Scribners, 1950), pp. 1–18.

446. Gowan, D. E., *The Triumph of Faith in Habakkuk* (Atlanta: John Knox, 1976).

447. Haak, Robert D., *Habakkuk* (Leiden; New York: E. J. Brill, 1992).

448. Hiebert, Theodore, "Habakkuk," *Books of the Bible,* I [9], pp. 391–96.

On Lamentations

449. Albrektson, Bertil, *Studies in the Text and Theology of the Book of Lamentations* (Lund, Sweden: Gleerup, 1963).

450. Ferris, Paul Wayne, Jr., *The Genre of Communal Lament in the Bible and the Ancient Near East* (Atlanta: Scholars, 1992).

451. Gottwald, Norman K., *Studies in the Book of Lamentations,* Studies in Biblical Theology 14 (Naperville, IL: Alec R. Allenson, 1954).

452. Hillers, Delbert R., *Lamentations: A New Translation with Introduction and Commentary,* 2nd rev. ed. (New York: Doubleday, 1992).

453. Westermann, Claus, *Lamentations: Issues and Interpretation,* trans. by Charles Muenchow (Minneapolis: Fortress, 1994).

CHAPTER 13: BY THE WATERS OF BABYLON

454. Anderson, Bernhard W., "A Stylistic Study of the Priestly Creation Story," in Coats and Long, eds., *Canon and Authority* [178], 148–62. Another study relevant to the Priestly Work is "Creation and the Noachic Covenant," in *From Creation to New Creation* [146], chap. 9.

455. Brueggemann, Walter, "The Kerygma of the Priestly Writers," *The Vitality of Israel's Traditions* [70], chap. 6.

456. Carley, Keith, *Ezekiel Among the Prophets,* Studies in Biblical Theology, 2nd series, 31 (London: SCM, 1971).

457. Cody, Aelred, *Ezekiel, With an Excursus on Old Testament Priesthood* (Wilmington, DE: M. Glazier, 1984).

458. Cross, Frank M., "The Priestly Work," *Canaanite Myth and Hebrew Epic* [129], 293–325. Fundamental for understanding the Priestly edition of the Pentateuch (or Tetrateuch).

459. Davis, Ellen F., *Swallowing the Scroll: Textuality and the Dynamics of Discourse in Ezekiel's Prophecy,* Bible and Literature 21 (Sheffield: Almond, 1989).

460. Eichrodt, Walther, *Ezekiel,* trans. by Cosslett Quin, Old Testament Library [26], 1970.

461. Galambush, Julie, *Jerusalem in the Book of Ezekiel: The City as Yahweh's Wife,* SBL Dissertation Series 130 (Atlanta: Scholars, 1992).

462. Greenberg, Moshe, *Ezekiel 1–20,* Anchor Bible [19], 1983. A creative work that moves in a new direction.

463. Haran, M., *Temples and Temple Service in Ancient Israel: An Inquiry into the Character of Cult Phenomena and the Historical Setting of the Priestly School* (London: Oxford University, 1978). A new slant on the Priestly tradition.

464. Joyce, Paul, *Divine Initiative and Human Response in Ezekiel* (Sheffield: JSOT, 1989).

465. Klein, R. W., *Israel in Exile: A Theological Interpretation,* Overtures to Biblical Theology (Philadelphia: Fortress, 1979).

466. Klein, R. W., *Ezekiel: The Prophet and His Message* (Columbia: University of South Carolina, 1988).

467. McEvenue, Sean E., *The Narrative Style of the Priestly Writer,* Analecta Biblica 50 (Rome: Biblical Institute, 1971). Emphasizes the rhetorical and dramatic qualities of the Priestly Writing.

468. Mettinger, Tryggve N. D., *The Dethronement of Sabaoth: Studies in the Shem and Kabod Theologies* [160], especially chap. 3 on "Kabod Theology."

469. Nelson, Robert D., *Raising Up a Faithful Priest: Community and Priesthood in Biblical Theology* (Louisville, KY: Westminster, 1993). One of the best books on the subject.

470. Noth, Martin, *Leviticus,* trans. by J. E. Anderson, Old Testament Library [26], 1965.

471. Raitt, Thomas A., *A Theology of Exile* (Philadelphia: Fortress, 1977).

472. Wevers, J. W., *Ezekiel,* Cambridge Bible Commentary [20], 1982.

473. Zimmerli, Walther, *Ezekiel,* 2 vols., Hermeneia [21], 1979, 1983. A monumental work. See also his essay, "The Message of the Prophet Ezekiel," *Interpretation,* 23 (1969), 131–57.

CHAPTER 14: THE DAWN OF A NEW AGE

474. Anderson, Bernhard W., "Exodus Typology in Second Isaiah," *Israel's Prophetic*

Heritage [174], 177–95; also "Exodus and Covenant in Second Isaiah and Prophetic Tradition," *Magnalia Dei* [179], 339–60.

475. Clifford, Richard J., *Fair Spoken and Persuading: An Interpretation of Second Isaiah* (New York: Paulist, 1984).

476. Clines, David J. A., *I, He, We, and They: A Literary Approach to Isaiah 53,* JSOT Supplement 1 (Sheffield: JSOT, 1976).

477. Conrad, Edgar W., "Second Isaiah and the Priestly Oracle of Salvation," *Zeitschrift für die Alttestamentliche Wissenschaft* 93 (1981), 234–46; "The 'Fear Not' Oracles in Second Isaiah," *Vetus Testamentum* 34 (1984), 129–52. See also, *Fear Not Warrior: A Study of 'al tira' Pericopes in the Hebrew Scriptures,* Brown Judaic Studies 75 (Chico, CA: Scholars, 1985).

478. Hanson, Paul D., *Isaiah 40–66,* Interpretation [22], 1995.

479. Knight, George A. F., *Deutero-Isaiah: A Theological Commentary on Isaiah 40–55* (New York: Abingdon, 1965).

480. McKenzie, John L., *Second Isaiah,* Anchor Bible [19], 1968.

481. Melugin, Roy F., *The Formation of Isaiah 40–55,* Beiheft zur Zeitschrift für die Alttestamentliche Wissenschaft 141 (Berlin: Walter de Gruyter, 1976). An illuminating literary study.

482. Mettinger, Tryggve N. D., *A Farewell to the Servant Songs: A Critical Examination of an Exegetical Axiom* (Lund, Sweden: Gleerup, 1983).

483. Muilenburg, James, "Introduction and Exegesis to Isaiah 40–66," *The Interpreter's Bible,* V [23], 1956. One of the best commentaries on Second Isaiah, emphasizing rhetorical criticism.

484. North, Christopher R., *Isaiah 40–55* (New York: Macmillan, 1964). His *The Suffering Servant in Deutero-Isaiah,* 2nd ed. (New York: Oxford, 1956) gives a good discussion of the various interpretations of the Servant.

485. Rowley, H. H., *The Servant of the Lord and Other Essays on the Old Testament,*

2nd ed. (Oxford: Blackwell, 1965), 3–60. A good review of various interpretations.

486. Smart, James D., *History and Theology in Second Isaiah: A Commentary on Isaiah 35, 40–66* (Philadelphia: Westminster, 1965). Places Second Isaiah in Judah, not Babylonia.

487. Stuhlmueller, Carroll, *Creative Redemption in Deutero-Isaiah,* Analecta Biblica 43 (Rome: Biblical Institute, 1970).

488. Waldow, H. E. von, "The Message of Deutero-Isaiah," *Interpretation,* 21 (1968), 259–87.

489. Westermann, Claus, *Isaiah 40–66,* trans. by D. M. G. Stalker, Old Testament Library [26], 1969. A major work using a form-critical approach.

490. Whybray, R. N., *Isaiah 40–66,* New Century Bible Commentary [25], 1975. The same author has produced a brief, valuable introduction: *The Second Isaiah,* Old Testament Guides (Sheffield: JSOT, 1983).

491. Wilson, Andrew, *The Nations in Deutero-Isaiah: A Study on Composition and Structure* (Lewiston, NY: E. Mellen, 1986).

492. Zimmerli, Walther, and J. Jeremias, *The Servant of God,* Studies in Biblical Theology 20 (Naperville, IL: Alec R. Allenson, 1957). Zimmerli's study on this subject now appears in Kittel's *Theological Dictionary of the New Testament,* V (Grand Rapids, MI: Eerdmans, 1968), 655–77.

On new attempts to understand the unity of the whole book of Isaiah, see Brevard Childs, *Introduction* [42], chap. 17; Edgar Conrad, *Reading Isaiah* (Minneapolis: Fortress, 1991); Katheryn Pfisterer Darr, *Isaiah's Vision and the Family of God* (Louisville: Westminster John Knox, 1994). *Interpretation* 36 (1982) is devoted to the book of Isaiah; especially the article by R. E. Clements, pp. 117–29. See the illuminating essay by Walter Brueggemann, "Unity and Dynamic in the Isaiah Tradition," *Journal for the Study of the Old Testament* 29 (1984), 89–107; also in the same journal, vol. 31, pp. 95–113, R. C. Clements, "Beyond Tradition-History: Deutero-Isaianic Development of First Isaiah's Themes."

CHAPTER 15: A KINGDOM OF PRIESTS

493. Ackroyd, Peter R., *The Chronicler in His Age*, JSOT Supplement 107 (Sheffield: JSOT, 1991).

494. Ackroyd, Peter R., *Exile and Restoration: A Study of Hebrew Thought of the Sixth Century B.C.* (Philadelphia: Westminster, 1968); also *Israel under Babylon and Persia* (London: Oxford, 1970). Important works by an authority in this field. See also his essays, "The Chronicler as Exegete," *Journal for the Study of the Old Testament* 2 (1977), 2–32, and "History and Theology in the Writings of the Chronicler," *Concordia Theological Monthly* 38 (1967), 501–15.

495. Clines, David J. A., *Ezra, Nehemiah, Esther*, New Century Bible Commentary [25], 1984.

496. Coggins, R. J., *First and Second Books of Chronicles*, Cambridge Bible Commentary [20], 1976.

497. Cross, Frank M., "A Reconstruction of the Judean Restoration," *Journal of Biblical Literature* 94 (1975), 4–18.

498. De Vaux, Roland, *Studies in Old Testament Sacrifice* (Cardiff: University of Wales, 1964). A perceptive discussion of how sacrificial worship was transformed in Israel's faith.

499. De Vries, Simon John, *1 and 2 Chronicles* (Grand Rapids, MI: Eerdmans, 1989).

500. Duke, Rodney K., *The Persuasive Appeal of the Chronicler: A Rhetorical Analysis* (Sheffield: Almond, 1990).

501. Freedman, D. N., "The Chronicler's Purpose," *Catholic Biblical Quarterly* XXIII (1961), 436–42. An illuminating essay.

502. Hanson, Paul, *The Dawn of Apocalyptic* (Philadelphia: Fortress, 1975). Discussion of the historical and sociological roots of apocalyptic, concentrating on so-called Third Isaiah and related literature.

503. Japhet, Sara, *I & II Chronicles: A Commentary*, Old Testament Library [26], 1993.

504. Kidner, D., *Ezra and Nehemiah: An Introduction and Commentary*, Tyndale Old Testament Commentaries (London: Inter Varsity Press, 1979). Conservative; sensitive to critical issues.

505. Myers, Jacob M., *I and II Chronicles*, 2 vols., Anchor Bible [19], 1965. See also his Anchor volume on *Ezra-Nehemiah* (1965).

506. Rowley, H. H., "Nehemiah's Mission and Its Background," in *Bulletin of the John Rylands Library*, XXXVII (1955), 528–61.

507. Rowley, H. H., *The Rediscovery of the Old Testament* (Philadelphia: Westminster, 1964). Chapter 7 gives an appreciative treatment of the ethos of Judaism.

On Haggai and Zechariah

508. Ackroyd, P. R., "The Book of Haggai and Zechariah 1–8," *Journal of Jewish Studies*, 3 (1952), 151–56; and "Studies in the Book of Haggai" in the same journal, 163–76.

509. Meyers, Carol L. and Eric M., *Haggai; Zechariah 1–8: A New Translation with Introduction and Commentary* (Garden City, NY: Doubleday, 1987).

510. Petersen, David L., *Haggai and Zechariah 1–8*, Old Testament Library [26], 1984. An up-to-date and helpful study.

511. Petersen, David L., *Zechariah 9–14 and Malachi*, Old Testament Library [26], 1995.

512. Redditt, Paul L., *Haggai, Zechariah and Malachi: Based on the Revised Standard Version* (London: M. Pickering/Harper Collins; Grand Rapids, MI: Eerdmans, 1995).

513. Stuhlmueller, Carroll, *Rebuilding with Hope: A Commentary on the Books of Haggai and Zechariah* (Grand Rapids, MI: Eerdmans; Edinburgh: Handsel, 1988).

On Joel

514. Prinsloo, Willem S., *The Theology of the Book of Joel*, Beiheft zur Zeitschrift für die Alttestamentliche Wissenschaft 163 (Berlin; New York: de Gruyter, 1985).

515. Kapelrud, A. S., *Joel Studies* (Uppsala: Almquist & Wiksell, 1948).

516. Wolff, H. W., *Joel and Amos*, Hermeneia [21], 1977. An excellent work.

CHAPTER 16: THE PRAISES OF ISRAEL

See the Akkadian and Egyptian hymns and prayers translated in J. B. Pritchard, ed., *Ancient Near Eastern Texts* [1], pp. 365–92. On worship in ancient Israel, see the following:

517. Clements, R. E., *God and Temple* (Philadelphia: Fortress, 1965). A study of the Jerusalem Temple as the center of Yahweh's presence in ancient Israel.

518. Cumming, Charles G., *The Assyrian and Hebrew Hymns of Praise* (New York: Columbia University, 1934). Treats formal parallels to Israel's hymnody.

519. De Vaux, Roland, *Ancient Israel* [130], especially Part IV which deals with Israel's sacral institutions.

520. Eaton, J. H., *Kingship and the Psalms*, Studies in Biblical Theology, 2nd series, 32 (London: SCM, 1976).

521. Harrelson, Walter, *From Fertility Cult to Worship* (Garden City, NY: Doubleday, 1970).

552. Johnson, Aubrey R., *Sacral Kingship in Ancient Israel*, 2nd ed. (Cardiff: University of Wales, 1967).

523. Kraus, H. J., *Worship in Israel*, trans. by Geoffrey Buswell (Richmond: John Knox, 1965). Especially helpful for understanding the Zion cult.

524. Rowley, H. H., *Worship in Ancient Israel: Its Forms and Meaning* (Philadelphia: Fortress, 1967).

525. Widengren, George, *The Accadian and Hebrew Songs of Lamentation* (Uppsala: Almquist & Wiksell, 1936). Helpful for understanding the genre of the laments.

On the Book of Psalms

526. Anderson, Bernhard W., *Out of the Depths: The Psalms Speak for Us Today*, rev. ed. (Philadelphia: Westminster, 1983). An introduction that uses a form-critical approach.

527. Barth, Christoph, *Introduction to the Psalms*, trans. by R. A. Wilson (New York: Scribner's, 1966). An excellent introduction, especially illuminating on theological issues.

528. Eaton, J. H., *Psalms: Introduction and Commentary*, Torch Bible Commentaries (London: S.C.M., 1967).

529. Gerstenberger, E., "Psalms," in *Old Testament Form Criticism* [71], 179–224.

530. Gunkel, Hermann, *The Psalms: A Form-critical Introduction*, trans. by Thomas M. Horner, with an introduction by James Muilenburg (Philadelphia: Fortress, 1967). A basic introduction to the genres of the Psalter by the great pioneer of form criticism and author (with Joachim Begrich) of *Einleitung in die Psalmen* (Göttingen: Vendenhoeck & Ruprecht, 1933).

531. Guthrie, Harvey H., *Israel's Sacred Songs* (New York: Seabury, 1966).

532. Kraus, H. J., *Psalmen*, Biblischer Kommentar, 2nd ed. (Neukirchen: Neukirchener, 1961). A major work on the Psalms.

533. McCann, J. Clinton, ed., *The Shape and Shaping of the Psalter,* JSOT Supplement 159 (Sheffield: JSOT, 1993).

534. Miller, Patrick D., Jr., *Interpreting the Psalms* (Philadelphia: Fortress, 1986); also his perceptive study, *They Cried Unto the Lord: The Form and Theology of Biblical Prayer* (Minneapolis, MN: Fortress, 1994).

535. Mowinckel, Sigmund, *The Psalms in Israel's Worship*, I–II, trans. by D. R. Ap-Thomas (New York: Abingdon, 1962). See also his earlier *Psalmenstudien* I–VI (Amsterdam: Verlag P. Schnippers, 1921–1924). The works of Mowinckel and Gunkel are fundamental to all modern study of the Psalter.

536. Ringgren, Helmer, *The Faith of the Psalmists* (London: SCM, 1963).

537. Terrien, Samuel, *The Psalms and Their Meaning for Today* (Indianapolis: Bobbs-Merrill, 1952).

538. Weiser, Artur, *The Psalms*, trans. by Herbert Hartwell, Old Testament Library [26] (1962). An important work which, however, overstresses the place of many psalms in covenant-renewal festivals.

539. Westermann, Claus, *The Praise of God in the Psalms*, trans. by Keith R. Crim (Richmond: John Knox, 1965). An important form-critical study which suggests a new way of classifying the types of psalms. See also *Praise and Lament in The Psalms*, trans. by Keith R. Crim and Richard N. Soulen (Atlanta: John Knox, 1981).

540. Wilson, Gerald H., *The Editing of the Hebrew Psalter*, SBL Dissertation Series 76 (Chico, CA: Scholars, 1985). A creative attempt to understand the book of Psalms as a whole.

CHAPTER 17: THE BEGINNING OF WISDOM

541. Blenkinsopp, Joseph, *Wisdom and Law in the Old Testament: The Ordering of Life in Israel and Early Judaism* (London; New York: Oxford University, 1983).

542. Bryce, Glendon E., *A Legacy of Wisdom: The Egyptian Contribution to the Wisdom of Israel* (Lewisburg, PA: Bucknell University, 1979). By an Old Testament scholar who was also an Egyptologist.

543. Crenshaw, James L., *Old Testament Wisdom: An Introduction* (Atlanta: John Knox, 1981). A valuable introduction by one of the authorities in this field.

544. Emerton, J. A., "Wisdom," *Tradition and Interpretation* [175], 214–37. A discriminating survey of discussions of the subject.

545. Gammie, J. G., et al., eds., *Israelite Wisdom: Theological and Literary Essays in Honor of Samuel Terrien* (Missoula, MT: Scholars, 1978). Valuable contributions; the essay by Hans-Jürgen Hermisson on wisdom and creation theology is reproduced in *Creation in the Old Testament* [132], pp. 118–34.

546. Gammie, John G., and Leo G. Perdue, eds., *The Sage in Israel and the Ancient Near East* (Winona Lake, IN: Eisenbrauns, 1990).

547. McKane, William, *Prophets and Wise Men*, Studies in Biblical Theology 44 (Naperville, IL: Alec R. Allenson, 1965).

548. Murphy, Roland, *Wisdom Literature*, Forms of Old Testament Literature 13 (Grand Rapids, MI: Eerdmans, 1981). See also Roland Murphy et al., eds., *Wisdom Literature & Psalms*, Interpreting Biblical Texts (Nashville: Abingdon, 1983), and the literature cited there.

549. Murphy, Roland, *The Wisdom Literature: Job, Proverbs, Ruth, Canticles, Ecclesiastes, and Esther* (Grand Rapids, MI: Eerdmans, 1981).

550. Noth, Martin, and D. Winton Thomas, eds., *Wisdom in Israel and in the Near East*, Supplement to *Vetus Testamentum* III (Leiden: Brill, 1955).

551. Perdue, Leo G., *Wisdom and Creation: The Theology of Wisdom Literature* (Nashville: Abingdon, 1994). See also Nicholson, E. W. *God and His People: Covenant and Theology in the Old Testament* (Oxford: Clarendon Press; New York: Oxford University Press, 1986). Excellent study of a familiar theme which brings to expression a distinctive understanding of the relationship between God, the chosen people, and the work.

552. Rad, Gerhard von, *Wisdom in Israel*, trans. by James D. Martin (New York: Abingdon, 1973). One of the best theological introductions to the subject.

553. Rylaarsdam, J. Coert, *Revelation in Jewish Wisdom Literature* (Chicago: University of Chicago, 1946). This valuable little book shows how Wisdom and Torah were eventually identified.

554. Scott, R. B. Y., *The Way of Wisdom in the Old Testament* (New York: Macmillan, 1971).

555. Whybray, R. N., *The Intellectual Tradition in the Old Testament*, Beiheft zur Zeitschrift für die Alttestamentliche Wissenschaft (Berlin: Walter de Gruyter, 1974).

On Proverbs

556. McKane, William, *Proverbs: A New Approach*, Old Testament Library [26], 1970. One of the best commentaries available.

557. Scott, R. B. Y., *Proverbs and Ecclesiastes*, Anchor Bible [19], 1965.

558. Whybray, R. N., *The Book of Proverbs*, Cambridge Bible Commentary [20], 1972. See also his earlier book, *Wisdom in Proverbs: The Concept of Wisdom in Proverbs 1–9*, Studies in Biblical Theology 45 (London: SCM, 1965).

On Ecclesiastes

559. Anthony, Perry T., *Dialogues with Kohelet: The Book of Ecclesiastes: Translation and Commentary* (University Park, PA: Pennsylvania State University, 1993).

560. Crenshaw, James L., *Ecclesiastes: A Commentary*, Old Testament Library [26], 1988.

561. Farmer, Kathleen Anne, *Who Knows What Is Good?" A Commentary on the Books of Proverbs and Ecclesiastes* (Grand Rapids, MI: Eerdmans, 1991).

562. Gordis, Robert, *Koheleth: The Man and His World* (New York: Jewish Theological Seminary of America, 1951; rev. ed., Schocken Books, 1967). A fresh translation with commentary.

563. Ogden, Graham S., "The 'Better'-Proverb (Tob-Spruch), Rhetorical Criticism, and Qoheleth," *Journal of Biblical Literature,*

96 (1977), 489–505. See also his various essays on passages in Ecclesiastes, e.g., *Vetus Testamentum,* 30 (1980), 27–37, 309–15.

564. Rankin, O. S., "Introduction and Exegesis to Ecclesiastes" *The Interpreter's Bible,* V [23], 1956.

On the Book of Job

565. Dhorme, Edouard Paul, *A Commentary on the Book of Job*, trans. by Harold Knight (London: Nelson, 1967). A classic commentary, first issued in 1926.

566. Gordis, Robert, *The Book of God and Man: A Study of Job* (Chicago: University of Chicago, 1965).

567. Gutierrez, Gustavo, *On Job: God-talk and the Suffering of the Innocent,* trans. by Matthew J. O'Connell (Maryknoll, NY: Orbis, 1987).

568. Habel, Norman C., *The Book of Job*, Old Testament Library [26], 1985. An illuminating, up-to-date commentary.

569. Jantzen, J. Gerald, *Job*, Interpretation [22], 1985.

570. Penchansky, David, *The Betrayal of God: Ideological Conflict in Job* (Louisville: Westminster/John Knox, 1990).

571. Perdue, Leo G., *Wisdom in Revolt: Metaphorical Theology in the Book of Job,* JSOT Supplement 112 (Sheffield: Almond, 1991).

572. Perdue, Leo G., and W. Clark Gilpin, eds., *The Voice from the Whirlwind: Interpreting the Book of Job* (Nashville: Abingdon, 1992).

573. Pope, Marvin H., *Job*, Anchor Bible [19], 1964. A fresh translation with notes.

574. Terrien, Samuel, "Introduction and Exegesis to Job," *The Interpreter's Bible,* III [23], 1954. An excellent commentary with respect to both literary analysis and theological interpretation. See also his book, *Job: Poet of Existence* (Indianapolis, IN: Bobbs-Merrill, 1958).

575. Van der Lugt, Pieter, *Rhetorical Criticism and the Poetry of the Book of Job* (Leiden; New York: E. J. Brill, 1995).

576. Westermann, Claus, *The Structure of the Book of Job: A Form-Critical Analysis* (Philadelphia, Fortress, 1981).

For a structuralist analysis of the book of Job, see the study by Robert Polzin [96].

On the Song of Songs

577. Fox, Michael V., *The Song of Songs and the Ancient Egyptian Love Songs* (Madison, WI: University of Wisconsin, 1985).

578. Gordis, Robert, *The Song of Songs and Lamentations,* revised and augmented (New York: KTAV, 1974).

579. Goulder, M. D., *The Song of Fourteen Songs* (Sheffield: JSOT, 1986).

580. Landy, Francis, *Paradoxes of Paradise: Identity and Difference in the Song of Songs* (Sheffield: Almond, 1983).

581. Murphy, Roland Edmund, *The Song of Songs,* Hermeneia [21], 1990.

582. Pope, Marvin, *The Song of Songs,* Anchor Bible [19], 1977.

583. Rowley, H. H., "The Interpretation of the Song of Songs," in his collected essays, *The Servant* [485], 195–245.

584. Sasson, Jack, "Unlocking the Poetry of Love in the Song of Songs," *Bible Review* I (1985), 11–19. An illuminating essay, which provides an excellent brief introduction.

CHAPTER 18:
THE UNFINISHED STORY

See editions of the Apocrypha and Pseudepigrapha listed above [5, 7], especially the work edited by James Charlesworth. For a selection of literature bearing on early Judaism, see the following:

585. Nickelsburg, George W. E., and Michael E. Stone, *Faith and Piety in Early Judaism: Texts and Documents* (Philadelphia: Fortress, 1983).

History and Literature of the Period

586. Metzger, Bruce, *An Introduction to the Apocrypha* (New York: Oxford, 1957).

587. Neusner, Jacob, *Invitation to the Talmud,* rev. ed. (San Francisco: Harper & Row, 1984); also *Midrash in Context* (Philadelphia: Fortress, 1983).

588. Nickelsburg, George W. E., *Jewish Literature Between the Bible and the Mishnah: A Historical and Literary Introduction* (Philadelphia: Fortress, 1981). An indispensable work by a leading scholar in the field.

589. Pfeiffer, R. H., *History of New Testament Times with an Introduction to the Apocrypha* (New York: Harper & Row, 1949).

590. Russell, D. S., *The Method and Message of Jewish Apocalyptic,* Old Testament Library [26], 1964. A comprehensive study of apocalyptic from 200 B.C.E. to 100 C.E. See also his paperback, *Apocalyptic Ancient and Modern* (Philadelphia: Fortress, 1978).

591. Schürer, Emil, *The History of the Jewish People in the Age of Jesus Christ* 1, rev. ed. by G. Vermes and F. Millar (Edinburgh: T. & T. Clark, 1973).

592. Tcherikover, Avigdor, *Hellenistic Civilization and the Jews,* trans. by S. Appelbaum (Philadelphia: Jewish Publication Society of America, 1959; New York: Atheneum, 1970).

On Eschatology and Apocalyptic

593. Brown, Raymond E., *The Semitic Background of the Term "Mystery" in the New Testament,* Facet Books, Biblical Series (Philadelphia: Fortress, 1968). Illuminates the motif of "secret" in prophecy and apocalyptic.

594. Frost, S. B., *Old Testament Apocalyptic* (London: Epworth, 1952). See also

"Apocalyptic and History" in *The Bible in Modern Scholarship* [185], 98–113.

595. Funk, Robert W., "Apocalypticism," the subject of the *Journal for Theology and the Church*, 6 (New York: Herder and Herder, 1969). An important discussion by outstanding scholars.

596. Hanson, Paul, "Jewish Apocalyptic against its Near Eastern Environment," *Revue Biblique*, 78 (1971); also "Old Testament Apocalyptic Reexamined," *Interpretation*, 25 (1971), 454–79. See also *Visionaries and Their Apocalypses*, Issues in Religion and Theology 2 (Philadelphia: Fortress, 1983), a collection of important essays edited by Hanson. See especially *The Dawn of Apocalyptic* cited above [502].

597. Koch, Klaus, *The Rediscovery of Apocalyptic*, trans. by Margaret Kohl, Studies in Biblical Theology, 2nd series 22, (Naperville, IL: Alec R. Allenson, 1970).

598. Mowinckel, Sigmund, *He That Cometh*, trans. by G. W. Anderson (New York: Abingdon, 1956). One of the most important works on Israelite eschatology.

599. Nicholson, E. W., "Apocalyptic," in *Tradition and Interpretation* [175], 189–213. A perceptive survey of recent scholarly discussions.

600. Schmithals, Walter, *The Apocalyptic Movement: Introduction and Interpretation*, trans. by John E. Steely (Nashville: Abingdon, 1975).

See also Gerhard von Rad's discussion of apocalyptic in his *Theology*, II [163]. He maintains that apocalyptic belongs primarily in the circle of wisdom, rather than of prophecy.

On the Book of Daniel

601. Collins, John J., *Daniel, with an Introduction to Apocalyptic Literature* (Grand Rapids, MI: Eerdmans, 1985). Discusses genre and structure of the book of Daniel.

602. Fewell, Danna Nolan, *Circle of Sovereignty: A Story of Stories in Daniel 1–6*, JSOT Supplement 72 (Sheffield: Almond Press, 1988).

603. Hartman, L. F., and A. A. Di Lella, *The Book of Daniel*, Anchor Bible [19], 1978.

604. Lacocque, Andre, *The Book of Daniel*, trans. by David Pellauer (Atlanta: John Knox, 1979).

605. Porteous, Norman W., *Daniel*, Old Testament Library [26], 1965.

606. Russell, D. S., *Daniel, An Active Volcano: Reflections on the Book of Daniel*, 1st American ed. (Louisville: Westminster/John Knox, 1989).

607. Towner, W. Sibley, *Daniel*, Interpretation [22], 1984.

On the Book of Esther

608. Anderson, Bernhard W., "Introduction and Exegesis to the Book of Esther," *The Interpreter's Bible*, III [23], 1954.

609. Berg, Sandra, *The Book of Esther: Motifs, Themes and Structure*. SBL Dissertation Series 44 (Missoula: Scholars, 1979).

610. Clines, David J. A., *Ezra, Nehemiah, Esther*, New Century Bible [25], 1984.

611. Clines, David J. A., *The Esther Scroll: The Story of the Story*, JSOT Supplement 30 (Sheffield: JSOT, 1984). Considers both the final form and the history of redaction.

612. Moore, Carey A., ed., *Studies in the Book of Esther* (New York: KTAV, 1981).

On the Dead Sea Scrolls

Of the voluminous literature that has appeared, only a few books can be mentioned.

613. Cross, Frank M., *The Ancient Library of Qumran and Modern Biblical Studies* (Garden City, NY: Doubleday, 1961). A comprehensive, perceptive treatment of the scrolls and their significance. See also "The Early History of the Apocalyptic Community at Qumran," in *Canaanite Myth and Hebrew Epic* [129], chap. 12.

614. Driver, G. R., *The Judean Scrolls: The Problem and a Solution,* rev. ed. (New York: Schocken Books, 1965). Discusses the significance of the scrolls for Old Testament study.

615. Dupont-Sommer, A., *The Essene Writings from Qumran,* trans. by G. Vermès (New York: Meridian, 1961). Introduction to and translation of Qumran literature.

616. Gaster, T. H., *The Dead Sea Scriptures,* rev. ed. (Garden City, NY: Doubleday, 1964). Introduction, translation, and notes.

617. Ringgren, Helmer, *The Faith of Qumran,* trans. by Emilie T. Sander (Philadelphia: Fortress, 1961).

618. VanderKam, James C., *The Dead Sea Scrolls Today* (Grand Rapids, MI: Eerdmans, 1994).

619. Vermès, Géza, *The Dead Sea Scrolls in English* (Baltimore: Penguin Books, 1962). Translation and illuminating introduction.

On the Canon

Especially the works of Brevard Childs [42, 150, 200, 238] and James A. Sanders [102–103] have called for a reconsideration of the canon.

620. Blenkinsopp, Joseph, *Prophecy and Canon: A Contribution to the Study of Jewish Origins* (Notre Dame, IN: University of Notre Dame, 1977).

621. Neusner, Jacob, *From Politics to Piety: The Emergence of Pharisaic Judaism* (Englewood Cliffs, NJ: Prentice-Hall, 1973).

622. Sanders, James A., *Canon and Community* [103]. An indispensable treatment of this subject.

623. Sundberg, Albert C., *The Old Testament of the Early Church.* Harvard Theological Studies XX (Cambridge, MA: Harvard University, 1964). A seminal reconsideration of the problem of canon.

624. Weingren, J., *From Bible to Mishnah: The Continuity of Tradition* (Manchester, England: Manchester University, 1976).

625. Wright, G. Ernest, "The Canon as Theological Problem" in *The Old Testament and Theology* [171], chap. 7.

See also James Barr, *Holy Scripture* [cited under 147].

INDEX

SUBJECT INDEX